"For anyone fatigued by the term 'sustainability,' Jane Penty breathes vitality back into the word – expanding its purview and animating its potential. Traversing multiple disciplines from material culture and artificial intelligence, to business frameworks, ethics, and social innovation, Jane Penty's *Product Design and Sustainability* may be the single most effective compendium for simultaneously defining a contemporary understanding of sustainability while providing an actionable toolkit for its practice. Required reading for design professionals, educators, and students; essential reading for anyone who needs to believe that we can find a way forward."

Allan Chochinov, Chair, SVA MFA Products of Design, NY;
Partner, Core77

"A book that is timely and urgently needed – revisiting the complex and fast-evolving relationships between design, consumption, economics and technology at a pivotal moment. *Product Design and Sustainability* will help answer questions we all have as designers, and help further close the gap between the work that we do and our lived experience of the world."

Hugo Jamson, Creative Director, New Territory, London

"Far from the tired, doom and gloom rhetoric peddled by so many academics on this topic, Penty's hopeful treatise lights the way toward a sustainable design future. Her clear and precise theoretical writing is further elucidated by a rich repertoire of case studies, methodological tools and practical examples. This important book will surely become an essential point of reference for anyone working at the intersections of design, sustainability and systems change."

Jonathan Chapman, Professor and Director of Doctoral Studies,
School of Design, Carnegie Mellon University, Pittsburgh

"A wonderfully comprehensive real-world guide through the maze of sustainability for anyone involved in new product creation. It manages to be both rigorous and pragmatic in equal measure and is the perfect starting point for designers, students and academics."

Alex Hulme, director, Map Project Office, London

"Through a very
us that product designers can play a major role in the transition to a more sustainable and meaningful tomorrow. For a whole new generation of designers ready and mobilised to engage on this course of action, this book offers a valuable tool to inform their thinking and practice."

Anne Marchand, Professor of Product Design, School of Design,
Université de Montréal

"*Product Design and Sustainability* is a resource primed for designers to tackle wicked global problems they are increasingly required to help solve. Penty sets the scene of humanity's 'unsustainability' from a vast body of knowledge, identifying practical environmental, economic and social levers for designers to use in response. Real world examples then contextualise frameworks that are life cycle based; systemic; efficiency-led; regenerative; regulatory; socially equitable; circular; and economically transformative, to assist designers in reorienting their practice to be sustainability-driven."

Simon Lockrey, Senior Lecturer, RMIT University,
Executive Director, Glowpear, Melbourne

"Jane Penty's book is a well-informed and engaging overview of the dramatic material challenges of our contemporary world we live in, as well as a useful and practical guide as to how design tools, methods and practice can be used to drive change."

Clare Brass, designer, circular economy expert
and director, Department 22, London

"In a world where doomsday scenarios paint alarming pictures while designers work on the next new trend, Jane Penty's voice is calm and points to a better world through design. She asks the difficult question – what problems are we solving and how? *Product Design and Sustainability* calls upon us to be conscious and responsible designers and shows us how. The mix of carefully put together information, insightful analysis, detailed examples and design strategy is valuable for both the student and practitioner of design. It is comprehensive and covers several design disciplines and their intersections."

Naga Nandini, Industrial Arts and Design Practices,
Srishti Institute of Art, Design and Technology,
Bangalore

Product Design and Sustainability

Whether it is the effects of climate change, the avalanche of electronic and plastic waste or the substandard living and working conditions of billions of our fellow global citizens, our ability to deal with unsustainability will define the twenty-first century. Given that most consumption is mediated through products and services, the critical question for designers is: How can we radically reshape these into tools for sustainable living?

As a guide and reference text, *Product Design and Sustainability* provides design students, practitioners and educators with the breadth and depth needed to integrate the most appropriate sustainable strategies into their practice. It establishes the principles that underpin sustainability and introduces a diverse range of social, economic and environmental design responses and tools available to designers. The numerous real-world examples illustrate how these strategies play out in different product sectors and reinforce the view that sustainability is the most positive opportunity and creative challenge facing designers today.

This book:

- delivers a comprehensive guide to the principles of sustainability and how they apply to product design that can readily be integrated into curricula and design practice

- reveals many of the issues specific product sectors are facing, and provides the depth and breadth needed for formulating and developing sustainable design strategies to address these issues

- empowers and inspires designers to engage with sustainability through its many examples and insightful interviews with practitioners

- is fully illustrated with over 300 photographs, graphs and diagrams and supported by chapter summaries, annotated further reading suggestions, and a glossary.

Jane Penty is a designer and educator focused on the creative challenge of transforming *how* and *what* we consume into tools for sustainable living. She is Sustainable Design Leader for BA Product Design at Central Saint Martins, UAL, London, UK.

Product Design and Sustainability

Strategies, Tools and Practice

Jane Penty

Routledge
Taylor & Francis Group

LONDON AND NEW YORK

First published 2020
by Routledge
2 Park Square, Milton Park, Abingdon, Oxon OX14 4RN

and by Routledge
52 Vanderbilt Avenue, New York, NY 10017

Routledge is an imprint of the Taylor & Francis Group, an informa business

British Library Cataloguing-in-Publication Data
A catalogue record for this book is available from the British Library

Library of Congress Cataloging-in-Publication Data
Names: Penty, Jane, author.
Title: Product design and sustainability : strategies, tools and practice /
  Jane Penty.
Description: New York : Routledge, 2019. | Includes bibliographical
  references and index.
Identifiers: LCCN 2019003362| ISBN 9781138301979 (hb : alk. paper) |
  ISBN 9781138301986 (pb : alk. paper) | ISBN 9780203732076 (ebook)
Subjects: LCSH: Industrial design--Environmental aspects. | Sustainable
  design.
Classification: LCC TS171.4 .P45 2019 | DDC 745.2--dc23
LC record available at https://lccn.loc.gov/2019003362

ISBN: 978-1-138-30197-9 (hbk)
ISBN: 978-1-138-30198-6 (pbk)
ISBN: 978-0-203-73207-6 (ebk)

Typeset in ITC Officina Sans
by Servis Filmsetting Ltd, Stockport, Cheshire

All Taylor & Francis books are printed on paper produced from certified
sustainable resources.

for the next generation of designers
to seize this pivotal moment to reshape how we will live
and reconnect us to our fellow humans and the generosity of our planet

Contents

Contents

Preface

Only a few years ago while researching for this book, a very experienced senior designer at one of the top global product design consultancies confessed to me off the record that he had never had a single brief from a client that explicitly mentioned sustainability as an outcome. Further conversations with many other designers and graduates at the time confirmed that, much to their frustration, this was by no means unusual.

Thankfully, as this book goes to print, the situation is very different. In a matter of a few years there has been a huge shift in public attitudes. Greta Thunberg has spoken and there is now an admission in many quarters that we are facing a climate emergency and mass species extinction. This is making businesses take sustainability, or the lack of it, much more seriously, as they see it hitting their bottom line directly or indirectly through brand reputation.

It seems that clients are now actively seeking direction and leadership in this area from designers, making this a pivotal moment that must be seized to reshape the nature of products and consumption for the next generation. But for this design input to lead to truly meaningful change, designers need to know more than the basics and be equipped to show their clients what a creative opportunity sustainability presents for the triple bottom line.

At the same time, sustainability has become one of the most overused, oversimplified and misunderstood words currently in circulation. Not only does it mean different things to different people, it is also being used for a range of different ends, from the blissfully naïve to the intentionally deceitful. Given the urgency of our global predicament, the only thing that might be worse than talking about sustainability is writing about it, because what it is really crying out for are 'deeds not words'. So why a book full of words, and why *this* book, when the very notion of sustainable product design is considered by many to be an oxymoron?

Even, or perhaps especially, in this age of digital connectivity and hyper access to information, you would be forgiven for questioning the choice of a book as a format for delivering and accessing this important content. The reason behind this choice is that, first, the sustained narrative of a book can establish the emotional connection needed for engagement in positive and confident action. Second, that to be effective, this action must be informed by sufficient analysis and detail to avoid the pitfalls of sound bites, greenwashing or inadvertently causing more harm than good. Third, through the platform of a book, it is possible to set out and synthesise the principles and the breadth and diversity of approaches and opportunities from which this subject can be tackled.

This book is the product of several years' extended research initially born out of my own frustration at not being able to point students and designers towards a reference text of sufficient scope and depth. But the writing of it is has also served to answer many questions, clarify many points, and get to the bottom of many assumptions, oversimplifications and contradictions that surround this subject and have been challenging my own design practice and teaching. In short, I hope this book will provide design students and practitioners alike with a coherent frame of reference upon which to confidently base their practice, and dare to imagine and create a more sustainable future.

Acknowledgements

Time, space, energy – and copious amounts of generosity, enthusiasm and dogged determination – these have all been essential ingredients in the realisation of this book. For this I have many to thank.

To my publishers. At Routledge, I am indebted to Jennifer Schmidt who championed the project and took time out to provide much needed editorial advice; to Fran Ford for so calmly and skilfully enabling the bigger picture; to Trudy Varcianna for always being at the end of an email with her detailed grasp of process; and to Ed Gibbons for his full commitment to shaping the manuscript into a book. For their earlier support with the book project I would also like to thank Jo Lightfoot and Sophie Drysdale for giving me the opportunity to begin the journey, and Anne Townley for her patient questioning and detailed editorial counsel.

At Central St Martins, to the very many art and design students over the years with whom I have had the privilege to work, inspire, and duly be inspired by. This book is a direct response to your appetite for more clarity on the subject and your desire to put your creative skills to good use. To the College, and the Product and Industrial Design Programme, for allowing me to take the time to give this project the focus it needed. I have discovered and learnt so much in the process. And in particular to my close colleagues in Product Design for your unswerving support over these past few years and your undiminished good humour.

To the Internet and our creative commons. Testament to our ability to collaborate.

To the hundreds of companies, organisations, designers and individuals for their generosity in freely sharing their knowledge, expertise, critical feedback and photographic material. In particular to my interviewees, all designers and practitioners in this field who have enriched the text with their personal experience and valuable insights. Making new connections with so many people who are genuinely committed to making a difference has given me fresh optimism.

In obtaining the very many images and requisite permissions, to my daughter Edith Penty Geraets for taking on the lion's share of this formidable task with such diplomacy, organisation and persistence over many months; to Saffie Pluck for her valued contribution to the collective effort; and to Sachiko Osawa, Ryo Terui and Hazuki Ysunaga for their assistance with Japanese permissions, interviews and translations.

To all my family and friends for proving the power and resilience of social capital by accepting my neglect over the past few years, yet always being ready to give me support when I have needed it – reading, suggesting, checking, editing, proofing, photographing, and photoshopping. And, most especially to Patrick, for always being there, unconditionally. It is more than thanks I owe you.

Y por fin, gracias Teresin por haber esperado. Este libro es testimonio de los valores que nos enseñaste. Creo que al final nos ha cundido.

Introduction

Today, whether we choose to or not, we are all unwitting observers and active contributors to the biggest collective existential challenge the human race has ever faced: climate change. And we are pushing hard towards the sixth mass extinction of our fellow living species. The fact that these are both man-made at least has the positive implication that reversing the course we are on is, for a few more years, largely in our hands.

As we explore in the book, climate change and species loss are *only two facets*, albeit very urgent ones, that design must address. The bigger question is: How can we as citizens and designers become a positive force in enabling a transition from our present state to a world where we all have an equitable share of the planet's physical and intellectual resources while living secure and meaningful lives within the Earth's biological carrying capacity?

On the face of it, the aim of sustainability is simple and uncontroversial: meeting our present needs without compromising the ability of future generations to meet theirs. Or, not taking out more than we put back in while sharing what there is within planetary boundaries. However, the deeper we dig into just how much would have to change practically on the ground, the more challenging it becomes to realise this vision.

Questions about *what* and *how much* we consume, *how* this is produced and *who* has *access* to it come up time and again in international discussions on sustainable development. In this regard, product designers are in a unique position to help catalyse the rethinking and reshaping of products and services into enabling tools for more sustainable lives. In order to do this successfully however, we must appreciate the constraints of the socio-economic web we have created that have locked us onto this destructive course, or we will merely continue adding to the problem.

In his 1971 book *Design for the Real World,* Victor Papanek accused industrial design of being one of the most harmful professions, mindlessly feeding consumption to keep business happy. If we, as product designers, connect this line of thinking with the view that products *are* the problem, then we are well on our way to talking ourselves out of doing what we are good at: designing transformative products and services. Given that by 2050 over 9 billion people will continue to need food, shelter, security, education, mobility, cultural connections and meaningful employment, *not* engaging in the design of 'better' products would be far worse.

Based on that conviction, this book confronts the real consequences of the products we produce and consume, their causes and the barriers that prevent them from being more sustainable, equitable and meaningful. It also seeks out new, and revisits old, lines of thinking and opportunities, be they mainstream or niche, local or global, that product designers can explore and exploit in shaping a more positive co-existence between ourselves and the biosphere.

This is approached in three parts. Part 1 sets the scene in terms of the global issues of unsustainability that most need addressing, the precedents of design activism upon which current attitudes and actions build, and the scope for sustainable product design. Part 2 looks at each of the three pillars – environmental, social and economic sustainability – in depth. It establishes the main issues, principles and objectives, and connects these with the key strategies and tools for sustainable product design. Part 3 turns some of the holistic principles espoused in earlier chapters on their heads when it looks at four product sectors in practice: short-use products and packaging, electronic and digital tools, furniture-related products, and transportation and mobility. Here, we delve into the particular problems, constraints, business models and technological developments and opportunities that each sector faces in delivering more sustainable products and services.

Throughout the book, topics and strategies are supported by interviews with practitioners offering diverse viewpoints and illustrated through a wide range of examples. These are consciously drawn from realised and commercially available projects in recognition of the considerable journey between a 'good idea', a 'good concept' and a viable, scalable and successful product or service. It also avoids being a catalogue of the latest potential innovations, as inspiring and fascinating as many are, and instead seeks to celebrate leading companies and designers active in this field and credit 'firsts' where possible to help give some context to their subsequent evolution and derivatives.

Dealing with the complexity of sustainability requires systems thinking, and producing a sustainable product requires the powerful combination of design thinking *and* systems thinking. Although no product has ever existed outside of a wider ecosystem, in today's digitally connected world the lines between product and service have melded. Product design now encompasses a range of activities that include the design of physically tangible artefacts as well as user experiences (UX) through user interfaces

(UI). Therefore, for the purposes of this book, a product designer includes anyone involved in the conceptualisation and realisation of product service systems (PSS) and their physical touchpoints.

While the principle of sustainability is simple, getting there successfully is complex but need not be complicated. Ultimately, *Product Design and Sustainability* aims to give designers the confidence to set their own sustainability agendas by helping them navigate some of this complexity and by revealing many of its true opportunities. From whatever angle or starting point we engage with sustainability, the only certainty is that it will lead us further in and alter our perception of the world around us and everything we do. What may start with a desire to design products that do less harm may one day evolve into the ability to create truly regenerative products and services that actively enable one-planet living.

PART 1

Concepts and context

CHAPTER 1
Sustainability and design in context

Chapter 1 sets out to contextualise and build an agreed understanding and vision of what a sustainable planet might look and feel like. Because sustainability is more of a goal than a tangible reality, it is easier to grasp by what it is not – the unsustainable. Thus we begin by focusing on some hard facts about the state of the planet, its biggest threats and their causes. From this perspective, we can construct a working definition of sustainable product design. We also look back at the inspiring actions of a few of the remarkable individuals and movements connected to design that have given physical form and voice to more equitable and sustainable ways of living. Finally, we identify the role of different actors in driving the necessary change forward and consider the particular contribution product designers can make in transforming our way of consuming, producing and doing business if we are to co-exist sustainably on the planet.

1.1 our unsustainability and major threats

Before we embark on designing more sustainably we need to grasp the nature and severity of the current threats that mankind and all life on the planet are facing in order to set clear priorities. We should also try to understand the underlying behaviours that cause them and be persuaded that changing these behaviours can and will make enough of a difference to reduce or even eliminate the dangers. Boxes 1.1 to 1.5 present the statistics behind the biggest man-made threats to life on the planet along with their causes and consequences. Although the threats are placed under environmental, social and economic headings, it quickly becomes apparent that their causes and effects are closely interconnected. These widely accepted headings, which we use throughout the text, are merely convenient constructs that allow us to break down the complexity of sustainability into manageable elements. They should not however be allowed to get in the way of considering the issues holistically.

Summarising the findings in Boxes 1.1 to 1.5, life on Earth is progressively being put under greater and greater stress. In the past 40 years population and CO_2 emissions have more than doubled, and in the mid-1970s human consumption of resources overtook the Earth's bio-capacity to replenish itself. The picture we have is of a planet struggling to cope. Over 7.7 billion very unequal human beings are consuming over 1.75 planets of resources annually. This rising level of overconsumption is destroying habitats and wildlife, and driving up the Earth's average temperatures. This in turn is creating disruptive and increasingly catastrophic weather events, causing ever-more deaths, displacement and economic losses.

By these accounts, climate change, also referred to as climate emergency, is considered the most critical threat. At its worst it is an existential threat to all life, and at its mildest it will continue to have increasingly significant socio-economic impacts across the globe. The message from the last Intergovernmental Panel on Climate Change's (IPCC) special report on the impacts of global warming of 1.5°C (2018) is clear. We must reduce emissions of greenhouse gases by 50% by 2030 and to *net zero* by 2050 to have a reasonable chance of limiting global warming to 1.5°C.[1]

The next 10 years will be absolutely crucial in determining what kind of world will exist in the decades beyond. If we act decisively, and innovate and invest wisely, we could both avoid the worst impacts of climate change and successfully achieve the sustainable development goals. If we do not, we face a world in which it will become increasingly difficult for us and future generations to thrive.[2]

One of the keys to resolving these big issues is the realisation that the world's environmental, social and economic problems do not recognise national boundaries. Floods in Thailand cause production problems for Japanese companies and customers globally. A banking crisis in America and Europe creates a slowdown across all economies. And rising commodity and food prices from droughts, floods, resource depletion, rising population demand and futures speculation cause economic and climate migration, political instability and conflict.[3] The world is so interconnected that global collective consciousness and local action are the first prerequisites for change. As we will see, denial is finally giving way to greater cooperation and action.

1.2 the concept of sustainability: definitions and models

Earth can provide enough for man's needs but not for every man's greed.[4]

Sustainability is both simple and complex – simple in its intentions but complex in its workings. While no concept can ever be fully defined by words, it helps to look at it from a range of perspectives to arrive at an understanding that resonates with us personally to inspire our work and act as a yardstick by which to measure our actions.

The most generic definition of sustainability is *the ability to self-maintain over a period of time.* Based on this definition, it seems self-evident that an ecosystem that is consuming over 75% more than it is able to replenish, and rising; that is, destabilising and destroying its own natural cycles and habitats through overproduction; and, where over half the population struggle to get by, let alone fulfil their potential because of deprivation or social injustice, is not self-maintaining over time and is therefore highly unsustainable.

Perhaps the most quoted definition for sustainable development and one that intuitively resonates with many people comes from *Our Common Future*, a UN report by the Commission on the Environment and Development (WCED) published in 1987, commonly known as The Bruntland Report:

> [Sustainable development is development that] [...] meets the needs of the present without compromising the ability of future generations to meet their own needs.[5]

Although this definition serves as a good starting point and is easy to relate to on a personal level, it does not give us any tangible leads as to what sustainability might look like or how we might begin to get there.

A useful way to understand sustainability is not as a static state, but rather as a system in dynamic equilibrium. For dynamic equilibrium to exist, the constituent parts compete *and* support each other, while allowing the whole system to change and evolve. This is known as a win-win strategy commonly used in decision-making, negotiations and conflict resolution. In a win-win scenario, each part seeks the best for itself but not at the expense of each other, since they recognise that they are all interdependent within the same system. In the same way, sustainability is about constantly seeking win-win-win outcomes between environment, society and economy through collaborative and creative thinking.

sustainable product design

How then does this translate into sustainable product design and what part might product designers play in creating this dynamic equilibrium? A superficial look at product design as an activity that just produces and encourages the consumption of more 'stuff' that we don't really need might lead to the conclusion that product design and sustainability are simply incompatible. But product design can and should offer much more. Without a doubt the rising billions of people living on the planet will need to eat, drink, dress, be sheltered, feel secure, communicate, travel, work and play. All these activities happen in some way in real time and space, and this is where product designers play an important role. *If those 'needs' can be met more intelligently by creatively balancing the planet's health while enhancing the human experience within a viable economic framework, then we will be approaching the idea of sustainable design.*

To achieve this, product designers need to shift their emphasis from creating objects to *meeting real needs.* The change of focus from the physical object to satisfying physical and emotional needs through the experiences, narrative and meaning that products can create is liberating for designers. This allows more holistic and therefore sustainable thinking that takes into account the wider context and interrogates the need. It does not assume that a product is the answer but, when it is, the whole 'product ecology' or 'product service system' (PSS) surrounding it comes into play. And because all products exist within their own 'product ecology', especially as the digital and physical worlds merge, in this text we will assume that a 'product' includes its product service system (PSS).

Thus, we begin to have sustainable product design when the experiences facilitated through products produce *net positive value* over their negative impacts. *Sustainable products are therefore products that create net value socially, economically and environmentally through their entire product ecosystem.* Put another way, sustainable products ultimately *give more than they take.* In this definition the word *net* is important, because it accepts that during the process of designing, the day-to-day social, environmental and economic balance sheets may fluctuate but, taken as a whole, our design actions should produce many more positives than negatives and ultimately lead us towards more ambitious restorative outcomes.

Box 1.1 environmental threat: global warming and climate change

Climate change isn't an "issue" to add to the list of things to worry about, next to health care and taxes. It is a civilizational wake-up call.

Naomi Klein, *This Changes Everything*

the basics

Global warming together with loss of natural capital are combining to create humanity's biggest existential threat. The average temperature of the Earth is rising at an unprecedented rate, with 75% of this increase in the past three decades, primarily due to human activity.[6] Unchecked, this will have catastrophic effects for life as we know it because human beings and the Earth's ecosystems cannot adapt quickly enough.

some facts

- average temperatures have already risen by 1.1°C (1.98°F) from pre-industrial levels (1850–1900) to 2017 with 16 of the past 17 years the hottest ever[7]

- extreme weather events and natural disasters have increased by 300% since the 1960s[8] with over 60% directly attributable to global warming[9]
- even when we reduce emissions to net-zero, temperatures will continue to rise because the GHGs we are producing today will still be in the atmosphere for between 100 to over 1000 years, making immediate action essential.[10]

causes

Exponentially increasing levels of greenhouse gases (GHGs), primarily from human activity, are trapping heat in the Earth's atmosphere, raising overall temperatures. GHGs and emission sources break down into:[11]

- 76% CO_2 carbon dioxide
  - 65% from burning fossil fuels
  - 11% from deforestation and decay
- 16% CH_4 methane from animal farming and waste
- 6.2% N_2O nitrous oxide from chemical fertilisers and fossil fuel burning.

Figure 1.1 Our main GHGs are intrinsically tied to our lifestyle. The choice is ours: burning coal for electricity; heat and air-condition buildings; deforestation for animal feed and palm oil; fossil fuels for transportation; methane from meat and dairy production (photo credits: CreativeNatureNl; Pattarapol Wesrungwit; Alf Ribeiro / Shutterstock.com; Rich Carey / Shutterstock.com; NotarYES)

consequences[12]

The effects of a 1°C rise are already a reality across the globe and worsening yearly:

- sea levels and the frequency of extreme weather events are rising, submerging islands and causing draughts, floods and water stress
- ecosystems are unable to adapt, causing bleached coral reefs and 30% of species facing extinction
- food production is decreasing in low latitudes and will eventually spread across the globe
- malnutrition, disease and deaths from heatwaves, floods and draughts are increasing.

If global temperatures rise over 2°C, all elements will worsen with a greater likelihood of sudden large irreversible and catastrophic events known as tipping points.

positive signs

- to avert a 2°C rise, 197 countries signed the Paris Agreement pledging to binding targets for 40 to 70% GHG reductions by 2050 and zero net CO_2 by 2100. Limiting the temperature rise to 1.5°C is now considered far safer, but that requires net zero CO_2 by 2050
- for the first time, energy-related CO_2 emissions levelled out between 2014 and 2016 despite economic growth thanks to renewables, but grew again by 1.4% in 2017[13]
- we have the answers: Project Drawdown outlines 100 solutions we can implement *today* to rapidly reverse global warming.

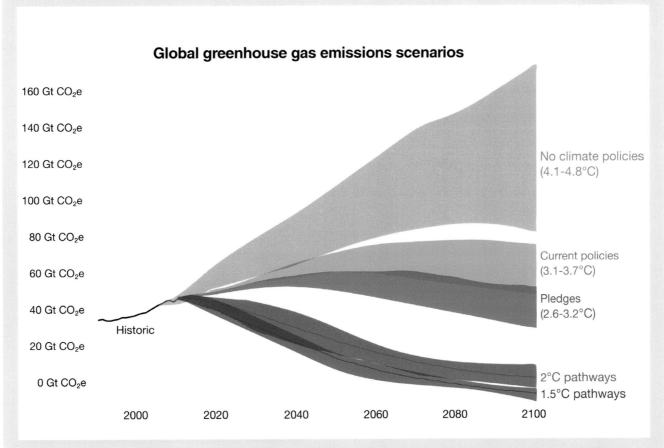

Figure 1.1b Predicted global temperature rises for four different potential future emissions pathways. (source: OurWorldinData.org. Visualisation Hannah Ritchie & Max Roser)

Box 1.2 environmental threat: loss of biodiversity and natural ecosystems

The 21st century presents humanity with a dual challenge of maintaining nature in all of its many forms and functions and creating an equitable home for people on a finite plane.
WWF Living Planet Report 2016

the basics

We are continuing to press forward with the sixth mass extinction of vertebrates.[14] Animal populations on the planet decreased by 60% from 1970 to 2014[15] and all species assessed are in a worse state due to the loss and degradation of natural habitats.[16] The most threatened are tropical rainforests, wetlands, and freshwater and marine environments.[17]

some facts

deforestation:[18, 19]

- 50% of the Earth's rainforests have already been destroyed and we are still losing an area the size of England or Oregon every year
- 80% of the world's land species live in forests

- 50,000 wildlife species become extinct each year in the rainforest
- it is the second biggest cause of global warming.

species loss:[20]

- 30% of all vertebrate species declined between 1970 and 2006
- 25% of the world's mammals and 30% of all amphibians are at risk of extinction
- freshwater wildlife has declined 83% in 40 years.

oceans and fish:

- 80% of the world's fish stocks are exploited beyond their sustainable limits and another 40 million tonnes of bycatch and 300,000 marine mammals are accidentally killed each year
- coastal deadzones (zero oxygen) have increased four-fold and open ocean low-oxygen areas ten-fold since 1950, and half of freshwater corals are dead.

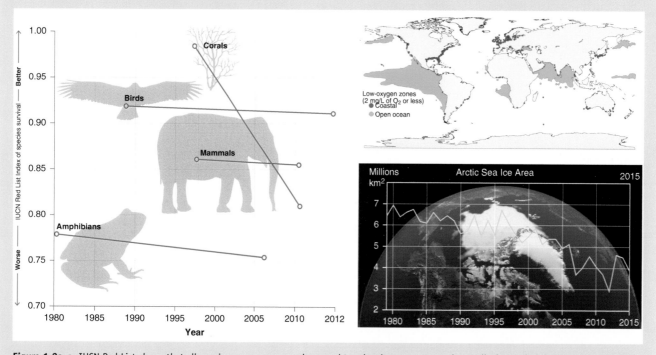

Figure 1.2a a. IUCN Red List shows that all species groups are on a downward trend as human consumption, pollution and global warming shrink their habitats. b. The Global Oxygen Network (GO2NE) maps out the exponentially growing coastal and open ocean dead zones globally c. NASA's satellites track the rapidly shrinking ice at the poles. (sources: IUCN; GO2NE 2018; NASA Scientific Visualization Studio)

causes[21]

The increasing demand for resources from a growing global population is putting all natural ecosystems under pressure. These include:

- rainforest clearance for agriculture, notably for animal feed and palm oil
- mining, oil and gas exploitation causing habitat loss and threatening fragile environments like rainforests, polar regions and deep seas
- overexploitation of wild species, especially overfishing
- climate change altering ecosystems faster than species can adapt
- thoughtless introduction of invasive alien species driving native species to extinction
- severe pollution, contamination and degradation of ecosystems from human activities.

consequences

Human beings are destroying the natural ecosystems they depend on for economic and biological survival.

- the supplies of food, fibre, medicines, freshwater, crop pollination, filtration of pollutants and protection from natural disasters by natural ecosystems are all being reduced by overconsumption
- rainforest destruction is driving up global warming and the loss of tens of thousands of species, many as yet unknown to humans
- at our current rates, wildlife loss will reach 67% by 2020
- extinction is irreversible.

positive signs

- the rate of deforestation decreased by half between 2010 and 2015 compared to 1990 to 2000.[22] This is thanks to a combination of reforestation, afforestation, carbon offsetting and net zero carbon initiatives, and an increased demand for certified forest products
- UN Convention on Biological Diversity (CBD) countries have pledged to protect at least 17% of land and freshwater and 10% of our oceans by 2020
- internationally, scientists are pushing for a post-2020 target of safeguarding 50% of the planet in order to protect the bulk of biodiversity from extinction.[23]

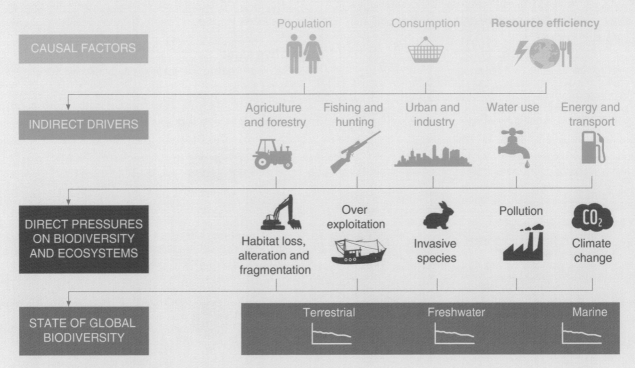

Figure 1.2b Interconnections between people, biodiversity, ecosystems health and provision of ecosystem services. (source: courtesy WWF Living Planet Report Rio+20)

Box 1.3 environmental threat: global overshoot and resource depletion

Humanity is living off its ecological credit card and it can only do this by liquidating the planet's natural resources.
Mathis Wackernagel, co-founder of Global Footprint Network

the basics
We have been living beyond the Earth's capacity since 1970. Most non-renewable resources, particularly fossil fuel and minerals, will run out this century at our current rate of overconsumption. Many natural resources are also being permanently lost.

some facts
- known reserves of non-renewable resources, many commonly used in consumer products, are running out, some quite rapidly
- using ecological footprint accounting, in 1970 our resource consumption surpassed the capacity of the Earth to support that consumption and has been getting worse ever since. This is known as overshoot[24]
- globally we need 1.75 earths to support our consumption, but a closer look reveals huge regional variations in how much we consume:[25]
  - 14.4 earths as Qataris
  - 5.0 earths as North Americans
  - 3.9 earths as Australasians
  - 2.8 earths as Europeans
  - 1.7 earths as South Americans

- 1.5 earths as Asians
- 0.8 earths as Africans
- 0.5 earths as Eritreans

causes
- the doubling of world population between 1970 and 2010, expected to reach 9.7 billion by 2050 and 11.2 billion by the end of the twenty-first century[26]
- continuing unsustainable levels of consumption in developed countries together with growing middle classes in emerging economies seeking to improve their standard of living.

consequences
- increasing scarcity of minerals and fuel will extend destructive exploration and extraction, damaging ever more ecosystems and threatening fragile environments like the deep sea, polar regions and even space
- energy will eventually need to come entirely from renewable sources, all metals and minerals will need to be completely recovered, and natural and renewable resources will become much more precious.

positive signs
- the global shift to renewable energy is reducing our reliance on fossil fuels
- the principle of circular economies and material recovery is gaining momentum with governments and business.

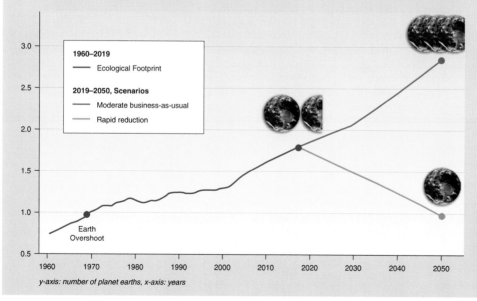

Legend:
1960–2019
— Ecological Footprint

2019–2050, Scenarios
— Moderate business-as-usual
— Rapid reduction

Earth Overshoot

y-axis: number of planet earths, x-axis: years

Figure 1.3a Planet Earth has been in environmental overshoot since 1970 and increasing ever since. Do we continue on this course or aim for One Planet Living by 2050? (source: Global Footprint Network 2019)

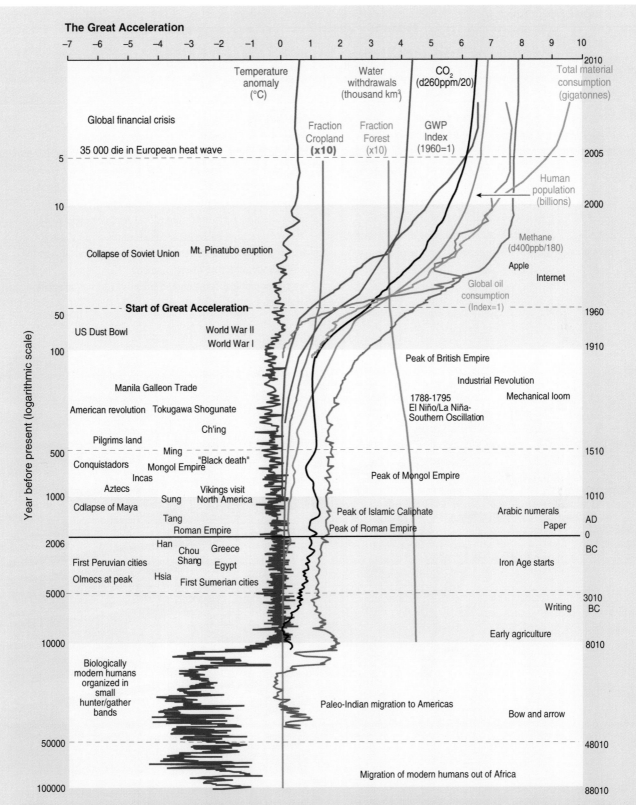

The Great Acceleration

Figure 1.3b The world has been experiencing a huge acceleration of consumption of renewable and non-renewable resources since the 1950s. Based on current known reserves and technology, even if we stabilise our current consumption rates we will only have between 10 and 100 years of many commonly used minerals and non-renewables. (source: GEO-5 / infographic courtesy of UN Environment, Nairobi)

Box 1.4 socio-economic threat: damage to economies, future prosperity and wellbeing from climate change, environmental degradation and resource depletion

The poorest countries will suffer earliest and most, even though they have contributed the least to the causes of climate change.

Nicholas Stern, *The Economics of Climate Change*

Our economies and our societies are dependent on nature, and once it's gone, so are we [...] the global economic system [...] continues to merrily saw away at the branch we're all sitting on.[27]

the basics

The social and economic cost of climate change and lost natural capital is growing year-on-year. Damage from rising sea levels, more frequent and intense extreme weather, mass species extinctions, toxic air and loss of essential supporting ecosystems directly affect economic outputs, productivity, infrastructure, agriculture and global resource supply chains. It also impacts negatively on social wellbeing in the form of displacements and threats to security, health and prosperity. It is already affecting developing countries the most due to their geographical location and inability to fund adaptation measures.

Figure 1.4a Bangladeshi farmers leaving their home with essential belongings in the 2017 floods. The increasing intensity of monsoon rains and cyclones in Bangladesh affects millions annually and costs the country over 5% of GDP. (photo credit: Farid_Ahmed)

Figure 1.4b Floods in Thailand in 2011 directly affected global supply chains and the delivery of goods around the world. (photo credit: Cpl. R. Maurer, US Marine Corps)

some facts

- between 1980 and 2016 hydrological events such as flooding rose 400%; climatological events such as extreme heat, droughts and forest fires, and meteorological events such as storms, cyclones and hurricanes rose more than 200%[28]
- damage from climate change already costs well over US$1 trillion annually and will grow exponentially as global temperatures continue to rise[29]
- there are already over 60,000 annual deaths from natural disasters and tens of thousands from extreme heat
- 150,000 additional deaths were attributed directly to climate change in 2014 and these are projected to rise to 250,000 annually from malnutrition, malaria and diarrhoea between 2030 and 2050[30]
- in 2015 alone, pollution cost over US$4.6 trillion and led to 9 million deaths.[31]

causes

- overconsumption and the lack of immediate tangible feedback on the environmental damage our consumption choices create
- short-termism, lack of visionary governance and insufficient collective responsibility or collaborative action to protect natural habitats, radically reduce GHG emissions and consume much more intelligently, especially in riche countries
- 'natural capital' has no monetary value in our current accounting systems, rewarding business-as-usual at the expense of the natural environment.

consequences

- the cost of not taking action will go up the longer we delay investing in a low-carbon economy, mitigation, protection and restoration[32]
- climate change and environmental degradation will also affect social cohesion and wellbeing through a reduced ability to grow food and access clean water, an increased spread of diseases and air pollution, and population displacement from extreme weather events[33]
- climate change has no national boundaries and will affect the poorest the most, creating migration pressures and aggravating tensions between individuals, nations and regions[34]
- average global incomes are predicted to be 23% less by the end of the century because of climate change.[35]

positive signs

- initiatives like the Global Footprint Network and Natural Capital Coalition are helping governments and businesses to measure, protect and enhance their stocks of natural capital
- over and above national targets, forward-thinking businesses are also leading the shift to 100% renewables (Re100) and net-zero carbon targets
- New Zealand has introduced the first Climate Refugee visa as neighbouring low-lying South Pacific Islands are submerged.

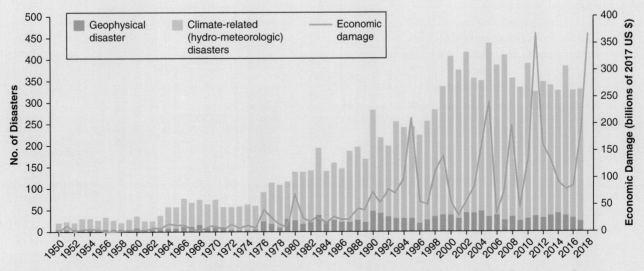

Figure 1.4c Climate-related disasters and their human and economic costs are increasing dramatically (source: EM-DAT The emergency Events Database www.endat.benote)

Box 1.5 socio-economic threat: inequality of income, wealth, social security and employment

Extreme wealth and inequality is:
economically inefficient
politically corrosive
socially divisive
environmentally destructive
unethical
not inevitable.[36]

Oxfam

If a free society cannot help the many who are poor, it cannot save the few who are rich.

J.F. Kennedy, 1961 Inaugural Address

the basics

Despite growing numbers of people on lower-middle incomes worldwide and extreme poverty being halved between 2000 and 2015, the gap between the richest and the poorest is still rising within countries. The wealthiest also consume the majority of the world's resources and generate most of the GHGs through their lifestyles.[37] In addition, underemployment, vulnerable employment, inequitable pay and poor working conditions affect nearly half of all workers. This waste of human potential impacts youth, women and the poor disproportionately and is a key barrier to sustainable development and social justice.[38]

some facts

In a world with a population of over 7.7 billion people, there are still:[39, 40]

- 1 in 10 living in extreme poverty/767 million
- 1 in 3 without access to sanitation/2.4 billion
- 1 in 4 using faecally contaminated water/1.8 billion
- 1 in 11 without access to clean water/660 million
- over 4 billion people (55%) in the world without any social security[41]

while

- the world's wealthiest 10% consume 60% of the world's resources and the poorest 10% consume only 0.5%[42]
- 82% of all wealth created in 2016 went to the top 1%, and the wealth of the bottom 50% (3.75 billion) stood still, continuing a growing trend.[43]

For those working:[44]

- 42% per cent of workers worldwide (1.4 billion) are in vulnerable employment mostly in developing and emerging economies
- in developing countries, up to 77% or 300 million workers are in extreme (<$1.90/day) or moderate poverty ($1.90–$3.10); in emerging economies this is 20% or 430 million
- in the world's poorest countries, around 1 in 4 children are engaged in child labour.[45]

causes[46, 47]

- the pace of technological change is increasing the gap between developed and developing economies
- technological advances and globalisation are focused on reducing human operators and moving to the cheapest labour supply point
- rich individuals and global corporations have ever greater leverage and power to protect their assets and profits
- poor governance, corruption and unregulated economies, especially in developing countries, obstruct more equitable employment conditions and distribution of wealth

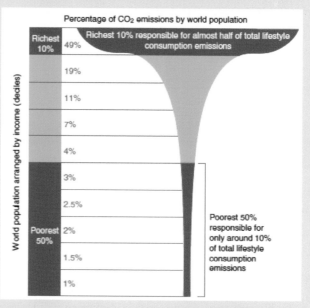

Figure 1.5a Through their consumption, the wealthiest 50% produce the majority of CO_2 emissions while the poorest will be the most affected. (source: Oxfam)

- the poorest countries have the highest population growth rates, making improving employment prospects and living conditions challenging.

consequences

- greater inequality in wealth within countries leads to higher levels of health and social problems and less social cohesion[48]
- growing economic migration is creating political tension and opportunities for human trafficking and modern-day slavery
- inequitable employment and unemployment lead to a waste of the world's greatest asset: human capital.[49]

positive signs

- awareness is growing: the World Economic Forum (WEF) ranked income inequality the top global development trend of the next ten years (2017–2027)[50]
- industry coalitions and better tracking are leading to more transparency of working conditions in supply chains
- the average UN Human Development Index improved substantially between 1990 and 2015 although this went hand-in-hand with a higher ecological footprint[51]
- looking ahead to 2015 to 2030, the UN Sustainable Development Goals are prompting governments, business and civil society to address many of the root causes.

Figure 1.5b Economic migrants and refugees crossing the Mediterranean rescued by an Irish Naval vessel (2015). (photo credit Irish Defence Forces)

Figure 1.5c Boys working in a traditional copper handcrafts factory, Bac Ninh, Vietnam (2015). (photo credit Asia Images / Shutterstock.com)

Since sustainable product design is often equated with 'eco design' and 'green design', it is important at this point to draw a distinction between them. Eco and green design are primarily concerned with lessening the environmental impacts of products. In this sense they connect mostly with the environmental dimension of sustainability, whereas sustainable product design takes a more holistic approach by addressing all the dimensions of sustainability, including the social and economic, and the many conflicts and compromises they create.

models and visualisation

From these definitions, it is clear that achieving sustainability involves a complex set of interdependencies. For the sake of simplification these are most commonly grouped into three principal dimensions or pillars – the environmental, social and economic – originating from the concept of sustainable development in the Bruntland Report. To make sustainability more accessible and directly measurable to the business community, John Elkington translated these pillars into accounting terms in 1994 with the Triple Bottom Line (TBL). In TBL accounting, the sustainability of a company or activity is measured by profit-and-loss balance sheets under the headings of social, environmental and economic capital (see Chapter 4.2). He went further to simplify the TBL into the 3Ps, summarising sustainability as 'Good for People, Planet and Profits', an easily understood slogan for a complex subject.[52] Other models or frameworks such as the Living Principles for Design include culture as a fourth pillar or stream. In the case of Stuart Walker's human-centric Quadruple Bottom Line of Sustainability,[53] a 'meaningful' material culture is achieved when personal, practical and social meanings are enabled by the right economic structures. For the purposes of this text we will stick with the three pillars as a working model given that the social pillar can encompass both the 'personal' and the 'cultural'.

Visual models are also very useful for appreciating the co-dependencies involved in sustainability and for setting priorities. Figure 1.6 shows some commonly used models based on the three pillars of sustainability. The stool and the house shown in Figures 1.6a and b are good metaphors for the crucial interdependency between environment, society and economy. The overlapping circles model (fig 1.6c) suggests that complete sustainability exists in the centre when all three elements are in balance. Finally, the concentric circles model (fig 1.6d) is perhaps the best representation of the ideal interrelationships we are aiming for with sustainability – an economy that works for society, and a society and economy that works for the whole planet within the boundaries of what the environment is capable of providing.

a. Stool

b. House

c. Overlapping circles

d. Concentric circles

Figure 1.6 Visualising interdependencies: graphic representations of sustainability a. stool b. house c. overlapping circles d. concentric circles.

1.3 a timeline: design and the sustainability movement

To help frame a personal position on sustainability and contextualise our actions as designers, we will now take a brief look at the evolution of the sustainability movement and its connections and influence on design. The current movement can be considered a direct evolution of the post-war environmental and human rights protest groups. These in turn draw from a longer tradition of concerned reaction against the damage caused to the natural environment and the wellbeing of people and society by economically driven technological 'progress' that began during the Industrial Revolution. In this sense the problems we face today are not new, but their global reach and scale are certainly unprecedented.

Intensification and *speed* are the key factors that changed our relationship with nature and the structure of society irreversibly in the 'first' Industrial Revolution. Beginning in Britain around 1760 and later spreading to Europe and North America, its prime catalyst was the shift from bio-fuels that humans had used for millennia, to fossil fuels as the main source of energy. The power intensity of fossil fuels enabled mechanisation that in turn drove production to rise exponentially. It also increased the speed and range of mobility as coal-driven railways replaced horses and carts.

The need for concentrated finance to fund these new technologies and enterprises spawned the capitalist system and also propelled the mass migration from the countryside to industrial centres. The rapid changes this created in social structures and work relationships left a vacuum of values, ripe for abuses. The horrors of working and living conditions for the lower classes, including women and children, led to the first labour laws and the birth of socialism as a response to the exploitation of workers in the new capitalist economic order.

Inspired by the writings of Ruskin and Pugin, artists, designers and architects were also critical of the effects of the Industrial Revolution on their material culture and social fabric. They came to see mass-produced goods as devoid of any real aesthetic value or cultural meaning, destroying nature in the process. They also reacted against the de-skilling and division of labour that they believed divorced maker from object, stripping away all sense of quality and pride in workmanship. The Arts and Crafts movement emerged from this critique. Among its leaders, William Morris, Edward Burnes-Jones and Charles Ashbee were unique in that they responded by setting up their own alternative educational and production models based on guild craftsmen, later leading to Guild Socialism. The Arts and Crafts movement became popular, and spread to Europe and the USA, developing their own regional

interpretations. Although ultimately they were never able to stem the tide of mass production, it is the fact that they chose to put their theory into practice through physical products that has given their cause a lasting voice (fig 1.7).

In contrast, this period also saw the birth of 'design' as a profession, as distinct from the maker-craftsperson. Unlike the Arts and Crafts movement that opposed the separation between the creation and making of artefacts and buildings, designers such as Christopher Dresser thrived on working across a range of industries, product typologies and materials, giving birth to Industrial Design. The Arts and Crafts movement saw this 'professionalisation' and detachment from the making process as a root cause of poor design, a point that is being revisited in current debates on the catalysts of unsustainable consumption and design practice[54] (fig 1.8).

Following the Arts and Crafts movement, several other design groups were also connected to socio-political and philosophical agendas. Among them, the Bauhaus, particularly under the direction of Hannes Meyer in the late 1920s and early 1930s, was a design and education experiment allied to socialist ideals. It had at its core the democratisation of design and production with an agenda to improve the quality of ordinary lives. To achieve this, they broke with traditional materials and methods of production and allied themselves with new materials and processes, including glass, steel, concrete and plywood. By liberating themselves from these cultural precedents, they were free to create a new aesthetic allied to new socialist values. Ironically, the Bauhaus 'style' was later mainstreamed into 'Modernism' and commercialised as the 'International Style', losing all connections to its original purpose and ethos of affordability and accessibility.

An example of one of their design objectives was to reduce the time women spent housekeeping through good organisation, as demonstrated in the Haus am Horn (1923) kitchen, one of the first built-in designs. Walter Gropius, head of the Bauhaus, stated that the goal of the house was "the greatest comfort with the greatest economy by the application of the best craftsmanship and the best distribution of form, size and articulation"[55] (fig.1.9a). This thinking was extended by other socialist designers such as Margarete Schutte-Lihotzky through her revolutionary Frankfurt Kitchen that perfected the built-in kitchen and made it available on a mass scale to the working classes[56] (fig.1.9b).

While the treatment of the working class in the first Industrial Revolution triggered the creation of labour and socialist movements to protect against the worst abuses of an unregulated capitalist system, the scars it left on the countryside were a growing, if lesser, concern. This changed during the second Industrial Revolution (1860–1914) when the *intensity* of

Figure 1.7 Block printing at Morris and Co.'s Merton Workshops: putting dignity and meaning back into the production of goods was central to the Arts and Crafts movement. (photo courtesy: William Morris Gallery archive, Walthamstow, London)

Figure 1.8 One of the first 'industrial designers', Christopher Dresser worked across a very wide range of products, materials and styles: cast iron Colebrookdale chair (1870); Linthorpe Pottery vase (1880); silver and ebony tea kettle and stand (1880–1890). (photo courtesy: ©Victoria and Albert Museum, London)

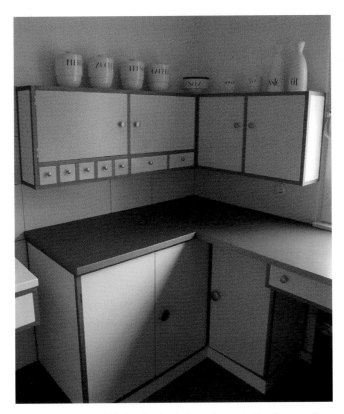

Figure 1.9a Restored kitchen in the Bauhaus demonstration Haus am Horn designed by Theodor Bogler (Weimar 1923). (photo credit Sailko 2011)

Figure 1.9b Restored Frankfurt kitchen designed by Margarete Schütte-Lihotzky (1926–1927). Over 10,000 kitchens of this design were built after 1927. (photo credit Christos Vittaratos 2008)

industrialisation deepened. Petroleum became the magical ingredient behind the development of new chemicals and materials such as plastics and fertilisers, and the invention of the internal combustion engine that led to the first mass-produced automobiles. Added to the increased *speed* of mobility with trains and motorcars was the *acceleration* in communication with the introduction of electricity, telephones and telegraphs.

It is in this context that the first grassroots 'environmental' protection and protest organisations were formed in America, Europe and Australia, including some of the largest and most influential today. In 1889 the Royal Society for the Protection of Birds (RSPB) was created by middle-class people in Britain outraged at the killing of birds for feathers used by the millinary industry for fashion hats. Shortly after, in 1892, John Muir, a pioneering conservationist in America, founded the Sierra Club, and their earliest success was the creation of Yosemite National Park to protect true wilderness. In Germany as well, the Nature and Biodiversity Conservation Union (NABU) formed in 1899 is still going strong. These few examples demonstrate how deeply ordinary people felt that business and politicians were failing to value and protect the natural environment at the end of the nineteenth century.

The conservation movement begun at the end of the nineteenth century then extended its focus onto agricultural practices as traditional methods of land and livestock farming intensified with the use of artificial fertilisers, mechanisation, and later pesticides and herbicides. Biodynamic farming began as early as 1928 in Germany with Demeter as the first organic label. It took over a decade longer for this to catch on elsewhere. In Britain, Lady Balfour published *The Living Soil* in 1942 and the Soil Association was founded in 1946. In 1942, Rodale in America published the first issue of *Organic Gardening Magazine* and the Australian Organic Farming and Gardening Society was founded in 1944. Meanwhile in Japan, Masanobu Fukuoka began experimenting with natural 'do-nothing' farming in 1938, leading to the publication of his *One Straw Revolution* in 1975 that inspired Bill Mollison and the permaculture movement across the world.

In the aftermath of the Second World War, the age of mass production and mass consumption promoted through mass media got into full swing. The United Nations (UN) was created and the Universal Declaration of Human Rights (1948) adopted by its member countries. The 'peace dividend' ramped up the scale of everything in industrialised countries: population, production, consumption, extraction of resources and GDP. Meanwhile, Japan and the Asian Tiger economies, namely Korea, Hong Kong, Singapore and Taiwan, made incredibly rapid transitions into industrialisation, with China joining in the 1980s.

Nowhere was mass consumerism embraced more than in North America. But it was not without its critics. Vance Packard articulated the unease felt by many in America in *The Hidden Persuaders* (1957) and *The Waste Makers* (1960), where he exposed the advertising machinery behind the relentless push for consumption of products with built-in obsolescence and no thought for its consequences.

> *The lives of most Americans have become so intermeshed with acts of consumption that they tend to gain their feelings of significance in life from these acts of consumption rather than from their meditations, achievements, inquiries, personal worth and service to others.*[57]

Out of this unfettered push on consumption and production, the consumer rights movement led by Ralph Nader emerged in the 1960s. His book *Unsafe at any Speed* (1965) established him as a relentless crusader demanding government regulation and forcing some responsibility from producers.

By this point the environmental price of mass consumption was starting to take its toll and did not go unnoticed. The World Wide Fund for Nature (WWF), now the world's largest and most influential international environmental NGO, was founded in

1961, and in 1962 Rachel Carson published *Silent Spring*, an exposé of the effects of the production and indiscriminate use of pesticides and herbicides, especially DDT, on the ecosystem. *Silent Spring* quickly became a bestseller and the rallying cry behind the growing environmental protests in the 1960s.

Widespread pollution and whole-scale poisoning of the landscape and communities increasingly made news headlines in the 1960s and 1970s: mercury poisoning in Minamata, Japan and the Great Lakes; oil tanker spills from Cornwall to California, Nigeria to Iran; acid rain falling over large swathes of Scandinavia and Canada; nuclear testing in the Pacific; and in 1979, the first big nuclear disaster, Three Mile Island. As the realisation of the scale of toxic poisoning and disregard for the environment grew, Friends of the Earth (FoE) (1969) and Greenpeace (1971) emerged, and 20 million people took part in the first Earth Day on 22 April 1970. The environmental movement was now truly international and newsworthy (fig 1.10).

The environment was not the only area where change was demanded. The anti-Vietnam peace and human rights movements in America and student protests in Europe united the 'hippy generation' and many more in rejecting establishment values and proving what people-power could achieve. In many ways the seeds of the 'sustainability movement' were sown in the 1960s with this mix of social, economic and environmental causes, although it was not until the 1980s that their interconnection was consolidated as 'sustainability'.

Figure 1.10 Ixtoc I oil spill (September 1979) caused by a blown-out oil well. The well ran wild for 9 months, spilling over 140 million gallons of oil into the Bay of Campeche, Mexico, only marginally smaller than Deep Water Horizon, the largest-ever spill. Oils spills are devastating for coastal and water wildlife and take decades to clean up. What have we learned? (photo credit Doug Helton, NOAA/NOS/ORR)

In 1968, the visionary designer and polymath Buckminster Fuller published *Operating Manual for Spaceship Earth* where he observed the wilful depletion of mineral resources and our inability to provide for all humans. The vision he proposed was of a 'World Game' where technological know-how and the infinite energy of the sun are put to the service of all mankind. It has taken several decades for the rest of the world to begin to catch up with him (fig 1.11).

In 1972, the publication of *The Limits to Growth, A Report for the Club of Rome's Project on the Predicament of Mankind* modelled the consequences for the planet of unrestrained economic 'development', triggering a worldwide wake-up call. Despite its shocking predictions, the book sold 12 million copies, adding to the weight of evidence and popular feeling behind the environmental movement. This now demanded international attention and the UN began to play a crucial role in bringing scientists, governments and activists together. In 1972 the United Nations Environment Programme (UNEP) was created and at the first UN Conference on the Human Environment (UNCHE), 112 countries agreed to the 'Stockholm Declaration', resulting in the first international environmental law that established the right to a healthy environment. It is only in hindsight that we know that the early 1970s also marked the moment when human activity first exceeded the Earth's bio-capacity known as 'overshoot' and this has been increasing ever since then.[58]

The ethos of the environmental movement conflated with the hippy counterculture of the 1960s and 1970s led to a younger generation rejecting consumerism and actively seeking to 'get back to the land' through 'alternative lifestyles', not only in America but also across Europe and Australia. Here, the shared, communal, handmade, ethnic, recycled, repaired and re-appropriated were celebrated, supported by game-changing publications such as Stewart Brand's *Whole Earth Catalog* (1968–1972) (fig 1.12). Many of these themes were and still are being revisited by the 'eco', 'green' and peer-to-peer maker movements.

It is in this context that two pioneers of socially conscious design emerged. Victor Papanek's *Design for a Real World* (1971) was a call to all industrial designers to reconsider their practice by responding to *real* needs and taking responsibility for their designs. This has gone on to be one of the most widely read design books of all time. Its aesthetics were captured in Hennessey and Papenek's *Nomadic Designs*, and later evolved into the Green movement with *The Green Imperative* (1995) (fig 1.13). Shortly after, Fritz Schumacher's *Small is Beautiful* (1973) called for a rethink of what we design and how we produce. He introduced the notion of 'intermediate' technology based on applying technology that is 'appropriate' for its context of use, particularly in relation to developing countries. Schumacher's legacy is still alive in the resurgence, local economies and transition movements as well as in design strategies for the base

Figure 1.11 Buckminster Fuller in front of two of his most iconic designs, the Dymaxion car and Snowmass geodesic dome in Colorado in 1980. Both were experiments in maximising energy and materials efficacy through the use of tension dynamics to provide affordable and comfortable shelter and mobility to the greatest number of people. (photo ©Roger White Stoller)

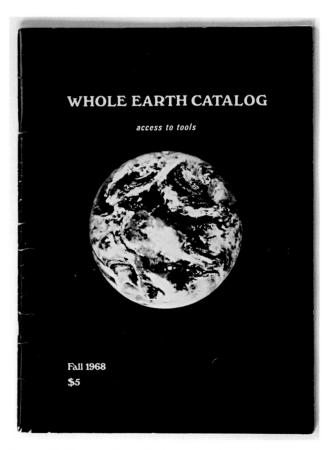

Figure 1.12 After campaigning for the release of images of the Earth, the cover of the first edition of Stewart Brand's *Whole Earth Catalog* featured the first NASA satellite photograph of the Earth from space (1967). Seeing the first images of the Earth from afar awakened a deep sense of its fragility and finity. (photo Stewart Brand / sb.longnow.org)

The late 1980s also saw the emergence of eco, organic and fair-trade labels to satisfy the growing demand of environmentally and socially conscious consumers, with Elkington and Haines' *Green Consumer Guide* (1989) selling by the millions. In 1993 Nigel Whiteley's *Design for Society* moved the socially responsible design agenda forward. In parallel, the work of Dutch Droog Design gave a narrative voice and form to questions around the relationship between our material culture and society that inspired a generation of designers to engage with wider social issues. Droog's Do Create project in 2000 illustrates this approach by inviting designers to explore more participative relationships between products and consumers. The outcome was a series of designs that call upon each owner to make the product unique to them, thus building-in greater personal meaning and longevity (fig 1.14).

Rapidly rising greenhouse gas emissions soon became the greatest cause of global environmental concern in the 1990s as the world population reached 6 billion, a 500% increase in 70 years, and the BRICCS economies were growing apace. This led to the UN Kyoto Protocol (1997) that set legally binding GHG reductions of 5% from 1990 figures between 2005 and 2012, and in 2012 the Doha Amendments set a target of 18% reduction between 2012 and 2020. Following on from Kyoto and Doha, the Paris Agreement on Climate Change (2016) achieved the greatest level of international consensus yet: 197 countries have agreed to binding CO_2 reduction targets and support mechanisms for poorer countries beginning from 2020, with the aim of keep warming below 1.5°C, or 2.0°C at worst. Despite some countries' official withdrawal, it seems that the rest of the world is moving forward with this objective.[60]

of the pyramid, including frugal design and the continuing work of the charity he established, Practical Action (formerly ITDG) (see Chapter 3.3).

The momentum of the 1970s led to greater international environmental cooperation, with one of the biggest successes being the UNEP-led Montreal Protocol in 1987 where 150 countries agreed to reduce and phase out ozone-depleting substances (ODS). The most recent official assessment concludes that the ozone layer is recovering and should reach 1980 levels by 2050.[59] In the same year, the Bruntland Report *Our Common Future* provided the seminal definition of sustainable development and clearly established the interconnection between the state of the environment and socio-economic actions. This report set the scene for the Rio Earth summit in 1992 where 154 countries signed the 'Rio declaration' that established the 'Polluter Pays' and 'Precautionary Principle' (see Chapter 2.1/2.4), the UN Framework Convention on Climate Change (UNFCCC) and Agenda 21, a global plan for local grassroots action.

Meanwhile, as the effects of climate change increased, its deep unfairness became clearer, with the poorest countries being most heavily affected due to their geographical locations and inability to mitigate. At the same time the realisation that large amounts of power had shifted from national governments to global corporations controlling the equivalent of half of the 100 largest economies was dawning.[61] Naomi Klein's *No Logo* (1999) exposed the rise of global corporate power, their unethical practices and pointed to the World Trade Organisation (WTO 1995) as the instrument for forcing trade agreements that favour the interests of large corporations over poorer developing countries and their workers. In the same year as her book appeared, the anti-globalisation movement protests started forcing positive concessions, but these advances were set back by the 9/11 attacks. Ultimately, the bailout of the banks by taxpayers during the global banking crisis of 2007 only served to prove the 'too big to fail' power of the financial corporations over national governments and citizens, sparking a new wave of protests through the Occupy movement (fig 1.15).

ENTERTAINING CUBE:

THIS WHOLE SERIES OF CUBES IS CONSTRUCTED OF 2"×2" DOUGLAS FIR OR PINE AND ¾" PLYWOOD PANELS, PLUS ROPE, FABRICS, DOWELS, ETC. ALL THE CUBES ARE 8×8×8 FEET.

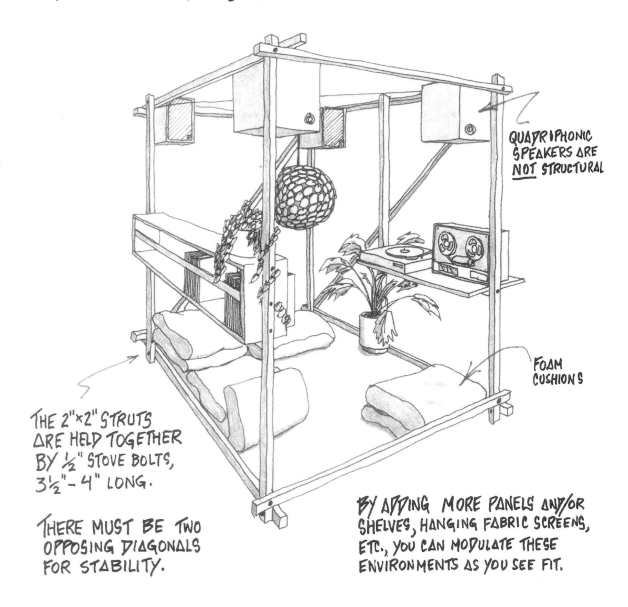

QUADRIPHONIC SPEAKERS ARE NOT STRUCTURAL

FOAM CUSHIONS

THE 2"×2" STRUTS ARE HELD TOGETHER BY ½" STOVE BOLTS, 3½"– 4" LONG.

THERE MUST BE TWO OPPOSING DIAGONALS FOR STABILITY.

BY ADDING MORE PANELS AND/OR SHELVES, HANGING FABRIC SCREENS, ETC., YOU CAN MODULATE THESE ENVIRONMENTS AS YOU SEE FIT.

note: FOR BUBBLE LAMP, SEE PAGE 111

Figure 1.13 The Entertaining Cube was part of a series of Living Cubes designed by James Hennessey and Victor Papanek (1973). They created spaces-within-spaces that could be self-built in rundown rentals, and knocked down for true low-budget nomadic living. (illustration Hennessey and Papanek courtesy Papanek Foundation, University of Applied Art, Vienna & James Hennessey)

Figure 1.14 In Do Break, part of Droog's Do Create exploration (2000), Frank Tjepkema and Peter van der Jagt invite the new owner of their vase to throw or crush it in order to create their own unique crazed surface. (photo courtesy Frank Tjepkema and Droog, Amsterdam)

In contrast, the new millennium was seized upon as a moment of optimism and change, with ambitious plans to improve the state of the world, particularly in developing countries. The UN Millennium Development Goal 1 (MDG1) achieved its target to halve poverty before 2015, largely due to China's rapid development. In the 2000s, sustainability in the form of Corporate Social Responsibility (CRS) became mainstream talk in boardrooms and the media, but significant change was still rare. As governments and businesses gave the excuse that cleaner technologies were 'too expensive' or 'not economic',

economist Nicholas Stern modelled the economic scenarios of global warming. In the *Stern Report* (2006), he demonstrated that early investment in low carbon technologies to reduce global warming would be by far the cheapest option compared with remedial actions. This report made many governments and business leaders sit up and take note, and in 2008 the world's first Climate Change Law setting national targets for GHG reductions and preparation for climate change risks was passed in the UK.

Figure 1.15 WTO protests, Seattle 1999, and Occupy Wall Street protests, New York 2011. (photo courtesy Seattle Municipal Archives and Joe Tabcaca / Shutterstock.com)

Figure 1.16 The UN's 17 Sustainable Development Goals set new targets from 2016 to 2030. The onus for achieving the SDGs shifts to collaborative business, government and NGO initiatives. (graphic courtesy United Nations)

Paul Hawken's *The Ecology of Commerce* (1993) and *Natural Capitalism* (1999), co-authored with Amory and Hunter Lovins, predicted the next industrial revolution. This would be governed by radical resource productivity, a shift from goods to services and investment in natural and human capital. Jeremy Rifkin elaborated this concept further in *The Third Industrial Revolution* (2011) into a clear plan to transition our energy infrastructure away from carbon dependence to green technologies governed by an Internet-enabled, post-carbon, distributed economy. Governments and companies, including the European Union (EU), are adopting aspects of this plan strategically. Like the two previous industrial revolutions, a shift in energy source and communication technology is the catalyst, but this time it is driven by the imperative of halting global warming (see Chapter 4.2).

Since the Rio summit of 1992, the UN has continued to play a central role in furthering sustainable development with the Johannesburg Summit 2002 and Rio+20 in 2012. This last summit resulted in the document *The Future We Want*, prioritising support for building green economies and finding new measures of wealth to replace GDP that recognise social and environmental capital. It has also followed up the successes of the MDGs with 17 ambitious Sustainable Develop Goals (SDG) agreed to by 193 nations. These include 'No Poverty', 'Zero Hunger' and 'Sustainable Cities and Communities' (fig 1.16). Finally, the monitoring reports on the state of the Earth produced by the UN's various bodies (IPCC, WHO, UNEP, FAO, ILO) have become authoritative tools in informing

policy and increasingly bringing pressure to bear on governments and companies around the world.

In assessing the current movement towards sustainability, we can certainly say that we have come a long way in awareness-raising and our understanding of what sustainable co-existence on the planet might entail. The major reports on climate change and the state of the planet (IPCC5, UNEP's GEO-5, WWF's *Living Planet Report*) are clear that as time progresses the possibility of restoration diminishes and we move to mitigation strategies. Despite this, they are also cautiously optimistic and unanimous in stating that strong action needs to be taken *now* through decisive leadership supported by universal participation from the citizens across the planet if we are to avert a catastrophe. It is up to designers to help make those actions easier and more effective.

In his book *2052*, Jorgen Randers, one of the original authors of the *Limits to Growth*, gives his own predictions of where we will be in 40 years' time. He concludes that we will live in a compromised world that he describes as a 'mild crash with our global limits' because we won't have taken decisive action early enough.

> *If I could persuade you of one thing, it should be this: the world is small and fragile, and humanity is huge, dangerous and powerful [...] this is the perspective we need to take if we're to be sure that sustainability emerges or, at least that the world as we know it survives for a couple of hundred more years.*[62]

1.4 obstacles, challenges and key players for change

With the earlier snapshot we took of the main threats to life on the planet and a historic perspective of the sustainability movement, it is now helpful to identify the main obstacles to sustainability and who holds the levers of power for change. Analysis of our current predicament suggests that the problem lies both at the level of the systems and attitudes we have locked ourselves into and of basic human nature. Time and again, we humans demonstrate a capacity for deep empathy, generosity, ingenuity and wisdom as well as singular short-sightedness and stupidity, often against our own best interests. However, since designers are very well trained in translating obstacles into creative opportunities, the following list of key impediments to greater sustainability goes hand-in-hand with some challenges designers may wish to explore.

- a lack of visionary leadership and governance able to prioritise long-term strategies and global collective benefits
  how can we foster and support long-term thinking strategies with collective benefits at all the interfaces of our design practice?
- a lack of a true understanding of the interdependencies between economic success and environmental and social wellbeing, and the ability to manage this complexity
  how can we foster and embed more whole-life systemic thinking at an intuitive and analytical level in our design process?
- an economic system that depends on 'growth' to work, effectively creating a Ponzi scheme where we pay for today's 'goods' with tomorrow's environmental and social capital
  how can design help decouple environmental damage from economic value creation, and natural and social capital be acknowledged in the costs and benefits of the products we create and consume?
- GDP used as the principal measure of economic development, and the assumption that wellbeing and prosperity are directly proportional to income
  how can society prosper without increased GDP or resource growth, and what might this look like?
- our sense of identity and 'happiness' is bound up with a culture of consumption and possessions
  how can we create a sense of personal self-worth and wellbeing disconnected from consumption and aligned with sustainable values?
- a lack of direct links between the effects of individual actions at a local level and their collective consequences at a global level
  how can we make the intangible more tangible to change behaviours and inform choices?

- an increasing lack of connection between people, the natural environment and the origins and impacts of what they consume
  how do we create a bond of understanding and appreciation between urban dwellers and the environment upon which they depend?

In order for designers to engage effectively in the transition to sustainability, they must understand where the real power and routes to change lie and where they can use their skills strategically to influence outcomes. Below we take a brief look at the key players, their spheres of influence and power, and the constraints acting upon them.

citizens and grassroots

At the base of the power structure is every individual person and citizen living on the planet. You and me. The grassroots. At over 7.7 billion people this is by far the biggest group and when we act collectively we are the most powerful. This power is expressed through individual daily actions as well as bigger life choices in what we buy or don't buy, what we support, and what we dedicate our lives to. Whether it is to walk or cycle rather than drive, turn the thermostat up or down, fly away for that weekend break, eat less meat or do a kindness every day, collectively these actions quickly add up. We elect governments in democratic countries, lobby through petitions and protests, and can be active at the grassroots level in our local communities. Our weakness is that we need to be watered, fed and sheltered. Our psychological make-up is also vulnerable to instruments of persuasion and manipulation, preying upon fear and self-gratification, but it can also call upon our higher instincts of fairness and collaboration. Our power is in our numbers and the collective impact of our choices. If we don't buy a product it fails; if we don't vote for a leader they aren't elected. If we all demand change it will happen, and the age of peer-to-peer communication is enabling that power. Every designer is also a citizen.

non-governmental and not-for-profit organisations

NGOs and NFPs are very important organisations for change, as they amplify grassroots voices most directly. They generally have humanitarian, social or environmental aims, often represent marginalised groups that don't have a voice in government or business, and take action in areas that fall between the cracks of social and economic support structures. For NGOs, independence from governments and business is crucial, as this allows them to focus on their primary goals and take a longer term view. For this reason, they enjoy a very high level of public trust. Because of their range of causes, they also involve a wide range of professions, including scientists, medics, lawyers, engineers, designers, politicians, economists, educators, media and the arts, etc. Traditionally, this group has been renowned for mobilising mass support, raising awareness and inspiring change through

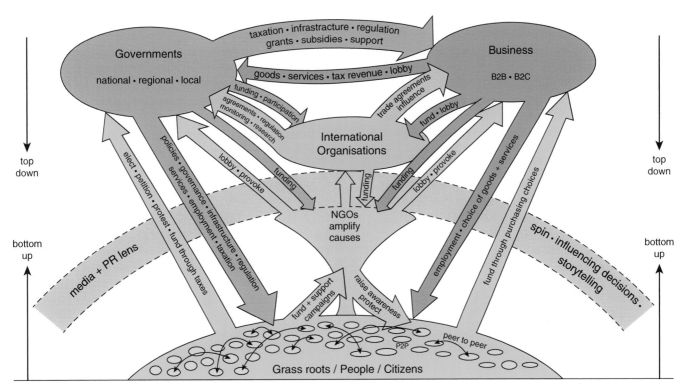

Figure 1.17 Key players for sustainability: spheres of influence and flows of power. (source: Jane Penty)

media stunts and campaigns. But more recently this sector has established relationships in hybrid organisations that are designing and delivering enabling products, technologies and training for more effective change for the base of the pyramid.

governments

Whether elected or imposed, local, regional or national governments provide a framework of common rules that regulate society and business. They are also responsible for infrastructure and services such as transport, energy, communication, justice, education and health. Directly or indirectly, this makes them the biggest consumer of products and services and their choices affect how we experience our day-to-day lives. Their purchasing power comes directly from the taxes they raise from ordinary people, businesses, transactions and national assets. Through their policies, taxation and regulation they have the power to incentivise change but they are also vulnerable to short-termism if they only think as far as the next election or sound bite. In the worst of cases, governments are self-serving and corrupt, and in the best, they can be a force for good. In any case, they have a difficult balancing act.

business

The majority of our daily activities and needs are met by goods and services provided by commercial companies (private or

shareholder owned), public services (taxpayer funded) or social enterprises and cooperatives (stakeholder owned) which we will call businesses. Private companies are seen as the source of innovation and enterprise but public trust in them is running very low. With maximising profits for shareholders seen as their primary objective, public image and accountability are becoming more and more important, and many businesses are engaging in Environmental, Social and Corporate Governance reporting. In reality, most trade happens business-to-business (B2B) and is subject to procurement policies. Many of these policies are pushing companies to meet higher environmental standards and have more transparent supply chains. In addition, government regulations for the supply of goods and services are there ostensibly to protect end users. However, the globalisation of companies has meant that many have more economic power than a good number of national governments, seriously compromising democratic processes.

inter-governmental organisations

International and inter-governmental organisations such as the UN play a very influential role in bringing issues into the public eye through their data gathering and monitoring reports and by creating high-level forums for discussion and collaboration between governments, businesses, scientists, academics and grassroots NGOs. Constrained by voluntary funding from national governments and donations, collaboration, information and an appeal to our humanity seem to be their strongest weapons. However, in extreme cases they also have the power of sanctions through international courts.

Poised as they are to take a global overview beyond national and regional self-interests, they have been a very strong force for change and a constant reminder around the world of the big ethical and environmental issues we have yet to resolve.

Figure 1.17 attempts to illustrate the interrelation between the different players. While this is inevitably an oversimplification, it shows how no single agent holds the balance of power. If anything, individual people acting collectively may have the greatest leverage. This implies that significant change can only happen if the key players develop and share common goals and collaborate in their execution. It is also a reminder that the very structures that are impediments to living within the planet's limits have been created by humans, and therefore can also be altered by humans. However, it will take grassroots action met by committed leaders, with 'big 'picture' thinking to effect this change.

co-designing sustainability

It is clear that designers alone will not change the world, but addressing issues and providing a physical expression of alternative values is important. The designers and design movements that have stood up for more equitable social, environmental and economic values were often ahead of their time with only some of their designs and attitudes percolating into the mainstream. However, they demonstrate that objects have powerful narratives and a lasting presence capable of influencing behaviours. Through artefacts, designers can give tangible expression and form to abstract collective ideas, philosophies and ideals, and make them the physical touchpoints of sustainable solutions.

In whatever context we work as product designers, from large corporations through to 'design activism', it is important to be aware of the particular skill set we bring through our design process. This fosters new ways of looking at problems, handling disparate demands and embodying these in physical touchpoints for these solutions. Our training is well suited to solving problems around sustainability thanks to the following capabilities:

- bringing a creative and intuitive mind that is curious, questions the 'obvious' and makes new connections to redefine the 'problem'
- generating insights through immersive research and empathic understanding of contexts people, needs and behaviours
- using redefinition and insights as the springboard for creative innovation

- using divergent thinking and synthesising of multiple demands to generate 'solutions'
- making it 'real', not being afraid to fail and getting it 'right' through physical experimentation, development, iteration, testing and prototyping
- involving stakeholders throughout the process to generate and validate new design ideas
- closing the loop by thinking in terms of whole product ecology with inbuilt service and support feedback loops that enable ongoing relationships with users
- creating new narratives and getting these to the right audiences

Looking at the big picture of key players (fig 1.17), where can product designers most influence sustainability? Traditionally designers have worked in or for private business and large corporations where their role is to increase commercial advantage through innovation and added aesthetic value. This is still the sector where product designers are most engaged and where a combination of small incremental changes peppered with more radical and disruptive innovations can make a very big difference over time.

Increasingly, however, as the world of products has shifted from stand-alone goods to product service systems (PSS), product designers are applying their skills not only to physical products but also to service design. This has opened up much greater involvement in other non-traditional sectors, including public service and infrastructure industries such as transportation, education, health and social care. NGOs and social enterprise sectors are another area where they are beginning to have a direct role in designing services and products for such areas as disaster relief, medical aid and sanitation. But perhaps the newest opportunities for designers to make a direct difference have come through the Internet with the peer-to-peer (P2P) access to audiences and finance, creating new scope for designers to become entrepreneurs. Designers need to harness all these opportunities to introduce more sustainable alternatives to our old models and imagine new ones.

In conclusion, acting sustainably is simple but difficult. Simple, because essentially it is about one-planet living; difficult, because our actions are constrained by economic, political, cultural and physical systems that are preventing these behaviours from becoming the norm. Even the simplest sustainable solutions involve a deep understanding of the complexity of the product's eco-system. Although product designers are trained in a robust design process that turns problems into opportunities and tangible solutions, this in itself does not create a sustainable practice. To become more sustainable as product designers, we need to question our practice, be informed and infuse every step of our design process with sustainable thinking. In Part 2 we look in more detail at sustainable strategies and approaches from a broad range of perspectives.

Finally, as designers, we need to have a vision to work towards. A vision where we contribute to a planet where 7.7 billion people live equitably from what the planet can produce and replenish, and in harmony with the other 30+ billion species. A vision where designers are more than just peons in the game of producing artefacts but active players in reshaping the nature and systems of consumption and production and the distribution of resources.

Chapter summary

1. We live in an unsustainable world caused by human activity. In the past 40 years, population and CO_2 emissions have more than doubled, wild species are down by over two-thirds and, since 1970, the human consumption of resources has exceeded the Earth's bio-capacity to replenish itself by 75%. Despite our overconsumption, over two-thirds of the world's population struggle to get by, let alone fulfil their potential owing to deprivation and lack of social security.

2. Climate change is our single biggest problem. It is now a climate emergency that threatens to destabilise all our economic, social and environmental systems. Its effects are growing exponentially, and unless global warming is kept below 2°C there is an increasing probability of an unpredictable catastrophic tipping point.

3. Together, global warming, resource depletion and loss of biodiversity are caused by overconsumption and destructive production. Yet we seem locked into these via an economic system that does not cost social or environmental capital and is led by short-term economic and political decision-making. If humans have created the problem they can also solve it, unless we let it go too far. However, this requires a globally and locally united vision of new ways to live on the planet supported by long-term strategies, regulations and collaboration, all of which designers can help shape.

4. The Earth and humans are part of a complex system, so achieving greater sustainability involves a complex set of interdependencies. For the sake of simplification these are most commonly grouped into three dimensions or pillars: environmental, social and economic. From this we can say that sustainable products are products that create net value socially, economically and environmentally. They are products that give more than they take.

5. In order to create more sustainable products, designers must shift their emphasis from the object to finding the best ways of meeting needs that may or may not be facilitated through products. This approach allows for more holistic thinking that encompasses the wider context of use and product ecosystem. And when the experiences facilitated through products produce *net positive value* over their negative impacts through their whole life, we begin to have sustainable product design.

6. The sustainability movement has its origins in the protests against unchecked environmental destruction and social injustices caused by the first Industrial Revolution. These concerns continued to grow throughout the twentieth century until the 1980s when connecting environmental, economic and social issues was recognised as essential for sustainable development.

7. Whether leading or following, from the Arts and Crafts movement to the Bauhaus, from the 'Back to the Earth movement' to eco, green and socially conscious design, many designers have and are challenging the reckless environmental destruction, social inequality, rampant consumerism and unthinking technological change by giving physical form and expression to alternative ways of living and consuming.

8. Significant change to a more sustainable planet can only happen if all key players, grassroots citizens, governments, private, public and not-for-profit sectors develop common goals and collaborate in their execution. While no single agent holds the balance of power, of all these groups, individual people acting collectively could ultimately hold the greatest leverage if they can unite and realise their power.

9. Product designers' unique contribution to sustainability over other professions lies in turning abstract theory and ideas into reality through the physical and psychological experiences afforded by objects. But this in itself does not create sustainable design. To become more sustainable, we need to question our practice and infuse every step of our design process with sustainable thinking. At the same time the range of non-traditional sectors and opportunities for designers to develop products is expanding and should be fully exploited.

Notes

1 IPCC (October 2018) Global Warming of 1.5°C.

2 Stern, N. (2018) We Must Reduce Greenhouse Gas Emissions to Net Zero or Face More Floods. Nicholas Stern | Environment | *The Guardian*, 8 October [online]. Available at www.theguardian.com/environment/2018/oct/08/we-must-reduce-greenhouse-gas-emissions-to-net-zero-or-face-more-floods (accessed 10 January 2019).

3 Burke, M.,S.Hsiang and E. Miguel (2015) Climate and Conflict. *Annual Review of Economics*, 7, pp. 577–561. doi: 10.1146/annurev-economics-080614-115430.

4 Gandhi, M. (1947) quoted in Pyarelal (1958) *Mahatma Gandhi – The Last Phase*, Ahmedabad: Navajivan Publishing House.

5 World Commission on Environment and Development (1987) *Our Common Future*, Oxford: Oxford University Press, section I, 3. 27 [online]. Available at www.un-documents.net/our-common-future.pdf/.

6 IPCC (2013) WG1 Summary for Policymakers. In *Climate Change 2013: The Physical Science Basis*. Contribution of Working Group I to the Fifth Assessment Report of the Intergovernmental Panel on Climate Change, ed. T.F. Stocker, D. Qin, G-K. Plattner, M. Tignor, S.K. Allen, J. Boschung, A. Nauels, Y. Xia, V. Bex and P.M. Midgley, Cambridge and New York: Cambridge University Press, p. 3. Available at www.ipcc.ch/report/ar5/wg1/ (accessed 2 July 2018).

7 World Meterological Organisation (2018) *WMO Statement on the State of the Global Climate 2017*. WMO No.1212. p.4.

8 WHO (2018) Climate Change and Health [online, 1 February]. Available at www.who.int/news-room/fact-sheets/detail/climate-change-and-health (accessed 10 January 2019).

9 Carbon Briefing (2017) Mapped: How Climate Change Affects Extreme Weather around the World [online, 6 July]. Available at www.carbonbrief.org/mapped-how-climate-change-affects-extreme-weather-around-the-world (accessed 4 July 2018).

10 IPCC (2013) IPCC WGI AR5 Summary for Policymakers, 2013, E8, p. 27.

11 IPCC (2014) IPCC Working Group III AR5 Summary for Policy Makers, p. 6 [online]. Available at http://report.mitigation2014.org/spm/ipcc_wg3_ar5_summary-for-policymakers_approved.pdf (accessed 2 July 2018).

12 IPCC (2014) IPCC Working Group II AR5 Summary for Policy Makers, pp. 11–20 [online]. Available at http://ipcc-wg2.gov/AR5/images/uploads/WG2AR5_SPM_FINAL.pdf (accessed 2 July 2018)

13 OEDC/IEA (2018) *Global Energy & CO$_2$ Status Report 2017*, Paris: International Energy Agency, p.1 [online]. Available at www.iea.org/publications/freepublications/publication/GECO2017.pdf.

14 Ceballos, G. *et al.* (2017) Biological Annihilation via the Ongoing Sixth Mass Extinction Signalled by Vertebrate Population Losses and Declines. *Proceedings of the National Academy of Sciences*. 201704949 [online]. Available at https://doi.org/10.1073/pnas.1704949114.

15 WWF (2018) *Living Planet Report – 2018: Aiming Higher*, ed. Grooten, M. and Almond, R.E.A., Gland, Switzerland: WWF.

16 IUCN (2015) The IUCN Red List of Threatened Species Summary [online]. Available at www.iucn.org/sites/dev/files/import/downloads/iucn_brochure_low_res.pdf (accessed 4 July 2018).

17 Secretariat of the Convention of Biological Diversity (2010) Global Diversity Outlook 3, Montreal [online]. Available at www.cbd.int/doc/publications/gbo/gbo3-final-en.pdf.

18 WWF (n.d.) Forests| *WWF* [online]. Available at www.panda.org/our_work/forests/ (accessed 4 July 2018).

19 Rainforest Foundation (n.d.) *Forest Facts* [online]. Available at www.rainforestfoundationuk.org/forest-facts (accessed 4 July 2018).

20 IUCN (2015).

21 Global Diversity Outlook 3 (2010).

22 FAO (2016) *2016 State of the World's Forests*, Rome: FAO.

23 See https://natureneedshalf.org/ and www.half-earthproject.org (accessed 4 July 2018).

24 Global Footprint Network (2010) *Ecological Footprint Atlas*, Oakland, CA, p.18 [online]. Available at www.footprintnetwork.org/images/uploads/Ecological_Footprint_Atlas_2010.pdf.

25 2016 data from Global Footprint Network (June 2019) *Open Data Platform* [online]. Available at http://data.footprintnetwork.org/#/countryTrends?type=earth&cn=2002 (accessed 16 June 2019).

26 UN DESA Population Division (2017) *World Population Prospects: The 2012 2017 Revision.Tables*, New York: UN [online]. Available at https://esa.un.org/unpd/wpp/Publications/Files/WPP2017_KeyFindings.pdf.

27 Teytleboym, A. *et al.* (18 May 2018) Natural Capital: Preventing the Economics of Mass Extinction [online]. Available at www.oxfordmartin.ox.ac.uk/opinion/view/408 (accessed 10 January 2019).

28 EASAC (March 2018) *Extreme Weather Events in Europe. Preparing for Climate Change Adaptation*. Halle, Germany: EASAC [online]. Available at https://easac.eu/fileadmin/PDF_s/reports_statements/Extreme_Weather/EASAC_Statement_Extreme_Weather_Events_March_2018_FINAL.pdf.

29 DARA and Climate Vulnerable Forum (2012) *Climate Vulnerability Monitor. A Guide to the Cold Calculus of a Hot Planet* (2nd edition) *Executive Summary*, Madrid: Fundacíon DARA International, p. 17 [online]. Available at www.daraint.org/wp-content/uploads/2012/10/CVM2-Low.pdf.

30 WHO (2018) Climate Change and Health [online, 1 February]. Available at www.who.int/news-room/fact-sheets/detail/climate-change-and-health (accessed 7 July 2018).

31 GAHP (2017) The Lancet Report on Pollution and Health. Summary [online]. Available at http://gahp.net/wp-content/uploads/2017/03/PE_InfoLancetSummary.pdf (accessed 5 July 2018).

32 Stern, Nicholas (2007) *The Economics of Climate Change. The Stern Review*, Cambridge and New York: Cambridge University Press, p. xv.

33 IPCC (2014) WGIIAR5 Technical Summary.

34 Rotman, D. (2016) Hotter Days Will Drive Global Inequality. MIT Technology Review [online]. Available at www.technologyreview.com/s/603158/hotter-days-will-drive-global-inequality/ (accessed 10 January 2019).

35 Soloman Hsiang, interviewed by David Rotman in *MIT Technology Review, December 2016* (based on Burke, M., Hsiang, S.M. and Miguel, E., *Nature* 527, pp. 235–239 (2015).

36 Oxfam (2013) *The Cost of Inequality: How Wealth and Income Extremes Hurt Us All*, Oxford: Oxfam Media Briefing, 18 January, pp. 2–4.

37 Milanovic, B. (2012) *Global Income Inequality by the Numbers: In History and Now – An Overview*, The World Bank: Policy Research Working Paper Series 6259, November, pp. 7–8, pp. 12–13 [online]. Available at http://elibrary.worldbank.org/doi/pdf/10.1596/1813-9450-6259.

38 ILO (2018) *Global Employment and Social Trends 2018*, Geneva: ILO, pp.1–3 [online]. Available at www.ilo.org/wcmsp5/groups/public/---dgreports/---dcomm/---publ/documents/publication/wcms_233953.pdf.

39 UNDP (2018) Poverty, United Nations Sustainable Development [online]. Available at www.un.org/sustainabledevelopment/poverty/ (accessed 10 January 2019).

40 UNDP (2018) Water and Sanitation, United Nations Sustainable Development [online]. Available at www.un.org/sustainabledevelopment/water-and-sanitation/ (accessed 10 January 2019).

41 ILO (2017) *World Social Protection Report*, 29 November, Geneva: ILO, p. xxix [online]. Available at www.ilo.org/wcmsp5/groups/public/---dgreports/---dcomm/---publ/documents/publication/wcms_604882.pdf.

42 Milanovic, B. (2012) *Global Income Inequality by the Numbers: In History and Now – An Overview*, The World Bank: Policy Research Working Paper Series 6259, November, pp. 7–8 and 12–13 [online]. Available at http://elibrary.worldbank.org/doi/pdf/10.1596/1813-9450-6259.

43 Alejo Vázquez Pimentel, D. *et al.* (2018) Reward Work, Not Wealth (for OXFAM) [online]. Available at http://hdl.handle.net/10546/620396.

44 ILO (2018) *Global Employment and Social Trends 2018*, p. 8.

45 UNICEF (2017) Child Labour [online, November]. Available at https://data.unicef.org/topic/child-protection/child-labour/ (accessed 10 January 2019).

46 WEF Global Risks (2014).

47 ILO, *Global Employment Trends* (2014).

48 Wilkinson, R. and K. Pickett (Eds.) (2010) *The Spirit Level. Why Equality is better for Everyone,* London: Penguin Books.

49 World Bank (2018) Year in Review: 2017 in 12 Charts [online]. Chart 4. Available at www.worldbank.org/en/news/feature/2017/12/15/year-in-review-2017-in-12-charts (accessed 3 January 2019).

50 WEF *Global Risks 2017 Report*, p.11.

51 See www.footprintnetwork.org/2018/04/11/three-visualizations-of-footprint-trends-1961-2014/.

52 Elkington, J. (1997) *Cannibals with Forks: The Triple Bottom Line for 21st Century Business*, Oxford: Capstone.

53 Walker, S. (2010) Stuart Walker Design – Quadruple Bottom Line of Sustainability [online]. Available at www.stuartwalker.org.uk/designs-2/10-quadruple-bottom-line-of-sustainability (accessed 28 June 2017).

54 Walker, S. (2006) *Sustainable by Design. Explorations in Theory and Practice*, London, and Sterling, VA: Earthscan, pp. 121–122.

55 Translated from Finsterbusch, S. (2016) Bauhaus Nr 1. *Frankfurter Allgemeine Sonntagzeitung*, Drinnen & Draussen, 12 August.

56 Anon (2018) Frankfurt Kitchen | Schütte-Lihotzky, Margarete (Grete) | V&A Search the Collections[online]. Available at http://collections.vam.ac.uk/item/O121079 (accessed 14 September 2018).

57 Packard, V. (1960) *The Waste Makers*, London: Pelican Books. p. 292.

58 Wackernagel, M. *et al.* (2010) *The Ecological Footprint Atlas 2010*,Oakland, CA: Global Footprint Network, p. 17.

59 World Meteorological Organization *et al.* (2015) Assessment for Decision Makers: Scientific Assessment of Ozone Depletion 2014 [online]. Available at www.esrl.noaa.gov/csd/assessments/ozone/2014/assessment_for_decision-makers.pdf (accessed 3 January 2019).

60 See United Nations Climate Change for Past and Current Agreements and Commitments [online]. Available at https://unfccc.int.

61 Akryoyd, Batt and Tolbert Thompson (2006) *The Oxford Handbook of Works and Organisation*, Oxford: Oxford University Press.

62 Adapted from Jorgen Randers' lecture in the tenth Annual Distinguished Lecture Series in Sustainable Development, University of Cambridge, 14 March 2012 [online]. Available at www.cisl.cam.ac.uk/resources/publication-pdfs/jorgen-randers-2052-a-global-forecast-for-the-next.pdf/view.

Key texts and further reading

a few seminal publications of the early environmental and sustainability movements

Brand, Stewart (1968–1972) *The Whole Earth Catalogue. Access to Tools*, Menlo Park,CA: Portola Institute. *The precursor to the Internet – 'the' sharing resource and 'access device' for the counterculture and those interested in living more in tune with the environment.*

Brown, Tim (2009) *Change by Design*, New York: Harper Business. *Extracts the essential qualities of the design thinking process used by product designers that can be applied more generally to problem-solving and innovation.*

Carson, Rachel (1962) *Silent Spring*, Boston, MA: Houghton Mifflin; London: Hamish Hamilton. *The bestselling seminal book exposing the disastrous effects of the widespread use of chemicals in agriculture and industry on wildlife, especially birds.*

Dresner, Simon (2002) *The Principles of Sustainability*, London: Earthscan. *Detailed account with good analysis of the beginnings and development of sustainable development.*

Fuad-Luke, Alistair (2009) *Design Activism*, London, and Sterling, VA: Earthscan. *A good overview of design as a force for social good with historic and current perspectives, case studies and possibilities for design activism.*

Fuller, Buckminster (1968) *Operating Manual for Spaceship Earth*, Carbondale: Southern Illinois University Press. *A cold, hard look at the Earth's dwindling resources and strategies for survival.*

Fuller, Buckminster (1981) *Critical Path*, New York :St. Martin's Press. *Fuller's summary of his lifetime's work and his concerns for the future of humanity.*

Hennessey, Jim and Victor Papanek (1974) *Nomadic Furniture 2*, New York: Pantheon Books (reprinted 2008 by Schiffer Publishing). *A collection of designs for furniture and lighting for flexible living that embody the ethos of the time by stepping lightly and being inventive and resourceful.*

Leopold, Aldo (1949) *A Sand County Almanac*, New York: Oxford University Press. *A compelling look at our relationship with nature and the necessity for a 'land ethic'.*

Meadows, Donella and Diana Wright (eds.) (2008) *Thinking in Systems. A Primer*, White River Junction,VT: Chelsea Green Publishing. *Covers the principles of systems thinking in an accessible and relevant way.*

Meadows, D., Randers, J. and Meadows, D. (1972) *Limits to Growth. Report to the Club of Rome*, White River Junction,VT: Chelsea Green Publishing. *Bestselling report that clearly demonstrated our level of environmental loss and resource depletion as unsustainable.*

Packard, Vance (1957) *The Hidden Persuaders*, New York: Pocket Books. *Exposes the psychological manipulation of the advertising industry to create ever more consumption.*

Packard, Vance (1960) *The Waste Makers*, New York: Vance Packard Inc. *Exposes America's relentless push for consumption of products with built-in obsolescence and no thought to its consequences.*

Papanek, Victor (1971) *Design for the Real World: Human Ecology and Social Change* (2nd edition 1985), New York: Pantheon Books. *The book that stirred up the design profession by advocating that product design should be a force for social and environmental good. Still inspirational.*

Papanek, Victor (1995) *The Green Imperative: Natural Design for the Real World*, New York: Thames and Hudson. *This book connects Papanek's earlier provocation on design for social good vs. unthinking consumption to sustainable design through product design and architecture.*

Ramakers, Renny (2002) *More + Less. Droog Design in Context*, Rotterdam: 010 Publishers. *An overview of Droog projects with insights into the designers' questioning and explorations.*

Schumacher, E.F. (1973) *Small is Beautiful*, London: Blond & Briggs. *Seminal book critiquing the unchecked pursuit of ever larger and more specialised industry and technology, and advocating Intermediate Technology (now known as Appropriate Technology) where 'Capital serves Man' rather than 'Man being enslaved to Capital'.*

Stern, Nicholas (2007) *The Economics of Climate Change. The Stern Review*, Cambridge and New York: Cambridge University Press. *Clear analysis and argument for the economic necessity to invest in stabilising temperatures by reducing GHG emissions, and investing in mitigation measures and the low-carbon economy.*

Whiteley, Nigel (1993) *Design for Society*, London: Reaktion Books. *A reaction to the 1980s design boom, this is a very good critique of design's weaknesses and its potential to create more value both socially and environmentally.*

World Commission on Environment and Development (1987) *Our Common Future*, Oxford: Oxford University Press. *Commonly referred to as the 'Bruntland Report' after Gro Harlem Bruntland, the Norwegian Prime Minister and Chair of the Commission. Provides a very clear and detailed analysis of the necessity to connect environment and human development that define the term 'sustainable development'.*

PART 2

Strategies, tools and approaches

The three chapters in Part 2 provide an overview of the principles underpinning sustainability, and the strategies, tools and approaches product designers can use to make their practice more sustainable, no matter what industry, level or stage of the design process they are involved in. In this sense, it is both an essential map and a menu which designers should be aware of and can use to select and adapt in the most relevant way to their practice. The strategies are grouped according to their environmental, social or economic focus. Although in reality design projects don't fit neatly into these categories, separating them helps break down some of the complexity around sustainability and shows how the same problem can be tackled from different perspectives. The examples chosen are primarily drawn from commercially available products, in recognition of the many challenges that must be overcome in developing a 'great concept' into a viable, more sustainable and successful product or service. While they serve to illustrate particular principles and approaches, above all they are there to inspire and to build upon in order to take the nascent practice of sustainable design forward.

CHAPTER 2
Environmentally led strategies

What makes a product environmentally sustainable and how can we tell if one design is more eco-friendly than another? The reality is that most impacts of a product are hidden from view in the story of its provenance, use and end of life, making this very hard to judge from appearances alone. This is why designers need to be armed with more than good intentions – they need a grasp of the essential principles that underpin products that are truly friends with the environment, how to make these a reality and communicate this at the point of purchase and later in use. From the early 'eco' and 'green' products of the 1990s, the understanding, science and tools needed to create more environmentally sustainable products and services have evolved considerably, from a focus on being *less bad* to one of creating *positive value* and of even being *restorative*.

This chapter introduces the essential principles and thinking for designing products that have a smaller footprint through to those that may positively benefit the environment. These practices are variously known as 'eco-design, 'green-design', Design for Environment (DfE) or Design for Sustainability (DfS). We also explore how these can be integrated into the design process with the help of some qualitative and quantitative tools. Finally, we contrast the potential of highly sophisticated emerging technologies and some of their simpler low-tech relatives to deliver the radical shift in resource intensity that we need if we are ever to have truly 'environmentally friendly' consumption for more than 9 billion people by 2050.

2.1 from less bad to better and positive: an overview of strategies and approaches

Over the past 40 years, two main schools of thought have evolved that may be applied to reducing the environmental impact of products. For the sake of simplicity these can be grouped under the umbrella terms of *eco-efficiency* and *eco-effectiveness*. In essence eco-efficiency is about reducing environmental impacts by achieving the same functionality with less energy and less material. Eco-effectiveness on the other hand takes a holistic systems approach to reduce impacts by eliminating all toxics and using circular models for energy and material flows that generate net environmental benefits in the long run. Table 2.1 compares the thinking behind both, and establishes their key principles and differences.

eco-efficiency: more with less

The term *eco-efficiency* was first coined in 1991 by the World Business Council for Sustainable Development (WBCSD), although the groundwork was laid in the 1980s. The practice and implementation of eco-efficiency, also known as resource-efficiency, has evolved considerably since then and is now considered a key strategy for Greenhouse Gas (GHG) emissions reduction and an important element of the 'low-carbon economy' (see Chapter 2.4). The main reasons why it has been widely accepted by business and governments are that it is readily quantifiable, offers obvious cost savings and, above all, does not significantly challenge existing business models or systems of consumption and production. This latter point is both its strength and its weakness.

To understand the basis of eco-efficiency we need to take a step back and look at the underlying causes of environmental damage. A good starting point is the well-established IPAT equation. Introduced by Paul Ehrlich and John Holden in 1991, it identifies the key sources of environmental impacts and sets out the relationship between them:

$I = P \times A \times T$
I = environmental impact
P = population
A = affluence or consumption / person
T = technology or impact / unit of consumption

Table 2.1 Side by side: eco-efficiency and eco-effectiveness

	eco-efficiency	eco-effectiveness
what	• maximise the resource efficiency of materials and energy through new technology to achieve the same functionality at a much lower environmental cost	• aim for net environmental benefit with zero waste and toxicity by modelling systems of production and consumption on natural cycles
why/rationale	• primarily a response to global warming, closely followed by depletion of non-renewable resources • there is a direct correlation between material and energy* consumption, carbon emissions and environmental damage • there are clear financial benefits • operates within existing economic mechanisms and relies on techno-solutions	• a response to our one-dimensional system of production and economics that does not account for socio-environmental consequences • looks beyond carbon emissions at all impacts on the biosphere where eco-destruction and toxicity are unacceptable • bases production and economic models on nature's intelligent systems to create maximum benefit for all
how/principles	• increase the efficiency and minimise the energy, material and resources needed for a given functionality • select the cleanest technologies, materials and processes that are economic • design-in the most optimal lifespan and lifecycle for a given function • minimise waste • design for disassembly and recyclability • continuously develop new technologies to achieve the same functionality more efficiently	• eliminate the concept of waste through circular biological and technological loops to preserve resources and protect the environment • remove all toxicity and develop beneficial substitutes • apply the precautionary principle before introducing any new materials • power with renewable forms of energy • rethink systems to create synergies between natural, human and economic needs • celebrate diversity • aim for abundance and not scarcity
subsets/related approaches	• eco-design, green design, design for the environment, radical resource efficiency: factor 4,10 and 20	• bio-mimicry, bio-thinking, cradle-to-cradle, circular economy, industrial ecology, regenerative design

*unless 100% renewable energy is used

If we interpret this equation at face value, it tells us that in order to reduce our environmental impacts we need to:

• reduce our population and hence overall demand
  and/or
• decrease consumption associated with affluence
  and/or
• reduce the intensity of our technologies and production

Because businesses hold little sway over population size **P**, and decreasing affluence **A** or consumption is not in their financial interests, they have naturally focused on what is in their control; that is, the choice of technology **T**. Eco-efficiency is effectively making technology and production processes cleaner and more efficient through design and innovation while still creating and satisfying demand for new products and services. From this point of view, eco-efficiency is a pragmatic solution for business that does not challenge the status quo. Likewise, product designers aren't in the business of reducing population but they can be instrumental in changing the nature and quantity of consumption by the 'affluent'.

It is worth noting that the IPAT equation does not give us solutions or apportion blame. Rather it points us towards the main levers we need to consider in addressing the problem. In this way, it allows room for different interpretations and multiple parallel approaches. As we see further ahead in the chapters on social and economic strategies, sustainably minded designers and economists are challenging the assumption that more affluence **A** must necessarily lead to higher environmental impacts. Instead it could depend on whether we can find alternative ways, through behaviour change and **T** (technologies), to meet our needs with lower impacts. Increasing consumption or GDP without increasing environmental impacts is known as *decoupling* (see Chapter 4.2) that we are beginning to see through the take-up of low-carbon technologies.

Another important question raised by the IPAT equation is: How much more efficient do we need to become to at least keep planet warming below 2°C? Factor 4 (75% reduction) and factor 10 (90% reduction) have been proposed at different times as necessary and achievable targets,[1] but where do these numbers come from? One way to calculate this is to use the IPAT equation and work backwards from our goal of delivering an acceptable quality of life to 9.7 billion people, the estimated peak population by 2050,[2] while reducing our CO_2 emissions to arrest global warming at 2°C, the maximum Paris Agreement target.

Joost Vogtländer[3] did just that by setting: our target for **I**mpact at 0.4 or 60% reduction in CO_2 from a 2004 baseline by 2050; peak **P**opulation at 9.7 billion;[4] and doubling **A**ffluence or wealth by allowing for the growth of middle classes in developing economies while remaining static in developed countries. The results show that we would need to reduce the carbon emissions of our technology by a factor of 7.7 by 2050 to arrest global warming at 2°C, without even considering the many other adverse environmental impacts of this consumption.

The big question for designers then is: What kinds of eco-efficiency improvements are achievable through products? Figure 2.1 looks at some of the most notable efficiency improvements in everyday products since 1990 from electric cars to LED lighting, laundry to music downloads, renewable energy to toilet flushing. It shows that apart from renewable energy and light bulb life, our best improvements are achieving between factor 1.3–7, somewhat short of the targets required to arrest global warming. It also tells us that renewably generated electricity has an efficiency factor of between 14 (solar PV Germany) and 91 (best case hydro Norway) over coal, giving an overall improvement of factor 20 to 30 over our current mix of electricity. This means that if we run lightweight electric vehicles and aircraft, LED bulbs and media downloads on renewable energy, *together* their factors would increase dramatically, making renewables the biggest eco-efficiency game changer related to products.

While this gives us a snapshot of how technology is working hard to reduce the impacts of consumption, we have to conclude that improving the resource-efficiency of products alone will not be enough to stop climate change, let alone begin to restore the biosphere. Experts agree that to not exceed the IPCC recommended target red line of 1.5°C, global emissions must halve by 2030 followed by a radical reduction to net zero by 2050.[5] In Project Drawdown, initiated by Paul Hawken, a team of researchers have modelled, quantified and listed in order the 100 most impactful *existing* technologies and initiatives that together can reverse our growing carbon emissions to net zero and even negative by 2050 and beyond.[6] These include measures for reducing and capturing carbon through electricity generation, food production, buildings and cities, land use, transport and materials. By also calculating the net cost to society and lifetime savings, Project Drawdown shows that these measures have the added benefit of improving lives, creating jobs, restoring the environment, enhancing security, generating resilience and advancing human health.

What is clear for designers is that we need to take every opportunity to include renewables and carbon-absorbing elements in our designs. But as we shall see, environmental impacts go far beyond just GHG emissions and techno-fixes. The IPAT equation makes it plain that we will also need to address 'how much', 'who', 'what' and 'how' we the wealthy consume, through behaviour change, the adoption of new lifestyles and new business models which we address in Chapters 3 and 4.

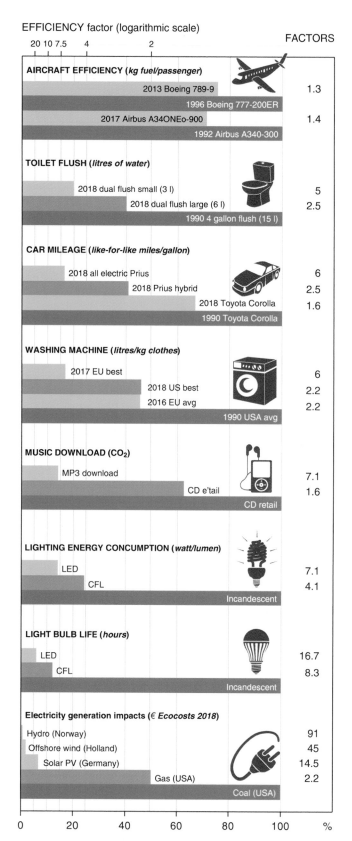

Figure 2.1 How much more eco-efficient have our everyday products become?

eco-effectiveness: eliminating negatives and generating positives

Many inspirational pioneers in sustainable thinking from business, design and science such as John Ehrenfeld, John Elkington, Paul Hawken, John Lyle and Walter Stahel,[7] to name a few, confirm the view that if we are to get anywhere near living within the planet's capacity, increasing our efficiency alone is not enough. In John Ehrenfeld's words:

> *Standard economic theory assumes that limitless resources will always be available as scarcity incentivizes sufficient innovation to produce substitutes. Carrying capacity simply does not enter the economic calculus. The present, clearly unsustainable state of the world trumps this theory, rendering eco-efficiency only a partially useful concept.*[8]

This analysis suggests that the problem is in the system itself, so we won't solve the problem by operating within the same system, as eco-efficiency attempts to do. Instead, eco-effectiveness says that if we are to design and live more sustainably, we need to look at all the drivers and their interrelationships that are locking us into unsustainable patterns of consumption and production. In short, we need to set ourselves more ambitious goals by applying systems thinking. The umbrella term *eco-effectiveness* encompasses a number of approaches each with their overlapping set of principles, including Industrial Ecology, Regenerative Design, Blue Economy, Circular Economy, Biomimicry and Cradle-to-Cradle (C2C). Here we will focus our attention on the last three, as they speak most directly to designers, and we will revisit the Circular Economy in Chapter 4.5.

"Unlike the Industrial Revolution, the Biomimicry Revolution introduces an era based not on what we can extract from nature, but on what we can learn from her."[9] Janine Benyus first introduced Biomimicry as a tool for designers in her highly influential book by the same name in 1997. It is defined as an approach to innovation that seeks sustainable solutions to human challenges by emulating nature's time-tested patterns and strategies.[10] Box 2.1 distils the ten design strategies of natural systems ready to be used as the ultimate model for sustainable design.

Walter Stahel first introduced the term Cradle-to-Cradle (C2C) in 1982 and together with John Lyle's complementary concept of Regenerative Design (1994)[11] it forms the foundations of what is now the Cradle-to-Cradle strategy. It was not until 2002 however that that these two elements were brought together and popularised by the chemist and architect team of Michael Braungart and William McDonough in their highly influential book *Cradle to Cradle* and further elaborated in *The Upcycle* (2013). The

Box 2.1 Biomimicry: the ten winning design strategies from complex, mature ecosystems

1. Use waste as a resource: *there is no waste in nature, everything is recycled*
2. Diversify and cooperate to fully use the habitat: *seek out and fill the gaps and niches in the system as opportunities to close loops*
3. Gather and use energy efficiently: *use nature's free and abundant source of energy, the sun, intelligently and efficiently*
4. Optimise rather than maximise: *shift the focus from quantity to quality*
5. Use materials sparingly: *only use what is needed and achieve the same with less*
6. Don't foul their nests: *production must be clean enough for us to live alongside it, leaving no room for toxics*
7. Don't draw down resources: *don't empty the bank account that took millions of years to build; instead work out how to build it up*
8. Remain in balance with the biosphere: *self-regulate human activity to a level compatible with our life-support system, the biosphere*
9. Run on information: *build in resilience through flexible and responsive feedback loops*
10. Shop locally: *connect and cooperate locally to reduce energy intensity and have a realistic chance of a circular economy*

source: Benyus, J. (1997) *Biomimicry*.

Cradle-to-Cradle framework and product certification program[12] that has emerged from this guides designers and manufacturers through a process of continual improvement in five categories: material health, material reutilisation, renewable energy and carbon management, water stewardship, and social fairness. Companies such as Method, Aveda, L'Oreal, Ahrend, Orange Box, Herman Miller and Steelcase have used whole company or product certification processes to develop and demonstrate their sustainability credentials.

What Biomimicry and Cradle-to-Cradle have in common is a strategy for design that models its systems of production on nature to create synergies between the different elements of the system, within and without. They share the principles of moving to zero toxicity, creating cycles that eliminate waste and using renewable energy to power all processes. But more importantly they challenge designers and anyone involved in the business of providing goods and services to seek collaborative opportunities to create net positives and abundance as nature already does by designing intelligent systems that can regenerate themselves. McDonough and Braungart named this eco-effectiveness.[13]

A good example of eco-effectiveness in action is the design of Interface's carpet tiles. Ray Anderson, their CEO, and designer David Oakley fully embraced the biomimicry model in a bid to become radically more sustainable. Interface's pioneering Entropy range (2000), which evolved into i2, imitates the random combination of patterns found in nature, allowing the tiles to be interchangeable. This reduces waste considerably at the laying stage and extends carpet life because the tiles can be rearranged to even out wear patterns. They also replaced the toxic PVC and fibreglass tile backing with 100% recycled nylon and eliminated adhesives so that they can be reconfigured, replaced and fed back into their REentry recycling programme since 1995. The result is a much more sustainable system and a game-changing aesthetic, product and business model that transformed the whole contract carpet industry[14] (fig 2.2).

Figure 2.2 By mimicking nature's random patterns, Interface's i2 carpet tiles extend product life and reduce waste through being randomly repositionable to even wear and allow individual replacement. (photo courtesy Interface Inc.)

2.2 thinking in systems and designing for lifecycles

Whether the intention is to be eco-efficient or eco-effective, one of the fundamental strategies that now underpins all environmentally minded design approaches is *lifecycle thinking*. Here, products and services are seen as a continuous flow of material and energy rather than as stand-alone objects. This is fully embodied in the concept of the *circular economy* that is rapidly gaining traction as a pragmatic business model. In China the notion of the circular economy appeared in official policy as early as 2002 and law in 2009, and in Europe it is now part of a phased action plan[15] (see Chapter 4.5 on the circular economy).

Using lifecycle information to guide and inform the design of products is known as Life Cycle Design (LCD). The lifecycle of a product is essentially an inventory of all the energy, materials and by-products that go *into* and come *out* of the creation and use of a product. To make it more manageable, it is normally broken down into *phases* and is typically represented by a lifecycle diagram. It begins at the *material phase* with the extraction and processing of raw materials that feed the *manufacturing phase* where product parts are made, assembled and packaged. That

is the cycle to the *factory gate*. From there, the lifecycle moves into the *distribution phase* that includes transportation and sales activity, and then into its active life, the *use phase*. Finally, once it has no useful life left, it moves to the *end-of-life* phase for repurposing, reprocessing or dumping. Figure 2.3 shows a generic lifecycle and highlights the main issues designers need to consider at each stage with recommendations for design actions. From this analysis we can conclude that the biggest elements preventing product lifecycles from being more environmentally sustainable are: water and fossil fuel energy inputs; the use and release of toxic substances through the specification of materials and processes; virgin material inputs, especially non-renewable; needlessly short product lives, and the lack of circular infrastructure for recycling materials back into new products.

mapping lifecycles and benchmarking

Ultimately, the purpose of Life Cycle Design (LCD) is to reduce the overall negative impacts of a product. This is achieved by first understanding *what* and *where* in the cycle they occur: this is known as *lifecycle mapping* or *hotspot* identification. Ideally, this should happen at the beginning of a project, so that it can be used as the basis for strategies to reduce or eliminate the worst

A generic product lifecycle

distribution & sales phase

includes all the energy, resources and damage to human health and
eco-systems damage from:
  marketing, distribution and product service
determined by:
  supply chain location, market and available infrastructure
choose:
  renewable energy powered transport
  lowest environmental and social impact mode of transport
  (see transportation rule of thumb)
avoid:
  only looking at distance travelled – transport mode may have a
  much bigger impact
compare:
  alternative geographical locations for suppliers and distribution
  modes available using LCIAs
consider:
  the 'last mile' of transport

manufacturing & assembly phase

includes all the energy, resources and damage to human health
and eco-systems from:
  manufacturing all the product parts, assembly and packaging
fixed during concept and detail design stages
  closely connected to material choice
  a balance between performance, aesthetics and costs
choose:
  least energy and water intensive processes
  lowest emissions
  renewable energy
avoid:
  processes that create toxic releases to air, water and land at
  any stage
compare:
  the impacts of your options using LCIAs
consider:
  factory location and working conditions
  impact of transportation between production, assembly and
  final destination

product use phase

includes all the energy, resources and damage to human health and
eco-systems from:
  the product in use
determined by:
  design and product quality, after sales service, the technology
  chosen, user behaviours
choose:
  most energy and resource efficient technologies
design in:
  interfaces that make the most efficient use the easiest and most
  pleasurable
  optimal or extended lifespan through:
  quality & classic aesthetics
  cultural resonance and meaning
  service support
  upgradability
  repairability
avoid:
  pollution to air, water or land in use
consider & compare:
  alternative user scenarios and their impacts

material processing phase

includes all the energy, resources and damage to human
health and eco-systems from:
  extraction, harvesting, recycling and processing materials
  ready for manufacturing
fixed during concept and detail design stages
  a balance between functionality, aesthetics and costs
choose:
  recycled over virgin
  renewable over non-renewable virgin
  recyclable over non-recyclable
avoid:
  non-recyclable
  materials with toxic releases at any stage
compare:
  the impacts of your options using LCIAs (Life cycle
  inventory databases)
  reference material selection, rules of thumb
consider material provenance:
  environmental record, conflict materials, labour conditions

end of usable life phase

includes all the energy, resources and damage to human health
and eco-systems from:
  the product after its usable life
determined by:
  material choices, product assembly details and
  infrastructure to support reuse and recovery.
choose:
  recyclable materials with supporting recycling infrastructures
design for, in order of benefits:
  re-use, multi-use, sharing
  remanufacture
  repair
  disassembly into biological, technical and toxic materials
  recycling: closed loop
  upcycling
  downcycling: open loop
  composting & anaerobic digestion
avoid:
  dumping, land fill & incineration
compare and consider:
  alternative existing end of life scenarios in the contexts of use

Figure 2.3 A generic product lifecycle with design and environmental considerations for each phase. (source: Jane Penty) of these impacts. If we are redesigning a product, mapping its lifecycle establishes a *benchmark* that the design team can use to pinpoint the specific places in the lifecycle over which they have some control and where there is most potential for improvement, so that they can focus their creative energy on these areas. Of course, these improvements also need to be integrated with the wider performance and marketing specification. Once established, the lifecycle benchmark acts as a reference throughout the design process to help keep sustainability targets on track. Similarly, when we are designing new products, mapping and comparing the lifecycle of products that offer a similar functionality can help spot opportunities for more radical innovation.

Not surprisingly, when we map the lifecycles of products that deliver similar functionalities, we find that they also share a similar distribution of impacts across their lifecycles. As figure 2.4 shows, regularly used electrical equipment, white goods and motorised transportation products have their biggest impacts in the *use phas*e while for furniture and packaging this is in the *material* and *production phases*. The comparison between the lifecycle impacts of the best- and worst-case washing machines also shows us just how much design and technology can help reduce a product's footprint. The other point designers should take away from these lifecycle comparisons is that the *how* and *where* the product is consumed or used can have a very big effect on the use and end-of-life phases. As we shall see in Chapter 3, there are important opportunities in the design of products to influence use behaviours. More specific issues associated with different product typologies are discussed in detail in Chapters 5 to 8.

For product designers, thinking in lifecycles fundamentally changes the way we approach design and the way we look at products forever. It does this by making us acutely aware of the hidden life and impacts of products, from the provenance of the materials to the labour in the supply chain, and from pollution in production and use to its fate when it is discarded. LCD acknowledges that all products and services are part of a much bigger system that includes the environment, technology, business models, supply chains and user behaviours, and that all the elements of the system need to play their part in supporting sustainable outcomes. It also points to the fact that strategic design decisions taken in the early stages of the design process that are informed by the bigger lifecycle picture have a much greater impact on how sustainable a product will be than decisions taken during later stages. By the detail design stage most factors, including cost, are locked in, leaving the designer with very little wriggle room. The bigger picture that LCD affords encourages us to set ambitious goals, but it also requires that we establish achievable intermediate targets and have quantifiable data on which to base our decisions.

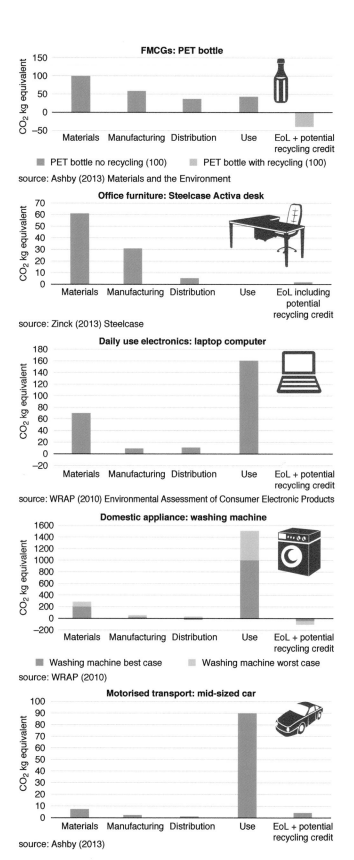

Figure 2.4 Typical CO_2 lifecycle impact distributions and hotspots for different product typologies.

from take, make, waste to circular economies

As the mountains of waste grow around the world, the end-of-life phase of products is coming under increasingly close scrutiny. It is quite salutary to consider that the concept of waste – that is, material that is neither reused nor recyclable – is in itself a very recent phenomena dating back to the second Industrial Revolution (see section 1.3). This is when we began producing synthetic compounds that could not be reabsorbed into our

natural cycles or recycled. The problem escalated after the Second World War when population growth and mass production exploded, firmly establishing the *take, make, waste* linear model of consumption that is largely still with us today (fig 2.5a). Taking plastic as an example of a recent manmade invention, production has increased 25-fold since 1960;[16] yet to date we have only recycled 9% globally. What happens to the remaining 91% accumulating in the environment year-on-year is not good news for the planet.[17]

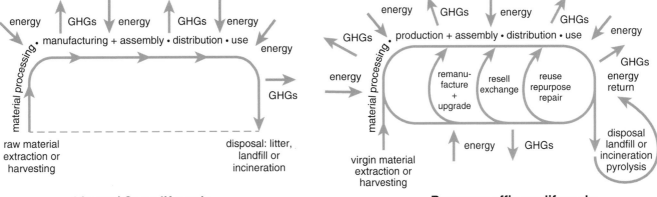

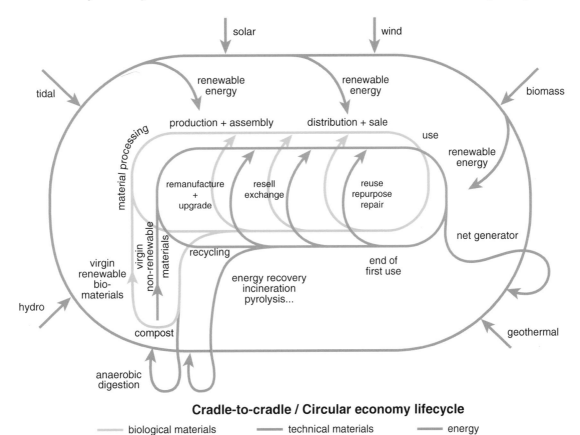

Figure 2.5 Towards zero waste: the evolution of product lifecycle thinking a. linear production and consumption model: take, make, waste b. resource-efficiency model: minimising energy and materials c. cradle-to-cradle model: a circular economy. (source: Jane Penty)

Today, *zero waste* is an ambition that is gradually gathering momentum, and designers are important partners in making it a reality. Lifecycle thinking, eco-effectiveness and eco-efficiency all share the principle of eliminating waste, although they have different interpretations of what this means. For the eco-efficiency-minded, converting waste into a resource, be it energy or materials, makes economic sense and forms part of the resource-efficiency strategy and circular economy. 'Waste management' has now become 'resource management', showing how important semantics can be in changing attitudes and making us more receptive to new behaviours (fig 2.5b).

Eco-effectiveness takes this further by using nature's ecosystems as the ultimate model of sustainability where the concept of waste does not exist, since one organism's waste is another's food. Nature is the ultimate *circular economy* we are trying to emulate. To create a truly zero waste cycle, *technical nutrients* – that is, manmade materials that can be recycled – need to be managed in separate closed-loop recovery systems from *biological nutrients,* substances that can be reabsorbed without harm back into biological cycles through processes such as composting and bio-digesting. Together, these parallel closed-loop cycles reabsorb all material flows to create the basis of the *Cradle-to-Cradle* and *Circular Economy* models. Materials that are neither biodegradable nor recyclable are what McDonough and Braungart term *monstrous hybrids* that are best avoided. These are non-recyclable manmade materials that have undergone one-way chemical reactions such as rubber used for tyres, polyurethane foams and resin fibre composites (fig 2.6). The circular material flows of the C2C or Circular Economy model powered by the renewable energy of the sun and the regenerative benefits of organic cycles is illustrated in figure 2.5c.

an anti-waste hierarchy: product-life strategies

Time is the other important factor for circular economies, but is much more difficult to illustrate in a two-dimensional diagram. Circular Economy models not only assume that materials will be recycled wherever possible, but that the life of a product and all its components will be optimised, saving hugely on energy. This can be done either by extending the product's life in as many ways as possible by designing in- longer use, reuse and repair for as long and in as many ways as possible or by making short-lived ephemeral products have the lightest of impacts. The waste hierarchy, first introduced in 1975,[18] is still a useful rule of thumb for designers that places product-life strategies and choices for consumers and designers in a cascade from best to worst. Figure 2.7 shows this revisited as an anti-waste hierarchy of strategies for designers. For maximum effectiveness, these strategies need to be considered as early as possible in the design process to find the best possible product lifecycle scenarios for delivering a particular function or service.

Figure 2.6 Billions of tyres that don't degrade and aren't recyclable are discarded annually. These 'monstrous hybrids' are at best turned into energy through pyrolisis or incineration, or shredded and used as a filler or substitute aggregate for products such as play surfaces and, fittingly, road asphalt. (photo credit mRm99)

closed- and open-loop systems: recycling, downcycling and upcycling

When a product can no longer be reused or repaired, ideally its materials will be recovered and recycled. Despite urban myths that may claim otherwise, recycling *always saves energy and resources* and *eliminates the environmental damage of extraction* compared with using virgin materials. Figure 2.8 shows the relative reduction in GHG emissions for a range of commonly recycled materials in closed-loop systems. At the top end, it shows the very dramatic benefits of recycling aluminium with a 90% reduction in GHGs. At the lower end, recycling glass still uses 28% less energy than virgin material. And this is *without* including the additional benefits from avoiding all the other forms of environmental damage caused during extraction that we shall see in Life Cycle Assessments (LCA). It is also worth noting that materials such as metals and glass can be almost infinitely recycled, whereas some plastics and fibre-based materials such as paper and cardboard lose some of their mechanical properties each time they are reprocessed and so can only be recycled a limited number of times.

While our recovery systems are still very far from being circular, designers play an important part in facilitating a C2C circular economy through the materials they specify and how the

A designer's anti-waste hierarchy

reduce

refusable	**dematerialise**	**resource efficient**	**shareable**
make near-zero impact alternatives the most attractive: ex: cycling or walking rather than driving; zero short-life packaging refill systems	find different ways of satisfying needs through new technologies and services that radically reduce consumption impacts	explore all the possibilities of introducing low water, energy and material consumption: ex handbasin water flushes toilet; LED light	design products specifically for the collaborative economy: games for toy libraries; bicycles for share schemes; cars for ridesharing...

reuse

resalable / reusable	**repairable**	**upgradable / adaptable**	**remanufacturable**
design products that retain their desirability through brand reputation, classic aesthetics and quality so that they keep being passed on	make consumables, wearing parts and components accessible and replaceable; provide parts, repair manuals, platforms and networks	design with upgradability, expansion or reconfiguration in mind; collaborate for industry standardisation	where products can be remanufactured, design this into the parts and service model to build client trust and lasting relationships

recycle

close loops	**upcycle**	**downcycle**	**renewable**
select materials that are from and can return to high-grade recycling systems or create your own designs for closed loop takeback systems	design high value products from discarded or beyond-repair products made of non-recyclable 'monstrous hybrid' materials	include as much downgraded recycled content as possible to save plastics, metals and paper from 'waste' streams	explore design uses for sustainably grown, versatile, fast growing, low water and disease resistant bio-materials like bamboo, wood,...

recover energy + nutrients

pyrolysise	**incinerate**	**anaerobically digest**	**compost**
waste plastics combusted at high temperatures (pyrolisis) produce hydrocarbon fuels including ethylene to make new plastics	some energy from burning non-recycled waste is recovered to produce electricity or direct heating but flue gases can be toxic	anaerobic microorganisms break down bio-waste (except wood), into bio-methane, CO_2 and fertilizer	all bio-materials can be aerobically broken down into rich fertilizer and humus to feed the next growth cycle of renewables

avoid

landfill	**litter**	**pollution**	**toxics**
unwanted products dumped on land producing GHGs, potentially toxic leachate and unrecyclable material detritus for centuries	byproducts of consumption, often packaging, discarded randomly into the environment and further dispersed via wind and water	the release of substances to air, water or land, intentionally or not, that cause damage to life as byproducts of any human activity	products or byproducts of production that may release or leach toxic substances lethal to life and cause environmental devastation

Figure 2.7 The anti-waste hierarchy provides a useful point of reference for setting strategic goals and design priorities in shaping new and more sustainable products and services. (source: Jane Penty)

Typical cradle-to-gate GHG emissions, Kg CO$_2$e/Kg

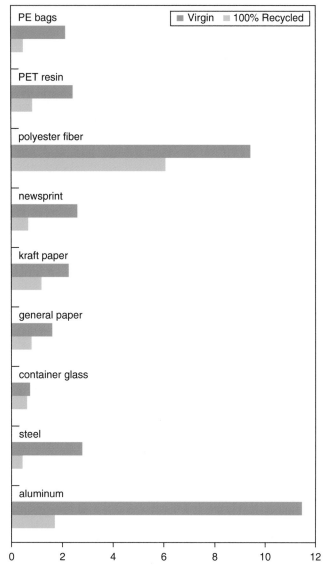

Figure 2.8 Cradle-to-gate comparison of GHG production emissions for common virgin and recycled materials. (source: CleanMetrics & EPA warm)

product is constructed. This needs to be informed by a good understanding of the different forms recycling takes, their relative benefits, and the possibilities and limitations of recycling particular materials.

In *closed-loop recycling*, post-consumer waste goes back into making the same category of products as many times as possible, such as with PET plastic bottles, aluminium drinks cans and some direct take-back schemes. Although this is the best outcome for any product, because *it directly displaces the use of virgin materials*, it is surprisingly still relatively rare.[19] Instead, the vast majority of products that are recycled end

up in *open-loop recycling*, where the materials recovered go on to produce a lower grade product either because the waste stream cannot be sorted or because the material naturally loses some of its performance properties when it is recycled, as in the case of paper fibres. This is also known as *downcycling* or *cascading*, and is still very valuable where *the recycled material displaces virgin content*. Examples of this include plastic downcycled into garden products, including rainwater collectors, or high-quality office paper downcycled into cardboard and newsprint.

Another term commonly used is *upcycling*. This is where the material recovered is used to create a product considered of greater value than the original. Upcycling materials that are already being recycled can be counterproductive, as it reduces the flow of recyclate stocks. However, upcycling is a particularly useful strategy for materials that are *not being recycled or non-recyclable* such as 'monstrous hybrids', thermoset plastics, composites, different materials bonded together and also natural materials that would otherwise be composted. Everyday examples in this category include sports footwear, carbon fibre frames, silicon products and car tyres. While some very beautiful and inspiring objects are being produced, such as Elvis and Kresse's accessories made from disused fire hoses, and Freitag bags from tarps (fig 4.29), upcycling does not address our waste problem significantly. This is because the volume of material upcycled does not come anywhere near matching the volume of non-recyclable 'waste' being generated. Although it can displace the use of virgin materials for the product in question, in the bigger picture the first strategy should be to avoid the production and specification of non-recyclable materials in the first place.

Where materials are not sorted or are not recyclable, the trend is to convert these into fuel or electricity through high-temperature *pyrolysis* or *incineration*, which are the least environmentally desirable options after landfill. A study comparing the whole lifecycle impacts of closed loop, open loop, incineration and landfill for one kg of recovered plastic in Belgium showed a recycling benefit rate of 55 to 60% for the closed loop, 15 to 22% for the open loop and 3 to 12% for incineration.[20]

As we can see, although we have the technology to recycle most materials, there are still some significant barriers to achieving zero waste. In the face of this, designers can play a significant part in improving the status quo by following some simple strategies:

1. displace the maximum amount of virgin material in your designs by specifying as much recycled content as possible to stimulate the supply and demand for recycled materials

2. design products for maximum material recovery by:
   - selecting materials that *are* being recycled rather than those that *can* be recycled
   - making products easy to disassemble and repair by end users
   - designing with as few different materials as possible
   - avoiding mixing technical and bio-materials
   - knowing what recycling infrastructure is in place for where your product is destined and communicating actions to take on the product
   - being informed about current and future recycling technologies and regulations
3. become an advocate for improving recycling and recovery infrastructures and the supply of high-quality recycled materials.

2.3 tools and metrics for better design choices

What we measure affects what we do. If we have the wrong metrics, we will strive for the wrong things.

Joseph Stiglitz [21]

Making the best decisions so that the products we are designing deliver functionality with as little impact as possible requires tools that enable us to compare alternatives. Equally, ambitious goals like zero waste, zero carbon and zero toxicity aren't arrived at overnight and are difficult to realise unless progress can be measured. For this, designers, companies and governments use a range of tools to monitor and achieve incremental targets. In relation to product design, environmental assessment tools can be *qualitative* or *quantitative*. These are used for the following purposes at different stages of the design process:

- **assessing** the current situation and **identifying** the main problems in order to **set strategic targets**, points of intervention and **benchmarks**
- **comparing** and **selecting alternative options** during the design process from early concepts through to specifying materials, manufacturing processes and technologies
- **monitoring** how our designs are *actually* used and how they *really* perform against the original design assumptions and benchmarks, and using this in a **reflective feedback** loop to learn from and improve future designs
- **communicating** a product's sustainable credentials, meeting regulations and achieving accreditation or certification.

Choosing the most appropriate tools will depend on the nature of the product, the quantities being produced and the capability

of the team. Generally, the higher the volume, the greater the consequences of design decisions and the greater the need for quantitative measurements.[22] As designers gain in experience and knowledge, they are able to assess situations much more quickly and informally, but even with experience it is important to use quantitative tools to check these judgements. Independently assessed metrics are also increasingly necessary for companies to meet internal Key Performance Indicators (KPIs) and external regulations and certification requirements such as Environmental Product Declarations (EPDs) that we will cover in Chapter 2.4. It is worth reminding ourselves however that tools should remain just that: help in delivering a vision rather than becoming goals in themselves.

basic concepts: functional and declared units

Whether we are using quantitative or qualitative tools, it is essential to compare like with like. To do this, there are two different reference units used to compare the impact of one product with another in delivering the same amount of functionality or service: *functional units* (FU) and *declared units* (DU).

A *functional unit* (FU) breaks down a product or service into the essential 'amount' of function that it delivers for a relevant unit such as time, distance and quality. For instance, a car and a train cannot be directly compared because they benefit different numbers of people. But if we define their common 'functional unit' as *distance travelled per person,* we can compare them by dividing their total impacts over the distance travelled by the number of passengers. Similarly, if we are comparing washing machines or refrigerators, the FU would be *per weight unit of clothes washed* or *cubic capacity for refrigeration*. The notion of the functional unit links with 'designing for need' covered in Chapter 3.2. Stripping back a product to its essential 'function' offers designers a high degree of freedom that allows them to step away from existing solutions to explore radically different and more sustainable ways of delivering a functionality or satisfying a need.[23]

The second type, *declared units* (DU), are typically used for redesigning products where the degree of freedom in what can be designed is restricted, often because of company, market, or commercial constraints. A DU is the specification of a product per relevant units and may include the scenario of use or time period. For example, the DU for a car could be *car for up to five people; < 1000c per distance travelled; city use; 10-year lifespan*. They are also used to make more accurate comparisons between similar products and for benchmarking Environmental Product Declarations (EPDs) required for some certifications[24] (see Chapter 2.4).

qualitative tools

rules of thumb

Rules of thumb, just as their name suggests, give a simple indication of better or worse environmental options for single issues that can be a very useful baseline from which to work. As a starting point, figure 2.9 proposes some top-level rules of thumb, based on a sliding scale of relative environmental impacts for materials, toxicity, electricity generation and goods and personal transport modes. Because each one only looks at a single issue there can be conflicts between different rules of thumb and design objectives. For instance, in designing a car to be as efficient as possible per mile/km, we may choose lightweight carbon composites that aren't fully recyclable to get the lowest carbon emissions. In this situation, the team needs to weigh up the relative benefits vs. impacts as well as alternative ways to achieve similar efficiencies such as through better aerodynamics and drive train technology. This is why every designer and company needs to learn to navigate the design conflicts between their environmental objectives and functional and commercial constraints to building up rules of thumb that are relevant to their particular field of design and priorities.

webs, wheels, compasses and checklists

The sustainable strategy and evaluation wheel in the form of a polar diagram is a popular tool for quickly identifying the areas that most need addressing in redesigning products to be more sustainable. Because of its clear graphic visualisation, it is also a very useful tool for teams to make quick and rough comparisons of alternative design concepts or as a trigger for brainstorming and strategic innovation. It was first developed in the 1990s and its many versions such as Sony's polar diagram, Dow Europe's eco-compass, E-concept's spider web, and Van Hemel and Brezet's LiDS or eco-design strategy wheel are a testament to the usefulness and flexibility of this format. The common element in these variations is a set of axes, each representing a strategic aspect of the product lifecycle that intersect a set of graded radiating circles. The further away from the centre of the wheel, the better the environmental score. As many of the questions are qualitative, the accuracy of the scoring and resulting diagram will depend on the experience of those completing it and how much data is available.

Eco-design checklists that also emerged in the 1990s are a useful complement to the strategy wheel. Essentially, they consist of a series of questions or prompts grouped by strategic headings that can be scored to provide a methodical point-by-point comparison of the environmental strengths and weaknesses of different concepts against benchmark designs. Figure 2.10 shows a strategy wheel combined with a shortened checklist of points that compares the disposable cup and reusable mug example used

in Box 2.3. Both products are given an average score for each strategic area and mapped directly onto the eight axes of the sustainable design wheel for a quick visual comparison.

The number of axes in the design wheel and the specific checklist prompts may be adapted to suit any stage in the design process, the level of analysis needed and the particular product type. For instance, the strategic emphasis for the design of furniture will be more focused on material inputs, lifetime extension and end-of-life strategies, whereas for electrical goods, the use phase and end-of-life will play a bigger part, reflecting their main lifecycle impacts. These tools and other variations are fully detailed in Tischner and Mosers' updated edition of *How to Do EcoDesign?*[25]

quantitative tools: LCAs and single-issue metrics

the LCA: lifecycle assessment

In line with the strategy of designing for whole lifecycles, Life Cycle Assessment (LCA) is a methodological tool that *quantifies and then interprets the damage from all the material and energy inputs and outputs of a product or product-service system* (PSS) *over any part of its lifecycle*. For example, this could be from raw material extraction to when the product leaves the factory gate or over its entire lifecycle from cradle-to-grave or from cradle-to-cradle. It is the most comprehensive method for quantifying the environmental burden of products and services, and it is increasingly expected for reporting Environmental Product Declarations (EPDs), and is also necessary for product benchmarking in line with the International Standards Organisation (ISO) 14040/14044 Environmental Management Lifecycle Assessment Guidelines (see Chapter 2.4).

The process of carrying out a LCA starts with deciding for which part of the product or service lifecycle we want to measure the impacts. We then draw a notional boundary around this part of the lifecycle called the *system boundary* and draw up a *system bill of material* (SBOM). The LCA then identifies and quantifies all the energy and resources *in* and works out all the emissions and resources that come *out* of the system boundary using data from Life Cycle Inventories (LCIs). These are huge databases that quantify all the inputs and outputs associated with most human activities broken down into great detail and specificity, including geographic provenance.

The next step is to carry out a Life Cycle Impact Assessment (LCIA). This takes the LCI data – that is, all the emissions, materials and land use associated with the activities in the system boundary – and applies environmental science to identify and quantify all the specific environmental mechanisms they trigger. These are called *midpoint indicators*. The final step is to interpret these midpoint indicators into *damage, prevention* or

Rules of thumb

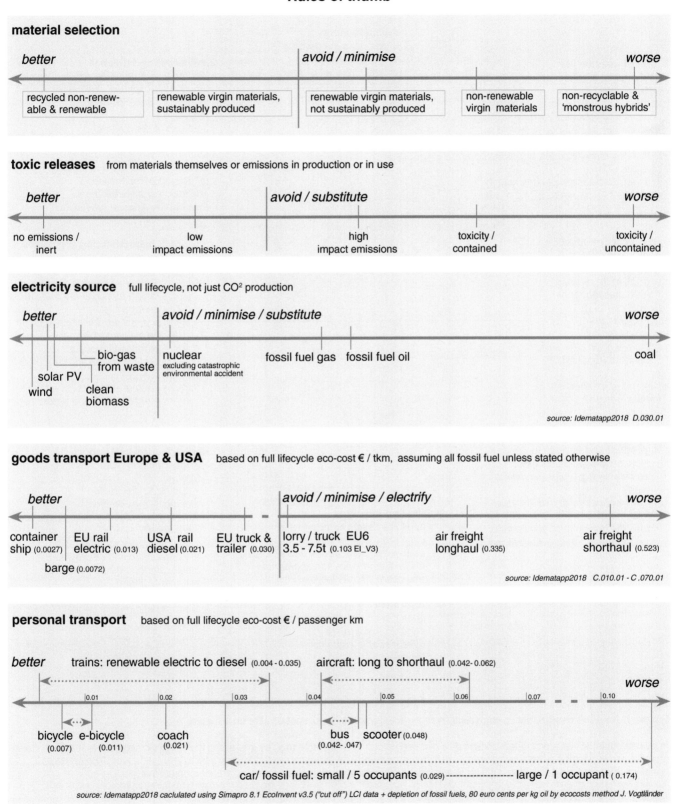

Figure 2.9 Some top-level rules of thumb for more sustainable products.

Sustainable design strategy & evaluation wheel*

1. needs and value
· how well does the product:
  · satisfy real needs?
  · enhance lives emotionally?
  · enhance lives physically?
  · add value to society?
· how safe is it?
· where does it sit between essential and superfluous?

8. end of useable life
· how close to cradle-to-cradle does the design come?
· is there a match between the material choices and the infrastructure available for closed loop recycling or composting
· is there re-manufacturing or product take back?
· is it easy to disassemble and identify materials?

2. materials and finishes
· best choice of materials for function and context: env impact vs. performance vs. design language?
· best use of the material properties?
· amount of material optimised?
· number of materials and parts minimised or rationalised?
· any toxic substances? could these be avoided or substituted?

7. lifecycle optimisation
· does it age well?
· is it durable or desirable enough to be re-used, shared, passed-on or re-sold?
· is it upgradable?
· is it repairable?
· is there a good after sales support for upgradability, or repair?
· if intended for short life, is impact benign?

3. manufacturing processes
· are the processes used the least impactful and most energy and resource efficient for the functions the parts must perform?
· is there any toxicity and can it be eliminated from the production process?
· can it be powered by renewable energy?
· are there any ethical employment issues in the production

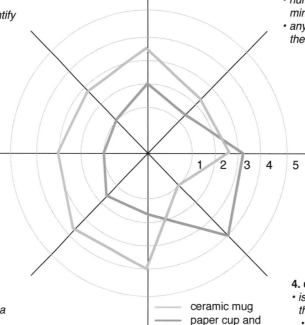

ceramic mug
paper cup and plastic lid

6. product and service in use
· does the design challenge or radically improve how we meet a need?
· is the technology in use the most energy and resource efficient?
· does the design interface foster or build-in the most resource efficient behaviours?
· is the product reliable?
· does its performance match expectation?

5. design impact
· does the design language and interface create emotional attachement and added value?
· is the design language appropriate and optimal for its lifcycle: classic longetivity or momentary enjoyment?
· does the quality of product and service create trust?
· does it enable sustainable lifestyles?

4. distribution and supply
· is the transport footprint minimised through:
  · optimized distribution?
  · minimised packaging?
  · most efficient renewable modes of transport?
  · minimised distances?
· are production and employment quality standards carried through the supply chain?
· is production sourced locally?
· are there community benefits?

Process: for each design, score each axis from 1 – 5 where 5 is most sustainable and 1 least

In this example, the strategy wheel compares a disposable cup and reusable mug by averaging the checklist scores and mapping these onto the corresponding axes. The superimposed diagrams clearly reveal each product's strengths and weaknesses. The strategic headings and prompts can all be modified to suit different product types, use scenarios and design objectives.

*derivative of the EcoDesign Strategy Wheel, Brezet and Van Hemel, 1997

Figure 2.10 Sustainable design strategy and evaluation wheel. (source: Jane Penty 2018)

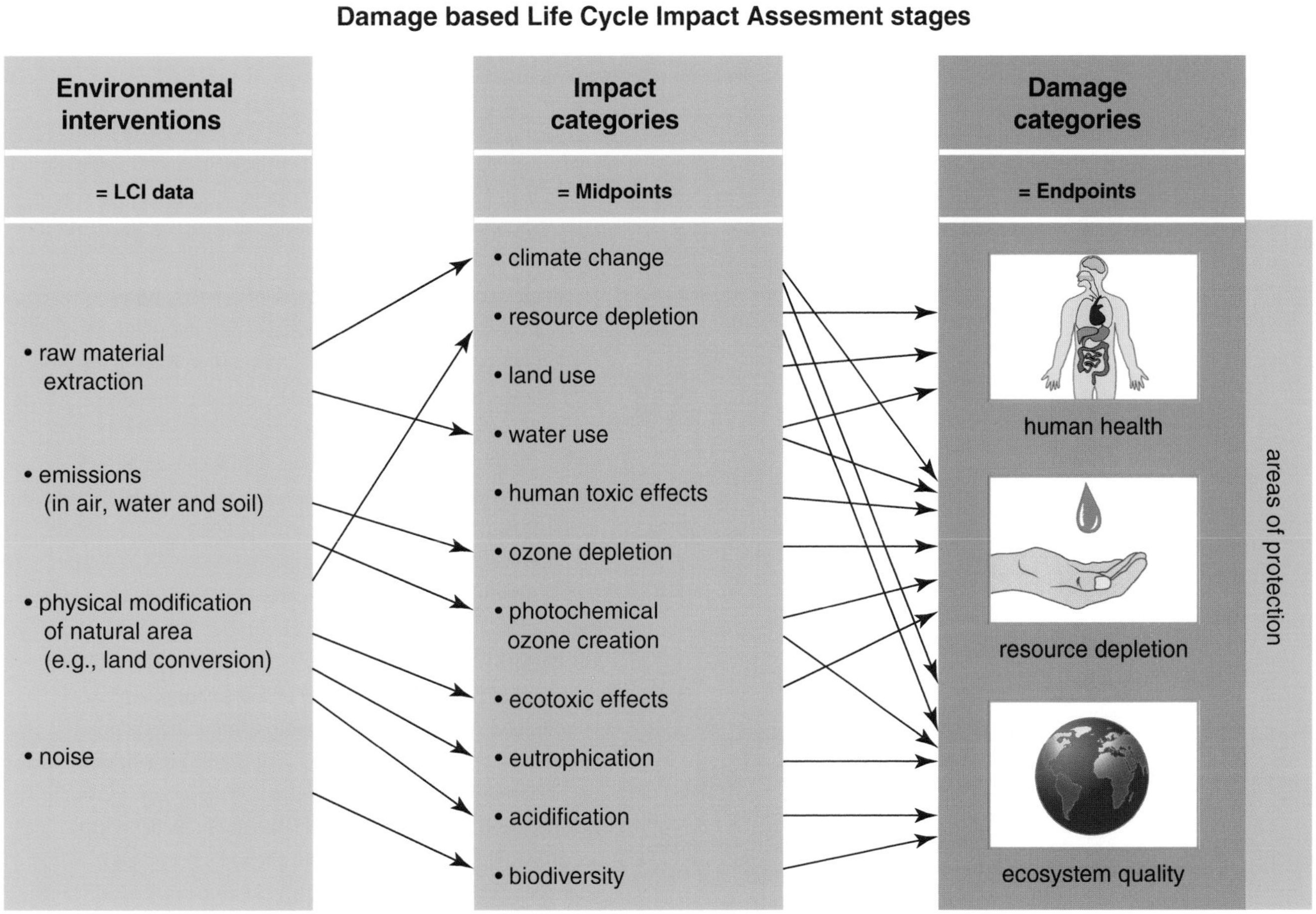

Damage based Life Cycle Impact Assesment stages

Environmental interventions	Impact categories	Damage categories
= LCI data	= Midpoints	= Endpoints

Environmental interventions (= LCI data)
- raw material extraction
- emissions (in air, water and soil)
- physical modification of natural area (e.g., land conversion)
- noise

Impact categories (= Midpoints)
- climate change
- resource depletion
- land use
- water use
- human toxic effects
- ozone depletion
- photochemical ozone creation
- ecotoxic effects
- eutrophication
- acidification
- biodiversity

Damage categories (= Endpoints)
- human health
- resource depletion
- ecosystem quality

areas of protection

Figure 2.11 The stages of a damage-based Life Cycle Impact Assessment (LCIA) starting from LCI data broken down into midpoint indicators and interpreted as endpoint damage. (source: UNEP/SETAC 2015)

single indicator LCA results, depending on the type of LCA you are carrying out. For a damage-based LCA, the *midpoint* indicators are translated into *endpoint indicators* grouped into three main categories: damage to resource availability (RA), damage to ecosystem diversity (ED) and damage to human health (DALY HH), as shown in figure 2.11.

Box 2.2 lists and explains the main indicators of environmental damage on which LCAs are based. By looking through this list it is easy to spot that the same causes repeat themselves: burning fossil fuels, using and not recycling non-renewable materials, overusing renewable resources, including water and deforestation, and creating, using and spreading toxic substances, especially connected with food, plastic and metal production, into the environment.

types of LCAs and terminology
LCAs fall into two main types, each with variants, but what they all have in common is that they measure all the inputs and outputs of a process or activity within a defined *system boundary*,

and assess the *net environmental impacts* they cause. In addition, to be able to make a fair comparison between products or services, LCAs are worked out for either a functional unit (FU) or a declared unit (DU) (see Chapter 2.2). Below is a description of the different types of LCAs.

the complete or rigorous LCA
This looks at the environmental burden of every aspect of a process from cradle-to-grave and increasingly from cradle-to-cradle. It requires detailed information in the form of SBOM on the exact composition, quantity, provenance, processing and transportation modes as well as use and EoL scenarios for all inputs. These figures are entered into lifecycle inventories databases (LCIs) to quantify their midpoint impacts. It then uses a Life Cycle Impact Assessment (LCIA) to translate these emissions into endpoint impacts on human health, resource depletion and ecosystem health. This level of LCA is generally needed for reporting and standards but can only be carried out when designs, processes and suppliers are known.

Box 2.2 what are we measuring? LCIA midpoint indicators

All human activity creates stresses on the environment to a greater or lesser extent. Below are the midpoint indicators that LCAs seek to quantify with a brief description of the problem, their main causes and the practical choices which product designers can make to reduce them.

1. **climate change:** caused by GHGs that create global warming. The primary manmade contributors are the burning of fossil fuels and deforestation (CO_2), meat and dairy production (methane CH_4), chemical fertilisers (N_2O) and F-gases.[26] GHGs take decades to break down, so the gases we produce today are building up in the atmosphere and will still have an effect in over 100 years' time.
   for designers: wherever possible use renewable energy for production, transportation and the use phase. Specify materials that are recycled, recyclable or sustainably renewable. Maximise connections to local recycling infrastructures. *Avoid* non-renewable energy and virgin materials.

2. **resource depletion:** finite resources (minerals, fossil fuels, freshwater and top soil) are being extracted faster than they can be replenished causing scarcity and ecological damage. As stocks diminish, extraction becomes more difficult, causing more habitat disruption and requiring greater energy.
   for designers: specify recycled, abundant or sustainably renewable materials, closed-loop recycling, regenerative practices, and minimise the use of water and non-renewable energy. *Avoid* virgin non-renewables and unsustainably produced renewables.

3. **toxic air, soil and water pollution:** toxic substances are discarded to air, water and land from industrial production, fossil fuel burning, waste 'disposal', incineration and pesticides in agriculture. Some have instant effects but many are bio-accumulative, increasing in concentrations as they move up the food chain with gradual but deadly effects on living organisms and entire ecosystems. For humans, toxic substances can be carcinogenic, mutagenic, cause foetal defects and disrupt or suppress endocrine systems and lower fertility.
   for designers: be informed before specifying materials and their finishes and processes. Start by substituting heavy metals, PCV and PTFE, toxic plasticisers and flame-retardants, with non-toxic materials. Specify sustainably and organically produced renewable materials wherever possible. If toxic materials are used in production processes, ensure that they are contained in a closed neutralising recovery system with no human exposure.[27]

4. **ozone depletion:** the ozone layer shields the Earth from the sun's harmful UV rays, which cause skin cancers. The main ozone-depleting gases (ODGs) are CFCs and halocarbons that have mostly been replaced with HCFCs and F-gases. But HCFCs and F-gases are GHGs thousands of times more potent than CO_2, adding to global warning. Substitutes have and are being developed.[28]
   for designers: do your research. *Avoid* specifying materials or processes that use ODGs or F-gases in production or hidden in cooling systems, air conditioning, heat pumps, propellants, inhalers, solvent-based finishes and gas-injected foams.

5. **smog:** summer or photochemical smog is caused by nitrogen oxides (NO_x) mostly from vehicles' exhausts, fossil fuel burning and volatile organic compound (VOC) solvents reacting with the sun to create ground ozone (O_3). Winter smog is caused by particulate matter (PM) and sulphur dioxide (SO_2) also from fossil fuel burning and incineration. For humans, smog causes chronic respiratory problems like asthma, long-term lung damage and premature deaths.
   for designers: maximise renewable energy and clean air releases. *Avoid* energy from fossil fuels and incineration, particularly in dense urban areas.

6. **acidification:** nitrous oxides (N_2O), sulphur oxides (SO_x), ammonia (NH_3) and VOCs form in the atmosphere and combine with rainwater to create 'acid rain' that falls on land and water, These are mostly produced by burning fossil fuels for electricity generation (especially coal) and transportation. Acid rain has devastating effects on terrestrial and aquatic life. It also corrodes concrete and metals, affecting buildings and structures. In addition, the higher levels of CO_2 from global warming are being absorbed into the oceans, creating mass acidification and coral bleaching.
   for designers: as for climate change.

7. **eutrophication:** caused by water pollution, mostly from run-off of phosphate and nitrogen fertilisers and untreated sewage. High levels of these nutrients in water increase plant growth and create algae blooms that take up all the oxygen, causing fish and aquatic organisms to die, known as 'dead zones'.
   for designers: specify renewable materials produced from the most sustainable land, water and agricultural management practices.

8. **land use (agricultural, urban, natural):** the damage caused by land occupation and transformation is a measure of how long it would take for an area to be restored to its natural state, connected with the ecological footprint.
   for designers: as for resource depletion, but also consider the area of land infrastructure needed for products in their use phase (e.g. cars need road networks and parking).

the streamlined LCA

This is a subset of the rigorous LCA. It still uses the same LCIs and LCIAs but reduces the system boundary to a particular process, phase or element in order to be able to make strategic decisions or assess alternatives while tweaking or redesigning specific parts of a product. Therefore, in practice we may want to consider different manufacturing processes known as (factory) *gate-to-gate*, or alternative materials *cradle-to-gate*, or the implication of different scenarios for the use or EoL phases of certain product parts. Developing LCIs and LCIAs is very detailed and costly, and many elements are geographically specific. Some LCI databases are commercial, such as Ecoinvent from the Swiss Centre for Lifecycle Inventories, one of the most comprehensive worldwide, while others are open or public and often country specific, such as the US LCI from NREL.

The complexity and scale of rigorous LCAs with their LCI databases and LCIA formulae make software and expertise necessary, adding to the cost for smaller businesses and designers. Some of the best-known commercial packages are SimaPro and GaBi, although free and open software and data are also available. In addition, commercial 3D modelling software packages are increasingly bolting on LCA screening that effectively create partial streamlined LCAs. While these can be very useful for initial comparisons of alternative designs or components, designers using these should check that the databases and assumptions used match their scenarios to avoid early misleading results. This 'black box' approach also makes it more difficult for designers to see the direct contribution of each element to the lifecycle, or to extend the analysis to include use scenarios.

the simplified or fast-track LCA with single indicator metrics

This method uses single indicator scores for material and process inventories derived from existing LCI and LCIA databases on 'look-up' tables. The steps to follow are the same as for the full LCA except that the amount of energy and materials for all processes are multiplied by a *single impact factor* and added up to give a total score. In contrast to rigorous LCA software packages, the *fast-track LCA* is not as costly and lends itself to quick comparisons and iterations so that it can be used much earlier in the design process and is much more transparent. By making all the elements and relative impacts visible on a single spreadsheet, designers can spot the critical elements and play with alternative production and use scenarios.

While this method is simple, it still leaves the important decision of choosing an indicator. *Single indicators* vary in what environmental impacts they assess. They can be *damage based*, *prevention based* or *single issue*. The choice of indicator will depend on the objectives of the assessment but fortunately, once

you have a systems bill of materials (SBOM), it is a simple matter to use a different indicator. Below is a summary of the most useful and better-known single indicators for use in a simplified or fast-track LCA calculation.[29]

damage based indicators: these models were first developed in the 1990s along with the LCA methodology and they are still the most common. They assess the damage in terms of human and ecological health and resource depletion, but rely on 'characterisation' and 'normalisation' models that carry levels of uncertainty and are difficult to equate to costs.

- **ReCiPe:** (points) the latest harmonised indicator LCIA method using 18 midpoint and 3 endpoint indicators. It replaces and combines eco-indicator 99 and CML2001 LCIAs.
- **Okala Impact Factors:**[30] (points) for North American datasets based on the EPA's TRACI midpoint impact characterisation[31] and the National Institute for Standards (NIST) weighting.

prevention indicators: this approach aims to eliminate much of the uncertainly of the damage-based approach by costing what it would take to *prevent* the damage in the first place. As an example, the damage from CO_2 emissions of electricity from a coal-fired power station can be prevented with the equivalent cost of producing power from a renewable energy source such as wind. The logic is that if we prevent damage, we eliminate the cost of putting it right.

- **eco-costs:** (€) this indictor takes the total environmental burden and calculates the cost of preventing it. Eco-costs are part of the Eco-efficient Value Creation design strategy and may one day approximate a real cost if environmental accounting becomes the norm.[32]

single issue indicators:

- **carbon footprint (CO_2e):** this is a measure of the total CO_2 equivalent emissions of an activity. It has become popular, as it correlates directly to climate change policy, is straightforward to calculate without the need for complex interpretation and is easy to communicate.
- **cumulative energy demand (CED):** previously termed embodied energy, this indicator looks at the impact of the total energy used throughout a product or service's lifecycle, but it does not account for other emissions or toxicity. It is more often used in the building industry or for more static and bulky products where materials and manufacturing make the largest contribution to the product footprint, rather than the use phase (MJ).[33]

Both carbon footprinting and CED do not fare well with more beneficial end-of-life scenarios such as C2C because they do not include toxic emissions or resource depletion in the first place. Other indicators that are often quoted are ecological footprinting

Box 2.3 Disposable vs reusable cups: a step-by-step 'fast track' LCA example

step 1. set your goals:
- *are you comparing alternatives or establishing a benchmark or baseline from which to improve designs?*
- *are you testing out the effects of different supplier, use or end of life scenarios?*

This example compares the impacts of two alternative choices for consuming coffee or tea in a real-life work situation where an internal coffee bar serves in disposable paper-based cups or personal mugs. Initially the calculation will be looking at the crossover point after which the reusable mug is more environmentally beneficial than the disposable option.

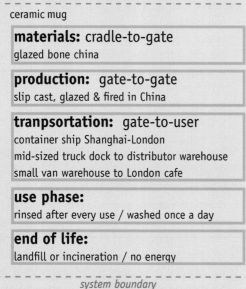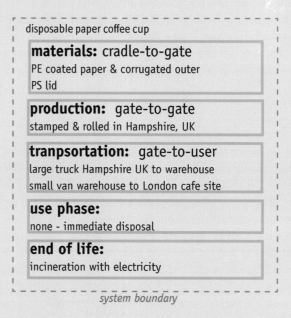

step 2. define your functional unit and system boundaries:
- *describe the function of your product or service – what it is delivering and over what period of time?*
- *draw / map your product system through all its phases as a process tree, flow diagram or other visualisation*
- *set the system boundary: what you include and what you leave out will depend on your goals and objectives*

functional unit (FU): both cups deliver up to 9 oz / 270 ml of a hot drink
period of time: the disposable cup is minutes and the ceramic mug can extend to years

product system and boundaries

ceramic mug

materials: cradle-to-gate
glazed bone china

production: gate-to-gate
slip cast, glazed & fired in China

tranportation: gate-to-user
container ship Shanghai-London
mid-sized truck dock to distributor warehouse
small van warehouse to London cafe

use phase:
rinsed after every use / washed once a day

end of life:
landfill or incineration / no energy

system boundary

disposable paper coffee cup

materials: cradle-to-gate
PE coated paper & corrugated outer
PS lid

production: gate-to-gate
stamped & rolled in Hampshire, UK

tranportation: gate-to-user
large truck Hampshire UK to warehouse
small van warehouse to London cafe site

use phase:
none - immediate disposal

end of life:
incineration with electricity

system boundary

step 3. create a system bill of materials (SBOM):
- *quantify all the materials, processes, transportation and energy going into your system*

step 4. create a spreadsheet and enter data:
- *fill in all known data and indicator multipliers for your SBOM*
- *where there is no data for an item, decide if it is significant and approximate or extrapolate from the most similar alternative. If it is a key element, seek expert advice and have it calculated. Apply this consistently across your design options*

Excel spreadsheet for 'Fast Track' LCA of mug & disposable cup in Eco-costs and Carbon Footprint single indicators using Idemat data

paper coffee / tea cup (capacity 270ml / 9oz; weight 15g / 0.53oz)		quantity	units	eco-cost €/ unit	ecocost C = C*E	kg CO2e / unit	carbon fpt = C*G
material: cradle-to-gate							
A.120.01.106 Idematapp 2018	cup 60% virgin uncoated FSC paper (inner cup)	0.009	kg	0.1770	0.0016	1.2100	0.0109
A.120.01.101 Idematapp 2018	cup 40% board and recycled paper (external kraft fluted liner)	0.006	kg	0.0730	0.0004	0.5000	0.0030
A.120.10.102 Idematapp 2018	LDPE coating (50µ) to inner cup virgin paper (20x30 cm2)	0.06	m2	0.0550	0.0033	0.1100	0.0066
manufacturing: gate-to-gate							
D.020.01.101 Idemat 2015	cup stamped, rolled, formed approximate to boxmaking plus gravure print	0.015	kg	0.0600	0.0009	0.3000	0.0045
transport:							
C.010.06.106 Idematapp 2018	produced in Hampshire, England transported by truck + trailer 100km	0.00987	m3km	0.0096	0.00009	0.0271	0.0003
C.060.01.204 Idemat 2015	15 km by light commercial vehicle	0.00023	tkm	0.4482	0.00010	1.9500	0.0004
use	none / nil						
end-of-life							
F.080.01.108 Idematapp 2018	paper cardboard municipal waste incineration with electricity	0.015	kg	-0.0900	-0.0014	-0.5900	-0.0089
total indicator scores for single paper cup					**0.0051 €**		**0.0169**

plastic lid (4g weight)		quantity	units	eco-cost €/ unit	ecocost C = C*E	kg CO2e / unit	carbon fpt = C*G
material: cradle to gate							
A130.04.124 Idematapp 2018	PS polystyrene general purpose	0.004	kg	1.5000	0.0060	3.6400	0.0146
production: gate-to-gate							
	vacuum forming: use thermoforming machine and production	0.004	kg	0.1160	0.0005	0.7180	0.0029
transport:							
C.010.06.106 Idematapp 2018	produced in Hampshire, England transported by truck + trailer 100km	0.00289	m3km	0.0096	0.000028	0.0263	0.0001
C.060.01.204 Idemat 2015	15 km by light commercial vehicle	0.00006	tkm	0.4482	0.000027	1.9500	0.0001
use	none/nil						
end-of-life							
F.090.01.117 Idematapp 2018	PS municipal waste incineration with electricity	0.004	kg	0.1700	0.0007	-0.5900	-0.0024
total indicator scores for single lid					**0.0072 €**		**0.0153**
total indicator scores for 1 cup + 1 lid					**0.0123 €**		**0.0321**

bone china coffee / tea mug (capacity 270ml / 9oz; weight 250g / 0.53oz)		quantity	units	eco-cost €/ unit	ecocost C = C*E	kg CO2e / unit	carbon fpt = C*G
material: cradle-to-gate							
A.020.01.106 Idematapp 2018	bone china: use porcelain	0.24	kg	0.0600	0.0144	0.3400	0.0816
A.020.01.105 Idematapp 2018	glaze (estimate 10g / 4% by weight)	0.01	kg	1.8900	0.0189	0.3400	0.0034
production: gate-to-gate							
A.040.03.102 Idemat 2015	slip casting and firing: approximate to refactory brick production (CED approx from CED/CO2 ratio for red bricks)	0.25	kg	0.2100	0.0525	1.0300	0.2575
transport:							
C.070.01.106 Idematapp 2018	produced in China & container shipped Shanghai - London 11866 nautical miles = 18986 km / 4000 cups / ton	4.7465	tkm	0.0027	0.01282	0.0081	0.0384
C.060.01.204 Idemat 2015	25 km by light commercial vehicle: 1 mug = 1/4000 ton 25 km/4000	0.00625	tkm	0.4482	0.00280	1.9500	0.0122
end-of-life (inert waste collected with general waste for incineration but as no energy is recovered / assume nil despite some energy being needed to process)							
total indicator scores for mug only without use phase					**0.1014**		**0.3931**
mug use: wash / rinse under tap / water heated by gas condensing boiler (Europe) from 10°C							
B.050.01.103 Idematapp 2018	**short cool wash:** quick rinse 0. 5l warm water 20°C	0.084	MJ	0.0096	0.0008	0.0700	0.0059
B.050.01.103 Idematapp 2018	**long hot wash:** full wash 2l hot water 40°C	0.252	MJ	0.0096	0.0024	0.0700	0.0176

LCA break even: number of uses after which the mug is less environmentally damaging than the disposable cup ± lid		ecocost C	carbon fpt
mug+short cool wash vs. cup+lid	(mug /((cup+lid) - short cool wash)) indicator points	9	15
mug+long hot wash vs. cup+lid	(mug /((cup+lid) - long hot wash)) indicator points	10	27
mug+short cool wash vs. cup only	(mug /(cup - short cool wash)) indicator points	24	36
mug+long hot wash vs. cup only	(mug /(cup - long hot wash)) indicator points	38	-512

data sources: *Idematapp2018.xlsx (with eco-costs 2017, carbon footprint, CED and ReCiPe2016, 1.5 MB) packaging data added, public version*
Idemat 2015: Ecocosts2012_V3.3_LCA_data_on_products_and_services_EI_V3_Idemat2015.xlsx / Idemat 2015 & full lit Ecoinvent V3_Idemat worksheets

step 5. calculate the indicator scores, analyse and prioritise action
- *add up all the elements, compare and analyse the results in terms of your original goals and what this means for design*
- *are there surprises, simple wins, or direct suggestions for different ways to deliver functionality with less impact?*
- *the hard work is done: use the set up to quickly test alternative material, production, supply and end of life scenarios*

observations and analysis from the fast track LCA results
1. material and product production
   - for the paper cup, the LDPE material layer has as much impact as the paper card: look for lower impact ways of waterproofing
   - the PS lid has more ecocosts than the paper cup and nearly as much CO_2 footprint: look for substitutes with lower impacts
   - for the mug, glazing and firing have heavy environmental burdens: explore single fire clays, vitrified ceramics and lower impact glazes
2. transportation
   - last mile choices matter: transporting 15 km by light commercial vehicle can have as much impact as 100 km by truck-trailer and shipping from China has only 5X more ecocosts and 3X more CO_2 than the final local transport by light commercial vehicle
3. use phase:
   - product longevity and how a reusable cup is washed has a very significant impact on the footprint break even. So much so, that the CO_2 for washing can be greater than for producing the whole the paper cup, hence the -512 (H47) result which essentially says that high water and energy washing can negate the CO_2 benefits of reuse
   - behaviour change in washing habits to reduce hot water and design for product longevity to minimise wear and breakages and maximise product attachment through aesthetic qualities are just as important as the other elements of the design

and water footprinting in sectors where these aspects are significant, such as textiles, mining and agriculture.

Box 2.3 shows a step-by-step fast-track LCA comparing the impacts of a disposable coffee cup and lid vs. a reusable ceramic mug with results for two single indicators: eco-costs and carbon footprint. Including all the contributing elements in a visible bill of materials (BoM) on a single spreadsheet makes it a very useful tool at the early strategic design stages to identify key factors and run quick iterations for different scenarios and design concepts.

From a broader perspective, the cup/mug example demonstrates how dependent LCA results are on how closely the LCI data 'fits' our particular scenarios. Where data that matches our processes is not available, best approximations need to be made, as used for the paper cup fabrication and mug slip-casting and firing in the example. This also exposes the fact that LCAs can be subject to wide margins of uncertainty, making them more useful as a tool for comparing alternatives and exposing the 'hotspots' to target through design and business strategies, as opposed to producing 'exact' or 'absolute' results. Equally, single indicators that reflect a wider range of midpoint impacts such as Ecocosts, Okala or ReCiPe give a better picture for human and environmental damage and toxicity than those that look at only a single issue such as CO_2 or cumulative energy demand (CED).

metrics as tools in the design process

LCAs are the most detailed and recognised method we currently have for quantifying and reporting environmental impacts, but complete LCAs are often not possible until a design is in its final detail stage and requires expert input. It is also the case that as a design project advances and decisions have been taken, the degrees of freedom of the design are reduced and, by implication, the possibility of any significant improvements. For this reason designers need to have tools that stimulate the process and give good insights into the relative impacts of different options right from the early strategic stages through to detail development. The simplified or fast-track LCA is useful because it gives transparency and allows rapid iterations and evaluation of alternative scenarios. Other useful tools include apps such as the IDEMAT Sustainability Inspired Materials Selection App and IDEMAT LightLCA that allow designers to compare the eco-costs and CO_2 footprint of materials and lifecycles to inform the early strategic stages of the design process. In commercial practice, particular industry associations share environmental data on materials and processes such as the Sustainable Apparel Coalition's Higgs Materials Selection Index (MSI) to help designers make informed choices from the outset. Nonetheless, when even this is too detailed for the initial stages of a project, qualitative methods like rules of thumb and the

sustainable design wheel supported by checklists can be very helpful for early brainstorming and strategic design directions.

In the end, design decisions for products are much more than a question of impact metrics – they also encompass the company's values and ethos, social and cultural acceptability, the types of behaviours and benefits they bring to people's lives and the ability to do so profitably. In this sense, choosing the best metrics to support a company's values and goals is very important, but so is ensuring that they remain just that: tools for measuring progress towards a goal and not goals in themselves. The creative challenge of having all of these elements succeed together *is* the challenge of designing sustainable products.

2.4 carrot and stick: voluntary or mandatory regulations and certification

Knowing the seriousness of our environmental predicament and having much of the technology to prevent it does not seem to be enough on its own to change the way we do things. With only a few exceptions, there is a fear among business and political leaders that unilaterally setting higher environmental standards will make them lose their competitive advantage on the global stage. What's more, trade agreements may actually hinder some initiatives. At the same time, environmental damage is not contained by political boundaries. International agreements combined with regulations and standards across large markets or regions are proving to be an effective way around this impasse because they create a level commercial playing field between businesses and countries.

In this, the UN has been instrumental in achieving scientific and political consensus for environmental protection through a long list of international treaties protecting biodiversity, natural habitats and human health. Among these there are a number that relate directly to the design and specification of products. They include: the Montreal Protocol (1989) restricting Ozone Depleting Gases; the Basel Convention restricting the transboundary movement of hazardous waste (1992); the Stockholm Convention restricting persistent organic pollutants (POPs) (2004); the Kyoto Protocol (1997), now superseded by the Paris Climate Agreement that sets binding national targets for the reduction of GHG emissions that affects all stages of a product's lifecycle from 2020.

Today, product designers must be aware of the essential role that mandatory and voluntary regulations, standards and international agreements play in curbing carbon and toxic emissions, over-exploitation and waste, and increasing resource efficiencies. The approach to standards and regulations can either be a 'stick' through penalties and taxes or a 'carrot' through incentives and voluntary accreditations or labels. Contrary to predictions of dire commercial consequences, history shows that setting ambitious environmental standards actually stimulates innovation and industry leadership, as demonstrated in California, China, Japan and the EU. One of the earliest examples of this were the pioneering regulations introduced to protect public health by the Air Resources Board in California from 1966 onward that led to innovations in cleaner vehicle exhausts and lead-free fuel.[34]

The first environmental laws in the 1960s and 1970s focused on *end-of-pipe* solutions where pollution is treated after it has been created but before discharge and the *polluter pays* principle where fines are imposed after discharge, ostensibly to help pay for the clean-up.[35]

> *End of pipe cleanups are like solving an unemployment problem*
> *by hiring half of the unemployed to smash windows and hiring*
> *the other half to repair broken windows. Create a problem [...]*
> *and then add to employment and the GDP by fixing it.*[36]

Since then, there has been a shift towards *prevention*. This is being tackled by greater accountability within companies through internal Environmental Management and Assessment Systems (EMAS), setting reduction targets through minimum energy performance standards for products (MEPS), incentivising cleaner technologies and extended producer responsibility (EPR) regulations where manufacturers or distributors are responsible for the waste their products produce. The EU and Japan have been leaders in EPR, particularly focusing on reducing the end-of-life (EoL) impacts for road vehicles, electrical and electronic waste (WEEE), toxic substances and packaging through direct or indirect forms of *product take-back*. This is now being reinforced through circular economy strategies and legislation, which will increasingly be coming into force over the coming decade.

At the very least, product designers need to be knowledgeable about the regulation frameworks in the regions their products are destined for and how these affect design and commercial decisions. However, a much better strategy for long-term economic viability and resilience is to be ahead of regulations through innovation and voluntary initiatives, including labelling and ISO standards. Table 2.2 summarises the main regulations and standards affecting product design by product category.

voluntary or mandatory, do regulations work?

There continues to be much debate about whether regulations work and whether they should be voluntary or mandatory, incentivised or punitive. Opinions are largely driven by business self-interest, political ideology and NGOs defending civil interests,

but also by variations in what is locally acceptable and the capacity of different countries to implement and enforce. Leaving ideology and politics aside, we will look at the effectiveness of different approaches.

In the case of the plastic bag (see Chapter 3.1), we see that charges and taxes have been hugely more effective than rewards in reducing their consumption. Equally, comparing packaging recycling rates between the USA with little EPR and EU countries with full EPR and minimum recycling targets indicates that these work.[37] The USA produces most packaging per head globally and in 2014 recycled 51% overall and 15% plastics,[38] while the EU's average was 66% overall with several Nordic countries at over 70% and 39% for plastics.[39]

Making the producer supply chain responsible for the cost of collecting and recycling the packaging waste they generate incentivises them to design packaging that is lighter and more recyclable. In this regard, design has been instrumental in the rethinking and redesigning of packaging formats and systems (see Chapter 5.2). The most obvious result has been widespread *lightweighting* mostly by substituting glass and card with plastics, and boxes and cans with pouches. Although this has undoubtedly reduced packaging's carbon footprint, looking at it more holistically it has not necessarily been the best environmental solution. As an example, replacing tins and cartons with plastic pouches made of non-recyclable laminated co-polymers and foils that end up in incinerators or land fill doesn't square with the notion of C2C or the circular economy. This is a clear example of regulations driving environmental trade-offs.

Offering direct incentives to consumers also seems to be highly effective. Areas that have mandatory deposit schemes on bottles and packaging for recycling or reuse, as in Canada, Denmark and Germany, have typical return rates well above 90% vs. curb-side collection rates of below 50%.[40] It also has the bonus of reducing litter, as deposit packaging tends to be picked up voluntarily by those needing extra cash, saving taxpayers millions. With the current plastic crisis, deposit schemes are at long last being reintroduced in many countries, states, provinces and cities across the world.

The efficiency of energy-consuming appliances, vehicles and buildings is another area that demonstrates good results through a mixed approach. The mandatory Canada EnerGuide (1978) and US EnergyGuide labels (1979) led the way in setting industry MEPS and communicating the energy efficiency of appliances to enable consumers to make informed choices (see Chapter 3.1). Energy labels now exist in most countries with the EU label being the most common model adopted. The A to G rating on these labels makes consumer comparisons very simple and drives competition

Table 2.2 Summary of leading environmental regulations and standards affecting the design of products

	country/start year/name	rationale	how it works	what it means for product designers
all production				
toxics	• EU: 2005/2007 REACH: Registration, Evaluation and Authorisation of Chemicals • USA: TSCA Toxic Substances Control Act (2010) • other countries have followed	REACH is based on the precautionary principle: all substances must be shown to be safe before release	requires industry to register all existing and future substances with the European Chemicals Agency and measure the potential risk to public health	• raises awareness of toxicity related to any materials and processes • flags substances to avoid and pressures suppliers to source or develop substitutes
EEE : electrical and electronic equipment				
EEE waste	EPR laws: • Japan (2001) Home Appliance Recycling Law • EU (2003/2005) WEEE directive • followed by many other countries, including South Korea, Taiwan, Canada, Australia and 25 US states, and more to follow	EEE is the world's fastest-growing waste stream. Shifts responsibility for waste to producers to: • reduce waste • make toxic materials safe • prevent illegal exports (Basel convention) • increase recycling • recover valuable non-renewable materials	WEEE in EU: producers, importers and distributors pay for schemes to collect, recycle and reuse based on WEEE as % of market share by weight • sets minimum recovery targets: 45%/2016, 65%/2019 WEEE in Japan: stakeholders share costs: • consumers pay for collection and recycling • retailers take back appliances • manufacturers recycle them	incentivises: • lighter and fewer materials for same functionality • design for recyclability and disassembly • longevity, as contributions are based on market share of sales, not repair
toxics in EEE	EU (2003/2005): RoHS Restriction of the Use of Certain Hazardous Substances in EEE • China 2006 • California 2007 • Japan: J-moss label	EU: restriction followed by safe substitution of: • heavy metals (lead, mercury, cadmium) • hexavalent chromium • flame retardants (polybrominated biphenyls (PBB) and ethers (PBDE))	• EU: producers must restrict and then substitute the six most common toxics in electronics • Japan: products exceeding target levels of toxic substances must have orange label listing their presence	• has forced R&D to develop safe alternatives • the global nature of the electronic industry has pushed these standards to be adopted worldwide
energy and resource efficiency	Energy Star label (1992) USA, Australia, Canada, Japan, New Zealand, Taiwan EU (office equipment only)	voluntary label: incentivise producers and reward leaders to continually improve the energy, and, more recently, water factor of EEE	• marks top performers in product category • 20 to 30% better than MEPS • covers products, buildings, plant • benchmark is raised when 50% of market has energy star rating	high international and over 80% consumer recognition rate in USA makes the label a strong motivator for designing efficiency-leading products
	MEPS: minimum energy performance standards • California (1978) • USA Dept of Energy (1988) • most countries since	force industry to continually improve efficiency standards	• mandatory • energy and increasingly water consumption • covers buildings, EEE, vehicles and plant • products below minimum standards fall out of market (e.g. incandescent bulbs)	knowledge of product category MEPS necessary
	mandatory energy performance labels: Canada (1978) EnerGuide USA (1979) EnergyGuide EU: (1992) Energy Label	help consumers and businesses make the best choices by communicating comparative performance and operating costs	• mandatory • hand-in-hand with MEPS • covers all energy and now water-using products, including buildings	big driver for designers and companies to place products in the top ratings

	country/start year/name	rationale	how it works	what it means for product designers
	EU (2009 /2011) ErP Ecodesign directive for energy-using and energy-related products (included MEPS)	stresses the importance of lifecycle thinking in the design process: aims to reduce energy and water use, polluting emissions, waste and increase recyclability through all the lifecycle stages at the design stage	• mandatory MEPS for more than 40 product groups and growing • all products covered must show CE compliance	for all lifecycles stages designers must predict: • consumption of materials, energy and other resources • air, water, soil emissions • pollution (noise, vibration, radiation, electromagnetic fields) • waste material • possibilities for reuse, repair, recycling and recovery of materials and energy
vehicles				
end-of-life of vehicles (EVL)	EU (2000/2002): EVL/EPR Japan (2005): EVL Recycling law Japan	reduce materials and maximise resource and toxic material recovery from the millions of vehicles scrapped every year	mandatory EPR EU: consumers have free take-back at EoL and producers must recover 95%; recycle 85% (by weight) Japan: car owners pay, recyclers and manufacturers share responsibility	• design for recyclability • substitute toxic materials • code all materials • provide instructions for dismantling, reuse, recovery
batteries				
	EU Battery and Accumulators Directive	safe disposal and phase out of some toxic substances	sets recovery and safe disposal targets	batteries must be removable from equipment/products
packaging				
waste and EoL	EPR • EU (1994): packaging and packaging waste directive/ essential requirements • Japan (2000): containers and packaging recycling law • followed by Taiwan, Australia, Canada (provincial), some US states and other countries	EU: the first EPR legislation led by Germany in 1991. • reduce volume and weight • maximise recovery • reduce hazardous materials • shift responsibility and cost of recovery from local government to producers and retailers	• mandatory targets for recovery • requires on-pack material information • embeds design for reuse or recycling • producer supply chain pays for recovery by % weight	• rethink materials and design of packaging and whole consumption systems towards recyclability and reusability • may encourage lightweighting rather than whole lifecycle thinking
international standards				
	ISO 14000 family of environmental management standards	provide tools for consistency and reliability in monitoring, comparing and reporting environmental standards	voluntary reporting and certification by ISO high standing and international recognition	designers must be aware of standards for product claims, LCA product comparisons, EDPs and reporting
ecolabels & independent certifications				
	some of the older and better-known product labels: • Blue Angel (1978) Germany • EcoMark (1989) Japan • Nordic Swan (1989) • C2C certified (1990) • EU Ecolabel (1992) • Ecomark (1991) India • FSC (1993) wood global • PEFC(1999) wood global • Global Green Tag (2003)	help consumers and business-to-business make more environmentally favourable choices and meet procuremant standards	generally voluntary, they are indicators of higher standards throughout product lifecycles, recognise top 20 to 25% in a product category and set benchmark standards	gaining independent label certification may be an important sales and communication tool in particular markets and avoids greenwashing

note: See www.ecolabelindex.com/ecolabel/ for listing of over 500 international labels.

to improve performance. On the other hand, the ENERGY STAR is a voluntary label awarded to the most efficient products in a particular category. It is also a continuous motivator for industry to improve efficiency as the MEPS benchmark standard shifts upward when 50% of market share in a product group achieves certification.[41]

how do regulations affect design?

EPR and Ecodesign regulations are having a significant impact on design. At its best, EPR encourages innovation in formats, materials and design for reuse, disassembly and recyclability. At its crudest, it leads to simplistic weight reduction of products that can inhibit better environmental material choices. Ecodesign regulations and ISO standards, on the other hand, cultivate a more holistic view of design by considering all aspects of a product's impacts throughout the lifecycle stages. Environmentally ambitious companies and designers are raising industry benchmarks by embracing voluntary environmental and ethical labels that have much higher standards than basic regulations. With consumers trusting independent labels far more than company claims, independent certification is having a big impact on consumer choices. It is also important for designers to be part of the discussions and formulation of regulations and standards so that these do not inadvertently produce unintended consequences or stifle more holistic and profound innovation.

2.5 radical rethinks: high tech, low tech, new tech and old tech

Up until now we have considered some overarching principles and strategies for environmental sustainability. But it seems that simply applying these to our current systems of production and consumption won't deliver the scale of impact reductions that the problem needs. We must therefore look to more radical step-change solutions. In this, there seem to be two strongly opposing pulls in what the nature of these radical changes should be. There are those who believe in less and slower combined with a profound change in the nature, quantity and distribution of our consumption. And there are those who have absolute faith that new high-tech developments will let us continue consuming our way out of the problem. In this section we will look at what both new and old technologies have to offer the pursuit of these two very different visions of a sustainable future.

technology will save us

The new technologies that have the greatest potential to radically transform product design and everyday life that we will look at

include synthetic biology and bio-engineering, nano-technology, distributive manufacturing and 3D printing and AI, big data and the Internet of Things (IoT). While the development of new technologies seems driven by an unstoppable economic and scientific momentum, the earlier designers and citizens can engage with them before they emerge from the 'laboratory', the more chance there will be of channelling their potential towards more radically sustainable outcomes.

biology, the new powerhouse of design: from collaboration to re-creation

The key realisation is that biology is a manufacturing capability.[42]

Tom Knight

For millennia humans have harnessed the power of nature for their own ends. For designers, this relationship ranges from working directly *with* nature and her materials, to redesigning and *reprogramming life* itself in the emerging field of synthetic biology. The following is a very brief summary of these relationships, describing the degree of intervention and some of the sustainable design possibilities and dangers they afford.

working with nature
- using nature as a materials 'factory'
- using nature as a production process
- using living organisms as a working part of a product.

Nature provides many materials with unique properties that we either use directly, reshape or reconstitute. Although they are renewable, the increasing demand from a growing population is directly reducing natural habitats. This makes growing biological materials more sustainably and using them more efficiently and effectively essential. Alvar Aalto's pioneering development of plywood for furniture in the 1920s and 1930s is an example of how design innovation leads to new ways of maximising the properties of natural materials while minimising the quantity of material required (fig 2.12).

Another way to use the efficiency of nature is to grow products directly into the desired form which eliminates waste and most manufacturing processes. While this practice has been in existence for centuries with fascinating results, it is being revisited and refined by companies like Full Grown to produce unique chairs and lighting. Their vision is to expand into a full 'furniture farm', although the long cycle times tend to limit the scale of production and affordability (fig 2.13). New techniques with faster growing organisms such as mushroom mycelium developed by Ecovative for packaging and insulation may be set to change the scale of production possible with growing organisms (see fig 5.34). Some

Figure 2.12 Pioneering innovative ways of working wood that maximises its strength and flexibility, Alvar Aalto's Paimio armchair demonstrates how this has also led to a radically new design language for wood and furniture (Finland 1932). (photo courtesy Artek.fi)

designers are taking this a step further by using living organisms as a working part of the end product. Recent concepts include luminescent bacteria for lighting in Philips' Microbial Home and Glowee's ephemeral lights. Living moss is also being integrated to create biophotovoltaics producing electricity in tables and radios[43] or to absorb air pollutants in Goodyear's Oxygene car

tyres and Sion cars' air filtering (see fig 4.19). Although not all of these projects are yet commercially viable, they do capture the imagination and point to the possibilities of a more active relationship between products and nature.

imitating nature: from biomimetics to biomimicry
- **biomimetics:** scientific and technological translation of natural systems to create radical innovations
- **biomimicry:** studying nature's systems and designs to inspire innovative sustainable solutions to human problems.

Biomimetics has brought us many everyday transformative inventions, from Velcro to human flight. Taking this a step further, biomimicry is specifically directed towards sustainable purposes. Unlike emerging biogenetics and synthetic biology, biomimicry, as Janine Benyus defines it, does not cross the genetic boundaries of natural biology. Because nature has evolved over many billions of years, it has reached a remarkable level of complexity, resiliency and elegant efficiency that biomimicry considers is a model that should be respected and emulated.

The use of biomimicry ranges from micro to macro scales, from imitating patterns and form to detailed structures, from complex systems to individual molecules. The C2C strategy is a prime example of whole-system biomimicry based on nature but it may also be used much more directly. For example, copying the uneven edges, or tubercles, of a whale's fin onto fan blades reduces noise and increases energy efficiency, or mimicking mussels' natural

Figure 2.13 Furniture farming: Full Grown's willow chairs in the making and the final product, Edwardes Chair (UK 2012 to 2017). (photos courtesy ©Full Grown)

adhesives we can replace toxic off-gasing glues used in plywood (see Chapter 7.3 on toxicity in furniture).

However, until recently it has been difficult for designers to understand, let alone copy, the complexity of some natural systems. The developing fields of nano-technology, computational analysis, AI and digital manufacturing combined are now making it possible to apply biomimicry at a molecular level and to apply this to the conception, design and fabrication of bigger, more complex structures. Assa Ashuach's Femur stool (fig 2.14) and STEM 45° chair (fig 2.27) are examples of new aesthetics that emerge from the radical optimisation of material and production energy (up to 70% less). This is achieved by copying the dynamic behaviours of bamboo microstructure growth (STEM) and bone structures (Femur) mathematically for the digital manufacture of artefacts.[45]

redesigning nature: from genetic engineering to synthetic biology

Imagine a world where biological fabrication replaces traditional manufacture, plants that grow products, and bacteria genetically re-programmed to 'biofacture' new materials, artefacts, energy or medicine.

Carole Collet, *En Vie exhibition, Paris 2013*

- **genetic engineering (GM):** modifying the genetic make-up of living cells to give them desired characteristics and behaviours such as algae and bacteria that produce fuel, vegan protein

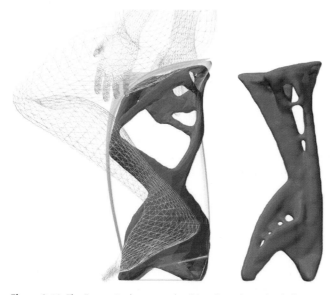

Figure 2.14 The Femur stool uses an algorithm that adapts the design form to different design loads based on human bone formation to optimise material, strength and laser sintering 'mileage' (UK 2013). (courtesy ©Assa Ashuach Studio)

and animal-free leather. The results are organisms that could not be created by nature because the new DNA crosses species boundaries.

- **synthetic biology:** a subset of GM where organisms or biological systems with programmable behaviours are created by assembling standard genetic components or 'biobricks', independently of cells.[46] The starting point of synthetic biology is that it is faster and more effective to design organisms from scratch than to modify nature.

If any technology has the potential to radically change our whole material culture and systems of production, then it is genetic engineering and its advanced form, synthetic biology. Just as the invention of the transistor in 1947 marked the beginning of the digital age, 2010 was an auspicious year when the first synthetically controlled cell capable of reproduction was created at the J. Craig Venter Institute in the USA. In the twenty-first century the whole nature of manufacturing, medicine, computing, food production and environmental management is set to be transformed by the quasi-infinite possibilities of recombining DNA/RNA life code to perform new functions in and out of living organisms. But will it make life more sustainable?

For the sustainably minded designer in the age of synthetic biology, the focus of design will shift to creating organisms that can bio-manufacture materials more sustainably, improving nutrition, and programming bio-sensors to detect and destroy disease pathogens or harmful environmental chemicals. The annual International Genetically Engineered Machines student competition (iGEM) is a good showcase for the many potentially positive uses to which synthetic biology can be applied. Participants must ensure that their projects are 'safe, responsible and good for the world'. A small sample of applications includes:

- **material bio-manufacture:** e-coli bacteria engineered to biosynthesise sustainable materials such as: natural rubber and palm oil substitutes to reduce deforestation; plastics from non-recyclable waste for closed-loop upcycling; compostable PLA plastic for 3D printing to reduce cost and non-renewables; a substitute for chemical indigo for dying jeans; enhancing the production of mycelium packaging.
- **environmental bio-sensing:** simple bio-sensors programmed to detect specific toxins to test drinking water safety, locate and degrade harmful herbicides, save bees from colony collapse, detect toxins and decontaminate water.

As the technology develops, sustainably literate product designers need to be working at the front end with biological engineers and entrepreneurs to shape radically beneficial product applications for the future and to ensure the safety of the natural environment. Designers at IDEO and scientists at the University of California in

Figure 2.15 IDEO and UCSF collaborated in this synthetic biology self-packaging biodegradable probiotic drink concept (2013). (photo courtesy IDEO.com)

San Francisco collaborated in the Synthetic Aesthetic project to do just this. They envisioned an extreme probiotic drink that forms its own biodegradable packaging around a light. It then lies dormant until water is poured inside to produce a healthy effervescent drink, many times over[46] (fig 2.15). In a more straightforward application, the Wyss Institute (Harvard) has demonstrated how a pocket-sized piece of paper printed with bio-programmed material can act as a simple diagnostics bio-sensor that could be used for diagnosing diseases such as Ebola in the field.[47]

Meanwhile, 'bio-facturing' is already a reality. As an example of the potential for more sustainable materials production, Algenol Biotech, started in Florida, have designed systems for bio-manufacturing a range of products, including natural food colorants, vegan proteins, spirulina, and bio-fuels using natural or modified algae (cyanobacteria). Their bio-ethanol produced from algae fed on waste CO_2, saltwater and sunlight has a carbon footprint 80% less than petroleum or crop-based fuels.[48]

The possibilities of synthetic biology inspire awe but they also provoke an equal share of fear, and raise important issues of safety and ethics in the short and longer term.[49] In bypassing the long-established safeguards of the natural evolutionary process, what risks are we running if they should be intentionally or accidentally released into nature? Are we overstepping the mark by interfering with nature and redesigning life? Who will have access to its benefits?[50] As with manmade chemicals, designers should apply the *precautionary principle* or risk irreversible damage to the very environment we are trying to protect. With sustainability in its broadest sense at the heart of ethical debates, in Chapter 3 we will see how designers can use design

activism and speculative design fictions to trigger debates on these issues with wider audiences.

nano-technology: material magic

As early as 1959, Richard Feynman and others anticipated the possibilities of a whole new nano-scale world in his famous presentation *There's Plenty of Room at the Bottom*. However, 'nano-magic' did not begin to emerge until after 1981 when the scanning tunnelling microscope (STM) made it possible to handle and observe materials at the scale of individual atoms and molecules. Today, nano-technologists are creating a palette of radically new materials for scientists and designers to play with. This is because at a nano-scale (1 nm = one-millionth of a mm) materials behave very differently from their familiar macro forms. Below 100 nm, the laws of Quantum physics take over from the familiar Newtonian physics, making the optical, electronic, physical and magnetic properties of materials change in unpredictable ways. For instance, at the nano-scale copper becomes transparent, silver becomes anti-bacterial, ceramics springy, clay flexible, metals plastic-like and gold can move like amoeba (fig 2.16).

applied nano-tech

Nano-technology is already being used to innovate a broad range of products, including electronics, sports equipment, cosmetics, UV protection, transportation, packaging, building materials and medicine. They offer designers a whole set of new possibilities for tackling sustainable issues such as material and energy efficiency, product longevity and self-repair with nano-versions of materials that in their conventional form have reached their natural physical limits.

Figure 2.16 Zinc oxide nanowire arrays seen through a scanning electron microscope and rendered to appear flower-like. (photo the Materials Research Society (www.mrs.org) and courtesy Hyun Wook Kang, Korea Advanced Institute of Science and Techonology (KAIST))

In transportation, materials like carbon nano-tubes (CNT) that have the highest strength of any material known – 100 times stronger than steel and 6 times lighter[51] – are being used in composites to lighten aircraft and vehicles, reducing material and energy consumption in use by up to 20%. The distance that electric vehicles can travel is also set to increase thanks to nano-enhanced lithium ion batteries and hydrogen fuel cells, while their newer competitor, super-capacitors, may also cut charging time dramatically (see Chapter 8).

For electronic products, nano-electronics have vastly increased the capacity for memory storage and the continued progress of miniaturisation with transistors and memory units down to

the size of a single atom in the lab.[52] With the move to mobile computing, cloud storage and big data, this will contribute to huge savings in energy as well as reducing the size of electronic devices and therefore electronic waste (see Chapter 6). Nano-materials are also enabling a whole range of wearable and portable bio-sensing products for monitoring fitness and health conditions. One example, Oxford Nanopore's field-ready MinION micro DNA/RNA sequencer, is revolutionising the surveillance of epidemics and environmental and medical field research by enabling real-time DNA analysis outside the traditional lab environment[53] (fig 2.17).

Nano-coatings also offer everyday sustainable benefits across all product sectors. These include extending product life with highly scratch-resistant coatings on lenses, product casings and car bodies. Self-cleaning coatings on buildings and outdoor products, and stain- and water-resistant fabric coatings for furniture, accessories and clothing also save on the use of water and chemical cleaners. In packaging, active and 'intelligent' materials with nano-coatings are extending the life of perishable foods and reducing food waste. With nano-clay linings, plastics can be made gas impermeable, helping plastic pouches to become recyclable and tennis balls to keep their bounce for longer.

Energy efficiency and the performance of renewables is also being boosted by nano-materials. OLED lighting, displays and solar cells can now be paper-thin and flexible thanks to nano-layers (fig 2.18). The efficiency of solar cells is increasing and their cost is coming down as nano-particles are printed onto flexible foils with self-cleaning surfaces. Flexible nano-printed foils are also helping to bring down the cost of applying organic photovoltaics

Figure 2.17 The revolutionary combination of Oxford Nanopore's pocket-sized minION gene sequencer and connected Fongle allow for real-time DNA data analysis directly from the field. (photos courtesy ©Oxford Nanopore Techonologies Ltd)

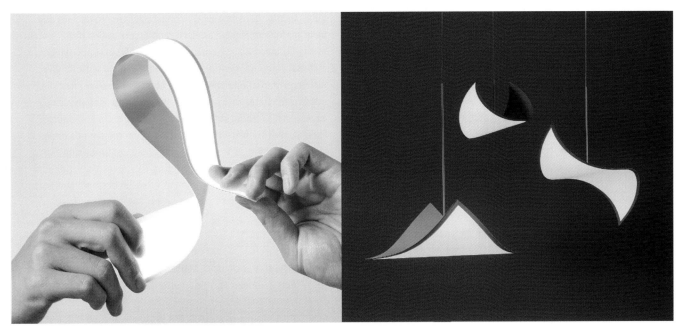

Figure 2.18 LG's flexible OLED panels free up lights to take to any shape or contour to any surface. (photos courtesy LG Display)

(OPVs) to buildings, aircraft, cars, clothing and off-grid products (fig 2.19). Producing these from non-toxic Copper Zinc Tin Sulphur (CZTS) materials on recyclable substrates rather than using rare earths and non-recyclable plastics will be an important piece of the sustainable energy jigsaw.[54] Wind turbines with CNT composite blades are also lighter, making them more efficient. Translucent eco-glazing made with silica aerogel – that is, 99% air – lets in light with over two to four times the insulating capacity of fibreglass bats. And furniture and walls embedded with phase-change materials that store and release heat can reduce space heating and cooling demands (fig 2.20).

Figure 2.19 Powerfilm Solar's portable LightSaver Max charging for off-grid use. (photo courtesy Powerfilm Solar)

Figure 2.20 Table Climatique, part of Zero Energy Furniture, absorbs and releases heat with phase change material (France 2015). (courstesy ZEF team / photo ©Clolombier Clier, VIA 2015)

nano futures

The future promises even more. If research in the lab becomes viable, we will see self-colouring dyeless nano-tube fabrics, self-healing and self-repairing polymers and metals for cars, bridges, aircraft and fabrics.[55] Wearable technology will continue to evolve, including clothing with conductive nanowires that gently keeps you warm instead of the room,[56] and electronics reduced to the size of single atoms. Two-dimensional materials like graphene with twice the strength and conductivity of CNT may one day transform energy storage, composite materials and photovoltaics. Mercedes' Vision G-code highly speculative concept car in 2015 with its multi-voltaic paint that could harvest solar and wind energy to produce its own hydrogen fuel lets us imagine a future where all cars passively generate the energy for their own propulsion.[57] This future may be closer than we think – the Sion, a flexible solar-panelled EV car by Sono motors, is already part-way to achieving the dream of endless clean mobility (see fig 4.20).

risks: too good to be true?

The possibilities for sustainable solutions may seem too good to be true, but we also need to understand the risks of nano-materials. Regulation of nano-materials is very recent and quite

light. In the USA since 2017, companies have to declare any nano-materials in their products and assert their safety,[58] while in the EU since 2012, cosmetics and food containing nano-materials require labelling and all must comply with REACH. Although the EU and the USA are continuing to monitor the need to regulate, this falls short of the precautionary principle, as research on their safety is only just beginning to emerge.[59] Early studies indicate that ingesting nano-compounds orally through the skin, digestion or lungs may not be benign. These concerns include CNT in lungs acting like asbestos,[60] zinc and silver oxides now commonly found in cosmetics, and sunblocks causing DNA damage to human cells[61] and nano-particles in processed blood causing clots, particularly dangerous during operations.[62]

Just as the risks to human health are little understood, so are the effects of releasing these materials into the environment. Currently, post-consumer waste containing nano-materials is mixed with other waste, with few protocols for recycling or handling products containing nano-materials separately. Equally there are no controls over their leaching out into water as is the case when cosmetics and sunblocks or clothing and other products with anti-bacterial nano-silver oxides are washed. The multi-award-winning Misoka toothbrush is a very good example of how applying lateral nano-thinking to simple products can help reduce some environmental impacts (fig 2.21). Its bristles are coated in nano-mineral ions that clean and protect teeth from staining without any need for toothpaste, eliminating the impact of toothpaste production, packaging and disposal in our water systems.[63] But while we solve one problem we need to be certain we aren't creating another. In this case it would involve ascertaining that ingesting the nano-oxides or releasing them into our water ecosystems is fully human and eco-safe. And we should still turn our design minds to dealing with the problem of what happens to all the toothbrushes at the end of their short lifespan.

From all the examples touched upon here and the many more that are emerging, the possibilities of nano-technology contributing to sustainable solutions are only limited by the imagination and their eco-safety. Designers will need to keep abreast as new research and regulations emerge about their safety and apply their own precautionary principles before specifying.[64, 65]

connected and smart: the IoT, big data and AI

In his book *When Things Start to Think* (1999), Neil Gershenfeld made a case for liberating people from the tyranny of 'stupid' technology by making it smarter and more ubiquitous. In this scenario, technology blends into the background to support

Figure 2.21 The nano-coated bristles of the elegant Misoka toothbrush designed by Kosho Ueshima do away with the need for toothpaste. Over three million have been sold globally since 2007. (photo courtesy Yumeshokunin Co. Ltd, Japan)

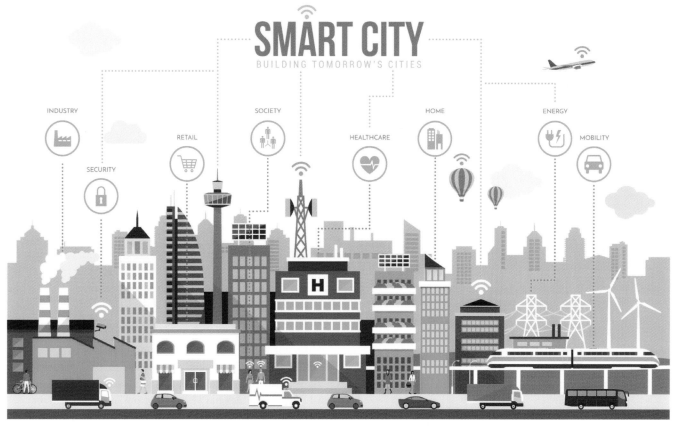

Figure 2.22 The IoT pervasive ecosystem will affect all personal, business and public products and services. (artwork credit elenabsl)

us rather than constantly demanding our attention. For this to happen, objects must be able to sense ambient conditions, start talking to us and to each other, share information and be responsive to their changing environment. That reality is with us now in the Internet of Things (IoT), a term coined by Kevin Ashton in 1999 in his Auto-ID lab at MIT.

The IoT or pervasive, ubiquitous, smart technology is essentially a network of 'things', connected locally or globally, with embedded technology that allows them to communicate, sense and respond accordingly. At the lowest level are objects with readable information tags such as radio frequency identification (RFID) or near-field communication (NFC). At the next level, objects are connected and can send and receive information from other objects or their environment. They can then use this data to adjust and optimise their responses by learning and even anticipating behaviours when they are enabled by different degrees of intelligent algorithms, including artificial intelligence (AI) and machine learning. At a domestic level, the Nest thermostat was an early example of this capability in the consumer market and reports 10 to 12% energy savings over un-programmed thermostats[66] (see fig 6.11). By monitoring outdoor conditions and learning our preferences, daily routines

and heating system response characteristics, it anticipates and reacts to set the optimal temperatures for comfort and energy efficiency.

To exist, the IoT depends on an ecosystem of physical objects, a communication network, 'intelligent' software and data storage. In many ways it is the confluence of the smartphone, wireless networks, machine-learning software, cloud storage and apps that have allowed it to finally take off. But beyond being the gadget lover's dream-come-true, is the IoT good for the planet or will it simply add to our electronic waste mountain? With over 27 billion 'things' or devices already connected in 2017 and forecast to rise to over 125 billion by 2030,[67] it is an important question for designers to ask themselves (fig 2.22).

For the environment, the IoT has enormous potential for energy and material savings. Billions of connected devices are producing and capturing information every moment of every day, generating big data. By using this data and learning from it, systems can operate more efficiently and improve experiences. The first and most basic sustainable gains from the IoT are in the world of manufacturing and logistics. By combining real-time information on stock location and using big data to predict demand,

Figure 2.23 On the Dutch Island of Texel, Tvilights's wirelessly controlled LEDs reduced lighting energy by 65% to make it Europe's first energy-neutral public lighting. The reduced light pollution from the intelligent dimming has enabled the rediscovery of magnificent night skies (2017). (photo courtesy ©Tvilight)

production can be tailored to this demand and the material and energy for production and transportation of goods can be substantially reduced.

Staying at the macro scale, cities are becoming 'smart' by using 'big data' collected from an array of fixed devices as well as from mobile devices to make transportation, lighting, utilities and other services able to anticipate demand and optimise infrastructure capacity in real time. Thus streetlights will only be switched on if there are people about (fig 2.23), traffic speed and lanes will be adjusted to create smoother flows, products will be serviced when they need to be and bins will be emptied when they are full. In transportation alone, one of our biggest and growing uses of energy, the IoT is at the centre of making Mobility as a Service (MAAS) possible which will radically reduce the number of vehicles needed (see Chapter 8.3). Cities like Songdo in Korea, designed from the outset to be 'smart', demonstrate how IoT integrated services can dramatically reduce GHGs, posting reductions of 40% compared with similar-sized cities. However, the level of control and automation may not make it everyone's ideal city.[68]

At a personal level, the IoT is already making big inroads in day-to-day life for those who live within its net. Smart homes controlled through interactive home hubs can save energy and improve ambient comfort and security while reducing the stress of dealing with so many interfaces. Social sustainability in the form of enhanced wellbeing and health care is also a major focus for the IoT allied to new nano-enabled sensing. Connected

health offers professionals and patients, especially the growing number of chronically ill and elderly, more control, independence and security, both in hospitals and at home (see figs 2.24 and 6.39). Wearable tech has also created the 'quantified self' for those wanting to increase their fitness and wellbeing by tracking anything from their physical activity and calorie intake to heart rate and sleep quality. Apps like Strava are encouraging competitively motivated runners, cyclists and swimmers around the globe to stay active. And, as we will see in more detail in

Figure 2.24 Measuring no more than 1x8x6mm, Philips' wearable biosensor can read and send vital medical data, including heart rate, respiratory rate, temperature, body posture as well as detect falls. (photo courtesy Philips)

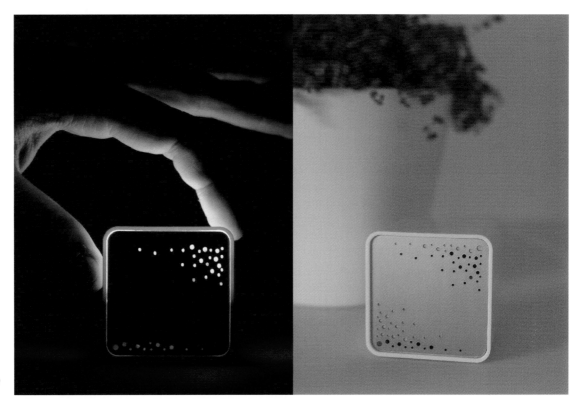

Figure 2.25 Koto Air monitors temperature, humidity, light, noise, air pollution and dust day and night to help maintain a healthy indoor environment. (photo courtesy Klevio Ltd)

Chapters 3 and 8, the IoT is also enabling the development of many monitoring and air-purifying products in response to the growing concern about air, light and noise pollution (fig 2.25).

Blockchain is another IoT-enabled technology that will increasingly contribute to sustainable consumption and production by providing a verifiable record of a product's environmental and ethical supply chain history.[69] This represents an important opportunity to rebuild trust between consumers and producers, especially for designers and companies that are genuinely 'doing the right thing' by their supply chain.

However, the IoT also has a more sinister side that may counteract its benefits unless designers and citizens play an active role in shaping and regulating it. With the smartphone, smart home and smart city, all our physical and digital movements and activities are continuously being logged and analysed in what were once personal or anonymous spaces. Apart from the obvious implications for loss of privacy, the information generated by this continuous surveillance is being channelled for highly targeted commercial and political interests. It also seems that Alexa, AliGenie, Google, Siri, Duer and colleagues are all there to 'help us' – by lowering barriers to consumption and reducing the space to question it. Is 'smarter' persuasion for political manipulation, more

consumption and loss of privacy progress towards the sustainability we want?

Much more inspiring is to look to the potential of the IoT to make the circular economy or cradle-to-cradle dream a reality. A large part of what hampers the creation of a truly circular economy is logistical. Simply capturing materials, getting them to the right place and identifying them so that they can be recycled in the correct waste stream has proved very challenging, especially for plastics, as our production and distribution systems weren't set up with this mindset. The IoT could be instrumental in changing this. At the logistics level it can provide a platform to track materials through formal and informal channels and direct them to the right processor. At the product level, materials and labels can be tagged with nano-optical or chemical markers that will give recycling feedstocks the integrity required for designers to use closed-loop recycling.[70] An example of a company working at both ends of this equation is Banyan Nation based in Hyderabad. They produce quality-assured recycled plastic granules for global brands starting from a supply chain of thousands of informal sector last-mile collectors integrated through a mobile Internet platform. Could a combination of IoT and nano-materials scenarios one day make our products resemble nature where every cell has its own ID in the form of DNA that allows it to organise itself down to the molecule? As Bruce Sterling clearly understood:

SPIMES [connected objects] are information melded with sustainability. Without sustainability, information is top-heavy, energy hungry and heading for a crash: while sustainability is impractical without precise, comprehensive information about flows of energy and materials.[71]

3D printing: additive and distributed manufacturing

Additive Manufacturing could be used in many ways, both good and bad for the environment. The outcome will depend strongly on the intentions of society and the incentives put in place to obtain the desired outcomes.[72]

Digital additive manufacturing (AM) via 3D printers and assemblers is the latest piece of the digital revolution jigsaw.[73] As the costs of AM falls, it is one of the top contenders for disrupting the possibilities of *what, who* and *how* we make physical objects, forcing product designers to re-examine their role. Its potential contribution to sustainability through democratisation, localisation of production and distributed manufacturing is discussed in Chapter 4.3, while here we focus first on its physical possibilities for environmental gains.

Digital fabrication in the form of subtractive manufacturing has been with us for several decades with CNC machines happily carving out complex and detailed 3D forms from solid material such as Apple laptop cases, while laser cutters make light work of profiling. 3D printers, on the other hand, build up or fuse materials, hence the generic term additive manufacturing (AM). AM can create anything from simple forms to highly intricate structures and even whole products, complete with moving parts, in plastics, paper, ceramic, metal, sand, salt, and almost any combination of composites, including food and living cells, without the need for expensive tool-making.

But why the revolution now, given that designers have been using rapid prototyping to develop products for some time? The rise of the maker movement, open-source technology, access to facilities through Fab Labs and maker spaces, and the development of affordable 3D printer technologies, have all contributed to its rapid expansion. With the possibility of moving manufacturing from the factory to local maker units, the studio, home or even the building site, there is an intense push by researchers and businesses to explore its potential applications and new business models.

Despite much hype, 3D printing has some way to go before it can replace mass manufacturing. The key limiting factors to date have been speed, hence unit cost, energy, size, finish quality and the ability to handle multiple materials, although all of these

Figure 2.26 The OpenHand project evolved into Open Bionics supplying highly affordable, lightweight, modular, adaptive robot hands and prosthetic devices. (photo courtesy OpenBionics)

factors are rapidly gaining ground.[74] However, it is undoubtedly revolutionising sectors that operate in low-volume, batch and one-off production, by enabling them to offer on-demand mass customisation, and specialised, localised, one-off products that were previously uneconomic. According to Neil Gershenfeld, *"the killer app in digital fabrication, as in computing, is personalisation, producing products for a market of one person".*[75] This is transforming industries that manufacture medical implants and prosthetics, aerospace, automotive specials, furniture and even architecture, not to mention fashion accessories and all manner of personalised products.

OpenBionics (fig 2.26) and Printhesis (see fig 4.25) are good examples of all the best aspects of 3D printing and the Open Design model (see Chapter 4.4). Started as the OpenHand Project, Joel Gibbard created a low-cost, openly available 3D printable bionic hand, Dextrus, with Indiegogo funding. The project has now grown into OpenBionics which supplies highly affordable bionic arms for children to the National Health Service (NHS) in the UK while still keeping the technology open.[76]

In terms of environmental sustainability, 3D printing has pros and cons around energy and resource consumption that designers should consider carefully if they want to produce more sustainable products. Starting with energy, studies to date show that most AM processes, especially sintering, use more energy than mass-production methods like injection moulding but are comparable to batch and one-off processes. However, when we look at whole-product lifecycles, we find that the situation can flip when the new forms possible through 3D printing reduce weight and therefore energy consumption in the use phase.

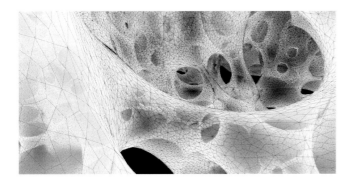

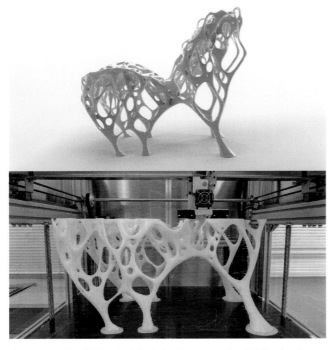

Figure 2.27 The STEM 45° chair design is generated and FDM printed using autonomous design scripts based on the logic of how bamboo grows to minimise production energy, materials and time, and to create its own unique aesthetic (Kyoto 2017). (photo courtesy ©Assa Ashuach Studio with KIT and Kyoto D-Lab)

Designers, engineers and architects are just beginning to explore some of AM's unique capabilities to create forms that were previously impossible to make. Super-efficient structures can now be faithfully produced following nature's rules by only putting material where it is needed. As we saw in Ashuach's STEM project, with the help of autonomous design scripts and algorithms, they were able to copy the efficiency of how bamboo structures grow that vastly reduces print time, energy and material[77] (figs 2.14, 2.27). If you apply these same autonomous design scripts to the design of lighter aircraft and cars, the savings during the use phase would greatly outweigh the extra energy in production compared with mass production.[78] This principle can also extend to architecture where light and insulating structures could be integrally fabricated to save on

embodied energy and heating or cooling during the lifetime of the building.

In terms of scale, the world's first 3D printed houses were demonstrated by WinSun in Sozhou, China in 2013 with a giant robotic arm extruding layers of concrete made from 50% construction or mining waste. Since then, 3D printing technology has been developed to build highly affordable houses. New Story's collaboration with Icon Build demonstrates how the entire structure of their low-cost houses can be fabricated in 24 hours for under $4000, leaving only the roof and windows to be added[79] (fig 2.28).

In terms of material sustainability, 3D printing has been heralded as a no-waste process.[80] This is actually quite far from reality. Many designs require extra material in the form of 'scaffolding' to support the piece while it is being made. This is discarded after the print and can amount to as much as 100% more material. In addition, the industry uses almost exclusively virgin plastics and many of the resins used are not recyclable, show levels of toxicity and some excess resin powders used in sintering cannot be reused.[81] Sandstone, metal and FDM filaments are much better in relation to recyclability.

Until more environmentally friendly resins are developed, designers can help a lot to reduce the impact of 3D printing by selecting recycled materials, less wasteful processes, and importantly by designing geometries that eliminate or reduce the need for scaffolding as demonstrated in the STEM work. Emerging Objects' experiments in formulating and printing with renewable and recyclable materials are inspirational examples of how designers can push the process and sustainability credentials of the materials used in 3D printing (fig 2.29). In her Soft Seat (2014), Lilian Van Daal began an exploration into how 3D printing could be combined with biomimicry principles to build in flexibility in order to replace environmentally problematic upholstery foams. In her follow-up Radiolara#1 chair (2018), she continues to explore the same theme and, in collaboration with OceanZ3D, has also succeeded in printing with 100% recycled Polyamide (fig 2.30).

The ability to manufacture locally for a local market has also been touted as environmentally beneficial through reduced transportation. However, if materials still need to be shipped to the printer, this may be far smaller than claimed.[82] It would be very interesting for designers to explore how products could be designed to be adaptable to the use of local materials to square the circle. Markus Kayser's project sintering forms from sand assisted by solar power and a Fresnel lens in the desert begins to unleash the possibilities of designing for 3D printing using abundant and free resources around us (fig 2.31). Similar thinking is being used in the European Space Agency's (ESA) design

Figure 2.28 New Story and ICON are working together to 3D print highly affordable housing in El Salvador (2019 roll-out). (photo courtesy New Story and ICON)

Figure 2.29 Emerging Objects' outdoor Pouf (2016), made from their specially formulated recycled rubber tyre powder and Bloom (2015), a tempietto made of over 840 printed blocks, are only a sample of the many natural and recycled materials and designs they have created for 3D printing (USA). (photos courtesy Emerging Objects; Bloom photo credit Matthew Millman)

Figure 2.30 Lilian Van Daal's biomimicry-inspired Soft Seat explores varying density and stiffness to replace upholstery (2014). (courtesy Studio Lilian Van Daal photo credit Martin Jansen)

concepts for 3D printing buildings and other products in situ that will make living on the moon 'feel like home'[83] (fig 2.32).

Extending product lifecycles through local repairing is another sustainable and empowering feature of 3D printing. As keeping stock of vast numbers of spare parts has become uneconomic, digital files of broken or worn-out parts can instead be sent out to be 3D printed by a local printer repair shop or at home by the DIY enthusiast. Currently however, many parts cannot be replaced with printed parts, so the approach to design would have to change

to make key components specifically replaceable by 3D printed parts.[84] Designing and self-printing also mean that people will be investing more personally in products, potentially creating greater product appreciation and attachment, leading to longer product lifespans.

Where we need to look more closely in the coming years is the desktop printing revolution.[85] Looking at the parallel world of 2D digital printing and the exponential increase in printed material it created, will cheap 3D printing also lead to mountains

Figure 2.31 Markus Keyser solar sand sintering in the desert: 3D printing products with free and abundant energy and materials. (photos courtesy Markus Keyser)

Figure 2.32 The European Space Agency (ESA) is developing building and product concepts for living on the moon 3D printed from lunar dust. (photo courtesy ©ESA)

of post-consumer waste?[86] What will happen to all those failed prints or the ones that were fun at the time but we have now tired of? Currently, most desktop printers (FDM) require you to buy proprietary material cartridges. Aside from the cost, most of these are virgin materials. Even the Ekocycle Cube cartridge has only 25% post-consumer recycled material.[87] One company working to shift this is Protoprint, a social enterprise in Pune, India. They are transforming plastic collected by waste-pickers into the world's

first fair trade filament.[88] Also promising are the development of open designs like Recyclebot[89] from the RepRap family and ReDeTec's ProtoCycler that now make it possible to create closed-loop 3D printing desktop systems by producing plastic filament directly from one's own FDM desktop printer waste.[90] By having consumption and production happening alongside each other, be it at home or at the local print shop rather than spread across the globe, 3D printing could one day lead the way in circular cradle-to-cradle production (fig 2.33).

a radical alternative: low tech and old tech

We have seen that while new and future technologies offer many potential benefits for efficiency savings, they may also come with unintended consequences. Several high-tech developments also fall short of sustainability in socio-economic terms by excluding a large part of the world population in their development, ownership and enjoyment due to the level of know-how, cost and investment required (see Chapters 3.3 and 6.2).

> *Technofixes are a pernicious cycle of problem generation designed to scratch the itch but never to find the reason for itching. It is precisely their inability to solve problems that makes them so attractive to big business.*[91]

Could there be an alternative answer in low-tech and appropriate technologies for meeting the needs of the many for a better quality of life with a radically smaller footprint? What happens if we could achieve the radical shifts we need by revisiting existing or even forgotten technologies? There have been and still are many advocates of smaller, more accessible and distributed models of technology and economy. Gandhi demonstrated it through his All India Village Industries Association (1936), and Fritz

Figure 2.33 Closing the 3D printing loop: ReDeTec's ProtoCycler, crowd-funded in 2014, recycles unwanted 3D prints back into FDM filament. (photo courtesy ReDeTec)

Figure 2.34 Medellin's Metrocable linea K (2004) not only makes commuting to work viable for Santo Domingo residents, it is also cleaner, more efficient and cheaper to install than other public transport options. (photo credit Robert Schrader (2012))

Figure 2.35 Texenergy's Infinite Orbit and Eton's American Red Cross Clipray wind-up chargers are produced by two companies committed to reliable off-grid human or renewably powered devices. (photos courtesy ©Texenergy Ltd and ©Eton Corp)

Schumacher disseminated and popularised it through his book *Small is Beautiful* (1973).

> *We shrink back from the truth if we believe that the destructive forces of the modern world can be 'brought under control' simply by mobilising more resources – of wealth, education, and research – to fight pollution, to preserve wildlife, to discover new sources of energy and to arrive at more effective agreements on peaceful coexistence.*
>
> E.F. Schumacher, Small is Beautiful

There are many inspiring examples of where refining existing low tech is proving to be the better and more sustainable option. One of the best examples of a sustainable shift made possible by low tech is the resurgence of the bicycle. Bicycles are increasingly being recognised and used as one of the best solutions for personal urban transport. They make cities more liveable and people-friendly, have zero emissions, save money and help keep people fit and healthy (see Chapter 8.2). Another example, led by Medellin's lateral thinking approach to improving access to

Figure 2.36 Dick van Hoff's hand-operated beater from his 'Tyranny of the Plug' series brings back physicality to kitchen appliances (2003, the Netherlands). (photo courtesy Dick van Hoff)

Figure 2.37 The tallest timber tower as of 2017: Brock Commons Tallhouse, 18 storeys of student accommodation, being built in Vancouver. (photo courtesy naturallywood.com)

AIDS, Trevor Bayliss revisited the kinetic mechanism of wind-up toys and adapted it to operate a radio where electricity was unavailable and replacing batteries unaffordable. His work has inspired many designers to create a new generation of human-powered, solar and wind-powered radios, flashlights, speakers and chargers for on-the-go and off-grid situations like the Eton and Texenergy product ranges (fig 2.35). The possibilities of kinetic power can also be used to question the need to electrify many everyday activities. In 'The Tyranny of the Plug' designer Dick van Hoff re-introduces simple and long-lasting human-powered tools that give us back a sense of direct involvement and control (fig 2.36).

Finally, humble wood is resurging as the sustainable choice for high-rise buildings. As more and more of the world's population moves to urban areas, high-density living will become the norm. Until very recently, these buildings could only be constructed from steel and concrete. With a carbon footprint 60 to 75% lower than steel and concrete[92] and the continued development of 'engineered wood' products like cross-laminated timber (CLT) and glulam beams, wood is now the 'new' wonder material. It also allows many building parts to be fabricated off-site, moving them into the realms of modular products. In 2017, the tallest wooden building was Brock Commons Tallhouse, standing at 18 storeys high in Vancouver (fig 2.37), surpassed in 2019 by the 85m-high Mjøstårnet building in Brumunddal, Norway. These are set to be dwarfed by projects for plyscrapers reaching 30 storeys high by 2020 while more fantastical proposals for plyscrapers over 300 m high in London and Tokyo may one day be a reality (fig 2.38).

These examples demonstrate instances of where rediscovering and refining existing low tech and traditional materials are proving to be the better and more sustainable option, not only in environmental terms but also bringing real social and economic benefits to create much-needed win-win-win scenarios. While this approach may not be the answer in every case, there is a huge opportunity for designers and engineers, planners and businesses to think laterally and spot the potential of simpler existing and past technologies to solve current issues. By reimagining them in ways that give them currency, product designers can be instrumental in making these new-old technologies relevant, desirable and viable for individuals and communities today.

Figure 2.38 Wooden plyscrapers redefining sustainable urban living: Jean-Paul Viguier's Hyperion in Bordeaux is set for completion in 2020 (France). (photo courtesy ©Jean-Paul Viguier et Associés)

employment for the barrios, is the introduction of cable cars as a much cleaner, more efficient and viable means of mass transport that is spreading to several other developing cities (fig 2.34). In Chapter 8.2 we explore how design can help propel cycling and other less impactful lower tech forms of mobility.

The wind-up radio is another example of rediscovering the usefulness of existing technologies. In 1992, looking for a way to bring radio to African communities to combat the spread of

Chapter summary

1. The environmental impacts of products are mostly hidden and can be very complex. Designers should seek to uncover these as best they can, and then decide which aspects they are in a position to change: immediately, in the near future or in the longer term. This forms the backbone of a sustainable design strategy. In order to formulate and implement this strategy, designers also need vision, information and tools coupled with the creative power of design thinking. For the sake of simplicity, the main strategic approaches to more environmentally sustainable products may be grouped under the umbrella terms eco-efficiency and eco-effectiveness.

2. Eco-efficiency is essentially about being *less bad* by doing much *more with less*. The eco-efficient product or service is designed to use less material, less resources, less energy and less water, causing less pollution and ecological damage for more functionality. How much more efficient does our consumption and production need to be? Experts consider that a factor in the order of 10 (90% less) is what is needed to avoid a climate change tipping point. Eco-efficiency is now widely accepted by governments and industry because it has obvious cost benefits and works within the prevailing economic system.

3. Eco-effectiveness sets the bar higher. It challenges designers to apply a systems approach by modelling our production and consumption on nature. In this scenario, all energy is clean, abundant and renewable, toxic materials are eliminated and zero waste is achieved through a circular economy cradle-to-cradle approach of closed-loop techno and bio-material flows. At its most ambitious, eco-effectiveness requires a shift in attitudes and priorities that goes beyond eliminating damage to actively considering how human activity could satisfy our needs and restore our eco-systems at the same time.

4. A lifecycle approach is now an essential part of designing more sustainably. It identifies all the inputs and outputs throughout the life of a product or service that contribute to its environmental impact: raw material supply, manufacturing and assembly, distribution and sales, product use, end of usable life, and return to raw materials. By understanding each phase, we can pinpoint a product or service's biggest impacts, or hotspots, and frame creative strategies that address these issues. Lifecycles are also very useful as benchmark references for keeping sustainability goals on track throughout the design process.

5. The concept of waste is gradually becoming less and less acceptable, with plastics, electronics and toxic waste being the most problematic. From the eco-efficiency perspective, waste is now recognised as a resource. For the eco-effective, zero waste is achieved through C2C or circular economies. With a very long way to go in delivering this vision on any significant scale, the waste hierarchy continues to provide practical strategies that designers can build in to extend product life and ensure that their products go on to be part of closed-loop bio- or techno-cycles.

6. Designers use tools to help: formulate strategies; assess and benchmark impacts; compare and select alternative design options; and monitor and communicate sustainable benefits. Tools can be qualitative or quantitative and should be introduced as early as possible in the design process to have the biggest impact on a product or service's sustainability. Generally, qualitative tools like rules of thumb, polar diagrams and checklists are useful for rapidly comparing alternatives and are also useful as early prompts to spur creative thinking. LCAs, on the other hand, are the most comprehensive and widely used quantitative tool available for assessing environmental impacts. They rely on large LCI datasets and detailed environmental science to interpret the impacts on human health, ecological health and resource depletion via LCAs. LCAs come in different levels of complexity and cost, from the complete or rigorous LCA, to the partial or streamlined LCA, and the simplified or fast-track LCA. In terms of the information they provide, LCAs can be: damage-based like ReCiPe and Oklala points; prevention-based like Eco-costs; or they may measure single issues like carbon, cumulative energy demand or water footprints.

7. Environmental standards and regulations are now accepted as necessary to create a level commercial playing field while protecting the environment and society. They also stimulate design innovation. In relation to products, these mostly address end-of-life, resource-efficiency, toxicity, emissions and, more recently, whole-product lifecycle assessments and EPDs. The early approach to regulation was end-of-pipe (EoP), but more recently extended producer responsibility (EPR) laws have spurred on lightweighting, efficiency and recyclability

in the packaging, electronics and vehicle industries. A combination of incentives and penalties, voluntary labelling and mandatory minimum energy performance (MEPS) are also shifting consumer behaviours and producer offer. In a global market, leaders in environmental regulation like the EU, California and Japan are raising standards across the world.

8. Living within the planet's carrying capacity or reducing our impacts by a factor of 10 cannot be achieved through incremental efficiency improvements alone. It demands radically rethinking our systems from both the consumption and production ends. The answer to how we achieve this lies anywhere between the high-tech camp that believes 'technology will save us' and the low-tech camp that advocates revisiting lower impact technologies combined with radical changes in the nature of our consumption.

9. Biology is an endless source of sustainable solutions from low tech to high tech. At its most traditional, nature can literally grow objects while its by-products can be transformed into exceptional materials and structures. Biomimicry applies nature's intelligent and sustainable rules to our design process. In contrast, synthetic biology and genetic engineering bypass the biological rulebook by creating human-designed organisms for bio-facturing, sensing, diagnosing and bio-computing. Its capabilities are being developed for food production, medicine, energy, environmental monitoring and computing. But creating new combinations of life so rapidly when biology has evolved over millions of years takes us into unchartered territory and is not without risks that designers and society must seriously consider.

10. At a nano-scale, familiar materials take on completely different properties. Nano-materials open up a world of new possibilities for designers to solve sustainability challenges such as: stronger and lighter materials that increase efficiency; coatings that extend life and reduce maintenance or produce energy; reactive packaging that reduces food waste; and flexible and miniaturised electronics for lighting, energy capture, ubiquitous and wearable tech. However, as research into the potentially harmful effects of some nano-materials on humans and the environment is only just emerging, designers should keep abreast of these developments and apply the precautionary principle in their decision making.

11. The Internet of Things (IoT) is about objects sensing, talking to each other and making decisions from the big data generated by using AI and machine learning. By constantly collecting data and feeding it back into responsive systems, we have everything from umbrellas that tell us when it will rain, to whole cities optimising their lighting, transport and waste collections according to demand. From personal fitness and medical monitoring to the smart house and smart city, the IoT certainly has the potential to increase the efficiency and wellbeing of everyday life. It could also be instrumental in realising a circular economy. But we will need to ensure that its beneficial uses do not come at the cost of privacy encroachment and stealth advertising aimed at driving yet more consumption or derailing democracy.

12. Additive manufacturing in the form of 3D printing is rapidly changing what, who and how we make physical objects. This is forcing product designers to re-examine their role and ask themselves: Can anyone be a designer? While 3D printing is not yet in a position to replace mass production in speed or efficiency, it is revolutionising the on-demand, low-volume and one-off production of medical implants and prosthetics, furniture, architecture, aerospace, fashion accessories and personalised products. AM also has the potential to create designs that are much more efficient in their use of materials, reduce waste in production and extend product life by printing parts for repairing. In spite of this, unless we build in recycling, recyclability and closed loops into our products and systems now, 3D printing has the potential to be another feedstock for our plastic waste mountains.

13. Revisiting existing and developing new low-tech options can prove to be the more sustainable and radical solution in many scenarios. For instance, the bicycle is making a comeback as the clean, healthy and cost-effective choice for urban transport. Low-energy devices can run on human and renewable power enabling off-grid access. Cable cars are providing mass transit at a fraction of the cost and energy in cities in emerging economies. And humble wood is now the sustainable wonder material for plyscrapers to house the growing urban populations of the future. Product designers are in a good position to spot the potential of new and existing low-impact technologies and give these currency, viability and desirability.

Notes

1 Factor 4 was proposed by L. Hunter Lovins, Amory Lovins and E. von Weizsaker in their book by the same name, *Factor 4* (1998); Factor 10 was put forward by Friedrich Schmidt-Bleek from the Wuppertal Institute, and more recently from the Factor 10 Institute.

2 UN DESA (2017) *World Population Prospects 2017. Key Findings*, New York: UN DESA, p.1 [online]. Available at https://esa.un.org/unpd/wpp/Publications/Files/WPP2017_KeyFindings.pdf (accessed 10 January 2019).

3 Vogtländer, J. (n.d.) *A Factor 4, 10 or 20?*, TU Delft [online]. Available at www.ecocostsvalue.com/EVR/model/theory/subject/1-general.html (accessed 21 June 2015).

4 The predicted 2050 population was updated to 9.7 billion from 9.3 billion in line with 2017 UN data.

5 Hausfather, Z. (2018) *New Scenarios Show How the World Could Limit Warming to 1.5C in 2100*. Carbon Brief, 5 March [online]. Available at www.carbonbrief.org/new-scenarios-world-limit-warming-one-point-five-celsius-2100.

6 Hawken, P., ed. (2017) *Drawdown. The Most Comprehensive Plan Ever to Reverse Global Warming*. New York: Penguin. Available at www.drawdown.org.

7 John Ehrenfeld (Industrial Ecology), John Elkington (SustainAbility & Volans/Breakthrough Capitalism), Paul Hawken (The Ecology of Commerce, Drawdown), John Lyle (Centre for Regenerative Design), Walter Stahel (Product Life Institute).

8 Ehrenfeld, J. (2006) Ecoefficiency. Philosophy, Theory and Tools. *Journal of Industrial Ecology*, 9(4), p. 7 [online]. Available at www.johnehrenfeld.com/Eco-efficiency%20JIE.pdf.

9 Benyus, J. (1997) *Biomimicry. Innovation Inspired by Nature*, New York: William Morrow, p. 2.

10 Biomimicry Institute (n.d.) What Is Biomimicry? [online]. Available at https://biomimicry.org/what-is-biomimicry/ (accessed 10 January 2019).

11 Lyle, J. (1994) *Regenerative Design for Sustainable Development*, Hoboken, NJ: Wiley.

12 see Cradle-to-Cradle Products Innovation Institute [online]. Available at www.c2ccertified.org.

13 McDonough, W. and M. Braungart (2002) *Cradle to Cradle. Remaking the Way We Make Things*, New York: North Point Press, pp. 68–91.

14 www.interfaceglobal.com/pdfs/Biomimicry_InterfaceFLOR_Case_Study-2.aspx (accessed 23 June 2016).

15 Mathews, John A. and Hao Tan (2016) Circular Economy: Lessons from China. *Nature News*, 24 March, 531(7595), p. 440. doi: 10.1038/531440a.

16 Geyer, Jambeck, Law (2017) Production, Use, and Fate of All Plastics Ever Made. *Science Advances*, 3(7), p. e1700782. doi: 10.1126/sciadv.1700782.

18 The European Union's Waste Framework Directive (1975/442/EEC).

19 Geyer, R. *et al.* (2016) Common Misconceptions about Recycling. *Journal of Industrial Ecology*, 20(5), pp. 1010–1017. doi: 10.1111/jiec.12355.

20 Huysman, S. *et al.* (2015) The Recyclability Benefit Rate of Closed-loop and Open-loop Systems: A Case Study on Plastic Recycling. *Flanders Resources Conservation and Recycling*, 101, pp. 53–60. doi: 10.1016/j.resconrec.2015.05.014.

21 Stiglitz, J. (2009) Towards a Better Measure of Well-being. *Financial Times*, 13 September. Available at www.ft.com/content/95b492a8-a095-11de-b9ef-00144feabdc0 (accessed 17 June 2017).

22 Fiskel, J. (2012) *Design for Environment*, 2nd edition, New York: McGraw Hill, p. 106.

23 Vogtländer, J.A. (2014) *Practical Guide to LCA*, 3rd edition, Delft: Delft Academic/VSSD. pp. 18–19.

24 Ibid., pp. 24–27.

25 Tischner, U. and H. Moser/UBA (2015) *How to Do EcoDesign?*, 2nd edition, Dessau-Roßlau: German Federal Environment Agency, pp. 113–114; 109–111; 153–166.

26 Blasing, T.J. (04/2016) *Recent Greenhouse Gas Concentrations*, The Carbon Dioxide Information Analysis Center (CDIAC) [online]. Available at http://cdiac.ess-dive.lbl.gov/pns/current_ghg.html (migrating to EES-DIVE, US DOE).

27 C2CCertified_Banned_Lists_V3_121113.pdf. Available at www.c2ccertified.org/resources/detail/cradle-to-cradle-certified-banned-list-of-chemicals.

28 EEA (2017) *Protecting the Ozone Layer While Also Preventing Climate Change* [online, 17 January]. Available at www.eea.europa.eu/themes/climate/ozone-depleting-substances-and-climate-change/protecting-the-ozone-layer-while (accessed 10 January 2019).

29 For a discussion on these different models see Vogtländer, J.G. (2014) *LCA. A Practical Guide for Students, Designers and Business Managers*, 3rd edition, Delft, the Netherlands: Delft Academic Press, and *'Fast Track' LCA for Dummies* [online]. Available at www.ecocostsvalue.com/EVR/img/LCA%20Guide-I02070_1011.pdf.

30 White, P., L. St Pierre and S. Belletire (2013) *Okala Practionner. Integrating Ecological Design*, Phoenix, AZ: Okala Team, pp. 44–48.

31 www.epa.gov/nrmrl/std/traci/traci.html.

32 Vogländer, J. *et al.* (2013) *Eco-efficient Value Creation. Sustainable Design and Business Strategies*, Delft, the Netherlands: Delft Academic Press.

33 ICE database available to download: Circularecology.com (n.d.) Embodied Energy and Embodied Carbon [online]. Available

at www.circularecology.com/embodied-energy-and-carbon-footprint-database.html (accessed 10 January 2019).

34 ARB (2014) arb 40th history [online, 22 October]. Available at www.arb.ca.gov/knowzone/history.htm (accessed 10 January 2019).

35 EPA Clean Air Act 1970 (USA).

36 Palmer, Paul (n.d.) Zero Waste Institute [online]. Available at http://zerowasteinstitute.org/?page_id=1067 (accessed 2 April 2015).

37 McKerron, C. (2012) *Unfinished Business*, Oakland, CA: As You Sow [online]. Available at www.asyousow.org/ays_report/unfinished-business-the-case-for-extended-producer-responsibility-for-post-consumer-packaging/.

38 US EPA (2015) Advancing Sustainable Materials Management: Facts and Figures [online]. Available at www.epa.gov/facts-and-figures-about-materials-waste-and-recycling/advancing-sustainable-materials-management-0 (accessed 10 January 2019).

39 EU (2018) Packaging Waste Statistics 2006–2015 [online]. Available at http://ec.europa.eu/eurostat/statistics-explained/index.php/Packaging_waste_statistics.

40 Thornton, E. (2017) Global Deposit Return Schemes. Edie.net [online, 3 October]. Available at www.edie.net/blog/Global-deposit-return-schemes/6098359 (accessed 11 April 2019).

41 energystar.gov (n.d.) How a Product Earns the ENERGY STAR Label [online]. Available at www.energystar.gov/products/how-product-earns-energy-star-label (accessed 8 December 2018).

42 Tom Knight, the 'father of synthetic biology', interviewed by Andy Coghlan, 5 December 2012.Biology is a Manufacturing Capability. *New Scientist* [online]. Available at www.newscientist.com/article/mg21628946.100-biology-is-a-manufacturing-capability.html#.VTkbgUiW_-F.

43 Cambridge University (2011) The Hidden Power of Moss, CambPlants Hub [online, 22 September]. Available at www.cambplants.group.cam.ac.uk/cambridge-bioenergy-initiative/the-hidden-power-of-moss-1/the-hidden-power-of-moss (accessed 11 March 2018).

44 Assa Ashuach Studio (n.d.) [online]. Available at http://assaashuach.com/learning-as-it-grows-designing-the-new-stem-objects-collection/ (accessed 11 March 2018).

45 iGEM open source registry catalogue of biological/DNA parts [online]. Available at http://parts.igem.org.

46 Anon (n.d.) Synthetic Aesthetics [online]. Available at www.syntheticaesthetics.org/ (accessed 10 January 2019).

47 Wyss Institute, Harvard (2014) Biology on Ordinary Paper, Results off the Page [online]. Available at https://wyss.harvard.edu/synthetic-biology-on-ordinary-paper-results-off-the-page/ (accessed 10 January 2019).

48 www.algenol.com/direct-to-ethanol/environmental-benefits (accessed 1 May 2015).

49 Sloan Report (2016) The Synthetic Biology Project at the Wilson Centre: Eight Years of Engagement and Analysis [online]. Available at www.synbioproject.org/site/assets/files/1402/stip_synbio_sloanreport_v2r5.pdf (accessed 10 January 2019).

50 Wintle, B.C., Boehm, C.R. *et al.* (14/11/2017) A Transatlantic Perspective on 20 Emerging Issues in Biological Engineering. *eLife*, 14 November. doi: 10.7554/eLife.30247.

51 http://phys.org/news/2013-01-nanotube-fibers-unmatched-combination-strength.html.

52 Fuechsle, M. *et al.* (2012) 'A Single-atom Transistor.' *Nature Nanotechnology*, 19 February, 7, p. 242. doi: 10.1038/srep31161.

53 Anon (n.d.) Oxford Nanopore Technologies [online]. Available at https://nanoporetech.com/ (accessed 10 October 2019).

54 University of New South Wales (27/04/2016) UNSW Takes Lead in Race for Non-toxic, Thin-film Solar Cells [online]. Available at https://newsroom.unsw.edu.au/news/science-tech/unsw-takes-lead-race-non-toxic-thin-film-solar-cells (accessed 10 January 2019).

55 Ridgeway, A., (11/10/2014) Wonder Stuff, Self-healing Polymers. *New Scientist*, 2990, p. 38.

56 Hsu, P-C. *et al.* (2015) Personal Thermal Management by Metallic Nanowire-coated Textile. *Nano Lett.*, 15(1), pp. 365–371. doi: 10.1021/nl5036572.

57 Templeton, G. (2014) Mercedes Hydrogen-electric Hybrid Harvests Solar and Wind Energy with its Paint Job. *Extreme Tech*, 7 November [online]. Available at www.extremetech.com/extreme/191336-mercedes-hydrogen-electric-hybrid-harvests-solar-wind-energy-with-its-paint-job (accessed 7 May 2015).

58 www.epa.gov/reviewing-new-chemicals-under-toxic-substances-control-act-tsca/fact-sheet-nanoscale-materials (accessed 14 March 2018).

59 http://www.nanoreg2.eu/ (accessed 14 March 2018).

60 Luanpitpong, S., L. Wang and Y.Rojanasakul (05/2014)The Effects of Carbon Nanotubes on Lung and Dermal Cellular Behaviors. *Nanomedicine*, 9(6), pp. 895–912 [online]. Available at https://doi.org/10.2217/nnm.14.42.

61 Liebert, M.A. (2015) Nanoparticles in Consumer Products Can Significantly Alter Normal Gut Microbiome [online, 4 May]. Available at https://phys.org/news/2015-05-nanoparticles-consumer-products-significantly-gut.html (accessed 10 January 2019).

62 Gaffney, A.M. *et al.* (2015) Blood Biocompatibility of Surface-bound Multi Walled Carbon Nanotubes. *Nanomedicine*, 11(1), pp.39–46. **doi.org/10.1016/j.nano.2014.07.005**.

63 Anon (n.d.) *YUMESHOKUNIN.CO., LTD. MISOKA Maison & Objet Paris January 2016* [online]. Available at www.yumeshokunin.jp/mo/ (accessed 10 January 2019).

64 Elsevier (n.d.) Uncovering Health and Environmental Risks of Nanomaterials [online]. Available at www.elsevier.com/connect/uncovering-health-and-environmental-risks-of-nanomaterials (accessed 10 January 2019).

65 Umweltbundesmamt (2017) Nanomaterial. Little is Known about the Risks [online, 7 November]. Available at www.umweltbundesamt.de/en/topics/health/environmental-impact-on-people/nanomaterial (accessed 10 January 2019).

66 This article reviews four reports: GreenBuildingAdvisor (20 May 2015) Does the Nest Thermostat Save Energy? Available at www.greenbuildingadvisor.com/articles/dept/building-science/does-nest-thermostat-save-energy (accessed 15 March 2018).

67 Howell, J. (2017) Number of Connected IoT Devices Will Surge to 125 Billion by 2030, IHS Markit Says. *IHS Technology* [online]. Available at https://technology.ihs.com/596542/number-of-connected-iot-devices-will-surge-to-125-billion-by-2030-ihs-markit-says (accessed 5 April 2019).

68 Garfield, L. (2018) South Korea Is Building a $35 Billion City Designed to Eliminate the Need for Cars. *Business Insider*, 14 July [online]. Available at http://uk.businessinsider.com/songdo-south-korea-design-2017-11 (accessed 10 January 2019).

69 IBM Blockchain Unleashed (2018) Why Blockchain and IoT Are Best Friends [online, 12 January]. Available at www.ibm.com/blogs/blockchain/2018/01/why-blockchain-and-iot-are-best-friends/ (accessed 10 January 2019).

70 A good summary of technologies in the pipeline for recycling plastics is Angeli Mehta, A. (15/09/2017) Recycling Is Taking Back Plastic. *Chemistry World*, 15 September [online]. Available at www.chemistryworld.com/feature/recycling-is-taking-back-plastic/3007943.article (accessed 10 January 2019).

71 Sterling, B. (2005) *Shaping Things*, Cambridge, MA: MIT Press, p. 43.

72 Holmström, Jan and Timothy Gutowski (2017) Additive Manufacturing in Operations and Supply Chain Management: No Sustainability Benefit or Virtuous Knock-on Opportunities?, *Journal of Industrial Ecology*, 1 November, 21(S1), pp. S21–S24 [online]. Available at https://doi.org/10.1111/jiec.12580, p. S24.

73 Lipman, H. and Melba Kurman (2013) *Fabricated: The New World of 3D Printing*, Indianapolis, IN: John Wiley, pp. 9, 14.

74 http://carbon3d.com/ addressed these points.

75 Gershenfeld, N. (2012) How to Make Almost Anything. *Foreign Affairs*. November/December [online]. Available at2 www.foreignaffairs.com/articles/2012-09-27/how-make-almost-anything (accessed 17 March 2018).

76 www.openbionics.com/blog/open-bionics-and-the-nhs-launch-worlds-first-trial-of-3d-printed-bionic-hands-for-children.

77 http://assaashuach.com/category/structures/ and video: KYOTO Design Lab, Learning as It Grows: Autonomous Design for Additive Manufacture [online]. Available at www.youtube.com/watch?v=KIBZzw5QC6g (accessed 19 March 2018).

78 Kellens, K. *et al.* (2017) Environmental Dimensions of Additive Manufacturing: Mapping Application Domains and Their Environmental Implications. *Journal of Industrial Ecology*, 1 November, 21(S1), pp. S49–S68 [online]. Available at https://doi.org/10.1111/jiec.12629.

79 newstorycharity.org (n.d.) 3D Printed Home [online]. Available at https://newstorycharity.org/3d-home (accessed 10 January 2019).

80 Reid, L. (2017) 3D Printing and Industrial Ecology. *Journal of Industrial Ecology*, 5 October, 21(S1), p.S8 [online]. Available at https://doi.org/10.1111/jiec.12669.

81 Jane.Penty, interview with D. Lim, 3D print operator, Chalk Studio, London. 29 January 2017.

82 Baumers, M. *et al.* (2017) Charting the Environmental Dimensions of Additive Manufacturing and 3D Printing. *Journal of Industrial Ecology*, 1 November, 21(S1), pp. S9–S14 [online]. Available at https://doi.org/10.1111/jiec.12668.

83 ESA (2018) What's Your Idea to 3D Print on the Moon – To Make It Feel Like Home? [online, 20 July]. Available at www.esa.int/Our_Activities/Space_Engineering_Technology/What_s_your_idea_to_3D_print_on_the_Moon_to_make_it_feel_like_home (accessed 10 January 2019).

84 Baumers *et al.* (2017).

85 Reid (2017), p. S7.

86 Kurman, M. and H. Lipman (n.d.) Is Eco-friendly 3D Printing a Myth?, *Green Manufacturing* [online]. Available at www.livescience.com/38323-is-3d-printing-eco-friendly.html (accessed 10 January 2019).

87 3dsystems.com (n.d.) Support | EKOCYCLE | FAQ | *3D Systems* [online]. Available at www.3dsystems.com/shop/support/ekocycle/faq (accessed 10 January 2019).

88 Holmström and Gutowski (2017), pp. 22–23.

89 Available to download from Thingiverse and Appropedia.

90 Kerns, J. (2017) Recycling PLA for 3D Printing. Machine Design [online, 21 September]. Available at www.machinedesign.com/materials/recycling-pla-3d-printing (accessed 10 January 2019).

91 Anon (n.d.) End-of-pipe | The Zero Waste Institute – Click to Start [online]. Available at http://zerowasteinstitute.org/?page_id=1067 (accessed 10 January 2019).

92 Gorvett, Z. (2017) 'Plyscrapers': The Rise of the Wooden Skyscraper [online, 31 October]. Available at www.bbc.com/future/story/20171026-the-rise-of-skyscrapers-made-of-wood (accessed 10 January 2019).

Key texts and further reading

design for environment: strategies and tools

Ashby, Michael (2013) *Materials and the Environment. Eco-informed Material Choice*, 2nd edition, Oxford: Butterworth Heinemann.

Comprehensive textbook of the science and factors influencing eco-efficient material choices introducing the eco-audit and material selector charts.

Benyus, Janine (1998) *Biomimicry. Innovation Inspired by Nature*, New York: William Morrow. *Sets out the rationale and principles for applying biomimicry to design.*

Friskel, Joseph (2012) *Design for Environment, A Guide to Sustainable Product Development*, 2nd edition. New York: McGraw-Hill. *A very comprehensive text on the principles of DfE and its systemic introduction in management and organisational processes of product development.*

McDonough, William and Michael Braungart (2002) *Cradle to Cradle. Remaking the Way We Make Things*, New York: North Point Press. *Establishes the rationale of a cradle-to-cradle approach and introduces the principles of eco-effectiveness for design.*

McDonough, William and Michael Braungart (2012) *The Upcycle: Beyond Sustainability-designing for Abundance*, New York: North Point Press. *Revisits the cradle-to-cradle and eco-effective approach a decade on with more examples of how this is being put into practice.*

Shedroff, Nathan (2009) *Design is the Problem: The Future of Design Must Be Sustainable*, New York: Rosenfeld Media. *Good mapping of strategies: broad coverage of subject with pointers for further investigation.*

Stebbing, Peter and Ursula Tischner, eds. (2015) *Changing Paradigms for a Sustainable Future*. Cumulus Think Tank Series no. 1, Helsinki: Aalto University. *Essential and comprehensive knowledge for designers and creatives to shift their practices to new design paradigms for sustainable production, consumption and lifestyles.*

Tischner, U. and Moser H./UBA (2015, 2nd ed) *How to do EcoDesign?*, 2nd edition, Dessau-Roßlau: German Federal Environment Agency. *Very comprehensive and practical guide to all the tools used in the practice of DfE. Downloadable interactive edition available from UBA: www.umweltbundesamt. de/sites/default/files/medien/376/publikationen/ecodesign_ eng_14_3.epub.*

Vezzoli, Carlo and Ezio Manzini (2008 translation of 2007 Zanichelli edition) *Design for Environmental Sustainability*, London: Springer Verlag. *Very thorough coverage of all aspects of DfE with added consideration for some social drivers.*

Vogtlander, Joost (2013, 2nd ed.) *A Practical Guide to LCA for Students and Designers and Business Managers*, Delft: VSSD. *Concise and informative introduction to fast-track LCAs and eco-costs.*

White, P., L. St Pierre and S. Belletire (2013) *Okala Practitioner. Integrating Ecological Design*, Phoenix, AZ: Okala Team. *Concise and informative summary of the principles and practice of eco-design with the Okala fast-track LCA method.*

new tech, old tech and sustainable design

Beukers, Adrian and Ed van Hinte (2005) *Lightness. The Inevitable Renaissance of Minimum Energy Structures*, 4th edition, Rotterdam: 010 publishers. *Inspiration for minimal and efficient structures and designs.*

Bezooyen, A. and P. Raché (2012) *It's not Easy Being Green*, self-published. *A direct account of the work of designers actively involved in 'greener' design from the author's travels around the world.*

Elvin, George (2015) *Post-Petroleum Design*, Abingdon, Oxon, and New York: Routledge. *A good summary of the need for fossil-free products supported by many innovative and diverse design examples.*

Gershenfeld, Neil (1999) *When Things Start to Think*, London: Hodder & Stoughton. *Argues for the need for more intelligent and less frustrating and dumbed-down technology, and gives insights into MIT media lab workings.*

Ginsberg, A., J. Calvert, P. Schyffer, A. Elfick and D. Endy (2014) *Synthetics Aesthetics. Investigating Synthetic Biology's Designs on Nature*, Cambridge, MA: MIT Press. *Introduces the science and questions what it might mean to 'design nature' through six collaborations between artists, designers and synthetic biologists from around the world.*

Leydecker, Sylvia (2008) *Nano Materials in Architecture, Interior Architecture and Design*, Basel, Boston, MA, and Berlin: Birkhauser. *Summary of the development and applications of nano-materials in these fields.*

Lipson, Hod and Melba Kurman (2013) *Fabricated. The New World of 3D Printing*, Indianapolis, IN: John Wiley & Sons. *Comprehensive overview of the technology and its potential to transform a wide range of applications.*

Mensvoort, K. van and H-J. Grievink (eds) (2011) *Next Nature. Nature Changes Along With Us*, Barcelona: Actar. *Compendium of the most thought-provoking observations from nextnature. net, questioning our relationship with nature and new possibilities.*

Sterling, Bruce (2005) *Shaping Things*, Cambridge, MA: MIT Press. *Sets the scene and contextualises the advent of the connected or smart networked world of objects.*

Templeman, E., B. van der Grinten, E-J. Mul and I. de Pauw (2015) Enschede, Netherlands: Boekengilde. Nature Inspired Design. *Principles and toolbox from the Nature Inspired Design (NID) team, TU Delft.*

Warnier, C. and D. Verbruggen (2014) 'Printing Things. Visions and Essentials for 3D Printing.' In S. Ehmann and R. Klanten (eds.), *Unfold*, Berlin: Gestalten. *Exploration of the creative potential of 3D printing.*

CHAPTER 3
Socially led strategies

what is social sustainability?

Although sustainability is most often associated with environmental issues and the health of the planet, it takes on a new meaning when we consider it from the human perspective. The social dimension of sustainability encompasses everything to do with the human experience of life, from the individual to the collective, the rational to the emotive and the physical to the psychological. It challenges what it is to be human in relation to each other and in relation to the planet through our values, practices and social norms.

We will have achieved social sustainability when all humans have the means to satisfy their basic needs and the possibility of self-fulfilment within the planet's limits. This is only achievable if the environment can sustainably supply sufficient natural resources for food, water and shelter, the economic framework facilitates its equitable distribution, and the political system provides a balance between freedom, opportunity and security. Under these conditions, people, cultures and societies thrive. This is what John Ehrenfeld describes as a condition of 'flourishing'.[1]

How does the aspiration of social sustainability compare with most people's reality around the world? Based on the snapshot we took in Chapter 1 (Box 1.5), for the majority in the world, social sustainability is a distant dream: 60% earn less than $4 a day, 55% have no social security while 1 in 11 have no access to safe water or enough food, and 1 in 3 have no sanitation. And as the consumption of the wealthiest 20% causes the Earth to overshoot its carrying capacity by over 75%, there will be fewer and fewer natural ecosystems to sustain future generations.

The connection between the environment and social wellbeing is clear: without environmental sustainability there can be no social sustainability. The elements of this relationship are illustrated in UNEP's GEO-5 report (fig 3.1). But wellbeing goes beyond meeting our physical needs and being financially solvent. It is also reliant on the supportive relationships and networks between people, be it families, friends, colleagues, communities, workplaces or associations. The collective wealth of all these intangibles is known as *social capital*.

As we will see, designers should be aware that through their products they can consciously help to build social capital or unwittingly erode it. Just as environmental sustainability is necessary but not sufficient for social sustainability, so it is with products. The most 'environmentally friendly' product in the world is not sustainable if it serves no positive purpose or does not create some form of social value. In fact it could even be harmful. As Allan Chochinov puts it:

> Designers would do well to remember that they are not in the artefact business. They are in the consequence business. And for design to truly be a force for positive change, we must always ask what consequences a design creates – from materials and energy use to toxicity, pollution and social inequality. [...] There now seems an urgent mandate to design for good – to understand the practice of design as an unequivocally interconnected, global, and consequence-creating endeavor.[2]

Given how far we are globally from achieving social sustainability leads us to the big question: Can we design our way to a better world? If the answer is in part 'yes', what can product designers contribute? While engineers can make products more efficient, and business can make them more profitable, designers sit in the fortunate position between users, technology and the wider social and economic context. This enables them to endow products with social relevance and cultural meaning while minimising their environmental burden.

As an example, a stove serves the purpose of cooking food. From an environmental impact point of view, we could redesign the most energy- and material-efficient model on the market. On the other hand, if we look at cooking as the creative, cultural and

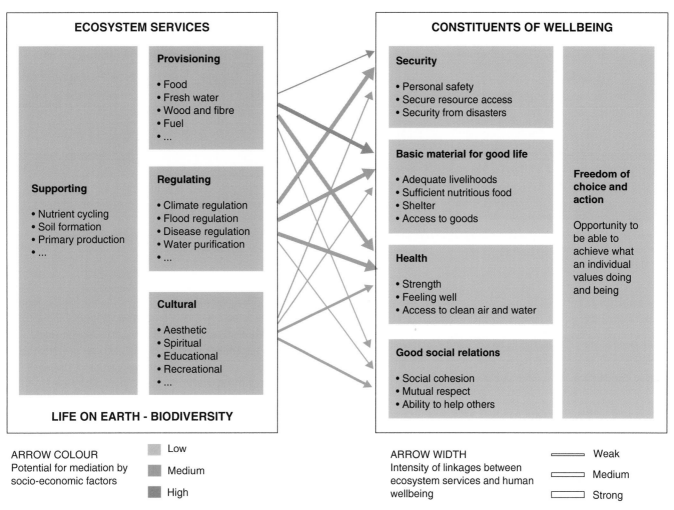

Figure 3.1 The dependence of human wellbeing on biodiversity and ecosystem services. (source: UNEP GEO-5 Report)

educational activity that it is, we could do much better. We could create a product that also fosters social bonding, cross-cultural appreciation and one that recognises the centrality of healthy eating to our wellbeing that connects with the reality of people's living spaces and lifestyle pressures. The outcome would naturally be quite different depending on who and where we are designing the stove for: a farming family in rural India, a time- and space-poor urban professional, etc. (fig 3.2).

measuring social impacts: the S-LCA

In Chapter 2 we looked at the importance of lifecycle thinking and the LCA as an established tool and methodology for measuring, and ultimately reducing the environmental product impacts of products. Measuring social impacts in such a rigorous way through a Social Lifecycle Assessment, or S-LCA, is far less straightforward or advanced, but nonetheless is being actively developed. Not only are the methodologies evolving but there is

also a very big task ahead of building the databases required to support the process.

Many certification bodies such as B Corps', which we will look at in Chapter 4.3, already use their own criteria and methodologies to measure social impacts, but these, like S-LCA's, most often apply to the activities of the whole company or business rather than to individual products. For this reason we will not go into detail about S-LCAs in this book, except to appreciate that they aim to measure the social impacts of a company's activities on their main stakeholders: workers, local community, society, consumers and others in their value chain. Each of these is measured against impact categories: human rights, worker conditions, health and safety, cultural heritage, governance and socio-economic repercussions.[3] While this is a very young and growing field, it will be interesting to see how the use of S-LCAs will impact upon business practices and regulations in the decade ahead.

Figure 3.2 Designing tools that build social capital: a traditional farmhouse stove in Brazil and IDEO's 'Table for Living' for IKEA's Concept Kitchen 2025 present contrasting approaches to creating 'the heart of the home'. (courtesy IDEO.com; photo credit Nick Polanszky)

key challenges in designing products for social sustainability

While many of the contributing factors of our unsustainability are outside a designer's control, the key challenges for the socially minded designer may be summarised as follows.

How can we create products and services that:

- put people at the centre of design?
- add true social value, authenticity and meaning?
- build social capital?
- assist the transition to lower impact lifestyles?
- reduce consumption while increasing quality of life?
- reconnect consumers with the environment and each other?
- challenge the direction of technology to produce value for society?
- have a positive impact through the whole supply chain and product lifecycle?
- address inequality by empowering individuals and communities?

In this chapter we will look at some socially led approaches that product designers can use to address these environmental and social sustainability challenges.

3.1 overconsumption: shifting the consumer society through behaviour change

If anything characterises affluent societies today, it is the drive to consume by those of us who have the means to do so and how integral this consumption has become to our identity. As we saw in section 1, post-war mass production went hand in hand with mass consumption to create our *consumer society*. What has changed since the post-war period is the sheer quantity and nature of what is consumed: while the population of the world doubled between 1970 and 2014, global production more than quadrupled[4] and we seem to be no happier for it. In fact mental health problems abound in the most affluent countries. Having saturated our world with physical objects, those of us at the top of the wealth pyramid are increasingly consuming experiences, both virtual and real, to define who we are.[5] Unfortunately, this shift to consuming experiences is not proving to be any kinder on the environment, as these experiences involve more travel and on-the-go consumption which are both energy- and waste-intensive activities, although they may be more personally rewarding and socially bonding than possessions.[6]

Fundamentally, overconsumption by 'the few' is at the heart of some of the most intractable problems facing humankind. Not only is it causing climate change and resource depletion, it also exacerbates the gross inequality of opportunity of the many. So, there are in fact two interconnected problems: one of *overconsumption* and one of *underconsumption*. We will start by looking at overconsumption while we address underconsumption in design for the base of the pyramid (Chapter 3.3).

Since designers are in the business of producing products and services that are 'consumed', it is essential that we understand the nature of this consumption and its drivers if we want to be in a position to offer more sustainable alternatives for satisfying physical and emotional needs. The strongest underlying driver of overconsumption is the prevailing economic system that requires continuous growth to succeed, usually measured by gross domestic product (GDP). Because GDP measures the consumption of goods and services, it is also closely linked to environmental damage and resource depletion. But it does not have to be this way. In Chapter 4 we take a look at the possibilities of *decoupling* economic growth from environmental damage and more helpful ways of measuring economic progress.

In this context, businesses need to grow to survive, and therefore so is persuading people to buy ever more of their products and services. In fact, the art of persuasion is so finely honed through the use of behavioural psychology throughout mass media and social media advertising that we feel compelled to buy things we do not 'need' and may even cause us harm. How does this happen? When people buy, they believe that they are buying more than a product: they are buying into what it represents, the rewards it promises, the status it confers, a sense of belonging, and even a part of the lifestyle it suggests. While they are constructing personal and collective meaning through what and how they consume,[7] they are unwittingly playing their dutiful part in an economic system set up for ever-increasing growth. Against such powerful forces, who can blame most consumers for succumbing to the persuasion and even believing that they are expressing their individuality through their consumption?

With consumerism so deeply embedded in our social and economic way of life, the notion of sustainable consumption implies not just technological and economic change, but also deep systemic societal change.

> [T]he insight that a certain amount of consumer behaviour is dedicated to an (ultimately flawed) pursuit of meaning opens up the tantalising possibility of devising some other, more successful and less ecologically damaging strategy for creating and maintaining personal and cultural meaning [...] this is fundamentally a social and cultural project.[8]

At the heart of this shift in consumption patterns is the creative challenge for designers to demonstrate that *less* and *different* can really be *more* and *better*. We will briefly look at how product designers who wish to join the 'sustainable consumption project' can influence behaviours and take part in defining what this new consumption may look and feel like.

why environmentally led strategies are not enough

In environmental strategies, we looked at the eco-efficiency model that focuses on reducing the impact of consumption by providing the same functionality using fewer resources (ex. lighting from LEDs vs. incandescents). However, studies have shown that efficiency improvements of existing technologies on their own will not be enough, for several reasons.[9]

the rebound effect

The rebound effect, also known as Jevons Paradox in economics, shows that when a product becomes more efficient, part of these efficiency gains are outstripped by higher demand and usage or displaced consumption. This happens in a number of ways. As an example, when cars are more fuel-efficient, the cost per mile of driving is lower, so people can afford to drive more. Alternatively, the money saved on fuel may be spent on other forms of consumption. If you take this across the economy as a whole, if transportation costs come down because of efficiency savings, so will the price of goods, fuelling a cycle of more activity and consumption. Studies estimate that the total direct and indirect rebound effect of more efficient technologies averaged across sectors is approximately 20%.[10] Although opponents of energy-efficiency regulations have used this as an argument against them, others argue that this makes an even stronger case for setting the price of carbon high enough to counteract these behaviours.

more people wanting a better life

The number of people in the 'global middle class' doubled between 2000 and 2015, and is expected to double again in the Asia Pacific region by 2030 dominated by growth in India, China and Indonesia.[11] Those joining the middle classes naturally seek to improve their standard of living, often emulating the models of consumption of the more affluent. In doing so, consumption of energy and resources will increase. Unless the affluent adopt new low-impact lifestyles, we are unlikely to change this trend. An example of where this is occurring is in the use of bicycles in urban areas. In most emerging economies, car ownership is a basic aspiration, while in developed countries, car ownership is in decline in urban areas and bicycle usage is increasing among the middle classes. This has helped with the image and take-up of cycle-share schemes in countries like China, Taiwan and Singapore, reversing decades of decline.

unchallenged fundamentals

Many energy-efficiency improvements do not question the inherent necessity or value of some products and their functionality. As an extreme example, improving the efficiency of an outdoor patio heater could be seen as beside the point. What line of thinking justifies a product that burns fossil fuels or other forms of energy to heat the outdoors to "*create a warm and cosy environment for entertaining*"[12] in the first place?

In conclusion, overconsumption needs to be tackled from the demand side as well as from the supply side. While designing more efficient products is very necessary, to be effective this must go hand in hand with other strategies. This means challenging both the quantity and the nature of our consumption. It also means creating low-impact, high-value lifestyles that are more attractive to current and future consumers and businesses than the old ways.

tools for behaviour change: designing in better choices

If you ask the average consumer or company from a developed economy if they care about the environment or the condition of workers, most will say that they do. Their intention is not to destroy the planet or create suffering and inequality through their production or consumption choices. Yet if you look in their shopping basket or the catalogue of products they manufacture, you will find that environmental and ethical credentials are most often not the top criteria for the choices they make. This lack of follow-through between what we say we believe in and what we do is known as the *value–action gap*. Designers can use insights from the study of behaviour change to help narrow the value–action gap in relation to sustainable consumption.

Value Modes: one size does not fit all
The first lesson from behaviour change is that when it comes to persuading people to do things differently, one size does not fit all. People's attitudes are underpinned by different values and, depending on these values, their actions will be motivated by different triggers. If we understand what these intrinsic motivators are, we can build sustainability into products and services to which different people will respond and connect positively.

The Value Modes system developed by Pat Dade and Les Higgins of CDSM uses Schwartz's theory of basic values[13] to divide people into three value mode groups – *pioneers, prospectors* and *settlers* – each driven by a set of common motivators. Based on extensive social surveys, these three value groups are further subdivided into value mode subgroups, each with their own psychographic characteristics[14] (fig 3.3). The important thing to realise is that people's value systems are rarely objective. Instead, they are closely tied to emotion and operate largely subconsciously.[15] In addition, unlike traditional marketing categories, these value groups cut across socio-economic groupings.

Table 3.1 shows how these different motivators translate into attitudes and behaviours towards sustainable consumption and the different design strategies to use for each group. Fundamentally it tells us that for two of the three groups, namely *prospectors* and *settlers,* sustainability for the sake of the greater good will not be a strong motivator in their purchasing decisions. For these groups, the more sustainable options will need to be designed into products that are attractive to them, and regulation will continue to play an important role. On the other hand, for those in the third group, the *pioneers*, the bigger picture of sustainability is important and they will scrutinise product and company information before buying, and demand change through their choices and support for pressure groups.

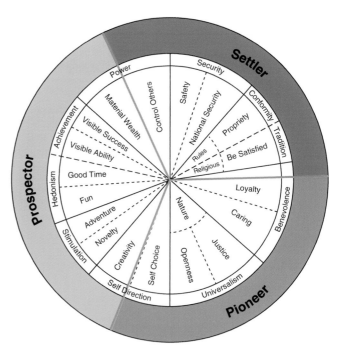

Figure 3.3 The Values Map: the three Value Mode groups superimposed onto the Schwartz basic value wheel. (source: Institute for Public Policy Research)

Nudge: designing in more sustainable choices
The second behaviour change lesson is that better choices, for our purposes the most sustainable ones, can be designed in. In their book *Nudge*, Thaler and Sunstein describe six principles of good choice architecture: *setting defaults, incentivising, understandable mappings, giving feedback, expecting error* and *simplifying complex choices*. For product designers, this connects well with Donald Norman's four principles of good, or more usable, design in *The Design of Everyday Things*: visibility, good conceptual models, good mappings and feedback. Both of these sets of principles overlap and can be applied in the design of products to influence decisions in favour of the most sustainable options at the point of purchase and during use.

Through this lens, overconsumption and its environmental consequences may be seen as the result of poor choice architecture. According to Thaler and Sunstein, the first problem the environment faces is that *incentives* to protect it *are not properly aligned*: typically, when we make choices that are environmentally costly, we are not asked to pay directly for the damage we cause to others and the environment. This leads to what is known as the 'tragedy of the commons' whereby individuals or organisations acting in their own self-interest go against the common good by spoiling or depleting collectively owned or shared resources.[16] The second weakness is the lack of direct

Table 3.1 Value modes of psychographic groupings and what this means for designing more sustainable consumption

core value groups	how this translates into their attitude to sustainability	how this translates into their consumption and lifestyle choices	designing for this group and activating sustainable consumption choices
pioneers: conviction led core motivators: • self-actualisation • exploration • bigger picture typical characteristics: • want to understand the wider context • strong sense of right and wrong, justice and fairness • sense of self-agency • believe in change if it is for the better • cautiously optimistic about the future	• are convinced of the need to be more sustainable by global consequences • actions will be motivated by the greater good • will galvanise others • principles rule their purchases and lifestyle decisions • are prepared to make sacrifices for their beliefs • believe in taking action rather than waiting for change	• will do their research on environmental and social impacts before purchasing • are looking for products and companies with similar values • will sacrifice convenience and pay a premium to be more sustainable • feel frustrated by the lack of real sustainable choices • some are independent and creative enough to opt-out and design their own sustainable lifestyles	• design products that are deeply sustainable and offer real alternatives that they can integrate into a sustainable lifestyle • trust and authenticity are essential • transparency, independent accreditation and labels work • favour commercial entities that share profits or 'do good' • use new technology where you can demonstrate its added sustainable value

prospectors: esteem led
 	
core motivators:
• success and status
• self-esteem
• esteem of others
 	
typical characteristics:
• need recognition and praise
• respond to competition
• natural networkers
• trend conscious
• hedonistic
• generally optimistic about the future
	• don't have deep convictions about sustainability but will be drawn in if it brings approval and recognition
	• their relationship with sustainability will be driven by what others will think of them and what it can bring them
	• once they come on board, they will champion sustainable behaviours to validate their choices and influence others
		• sustainability is not the top driver for their consumption and lifestyle decisions but if it's wrapped up with trendy, new and desirable, they will be attracted to it
		• peer pressure to be seen to be 'greener' may influence their choices
		• brand image is important in their purchases
		• they are early adopters of new technologies and products
			• sustainable products need to be the most desirable, seductive and even enviable they can afford
			• leverage their enthusiasm as early adopters to make new sustainable products or lifestyles 'cool' and more visible
			• consider motivating more sustainable choices through:
			  – rewards and competition
			  – fun and impulse
			  – status and recognition
			  – brand image and trendiness

settlers: security and comfort led
 	
core motivators:
• basic physiological needs
• safety and security
• belonging
 	
typical characteristics:
• like stability and routine
• life revolves around family, friends and home
• fear loss and find change threatening
• loyal to their own
• concerned about what the future holds
	• they are not swayed by bigger picture facts but respond to personal stories that demonstrate how unsustainability affects people's lives in tangible ways
	• sustainability will only be a motivator if it threatens them and their immediate world: it needs to speak to them personally
		• sustainable behaviours for this group will be mostly unconscious
		• they will 'buy into' sustainability if it feels familiar and has obvious and immediate benefits
		• once they have made a change, it will become part of their routine and they will remain very brand loyal
		• often they will be forced into more sustainable consumption through regulation, peer pressure, shame, or when it becomes the new norm
			• sustainability needs to be embedded and part of new behaviour norms
			• sustainable products need to:
			  – speak through personal stories
			  – show immediate personal benefit
			  – be the most convenient, cheapest or best performing option
			  – resemble 'normality'
			  – feel safe
			  – introduce change through small steps

source: Based on on Pat Dade and Les Higgins' *CDSM Cultural Dynamics Strategy and Marketing 'Values Modes'.*

feedback. In most cases we cannot see or feel the consequences of our actions such as the air and water pollution caused by the production of the electricity our appliances consume or the CO_2 emissions from the flight we have just taken, so we are not directly motivated to change our behaviour.

Short of redesigning our accounting systems, which we look at in *economic strategies*, here are a few illustrations of how applying better choice architecture in design can modify behaviours to lessen environmental impacts. One of the simplest ways is to design in *defaults* in favour of the least environmentally harmful

Figure 3.4 A keycard-activated light and power switch defaults to off when leaving your hotel room. (photo credit tiffanystock)

like thermostats increasingly allow designers to take default and feedback integration a step further by writing them into the algorithms which optimise efficiency.

The IoT is also providing more and more opportunities for electronic products to *feedback* on our immediate and less visible impacts. Examples of this are car displays that constantly let you know how efficiently you are driving and make suggestions on how to improve (fig 3.6), and smart meters that help us visualise our energy consumption, *aligning* money saving *incentives* with energy saving. Some utility companies are taking the use of smart meters one step further by comparing a customer's energy consumption with their neighbours' on their bills.[19] This is having positive results that we can explain through value modes. For *settlers*, this can signal a shift in norms and shame them into action: *"If my neighbours are saving energy, should I?"* Others are *incentivised* by being shown potential or realised savings on their bills, and finally some, especially *prospectors*, are motivated by the competition.

option. The hotel keycard and power switch that defaults to 'off' when the user leaves the room is an excellent example (fig 3.4). This has reduced hotel room power consumption by 20 to 30%.[17] Other examples of defaults that can save substantial amounts of energy, water and CO_2 include taps that default to cold water (fig 3.5), toilets to small flushes and kettles that only boil the water that is needed.[18] Meanwhile, IoT connected smart products

As we have seen with value mode groups, *pioneers* who want to make the greenest choices will be looking for information disclosure and transparency. But even with the best will in the world this information needs simplifying. Labels are a very good example of helping with complex decisions by providing *better mapping* and *aligning incentives*. If we look at energy performance labels for appliances, we can see how they help. First, these labels do the calculation and comparison between

Figure 3.5 Roca's innovative Cold Start tap technology: making the most environmentally friendly setting the default saves considerable energy and carbon. (photo courtesy Roca, Spain)

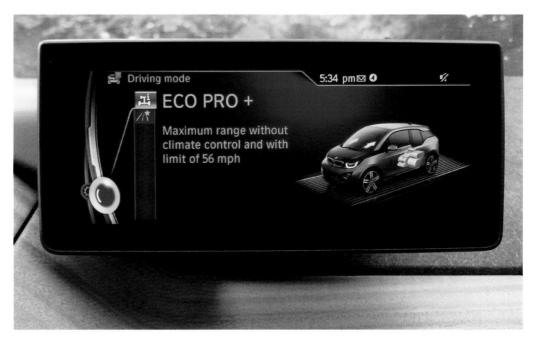

Figure 3.6 The EcoPro+ modes on the BMW i3 electric car actively encourage maximum driving efficiency through the display and accelerator feedback. (photo credit Jane Penty)

products for the consumer, so we have *better mapping*. But how this information is presented can also make a big difference.[20] The US Energyguide label (fig 3.7) emphasises the annual running cost of the appliance and compares it with others in its class. Here the intention is to incentivise money savings. The EU energy label on the other hand gives all products in the same class a single energy-efficiency ABC score to make it easier to choose the

most efficient. Both provide *good mapping* but presume different consumer motivators and therefore incentives.

Fogg Behavior Model: how to change habits
The third behaviour change lesson is around understanding how the design of products might help to change 'bad habits' into 'good habits'. We already know that for a large segment of the

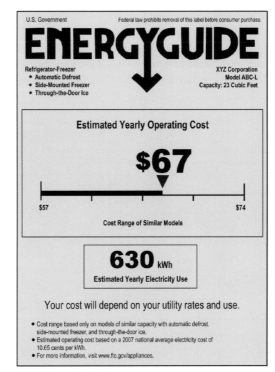

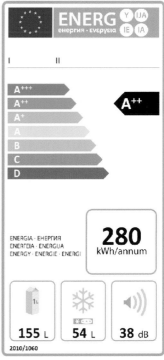

Figure 3.7 The US and EU appliance energy-efficiency labels facilitate better consumer choices but are based on different motivators. (source: US Federal Government and European Union)

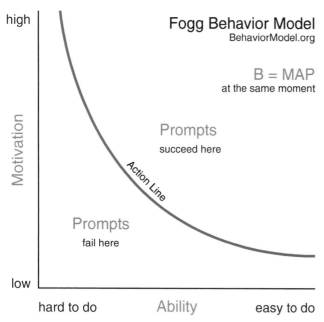

Fogg Behavior Model
BehaviorModel.org

$B = MAP$
at the same moment

Motivation — high / low

Ability — hard to do / easy to do

Prompts
succeed here

Action Line

Prompts
fail here

Figure 3.8 Fogg Behavior Model. (source: BJ Fogg BehaviorModel.org)

population acting more sustainably is not their prime motivator so *the most sustainable option needs to be either the easiest, correctly incentivised or the default*. Even then, changing habits is hard for everyone, especially for *settlers* who are creatures of routine. According to the Fogg Behavior Model (fig 3.8), to change a behaviour we need be motivated to change, we need to have the agency and ability to change, and we need *positive triggers or prompt*s that encourage us to keep on track. If all three are not present then the initiative is likely to fail. In addition, everyone naturally has cycles of high and low motivation. These dips in motivation are at the heart of the value–action gap. As designers we need to anticipate the moments that may be 'too much' for someone to continue with the new behaviour if their

motivation dips and use design to lower the barriers at these moments.

As an example, imagine you are a person who has recently been persuaded that cycling is the best way to get around: it's healthier, it's cheaper and it's better for the environment. Your motivation is high and you are captivated by a great-looking bicycle that you buy with the intention of commuting regularly to work. When your motivation is low, your determination will weaken when an obstacle arises [...] *I can't take my toddler to the nursery on the way to work, I can't carry my shopping back, I want to wear smart clothes, it's raining, its dark and my lights are out of battery.* This is where designs or features that help someone overcome these obstacles will make the new behaviour easier to adopt and turn it into a habit. In addition, steps like working out a good route, or having a cycling buddy, will ensure that there are fewer reasons to give up when motivation flags. Once the habit is established, it is less vulnerable.

In Chapter 8.2, active transport, we look into how design can and does anticipate these moments of low motivation, particularly in relation to supporting the possibility of making cycling the main form of transport for urban commuting through a range of products that support this move. Figure 3.9 gives one such example of how the rain- and snow-proof cargo bicycle becomes the tool that allows working parents to take their children to nursery in all weathers.

The behaviour change models we have looked at thus far make it clear that how a product or service is designed influences our behaviour. A good complement to these is Dan Locton's *Design with Intent – 101 Patterns for Influencing Behaviour through Design*. This highly insightful toolkit is intended to inspire and provoke designers to be more aware and in control of this potential power. Drawing on existing knowledge and practices

Figure 3.9 Anticipating barriers to more sustainable behaviours: cargo bikes and their accessories allow commuters to transport children, shopping and more in all weathers. (photo credits Greg Perkins/ Shutterstock.com; Peter Mooij)

across disciplines, it groups visual examples of how behaviours are currently being steered towards desired outcomes ready for their creative reinterpretation into new design scenarios.[21]

breaking the bag habit

The story of the short-life or 'disposable' plastic bag is a good example to illustrate different attitudes and approaches to changing behaviours. It is estimated that over one trillion bags are 'used' every year with worldwide consumption as high as 400 per person in Eastern Europe[22] and as low as 4 in Denmark. Of these, only 1 in 200 is recycled, with most ending up as litter, in landfill, incinerated, or joining the giant plastic gyres defacing our oceans. At sea and on land they are a visual blight and, when mistaken for food, cause the slow death by choking and asphyxiation of over 100,000 marine and land animals every year.[23] (fig 3.10). As litter, plastic bags do not biodegrade, but rather photodegrade over years, breaking down into smaller and smaller toxic bits, known as micro-plastics that enter the food chain where their disruptive effects are only just beginning to be understood[24] (see more in Chapter 5.1).

The fact that plastic bags have only been around on a mass scale since the 1980s in itself proves that they are far from essential. And yet, despite us knowing the damage they cause to the environment, the non-renewable resources they waste and the fact that they are mostly unnecessary, their use has become the norm. Effectively they are a 'bad habit' we need to kick.

From the Value Mode perspective, conviction-led *pioneers* responded to the facts from media campaigns years ago. They are the ones who for years have packed their reusable bags, generally not plastic, when they go shopping and carry one around with them for the unplanned purchase. For the other two groups however, it takes more to kick the habit. Esteem-driven *prospectors* respond when a fashionable alternative is offered such as We are What We Do's *'I'm not a plastic bag'* campaign in 2007 (fig 3.11). Endorsed by celebrities, the campaign hit fashion magazines and made headline news globally thanks to Anya Hindmarch's limited edition design that had the fashion-conscious queuing up for one in the UK, USA, Japan and Hong Kong: *"it doesn't matter why people buy it [says one marketing expert], what's important is the huge amount of publicity the bag generates."* [25]

Although this campaign raised awareness, it did little to change regular habits. Ultimately, most people behave like *settlers* and let convenience and the irresistibility of something 'free' trump their rational knowledge when offered a plastic bag at the checkout. This is a clear illustration of the yawning value–action gap. To date, the only methods that have proven to have significant impact in cutting plastic bag consumption are the choice architecture strategies of *aligning incentives* and making 'no bag'

Figure 3.10 Ingesting plastic bags from street litter is not only a danger to cows; it is also producing toxic milk in India. (photo credit Tim Graham/robertharding/Shutterstock.com)

Figure 3.11 Anya Hindmarch's limited edition 'I'm Not a Plastic Bag' for We Are What We Do in 2007 reached celebrity status. Shown here: hundreds queuing for their own bag at the Hong Kong launch. (courtesy Shift, formerly We Are What We Do)

the *default*. Some countries, like Kenya, have introduced outright bans while others, like Australia, China and a growing number of states in the USA, EU and India, are having success with taxes. Most notably, Ireland's PlasTax is proof that taxing works. Since its introduction in 2001, bag usage dropped by 90%, but it started to creep up again after a few years, so that in 2007 they increased the tax and brought it back down. Unlike outright bans, the tax *aligns incentives* while still giving people a choice. The PlasTax also decreased plastic bags' overall share of litter in Ireland from 5% to 0.2%, saving taxpayers a considerable amount of money. What is also very interesting is the shift in attitude that the tax has created. Using disposable plastic bags has become socially unacceptable in many countries, making reusable bags the new social norm.[26] This makes *settlers* comfortable following a new 'norm' and *prospectors* don't need to worry about being 'un-cool'. However, well before these taxes, retailers like IKEA and Lidl, who stopped offering bags altogether many years ago, had already discovered that customers adjusted their behaviours to the 'no-bag' *default* without it affecting their business.

3.2 better products and real needs: human-centred and socially responsible design

Having looked at how design can influence the nature and quantity of consumption from the consumer demand side through behaviour change, we will now consider sustainable consumption from the supply side. This puts designers in the spotlight, as they play an important role in the creation of the products that surround us and shape our daily lives. This is no small responsibility, as Victor Papanek recognised: *"regardless of political systems or religious beliefs, the designer is accepted everywhere as an essential contributor to society."*[27]

Socially responsible designers use their skills to craft better products. But what is a *better product* in the context of sustainability? First, better products address *real needs* as opposed to *wants* and *desires* fabricated for the sake of increasing consumption. Better products innovate to meet these needs while improving life and wellbeing. Better products build social capital, facilitate positive interactions, lighten loads, express our values, and keep us safer but not cotton-wooled. Better products delight beyond the first moment. Better products enable us to challenge ourselves. Better products do not overburden us, society or the planet. In short, they are the tools for meaningful lives in balance with a shared environment.

In order to design better products we must begin by asking the fundamental questions: *Why?* and *What?* Why do we need a new product or service and what value could it bring? For a designer, believing in a project goes a long way in achieving design success. Once a real *need* is established, then the design process should

lead to the best possible outcomes in terms of functionality, interface, aesthetics and cultural connections with the context of use and all its stakeholders.

Applying a human-centred design (HCD) approach to the creative process is a good way to achieve more value and relevance for products. As we see throughout the book, this approach can and is being applied across the spectrum of product and service design, within both commercial and not-for-profit organisations. The powerful combination of HCD and design thinking can be used for relatively straightforward design problems through to more 'wicked' or complex and intractable social problems, such as how best to care for an ageing population with limited budgets, build social capital and community engagement, widen access to education, and reduce obesity.

This moves designers into the realms of Design for Social Innovation (DSI) where they are increasingly involved in applying their 'expert' skills. Solutions to many of these issues are being enabled by software solutions by what are variously termed the 'Digital Social', and 'Tech for Good' (see fig 6.29). But there are still many instances where physical touchpoints and artefacts play an important role in successfully delivering these services. While it is beyond the scope of this book to explore in any detail, Ezio Manzini's *Design, When Everybody Designs* offers good insights into the designer's role as 'expert' within social innovation teams. In addition, organisations such as IDEO.org, FrogDesign, the Hamblyn Centre for Design and Index: Design to Improve Life have developed, championed and shared their methodologies, courses, toolkits and case studies in this field.

HCD is inherently a collaborative process involving varying degrees of co-design. It is based on the premise that users hold the key to solving their own problems. Therefore all the people or organisations implicated in a project – its key stakeholders – must be at the centre of the design process. Not only does this ensure a deeper understanding of the 'problem', it also ensures greater success in implementation, as the stakeholders all have ownership of the problem and the solution. Depending on the complexity and the nature of the problem, the HCD team is often multidisciplinary or transdisciplinary and may call on input from a range of different expertises. The final crucial ingredient of the HCD approach is the design team's attitude: HCD requires an open, empathetic, inclusive, proactive and always creative mindset.

the human-centred design process: a collaborative and empathic model

Below is a brief summary of the phases in the design process through a human-centred lens.[28] It is made up of divergent activities that open up new possibilities and connections, and convergent activities that narrow down and synthesise the ideas and insights generated to move towards implementable solutions.[29]

- **research gathering:**
  sometimes called the discovery or inspiration phase, this is heavily based on primary research.
  aim: to understand the problem and context of use through the eyes of the stakeholders: their core values, aspirations, environment, constraints, day-to-day life, pressures they are under, current coping strategies, etc.
  methods: involves working directly with stakeholders in immersive and ethnographic information gathering, including shadowing, fly on the wall, observations, interviews, diaries, cultural probes. Should include mainstream and extreme users.

- **research analysis:**
  aim: making sense of the data and experiences gathered to provide an informed design direction.
  methods: share information, present highlights, select most notable, group by themes or issues and map as frameworks, extract key insights and opportunities for addressing the problem.

outcome: formulate the most promising (3–5) insight statements for each theme framed as a 'How might we … ?' question.

- **ideas to developed concepts:**
  aim: to convert key insights into ideas and then develop into concepts.
  methods: generate ideas through co-creation, explore and test ideas through role-play, storyboard scenarios with rough-and-ready prototyping; develop and validate through iterative field testing with integrated feedback; explore potential business models.

- **realisation and implementation:**
  aim: make the project a viable reality.
  methods: develop the business model and roadmap, bring in expertise, build partnerships and teams for delivery and funding, run live pilots, refine, assess feasibility, build in continuous feedback and monitoring; launch.

Figure 3.12 illustrates the human-centred design (HCD) process in action during the Safe Agua Peru project in 2011.[30] This was a co-creation project between Cerro Verde campamento residents in

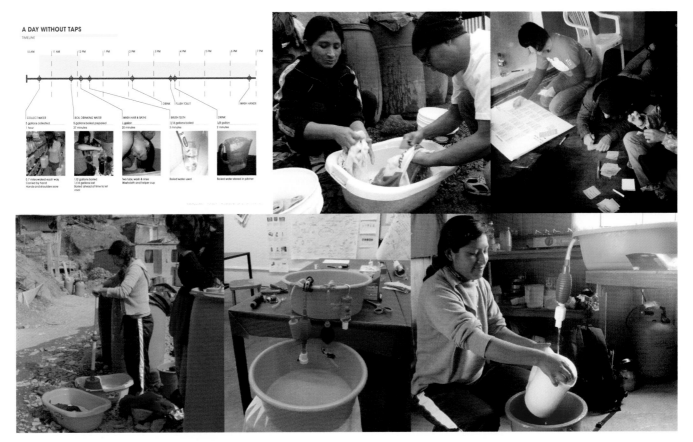

Figure 3.12 HCD in action during the Safe Agua Peru project in Cerro Verde, Lima: immersion; observations; information gathering; insight analysis; iterative prototyping; field testing. (photos courtesy Designmatters at Art Center College of Design)

Lima, Techo, a Latin American NGO and Art Center's Designmatters. Its aim was to overcome the residents' water poverty challenges. Building on experience from two previous collaborations in Chile and Colombia the process was well honed, leading to a valuable learning experience for all and positive outcomes for the residents.

ergonomics and inclusive design

As a complement to the emphasis on inter-human interfaces of HCD, *ergonomics,* or *human factors,* operate at the physical and, more recently, digital interfaces between products and humans. The science of ergonomics offers valuable research, data and tools informed by physiology and psychology for improving our interactions with products to make them safer and much more usable. In particular, ergonomics has been successfully applied to reducing long-term work-related health problems and accidents in work environments, vehicles, as well as to sports and medical equipment, user experience (UX) and user interface (UI) design. As Niels Diffrient, co-author of *Humanscale,* the anthropometric bible for ergonomic design, put it: *"Why would you design something if it didn't improve the human condition?"*[31] His range of chairs for Humanscale illustrates his point elegantly (fig 3.13).

Beyond the work environment, ergonomics is used to reduce sports injuries, helping people to stay fit for longer. As an example, the Specialized Body Geometry bicycle saddle range was specifically designed to reduce saddle pressure for riders in response to the problem of erectile dysfunction and lower fertility in male cyclists caused by reduced blood flow. The design solution of creating an opening in the saddle was informed by scientifically based ergonomic research and testing. This is a good example of how a significant physiological problem can be overcome through an ergonomic redesign and how this can redefine the form and aesthetics of an entire product category, in this case, bicycle saddles (fig 3.14).

The concept of *inclusivity* is another important principle for better design. *Inclusive* or *universal design* aims to make mainstream products and services accessible to as many people as possible. This moves away from the notion of 'design for disability' to 'design for all' by recognising that the population as a whole is a continuum of physical and mental ability, from the young to the old, male or female. What began as an equality issue has in fact turned out to have wider benefits. Designers and users soon discover that a product that is easier to use for those with less ability is usually better for all. OXO 'good grips' set out to make kitchen tools easier for arthritis sufferers and the elderly to use. One of their first products was the jar opener (1989 Smart Design) which became an icon for how inclusive products could not only make life easier for everyone but they could also be highly desirable and commercially successful (fig 3.15). Lifts and ramps

Figure 3.13 Humanscale's Freedom Chair designed in 1998 and still in production by Niels Diffrient, the grandfather of human factors, demonstrates the ultimate simplification of a complex problem into a natural and intuitive interface (USA). (photo courtesy Humanscale)

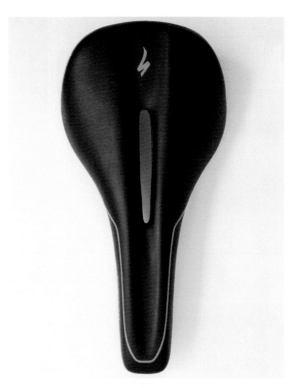

Figure 3.14 Specialized's Body Geometry range redefined the design language of bicycle saddles in response to ergonomic research into lower male fertility. (photo credit Jane Penty)

Figure 3.15 OXO Good Grips led the way in making inclusive design mainstream and desirable. Shown here are OXO's jar opener and angled measuring jug that allows you to read measurements as you fill. (photos courtesy OXO)

installed for wheelchairs are another good example of this, as they also benefit people with injuries, baby buggies, bicycles and luggage, to mention a few. With the global trend of an ageing demographic predicted to increase to the end of the century, inclusivity will need to be embedded in all our design thinking and outcomes.

To conclude with a word of caution: a human-centred, ergonomic and inclusive design approach on its own does not make a product 'sustainable'. However, when properly applied, it will certainly go a long way to making a product more socially beneficial. Designers should, however, avoid straying into the notion that making everything in life frictionless is always better or more sustainable. Humans also thrive on challenge within reasonable bounds, especially when it is their choice.[32]

3.3 the other 70%: design for the base of the pyramid

More than one in ten people worldwide – that is, over 750 million – live in extreme poverty (below $1.90/day, 2011 PPP) and half of those live in Africa.[33] The good news is that this is less than half what it was in 1990 and falling, with improvements

in China accounting for most of this uplift. The UN Millennium Development Goal to halve extreme hunger and poverty was reached five years ahead of time in 2010 and the new Sustainable Development Goals aim to eradicate extreme poverty by 2030.[34] However, while extreme poverty has halved, the number of people living below their national poverty line is barely down since 1981, at well over 2 billion.[35] Figure 3.16 shows the distribution by income below $2 (poor) and $10/day (low income) globally that make up over 70% of the world population.

Put another way, more than one in six (or 15%) of the world live on less than $2 a day and 70% of the world, nearly three in four, have an income of under $10/day. $10/day is the level that some economists suggest is needed to have secure access to food, clean water, sanitation, education and health care.[36] From a humanitarian point of view, these statistics show that nearly three out of four on the planet are at best subsisting. Only 16% worldwide have daily incomes of over $20/day, while for the top 7% earning over $50/day all these privileges are assumed, as they decide whether to holiday abroad or at home, eat in or out, buy a new car or put in a new kitchen. Not surprisingly, this is the target market of most product design and also where most of the overconsumption we looked at earlier is concentrated. In response, this section will shift the focus of design from the wealthiest to the base of the pyramid (BoP) which is made up of the extremely poor, the poor and those on a low income which, depending on definitions and boundaries, make up between half and two-thirds of the world population.[37]

But what do poverty and low income have to do with sustainability? The vicious circle between poverty, overpopulation and environmental degradation is well known. We now add to this the fact that climate change caused by the richest will continue to hit the poorest regions in the world hardest (Chapter 1, box 1.5). These factors are all increasing migration pressures, as those with nothing to lose risk all to enter countries where they may have hope. So whether we look at it from a humanitarian, environmental or more self-interested point of view, global poverty and income inequality are unsustainable and are very much *our* collective problem.

Given the complexities, can designers have any impact on the lives of the billions living at the base of the pyramid? In his book *Out of Poverty*, Paul Polak, founder of iDE, demonstrates that they can. He suggests that designers and entrepreneurs should consider the *design of successful products for the base of the pyramid as the ultimate challenge and business opportunity of our time*.[38] Although there is much debate about how best to achieve this, he and many others involved with development NGOs at least agree that what the very poor most need is the means to increase their income and independence.

World Population by Income
How Many Live on How Much, and Where

World Population by Income
How Many Live on How Much, and Where

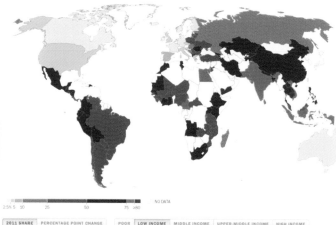

15% of people globally are **poor**

People living on $2 or less daily are classified as poor

56% of people globally are **low income**

People living on $2.01-10 daily are classified as low income

Figure 3.16 Pew Research Center interactive maps showing world totals and proportion of people in each country who live on less than $2/day (poor) and those who live on $2.01 to $10/day (low income). (source: 'World Population by Income', Pew Research Center, Washington, DC, 2015. Available at www.pewglobal.org/interactives/global-population-by-income/)

For designers, the key to helping people out of poverty is to design the tools they need and can afford, provide the know-how to use and maintain them, and build the physical and commercial infrastructure for these products to get to market. However, designing for the BoP presents a unique set of challenges and constraints. It means designing *"better solutions for more people by using fewer resources by doing things completely differently"*. [39] *Frugal* design and innovation and making things technologically *appropriate* and extremely *affordable* are recurring approaches in designing for the BoP.

Experience on the ground also shows that the design process for the BoP must be grounded in a deep understanding of the people and context. Here more than anywhere, a human-centred design approach is essential and leads to the most appropriate solutions that go hand-in-hand with technical ingenuity. In addition, the right design may not be enough. Business models from wealthier countries do not work in poor communities where wages are paid daily, if and when you are able to work. This means that new business models and commercial networks often need to be developed alongside the products to make them viable and successful.

Let us take a look at some key characteristics and examples of product design for the BoP.

who and where?

Over 75% of the poorest live in rural areas in developing countries, often as subsistence farmers. The other 25% are the urban poor living in slums or informal settlements in and around cities. They also have the lowest levels of education and are predominantly young with the biggest concentrations in Africa, India and Southeast Asia.[40] Although these urban and rural contexts are very different, the design approach is similar.

what products?

Designs for the BoP focus primarily on products and services that:

- contribute to basic needs for sanitation, clean water and health like toilets, latrines, water filters, eyeglasses and prostheses (Boxes 3.1/3.2/3.3)
- enable small farmers to grow more food reliably to earn a living using treadle pumps, micro-irrigation systems, and other tools for climate change resilience in flood- and drought-stricken areas (Box 3.5)
- enable these farmers and cooperatives to create products with more added value with processing and packaging equipment and access to markets and supply chains
- reduce respiratory diseases, fuel costs, carbon emissions and mass deforestation with more efficient cookstoves (Box 3.6)

- enable small craft enterprises to grow through access to clean energy that saves on kerosene costs, improves productivity, and opens access to markets through digital communication and solar lighting and electricity (Box 3.4)
- provide basic transportation to get their products to market and access education and health care with carts, bicycles, trailers, or even aerial ropeways in mountainous regions (Box 3.7)
- provide emergency and disaster relief: shelter, sanitation, cooking, lighting, security, etc. (Box 3.8).

what characteristics?

Products for the BoP need to be:

- innovative, ingenious yet highly functional
- most appropriate to the context and user
- extremely affordable
- sufficiently reliable but not overdesigned to keep costs down
- upgradable or expandable as income improves
- culturally acceptable
- transferrable and scalable

Sometimes the solution can be found by looking back at earlier or simpler technologies that accomplish the same function such as the treadle pump and the multiple uses of bicycles. And sometimes this means looking forward or 'leapfrogging' to new technologies such as solar energy, mobile phones and Internet connectivity where dirtier and costlier technologies are bypassed. The key is: What is *appropriate* and *affordable*?

how?

In the words of Fritz Schumacher, "*find out what people are doing and help them to do it better*".

- spend time with and involve the people in the communities and supply chains that you are designing for to deeply understand their situation and constraints. Let them tell you what their problems are and what they need.
- once you've identified the need and problem, apply ingenuity in design, and develop, prototype and test to get the product right with the users
- develop the business model and supply chain
- promote, inform and demonstrate to get product take-up

In many ways it's even more important that you involve the user heavily in the design process when you're targeting the product or service towards an emerging market or BoP

customer, because there's less wiggle room in getting the value proposition right. [...] They're unable to take lots of new technology risks, so you need to make sure it's the perfect product for the customer before you sell it to them.

Peter Frykman, founder of Driptech. [41]

business models for the BoP

In developing countries the basic business assumptions of industrialised economies are turned on their head. At the BoP people are plentiful and labour is cheap but access to capital or money is scarce or non-existent. So solutions can be labour intensive with the lowest capital cost. However, to create change, people at the BoP need help to make their first investment – for instance, in a water pump – that will allow them to grow crops in the dry season. Micro-finance schemes pioneered by the Grameen bank, and taken further to the mobile world by groups like Kiva, have been instrumental in overcoming this barrier. By providing micro-loans to the very poorest, they make it possible for them to buy the critical products to improve their production and stay healthier as the first step towards a sustainable income. In Chapter 4 we look at hybrid business models for the BoP in more depth and their implications for design.

In this context, from the designers' point of view, getting the business model right is just as important as designing the right product. Paul Polak's '*Don't Bother Trilogy*' sets the strictest of tests in designing for the billions at the BoP. Based on his years of experience in this field, it reflects his deeply held belief that these products need to be functionally *and* economically viable with their own robust supply chains, free of subsidies or brokering through governments that are all too often subject to bribery and corruption.

1. *if you haven't had good conversations with your eyes open with at least 25 poor people before you start designing, 'don't bother'*
2. *if what you design won't at least pay for itself in the first year, 'don't bother'*
3. *if you don't think you can sell at least a million units at an unsubsidized price to poor customers after the design process is complete, 'don't bother'* [42]

Awareness and experience of designing for the base of the wealth pyramid is a growing field for designers in developing and industrialised countries alike. While it presents many unique challenges that cannot be underestimated, when they succeed, their transformative effects and the sense of achievement this produces justifies the commitment and reaffirms the motivation. Sharing these success stories for them to be replicated and

Box 3.1 designing for basic needs: sanitation

An estimated 2.3 billion people – one in every three in the world today – live without access to basic sanitation, and of these approximately 900 million still defecate in the open on a daily basis. This lack of access to adequate sanitation is estimated to contribute to 10% of the global disease burden, mostly through the spread of diarrhoea, cholera, dysentery, hepatitis A, typhoid and polio. This in turn impacts very negatively on their social and economic prospects.

Millions of people have to defecate in open-pit latrines daily, exposing them to deadly diseases, not to mention very bad odours. To combat this problem, a LIXIL/American Standard team developed the SaTo self-closing pit-latrine pan that shuts out odours and disease-spreading insects. The first model, funded by the Gates Foundation and developed in collaboration with iDE, was launched in Bangladesh in 2013. It has since been deployed in 14 countries, including Uganda, Haiti, Malawi, Nigeria and the Philippines. (fig 3.17a)

Clean Team Ghana is a social enterprise originally developed by WSUP with support from Unilever and design input from IDEO. They offer a home toilet service as an alternative to public toilets since buckets were banned in urban areas. This includes the lease of the specially designed toilet, regular waste cartridge collection and frequent payment collection to keep cash flow manageable. (fig 3.17b)

Sanergy's FreshLife is a circular clean public toilet service that takes a sustainable systems-based approach to tackle the sanitation crisis in informal urban settlements in Africa. FreshLife began as an MIT d-lab spin-off and now operates in the slums of Nairobi building low-cost toilets, franchising operations and transforming the collected waste into affordable 'Evergrow' organic fertiliser used by local farmers. (fig 3.17c)

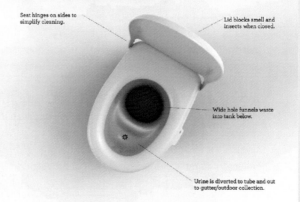

Figure 3.17a The SaTo self-closing pit latrine pan in a communal latrine Bangladesh (photos courtesy LIXIL / American Standard)

Figure 3.17b Clean Team Ghana's urine diversion toilet, designed with IDEO.org attracts the attention of school children. (photos courtesy IDEO.org)

Figure 3.17c Sanergy's Fresh Life clean public toilet circular service model in action in Nairobi: toilets and users; cleaning, collection and servicing; affordable Evergrow organic fertiliser at work in the fields. (photos courtesy Sanergy)

Box 3.2 designing for basic needs: health care

eyesight

More than 2 billion people worldwide have poor eyesight that can be corrected with lenses. Of these, at least 100 million are school-age children and 60% do not wear glasses because the eye testing and annual lenses fitting they would need is neither available nor affordable to them. This impacts heavily upon their education and life prospects. Professor Joshua Silver's highly innovative self-adjusting lenses with adaptive optics overcome the need for specific power lenses, and the cost and logistics associated with these. Instead, the lens power is adjusted by turning the syringe side dials during fitting, which are then removed for everyday wear. The Centre for Vision in the Developing World (CVDW) and Dow Corning collaborated in the development and design of the commercially viable Child Vision glasses. (fig 3.18a)

maternal mortality

Globally, more than 300,000 women die annually from complications of pregnancy and childbirth. This is known as maternal mortality and 99% occurs in developing countries, especially in sub-Saharan Africa and Southern Asia.[43] Reducing maternal mortality is one of the UN Sustainable Development Goals.[44] In 2008 Dr Laura Stachel went to Northern Nigeria to study ways of lowering hospital-based maternal mortality. She observed that sporadic electricity supply was impairing the ability to provide life-saving care, as critical procedures were delayed, cancelled or conducted in near-darkness.

This led to the design, development and field trials over a number of years of the Solar Suitcase, a robust, institutional grade solar electric system for health workers. Originally designed as a tool for midwives in Nigeria, demand for this innovative power solution now comes from clinics, medics and health workers around the world.[45] As of early 2018, over 3500 suitcases were in use in 27 countries with the help of UN and NGO regional partners. (fig 3.18b)

Figure 3.18a A pair of Centre for Vision in the Developing World (CVDW) glasses that users can self-adjust by turning the side dials to regulate the fluid between two lenses. Once the correct power is confirmed, the adjustable mechanism is removed. Shown here in eye tests and fitting in Uganda and eye tests in Nepal (photos courtesy Centre for Vision in the Developing World)

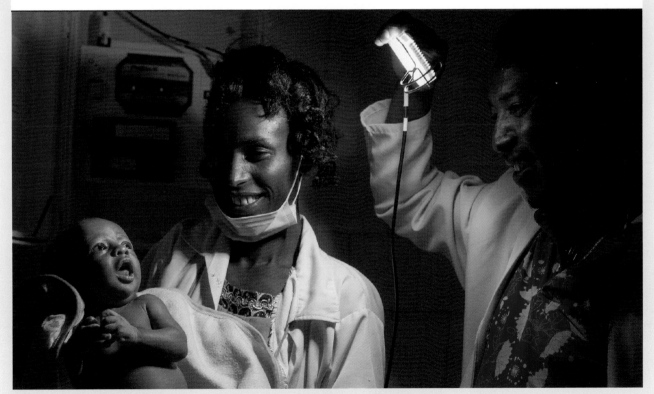

Figure 3.18b The Solar Suitcase includes a control panel, customised solar panels, long-lasting break-resistant medical-grade lights, lithium batteries, a foetal Doppler and phone charging. Also shown, a baby delivered by solar light in Ethiopia. (photos courtesy We Care Solar)

Box 3.3 designing for basic needs: clean drinking water

Some 2.1 billion people don't have clean water at home and one in nine (or over 800,000 million) people still do not have access to basic clean water.[46] These are figures with a devastating human cost, especially for infant mortality: 700 children under 5 years of age are estimated to die *every day* from diarrheal diseases caused by a lack of clean water and sanitary living conditions. Ceramic pot water filters are an affordable solution that can also be locally produced.

With a goal of reaching 1 million Guatemalan homes by 2020, Ecofiltro started producing ceramic drinking water filters as a social enterprise 30 years ago but is now a hybrid for-profit company with its own manufacturing and distribution facilities

in Guatemala. While the most basic model is highly affordable, the more decorative traditional and modern designs are aspirational products, removing any stigma of poverty. Sales of the high-end products subsidise rural sales and Ecofiltro's charitable work. (fig 3.19a)

Hydrologic is a social enterprise that began working with NGOs to bring clean water to the poorest households in Cambodia using the Tunsai ceramic water filter originally designed by iDE. However, as purchasing power has doubled in Cambodia, they have also developed the Super Tunsai design as a desirable consumer product that they manufacture in Cambodia and sell as a successful commercial product. (fig 3.19b)

Figure 3.19a Ecofiltro's range of ceramic filter pots from budget to modern and traditional aspirational models. (photos courtesy Ecofiltro, Guatemala)

Figure 3.19b Hydrologic's Super Tunsai ceramic filter pots sells well alongside their original budget Tunsai model. (photos courtesy Hydrologic, Cambodia)

Box 3.4 cleaner affordable electricity and lighting

Over 1 billion people in the world do not yet have access to electricity and, for another billion, electricity supply is very erratic. Eighty per cent live in sub-Saharan Africa.[47] Having access to reliable electricity and light allows households and businesses to increase their incomes by boosting their productivity and extending working hours. This makes it a key factor in lifting households out of poverty and also provides children with light for study, further improving their future prospects. The UN Sustainable Development Goal 7 is for everyone to have access to affordable, clean and reliable energy by 2030. This can be met by leapfrogging costly and dirty old technologies with renewably powered distributed models in the form of community micro-grids or stand-alone installations. Established social enterprises like SELCO, d-light and Green Planet (see fig 6.35) and newer players like BioLite design and distribute successful products that do just that.

Started in 1995 in Bangalore, SELCO is a pioneer in this field committed to bringing clean, affordable and reliable renewable power to the poorest off-grid communities in remote villages and urban slums dependent on expensive and dirty kerosene. Their success is based on the complete service package that they provide – custom installation, maintenance support and affordable micro-finance packages. (fig 3.20a) d.light is another hybrid social enterprise on a mission to improve the lives of 100 million people in the developing world by 2020 by providing the most reliable, affordable and accessible solar lighting and power systems. From stand-alone solar lights to solar home systems and pay-as-you-go offer, d.light have sold over 20 million products in 64 countries, and make a science of measuring their impacts and adapting their products. (fig 3.20b)

Figure 3.20a SELCO India's solar electricity and lighting products at work: a rural potter's workstation with a solar-powered pottery wheel in Udupi, Karnataka, and an entrepreneur using a solar-powered sewing machine in Chitradurga, Karnataka. (courtesy SELCO Foundation, India)

Figure 3.20b d. Light's S100 solar lantern and charger making homework possible. (courtesy d. light design)

Box 3.5 growing food to earn a living

The majority of the poorest people at the base of the pyramid are small-plot farmers in rural areas, so helping them increase their yields is a key strategy for improving their incomes. Having enough water to grow crops is one of their most basic needs. The humble treadle pump may have helped more farmers out of poverty than any other single design.[48] In Bangladesh alone, iDE estimate that they have sold over 1.4 million. This very simple human-powered design allows farmers to extract water from wells with much less effort than hand pumps and cost than motorised pumps. The treadles are also easily adapted to local production and materials. (fig 3.21a)

Water also allows farmers to grow crops in the dry season, including high-value out-of-season crops. In particular, drip irrigation systems consume one-third of the water of traditional systems. Driptech, an offshoot from Stanford's Design for Extreme Affordability, developed a highly affordable and easy-to-use system through a thorough user-centred process of rationalisation and testing.[49] With a payback of six months and increased income for the next three to five years, its success has led to Driptech being bought by India's largest irrigation company, Jain Irrigation, thereby spreading its market and reach. (fig 3.21c)

Proximity Designs are another human-centered design social enterprise company designing for BoP farmers in Myanmar. They began by designing robust and highly affordable physical products needed on the ground such as treadle pumps and irrigation systems, which they continue to evolve. More recently they have extended their offer to agronomy and farm finance services to help farmers establish secure businesses and livelihoods. They also monitor the impressive social impact of their products and services very closely.[50] (fig 3.21b) (fig 3.21d)

Figure 3.21a A Practical Action treadle pump in use in Pithauli, Nepal. (photo courtesy Practical Action / Peter Crawford)

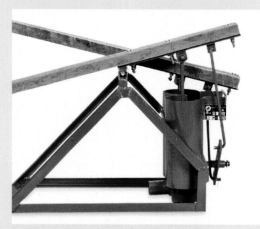

Figure 3.21b Proximity Designs' robust Red Rhino mobile treadle pump mechanism still going strong since 2004. (photo courtesy Proximity Designs, Myanmar)

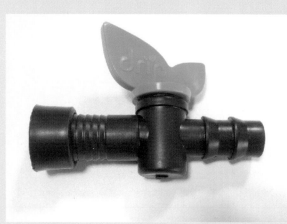

Figure 3.21c Driptech's drip irrigation feeder valve and the system working in the field (photo courtesy Driptech, India)

Figure 3.21d Proximity Designs' Sturdy Boy 250-gallon water storage tank filled by their Baby Elephant gravity water pump feeds their Drip irrigation system in a field in Myanmar. Drip irrigation system components shown top and Baby Elephant gravity pump components shown bottom. (photos courtesy Proximity Designs, Myanmar)

Box 3.6 cleaner and more efficient cooking

Three billion people, nearly half the world's population, cook with solid fuels, mostly wood and charcoal. Of these, more than one billion cook over three stone open fires. This is one of the biggest global risks to human health and the environment which affects the poorest most. It accounts for 15% of CO_2 emissions and causes deforestation and soil erosion. As wood becomes scarcer, rural women spend up to three hours a day searching for fuel, often in the form of charcoal, often risking attack. In urban situations, fuel costs up to 30% of their income. In addition, the smoke from cooking causes over 4.3 million deaths a year from respiratory diseases, mostly to women and children.[51, 52]

Designing more efficient and smokeless stoves has been a focus for over 30 years with many ingenious improvements. From the early Kenya Jiko ceramic stoves to the newer fan-assisted or solar models, cookstoves are now 50 to 90% more fuel-efficient, reduce smoke and toxic emissions by up 80%, cut cooking time in half and some can even charge the ever-more essential mobile phone and provide lighting. The biggest issue is not the existence of designs but increasing their adoption. Although relatively expensive, they can pay for themselves in less than a year through the fuel savings, especially in urban areas. Thus developing strong local distribution networks and micro-finance is essential for their adoption. Figures 3.22c and fig 3.22d show two successful social enterprises, Envirofit and BioLite's stoves in location in Kenya.

Figure 3.22a Women in Nyaung Shwe, Myanmar, carrying wood to market. (photo Patrik Dietrich/Shutterstock.com)

Figure 3.22b Young women return home after collecting wood in the forest, Nkhata Bay, Malawi. (photo Martin Mwaura/ Shutterstock.com)

Figure 3.22c Envirofit's SuperSaver Wood cookstove in use in India. With over a dozen user-designed, locally produced products and 1.6 million clean stove sales, Envirofit International is an economically sustainable social enterprise that proves the success of market-based solutions for creating large-scale sustainable impact. (photo courtesy Envirofit International)

Figure 3.22d Driven by the motto 'energy everywhere', BioLite HomeStove's innovative technology uses a heat-driven fan and mini-generator for ultra-efficient cooking and powering phones and lights. Biolite have now extended their range of products to solar lighting systems with their outdoor and camping sales subsidising emerging market sales. (photo courtesy Biolite)

Box 3.7 transportation: accessing markets, education and health care

Improvements in productivity are of little use if you cannot get your products to market. The World Bank estimates that over 1 billion of the world's rural population in developing countries don't have adequate access to transportation, and this correlates directly to poverty, child mortality, gender inequality and low levels of education. But all these indicators have been shown to improve with better access to mobility.[53]

For poor rural and urban communities, the first mile is just as crucial as the last mile. A staggering 70% of all agricultural output in sub-Saharan Africa is still headloaded by women and children[54] and this practice is also prevalent across South Asia. (fig 3.23a) The lack of transportation is also the cause

of the high proportion of food wastage between field and market. Here more than anywhere, appropriate and affordable are the only way forward. Alongside building and maintaining a good road system, BoP designs focus on what are known as Intermediate Means of Transport (IMTs). These take the form of wheelbarrows, bicycles, motorbikes, animal power and innumerable ingenious adaptations of two- and three-wheeled vehicles for almost any function imaginable. Even these low-cost solutions however are unaffordable to most, giving rise to micro-businesses either designing, making, maintaining or offering 'taxi' services through many ingenious adaptations of the bicycle (see also Chapter 8.2). (fig 3.23b / fig 3.23c)

Figure 3.23a Walking together with headloading remains the main form of mobility and transportation in many rural areas of Sub-Saharan Africa and South Asia, as seen here in Karawa, Democratic Republic of Congo (2013) and women headloading their goods to market in Orissa, India (photo credits gunterguni; Steve Estavnick)

Figure 3.23b In very mountainous regions like Nepal, roads are too expensive and prone to washing away. Lateral thinking at Practical Action introduced gravity ropeways and tuins. The ropeway shown takes five minutes to lower produce for market that used to take three hours to carry down on foot. The tuin in Gordi, Nepal allows many marginalised households to cross the Trishuli River to sell their produce and access schools and hospitals.

Figure 3.23C Several banana links transported to market on a bicycle in Kisoro, Uganda (2013); a fully loaded rickshaw in New Delhi (2018); traditional street vending by bicycle in Hanoi, Vietnam (2016); a bicycle ambulance prototype being trialled in Oshikuku, Namibia (2007). (photo credits clockwise: GUDKOV ANDREY /Shutterstock.com; MindStorm; Asia Images; Aaron Weiler)

Box 3.8 design for emergency and disaster relief

According to the UNHCR, in 2018 there were 68.5 million forcibly displaced people worldwide of whom 40 million are internally displaced, 25.5 million official refugees, 10 million stateless people and 3.1 asylum seekers.[55] As climate change and natural disasters increase alongside conflicts, the need for emergency, short and long-term refugee accommodation has never been greater. Designers continue to contribute their skills to these efforts in many different ways, but it requires very considered, informed and participative approaches.

Established by Shigeru Ban in 1995, the Voluntary Architects' Network provides post-disaster design, resulting in many famous and influential paper houses, bridges, and temporary schools, concert halls and museums. More recently, in response to the Eastern Japan Earthquake and Tsunami, Shigeru Ban and a team of students developed a Paper Partition System for rapid deployment in halls and large spaces. Easily assembled without the need for wooden joints or braces, it can be delivered to site within a week (Japan 2011). (fig 3.24a)

Given that the average length of time refugees live in camps is 17 years,[56] fly-in housing solutions are only useful in emergencies. For longer-term housing, development workers advocate a more participative approach known as Creative Capacity Building (CCB) where designers work with camp residents to develop their own capabilities and skills for them to create their own housing solutions based on their building traditions.[57]

Maidan Tent (fig 3.24b) is an example of a design outcome for a sheltered communal space developed through a participatory approach. The social enterprise Better Shelter, supported by IKEA and UNHCR, has designed a modular flat-pack shelter as a longer lasting option to the current emergency tents. With the logistical advantages and adaptability of modularity, tens of thousands have been deployed in camps by the UNHCR since 2015. (fig 3.24c)

Figure 3.24a Established by Shigeru Ban in 1995, the Voluntary Architects' Network provides post-disaster design, resulting in many famous and influential paper houses, bridges, and temporary schools, concert halls and museums. More recently, in response to the Eastern Japan Earthquake and Tsunami, Shigeru Ban and a team of students developed a Paper Partition System for rapid assembly in halls and large spaces. It is easily assembled without the need for wooden joints or braces and can be delivered onsite within a week (Japan 2011). (photos courtesy Voluntary Architects Network)

Figure 3.24b Maidan tent is a covered communal space to enable the hosting of a range of social activities in refugee camps. It was designed collaboratively specifically at, and for, the Ritsona refugee camp in Euboea, Greece 2018. Lead designers were Bonaventura Visconti and Leo Bettini Oberkalmsteiner with Eco 100 Plus IOM (UN Migration Agency), ARUP community engagement, LEAP (Laboratory for effective an@-poverty policies), Boa Mistura and the support of some crowd funding. (photos courtesy Maidan Tent /maidantent.org / credits Delfino Sisto Legnani and Marco Cappeletti)

Figure 3.24c The social enterprise Better Shelter, supported by IKEA and UNHCR, has developed a modular flat-pack shelter as a longer lasting option to the current emergency tents. With the logistical advantages and adaptability of modularity, hundreds of thousands have been deployed in camps by the UNHCR since 2015. Shown here: units in Kara Tepe transit camp, Lesvos (Greece 2015). (photos courtesy Better Shelter / Jonas Nyström)

built upon is part of the process of shaping an open library of possibility and optimism.

3.4 ethics and sustainability: design as a tool for change

If achieving sustainability means balancing who, what and how much is consumed in relation to what the planet can provide and replenish, then it is inevitably connected to questions of ethics. In many of the sustainable design strategies we have looked at to date, these ethics have been more implicit than explicit. Now, we will explore the ethical dimension of sustainability more directly and areas of design where questions of ethics and values are central to the practice, such as design activism and speculative and critical design.

Justice, in its many forms, together with the responsibility of stewardship that it entails, is the ethical principle most closely connected to sustainability. This is specifically articulated through the concept of *eco-justice* that links environmental, social and economic justice:

> *Eco-Justice ethics seek the common human good in harmony with nature, coupling human-centered imperatives with eco-centered imperatives for earth citizenship.*[58]

Defining sustainability as 'meeting our needs without compromising the needs of future generations' then implies the notion of *inter-generational justice*. Instead, what we currently have is one generation's overconsumption robbing future generations of an equal opportunity for wellbeing, a situation that is neither ethical nor sustainable. But this overconsumption by the few is not only at the expense of future generations; it is also at the expense of their fellow humans today. This unequal distribution and consumption of resources further raises issues of *distributive justice* and basic *human rights*. And the fact that the consequences of climate change will be felt most by those who have least contributed to it and have the least power to shape the future and adapt is central to the cause of *climate justice*.

The *eco-justice* response to overconsumption is the concept of *sufficiency*. But how much is 'sufficient' to satisfy our needs and how much is our 'fair share'? The answer in eco-justice terms is *that people and the planet will thrive when all humans have sufficient to lead fulfilling lives at a level that the natural environment can sustain within the Earth's carrying capacity.* Ultimately, eco-justice questions the greater right of some people over others to *the commons* and demands equity between humans

and other species. What part of that responsibility do designers bear?

taking responsibility

Papanek's accusation in 1971 that there were few professions more harmful than industrial design was certainly a wake-up call for more than one generation of designers. While this condemnation was largely justified at the time and is still true in large part, designers have increasingly come to accept their environmental responsibility and broadened where and how they apply their design skills as a tool for equitable change and 'social good'.[59]

Designers' acceptance of their responsibilities closely linked to sustainable values has been explicitly stated through design manifestos and ethical codes of practice for over 100 years, as compiled by the design activist John Emerson.[60] To give a flavour of these, the Ahmadabad Declaration on Industrial Design for Development (UNIDO and ICSID 1979) was an early manifesto setting out appropriate industrial design practice in developing contexts. It states "that designers in every part of the world must work to evolve a new value system which dissolves the disastrous divisions between the worlds of waste and want, preserves the identity of peoples and attends the priority areas of need for the vast majority of mankind".[61] The Hannover Principles were an early code for environmental sustainability used for the Hannover 2000 world expo based on William McDonough and Partners' working principles from 1992.[62] Below are three more recent collective initiatives that illustrate the breadth of designers' concern to integrate ethics and sustainability in their practice:

- the Designers Accord (2007): a code and guidelines that call upon its members to activate sustainable values in their practice and engage a wider audience, including clients, in conversations about these values. The Accord was integrated into AIGA's standards of professional practice in 2008.
- the Kyoto Design Declaration (2008): a six-point statement of commitment by the members of Cumulus (124 art and design education institutions around the world) to share the global responsibility for building sustainable, human-centred, creative societies.
- the Utrecht Manifesto (2015): the legacy of five inspiring biennials on the theme of 'Design for the Good Society', sets out ten action frames for achieving this. To quote the introduction, "*The 'good society' is a dream of a world that is fair and just, a utopian concept, which provides direction and enables us to join forces. By virtue of their powers of imagination and expertise, designers are well placed for expressing this dream of 'the good society' in an appealing way and to help translate it into practice.*"[63]

Figure 3.25 Occupy George: a sample dollar bill printed with one of the freely downloadable templates designed to spread the message of wealth inequality using the establishment's own distribution system for Occupy Wall Street protests, 2011. (photo Jane Penty/design Occupy George 2011)

But what can words achieve? These codes, guidelines or principles have all emerged from collective debates between concerned designers who want to see change. They act as a reminder of shared values while providing solidarity and concrete ways of activating these values. Equally, they are not so naïve as to suggest that designers alone can change all. They also acknowledge that successful design interventions can only happen through cross-disciplinary and co-design approaches *with* the political, social and economic will at leadership and grassroots levels.

design activism: deeds not words

> *Once the practical things start happening that people can see and touch, something changes in the culture.*
> José Martin, Coin en Transición[64]

Activism occupies the space where words are transformed into deeds. Alistair Fuad-Luke defines activism as: "*taking actions to catalyse, encourage or bring about change, in order to elicit social, cultural and/or political transformations.*"[65] As designers are by nature doers, linking the term design to activism is a fairly natural alliance. In seeking to redress ethical injustice, design activism goes beyond 'good' design's mission to improve the experience of daily life.[66] Applied to sustainability, *design activism identifies unsustainable practices or inequities and their root causes, and uses design as a tool to instigate change and give shape to new systems and ways of doing and being.*

By implication, 'new ways' of doing or being require agency to challenge the political, economic, social and cultural status quo. Fundamentally, design activism supports change from the ground up and most often operates on the fringes or outside the systems it is attempting to change. Being a design activist calls for a high level of commitment, imagination and risk-taking. While this may not be for every designer, it can provide a significant degree of satisfaction and a supportive community through its co-design and collaborative approaches.

In the world of activism, graphic communication and social media are well-known NGO campaigning tools, capturing attention through their cleverness and wit. The Occupy George dollar stamps illustrate this well. As part of the Occupy Wall Street protests in 2011, five 'Occupy George' stamps or over-prints were designed for the $1US bill to communicate wealth inequality through simple infographics. The designs are freely downloadable and the dollars remain legal tender, thereby using the money system itself to spread the message[67] (fig 3.25).

The role of the physical object however is less recognised, although artefacts have been fashioned for direct action, including protests and acts of civil disobedience, for a long time and have even achieved official recognition in exhibitions and publications like *Disobedient Objects*.[68] In fact, for certain forms of activism it is becoming the preferred tool, presenting interesting new opportunities for product designers and others like them who can turn shared ideas into physical reality.

artefacts as tools for protest and urban activism

> *Provisional, informal, guerrilla, insurgent, DIY, hands-on, unsolicited, unplanned, participatory, tactical, micro, open-source – these are just a few of the words floating around to describe a type of interventionist urbanism sweeping through cities around the world. Worth highlighting are four overriding themes that seem to pervade [...] [the] projects: Citizenship, Equity, Protest, and Participation.*[69]

Examples of physical artefacts for protest include the 123 Occupy set of prototypes with downloadable instructions designed by Common Practice to "*connect strategies for occupation and protest with reproducible physical actions*".[70] Each design is based on a temporary structure that can be easily constructed and speedily deployed and adapted on a minimal budget to suit particular protest or occupation requirements (fig 3.26).

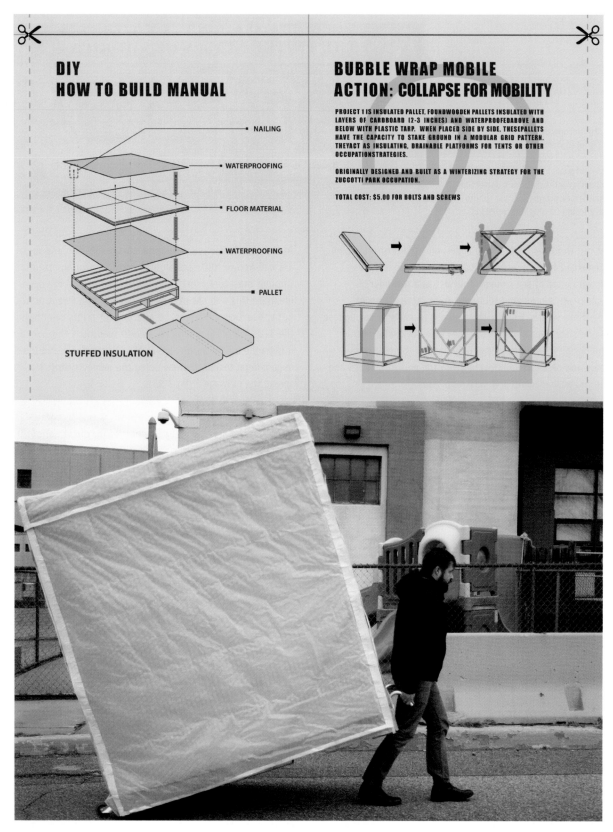

Figure 3.26 123 Occupy: Collapse for Mobility by Common Practice is a set of low-cost structures with downloadable instructions for rapid deployment shown at Venice Biennale and NY Storefront for Art and Architecture 2012. (photo courtesy Greta Hite Hansen, Common Practice)

Figure 3.27 paraSITE by Michael Rakovitz has built over 30 paraSITES with and for homeless people in Boston, New York and Chicago (1998 -ongoing). (photo courtesy Michael Rakovitz)

Michael Rakovitz's interventions use the tent typology to address social issues such as homelessness and the loss of public space to 'store cars' known as parking. His paraSITES are inflatable tents each co-designed and built specifically *with* and *for* a homeless person. They attach to the HVAC of specific buildings and use the exhausted hot air to inflate and add warmth (fig 3.27). In his P(LOT) series he *"questions the occupation and dedication of public space [to cars] and encourages reconsiderations of 'legitimate' participation in city life"*[71] by demonstrating alternative uses for metered parking spaces by disguising tents as cars.

This theme of reclaiming urban space for public use and community building over cars continues to be a rich seam for

Figure 3.28 Public Parklets all over the world are a legacy of the PARK(ing) activism instigated by Rebar's first PARK(let) in 2005. Shown here San Francisco's Planning Department engaging the community in conversation at their MSPF idea lab, and the Haight Street Market Parklet in San Francisco. (photos courtesy San Francisco Pavements to Parks, SFP)

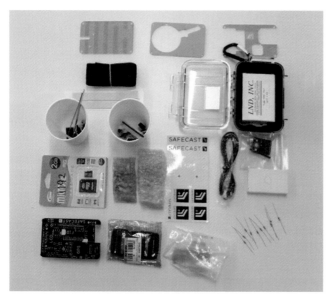

Figure 3.29 The bGeiger Nano portable open source radiation detector kit with GPS was developed in response to Fukashima for citizens to be able to take and share location-specific radiation measurements that official data was not providing. (photo courtesy safecast.org)

Figure 3.30 Libelium's family of solar-powered Waspmote Plug & Sense radiation and pollution sensors evolved from their initial remote sensing platform developed in response to the Fukashima nuclear accident (2011). (courtesy ©Libelium Communicaciones Distribuidas S.L./libelium.com)

design activism. It was brought to prominence by the Reclaim the Streets direct action movement started in London in the early 1990s and had spread across the world by 1997. An example of this is Rebar's first PARK(ing) action in 2005. With over 70% of downtown San Francisco's outdoor space dedicated to cars, it set out *"to transform a parking space into a PARK(ing) space, thereby temporarily expanding the public realm and improving the quality of urban human habitat, at least until the meter ran out"*.[72] Since Rebar's first action in 2005, PARK(ing) has become an annual worldwide event and has led to real change. In 2010, San Francisco's planning department formalised a route for communities to self-identify parking spaces for co-design conversions into 'parklets' through their Urban Protoyping and Parklet grants. The result has been the creation of several distinct and imaginative parklets and this model has since spread to many other cities all around the world (fig 3.28).

citizens as environmental vigilantes

Open platforms, citizen science, hacker groups and the IoT are facilitating the growth of another area of activism: citizen 'policing' of environmental data, including air quality, noise levels, contamination and radioactivity. Together, citizens, scientists, designers and coders are collaborating in the creation of products for sensing, collecting and sharing data, particularly where official information is not forthcoming or insufficiently localised, detailed or transparent.

An early example of this that catches the imagination is Natalie Jeremijenko's Feral Robotic Dog Project where toy robotic dogs were 'hacked' for higher purposes than begging for plastic bones. The dogs were modified and reprogrammed to literally sniff out dangerous toxins on suspect sites. Started at New York University with engineering design students in 2002,

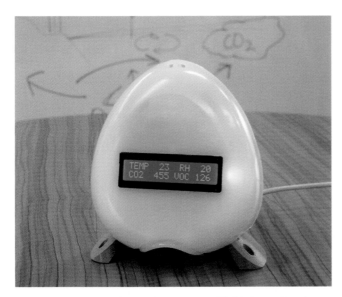

Figure 3.31 The Air Quality Egg in Internet-enabled indoor and outdoor pollution sensor for CO, CO2, SO2, NO2, PM, O3 and VOCs. Originally developed by IoT Meetup groups as a citizen science tool in 2012, it is now educating and connecting classrooms around the globe about air quality. (photo courtesy Wicked Device/photo Joshua Fidanque)

Figure 3.32 Buggy Air: on the go, real-time air quality monitors to inform direct local action. (phtotos courtesy Superflux)

this spread to workshops in many other inner cities. It also had the double purpose of empowering underserved youth with physical computing skills and raising awareness about toxic pollutants in their own neighbourhoods, potentially some of the very same chemicals released in the production of the robot dogs and similar high-tech toys they were repurposing.[73]

Immediately after the Fukashima nuclear disaster in 2011, a spontaneous network of concerned international scientists and designers joined forces at the Tokyo Hackerspace. This gave birth to Safecast, *"a global volunteer-centered citizen science project working to empower people with data about their environments"*,[74] With Kickstarter funding, they developed the *bGeigie nano*, an arduino-based radiation meter in kit form that could be attached to cars or statically positioned for citizen groups to do their own localised monitoring (fig 3.29). Other companies like Libelium in Spain also responded to the emergency and within a few weeks developed their initial Waspmote Wireless Radiation Sensor Platform. This eventually evolved into a commercial family of solar-powered plug and sense remote radiation and pollution sensors that are easily attached to existing infrastructure (fig 3.30).

The high levels of air pollution from vehicle traffic in many cities around the world are now at crisis level (see Chapter 8.1). This is another area that citizens have taken into their own hands as a means to protect themselves and those most vulnerable – the elderly, children and asthma sufferers – as well as to hold authorities to account.[75] A good example of this is Sensemakers' Air Quality Egg, a product originally developed as a community-led crowd-funded product initiated by New York City and Amsterdam IoT meet-up groups in 2012 to measure indoor and outdoor air quality. The Air Quality Egg, now produced by Wicked Device, has evolved into a commercial educational tool to actively learn about air pollution. By sharing their real-time local data, connected classrooms across the globe become part of a community helping to raise awareness and make air pollution more visible (fig 3.31).

Concerns over how much worse air pollution from vehicle traffic is close to the ground and how this puts babies and young children at risk led to the BuggyAir project in 2016, a monitor you attach to your baby's pram. Despite the high demand from anxious parents and offers of equity finance, the BuggyAir team changed tack and broadened the product to avoid falling into the trap of "selling sensors that might ultimately dissuade parents from going outdoors without solving the root problem, reducing air pollution".[76] The second-generation BuggyAir is designed to be used by people across different modes of transport in order to create a dynamic air quality map that can be shared with local councils, school and other institutions for direct local action[77] (fig 3.32). In Chapter 8, Box 8.1 we also discuss Brizi, a commercialised buggy air quality monitor and purifier with a shared data platform.

critical and speculative design: envisioning and challenging the ethics and sustainability of emerging technologies

As we saw in 'technology will save us' (Chapter 2.5), emerging technologies hold within them both the hope of utopias and the fear of dystopias. The rapid advances in the fields of bio-engineering and artificial intelligence (AI) into uncharted territories for humankind and life on the planet raise many philosophical and ethical questions. Among these is the question of how we want to live on a shared planet and what it means to be human. Sustainability and its underlying ethics can provide both a lens for challenging new scenarios and a compass for steering emerging technologies towards sustainably beneficial outcomes.

As citizens and even designers, we may see the development of these technologies as the inevitable march of 'progress' outside of our control, shaped by scientists and entrepreneurs: *"Today most non-specialists have little say in charting the role that robots will play in our lives. We are simply watching a new version of Star Wars scripted by research and business interests in real time, except that this script will become our actual world."*[78]

Or we may take a more optimistic view and seize the opportunity to interrogate and shape these technologies positively before they emerge from the laboratory. This is where *speculative* or *critical design*[79] is a useful tool for engaging critically yet constructively with new technologies and their socio-environmental implications. If the key to design activism is 'doing', then for speculative design 'doing' happens through imagining, envisioning and creating physically tangible future scenarios, ranging from the utopian to the dystopian, to provoke debate and allow us to examine our own moral and ethical boundaries.

As designers practising in this field for many years, Dunne and Raby are careful to point out that speculative designers should not define or moralise about these futures but work "with experts including ethicists, political scientists, economists and so on, [to] generate futures that act a catalysts for public debate and discussions about the futures people really want".[80] In Chapter 8 (fig 8.62), we see how they put this into practice in their United Micro-Kingdoms thought experiment on future mobility scenarios in a post-fossil fuel era.

But designers by no means hold a monopoly on imagining futures. Science fiction writers and filmmakers are already very successful at creating influential future narratives in books and on screen that provoke debate and reflection, including such classics as *Brave New World*, *Nineteen Eighty-Four*, *Blade Runner* and the more recent *Black Mirror* series. What product designers contribute to this field are the physical props that interpret and enhance the narratives

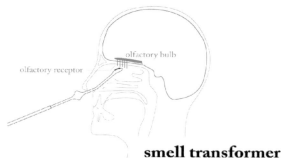

smell transformer
Genetically modified Synsepalum dulcificum (miracle berry) which releases enzymes which binds to smell receptors, changing all smells including the smell of rotten food into a sweet smell.

Figure 3.33 Paul Gong's Human Hyena tools, the hyena inhaler, smell transformer and taste transformer, address the issue of food waste by giving humans the capacity to eat rotting food. (courtesy ©Paul Gong)

and interactions, often using the power of the unfamiliar, the fantastical and the magical to help us consider preferable futures.

While the twentieth century has seen some product designers engaging in futurist concepts such as Norman Bel Geddes, Luigi Collani and the radical design groups of the 1960s and 1970s, Buckminster Fuller stands out for his anticipation of sustainability issues. Through his products and buildings he embodied his visionary philosophy of designing for a world of limited resources. His 1933 Dymaxion prototype car (fig 1.11) was a realisation of his principle of *"maximum efficiency of time and resources for minimum energy input"* – essentially eco-efficiency 60 years before its time.[81] He was also a great believer in the social construction of technology through his annual World Game where participants co-imagined a future using technology to create a sustainable and equitable world.

Philips Design's inspiring 'Visions of the Future' programme is a rare example of the corporate world's commitment to open speculation. While their designs probe new applications for emerging technologies, the Microbial home specifically set itself a

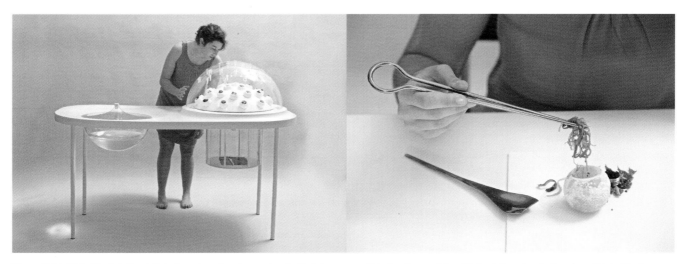

Figure 3.34 Livin Studio's Fungi Mutarium: transforming waste plastic into a new edible fungi, complete with tools to enjoy it. (courtesy ©Livin Studio www. livinstudio.com)

sustainable agenda for *"the home [...][to be] viewed as a biological machine to filter, process and recycle what we conventionally think of as waste – sewage, effluent, garbage, waste water"*.[82]

Staying on the subject of waste, speculative design pushes the boundaries of acceptability. Paul Gong's Human Hyena project addresses the problem of food waste by providing humans with transhumanist synthetic biology tools to become scavengers. Genetically altered bacteria and enzymes delivered by these tools enable us to eat rotting food by modifying our digestive systems and sense of smell to overcome our natural revulsion (fig 3.33). Katrina Unger's Livin Studio tackles a different waste problem:

plastic. Their Fungi Mutarium protoype design grows and harvests edible fungi that feed on plastic waste and agar to transform it into a new type of food (fig 3.34).

Beyond the purely speculative, outstanding designers such as Jurgen Bey and Marti Guixé demonstrate that it is possible to maintain a stream of critical explorations alongside their commercial practices that inevitably touch on many aspects of sustainability. In *Critical Design in Context,* Matt Malpass reminds us that faced with the complex socio-technical, environmental and ethical issues of today, critical design offers us the tools to question our design practice and its impacts.[83]

Chapter summary

1. Social sustainability challenges what it is to be human in relation to each other and in relation to the planet through our values, practices and social norms. It will exist when all humans have the means to satisfy their basic needs and the possibility of self-fulfilment, within the planet's limits. As a key pillar of sustainability, it is highly connected to ethical concepts of justice and reliant on a healthy environment.

2. Many of the root causes of unsustainability are socio-political and economic in nature, particularly the grossly unequal distribution of wealth and power. While designers may feel impotent in shifting the wider framework, sustainably minded designers recognise that products can have both positive and negative social, environmental and economic consequences and accept that responsibility.

They seek to design products that address real needs, build social capital and improve life and wellbeing with the least negative impacts, and not just for the richest. These 'better' and more sustainable products are the tools for meaningful lives in balance with a shared environment.

3. Overconsumption by the most affluent is undeniably one of the major causes of environmental damage the world is facing. It is the logical consequence of the 'consumer society' created by the need to continuously feed GDP growth. Shifting to a model of 'sustainable consumption' cannot be achieved through techno-fixes and eco-efficiency alone – it also requires significant behaviour change. In this sense, a move to 'sustainable consumption' is largely a social and cultural project that involves developing new

values and exploring new ways of living. For designers, it presents an opportunity to be part of the biggest creative challenge of our time.

4. The benefits of eco-efficiency measures set up to reduce the impacts of consumption are being offset by the rebound effect, a growing middle class quite naturally seeking a better standard of living, and the unchallenged existence of products simply created to gratify desires and increase profits with no thought to their consequences. To be effective, products with lower environmental impacts need to go hand in hand with behaviour change strategies in order to address overconsumption from both the demand and the supply side.

5. In designing products that lead to more sustainable lifestyles, designers need to understand that one size does not fit all because people's consumption patterns are heavily motivated by their personal values. The Value Modes model categorises people into distinct psychographic groups based on personal values and motivators which designers can use to make products for more sustainable consumption and lifestyle choices attractive to these different value groups.

6. Choice architecture is the way in which consumers are presented with options. By applying the NUDGE principles of good choice architecture, designers can build in more sustainable consumer behaviours, not only at the point of purchase but also during the use phase of products. These principles are to *provide feedback, align incentives, set defaults, understand mappings, structure complex choices* and *anticipate error*.

7. The value–action gap is a well-documented disconnect between what we say we believe in and what we actually do. Quite often this happens because there are inbuilt barriers that make it hard to change our habits and routines to more sustainable behaviours, especially at moments when our motivation dips. As designers, if we can anticipate the moments of low motivation, we can design-in solutions that help overcome the obstacles to living more sustainably.

8. A human-centred design (HCD) approach is fundamental to the design of better products. It is used across the whole spectrum of design from stand-alone products to the design of services for social innovation. As its name implies, it puts people and their needs at the centre of the design process either directly in co-design scenarios or through consultation during the design process. It is stakeholder engagement and the open, empathetic and creative attitude required that ensure a higher rate of success in addressing the complex social issues and 'wicked' problems that often lie at the heart of unsustainable and inequitable behaviours.

9. When 60% of people globally earn less than $4 a day, 1 in 11 have no access to safe water or enough food and 1 in 3 have no sanitation, it is clear that the current disparities in income are neither equitable nor sustainable. Designing products that empower the poorest to lift themselves out of poverty to reduce inequality is a real and growing area of endeavour for product designers and one that is yielding significant results. Products for people at the base of the pyramid focus on: increasing livelihoods and employment opportunities; improving hygiene and health; accessing to clean water and connectivity; and responding to humanitarian emergencies and the growing number of displaced people. HCD, frugality, extreme affordability and the appropriateness of the technology and business models to the local context are the hallmarks of design for the BoP.

10. Justice, in its many forms, and the responsibility of stewardship that it entails, is the ethical principle that runs through all aspects of sustainability. This is specifically articulated through the concept of eco-justice that links environmental, social and economic justice. In our Anthropocene epoch, eco-justice puts humans squarely in the position of environmental stewards rather than overlords, fully responsible for the state of life on the planet. A number of ethical manifestos and design codes of practice that embrace sustainability demonstrate the design community's concerns and their willingness to accept this responsibility.

11. Design activism is about doing. Doing something about unsustainable practices and social inequality armed with design as its tool. It supports change from the grassroots and often operates on the fringes or outside the systems it is attempting to change. For certain areas of activism such as contesting the use of public space or citizen monitoring of pollution and contamination, the physical artefact is becoming the preferred tool, presenting interesting new opportunities for product designers.

12. The rapid advances in the fields of bio-engineering and artificial intelligence (AI) raise deep questions of ethics and sustainability. Speculative or critical design fictions can be used as tools to interrogate and shape these technologies for environmentally safe and socially positive ends before they emerge from the laboratory. This happens through imagining, envisioning and creating physically tangible future scenarios ranging from the utopian to the dystopian, to stimulate debate and allow a wider audience to examine their own moral and ethical boundaries.

Notes

1 Ehrenfeld, J. and A. Hoffman (2013) *Flourishing. A Frank Conversation about Sustainability*, Sheffield: Greenleaf.

2 Chochinov, A. (2009) *A Good Long Tradition*. In foreword to E. Pilloton, *Design Revolution*, London: Thames & Hudson, p. 9.

3 UNEP (2018) Social Life Cycle Assessment (S-LCA) – Life Cycle Initiative [online]. Available at www.lifecycleinitiative.org/starting-life-cycle-thinking/life-cycle-approaches/social-lca/ (accessed 14 January 2019).

4 UN population data 1970: 3.70 billion; 2014: 7.3 billion. GDP data: 1970:18.3 trillion; 2014: 74.8 trillion (both $2016 PPP); World Bank data available at https://data.worldbank.org/indicator/NY.GDP.MKTP.CD and real worth calculator: com/uscompare/relativevalue.php (accessed 10 January 2019).

5 Harris survey results: Eventbrite Report (2014) *Millennials. Fueling the Experience Economy* [pdf]. Available at https://eventbrites3.s3.amazonaws.com/marketing/Millennials_Research/Gen_PR_Final.pdf (accessed 11 January 2019).

6 Jay Cassano (2015). The Science of Why you Should Spend Money on Experiences and not Things. *Fast Company,* 30 March [online]. Available at www.fastcompany.com/3043858/the-science-of-why-you-should-spend-your-money-on-experiences-not-thing (accessed 01 March 2018).

7 Jackson, T. (2006) Readings in Sustainable Consumption. In T. Jackson, ed., *The Earthscan Reader in Sustainable Consumption*, London, and Sterling, VA: Earthscan, p.1.

8 Ibid., p.20

9 Dahmus, J. (2014) Can Efficiency Improvements Reduce Resource Consumption? *Journal of Industrial Ecology*, 18(6), pp. 883–897. doi: 10.1111/jiec.12110.

10 Nadel, S. (2012) *The Rebound Effect: Large or Small?*, American Council for an Energy-Efficient Economy white paper, Washington, DC: ACEEE, August, p. ii. Available at https://aceee.org/sites/default/files/pdf/white-paper/rebound-large-and-small.pdf.

11 Karas, H. (Feb 2017) *The Unprecedented Expansion of the Global Middle Class: An Update* [pdf]. Global Economy and Development Working Paper 100, Washington, DC: Brookings Institute, p.11. Available at www.brookings.edu/wp-content/uploads/2017/02/global_20170228_global-middle-class.pdf.

12 Calor.co.uk (n.d.) *Patio Heaters – Outdoor Living – Shop* [online]. Available at www.calor.co.uk/shop/outdoor-living/patio-heaters.html (accessed 11 January 2019).

13 Schwartz, S.H. (2012) An Overview of the Schwartz Theory of Basic Values. *Online Readings in Psychology and Culture,* 2(1). http:// dx.doi.org/10.9707/2307-0919.1116.

14 Cultural Dynamics (n.d.) CDSM Values Modes [online]. Available at www.cultdyn.co.uk/valuesmodes.html (accessed 11 January 2019).

15 Rose, C. (2011) *What Makes People Tick. The Three Hidden Worlds of Settlers, Prospectors and Pioneers*, Leicester: Matador, p. 235.

16 Hardin, G. (1968) The Tragedy of the Commons. *Science*, 162(3859), pp. 1243–1248. doi:10.1126/science.162.3859.1243. Available at http://science.sciencemag.org/content/sci/162/3859/1243.full.pdf.

17 Hotel Energy Solutions (2011) Key Card Systems to Switch Off Electricity [pdf]. Available at www.hes-unwto.org/HES/files/HES_Key_EE_Technology_11_EN.pdf (accessed 11 January 2019).

18 Sherwin, C. (20/11/2012) Sustainable Behaviour by Design [online]. *The Guardian*, 20 November. Available at www.theguardian.com/sustainable-business/blog/sustainable-behaviour-design-toolkit (accessed 11 January 2019).

19 Allcott, H. (2011) Social Norms and Energy Conservation. *Journal of Public Economics*, 95(9–10), pp. 1082–1095. doi: 10.1016/j.pubeco.2011.03.003.

20 London Economics/ =IPSOS (2014) *Impact of Energy Labels on Consumer Behaviour*. Report commissioned by EU, October. London: London Economics. Available at https://ec.europa.eu/energy/sites/ener/files/documents/Impact%20of%20energy%20labels%20on%20consumer%20behaviour.pdf (accessed 11 January 2019).

21 Lockton, D., D. Harrison and N.A. Stanton (2010) *Design with Intent: 101 Patterns for Influencing Behaviour Through Design v.1.0*, Windsor: Equifine.

22 Earth Policy Institute (2014) The Downfall of the Plastic Bag: A Global Picture [online]. Available at www.earth-policy.org/plan_b_updates/2014/update123 (accessed 31 October 2015).

23 United Nations Educational, Scientific and Cultural Organization (n.d.) Facts and Figures on Marine Pollution [online].Available at www.unesco.org/new/en/natural-sciences/ioc-oceans/focus-areas/rio-20-ocean/blueprint-for-the-future-we-want/marine-pollution/facts-and-figures-on-marine-pollution/ (accessed 11 January 2019).

24 Kärrman, A., A. Schönlau and M. Engwall (2016) *Exposure and Effects of Microplastics on Wildlife. A Review of Existing Data*, 1 March, Orebor, Sweden: MTM Research Centre. Available at www.naturvardsverket.se/upload/miljoarbete-i-samhallet/miljoarbete-i-sverige/regeringsuppdrag/2016/mikroplaster/report-orebro-university-160405.pdf.

25 BBC (2007) It's in the Bag, Darling. *BBC Sec.Magazine*, 25 April [online]. Available at http://news.bbc.co.uk/1/hi/magazine/6587169.stm.

26 Rosenthal, E. (2/02/2008) Motivated by a Tax, Irish Spurn Plastic Bags. *The New York Times*, Sec., 2 February. International/Europe. Available at www.nytimes.com/2008/02/02/world/europe/02bags.html.

27 Paṗanek, V. (1995) *The Green imperative. Ecology and Ethics in Design and Architecture,* London: Thames & Hudson, p. 8.

28 Design Matters (2010) *Safe Agua,* Pasadena, CA: Arts Center California.

29 Ideo.org (2015) *The Field Guide to Human-centered Design*, San Francisco, CA: IDEO.

30 Design Matters (2012) *Safe Agua Peru.* Available at https://designmattersatartcenter.org/proj/safeaguaperu/.

31 Viladas, Pilar (2003) Questions for Niels Diffrient. A Machine for Sitting. *The New York Times Magazine*, 30 November. Available at www.nytimes.com/2003/11/30/magazine/the-way-we-live-now-11-30-03-questions-for-niels-diffrient-a-machine-for-sitting.html (accessed 6 January 2016).

32 Frogdesign (2015) Human-centered Design: Why Empathy Isn't Everything. frog [online]. Available at https://designmind.frogdesign.com/2015/05/human-centered-design-why-empathy-isnt-everything/ (accessed 11 January 2019).

33 All income figures including PEW data in this section are based on World Bank 2011 US Purchasing Power Parity (PPP). Extreme poverty was updated in 2015 to $1.90/day (2011 PPP), although the new UN Sustainable Development Goals are using the older 2005 figure of $1.25/day. For a full explanation of how this is calculated see Ferreira, F. (2015) http://blogs.worldbank.org/developmenttalk/international-poverty-line-has-just-been-raised-190-day-global-poverty-basically-unchanged-how-even, 4 October.

34 Latest figures available: World Bank (2016) *Poverty and Shared Prosperity 2016. Taking on Inequality*, Washington, DC: World Bank, pp. 35–45. doi: 10.1596/978-1-4648-0958-3.

35 Kochhar, R. (2015) *A Global Middle Class Is More Promise than Reality: From 2001 to 2011, Nearly 700 Million Step Out of Poverty, but Most Only Barely*, Washington, DC: Pew Research Center.

36 Kenny, C. (2013) Why Ending Extreme Poverty Isn't Good Enough. *BloombergView*, 29 April. Available at www.bloomberg.com/bw/articles/2013-04-28/why-ending-extreme-poverty-isnt-good-enough (accessed 11 January 2019).

37 Rangan, V,, M.C. Kasturi and Djordjija Petkoski (2011)The Globe: Segmenting the Base of the Pyramid. *Harvard Business Review*, 1 June. Available at https://hbr.org/2011/06/the-globe-segmenting-the-base-of-the-pyramid (accessed 5 May 2018).

38 Polak, Paul (2008) *Out of Poverty. What Works When Traditional Approaches Fail*, San Francisco, CA: Berrett-Koehler Publishers.

39 Leadbeater, Charles (2014) *The Frugal Innovator. Creating Change on a Shoestring Budget*, Basingstoke: Palgrave Macmillan, p. x.

40 World Bank (2016) *Poverty and Shared Prosperity 2016.*

41 Gangemi, J. (2010) Irrigating the 'Perfect Solution' with DripTech's Peter Frykman [online]. Available at http://gangemithinkingdesign.blogspot.com/2010/09/interview-with-driptechs-peter-frykman.html (accessed 8 September 2015).

42 Polak (2008), p. 75.

43 WHO(2018) Maternal Mortality [online, 16 February]. Available at www.who.int/news-room/fact-sheets/detail/maternal-mortality (accessed 20 December 2018).

44 Maternal Health Task Force (2018) The Sustainable Development Goals and Maternal Mortality [online]. Available at www.mhtf.org/topics/the-sustainable-development-goals-and-maternal-mortality/ (accessed 11 January 2019).

45 wecaresolar.org (n.d.) We Care Solar Suitcase® [online]. Available at https://wecaresolar.org/about/our-story/ (accessed 20 December2018) and email correspondence with Dr Stachel, December 2018.

46 WHO (2019) UN-Water: World Water Day 2019 Factsheet [online]. Available at www.worldwaterday.org/theme/ (accessed 8 April 2019).

47 Daly, H. (2018) 1.1 Billion People Still Lack Electricity. This Could Be the Solution [online, 20 June]. Available at www.weforum.org/agenda/2018/06/1-billion-people-lack-electricity-solution-mini-grid-iea/ (accessed 29 September 2018).

48 Shah, T. *et al.* (2000) *Pedalling Out of Poverty: Social Impact of a Manual Irrigation Technology in South Asia. Research Report 45*, Colombo, Sri Lanka: International Water Management Institute.

49 bevi.co (2018) Interview with Social Entrepreneur & Driptech Founder Peter Frykman [online, 15 January]. Available at www.bevi.co/blog/interview-driptech-founder-peter-frykman/ (accessed 11 January 2019).

50 proximitydesign.org (n.d.) Farm Tech [online]. Available at https://proximitydesigns.org/service/farm-tech/ (accessed 11 January 2019).

51 cleancookingalliance.org (n.d.) Impact Areas [online]. Available at http://cleancookingalliance.org/impact-areas/ (accessed 11 January 2019).

52 envirofit.org (n.d.) Cookstoves | Clean Energy Initiatives | Social Impact Investing [online]. Available at http://envirofit.org/ (accessed 11 January 2019).

53 WorldBank.org (2015) A New Measure of Rural Access to Transport: Using GIS Data to Inform Decisions and Attainment of the SDGs [online]. Available at www.worldbank.org/en/topic/transport/brief/connections-note-23 (accessed 11 January 2019).

54 IFRTD (n.d.) Agriculture [online]. Available at www.ifrtd.org/index.php/component/content/article/27-ifrtd/main-programme-areas/118-agriculture (accessed 11 January 2019).

55 Refugees, U.N.H.C. for (n.d.) Figures at a Glance [online]. Available at www.unhcr.org/figures-at-a-glance.html (accessed 11 January 2019).

56 Devictor, X. (2016) How Many Years Do Refugees Stay in Exile? World Bank, Dev4peace, 15 September. Available at http://blogs.worldbank.org/dev4peace/how-many-years-do-refugees-stay-exile (accessed 6 March 2018).

57 D-lab (2016) Creative Capacity Building. MIT D-Lab [online, 30 June]. Available at https://d-lab.mit.edu/category/class-research-fieldwork/creative-capacity-building (accessed 11 January 2019).

58 Hessel, D.T. (2010) Eco-justice Ethics. *Intersecting Disciplines, Yale Forum On Religion and Ecology* [online]. Available at http://fore.yale.edu/disciplines/ethics/eco-justice/ (accessed 20 March 2016).

59 Bruinsma, M. and J. Kirkpatrick (eds) (2015) *Design for the Good Society*, Rotterdam: nai010.

60 Emerson, J. (updated 2014) 100+ Years of Design Manifestos – Social Design Notes [online, 5 March]. Available at https://backspace.com/notes/2009/07/design-manifestos.php#more (accessed 11 January 2019).

61 UNIDO/ICSID (1979) *Ahmenabad Declaration on Industrial Design for Development.* NID, India: UNIDO/ICSID Design for Development Conference, 14–24 January 1979 [pdf]. Available at www.designinindia.net/resources/publications/reports/Ahmedabad-declaration-on-industrial-design-6-2009.pdf (accessed 22 March 2016).

62 Krista Sykes, A.K. (ed.) (2010) *Constructing a New Agenda: Architectural Theory 1993–2009,* San Francisco, CA: Chronicle Books, p. 216.

63 Anon (n.d.) Utrecht Manifest [online]. Available at www.utrechtmanifest.nl/ (accessed 11 January 2019).

64 Hopkins, R. (2013) *The Power of Just Doing Stuff. How Local Action Can Change World*, Cambridge: UIT/Greenbooks, p. 86.

65 Fuad-Luke, A. (2009) *Design Activism: Beautiful Strangeness for a Sustainable World*, London, and Sterling, VA: Earthscan, p. 6.

66 Thorpe, A. (2012) *Architecture and Design versus Consumerism. How Design Activism Confronts Growth*, Abingdon, Oxon, and New York: Earthscan, p. 4.

67 occupygoerge.com (n.d.) Money Talks for the People [online]. Available at http://occupygeorge.com(accessed 11 January 2019).

68 Flood, C. and G. Grindon (2014) *Disobedient Objects*, London: V&A.

69 Anon (n.d.) Reading | Spontaneous Interventions [online]. Available at www.spontaneousinterventions.org/reading (accessed 11 January 2019).

70 Kim, K-J. (n.d.) Work 1 [online portfolio]. Available at http://www.kimkyungjae.com/work-i. (accessed 1 April 2016).

71 Rakowitz, M. (n.d.) (P)LOT: Proposition I [online]. Available at www.michaelrakowitz.com/plot-proposition-i/ (accessed 11 January 2018).

72 PARK(ing) | Rebar Art & Design Studio | San Francisco (n.d.) [online]. Available at http://rebargroup.org/parking/ (accessed 1 April 2016).

73 Norton, Q. (2005) Inside IT: Robots with a Nose for Trouble. *The Guardian*, 19 October [online]. Available at www.theguardian.com/technology/2005/oct/20/hacking.internetcrime.

74 Safecast (2011) *History,* 31 January [online]. Available at http://blog.safecast.org/history/ (accessed 2 April 2016).

75 Marsh, S. (2017) UK Citizens Are Taking Air Pollution Monitoring into Their Own Hands. The Guardian, 1 September [online]. Available at www.theguardian.com/environment/2017/sep/01/uk-citizens-are-taking-air-pollution-monitoring-into-their-own-hands (accessed 6 March 2018).

76 Fildes, N (2017) Grassroots Groups Use 'Internet of Things' Data to Tackle Damp and Noise. *Financial Times*, 26 September [online]. Available at www.ft.com/content/2a81afcc-7204-11e7-93ff-99f383b09ff9 (accessed 7 March 2018).

77 Superflux blog (2017) Buggy Air at Design Frontiers. [online, 15 September]. Available at http://superflux.in/index.php/buggy-air-design-frontiers/ (accessed 7 March 2018).

78 Nourbakhsh, I.R., (2013) *Future Robots*, Cambridge, MA: MIT Press, p. xxi.

79 I use the term to encompass design activity that is variously labelled: *speculative design, critical design, design fiction, design for debate, design futures, antidesign, radical design, futurescaping, design as provocation*, etc.

80 Dunne, A. and F. Raby (2013) *Speculative Everything. Design, Fiction and Social Dreaming*, Cambridge, MA: MIT Press, p. 6.

81 Nye, D. (2009) Energy in the Thought and Design of Buckminster Fuller. In H. Chu-Y and R.G. Trujillo (eds), *New Views on Buckminster Fuller*, Stanford, CA: Stanford University Press. pp. 86–98.

82 Philips 90 Years of Design [online]. Available at www.90yearsofdesign.philips.com/ (accessed 7 March 2018).

83 Malpass, M., (2017) *Critical Design in Context*, London: Bloomsbury, p.132.

Key texts and further reading

overconsumption and behaviour change

Chapman, Jonathan (2015) *Emotionally Durable Design*, 2nd edition, Abingdon, Oxon, and New York: Routledge. *Establishes the concept of emotional durability as a positive strategy for product life extension supported by meaningful narratives.*

Jackson, Tim (ed.) (2006) *The Earthscan Reader in Sustainable Consumption*, London, and Sterling, VA: Earthscan. *A selection of extracts from books, articles and institutional publications that examine consumption, the possibility of sustainable consumption and how this might be framed.*

Lockton, D., D. Harrison and N.A. Stanton (2010) *Design with Intent: 101 Patterns for Influencing Behaviour Through Design v.1.0*, Windsor: Equifine. *A card toolkit of 101 possible design approaches for prompting desired behaviours through digital and physical products, services and environments.*

Rose, Chris (2011) *What Makes People Tick*, Leicester; Matador. *Further material available at www.cultdyn.co.uk. An introduction to the 'Value Modes' system which identifies and groups personal attitudes and beliefs that motivate people's actions.*

Schor, Julliet and Douglas Holt (eds.) (2001) *The Consumer Society Reader*, New York: The New Press. *Builds an understanding and critique of the consumer society from a range of viewpoints from experts in the field.*

Thaler, Richard and Cass Sunstein (2009) *Nudge. Improving Decisions about Health, Wealth and Happiness*, London: Penguin Books. *Introduces the notion of choice architecture and how its principles can be used to influence 'better' decisions.*

Weinschenk, Susan (2013) *How to Get People to Do Stuff*, San Francisco,CA: New Riders, Peachpit. *Identifies specific drivers and strategies to effect change.*

HCD, inclusivity and social innovation, and designing better products

Amatullo, M., Boyer, B., Danzico, L. and Shea, A. (eds) (2016) *LEAP Dialogues: Career Pathways in Design for Social Innovation*, Pasadena, CA: Design Matters at Art Centre College of Design. *Presents the what, why and how of designers' practice in social innovation.*

Boeijen, A. van, J. Daalhuizen, J. Zijlatra and R. van der Schoor (2014) *Delft Design Guide*, 2nd edition, Amsterdam: BIS. *Presents the many steps, methods and tools used for better design and better products.*

Design Matters (2010) *Safe Agua*, Pasadena, CA: Arts Center California. *A summary of the HCD process used in the first in a series of design collaborations for water provisioning in campamento settlements in South America with Un Techo.*

Design Matters, (2011) *Safe Agua Peru Method cards*. Arts Center, Pasadena, CA: Arts Center California. *Cards for field research methods and processes [online download] https://4eyos01khlgv2ccw28adjy2x-wpengine.netdna-ssl.com/wp-content/uploads/SAP-METHOD-CARDS.pdf.*

FrogDesign (2012) Collective Action Toolkit. San Francisco, CA: FrogDesign. Downloadable from www.frogdesign.com/work/frog-collective-action-toolkit. *Frog's tried and tested universal framework translated into a stand-alone toolkit designed to lead 'anyone, anywhere' through a dynamic problem-solving process.*

Helen Hamblyn Centre for Design (n.d.) Designing with People | Putting People at the Heart of the Design Process [online]. Available at http://designingwithpeople.rca.ac.uk/. *A web-based resource of ways to design with people, including insights into real people's lives, activities, design methods and ethical practice protocols.*

ideo.org (2015) *The Field Guide to Human-centered Design*, San Francisco, CA: IDEO. Downloadable from www.designkit.org/resources/1. *A step-by-step guide to IDEO's human-centred design approach, including the thinking behind it, the stages and methods, underpinned by examples.*

Index Awards (n.d.) Compass | Design to Improve Life Education [online]. Available at http://designtoimprovelifeeducation.dk/en. *Inspiration from the Index Award back catalogue since 2005, clearly presented case studies and Design to Improve Life Compass HCD methodology.*

Manzini, Ezio (2015) *Design, When Everybody Designs*, Cambridge, MA: MIT Press. *An insightful introduction to design for social innovation and the changing role of designers and citizens in new collaborative scenarios.*

Martin, Bella and Bruce Hannington (2010) *Universal Methods of Design*, Beverly, MA: Rockport Publishers. *125 ways to enhance usability, influence perception, increase appeal and make better design decisions.*

Resnick, Elisabeth (2019) *The Social Design Reader*. London: Bloomsbury Visual Arts. *Although not specific to product design, this book brings together many of the writings by the originators of Socially Responsible Design through to those exploring the necessary paradigm shifts in design focus, approaches and outputs to deal with our current social, economic and environmental challenges.*

design for the BoP

Leadbeater, Charles (2014) *The Frugal Innovator. Creating Change on a Shoestring Budget*, Basingstoke: Palgrave Macmillan. *A broad-minded and inspiring read full of examples and ways to approach 'frugality' in innovation.*

Pilloton, Emily (2009) *Design Revolution. 100 Products That Are Changing People's Lives*, London: Thames & Hudson. *A* compendium of product designs that share an intention of improving lives by the founder of Project H.

Polak, Paul (2008) *Out of Poverty. What Works when Traditional Approaches Fail*, San Francisco, CA: Berrett-Koehler Publishers. *Personal approach to lifting the poorest farmers of the world out of poverty through design and effective business models.*

Smithsonian Institute (2007) *Design for the Other 90%*, New York: Cooper-Hewitt National Design Museum. *A selection of views and inspiring case studies of designs for the BoP (also exhibition).*

sustainable ethics, design activism and speculative design

Bruinsma, Max and John Kirkpatrick (eds) (2015) *Design for the Good Society*, Rotterdam: nai010 publishers. *A series of essays and interviews representing ten years of the Utrecht Manifest biennials that sets out an agenda for the future of design in society.*

Dunne, Anthony and Fiona Raby (2013) *Speculative Everything. Design, Fiction and Social Dreaming*, Cambridge, MA, and London: MIT Press. *A review of design as a tool for imagining different futures ranging from utopian to dystopian as provocations to engage debate and critique.*

Extinction Rebellion (2019) *This Is Not a Drill. An Extinction Rebellion Handbook*. London: Penguin. *A book setting out the facts about why we must act now and demand democratic government action to address our climate emergency together with a how-to activists' toolbox to achieve these aims.*

Flood, Catherine and Gavin Grindon (2014) *Disobedient Objects*, London: V&A Publishing. *Companion to the exhibition by the same name, this book takes a look over time at the use of artefacts as tools for protest and social activism.*

Hopkins, Rob (2013) *The Power of Just Doing Stuff. How Local Action Can Change World*. Cambridge: UIT/Greenbooks. *A book of how-to examples to inspire action to create stronger communities and local economies.*

Malpass, Matt (2017) *Critical Design in Context. History, Theory and Practices*, London: Bloomsbury Academic. *An introduction to critical design and its potential to address societal issues through interrogation and more radical practice.*

Nourbakhsh, Illah Reza (2013) *Robot Futures*, Cambridge, MA, and London: MIT Press. *Robotics scientist Nourbakhsh explores how sharing our world with AI-empowered robotics may play out through progressively more extreme scenarios of daily life.*

Tegmark, Max (2017) *Life 3.0. Being Human in an Age of Artificial Intelligence*, London: Allan Lane. *An exploration of what AI is capable of, and the sorts of relationships we have and might want to have with it.*

Thorpe, Anne (2012) *Architecture and Design. How Design Activism Confronts Growth*, Abingdon, Oxon, and New York: Earthscan Routledge. *A good overview of where and how design can be used to create real wellbeing outside of the consumerist model.*

Thunberg, Greta (2019) *No One Is Too Small to Make a Difference*. London: Penguin. *An inspiring collection of speeches that remind us and leaders of the intergenerational injustice of climate change caused by our actions and of their responsibility to act urgently to reverse the course we are on if planet Earth and all its inhabitants are to have a future.*

CHAPTER 4
Economically led strategies

For better or for worse, all design operates within an economic framework involving some form of transaction. For designers who want to create a more sustainable offer, a basic awareness of the constraints and opportunities that different economic and business models have for enabling sustainability is essential. In response, this chapter first seeks an understanding of what 'the economy' is and the role it could play in supporting sustainability. It then analyses the problematic aspects of our current systems and considers alternative economic models that address these shortcomings. Finally it takes a more pragmatic look at the possibilities that existing and emerging business models have for delivering more sustainable products.

4.1 introduction to economy and sustainability

A simple definition of 'economy' is the system governed by a set of rules which the various 'agents' (businesses, governments, institutions, citizens) agree on for how resources are allocated, used, produced, distributed, managed and controlled.[1] The important point here in relation to sustainability is that economies are the particular set of rules that we as a society construct and choose to play by. In this sense they can be shaped into a tool that reflects society's values and serves the environment's best interests in the way resources are exploited and distributed.

By extension, if we have a society that shares the principles and values of sustainability, then its economy should be an instrument that enables and supports society to meet its needs fairly and equitably within the natural boundaries of the biosphere. This relationship is best illustrated by the three nested circles model in Chapter 1 (fig 1.6c). In this representation of sustainability, the economy is a sub-system of human society that enables people to meet their needs while society is in turn a sub-system of the environment or biosphere that supports all the most

fundamental aspects of life by providing air, water, food, energy and raw materials. The economist Kate Raworth has extended the concept and visualisation of what a sustainable economy fit for the twenty-first century looks like and must achieve. The economic doughnut defines a sustainable economy as one that keeps us within planetary boundaries while providing all of humanity with the essential resources and freedoms in line with the UN Sustainable Development Goals. Figure 4.1 gives a snapshot of what our current global economy doughnut looks like.[2]

our current economic model

Since the beginning of the Industrial Revolution in England at the end of the eighteenth century, capitalism has gradually grown to be the dominant economic system across the world, although this was seriously challenged by planned economies in the twentieth century. While pure capitalism believes in the absolute efficiency of competitive free markets through the laws of supply and demand, what we have in practice across the world are mixed market economies with varying levels of government regulation ranging from light-touch neoliberal approaches through to state-controlled capitalism.

The basis of the capitalist economic model is the *accumulation of financial capital*. To accumulate capital one must make a *profit* either by selling at a higher price than it costs to produce or by earning interest from *invested or borrowed capital*. This means that for the capitalist system to work, financial capital must grow continuously to show a return on investment (ROI). In addition, only goods and services that can be expressed in monetary terms have a value, which excludes any social or environmental value that cannot be monetised. The size of a country's economy is most commonly measured by its gross domestic product (GDP) which is the sum of the monetary value of all goods and services produced in that country over a period of time. The widely accepted rule is that if a country's GDP is increasing, its economy is said to be healthy, and if it is negative, the economy is in recession.

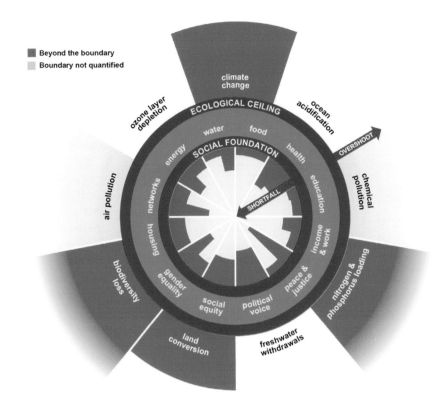

Beyond the boundary
Boundary not quantified

Figure 4.1 Kate Raworth's economic doughnut provides a snapshot of how our current economy is exceeding planetary boundaries and failing to deliver a basic social foundation for all (2017). (source: Kate Raworth (2017) 'A Doughnut for the Anthropocene: Humanity's Compass in the 21st Century'. The Lancet Planetary Health, 1(2), pp. e48–e49)

capitalism, the cynical system that knows the cost of everything and the value of nothing?[3]

However, all is not well in the world. The simple fact that traditional capitalism does not include the environmental or social costs of its activities, which it considers as externalities, has created a deep disconnect between our economic and environmental systems. This is considered by many to be the root cause of the current environmental and social crises we face, leading many business leaders and economists to openly state that "our current economic model is broken".[4] Let us therefore look into these incompatibilities and possible alternatives.

The biggest but by no means the only incompatibility between sustainability and capitalism is its requirement for continuous compound growth and belief that this is both possible and desirable. As Manfred Max Neef, Herman Daly and many other economists have pointed out, the basis of real wealth is the energy and matter provided by the biosphere.[5] The Earth is a steady-state system where matter in the form of atoms is neither created nor destroyed and all its energy is supplied directly or indirectly by the sun. Because it operates within the limits of physical and biological laws it cannot grow indefinitely.

In contrast, the monetary 'wealth' (or debt) of our economies has no growth limits because it is an imaginary construct.[6] The use of fossil fuels, latent sources of intense energy

created over millions of years that were the basis of monetary wealth creation during the Industrial Revolution, exemplifies this relationship. They have given the illusion that continuous growth is possible while in fact we have been depleting our bank of resources, and their use has left us with a huge environmental and social deficit in the form of global warming and pollution.

Closely connected with the need for capital growth is the political pursuit of national GDP growth on the basis that the higher it is, the greater the economic benefits to society through shared prosperity, happiness and wellbeing. On the point of shared prosperity, Thomas Picketty demonstrates in his book *Capital* that without considerable counterbalancing restraints, capitalism is a poor model for wealth distribution. On the contrary, inequality grows as unconstrained capital wealth increases (see Box 1.5). Oxfam's findings confirm this. They found that the richest 26 billionaires owned as much as the poorest half the world in 2018 and this number has been decreasing year-on-year since 2010, while the richest 1% own more than 50% of the world's wealth[7] (fig 4.2). In their book *The Spirit Level,* Richard Wilkinson and Kate Pickett's research also shows that the greater the inequality across a country or region, the greater the social problems that arise, and the greater the financial cost to society and loss of wellbeing (fig 4.3).

The second assumption, namely that continuously rising GDP correlates to greater happiness and wellbeing, is only true up

Billionaires who own the same wealth as half the world

And what transport they would fit on (source: Oxfam 2016/2018)

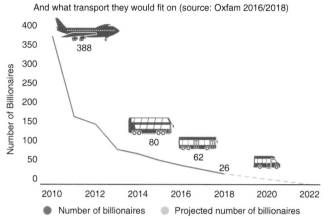

Figure 4.2

Index of health and social problems vs. Income inequality

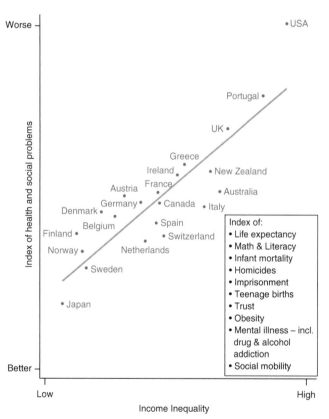

Figure 4.3 A country's health and social problems worsen with income inequality. (source: Wilkinson and Pickett (2009) 'The Spirit Level')

to a point. Research has shown that there is a threshold of per capita income in the region of $15 to 20k (2002 PPP) beyond which there are no significant gains in perceived happiness or wellbeing. This phenomenon is known as the Easterlin Paradox[8]

(fig 4.4). It seems that once personal and economic security is attained and basic needs are met, the pursuit of happiness is directed towards having free choice and a sense of control over one's life.[9]

The lack of connection between GDP and social and environmental wellbeing has been troubling ecological economists and sustainability development experts for some time.[10] This has led to the introduction of a number of alternative indicators, including the Human Development Indicator (HDI), the Index of Sustainable Economic Welfare (ISEW), the Genuine Progress Indicator (GPI) and various happiness indexes, including Bhuttan's Gross National Happiness index that forms the basis of their government policy. Of these, the GPI comes closest to measuring a 'sustainable' economy by balancing financial gains or losses against environmental and social ones and is beginning to be used internally in a number of countries.

So why, if we know that the natural environment cannot increase supply exponentially, that equality of income is better for society and that beyond a certain point more money does not make us any happier, do we seem locked into this self-destructive course? Besides the fundamental problem of unaccounted externalities, there are two other important factors creating this lock-in. The first is short-termism. Political and financial decisions are taken and judged on a very short timeframe of months stretching to at most a few years. This fails to acknowledge or reward the longer term cycles and vision needed for effective environmental and social stewardship.

The third is the erosion of national democratic control to powerful individuals and trans-national corporations (TNCs). This comes about because corporations are accountable to shareholders for returning maximum profits and not to the citizens of the countries in which they operate.[11] This loss of democratic control is not surprising, as 69 of the top 100 economic entities globally by revenue are corporations and only 31 are governments. These powerful businesses also invest heavily in protecting their interests through government lobbying.[12] Among the ten largest companies in the world, five are petrochemical companies and four are product manufacturers: Wal-Mart, Toyota, Volkswagen and Apple[13] (see Box 1.4 and fig 4.5). The UN Human Rights Council's agreement in 2017 to negotiate a binding treaty to regulate the activity of TNCs and other business enterprises (OBEs) is a big step forward in acknowledging their human rights impacts.[14]

alternative economic models

decoupling and natural capitalism

If the current economic and political system is broken in terms of supporting the environment and society, what other options are

GDP per Capita and Life Satisfaction: On Average, Life Satisfaction Higher in Richer Nations, Up to a Point

On a ladder of life from 0 to 10, on which step do you stand at the present time?
Percent saying 7, 8, 9 or 10

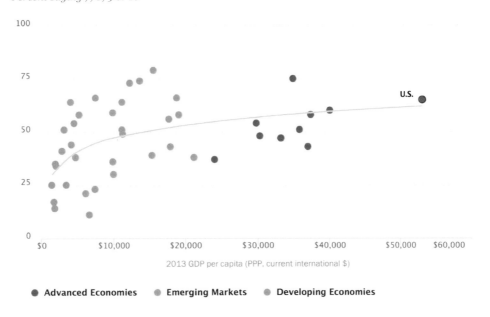

2013 GDP per capita (PPP, current international $)

● Advanced Economies   ● Emerging Markets   ● Developing Economies

Source: Data for GDP per capita (PPP) from IMF World Economic Outlook Database, April 2014.
Note: Data not available for the Palestinian territories.

PEW RESEARCH CENTER

Figure 4.4

there? Here we look very briefly at some alternative models and measures that are currently advocated to resolve the impasse we are in where a healthy environment is pitted against a healthy economy.

Beginning at the least disruptive end, we have the concept of eco-economic *decoupling*. Essentially, *decoupling* means breaking the direct connection between economic growth and environmental damage. Thus, as GDP goes up, environmental damage stands still or reduces. The principal tool for eco-economic *decoupling* is a shift to a low-carbon economy based on renewable energy, carbon-capture and eco-efficiency measures. Added value of the sort that design can provide is also an example of decoupling where a well-designed and desirable product generates greater profit for the same level of functionality and less environmental damage.

But is decoupling achievable? It would seem like having our cake and eating it too. The answer is both yes and no. It appears that we may be moving towards *relative* decoupling. The positive signs are that 2014 to 2016 were the first years recorded where global GDP rose while *energy*-related CO_2 emissions stood still.[15] However, these were up again by 1.4% in 2017 and by 1.8 in 2018[16] (fig 4.6). This relative decoupling

or de-intensification of our activities has not been thanks to the free markets but rather to concerted international commitments to nationally binding reductions in CO_2 levels through the Kyoto Protocol and the most recent Paris Agreement effective from 2020. With global emissions still rising, it is very hard to see how we will meet the 45% reduction in CO_2 emissions by 2030 and *net-zero* CO_2 by 2050 that the IPCC states is necessary to avert a highly damaging 1.5°C rise.[17]

While these relative reductions in some areas are encouraging, achieving sustainability requires *absolute decoupling*.[18] This is when our impacts reduce to within planetary limits. As we saw in environmental strategies (Chapter 2.1), to reach a sustainable level of global wealth distribution for 9.7 billion, our efficiency and low-carbon gains would need to meet reduction factors of at least 7.7 based on the IPAT equation. But if GDP is to grow year-on-year, efficiencies would have to also increase year-on-year, making *absolute decoupling* a physical impossibility. So while *relative decoupling* through the continued investment in a low- and even net-zero carbon economy is essential, eco-efficiency measures alone will never be enough for *absolute decoupling*.[19] This means that we still need a rethink of our economic and business models.

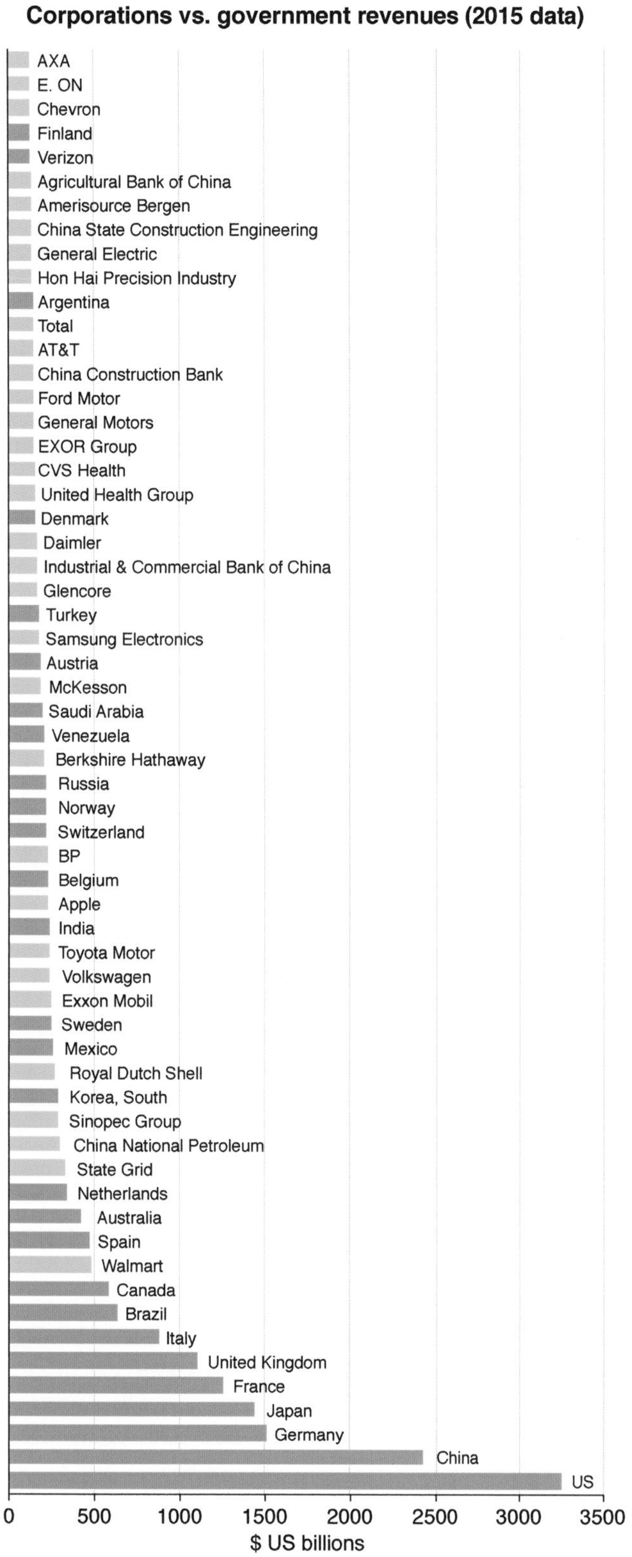

Corporations vs. government revenues (2015 data)

AXA
E. ON
Chevron
Finland
Verizon
Agricultural Bank of China
Amerisource Bergen
China State Construction Engineering
General Electric
Hon Hai Precision Industry
Argentina
Total
AT&T
China Construction Bank
Ford Motor
General Motors
EXOR Group
CVS Health
United Health Group
Denmark
Daimler
Industrial & Commercial Bank of China
Glencore
Turkey
Samsung Electronics
Austria
McKesson
Saudi Arabia
Venezuela
Berkshire Hathaway
Russia
Norway
Switzerland
BP
Belgium
Apple
India
Toyota Motor
Volkswagen
Exxon Mobil
Sweden
Mexico
Royal Dutch Shell
Korea, South
Sinopec Group
China National Petroleum
State Grid
Netherlands
Australia
Spain
Walmart
Canada
Brazil
Italy
United Kingdom
France
Japan
Germany
China
US

0   500   1000   1500   2000   2500   3000   3500
$ US billions

Figure 4.5 When 69 of the top 100 economic entities in the world are Transnational Corporations (TNCs) free to take their business elsewhere, how can vulnerable and less vulnerable countries protect their citizens' interests? (source: Global Justice Now 2016)

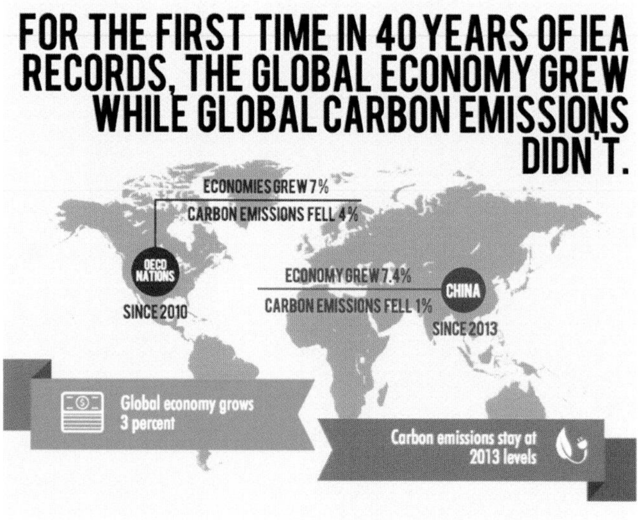

FOR THE FIRST TIME IN 40 YEARS OF IEA RECORDS, THE GLOBAL ECONOMY GREW WHILE GLOBAL CARBON EMISSIONS DIDN'T.

ECONOMIES GREW 7%
CARBON EMISSIONS FELL 4%
OECD NATIONS
SINCE 2010

ECONOMY GREW 7.4%
CARBON EMISSIONS FELL 1%
CHINA
SINCE 2013

Global economy grows 3 percent

Carbon emissions stay at 2013 levels

Figure 4.6 Relative decoupling in action: global energy-related CO_2 emissions remained static between 2014 and 2016 while GDP rose. This trend is still very precarious, with carbon emissions on the rise again from 2017. (source: Nexus Media/IEA 2017. Available at www.huffingtonpost.com/climate-nexus/conscious-decoupling-divorcing-economy-and-emissions_b_6866556.html; data source: IEA International Energy Agency 2015 report)

In *Natural Capitalism* (1999), Paul Hawken and Amory and Hunter Lovins proposed an alternative capitalism 'as if living systems mattered'. Building on Hawken's highly influential work *The Ecology of Commerce* (1993) and that of other ecological economists like Robert Costanza,[20] they address the problem that currently, all our shared life-supporting eco-systems, known as natural capital, have no financial value[21] (fig 4.7).

> *Capitalism, as practiced is a financially profitable, non-sustainable aberration in human development. What might be called 'industrial capitalism' does not fully conform to its own accounting principles. It liquidates its capital and calls it income. It neglects to assign any value to the largest stock of capital it employs – the natural resources and living systems, as well as the social and cultural systems that are the basis of human capital.[22]*

In 1997 when they wrote this book, the Earth's ecosystem services were valued at over three times the Global GDP. By 2011 their value had dropped by 20% while GDP rose, representing only 1.7 times global GDP.[23] These findings indicate the urgency of accounting for natural capital. By attaching a financial value to ecosystem services, any damage or improvement to them is added to a company's balance sheet and thereby modifies business behaviour. This new form of accountability is closely aligned with eco-effectiveness and regenerative design, helping to keep economic activity within the bounds of the natural capital

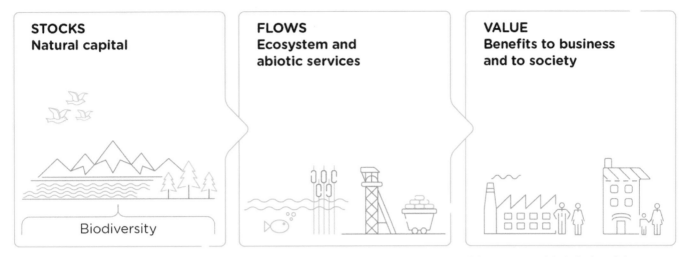

STOCKS
Natural capital

Biodiversity

FLOWS
Ecosystem and
abiotic services

VALUE
Benefits to business
and to society

Figure 4.7 Business and society are acutely dependent on maintaining and replenishing natural capital but it is not accounted for in business balance sheets. (graphic courtesy Natural Capital Coalition 2016.–)

available, while incentivising investment in restoring ecosystems and preserving resources.

Carbon pricing may be considered one of the first steps in global natural capital accounting. By limiting or taxing the production of GHGs, we are placing a value on the ecosystem service our atmosphere provides in regulating the Earth's temperature. Figure 4.8 illustrates natural capitalism in action through the conceptual redesign of a sardine fishing boat. The boat includes a facility for cultivating and releasing as many kilos of phytoplankton as kilos of sardines caught, transforming fishermen into custodians of the sea, their main source of livelihood.

Since the publication of *Natural Capitalism* in 1999, businesses, governments and institutions have moved forward to make natural capital accounting a reality by establishing a framework and valuation based on The Economics of Ecosystems and Biodiversity (TEEB/UNEP) studies. In 2016 the Natural Capital Coalition released the Natural Capital Protocol that finally gives businesses a methodology and tools to integrate natural capital accounting into their strategy and operations.[24]

limits to growth: transitioning to steady-state or de-growth economies

Let us now review how closely a decoupled economy and natural capitalism come to delivering a sustainable economy, one that enables society to meet its needs fairly and equitably within planetary boundaries. The first, the decoupled 'low-carbon economy', accepts the capitalist model with its necessary year-on-year growth and hopes that through energy and material de-intensification and new technology we can somehow do sufficiently less harm. However, taken to their natural conclusion,

Figure 4.8 Natural capitalism in action: Inês Ferreira's Post-fishing boat is designed to make fishermen custodians of the sea by growing and releasing phytoplankton to replenish the fish stock they catch. (courtesy Inês Ferriera Marques /photo Tom Manion)

the laws of physics, chemistry and biology state that the infinite de-intensification necessary is physically impossible. So this can only help up to a point. The second, natural capitalism, has much more scope for rebalancing the relationship between human activity and the ecosystem by including the externalities in the balance sheet, but it does not go so far as to challenge the growth model directly, only the basis of its accountancy. However, there are critics of natural capitalism who consider that attaching a monetary value to the natural world and the commons debases their intrinsic value.

In addition, both of these alternatives deal primarily with environmental sustainability. Where does that leave the social dimension of the economy? From this perspective, the biggest shortcoming of both is that neither addresses the failure of the current model to serve society (fig 4.9).

> By itself, the market cannot guarantee integral human development and social inclusion (109) [...] the present world system is unsustainable [...] for we have stopped thinking about the goals of human activity (61).
>
> Pope Francis, *Encyclical letter Laudato Si*, 2015

The inclusion of the social dimension of sustainability leads to a more radical transformation of our economic model. Abandoning the growth 'at-all-costs' model and reducing our consumption and production to within planetary limits can only be achieved through a fundamental transformation of our social values and priorities where the end game is no longer material or monetary acquisition but quality of life.[25] In short, what is needed is a new socio-economic relationship with the environment that will offer a better quality of life for all.

The *steady-state economy* proposed by Herman Daly and other ecological economists calls for an overall freeze on growth and a fairer distribution of wealth. In this scenario, industrialised countries currently living well beyond their ecological means would undergo a process of *de-growth* while regions that are underconsuming could grow to meet their needs.[26] The proponents of *de-growth*[27] envisage a complete political and social reorientation where the economy serves the biosphere and society.

The overarching move is towards a *social capitalism* based on a deep culture of participation and cooperation. As accumulating wealth and using resources is no longer the objective, people would spend less time in paid work and have more time to build supportive and culturally rich lives and communities within the boundaries of sufficiency.[28] With the advent of AI and robotics and the prospect of many jobs losses from it, the notion of a universal basic income is gaining traction and being piloted in several countries.[29] The thinking is that it would free us up for greater self-development through social and environmentally oriented activities. Gar Alperovitz suggests, *"We need to design a system in which the exchange of commodities facilitates development of community, not its destruction".*[30]

the relevance of economics and business models to designers

From decoupling, to natural capitalism, zero growth and de-growth, there is no doubt that getting the planet back on a sustainable footing calls for some radical changes to how we go about living,

Figure 4.9 Poverty and wealth side-by-side: urban homelessness, food banks, tent cities, slums or campamentos. Is our economy working for society? (photo credits epicurean and Fred Cardoso)

and the businesses and institutions that will support this. But why should economics or business models matter to designers?

First, because designers wishing to make a more sustainable contribution through their work must understand the system they are working in and the constraints and opportunities this imposes upon their design outcomes. It is essential to appreciate that companies will develop and sell products that align with their values, but only within the limitations of the business model and regulations within which they operate. As we will see, this can and does create conflicting demands for designers and the company itself.

Second, designers have a key role to play in making new and existing more sustainable business models successful. Their design training and creative thinking often lead to unexpected and innovative solutions in response to seemingly conflicting stakeholder needs. More specifically, product designers can provide a more tangible and human-centred, desirable and persuasive face to the transition to more sustainable lifestyles.

Third, research has found that for millennials, working in organisations or communities where they can grow personally, share values and can see the benefit of their contribution is more important than earning the top salary.[31] Designers are very much included in this desire to find meaningful work[32] and will have to become proactive in finding the types of companies whose values align with theirs or embarking on their own enterprise with other like-minded people.

4.2 the rise of more responsible business

Either we see business as a restorative undertaking, or we, businesspeople, will march the entire race to the undertaker. Business is the only mechanism on the planet today powerful enough to produce the changes necessary to reverse global environmental and social degradation.[33]

Paul Hawken, 1992

While we wait to see if more radical or transition economies take hold, for most designers who genuinely want to contribute to a more sustainable planet through their work, the choices before them may seem limited. In this subsection we will ask ourselves: Are there business models and structures that inherently have more scope for sustainability than others? What behaviours and practices do more sustainable companies have in common, and how do designers fit in and contribute to its realisation?

businesses taking the lead

Given capitalism's track record to date, would it be unfair to ask if sustainable business is an oxymoron? Although not the perfect marriage, some highly commercial and successful companies are proving that they do not have to be mutually exclusive. In fact, many business leaders believe that *only* business can deliver sustainability on a large enough scale, albeit through new partnerships with governments, not-for-profits and all their stakeholders.[34]

As we have already observed, most companies do not intentionally set out to destroy the planet or make people's lives a misery. Rather, these come about as the unintended consequences of doing business where the object of the game is maximising short-term profit while the costs of their impacts, or 'externalities', are not included on the balance sheet. However, pressure is mounting for companies to take responsibility for their wider impacts not only from consumers, citizens, NGOs and governments but also from leaders within the business community itself (see fig 1.7). This is evidenced through the voluntary creation of influential organisations over the past 40 years. These include the World Economic Forum (WEF) (1971); Ceres (1989); the World Business Council for Sustainable Development (WBCSD) (1995); the UN Global Compact (1999); Sustainable Brands (2006); and B-Lab (2006).

The seeds for change in mainstream business practice were planted in the late 1990s by John Elkington with the introduction of the *triple bottom line* (TBL).[35] Also referred to as the 3Ps, *people, planet and profit*, it involves businesses measuring their performance not only in economic terms but also socially and environmentally, thereby seeking win-win-win outcomes. By the turn of the millennium, TBL had grown into *corporate social responsibility* (CSR). Although CSR reporting has become firmly established as a norm for publicly facing businesses, it has quite rightly been subject to accusations of greenwashing. It has taken robust externally verifiable reporting standards such as the Global Reporting Initiative (GRI) or B Corps certification to achieve parity and transparency in how sustainability claims are measured and reported for genuinely engaged companies not to be tarred with the greenwashing brush.[36] Blockchain is also emerging as a promising tool for validating companies' supply chain claims and restoring consumer trust.

As we see from these changes to practice and initiatives, many business pioneers are several steps ahead of governments in demanding regulation and support for more responsible corporate behaviour. Since the 2015 COP21 climate change talks in Paris, it is enlightened leaders of the business community and NGOs who are pressing their electorally constrained or risk-adverse governments to stand by their commitments to binding CO_2 reductions. At the same time, the onus for delivering the UN 2015-2030 SDG has shifted from governments to business-government-NGO collaborations pushing to the fore design solutions that help meet environmental and social goals.

sustainability: a strong business case

While the level of understanding and engagement in sustainable practices varies hugely between companies today, the more enlightened business leaders appreciate that *the best interest and long-term viability of their business is inseparable from the health and wellbeing of their workers, their community, their supply chain and the state of the natural capital upon which they depend.* Irrespective of whether companies are motivated by conviction, public image, compliance, cost savings or the very tangible business opportunities of the growing low-carbon economy, there are very real internal and external motivators and drivers for integrating sustainable behaviours that even the most hard-headed business people ignore at their peril. Table 4.1 summarises the most important.

Surveys of businesses confirm that while sustainability is rising on corporate agendas, it is still far from being universally embedded. The GlobeScan/BSR *State of Sustainable Business survey* (2017/ninth year) shows that sustainability continues to rise in CEOs' top-five agenda priorities from 37% (2015) to 52% (2017). This is being driven by customer and investor expectations, followed by employee expectations and government regulation. More significantly for designers, results also indicate that sustainability is now viewed as either a significant (13%) or a partial (56%)

Table 4.1 The business case for integrating sustainable practices

internal motivators

- increasing employee motivation, recruitment and retention
- satisfying a collective sense of ethical responsibility by 'doing the right thing'
- seeing sustainability as the inspiration and driver for innovation
- reducing costs and improving margins through efficiency savings
- future proofing the business by reducing risks and increasing resilience

external drivers

- meeting consumer and investor expectations
- complying with standards and regulations throughout the supply chain
- standing up to public scrutiny through open and transparent disclosure practices
- building and maintaining brand trust by exceeding regulations and signing up to voluntary codes of practice
- creating competitive advantage and sector leadership through environmentally and ethically led innovation and initiatives.

enabler of growth and innovation[37] (fig 4.10). However, on reviewing survey results from 2009 through to 2016, the MIT Sloan/BCG Report, *Corporate Sustainability at a Crossroads*, concludes less optimistically that only a small proportion of companies are really embracing sustainability as a key business strategy. Just as with consumers, companies have a big value–action gap:

> One reason for this state of affairs is that identifying profitable sustainability opportunities typically involves looking at one's business in a new way and then erecting new organizational structures, developing new expertise and processes, and shifting mindsets. [...] Few companies are willing to make this massive shift.[38]

In *The Zeronauts*, John Elkington describes the extremes in levels of engagement in the business community as 'weak sustainability' and 'strong sustainability'.[39] At the 'weak sustainability' end of the spectrum we have companies which continue largely business-as-usual, using CSR reporting as a public relations exercise to demonstrate how they are 'giving back'. In the worst cases this amounts to 'greenwashing' or even 'bluewashing', where UN institutions are involved.

At the other end of the spectrum we have 'strong sustainability' inspired by early pioneering companies such as Interface, Patagonia, Herman Miller, Xerox, Seventh Generation, Ecover and The Body Shop to name a few, led by inspirational leaders like Ray Anderson, Yvon Chouinard, Anita Rodick and Gunter Pauli. Their ranks are growing year-on-year to include newer leaders like Unilever, IKEA, M&S, Dell, BMW, Tesla, Natura, and many other smaller companies where much of the real innovation starts. All these businesses and their leaders have embedded sustainable values and goals and embraced deep systemic change in their organisations while recognising that they are on a journey *towards* sustainability.

from less harm and zero impact to net positive and restorative businesses

Companies that began the journey in the 1990s with eco-efficiency measures have now moved far beyond this to more ambitious goals. These include targets for net-zero waste, carbon, fossil fuel, toxics, and a strong sense of social and ethical responsibility towards all their stakeholders. These are evidenced through the engagement of influential companies in cross-industry initiatives, including: RE[newable]100, Sustainable Apparel Coalition (SAC), Sustainable Packaging Coalition (SPC), Sustainability and Health Initiatives for Net Positive Businesses (SHINE), Carbon Disclosure Project (CDP), Natural Capital Coalition and the Net Positive Project.[40]

Influence on Sustainability Agenda at Company, 2017
(Percentage of all respondents identifying groups as "influential")

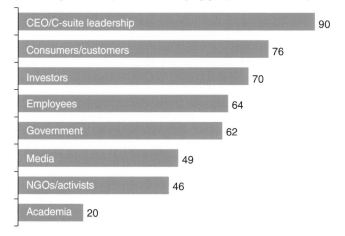

CEO/C-suite leadership	90
Consumers/customers	76
Investors	70
Employees	64
Government	62
Media	49
NGOs/activists	46
Academia	20

CEO Corporate Agenda Priorities, 2017
(Percentage of company-level respondents)

☐ Highest priority ☐ Top-three priority ☐ Top-five priority

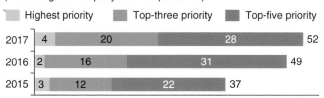

2017	4	20	28	52
2016	2	16	31	49
2015	3	12	22	37

How Sustainability Is Viewed by Those Outside the Company, 2017 (Percentage of all respondents)

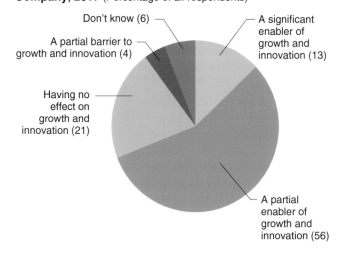

- Don't know (6)
- A partial barrier to growth and innovation (4)
- Having no effect on growth and innovation (21)
- A significant enabler of growth and innovation (13)
- A partial enabler of growth and innovation (56)

Figure 4.10 Key results for designers from the GlobeScan-BSR State of Sustainable Business 2017 survey.

Choosing from a number of remarkable sustainability pioneers, figure 4.11 illustrates the inspiring leadership and achievements of four quite unique companies. They are Patagonia, Seventh Generation, Fairphone and Tesla. Despite

being in very different sectors, they share a set of common characteristics:

- sustainability is embedded as a mindset and integral to how they approach their whole business at all levels and across all activities
- shared sustainable goals drive continuous innovation and excellence in their product offer and forward-thinking business models
- a clear vision that encompasses sustainability, demonstrated through actions
- inspiring leadership and wider engagement in delivering change
- a desire to leave a positive legacy

Even the most cynical will accept that a tangible shift is permeating business thinking, and that sustainable products and innovation are an integral part of the most forward-thinking companies committed to creating value.

the sustainable potential of different business entities

Since the millennium, the notion of businesses as a force for good has been growing steadily. Mission-driven companies, businesspeople and entrepreneurs aren't waiting for other companies or governments to act. They are developing new company types, business models, cross-sector collaborations and setting their own voluntary standards with like-minded and complementary organisations. However, a lesser known but very important fact is that a company or organisation's legal status will constrain or facilitate how much social or environmental 'good' they can achieve. We will therefore briefly look at how the different forms of business entities – corporations, limited liability companies, cooperatives, social enterprises and benefit corporations – lend themselves to achieving sustainable goals and producing sustainable products.

private and publicly owned for-profit companies
By far the largest and most dominant business type across the world is the private or publicly owned *for-profit* company or corporation. This group covers the spectrum from huge transnational company networks that singly have larger economies than many countries [41] through to small and medium enterprises (SMEs) and start-ups that are often privately and locally owned by families (see fig 4.4). As this group generates and delivers the majority of industrial production, most product designers will find themselves working in, or for, this type of company. And because this business type also encompasses sustainability's most inspiring and celebrated heroes through to its worst offenders, it is an important one to understand.

DON'T BUY THIS JACKET

Patagonia

1973: family-owned owned FP; 2012 Benefit Corporation; 2014: B Corps certified

mission & about: one of the most respected outdoor apparel companies in the world committed to *'creating the best product'* and *'causing the least harm'*

sustainable design leadership and firsts:
- 1986: donates 1% of profits to grassroots environmental NFPs and founds 1% for the Planet (2002)
- 1990: moves to 100% organic cotton
- 1993: develops first fleece from recycled post-consumer waste
- 2005: Worn-Wear take-back garment resale or recycling
- 2008: begins co-development of plant-based alternative to wetsuit neoprene, leading to Yulex 2016
- 2013: sets up $20 Million & Change Fund, Tin Shed Ventures

Seventh Generation

1989-2016 publicly owned FP producing cleaning and personal care products; 2016 bought by global transnational Unilever
2007 B Corporation founding member and B Corps Certified

about & mission:

'Inspire a consumer revolution that nurtures the health of the next seven generations'

sustainable design leadership and firsts:
- first chlorine-free baby and feminine care products in North America
- first company to disclose ingredients on pack (2008)
- successful advocacy for consumer protection standards and transparency: phosphate-free dishwasher cleaners; zero VOCs; ingredient disclosure
- first North American homecare company committed to Roundtable on Sustainable Palm Oil
- design recyclable packaging from recycled materials

Fairphone

2013-: FP Social enterprise, producing smartphones;
2015: B Corps Certified

mission & about:

'Together we can change the way products are made'
Started as an awareness campaign by Bas van Abel about conflict minerals in electronics, and still consider themselves more a movement than a company

sustainable design leadership and firsts:
- 2015: launched the Fairphone 2, the world's first ethical, modular repairable, upgradable and recyclable - designed-to-last phone
- world's most ethical and transparent smartphone making a positive impact across mining, design, manufacturing and lifecycle
- first smartphone to be awarded an iFixit 10/10 repairability score

Tesla Inc.

2003-: FP publicly listed company producing electric vehicles producing renewable energy generation and storage products

mission & about:

Accelerate the world's transition to sustainable energy. Led by the ambitious visionary leader, Elon Musk

sustainable design leadership and firsts:
- enabling a joined-up zero emission lifestyle and demonstrating that it need not be a compromise
- 2008-2012: Roadster, first highway-legal serial production lithium ion battery powered car to travel over 200 miles (320 km) per charge
- 2017: builds Giga Factory1, the highest volume battery plant in the world, to supply their products and bring down the cost of EV

Figure 4.11 Some notable sustainability pioneering mainstream companies and their commitment to business with a better purpose. (photos courtesy Patagonia, Seventh Generation, Fairphone and Tesla Inc.)

The essential goal and even responsibility of a for-profit company is exactly as its name spells out, namely to deliver a financial profit or return on investment (ROI) for its investors and owners. Beyond complying with regulations, there is nothing that stipulates how companies should do this, so it is up to each one whether they embrace sustainable and ethical goals or not, provided they maximise profits. Otherwise, investors who have no other personal stake or responsibility in the success of a company are free to take the board to task and their money elsewhere.

Yet, while the capitalist profit motive is often blamed for unsustainability, companies with a strong commitment to 'doing good' will not be in a position to 'do good' unless they have a healthy profit margin. Without this they cannot invest in the new technologies, R&D, design, business and employment practices that will allow them to create social and environmental value. *Therefore running a profitable and healthy business is a necessary condition for sustainability*. And well-designed, relevant and desirable products supported by good service are the basis of profitable companies.

What is perhaps less well known is that 80 to 90% of all for-profit firms worldwide are family owned or controlled. Some of these are among the biggest and most successful in the world. They include the following physical product-focused companies (in order of size): Walmart, Volkswagen, Ford, BMW, Dell, LG, Peugeot, Tata Motors, LVMH, IKEA, Mars, Nike, L'Oréal, Porsche, Heineken, Suntory, Bombardier, Porsche, Liebherr, Canadian Tire, Decathlon, Swatch, Wipro, Kohler, Miele, JCDecaux and Lego. The 500 largest family-controlled businesses are equal to the third largest economy in the world after the USA and China. Of these, 18% are in retail, 17% industrial product and 15% consumer products, all sectors relevant to product designers.[42] Although privately controlled companies are not necessarily more sustainable, many private owners are clear that not having to show quarterly results to shareholders gives them much more freedom to prioritise their values and longer term financially and sustainably beneficial strategies.

cooperatively owned companies
As business ethics have increasingly come under the spotlight in recent years, the cooperative business model has regained favour for its equitable and socially sustainable qualities. This includes praise from the UN for its "contribution to socio-economic development, particularly their impact on poverty reduction, employment generation and social integration".[43] Cooperatives or mutuals are for-profit companies owned and run democratically for the benefit of their members with a shared common purpose set out in their governing documents. Members can be exclusively employees, producers, customers, other cooperatives, or a mix of these. The cooperative movement began in Germany in the mid

nineteenth century as an alternative to ownership by capitalist investors and has since spread around the globe. Today, the sum of all cooperatives' turnover worldwide is over 2.4 trillion, making them bigger than Brazil, the seventh largest economy.[44]

Through their democratic structures and shared values of self-help, equality and solidarity, cooperatives are inherently more socially sustainable and economically equitable than private or shareholder-run companies. But this does *not necessarily make them more environmentally sustainable*, although many do also prioritise environmental values. Their ethical strength is also their business strength through the effect of shared ownership. Having a stake in the business increases engagement from their members, be they employees, customers or producers, as they have a greater appreciation of how their actions align with the success of the business and their personal benefit.

In the world of product design, cooperatives range from huge industrial conglomerates such as the Mondragon group of cooperatives, the seventh largest corporation in Spain that produces capital goods and production machinery, through to micro-community-based initiatives employing disadvantaged groups or providing market outlets for small producers and crafts people. In emerging economies, cooperatives can be a lifeline for designer-makers by providing them with a means of getting their products to market and are often connected with Fair Trade.

In developing and emerging economies, agricultural cooperatives play a very important role in helping small farmers bring their products to market through economies of scale and achieving a fair price. One of the most famous is the Gujarat Co-operative Milk Marketing Federation that trades under the Amul brand. Started up in India in 1946, it rapidly gained popularity by making it possible for small rural farmers with as little as a single cow to have a fair and reliable income. Closely in tune with Gandhi's Khadi and Village Industries movement, its success made it the main model for milk production across India (fig 4.12).

In industrial economies, product design is most closely connected to cooperatives in the retail sector because many own-brand ranges are designed in house. Some of the best-known retail groups include ReWE/Germany; LeClerc & Systeme U/France; Migros/Switzerland; SOF/Finland; Fairprice/Singapore; JCCU/Japan; REI/USA; MEC/Canada, and the John Lewis Partnership/UK.[45] As many of these originate their own product ranges their design and supply chains are strongly influenced by the ethos of the cooperative movement.

The story behind John Lewis beautifully illustrates this ethos and the innovative approach of the cooperative movement. As early as 1914 John Spedan Lewis, son of the founder, connected with

Figure 4.12 Amul, a pioneering brand of the cooperative movement in India, makes it possible for villagers with as little as a single cow to earn some income. (photo credits Abir Roy Barman, Silar)

the notions of *equity* and *sufficiency*, both important principles of sustainable ethics, when he realised that the profit he and his family extracted from the business equalled *all the employees' wages put together*. Gradually, he transformed the business from a private company into an employee-owned business by 1957. Today, John Lewis is the largest department store group in the UK and each member of staff is a 'partner' in the business and shares in the profits. This results in strong employee engagement that is felt by the customer through a very high level of service and product quality, which in turn results in strong customer loyalty and trust.

In North America, REI in the USA with 6 million members and MEC in Canada with 4 million are two retail cooperatives that stand out for their commitment to protecting the environment and leading in sustainable design practices. Both cater to the outdoor-active and design between 30 and 40% of their own product ranges in-house. Their mission is to design and sell *the best-quality products* that *do least harm* that encourage and make it possible for people to enjoy and explore the outdoors, both as a means to healthier lifestyles but also for the understanding of and support for environmental conservation that this creates.

Their design teams tackle this by measuring all their impacts as a business to minimise their footprint, eliminate toxicity and create maximum benefit. In the design and specification of their products, the use of LCAs and the Higgs Index design tools are embedded in their process,[46] and as members of the Fair Labor Organisation (FLA) and the Sustainable Apparel Coalition (SAC) they continually

work with their suppliers to develop better materials, processes and fair labour conditions. Product longevity by design is another cornerstone of REI and MEC's product sustainability, but in this, MEC goes one step further by offering a return-and-repair service for *any* products that members feel should still be usable, over and above any warranty period (fig 4.13).

John Lewis, REI, MEC and Amul are only a few examples which demonstrate the scope within the cooperative model to set higher standards across their industries and live by their ethos of *"think[ing] beyond profit"*.[47] The hope for the future is that cooperativism will find strong leadership and support to unleash its potential for more equitable business models across digital platforms through the power of the Internet.

Figure 4.13 MEC's classic duffle bag illustrates their mission to 'produce the best-quality products that do least harm'. As one of their most popular bags, they replaced the main fabric with a nylon fabric made from 100% discarded fishing nets chemically recycled into virgin nylon. (courtesy MEC)

social enterprises

The idea that businesses should and can be a force for good, existing for more than just maximising financial profits for investors and owners, has grown considerably both in response to public pressure but also from a new generation of entrepreneurs and investors. At the same time, many charities and not-for-profits are finding that they need new income streams and new ways to deliver and accelerate change effectively.

From this new sense of social purpose in business, the concept and working model of the social enterprise or 'mission-led business' is rapidly evolving. Organisations like Ashoka, Schwab, and Skoll Foundations have been instrumental in helping to support and promote the expanding field of social entrepreneurship. But what is a social enterprise? In essence, it is a business whose *main purpose* is to deliver stated social or environmental benefits *directly* through the products and services it trades and the profits these generate in a measurable and transparent way.[48]

In itself, the term 'social enterprise' is not defined by a single legal entity or type of company and the options available vary from country to country around the world. Social Enterprises can take the form of traditional organisations like not-for-profit charities (NFP), for-profit (FP) companies, cooperative societies, community benefit companies, or hybrids of these. More recently, there has been a flurry of new legal business entities that bridge the gap between not-for-profit and for-profit companies that better fit the purpose of a social enterprise through their articles of association. These include Community Interest Companies or CICs (UK 2005), Low Profit Limited Liability Companies or L3C (2008 USA), Community Contribution Companies or 3C (2013 Canada) and Benefit Corporations (USA 2010; Italy 2015; Puerto Rico 2015). In addition, another 15 countries across Europe have legal forms of social enterprises and social cooperatives.[49] Among these, the benefit corporation is of particular interest to product designers.

benefit corporations

It is not uncommon for traditional for-profit companies that are 'socially driven', or have a mission to 'do good through business', to describe themselves as 'social enterprises'. Although many of these companies do create positive social and environmental benefit through their CSR practices, that may include funding charitable projects and foundations, paying fair wages, being environmentally responsible and engaging employees in community activities; they are not strictly social enterprises, as their main legal responsibility remains to maximise profit for their owners and investors.[50]

The creation of the new legal entity, the benefit corporation, however, finally removes the main obstacles preventing mission-driven for-profit companies from following through with their aspirations by having their broader social and environmental objectives enshrined in the company articles. Benefit corporations are in fact for-profit companies, privately or publicly owned by shareholders that could be considered on the edge of the definition of a social enterprise in that they do not need to be democratically owned, run or held in trust by the benefiting stakeholders. But what makes them radically different from the traditional for-profit company is that their directors have a legal duty to deliver stated measurable social or environmental benefits to a wider public as well as maximising profits for their owners and shareholders. This new type of company suits businesses that are genuinely values-driven but still want the freedom of the for-profit business model. Some of the better-known public benefit companies involved in physical products include Patagonia, Method, Klean Kanteen and Kickstarter.

As of 2019, the benefit corporation model is only available in 35 US states as well as Italy and Puerto Rico, although legislation is in process or being considered in several other countries around the world.[51] Equally, existing companies that are mission-driven may not be in a position to change their company's legal status. In both of these cases and more widely for any organisation, there are two further options available for businesses that want to demonstrate their commitment to creating wider environmental and social benefits. One is *independent certification* as a B Corps and the other is to adopt a *hybrid* business model where connected FP and NFP companies work together.

certified B Corps

Hailed as the fair trade of socially minded corporations, B Labs introduced B Corps certification in 2006 in the USA. From the first 19 pioneering companies to be certified in 2007, as of mid-2019 it has grown to over 2800 certified companies in 64 countries across more than 150 industries.[52] To become certified, a company or organisation needs to score a minimum of 80 out of 200 points on their B Impact Assessment covering their employee, community, long-term environmental and core impacts.[53] Take-up in Latin America has been second only to North America where it goes under the name of Sistema B. The Brazilian company Natura was the first and largest publicly traded company to become B Corps certified in 2014 and in 2018 Danone North America the largest. [54] Other B Corps include high-profile names like Method, Etsy, Seventh Generation, Ecover, Parker Warby, UncommonGoods as well as Patagonia, One Earth Designs and Klean Kanteen that are both B Corps and legal benefit corporations. Being a B Corps or a benefit corporation are two different ways for for-profit companies to signal to their customers and employees that they are really serious about creating value beyond the financial bottom line.

hybrid models

The hybrid model is yet another business model gaining popularity with mission-driven enterprises based around the design and distribution of consumer products.[55] Envirofit, Biolite, Selco, D-light, Eco-filtro, Proximity, We Care Solar that we saw in Chapter 3.3, as well as Raspberry Pi, Buffalo Bicycles, Motivation and Whilrwind Wheelchairs International, are all examples of successful product-based social enterprises that operate hybrid models. In the hybrid model, a charity or NFP organisation creates and controls a for-profit company that acts as its trading arm or vice versa. Typically, the profit generated by selling a product into affluent markets or to other NFPs is channelled back into their NFP. Together with charity donations, these profits are then used to subsidise the cost and distribution of the same or similar product to more remote and low-income users, and to fund other activities such as R&D and education programmes. The reason hybrid models can be very effective is because the NFP and the FP arms each attract different types of funding and investment that are necessary to scale the enterprise on a sustainable economic basis.

the growing role for product design in social enterprise

While products are not the most obvious solution to problems of social equity or environmental restoration, as the physical touchpoints of wider strategies and services they represent a growing part of social enterprise activities, bridging industrialised, emerging and developing economies.[56] In Chapter 3.3 we saw many examples of how designing highly affordable, scalable and truly useful products can make all the difference for the billions at the base of the economic pyramid (BoP). As the impact and success of these products spreads, social enterprises are becoming a growing sector of employment and entrepreneurial opportunities for product designers.[57]

In this context, *the design and implementation of the right business model becomes just as important as the physical design* for the success of a product. Making life-improving products a feasible proposition for the BoP relies on strong local distribution networks. These networks need to build trust and reach target groups, often in remote areas, to demonstrate a product's benefits and make them accessible and affordable through micro-finance partnerships.

Typically, people living on less than $2 a day don't have money to pay for products upfront. They need products that have a short pay-back and access to purchasing finance through a combination of micro-loans for initial payments followed by smaller regular 'micro-payments'. A lot of social enterprise work has been focused on precisely this: the design of financial services specifically

for the BoP. These were spearheaded by the Grameen bank's micro-loans in Bangladesh as early as 1983, and have evolved into myriad different micro-payment services now enabled by smartphones such as Kiva.

IDEO.orgs' work with Mercy Corps and BankO to offer banking facilities for the victims of Typhoon Haiyan in the Philippines in 2014 is one of many examples of designers getting involved in the design of the essential services for recovery. With 80% of the Philippine population not having bank accounts, their task was to design a banking product that could work for the victims to access immediate financial support and provide them with longer-term security to rebuild sustainable livelihoods.[58]

In developed economies, social enterprises that directly benefit local stakeholders based around the sale of products play a smaller role and are generally at the low or non-profit end of the sector. Where they do exist, they are often connected with providing employment for socially excluded or vulnerable groups while offering products that support sustainable lifestyles. An early and inspiring example of a successful product-focused social enterprise was Remploy.[59] It was set up in the UK in 1945 as a socio-industrial innovation initially to provide employment and training for people injured during the Second World War and disabled miners. At its height, it had over 10,000 disabled employees and 94 factories. Although it was best known for its furniture, the company produced a very wide range of products, from knitwear to medical products, automotive parts to electronics (fig 4.14). However, Remploy's last remaining factory closed in 2013, as it had to adapt its business model in response to the competition from cheaper imports, changing attitudes towards disability and the loss of government support in a new political regime.

Figure 4.14 Remploy was a UK post-war social enterprise employing over 10,000 disabled workers that was closed in 2013. Its furniture was popular in homes, schools and community halls up and down the country, and today these items are sought-after vintage classics. (photo courtesy Scarmangashop.co.uk)

common traits and approaches for sustainable businesses and products

At the beginning of this section we asked ourselves a number of questions around whether business could be sustainable, if certain business entities are inherently more sustainable and what practices the most sustainable companies have in common. Based on our findings to date, it seems that company type alone is not the defining element for sustainability, although it can signal strongly a business's motivations and constraints. To summarise, privately owned FP companies have more freedom to prioritise longer term benefits over publicly owned businesses, an important foundation for sustainability. The new FP benefit corporation entity enables mission-driven companies to operate by their principles. Cooperatively owned companies are inherently more economically and socially ethical, as they share their profits. They also have greater stakeholder engagement but this does not determine their environmental credentials and ability to innovate. Finally, social enterprises, in their many forms, are by definition set up for the purpose of benefiting defined causes through their constitutions and are the fastest-growing and perhaps the most innovative business category.

We also found that commercially successful companies of whatever type that have sustainability and value creation high on their agendas share the following common traits:

- first, they embed a culture of sustainable values through inspiring leadership and vision that extends to their employees, customers and partners
- second, they set ambitious internal goals with measurable targets that are achievable through cooperation between employees, operations and supply chain
- third, they collaborate with other businesses and NGOs to share and develop best practice and extend the reach of the value they can create
- fourth, they believe and invest in design and innovation as systemic tools for achieving sustainability and maintaining profitability

On this fourth and last point, a company that aspires to be sustainable must also have sustainable products and, conversely, a product that purports to be sustainable can only emerge from a sustainable process and organisation. Thus sustainable products and sustainable companies go hand-in-glove. The centrality of product offer in the achievement of sustainability for a company is perfectly articulated in Patagonia's mission statement:

> Build the best product,
> cause no unnecessary harm,
> use business to inspire and implement solutions to the
> environmental crisis.

In *The Responsible Company*, Yvon Chouinard and Vincent Stanley offer a number of checklists for companies wanting to minimise damage and maximise value. In relation to the customer product offer they put forward the following checklist as a recipe for *'building the best product'*:

- make useful things that have an identifiable benefit to the user
- make things that benefit the commons
- make things that benefit health or healthy activities
- make things that are multifunctional
- make long-lasting products whose parts can be repaired
- vigilantly avoid unnecessary product proliferation (including excessive options for popular products)
- have production and manufacturing processes screened by third parties (e.g. FSC, bluesign, LEED) to reduce environmental harm
- be progressively transparent about the social and environmental impact of what you make and participate in any manufacturer- or brand-facing indexes in the industry you work in
- guarantee your product unconditionally
- serve the underserved; donate what you no longer need to those who do[60]

While this may sound relatively tame for designers, its interpretation need not be so. They suggest that the journey towards sustainable business and products can be a combination of regular incremental improvements and periodic 'breathtakingly bold' moves that disrupt accepted practices and inspire and motivate further discoveries.

From the point of view of employment, sustainable companies also score highly with employee retention and satisfaction, as we saw earlier with millennial motivators. Designers who understand sustainability deeply and can approach it pragmatically will be a valuable contributor to companies where this culture already exists. Where it is still nascent, they can become tomorrow's change leaders and innovators.

4.3 emerging business models: the collaborative economy

Designers are trained to use 'design thinking' and increasingly to work collaboratively with stakeholders to turn problems into creative opportunities with positive outcomes. But it would be naïve in the extreme to consider that these skills and approach alone are sufficient to get us out of the predicament we are in. In tackling even a small part of our biggest challenge – how over 9 billion people can live well within the Earth's limits

New and emerging business models and design approaches for sustainability

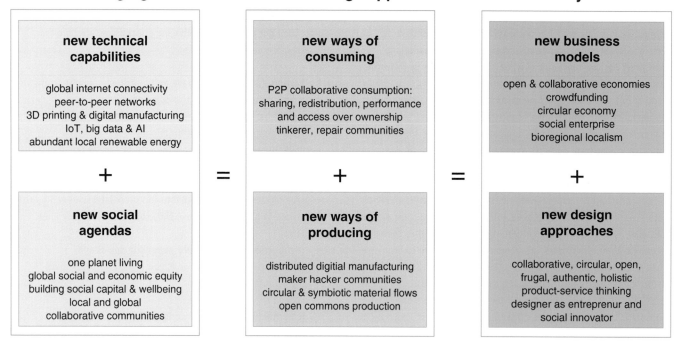

Figure 4.15 New more sustainable business models and design approaches are being enabled by emerging technologies and driven by new rapidly evolving socio-environmental agendas. (source: Jane Penty)

by 2050 – designers will inevitably come up against systemic barriers that are outside of their control. A paradigm shift to a more desirable and viable economic system assisted by new business models will be just as essential as applying design thinking to wicked problems and harnessing new design opportunities for navigating a transition to sustainability.

One of the systemic barriers that directly affects the development of sustainably innovative products is the concentration and protection of investment capital by large corporations. There continue to be many instances where industries that control a large segment of a market wilfully hold back the development of more environmentally and socially favourable solutions. They do this by buying up and holding onto banks of intellectual property design rights or skewing markets and regulations in favour of their technologies and methods of production for the sake of protecting their capital investments and maintaining their market dominance. This has been particularly notable in relation to technologies that are reliant on fossil fuels and processes that involve unnecessary toxic substances. These include obstructing the development of distributed renewable energy, cleaner and more efficient forms of mobility, less impactful packaging solutions, toxic substitution, closed-loop recycling systems and consumer safety (see Chapter 7.2 on fire retardants and Chapter 8.2 on electric cars).

While we have looked at a number of ways in which established businesses are *gradually* embedding more responsible attitudes, today we have before us a number of opportunities created by socio-technical changes that promise a much faster route to market for sustainable products. In figure 4.15 we see that technical capabilities in the form of accessible mobile networks, the IoT, digital manufacturing and abundant renewable energy are converging with new social and environmental agendas across the world to create the possibility of consuming and producing more sustainably while building social capital through new and disruptive business models.

In this section we will look at the new business models that offer most opportunities for designers to rethink and reshape the nature of products and services to meet our needs that spring from digitally enabled collaboration. These are collaborative consumption, crowd-funding, open and distributed production, including the maker movement, and the circular economy that we will group under the umbrella term of collaborative economy.

the 'collaborative' economy in context

Rising out of necessity and the loss of trust in institutions caused by the 2007/2008 financial crisis, ordinary citizens joined together to develop new ways of transacting and new types of transactions, initially between themselves and later joined by businesses and institutions. This was made possible by the creation of platforms enabled by the connecting power of the Internet and further boosted by the introduction and mass take-up of the smartphone at about the same time. The new business models to which this has given rise go variously under the names *collaborative consumption, sharing, peer-to-peer, distributed, open and social economies.*

Collaborative 'economies' in themselves are not new. They have existed for as long as humans and play an important role in building social capital and the wellbeing that comes with it. While competition is considered a necessary ingredient for success in a market economy, in interpreting his evolutionary theory, Darwin considered humankind's capacity for empathy and collaboration just as important for survival as competitiveness.[61] And so it is that face-to-face collaborating, sharing, swopping, borrowing, bartering and gifting of information, ideas, goods and services have existed for millennia and are alive and well today, especially in more disadvantaged communities.[62] What *is* new in the twenty-first century is that this sharing, collaborating and all manner of 'economic' transacting is being done on a mass scale largely between strangers, both locally and globally, via digital platforms, thanks to newly developed systems of trust borrowed from social media.

Inspired by books like Charles Leadbeater's *We Think* (2009) and Botsman and Rogers' *What's Mine is Yours* (2010), the collaborative economy was heralded in its early years as the long-awaited means to break away from our top-down, centralised, consumption-led capitalist economy to a more horizontal and distributed sharing of wealth. In addition, its peer-to-peer nature promotes a greater sense of community, and importantly for sustainably minded product designers, a reduction in consumption of products by enabling a shift from ownership to access and product life extension through resale. From this point of view, Rachel Botsman defines the collaborative economy as: *"An economy built on distributed networks of connected individuals and communities versus centralized institutions, transforming how we can produce, consume, finance, and learn."*[63]

Ten years on, however, the lines between the peer-to-peer 'collaborative' economies and yet another channel for 'business as usual' are becoming increasingly blurred. Collaborative economies have grown to encompass all manner of transactions of goods and services and now include not just peer-to-peer but also business-to-consumer and business-to-business. Figure 4.16 illustrates the collaborative economy as a honeycomb, showing how it now extends well beyond the initial key sectors of mobility, space, money, goods, food and personal services into education, logistics, energy, health, local services and beyond.

This rapid expansion of Internet platforms has also seen the highest market value and volume of transactions move from the more collaborative and altruistic founding platforms (Freecycle, Craigslist, Couchsurfing, Wikipedia, Gumtree, Fairmondo, Streetbank and many more) to whole sectors being dominated by a few highly profitable players such as Uber, Didi Chuxing, Airbnb, Ebay and Alibaba that take a healthy percentage of each transaction. These dominant platforms are now effectively owned by billionaire venture capitalists at the start-up stage and later joined by their billionaire founders when they become publicly listed. And so, ironically, from a movement that grew from the sense of outrage and betrayal created by the financial crisis, the largest enabling platforms of the 'collaborative economy' are now companies owned by the 1%, growing at rates of between 15 to 60% annually across different parts of the globe.[64, 65] Even mainstream companies such as BMW and Walmart with Drive Now and CExchange are adding collaborative business models to their portfolio of customer offer.

There are many, including Doug Rushkoff, Trebor Scholtz and Michael Bowens, who consider the dominant direction the 'collaborative economy' has taken as a huge missed opportunity for the creation of a more socially cohesive, democratic, equitable and sustainable economy the world is crying out for. At the very least, as we saw earlier in this chapter, there is nothing preventing these dominant platforms from adopting cooperative or benefit company structures. Kickstarter demonstrated that this was possible when it became a public benefit corporation in 2015. In short, the financial instruments now enhanced by technology exist to create a collaborative economy that supports more sustainable living, but will we seize the opportunity? This debate should continue. Advocates of a more sustainable vision on sites like Ouishare.net, Collaborative Consumption.com (2011–2016), Shareable.net, Peers, Share the Worlds Resources (sharing.org) and the P2P Foundation are actively inspiring and supporting the work of a very large number of platforms that are not only more egalitarian in structure but are also creating the opportunities for local and smaller businesses, including designers, to exist and flourish.

We introduced the collaborative economy as a disruptive force in business whose main claims to sustainability are its ability to build social capital, provide a fairer distribution of economic benefits and reduce consumption through reuse and multiple users.

While we have exposed some of its contradictions,[66] we will now focus specifically on collaborative models that involve the use of products and PSS that can claim to be more sustainable,[67] and look for the design opportunities there are to amplify these sustainable benefits. These include *collaborative consumption,*

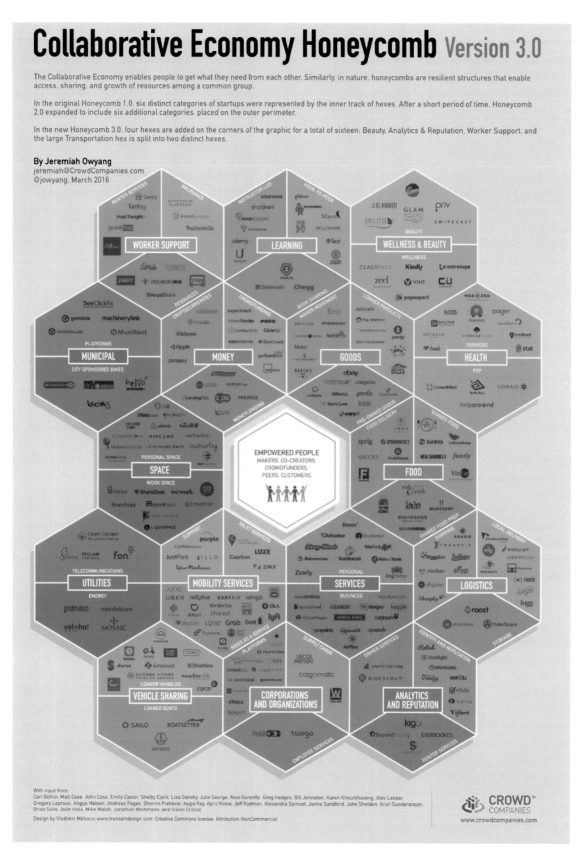

Figure 4.16 Collaborative Economy Honeycomb (courtesy Jeremiah Owyang, design Vladimir Mirkovic)

crowd-funding, the maker movement, open design, distributed production and *the circular economy*.

collaborative consumption

Collaborative consumption is an umbrella term that encompasses all the platform modes of sharing, swapping, trading, or renting products and services. The two main models that can claim to reduce consumption are *redistribution* and *access over ownership*. We will focus on what implications these have for product design and how their sustainable benefits might be amplified.

redistribution: one product, serial ownership

The many trading and gifting platforms around the world (ex. eBay, Freecycle, Craigslist, Gumtree, Pre-loved, CQout, Rakuten, Alibaba, Linio, Tokopedia, Flipcart) have made finding new owners for all the possessions we no longer need or want much easier than it used to be through classified ads, local notice-boards or word of mouth. It has also vastly extended the geographical range of potential buyers and products that are exchanged, especially smaller items, including spare parts. Resale markets are growing even more rapidly in Asia and Latin America as second-hand markets in these regions 'catch up'.[68] In this regard, Internet blogs and forums are also helping develop a culture of appreciation for older and used products through their shared stories. Together with the prevalence of the platforms, they are vastly reducing the stigma of buying second-hand goods, helping to shift norms and increasing accessibility to products for many lower income households.

Reuse through redistribution is a clear example of a sustainability win-win-win. Not only do you acquire what you need, you save money, the seller or gifter makes money or has the satisfaction of finding a home for their unneeded goods and, all the while, product lifecycles are being extended. Additionally you may also make a personal connection with the previous owner and find out the story behind what you have bought that creates an emotional connection with the product, that may extend its life even further. Redistribution is also an integral part of a circular economy.

The main sustainability gain in reselling goods lies in the assumption that by buying second-hand we are avoiding the

purchase and therefore the production of a new product. Looking back at product lifecycles (Chapter 2.2), reselling clearly extends the useful life of a product. While this does not change its initial impact in terms of materials extraction or manufacturing, it does *reduce the intensity of its production and disposal impacts* by spreading these over a longer period of time. One exception to this rule are products whose main impacts are in their use phase and where there is a new technology that is significantly more efficient than the old technology, such as with lighting, appliances and electric cars (see fig 2.1). In this case, buying new rather than second-hand can be the better environmental choice, depending on how old the product is and how radically the technology has improved over those years[69] (see also Chapter 6.2 on optimal product lifespans).

Although there is still very little hard data on the impacts of collaborative consumption, a study conducted by IVL Swedish Environmental Research Institute for Schibsted media group, *The Second-hand Effect Report 2017*, gives us some early insights. It quantifies the GHGs saved of *not producing* an equivalent new product and *not disposing* of the old one, *less* the emissions produced from transporting the goods from seller to new owner for all the second-hand products traded across eight of their marketplaces in 2016. These include Vibbo (Spain); Leboncoin (France); Subito (Italy); Jófogás (Hungary); Blocket (Sweden); Finn (Norway); Tori (Finland), and Avito (Morocco). Figure 4.17 shows that second-hand sales across these platforms saved a total of 16.3 million tons of CO_2e GHGs in just one year. That is the equivalent of 16.4 million return flights between Western Europe and New York or 66 million new sofas, or the traffic in Paris standing still for six years for these eight trading platforms alone.[70]

However, in calculating the overall environmental benefits of redistribution, we cannot simply assume that every second-hand product traded is one less product purchased.

Knowing what we know about the rebound effect (Chapter 3.1), we have to ask ourselves: Do cheaper second-hand goods and the additional cash raised drive people to increase their consumption of other goods or spend it in other areas? Or does it mean that people can live better on smaller incomes? These and other questions are waiting for more data-based research to be

Figure 4.17 GHG savings across eight of Schibsted's P2P resale marketplaces across Europe and Morocco in 2016 alone. (courtesy Shibsted.com)

answered. But even without having answers to these questions yet, we can still safely conclude that there is a net positive environmental, economic and sometimes social effect of reselling and reusing goods.

designing for multiple owners and multiple sales
From the design perspective, does the growth of the resale market affect the design of products and how can product design contribute further to its positive effects? In terms of durable goods, looking across peer-to-peer resale markets, we find that cars still represent the biggest share in monetary value while books and smartphones are the highest by volume followed by furniture, bicycles, laptops and small electronics, appliances, baby goods and toys.[71] We also find that products from brands with a reputation for reliability and desirability resell better and hold their value.

Strong brands often go hand-in-hand with well-designed products. Over and above their inbuilt kudos, they typically include classic aesthetic appeal, well-considered innovations and functionality, higher quality materials and finishes, reliability and repairability. In relation to resale and reuse, designs should also include flexible product architecture that will allow the product to be disassembled and reconfigured to adapt to different contexts of use, shipping and ultimately recycling. The added value that design-led products offer also links directly to the concept of *decoupling* that we touched upon in section 4.1, commanding higher prices and profits for fewer resources.

Beyond the product itself, designers can also add value in the resale market through product presentation, packaging and storytelling. The quality of product photography and graphic design on the Internet and thoughtful on-brand packaging and storytelling in face-to-face platforms like markets and pop-up stalls can really increase their appeal and achieve higher value sales. The Toy Project's Loved Before range is an example of this. The charity raises income by upcycling and reselling donated toys to provide toys for a range of social needs such as children's hospital wards and hospices, child bereavement therapy or toys for prisoners to give to their children. Their experience has shown that the perceived value and sales of second-hand toys can be vastly increased by sharing the stories behind them, supported by carefully designed packaging, curation and online presence. At the same time, all their packaging designs need to be highly cost-effective (fig 4.18).

Designers should also be aware that other aspects that may seem ancillary to the main design such as instructions for use, maintenance, warnings and safety certifications can have a significant effect on whether a product can be resold or

will be reused. An example of this that has big implications for waste furniture (Chapter 7.1) is that a second-hand sofa or mattress without a fire safety label cannot be resold, purchased or used by commercial bodies or charities. With sofas and mattresses representing the largest amount of household waste by volume,[72] resolving how safety test labelling remains integral to the product should not be an afterthought.

Generally, the further a product gets from its original point of sale, the more information about the product is lost, and this can be crucial to its reusability and longevity. To avoid this, designers must consider how critical information for using the product safely and efficiently for as long as possible can remain available. At the very least, model numbers and all certification and critical information for safe use should either be printed onto, attached or moulded into the product. In addition, safe operation, maintenance and repair instructions should be available online. This is a very good example of where P2P sharing and open information through online forums and videos such as iFixit (see Box 6.1) have helped tremendously in making it possible to repair, optimise and extend the life of many products.

new resale and re-manufacturing markets
Whether it is thanks to the growing momentum of the circular economy and concerns for sustainability or simply the logistical enabling of technology, a growing number of brands and retail companies are offering trade-ins, buy-backs, take-backs and refurbished products alongside the peer-to-peer platforms. Brands and retail companies are realising that by doing this they are not only tapping into an additional revenue stream, this is also helping them to retain customers and build loyalty by creating more touchpoints, a better service and aligning sustainability values. We will look at this in more detail as part of the circular economy.

access over ownership or pimping your assets: one product, one owner, many users
> *New technologies enable us to unlock the 'idling capacity' of resources – the untapped social, economic, and environmental value of underutilized assets.*[73]
>
> Rachel Botsman

Access over ownership is one of the most distinctive offerings of collaborative consumption and the most disruptive and challenging to existing business models. It is now the basis of many platforms where anything from cars to baby equipment, tools to yachts, accommodation to workspace are given, swopped, borrowed, loaned, hired, or rented out. Essentially this means that instead of owning these 'assets' you can have use of one when you need it. This sits particularly well with urban millennials, as they

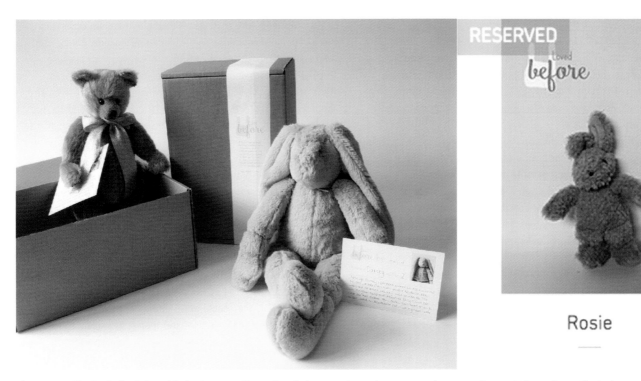

Figure 4.18 The Toy Project's 'Loved Before' range online and ready for a new home demonstrates the power of presentation and narrative to increase the perceived value and reuse of second-hand products. (courtesy ©Charlotte Liebling)

are pushed into living in smaller and smaller spaces and they find that having too many possessions, especially cars, can become more of a burden than a utility.[74]

From the point of view of sustainability, access over ownership has been hailed as the breakthrough we were waiting for to reduce consumption while still enjoying the benefits of many products and spreading out the financial benefits. The environmental case assumes that by using products or services when we need them we will buy fewer products, while the products we do produce will have a much higher utilisation rate, rather than entrapping valuable resources while they sit idle for most of their lives. For people with assets, it means that they can earn extra income by renting or 'sharing' their underused assets. For the 'borrowers', it means that they don't need to commit nearly as much money or time to have the use and convenience of products and may even indulge in occasional luxury and frivolity, such as yachts, jets or designer fashion, creating a sense of abundance and possibly with a smaller footprint. Some forms of asset sharing, such as carpooling, space sharing, neighbourhood goods sharing and Libraries of Things (LoT), have also been shown to provide a richer social experience, creating new personal connections.[75]

Like the redistribution markets, short-term rental, borrowing, loaning and pooling of goods, spaces and services has been around for some time both informally and formally. The first public libraries date back to the fifteenth century in England and were widespread by the nineteenth century; toy libraries date back to 1935 in Los Angeles to support parents with disabled children and spread to Europe in the 1960s; tool rental businesses started in the 1950s; car sharing in the form of Jitneys appeared in San Francisco in 1914 and carpooling reached a peak in the USA in the late 1970s during the 'oil crisis'. But the breadth of services, product types, geographical range, ease and convenience made possible by clever algorithms and carefully designed interfaces have taken this to another order of magnitude.

Businesses based on the 'access over ownership' model are taking many forms, from community NFPs to seriously high capital-value FPs offering purely transactional exchanges. Research to date shows that whether implicitly set up to create sustainable benefits or to be purely profit centred, access over ownership models can still offer environmental benefits. In surveys across all platforms, *convenience* and *price savings* top the list of motivators in shifting to this model with sustainability coming further down the list.[76, 77] This is a very important observation for designers to note in designing successful sharing models that connects back to the value modes and behaviour change strategies that we saw in Chapter 3.1. As an illustration of this, a survey of library of things (LoT) users uncovers their motivations:

People say [...] the models are friendlier and build a sense of community compared to conventional tool rental companies. The financial incentive of affordable access was less important [...] than the human element. Interestingly, while LoT provide huge conservation and sustainability impacts, those were the least cited reasons that people chose to become members.[78]

However, just as we saw with different business types, the socio-economic benefits are far greater in organisations specifically set up with these goals in mind, even if it is not their users' main motivation.[79] In terms of socio-economic sustainability, the pros and cons of the gig economy that these models have introduced are being hotly debated, with some of the larger profit-intensive platforms being accused of actively eroding hard-won workers' rights. Some researchers go so far as to describe the gig economy as neoliberalism on steroids.[80]

What is also clear is that the sustainable benefits of access over ownership models are very sector specific. On this basis we will touch on the specific product-centred sectors where access over ownership is proving to be most conducive to greater sustainability, and suggest the opportunities these present for product design.

sharing smaller durable products: the Netflix of stuff

> *Is your home just a place to store stuff [...] while you're getting more stuff?*
>
> George Carlin

Infrequently used products like tools, and leisure equipment or products that are only needed for specific periods of time such as baby equipment, toys, temporary disability equipment, musical instruments, and countless others, seem ideally suited to the 'access over ownership' model. The fact that our homes are filled with so many products that we rarely use, combined with the benefits of building relationships with our neighbours, led to the creation of many environmentally and socially motivated P2P lending and renting sites between 2007 and 2012 (fig 4.19). These include Ecomodo (2007); Crowd Rent, NeighborGoods, Share some Sugar (2009); Thingloop, OhSoWe, Snapgoods, Streetbank (2010); Spinlister (2011); and Peerby (2012).[81] Interestingly and regrettably, of all these platforms, only Streetbank, Spinlister and Peerby are still operating as of early 2019.

In conversation, Daan Weddenpohl, founder of Peerby, explained why creating a successful sharing platform for smaller consumer goods is so challenging compared with platforms for higher value transactions such as mobility and accommodation. For these high-value 'products' the sharing model breaks the scarcity model whereas we are awash with smaller products because they have

such a low monetary cost. As an example, there are estimated to be 17 million power drills in the Netherlands alone, hardly used and adding up to 3000 unused years of service – all because they are so cheap and convenient. Peerby has demonstrated that people are more than willing to share – they have over 1 billion products on offer – but there is a lack of demand because the low cost of smaller items often makes it more convenient to purchase.[82]

Toys are another product group that naturally lends itself to sharing, as children look for new challenges as their abilities and interests develop. Toy-sharing platforms generally offer a subscription service where the child receives new toys at regular intervals. Although several start-ups like Toyaroo and Spark Box Toys have also failed, Pley (2012) in the USA and Ludobox AG (2014) in Switzerland seem to have found models that work. Pley started by offering LEGO sets exclusively, on the basis that if they could get their model to work with one of the most challenging toys to share, then it was likely to work for the easier toys.

In an interview, Stefan Keller, the CEO of Ludobox, shared his insights into what designers could do to make toys more appropriate for sharing commercially. To contextualise his comments, Ludobox's biggest markets are 1- to 4-year-olds and their most commonly rented toys are play tents, bobby cars, LEGO, Brio sets and remote controlled cars. He revealed that they have surprisingly few problems with the toys because they mainly have very high-quality toys (often wooden) that generally don't break. He advises designers:

> *The number of pieces and the quality of the material are key for good lending toys, as well as shipping size and ease of sanitizing. But first and foremost it is important that the toys have a high fun-factor for the kids and an educational factor [for the parents].*[83]

With toy recycling being almost non-existent, getting more use out of the ones we do produce and reducing the purchase of new ones should make a small dent in the toy waste mountain. Another clear benefit of toy sharing is introducing children at a young age to the idea that they don't need to own a product to enjoy it. As one Ludobox parent put it:

> *My kids love being able to pick new toys on a regular basis. [...] For me as a parent it is nice not having to buy new toys and there is an educational factor. My children learn how to take care of the toys while learning about sharing.*[84]

Another formula for sharing small durable products that is growing all over the world are community-based Libraries of Things

Figure 4.19 Streetbank (UK & Egypt) provides a platform for people living near each other to request, share or give away 'stuff' and skills. It has also proven to lead to new and friendlier relationships within neighbourhoods. (photo courtesy ©Sam Stephens for Streetbank)

(LoT) and Toy Libraries. These mostly take the form of a local face-to-face service supported by an online presence.[85] While Toy Libraries have existed for many decades, often attached to public book libraries, the wider object library is newer. As we will see in section 4.4 when we cover open design and the maker movement, the creation of maker spaces where tools are accessible is in many ways an extension of this concept.

These examples demonstrate that while the idea of sharing and borrowing products we only need occasionally seems to make perfect sense as a win-win-win in terms of sustainability, the challenges of turning these into viable PSS business models for sharing goods are still very great. There are many lessons to be learnt from these examples for setting up successful sharing platforms. They include getting the offer and service right, carrying out proper human-centred research and testing, building the critical mass of members needed as well as having strong tech support and financial backing.[86] Where relatively small sums of money or savings are involved, the question is: What would

motivate me to travel a few blocks away to borrow the screwdriver set, backpack, party awning, etc. and to return it again, when a delivery from Amazon can be on my doorstep within an hour with only the bother of a few clicks?

Could it also be that we won't be able to change our consumption patterns significantly until we deal with the issue of our lives being busier and busier than ever, virtually and physically? Will it take moving to a shorter working week or a minimum universal wage with less money for us to have time to engage with our communities and more sustainable consumption patterns? Is it just a case of having a better business proposition that aligns with behaviour change theory (see Chapter 3.1)? Or is the core of the problem, as Daan Weddenpohl believes, the fact that our economic system incentivises the 'sell once' and 'as many as possible' model by not having business pay for their real impacts? If we had a level playing field, then sharing, leasing and repair models would become very competitive.

Figure 4.20 Crowd-funding sustainable projects **a.** Environment: Flow Hive provides on-demand honey harvesting while disturbing bee life as little as possible to support healthy hives. It became Indiegogo's most successful campaign by surpassing its target by 17380% in 2015. It is also testament to highly user-centred and environmentally considered design, simply and honestly presented. **b.** Food: Livin Farms Hive is a complete mealworm farm in your kitchen fed off food scraps. Their mission is to facilitate the transition from meat to more sustainable diets from high-quality nutritional protein (Kickstarter 2015/2016). **c.** Water: Nebia is a shower that saves up to 70% of water by atomising water to increase the effectiveness of every drop (Kickstarter 2015) **d.** Sion Car by Sono Motors is the first-ever production EV solar car fulfilling their vision of 'endless mobility' in an affordable family electric car (Indiegogo prototype 2016/Seedrs and Wiwin crowd-investing for full production 2017/5000 pre-orders 2018) **e.** Energy: Orison is a smart home energy storage system

collaborative mobility

Mobility is perhaps one of the sectors most impacted by the 'access over ownership' models, with cars, vans and bicycles being the most prominent products, soon to be joined by passenger drones. Interestingly, as one of the biggest contributors to our individual footprint, transportation seems the perfect sector to apply this to if it can provide better options for reducing our footprint while improving the quality of life. In Chapter 8.3 we look in greater detail at the sustainability pros and cons of current collaborative mobility models for cars and bicycles, and consider how product design can enhance the experience and uptake of the most beneficial models. Extending this into the future, we also look at its implications for sustainable mobility and the design of driverless automotion and Mobility as a Service (MaaS) scenarios.

sharing space

The final sector that is being radically affected by the access-over-ownership model of collaborative consumption is space for living and working. While this is having very significant positive and negative socio-economic impacts on urban communities, tourism, the traditional accommodation sector and people's ability to earn additional income, most of this sits beyond the scope of product designers to affect. However, one product area it is having an impact on is the design of furniture, fittings and lighting for shared co-workspaces that are springing up all over the globe. In Chapter 7.3 we look at some specific design responses to these new workplace scenarios and also touch upon open and collaborative design practices in section 4.4.

crowd-funding: opening doors for successful sustainable products

Few business models have revolutionised the world of new product development as much as crowd-funding. Through Internet platforms, it has brought mass collaborative consumption to the world of finance, enabling the realisation of a great many projects for groups and individuals as diverse as artists, writers, inventors, designers, community groups, social enterprises, start-ups, NGOs, charities as well as commercial companies. Many of these projects that would otherwise never have been possible are delivering cultural, social and environmental benefits through an open voluntary process. Where this is the case, crowd-funding can be held up as an example of a business model working for the benefit of society and the environment.

For product design, crowd-funding is a way to raise money for the development, production and marketing of new products

and technologies. It works either by donation, or by exchanging rewards or company equity for money or convertible loans. The beauty of crowd-funding for the designer is that it contributes much more than just finance to the success of new products. The crowd-funding platform is also a low-risk route for testing the market while exposing projects to a wider audience, building a community and a 'buzz' around the product. Running a successful campaign not only confirms that the design has a market; it also has the added bonus of providing a direct relationship with your donors or investors by involving them in the ongoing success of your project.

In less than a decade, crowd-funding has unquestionably transformed the landscape of product development and opened an exciting new door of possibility for product designers. So much so that many designers now find themselves propelled into the world of entrepreneurship and start-ups, either as originators or as part of a team where a designer's ability to develop concepts into viable and desirable products has become a very valuable asset. With crowd-funding continuing to grow exponentially, this is also a unique opportunity for the sustainably minded designer.[87]

Interestingly, from the demand side, the take-up of crowd-funding has clearly demonstrated what an appetite people have to connect with new ideas, products and causes. By giving exposure to a great number and range of initiatives, it has empowered people all over the globe to exercise their judgement and actively demonstrate their support rather than having to be passive and often frustrated receivers of the products that traditional companies choose to offer them.

Crowd-funding platforms also come in many forms, from not-for-profits, for-profits and benefit corporations such as Kickstarter. Some are open to any type of campaign and category (Indiegogo, Crowdfunder, Crowdcube), while others curate their offer (Startnext, Kickstarter) or specialise in particular fields, including sustainability (OneplanetCrowd (Netherlands), Pozible (Australia), Kiva (global), Greencrowd (Netherlands).[88]

Both general and specialist platforms have brought to life many product-oriented sustainable solutions across a range of areas, including the following:

- water and energy savings
- renewable energy
- medical devices and services
- sustainable mobility

that supports self-generation and a renewable, distributed energy grid by optimising charging and discharging times (Kickstarter 2016) **f.** Shetler: Maidan tent, designed by Bonaventura Visconti and Leo Bettini with Eco 100 Plus, provides a communal covered space for hosting a range of social activities at Ritsona refugee camp, Euboea, Greece 2018 (Generosity 2017). (courtesy ©Beeinventive, ©Livin Farms, ©Nebia, ©Sono Motors GmbH, Orison, ©Maidan Tent)

- products for the base of the pyramid
- urban and rural agriculture
- environmental protection
- product- and service-sharing platforms
- … and many community cohesion and social innovation projects

Diversity of intent, audience and geographical location is another positive quality of crowd-funding as demonstrated through the wide range of projects it supports. Figure 4.20 illustrates a very small selection of successful sustainably oriented product campaigns across different product sectors. Interestingly, a high percentage of the products used as examples throughout this book on design for the BoP, design activism and mobility were at least partly crowd-funded. These include Parklets, the Air Quality Egg, Sion Car, Nucleo Terra2, Puzzlephone, Safecast bGeigie, and products from Biolite, Fairphone, Kano, littleBits, Ooho, as well as sharing platforms like Snapp Car and Peerby aimed at changing our consumption models.

the maker, tinkerer, repairer, hacker movement

There has never been a better time for anyone with the inclination to shape the physical world around them to share and realise their ideas. From the crafted object to the batch or pre-mass-produced product, from yarn bombs to personalised prosthetics, from planet-saving energy to life-saving medical devices, the creative possibilities of 'making' is coming back into people's lives. Today's new maker culture invites anyone to explore and reshape the products we live with as a hacker, tinkerer, repairer or maker.

The maker movement is fundamentally a grassroots phenomenon that believes in the power of doing. It has emerged from the well-established DIY and craft cultures crossed with the clever and playful hacker mindset of improving what we have in meaningful ways, enhanced by twenty-first-century tools and a new spirit of entrepreneurship. A number of factors have come together to ignite, inspire and enable the maker movement.

A key provocation is the ever-increasing frustration 'consumers' experience at being forced to accept the limitations of the existing product offer. This includes being 'locked out' of repairing, modifying or improving the products they own and use through manufacturers' 'black box' approach and warranty voiding. This also extends to the very limited choice of products that genuinely enable more sustainable living which feeds the urge to produce products that have more value for society and the environment. The maker movement provides the tools for enterprising people to take these issues into their own hands.

On the flip side of these frustrations stand several enablers without which the maker phenomena would not be possible. An important one is the ongoing evolution and availability of digital manufacturing technologies (see Chapter 2.5). This has spurred a curiosity to explore the potential of these new technologies and made possible the production of forms that were previously out of bounds to the lone maker. The second enabler is having the space and equipment to be able to create. Known as makerspaces, these are essentially open-access workshops that provide the tools for making and prototyping, the space for playing and experimenting, and the community for learning and collaborating. The makerspace concept has evolved from hacker spaces (c-space Berlin 1981) and the Fablab movement led by Neil Gershenfeld from the Centre for Bits and Atoms at MIT Media Lab (2001),[89] and their vision to *"creat[e] opportunities to improve lives and livelihoods around the world"*.[90] Although most often associated with non-profits like schools, universities and community organisations, today they also take the form of for-profit businesses like Techshops (2006).

Financial viability is the next challenge. While makerspaces are often publicly funded, the growth of the maker movement as a significant disruptor has gone hand-in-hand with incubators, accelerators, crowd-funding and direct sales. Platforms like Etsy and Shapeways are demonstrating how collaborative platforms and digital fabrication can democratise creativity, innovation and production by providing the marketplace for small-scale 'makers' to earn a living from the sale of their designs.

But perhaps the most important element in facilitating this to grow as a truly grassroots mass movement is the building of maker and repairer communities. DIYers, tinkerers, crafters, etc. are no longer isolated working in their shed, basement, or bedroom thanks to the digitally and physically connected communities. All types of creations, hacks, repairs, skills, knowhow and feedback can be shared through online videos and blogs, instruction manuals, magazines, maker fairs and meet-ups. This also extends to co-creation opportunities in shared workspaces and global open innovation platforms working on solving some of the world's most pressing issues.

Although not all of the methods and outputs from the maker movement could be called sustainable by any means, it has many overlaps with sustainability and its values. The most direct is that through the act of making, repairing or simply taking the time to select a product directly from a maker, we are engaging with our possessions and will tend to care for and value them more and keep them for longer. Thus, from the environmental point of view, this change in the relationship with products could help increase their longevity.

Figure 4.21 iFixit's Repair Manifesto clearly expresses all the social, economic and environmental values of a repair culture. (courtesy ©iFixit/iFixit.com)

The ability to repair is also a very important strategy in extending product life and feeding local economies as fully articulated in iFixit's Repair Manifesto (fig 4.21). The global popularity of repair cafés, parties and websites offering open access to hundreds of thousands of repair guides and teardowns has proven that people *want* to fix their products and share their knowhow. The repair movement has also exposed how manufacturers are actively preventing repairing and has thrown its weight into lobbying governments for 'the right to repair'. This would force manufacturers to provide access to diagnostic software, service manuals, product information and spare parts. The car industry in the USA was the first to win the 'right to repair' in 2012. With legislation in the pipeline in many US states and an element of the EU circular strategy, it is hoped that the electronics and other product sectors will soon follow. Meanwhile, designers can make a big contribution to the growing repair movement by designing repair-friendly products, affordable quality tools and support services (see Box 6.2, Interview with Kyle Wiens).

From the perspective of social sustainability, empowering a greater number of people to integrate creativity in their lives starting at school and perhaps even going on to earn a living from it takes them a step up on Maslow's hierarchy of needs. Being engaged in creative work with tangible outcomes supported by a strong community feeds esteem and self-actualisation, producing a sense of purpose and belonging. The growing number of Men's Sheds across the world is also proving the power of the workshop as a vehicle for mental wellbeing. On the economic front, the maker movement is closely connected to more egalitarian business models of crowd-funding, open design and distributed digital manufacturing. This is because these are generally flatter structures where a higher percentage of revenue feeds back directly to the designers and makers rather than to middlemen.

Not only does much of the intent and participatory nature of the maker movement align with sustainable values, but many socially and environmentally beneficial products have emerged as outputs, as we've seen with crowd-funding and will see in open innovation. It seems however that there is still a lot that the maker movement could contribute if more of this energy and enthusiasm could be directed at making the world a better place, starting in their local communities.

4.4 emerging business models: open design and distributed production

The concept of open design has its roots in the Free Software movement started by Richard Stallman and fellow hackers at MIT in the early 1970s. It is based on the principle that software should be free to access, share and build on so that it can be customised, adapted and improved, as opposed to the closed proprietary models that emerged from Microsoft and Apple. This is based on their belief that the more minds working on a 'problem' collaboratively, the better the solution and the more resilient the system, whereas proprietary software leads to monopolies, inflexible products and poor service.

This led to the creation of the 'free' operating system, GNU-Linux in the early 1990s that today has over 91 million users, and later, to the Open Source Initiative led by Bruce Herons and co. in the mid-1990s. Where Free and Opensource software differ is that the latter believes that open and proprietary software can co-exist mainly for financial benefit while the Free Software movement maintains that is should remain 'free', as in freely accessible, not gratis, for its contribution to quality of life and 'good society'.[91]

Inspired by the ethos of the free and open software movement, the hardware version is *open design* and innovation. It is also the result of tumbling costs of distributed digital fabrication, the momentum of the maker movement and the ease with which designs from concepts through to detailed product specifications can be shared digitally. Just as crowd-funding has completely changed the landscape of *who* can finance and develop new designs and services, by turning the prevailing business model of proprietary IP on its head, open design is probably the most radical change in *how* we design.

In the current model of Intellectual Property (IP), copyright, design or patent rights are owned by the person or entity that originates or registers them. They can only be used by the owner or by someone to whom they grant a licence. This allows the IP owners to protect their designs and be rewarded financially should they be developed, licensed or sold on. This system has also led to abuses ranging from market monopolies (e.g. retroviral drugs) to companies purchasing and sitting on IP banks that they have no intention of using in order to control the market by preventing the development of competing technologies. Proponents of open versions of IP would also argue that proprietary IP is an obstacle to co-creating better solutions and tackling some of the world's really pressing problems more efficiently and effectively.

The alternatives to the current copyright system are the copyleft GNU General Public License (GPL) originating in 1989 and Creative Commons (CC) licensing agreements born in 2006. GNU licenses are based on the principle that if you distribute content you have created, whether gratis or for a fee, *"you must pass on to the recipients the same freedoms that you received".*[92] Creative Commons offers licences with different levels of permissions for any copyright IP, including attribution only, share alike, no derivatives and non-commercial. In all cases, if someone wishes to use work differently to the licence, then they must have the originator's permission.

With little more than a decade behind it, open design is still finding its way towards viable business models across FP and NFP sectors by testing different formats in the fields of mobility, prostheses, furniture, buildings and environmental monitoring. We will look at how it is evolving through some of these 'live experiments'.

co-creation design and open innovation challenge models

Vehicle design is one of the earliest industries to have developed commercially successful open co-creation models. Since their first co-created car in 2009 and the first 3D printed car Strati (2014), to the Olli autonomous EV shuttle (2016) controlled by IBM's Watson (fig 4.22), Local Motors have become a leader in using co-creation challenges as the basis for their product offer.

Figure 4.22 #Accessible Olli is Local Motors' open design challenge to make their autonomous EV shuttle Olli as accessible as possible. (courtesy Local Motors. All rights reserved.)

Essentially, Local Motors set and manage co-creation 'challenges' from which they go on to refine and produce the co-selected designs via their distributed micro-factories.[93] While these designs remain open source, they generate income from producing the designs and providing design services for customisations, such as the Domino's Ultimate Delivery Vehicle. Interestingly, by being pioneers of co-creation, they also sell their expertise in setting up and managing co-creation challenges working with the likes of DARPA, Airbus and GE–FUSE.

In the NFP sector, the open innovation or co-creation challenge model has also been gaining momentum. OpenIDEO was set up in 2010 specifically to engage the widest community in global challenges spanning social and environmental issues. It works through a network of local chapters and long-term partnerships that sponsor a range of specific challenges in fields as diverse as health, ageing, community building, equity, human rights, consumption and production. This model is also being used to tackle the UN Sustainability Goals through cross-sector partnerships and mass participation.[94]

open design sales and custom service models

Beyond the open challenge and co-creation models, there are a number of approaches where open design forms part of viable businesses. The most straightforward is where designers offer free downloads of their design files for non-commercial uses but also earn a living by selling the product ready-made.

Opendesk have developed the open and distributed business model much further through their global network of designers and fabricators. From their website you can select a furniture design to either download for personal use or order to be made by your nearest affiliated CNC fabricator. Offering customised designs for workspaces is another essential side of the business proposition. This model introduces two sustainable innovations. The first is that the product is made locally, reducing transport costs and boosting the local economy. The second is an intentionally more equitable and transparent split of the proceeds between makers, designers and platform, as opposed to the current system where retailers keep the biggest share of the earnings (fig 4.23).

Open Motors is another mobility company operating an open design model. Their first product was the Tabby Evo, a basic off-the-peg EV car rolling chassis that radically cuts down new vehicle R&D time. It is being used to build 'specials' for parking patrols, last-mile delivery, car sharing, self-driving fleets, agriculture, off-road and low-speed vehicles. Their more recent offering is the Edit (fig 4.24), a white-label customisable, modular, upgradable EV mini-van platform consciously designed for a circular economy. While all designs are open source, their business model consists of supplying the generic platform parts and supporting their clients in adapting them to their needs. Local Motors and Open Motors are demonstrating the speed with which new designs can be developed and customised through a combination of open design and digital fabrication, and

Figure 4.23 Opendesk's pioneering global manufacturing platform is based on an open design and distributed manufacturing business model. Shown here: desk components being made in a local workshop and locally made Lean desks in use at Old Oak, a co-living and co-working development in London. (courtesy Opendesk/photo Amandine Alessandra)

the positive impact this is having on the take-up of EV across specialist applications.

Beyond this, open design is also being widely used in NFP organisations and spontaneous communities of practice to develop medical, agricultural, environmental and housing products through online platforms, meet-ups and hackathons. Some of the more notable examples are openprosthetics.org's support for the Printhesis printable prosthetic arm (fig 4.25); Open Bionics' Open Hand project (see fig 2.26); disruptdisability.org's push to find open printable solutions for customising wheelchairs; Open Source Beehive's BussBox for monitoring hive health; citizen science

and meet-up groups taking control of their neighbourhood's air quality (see fig 3.32) and radioactivity data (see fig 3.30); Wikihouse Foundation's open source building designs; the incredibly ambitious Global Village Construction Set from Open Source Ecology (fig 4.26); the pioneering RepRap designed to give everyone access to 3D printing; and open source design libraries like Thingiverse and Appropedia.

Through the many manifestations of open design we can see the reshaping of the designer's role and glimmers of more sustainable business models. In the case of open innovation challenges, product designers can use their traditional skills of ideating and

Figure 4.24 Open Motors' Edit is an open source white label customizable, modular, upgradable EV mini-van platform consciously designed for a Circular Economy. (courtesy ©Open Motors® (formerly OSVehicle®) 2018 ALL RIGHTS RESERVED)

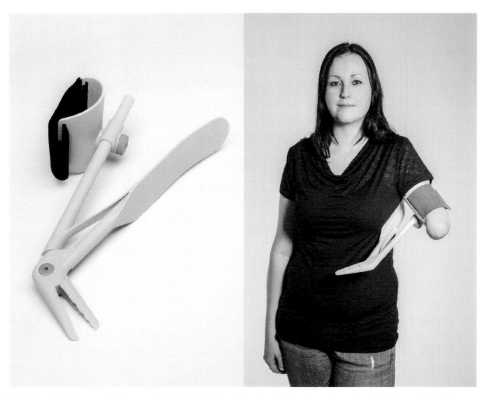

Figure 4.25 Printhesis is a 3D printable open design prosthesis tool designed by Roel Deden to make craft activities possible. It was supported by Kickstarter and Open Prosthetics. (courtesy ©Roel Deden/photo Bart van Leersum)

Figure 4.26 The Global Village Construction Set from Open Source Ecology is an ongoing project to design and share designs for the 50 most essential industrial machines that make small, sustainable communities with basic modern comforts viable. (source: Open Source Ecology)

developing design concepts, but to become active participants they will also need collaborative skills to build on others' ideas and be responsive to wide-ranging feedback. Equally, they may themselves be designing co-design challenges that involve establishing key partnerships and defining the strategic vision, framework and processes. Or, as in the case of Opendesk, they may be designing whole new platforms for more equitable relationships between designers, makers, consumers and their consumption. Jos de Mul[95] and John Wood[96] refer to this new role as 'metadesign' performed by what Ezio Manzini refers to as 'expert designers' in a world where "everyone can be a designer".[97]

By its very nature open design is inclusive and collaborative, and from these stem diversity and feedback loops that add resiliency to the design process. As these are all characteristics of more sustainable systems, it would seem that the open design approach coupled with a sustainable vision needs a concerted effort in developing viable business models to be an effective route for change. As this 'change' is facilitated through a more distributed form of design and manufacturing, it could hold the key to flourishing local economies. It also has the capacity for designs to be adapted to the constraints of local regions, keeping designers, producers and consumers more in tune with their local environmental and cultural conditions.

4.5 emerging business models: the circular economy

The term *circular economy* has gained a lot of momentum over the past decade as the business face of eco-effectiveness discussed in environmental strategies (Chapter 2.1). This has been largely spurred by its recognition at national policy level in China as early as 2002 and its active promotion by the Ellen MacArthur Foundation from 2012 with businesses and governments around the world. Rather than being a specific business model, the circular economy is more of an umbrella term that feeds back into a suite of economic, business, policy and design strategies.

The concept of a circular economy derives from industrial ecology, and seeks to put into practice many of the principles of cradle-to-cradle, natural capitalism, biomimicry and regenerative design. The Ellen MacArthur Foundation succinctly illustrates the C2C flow of materials in the circular economy (fig 4.27) and defines it as:

an industrial system that is restorative or regenerative by intention and design. It replaces the 'end-of-life' concept with restoration, shifts towards the use of renewable energy, eliminates the use of toxic chemicals, which impair reuse, and

aims for the elimination of waste through the superior design of materials, products, systems, and, within this, business models.[98]

Fundamentally, the circular economy asks for true systemic change through a comprehensive shift from linear to circular mindsets. In the circular system, products no longer have an 'end-of life' per se but become feedstocks for new products after their lives have been extended for as long as possible. It is the systemic embodiment of the anti-waste hierarchy we saw in figure 2.7 that requires the engagement from all players, at all levels.

One of the key attractions of the circular economy is that it speaks to business by offering a level of decoupling of environmental damage from economic growth. In theory, companies producing goods from circular loops should be able to cut costs and increase margins while reducing their environmental impacts. However, not unlike the critique of eco-efficiency measures from the 1990s (see Chapter 2.1), some critics believe that while its tacit acceptance of growth as a measure of economic success ensures take-up by business and governments, it is also a barrier to facilitating a true transition to a sustainable ecosystem.[99] This critique does not however call into question that it is a necessary step in the right direction.

Where the circular economy seems to be quite light is on the question of social sustainability – wellbeing, eco-justice and equity – apart from job and wealth creation. Walter Stahel, one of the original architects of circular economies, addresses this by including 'work by humans' as an abundant renewable resource to be promoted alongside renewable energy and materials. However, this human dimension does not appear explicitly in the policies currently being implemented and would seem at odds with the current push to replace human tasks with AI and robotics.[100]

As a unified proposal that offers clear economic gains, the circular economy has been endorsed by some big industry players and is making its way into government policy. This should create clear incentives for a shift to circular economy practices. China was the first country to take steps to integrate the term *circular economy* into its policy by defining it in legislation as early as 2002. It then introduced the Circular Economy Promotion Law in 2009, a State Council national strategy for achieving a circular economy in 2013, and has made it an important element of its five-year plans from 2006 through to 2020. Examples of this in practice are the creation of a number of eco-parks where a few thousand businesses create feedstocks for each other through their waste, such as in the production of circuit boards from recycled copper and gold.[101] Although China has a long way to go in terms of lowering their carbon emissions and improving their resource efficiency, which is five times less than OECD countries, they also

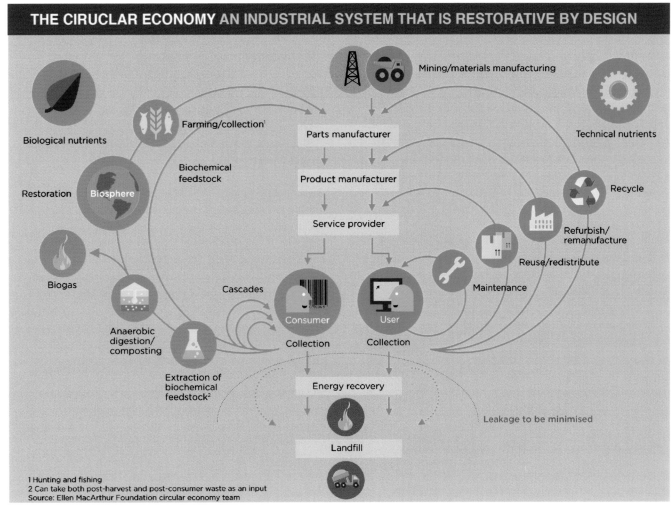

Figure 4.27 The Ellen MacArthur Foundation diagram of the Circular Economy. (source: Ellen MacArthur Foundation, Towards the Circular Economy Vol 1 2012)

demonstrate a great commitment to achieving these goals from their current baseline.[102]

Europe's extended producer responsibility regulations (EPR) first introduced in the 1990s and Japan's Basic Law to Promote the Establishment of A Recycling-oriented Society from 2000, designed to make producers responsible for recycling their waste, mark the beginnings of circular economy regulations, although on their own they have not proven to be sufficiently transformative. More recently the EU Commission adopted a Circular Economy Package and implementation Action Plan in 2019, which introduce a mix of regulations and incentives to "*retain precious resources and fully exploit all the economic value within them*". The package includes the following measures that will have a direct impact on business models and product design, including:

- extending the EU Ecodesign Directive 2009 (EuP) to promote repairability, durability and recyclability

- developing quality standards for secondary raw materials
- developing a plastics strategy to address issues of recyclability, biodegradability hazardous substances and reduction of marine litter
- revising waste legislation to increase recycling targets, promote reuse and industrial symbiosis
- creating economic incentives for 'greener products' on the market

These measures should help designers specify more sustainably by creating reliable recycled materials supply streams. It will also influence the fundamental product concept and business model by incentivising repairability and durability and more generally 'greener products'.

Fundamentally the circular economy is about integrating big-picture *systemic thinking* in how we deliver products and utility from the outset. At this is point we should remind ourselves that in the perfect world of sustainable design, strategic thinking begins first and foremost by being prepared to question a product or service as a means to deliver a certain functionality and social value. If, for a given need, the conclusion is that a product or product service system is the most appropriate, then lifecycle thinking should be integrated from the outset. While it is in fact rare to have the luxury of a blank slate, there are still many points of intervention in the process of shaping and realising a product where circular thinking can be integrated. Many of the environmental design strategies covered in Chapter 2.1 as well as better business practices and the emerging business models discussed in this chapter feed directly into realising a circular economy.

Just as the circular economy demands a change of mindset for designers, producers and consumers, it also requires new business models to support it. Many of the new emerging models that we have looked at, collaborative consumption, access over ownership, distributed production, open design and the maker-repair movements are all important contributors to the wider notion of the circular economy by helping reduce the demand for new goods. As we saw earlier, they do this by increasing the intensity of use of idle assets; lengthening product life; and in the best of cases, creating social capital and 'prosperity' by reconnecting with local and regional skills, materials and cultures.

selling performance, hybrids and take-back

In addition to the emerging business models already discussed, there are two others directly related to products that align very well with the goals of a circular economy. The first is *selling performance* whereby the product manufacturer sells the functionality that their product offers through leasing and use monitoring, which also relates to the access-over-ownership model. Unlike the one-off sales model where more sales mean more profit and the buyer takes away the product and the risk, in the performance model the manufacturer takes on the future risk. This makes it in the manufacturer's best interests to design products that excel in performance, quality and reliability, and are easily maintained, refurbished or remanufactured. This also naturally leads to rationalising the number of parts, and having common parts across product platforms. It also provides continuous opportunities to build relationships with customers.

Xerox was one of the pioneers of the performance and service model as early at the 1990s and transformed the reprographics market. Rolls Royce Engines selling flying time and service is another notable example in the B2B sector. Despite the obvious logic of this model there have also been a lot of attempts ending in failures in the consumer market, but its moment may

finally have arrived. Companies like Bundles in the Netherlands provide an IoT-enabled pay-as-you-wash (or dry) subscription service using Miele products renowned for reliability and long life.[103] Riversimple's Rasa is another good example of the usefulness of the product service model for de-risking the early adoption of new, more sustainable technologies, a hydrogen fuel cell car. By consciously 'building a car that will never be sold' they are linking company profits to the sustainability of their design – performance efficiency and reliability[104] (see fig 8.29, Rasa business model).

There are also hybrid models where the product is sold but the manufacturer continues to take responsibility for its maintenance and supply of consumables like ink cartridges and coffee capsules. As one of the earliest and most prevalent adopters of C2C systems (see fig 7.18), the office furniture market is an example which includes maintenance and take-back. A hybrid pay-for-performance model has also been introduced by car manufacturers for their batteries to encourage early adoption of EV cars by de-risking the rapid improvements in battery technology. The customer buys the car but leases the battery which can be upgraded and pays on mileage.

Product take-back is not new, but has been actively eroded since the post-war mass-consumption/production push. Deposit bottle schemes are one example that have just managed to survive and are now returning into favour. There is also a noticeable move by leading retail manufacturers like IKEA, Patagonia, Apple and Nike, to name only a few, towards a product take-back model as they realise its commercial and reputational advantages. The most basic level is taking back their own products to be either reused or recycled appropriately. The next level of offering is to recycle the take-back products into new products, sometimes paying the customer in part-exchange. The final level is to buy back and resell their used products. This is often achieved by collaborating with charities and experts in the field, like Patagonia and Eileen Fisher's partnerships with Yerdle's Recommerce (fig 4.28). All these forms of take-back business models have a significant impact on how products are conceived and designed from the outset as resources to be recovered for closed-loop recycling or resale.

one company's waste is another's food

Finally we have the symbiotic upcycling or downcycling models, where one company uses another's non-recyclable waste as the basis for their products. This model is much more prevalent between businesses and in the agricultural by-products sectors, but it is becoming more common in the consumer world. Two early trailblazers in bringing this approach to the consumer world are Remarkable (Pencil Co/UK) and Freitag (Switzerland). Remarkable understood the potential of circular thinking and the power of

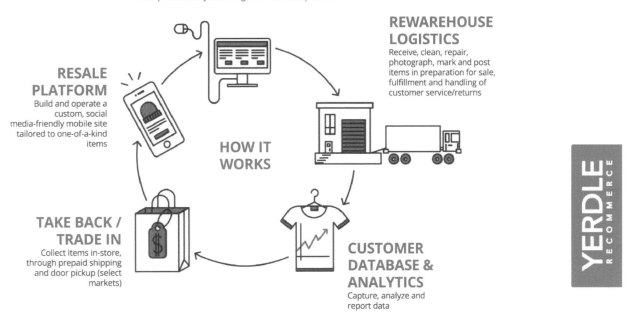

PROGRAM DESIGN, LEARNING & ITERATION
Develop the identity and design for the resale platform

REWAREHOUSE LOGISTICS
Receive, clean, repair, photograph, mark and post items in preparation for sale, fulfillment and handling of customer service/returns

RESALE PLATFORM
Build and operate a custom, social media-friendly mobile site tailored to one-of-a-kind items

HOW IT WORKS

TAKE BACK / TRADE IN
Collect items in-store, through prepaid shipping and door pickup (select markets)

CUSTOMER DATABASE & ANALYTICS
Capture, analyze and report data

YERDLE RECOMMERCE

Figure 4.28 Yerdle's Recommerce expertise supports businesses like Patagonia, REI and Eileen Fisher to offer a take-back and resale service. (courtesy ©Yerdle Recommerce)

narrative very early on. Starting in 1996 they collected used office coffee cups that would have been landfilled and transformed them into pencils and stationery for the same office workers to use.

Still earlier, in 1993 Freitag started transforming spent truck tarps, inner tubes and seatbelts into desirable bags for cycle messengers[105] and anybody else who liked the look of them,

which turned out to be quite a few people (fig. 4.29). Freitag have continued to extend their exploration of sustainable sources, ranging from developing their own biodegradable fabric and garments to collaborating with DLL, a finance company, and Smidtz Cargobull, a trailer manufacturer, to advise them on preferred colourways to increase the repurposing of tarps into their bags.[106]

Figure 4.29 Freitag's upcycling journey started in 1993 with their F13 TopCat messenger bag made of spent truck tarps. It has continued into a full range of products, including their recent Zippelin that also addresses material reduction and coping with smaller living spaces. (photos courtesy Freitag Lab AG)

Figure 4.30 Bureo's Ahi performance cruiser skateboard designed in collaboration with Carver Skateboards has a deck made from 50 ft²/5 m² of fishing nets. (courtesy Bureo Inc)

As an example of a newer player, Bureo started collecting discarded fishing nets and turning the nylon into their Minnow skateboards in 2013 in response to the 700,000 US tons of fishing gear dumped into the oceans every year. With support from Patagonia's $20 Million and Change Fund, they have gone on to establish the 'Net Positiva' collection programme operating in fishing communities in Chile to prevent nets from entering the oceans. Their product range has also expanded to include their Netplus recycled nylon pellets, sunglasses, Frisbees and a new range of performance skateboards (fig 4.30).[107]

challenges ahead

The complexity of replacing our linear system and embracing a truly circular mindset cannot be underestimated. It calls for systemic change in all aspects of how we produce and consume, and therefore how we design. It will certainly require considerable resources to be channelled into technological systems to monitor and track energy and materials through IoT and blockchain-enabled supply chains, smart logistics, reverse distribution systems and comprehensive de-manufacturing. But perhaps one of the most essential ingredients in getting the circular economy to work is collaboration. Without developing new partnerships it will be impossible for businesses and consumers to meet the challenges of a circular economy that relies on symbiosis. It should however make designing much more interesting, rewarding and diverse.

Chapter summary

1. A fundamental pillar of sustainability is an economic system that works for the environment, equity and people. Although not immediately obvious, economics and business models are very important factors affecting the ability to develop sustainable products. This makes it important for designers to understand the constraints and opportunities that different business models impose upon their design outcomes. With new values-led and entrepreneurial business models emerging, sustainably minded designers are poised to direct their creativity, skills and design thinking towards a transition to more sustainable lives.

2. Economies are the systems that we put in place to manage how resources will be used, distributed and controlled based on an agreed set of rules. From a sustainable point of view, economies are there to ensure the most equitable distribution of these resources and opportunities, while safeguarding the environment that supplies them. As they are constructed by society, they can and should

be adapted by society to reflect changing values and priorities.

3. Emerging from the Industrial Revolution, capitalism is the current dominant economic model across the world, implemented with varying degrees of regulation. As a system, it expresses value through money and requires the growth of capital to succeed. Currently, the health of an economy is measured in terms of GDP growth with the prevailing assumption that higher GDP means greater prosperity and wellbeing for all. In sustainable terms, this assumption is highly contested, with alternative indexes such as the Genuine Progress Indicator (GPI) and the Human Development Indicator (HDI) considered better measures of an economy's success in delivering sustainable prosperity and wellbeing.

4. There are three main conflicts between the form of capitalism we currently operate and sustainability. These are the lack of accountability for its social and environmental

damage known as externalities, its need for continuous growth, and its inability thus far to achieve an equitable distribution of resources, prosperity and wellbeing across national populations or between countries. Alternative economic solutions proposed to address these conflicts include decoupling, natural capitalism and steady state or de-growth economies. These all require increasing degrees of consensus on the urgency of living equitably within our planet's limits, as well as a redefinition of wellbeing and what constitutes sufficiency.

5. Since the millennium, the notion of 'business for good' has been gaining momentum. More businesses are taking responsibility for their impacts and developing ways of creating greater value through the products they sell and the lives they touch. Enlightened business leaders, entrepreneurs and NGOs are taking the lead in spearheading a shift from a *shareholder economy* to a *stakeholder economy* through the creation of social enterprises, benefit corporations, B Corps and creative hybrids of FPs and NFPs. While company type alone is not the defining element, it is a strong indicator of a business's motivations and an important factor in making sustainable products possible.

6. Regardless of business type, the most successful sustainably oriented companies share key traits. First, they are led by inspiring leaders with vision and commitment that gives the business and its staff a clear purpose beyond profit-making. Second, they embed a culture of sustainability and cooperation throughout the organisation by setting common and measurable goals. Third, they develop and share best practices to extend the reach of the value they can create through collaborations with other businesses and NGOs. Finally, they believe and invest in design and innovation as systemic tools for achieving sustainability and profitability.

7. The collaborative economy is a disruptive business model that encompasses all forms of accessing and providing goods and services between connected individuals and organisations through distributed networks. From the double lenses of sustainability and product design, its main sustainability claims lie in its ability to build social capital through P2P connections, provide a fairer distribution of economic benefits and reduce environmental impacts of consumption through higher product utilisation rates and greater longevity.

8. The collaborative consumption of durable goods has two main mechanisms for enabling more sustainable consumption: resale and redistribution markets, and access-over-ownership. Resale extends the life of products

through multiple owners and saves on the production of new items and delays the disposal of unwanted ones. Product design can contribute to these positive effects through 'well-designed' products that increase resale potential through their inbuilt quality, durability, reputation and desirability. The effect of access-over-ownership is to increase the utilisation rate of products and in some cases decrease the purchase of new products and create shifts to more sustainable behaviours. This has led to some products being redesigned to work as part of new product service systems, as in the case of car- and bicycle-sharing schemes. Both mechanisms also have the economic benefit of redistributing income for asset owners.

9. Few business models have revolutionised the world of product development as much as crowd-funding, the collaborative consumption form of investment. By giving designers direct access to capital and customers, it has enabled the realisation of a very diverse range of projects. These are delivering cultural, social and environmental benefits through a more open and participatory process. It has also propelled many product designers into the world of entrepreneurship and start-ups, either as originators or as contributors, making this an exciting time for the sustainably minded designer.

10. The maker movement is fundamentally a grassroots phenomenon made up of hackers, tinkerers, repairers and makers provoked in part by the ever-increasing frustration of being forced to accept the limitations of our current products. While the accessibility of digital manufacturing and the creation of maker spaces, accelerators, incubators and sales platforms have made this feasible, it is the strength of the maker community's support network, on- and offline, that is at the heart of the movement's success. Its influence is being felt in the design of mainstream products: manufacturers are being forced to make their products more repairable and some are emulating incubator models for rapid product innovation.

11. Open design and innovation is the hardware version of free and open software inspired by the same belief that open and collaborative innovation leads to better solutions, faster. Just as crowd-funding has completely changed the landscape of *who* can develop new designs and services, open design is probably the most radical change in *how* we design by turning the prevailing IP business model on its head. While it is still finding its way to commercially viable formats, it is showing very promising outcomes as an approach for tackling both small- and large-scale social and environmental issues through open innovation and

co-creation challenges. In open innovation scenarios, the role of product designers has the scope to expand into that of 'metadesigners', or enablers of successful participatory co-creation.

12. The concept of the circular economy stems from industrial ecology as a holistic way of integrating and managing our consumption and production in greater harmony with the environment with the longer term objective of becoming regenerative. This represents a shift from the product as a stand-alone to the integrated product service eco-system.

To succeed, it will require new systems, technologies, infrastructure and regulations but above all full participation from consumers, manufacturers, retailers, and, of course, designers. As a unified proposal that offers clear economic gains, the circular economy has been endorsed by some big industry players and is increasingly being integrated into government policy. This should ultimately be highly favourable to more sustainable product design in the coming years.

Notes

1 James, P. *et al.* (2015) *Urban Sustainability in Theory and Practice: Circles of Sustainability*, London: Routledge, p. 5.

2 Raworth, K. (2017) A Doughnut for the Anthropocene: Humanity's Compass in the 21st Century. *The Lancet Planetary Health*, May, 1(2), pp. e48–e49. doi: 10.1016/S2542-5196(17)30028-1.

3 Paraphrasing Lord Darlington's definition of a cynic in Oscar Wilde's *Lady Windermere's Fan*.

4 WEC (2016) Our Economic Model Is Broken. So How Can We Fix It? *World Economic Forum*, April [online]. Available at www.weforum.org/agenda/2016/04/our-economic-model-is-broken-so-how-can-we-fix-it/ (accessed 5 May 2016). See also Ki-Moon, B. (2012) Secretary-General's Remarks to Rio+20 Conference Ceremonial Opening Session – As Delivered [online]. Available at www.un.org/sg/en/content/sg/statement/2012-06-20/secretary-generals-remarks-rio20-conference-ceremonial-opening (accessed 2 January 2019).

5 Lasn, K. and Adbusters (2012) *Meme Wars. The Creative Destruction of Neoclassical Economics*, London: Penguin.

6 Smith, P.B. and Manfred Mann-Neef (2011) *Economics Unmasked: From Power and Greed to Compassion and the Common Good*, Totness, Devon: Green Books.

7 Chan *et al.* (2019) *Oxfam Briefing Paper: Public Good or Private Wealth*, Bambury, Oxon: Oxfam, p.12. doi 10.21201/2019.3651.

8 Dalton-Smith, A. (2010) Too Much of a Good Thing: The Relationship between Money and Happiness in a Post-industrial Society [online, 7 March]. Available at www.thesustainabilityreview.org/articles/too-much-of-a-good-thing-the-relationship-between-money-and-happiness-in-a-post-industrial-society (accessed 31 December 2018).

9 Inglehart, R., Foa, R., Peterson, C. and Welzel, C. (2008) Development, Freedom, and Rising Happiness: A Global Perspective (1981–2007). *Perspectives on Psychological Science*, 3, pp. 268 and 271. doi: 10.1111/j.1745-6924.2008.00078.x.

10 Stiglitz, J., A. Sen and J-P. Fitoussi (2009) *The Measurement of Economic Performance and Social Progress Revisited*, OFCE – Centre de Recherche en Économie de Sciences Politiques, p. 4, pt. 8 [online]. Available at www.ofce.sciences-po.fr/pdf/dtravail/WP2009-33.pdf (accessed 2 January 2019).

11 George, S. (2015) *Shadow Sovereigns: How Global Corporations Are Seizing Power*, London: Polity.

12 globaljustice.org (2016) 10 Biggest Corporations Make More Money than Most Countries in the World Combined [online, 12 September]. Available at www.globaljustice.org.uk/news/2016/sep/12/10-biggest-corporations-make-more-money-most-countries-world-combined (accessed 2 January 2019).

13 Fortune's Global 500 2018, 11 October 2018/ http://fortune.com/global500/.

14 Barro, V. (2018) *Ending Corporate Impunity. Briefing Paper*, 29 July. London: Global Justice Now.

15 IEA (2017) EA Finds CO_2 Emissions fFlat for Third Straight Year Even as Global Economy Grew [online, 17 March]. Available at www.iea/newsroom/news/2017/march/iea-finds-co2-emissions-flat-for-third-straight-year-even-as-global-economy-grew.html (accessed 5 October 2018).

16 IEA (2019) Emissions [online, March]. Available at www.iea.org/geco/emissions/ (accessed 9 April 2019).

17 IPCC (2018) *Global Warming of 1.5°C. Special Report. Summary for Policymakers*. SR1.5 UNEP/WMO. C1 [online, October]. Available at http://report.ipcc.ch/sr15/pdf/sr15_spm_final.pdf.

18 For a distinction between relative and absolute decoupling see T. Jackson (2009) *The Myth of Decoupling. Prosperity without Growth*, London: Earthscan, ch. 5.

19 Fletcher, R. and C..Rammelt (2017) De-coupling. A Fantasy of the Post-2015 Sustainability Agenda. *Globalizations*,14(3).

Available at https://doi.org/10.1080/14747731.2016.
1263077

20 Costanza, R. (1992) The Ecological Economics for
Sustainability: Investing in Natural Capital. In R. Goodland,
H.E. Daly and S. El Serafy (eds), *Population, Technology and
Lifestyle. The Transition to Sustainability*, Washington, DC, and
Covelo, CA: Island Press.

21 naturalcapitalforum.com (n.d.) What Is Natural Capital?
[online]. Available at https://naturalcapitalforum.com/
about/ (accessed 2 January 2019).

22 Hawken, P., A.L. Lovins and H. Lovins (1999) *Natural
Capitalism*, London: Earthscan, p. 5.

23 UNEP TEEB and R. Costanza *et al.* (2014) Changes in the
Global Value of Eco-system Services. In *Global Environmental
Change*, Vol. 26, London: Elsevier, pp.152–158.

24 The Natural Capital Protocol [online]. Available at https://
naturalcapitalcoalition.org/natural-capital-protocol/
(accessed 2 January 2019).

25 Jackson (2009).

26 CAASE (n.d.) Steady State Economy Definition. Center for the
Advancement of the Steady State Economy [online]. Available
at https://steadystate.org/discover/steady-state-economy-
definition/ (accessed 2 January 2019).

27 Kallis, F. (2015) The Degrowth Alternative, Great Transition
Initiative [online, February]. See also writings by Bruno
Latour, Serge Latouche, Giacomo d'Alisa.

28 See Schor, Juliet (n.d.) *Visualising a Plenitude Economy* [online
video]. Available at www.newdream.org/programs/redefining-
the-dream/plenitude. See also Schor, J. (2010) *Plenitude. The
New Economics of True Wealth*, New York: Penguin.

29 BIEN (n.d.) *Basic Income Earth Network* [online]. Available at
http://basicincome.org/ (accessed 5 October 2018).

30 Alperovitz, G. (2015) A Social Capitalism. *RSA Journal*,
CLXI(5562), Issue 2.

31 Jenkins, M. (2015) Millennials Want to Work for Employers
Committed to Values and Ethics. *Guardian Sustainable
Business, The Guardian*, 5 May [online]. Available at www.
theguardian.com/sustainable-business/2015/may/05/
millennials-employment-employers-values-ethics-jobs
(accessed 2 January 2019). See also
Deloitte (2018) Millennial Survey 2018 | Deloitte | Social
Impact, Innovation [online]. Available at https://www2.
deloitte.com/global/en/pages/about-deloitte/articles/
millennialsurvey.html (accessed 2 January 2019);
Solomon, M. (2016) You've Got Millennial Employees
All Wrong [online]. Available at www.forbes.com/sites/
micahsolomon/2016/01/26/everything-youve-heard-about-
millennial-employees-is-baloney-heres-the-truth-and-how-to-
use-it/ (accessed 2 January 2019.)

32 Amatullo, M., B. Boyer, L. Danzico and A. Shea (eds)
(2016) *LEAP Dialogues: Career Pathways in Design for Social

Innovation*, Pasadena, CA: Design Matters at Art Centre
College of Design.

33 Speaking in 1992 at the Commonwealth Club, San Francisco,
CA.

34 Porter, M. (2013) Why Business Can Be Good at Solving Social
Problems. TED talk, 7 October [online]. Available at www.
youtube.com/watch?v=0iIh5YYDR2o.

35 Although first attributed to Freer Spreckley in 1981, it is
John Elkington who popularised and made it relevant to the
wider business community in *Cannibal with Forks (*1997).

36 GRI sustainability reporting standards are continually updated
to keep up with improving practices. Available at www.
globalreporting.org/information/sustainability-reporting/
Pages/gri-standards.aspx.

37 Globescan/BSR (2017) The State of Sustainable Business
2017. Survey of Sustainable Leaders [online, July]. Available
at www.bsr.org/reports/2017_BSR_Sustainable-Business-
Survey.pdf.

38 Kiron *et al.* (2017) Corporate Sustainability at a Crossroads.
Summary Finding of the Global Executive Studies 2009–2016.
*MIT Sloan Review and Boston Consulting Group Research
Report*, May, pp.19–20.

39 Elkington, J. (2012) *The Zeronauts. Breaking the Sustainability
Barrier*, Abingdon, Oxon, and New York: Earthscan, pp. 33–34.

40 See www.netpositiveproject.org; http://there100.org;
https://apparelcoalition.org/; https://sustainablepackaging.
org/; SHINE: https://globalhealth.harvard.edu/links/
sustainability-and-health-initiative-netpositive-enterprise-
shine.

41 147 transnational corporations (TNCs) super entities
control 40% of the total wealth in the network of TNCs and
1318 own 60% of global revenues. From *New Scientist*, 19
October 2011. Available at www.newscientist.com/article/
mg21228354-500-revealed-the-capitalist-network-that-runs-
the-world/.

42 Where control is defined as family members having over 50%
of voting rights for private and 32% for public companies:
HSG (V1.2, June 2017). *Global Family Business Index* [online].
Available at http://familybusinessindex.com/ (accessed 2
January 2019).

43 UN (2012) United Nations International Year of Cooperatives
(IYC) [online]. Available at https://social.un.org/coopsyear/
get-involved.html (accessed 2 January 2019).

44 ica.coop (n.d.) Cooperative Identity, Values and Principles
[online]. Available at www.ica.coop/en/cooperatives/
cooperative-identity (accessed 2 January 2019).

45 Co-operative News (2014) View the Top 300 Co-operatives
from Around the World [online]. Available at www.thenews.
coop/49090/sector/view-top-300-co-operatives-around-
world/ (accessed 31 December 2018).

46 Developed and piloted with the Sustainable Apparel Coalition (SAC).

47 Strizke, J. (2015) President's Message, *REI 2015 Stewardship Report*, p. 3.

48 SEI (n.d.) Social Enterprise | Social Enterprise International [online]. Available at http://sei.coop/definition/ (accessed 2 January 2019).

49 Bates Wells & Braithwaite (2015) Social Enterprise in Europe. Developing Legal Systems which Support Social Enterprise Growth. European Social Enterprise Law Association [online]. Available at https://esela.eu/wp-content/uploads/2015/11/legal_mapping_publication_051015_web.pdf.

50 Anon (2014) About the SECC [online]. Available at http://secouncil.ca/index.php/about/ (accessed 2 January 2019).

51 Benefit Corporation (n.d.) International Legislation [online]. Available at http://benefitcorp.net/international-legislation (accessed 9 April 2019).

52 Anon (n.d.) Certified B Corporation [online]. Available at https://bcorporation.uk/ (accessed 27 June 2019).

53 Honeyman, R. (2014) *B Corps Handbook. How to Use Business as a Force for Good,* San Francisco, CA: Bennett-Koeler.

54 Antunes, A. (2014) *Brazil's Natura,* The Largest Cosmetics Maker In Latin America, Becomes a B Corp [online, 16 December]. Available at www.forbes.com/sites/andersonantunes/2014/12/16/brazils-natura-the-largest-cosmetics-maker-in-latin-america-becomes-a-b-corp/#5da9c3e025a2 (accessed 2 January 2019).

55 Battilana, J. *et al.* (2012) In Search of the Hybrid Ideal (SSIR) [online]. Aailable at https://ssir.org/articles/entry/in_search_of_the_hybrid_ideal (accessed 2 January 2019).

56 British Council (2016) The State of Social Enterprise in India [online]. Available at www.britishcouncil.org/sites/default/files/bc-report-ch4-india-digital_0.pdf (accessed 2 January 2019).

57 Amatullo, M. *et al.* (eds) (2016).

58 Long, A. (2014) *After Typhoon Haiyan, New Financial Products Speed Recovery for Philippines' Hardest Hit* [online, 6 May]. Available at www.mercycorps.org.uk/press-room/releases/after-typhoon-haiyan-new-financial-products-speed-recovery-philippines-hardest (accessed 2 January 2019).

59 ITV.com (2013) *Remploy's History as Specialist Disabled Employer Remembered as Final Factories Close* [online, 31 October]. Available at www.itv.com/news/2013-10-31/final-remploy-factory-closes/ (accessed 2 January 2019).

60 Chouinard, Y. and V. Stanley (2012) *The Responsible Company. What We've Learned from Patagonia's fFirst 40 Years*, Ventura, CA: Patagonia Books, pp. 102–103.

61 Rifkin, J. (2014) T*he Zero Marginal Cost Society*, New York: Palgrave Macmillan.

62 Frenken, K. and J. Schor (22/01/2017) Putting the Sharing Economy into Perspective. *Environmental and Societal Transitions*, 23, pp. 3–10. http://dx.doi.org/10.1016/j.eist.2017.01.003.

63 Botsman, R. (2013) The Sharing Economy Lacks a Shared Definition. *Fast Company*, 21 November [online]. Available at www.fastcompany.com/3022028/the-sharing-economy-lacks-a-shared-definition (accessed 3 June 2017).

64 PricewaterhouseCoopers (n.d.) UK Sharing Economy to Get £8bn Boost in 2017 [online]. Available at www.pwc.co.uk/who-we-are/regional-sites/northern-ireland/press-releases/P2P.html (accessed 2 January 2019).

65 WEF (2016) *Understanding the Sharing Economy Report*, December, Geneva: World Economic Forum. Available at www3.weforum.org/docs/WEF_Understanding_the_Sharing_Economy_report_2016.pdf.

66 OCU, Altroconsumo, Deco Proteste and Test-Achats/Test- Aankoop, Cibersomosaguas, Ouishare (22/02/2016) *Collaboration or Business? Collaborative Consumption: From Value for Users to a Society with Values.* Report by four European consumer associations, 22 February, Madrid: OCU Ediciones. Available at Collaboration or Business_ CC P2P 2016.pdf www.ocu.org/organizacion/~/media/lobbyandpressocu/images/que-hacemos/nuestras-acciones/2016/informe%20ocu%20economia%20colaborativa/informe%20ocu%20consumo%20colaborativo/collaboration%20or%20business_%20cc%20p2p%202016.pdf.

67 Martins, C.J. (2016) The Sharing Economy: A Pathway to Sustainability or a Nightmarish Form of Neoliberal Capitalism? *Ecological Economics*, 121, pp. 149–159. Elsevier BV, http://dx.doi.org/10.1016/j.ecolecon.2015.11.027.

68 Bharadwaj, M. (2014) *India's Shining Second-hand Market* [online, 21 March]. Available at www.aljazeera.com/indepth/features/2014/02/india-shining-second-hand-market-2014211947815757.html (accessed 2 January 2019).

69 Ashby, M. (2013) *Materials and the Environment,* Oxford: Butterworth Heinemann, pp. 425–427.

70 Schibsted Media Group (2017) *The Second-hand Effect Report 2017*. Oslo: Schibsted. Available at https://secondhandeffect.schibsted.com/wp-content/uploads/2017/04/PDF-Rapport_2017.pdf.

71 Fremsted, A. (2015) *Online Platforms for Exchanging and Sharing Goods*. Portland: Ecotrust and E3, 2 February.

72 WRAP (2012) Composition and Re-use Potential of Household Bulky Waste in the UK. MPD006-002 [online].Available at www.wrap.org.uk/sites/files/wrap/UK%20bulky%20waste%20summary.pdf.

73 Botsman (2013).

74 Reinvent Staff (2017) Millennials, Worried about Climate Change, Look to New Ideas and Companies for Solutions

[online, 17 May]. Available at https://medium.reinvent. net/millennials-worried-about-climate-change-look-to-the-sharing-economy-for-solutions-e188bc22aab4 (accessed 2 January 2019).

75 Himiki, C. (2017) Lessons from the Second Annual International Lending Library Symposium [online, 27 June]. Available at www.shareable.net/blog/8-lessons-from-the-second-annual-international-lending-library-symposium.

76 Owyang, J., A. Samuel and A. Grenville (2014) *Sharing is the New Buying*. VisionCritical and Crowd Companies [online]. Available at http://info.mkto.visioncritical.com/rs/visioncritical/images/sharing-new-buying-collaborative-economy.pdf (accessed 2 January 2019).

77 Böcker, L. and T. Toon Meelen (22/01/2017) Sharing for People, Planet or Profit? Analysing Motivations for Intended Sharing Economy Participation. In *Environmental and Societal Transitions*, Vol. 23, pp. 28–39, Elsevier. http://dx.doi.org/10.1016/j.eist.2016.09.004.

78 Himiki (2017).

79 Stark, K. (n.d.) Q&A with Scholar Juliet Schor on the Striking Differences between Nonprofit and For-profit Sharing Enterprises [online]. Available at www.shareable.net/blog/qa-with-scholar-juliet-schor-on-the-striking-differences-between-nonprofit-and-for-profit (accessed 2 January 2019). See also OCO *et al.* (2016).

80 Martins (2016) and Rushcoff, D. (2016) *Throwing Rocks at the Google Bus*, New York: Penguin, pp. 93–97.

81 Kessler, S. *et al.* (2015) The 'Sharing Economy' Is Dead, And We Killed It [online]. Available at www.fastcompany.com/3050775/the-sharing-economy-is-dead-and-we-killed-it (accessed 2 January 2019).

82 Penty, J. and Daan Weddenhohl, Peerby (2017) Telephone interview with Daan Weddenhohl, founder of Peerby, NL, 31 September.

83 Keller, Stefan (CEO, Ludobox AG) (2017) Email interview, 4 August.

84 Testimonial from Ludobox user 'Paula' in Stefan Keller (CEO, Ludobox AG) (2017) Email interview, 4 August.

85 Himiki (2017).

86 McKewan, C. (2013) Why It's so Hard to Build a Peer to Peer Marketplace [online, 28 March]. Available at www.ouishare.net/article/why-its-so-hard-to-build-a-peer-to-peer-marketplace (accessed 2 January 2019).

87 Calic, G. and E. Mosakowski (2016) Kicking Off Social Entrepreneurship: How A Sustainability Orientation Influences Crowdfunding Success. *Journal of Management Studies,* 53(5), pp. 738–767.

88 REconomy Project (2012) *Top 40 Platforms for Crowdfunding Social Change* [online]. Available at http://reconomy.org/top-40-platforms-for-crowdfunding-social-change/ (accessed 2 January 2019).

89 Gershenfeld, N. (2005) *FAB*, New York: Basic Books.

90 Anon (n.d.) Fab Foundation – About Fab Foundation [online]. Available at www.fabfoundation.org/index.php/about-fab-foundation/index.html (accessed 2 January 2019).

91 Stallman, R. (2016) Why Open Source Misses the Point of Free Software [online, last update 18 November]. Available at www.gnu.org/philosophy/open-source-misses-the-point.html (accessed 2 January 2019).

92 www.gnu.org/licenses/gpl-3.0.en.html (accessed 2 January 2019).

93 List of Local Motors challenges to date: LM Labs (n.d.) Discover Projects | [online]. Available at https://launchforth.io/discover/ (accessed 2 January 2019).

94 Martin (2016) Design Leaders Launch Collaborative Platform to Support SDGs [online]. Available at www.un.org/sustainabledevelopment/blog/2016/11/design-leaders-launch-collaborative-platform-to-support-sdgs/ (accessed 2 January 2019).

95 de Mul, J. (2011) Redesigning Design. In Bas van Abel *et al.*, *Open Design Now. Why Design Cannot Remain Exclusive*, Amsterdam: Bis.

96 Wood, J. (2007) *Design for Micro-Utopias*, Aldershot, Hants: Gower.

97 Manzini, E. (2015) *Design, When Everybody Designs. An Introduction to Design for Social Innovation*, Cambridge, MA: MIT Press.

98 Ellen MacArthur Foundation (2012) *Towards the Circular Economy Vol. 1: An Economic Business Rationale for an Accelerated Transition*, Cowes, UK: Ellen MacArthur Foundation, p. 8. Available at www.ellenmacarthurfoundation.org/ publications.

99 Skene, K.R. (2017) Circles, Spirals, Pyramids and Cubes: Why the Circular Economy Cannot Work. *Sustainability Science*; Springer Japan, pp. 1–14. Available at https://doi.org/10.1007/s11625-017-0443-3.

100 Stahel, W. (2017) Consumer to User. In Ken Webster (ed.), *The Circular Economy. A Wealth of Flows*, 2nd edition, Cowes, UK: Ellen MacArthur Foundation.

101 Mathews, John A., and Hao Tan (2016) Circular Economy: Lessons from China. *Nature News*, 24 March, 531(7595), p. 440. doi:10.1038/531440a.

102 Murray, A., K. Skene and K. Haynes (2015) The Circular Economy: An Interdisciplinary Exploration of the Concept and Application in a Global Context. *Journal of Business Ethics*. doi: 10.1007/s10551-015-2693-2.

103 Bundles.nl (n.d.) Miele Washing Machine, Miele Tumble Dryer and Miele Dishwasher in a Subscription [online]. Available at www.bundles.nl/en/ (accessed 2 January 2019).

104 Riversimple.com (n.d.) *How the business works* – Riversimple Hydrogen Car Company [online]. Available at www.

riversimple.com/how-the-business-works/ (accessed 25 November 2018).

105 Gemperle, O. (n.d.) The Birth of FREITAG [online]. Available at www.freitag.ch/en/about/history (accessed 2 January 2019).

106 Wills, J. (2015) DLL Finds the Value in Lorry Trailers – and Makes Some Handbags. *Guardian Sustainable Business | The Guardian*, 30 March [online]. Available at www.theguardian.com/sustainable-business/2015/apr/30/dll-finds-the-value-in-lorry-trailers-and-makes-some-handbags (accessed 2 January 2019).

107 bthechange.com (2016) How Bureo's Recycled Skateboards and Sunglasses Are Making Oceans Cleaner [online]. Available at https://bthechange.com/how-bureos-recycled-skateboards-and-sunglasses-are-making-oceans-cleaner-6b7ce2c92755 (accessed 4 January 2019).

Key texts and further reading

economy and sustainability

Dorling, Danny (2017) *The Equality Effect. Improving Life for Everyone*, Oxford: The New Internationalist Publications. *Details the damage caused by inequality, and the benefits we all derive from more equal societies.*

Goodland, Robert, Herman E. Daly and Salah El Serafy (eds) (1992) *Population, Technology and Lifestyle. The Transition to Sustainability*, Washington, DC, and Covelo, CA: Island Press. *A seminal text that laid the ecological economics ground for Rio in 1992.*

Hawken, Paul (1993, revised 2010) *The Ecology of Commerce.* (revised edition), New York: Harper Business. *Hawken's book was ground-breaking in 1993 and is even more relevant today. He argues that business is at the heart of most of our ecological disasters but also offers the best hope of remedy.*

Hawken, Paul, Amory Lovins and L. Hunter Lovins (1999) *Natural Capitalism. Creating the Next Industrial Revolution*, London: Earthscan. *Proposes natural capitalism, a system that values the world's natural capital, as a solution to the conflict between capitalism and ecology.*

Jackson, Tim (2009) *Prosperity without Growth. Economics for a Finite Planet*, London: Earthscan. *A clear account of the need to transform our economic objectives and a credible vision of the alternative no-growth model for planet and society to flourish.*

Klein, Naomi (2015) *This Changes Everything. Capitalism vs the Climate*, London: Penguin. *Clearly sets out the destruction that our current economic model is waging against life on Earth and offers a way out.*

Lasn, Kalle and Adbusters (2012) *Meme Wars. The Creative Destruction of Neoclassical Economics*, New York and London: Penguin. *Using the Adbusters mix of provocative graphics interspersed with short texts from key thinkers and contributors, this book pits neoliberal capitalism against an alternative sustainable economic vision.*

Picketty, Thomas (trans. Arthur Goldhammer) (2014) *Capital in the Twenty-first Century*, Cambridge, MA, and London: Harvard University Press. *Traces the distribution and accumulation of wealth since the beginning of capitalism showing a disturbing trend in rising inequality and offers a rebalancing solution through state intervention.*

Rawworth, Kate (2018) *Doughnut Economics. Seven Ways to Think Like a 21st-century Economist*, London: Penguin Cornerstone. *A new economic model that addresses the problems of the old and balances our needs with what the environment can sustain.*

Stieglitz, Joseph (2012) *The Price of Inequality*, New York: W.W. Norton. *Analyses the causes of inequality, its rapid growth and economic and political impacts, and offers 'another way'.*

Wilkinson, Richard and Kate Pickett (2010) *The Spirit Level. Why Equality is Better for Everyone*. London: Penguin. *Draws upon years of research data on social problems and correlates this to income distribution and level of inequality across countries and states.*

business and sustainability

Anderson, Ray (2009) *Confessions of a Radical Industrialist*, London: Random House Business Books. *Ray Anderson uses his experience of transforming Interface into a world leader of sustainable manufacturing to share the principles and vision for a new way of making and doing business.*

Chouinard, Yvon (2016) *Let My People Go Surfing. The Education of a Reluctant Businessman*, 2nd edition, New York: Penguin Books. *Chouinard's personal journey with Patagonia into what a responsible business might be like.*

Chouinard, Yvon and Vincent Stanley (2012) *The Responsible Company. What We've Learned from Patagonia's First 40 Years*, Ventura, CA: Patagonia Books. *Complete with recommendations and checklists for other businesses that may be starting out, changing course or checking their position.*

Elkington, John (1997) *Cannibals with Forks. The Triple Bottom Line of 21st Century Business*, Oxford: Capstone. *The book that established the case for a new approach to business accounting, the triple bottom line: economic prosperity, environmental quality and social justice.*

Elkington, John (2012) *The Zeronauts. Breaking the Sustainability Barrier*, Abingdon, Oxon, and New York: Earthscan Routledge. *Homage to the pioneering innovators tackling global problems of carbon, waste, toxics and poverty, and driving them to zero.*

design for new and emerging economic and business models: open, collaborative, distributed, circular

Abel, B. van, L. Evers, R. Klaasen and P. Troxler (2011) *Open Design Now. Why Design Cannot Remain Exclusive*, Amsterdam: BIS. *An early and inspiring guide to the emerging world of open design from multiple points of view, practices and case studies.*

Bakker, C., M. den Hollander, E. van HInte and Z. Zljsta (2014) *Products that Last. Product Design for Circular Business Models*, Delft: TU Delft Library. *A guide to business and design strategies for more intensive use and longer lived products.*

Gershenfeld, Neil (2005) *FAB*, Cambridge, MA: Basic Books. *The book that heralded the personal fabrication/maker space revolution.*

Grima, Joseph (curator), V. Sacchetti, A. Rajagopal and T. Shafrir (eds) (2012) *Adhkrasi/Adhocarcy. 1st Istanbul Design Biennal Catalogue*, Istanbul: Istanbul Foundation for Culture and Arts. *An exhibition that explores the transformational impacts of digital networks and open-source thinking on the way objects will be designed, look and be made.*

Hatch, Mark (2014) *The Maker Movement Manifesto. Rules for Innovation in the New World of Crafters, Hackers and Tinkerers*, New York: McGraw Hill. *Insights into the power of the maker movement to lead successful innovation through new business models.*

Leadbeater, Charles (2009) *We-think. Mass Innovation, not Mass Production*, 2nd edition, London: Profile Books. *Early book about the new possibilities of digital collaboration and creativity.*

Mau, Bruce and the Institute Without Boundaries (2004) *Massive Change*, London: Phaidon. *Part of an ongoing project, illustrating new inventions and technologies affecting the world to provoke debate about the future of design culture.*

Millstone, Carina (2017) *Frugal Value. Designing Business for a Crowded Planet*, Abingdon, Oxon: Routledge. *A re-imagining of what truly sustainable business must look like to be fit for the twenty-first century.*

Rifkin, Jeremy (2014) *The Zero Marginal Cost Society. The Internet of Things, the Collaborative Commons and the Eclipse of Capitalism*, New York: Palgrave Macmillan. *A theory of how collaborative platforms and an IoT connected world may radically change our economic systems and society.*

Schwarz, M. and D. Krabbendam (2014) *Sustainist Design Guide. How Sharing, Localism, Connectedness and Proportionality are Creating a New Agenda for Social Design*, Amsterdam: BIS Publishers.

Stahel, Watler H. (2019) *The Circular Economy*. A user's guide. Abingdon, Oxon: Routledge. *By one of the founders of the circular economy, this book sets out the framework and how to apply it to industrial production.*

Thackara, John (2015) *How to Thrive in the next Economy. Designing Tomorrow's World Today*, London: Thames & Hudson. *A book that leads by example, showing how ground-up initiatives based on restorative stewardship are meeting local needs around the world.*

Turner, F. (2008) *From Counterculture to Cyberculture. Stewart Brand, the Whole Earth Network, and the Rise of Digital Utopianism*, Chicago, IL: Chicago University Press. *The story of counterculturalists and technologists joining forces in the 1990s to reimagine computers as tools for personal liberation, building virtual and alternative communities, and exploring new social frontiers.*

Webster, Ken (2017) *The Circular Economy. A Wealth of Flows*, 2nd edition, Isle of Wight: Ellen MacArthur Foundation Publishing. *An overview of the circular economy, from principles to activation, as an opportunity to rethink the relationships between people, resources and products.*

PART 3

In practice

Part 3 turns many of the principles explored in Part 2 on their heads by looking at sustainable product design from inside existing industry practices and constraints as opposed to the ideal scenario of a blank sheet of paper. This is in recognition of the fact that most designers find themselves in this position, but that this need not stand in the way of a shift to more sustainable practices. Each chapter looks in detail at the particular sustainability issues faced by one of four sectors: packaging and consumables, electronics and digital tools, furniture, and mobility. While this does not encompass all product sectors, these four sectors were chosen specifically because the nature of their considerable environmental and social impacts lends itself most to design interventions. It covers the main trends and technologies that impact upon the sector, their biggest negative and positive effects, and the main strategies designers can employ to guide them towards more sustainable outcomes. This is fully supported by numerous and wide-ranging examples from across the globe, as well as interviews with designers who are actively pioneering change in their sectors.

CHAPTER 5

Short-use products: packaging, consumables and disposables

Ana simply adds hot water to a porridge-pot and her breakfast is ready. Tom packs a zip-locked sandwich, yoghurt tub, snack bar and juice carton for his school lunch. Sophie picks up a coffee and smoothie on her way to work. Win brings back tomyum soup from a street vendor in a bag with plastic cutlery for lunch at the office. Hinako has her regular bottle of iced tea and bento box complete with chopsticks and finger wipes for lunch with colleagues. After working late, Pat picks up a take-out burger, chips and soft drink on the way home. Studying late into the night, Shin microwaves some instant noodles in a cup to keep himself going.

Meanwhile there is an area in the middle of the Pacific bigger than France created by floating plastic waste and debris. Its scale is so shocking that citizens around the world have campaigned to have it officially recognised as a UN member country, the Trash Isles. This would force the UN's Environmental Charter to come into action: *"[for] All members [to] co-operate in a spirit of global partnership to conserve, protect and restore the health and integrity of the world's ecosystem"*.[1]

In less than two generations we have moved from a world of reuse and forethought to a world of single-use convenience and instant gratification. In this 'throw-away society' we have created, all the products that surround us have been designed to give us maximum convenience and sold to us as the obvious answer to a 'carefree modern lifestyle'. They have also been carefully designed to generate maximum psychological dependency and repeat sales. Even if we do not particularly want this lifestyle, in many instances we have little or no alternative.

So we could ask ourselves: Who really benefits from this 'convenience' and at what cost? Unlike what the adverts have been telling us, it seems that single-use, short-life, disposable products are the key ingredient of a highly lucrative business model that locks producers, consumers, designers and retailers into the consumables industry. In this chapter we will look at this sector and the enormous environmental problems it is causing against the benefits it provides and how designers can contribute

to rethinking these products and systems in sustainable terms to benefit all.

the business of convenience

From being almost non-existent before the 1950s,[2] the notion of 'short-life' disposable products has crept into all areas of our lives hand-in-hand with the development of plastics. Vance Packard clearly foresaw these developments and their motivations in *The Hidden Persuaders* (1957) and in his imaginary Cornucopia City in *The Waste Makers* (1960).

Today this trillion-dollar global industry touches every aspect of our lives emotionally and physically on a daily or even hourly basis, from food and drink to personal care, household cleaning to stationery, baby products to drugs and alcohol. Disposable and short-life product lines have also grown steadily in the medical, building, manufacturing, agricultural and office supply sectors, providing them with a lucrative new stream of steady income.

As a market, short-life products account for well over half of all consumer spending[3] and this is on course to double to $14 trillion between 2014 and 2025.[4] The biggest supplier of these products is the Consumer Packaged Goods (CPG) industry, also known as Fast Moving Consumer Goods (FMCG) and the packaging industry that supports it.[5] It encompasses some of the best-known global and regional brands in the world, including Nestlé, Pepsi, Unilever, P&G, Cadbury, Parle Agro, Godrj and Amul (India), Natura (Brasil), Yakult, Ajinomoto and Nissin (Japan), and many, many more household brands.

The sheer size and scale of the CPG and packaging sector and its negative impacts on global environments make it a natural focus for sustainably oriented systemic redesign. There is also fierce competition in this market driving the introduction of new consumer products in the USA from 3000 in 1980 to a staggering 40,000 per year in 2013 and rising every year.[6] The fact that product designers already work closely with brands in the

Figure 5.1 In 1955 *LIFE* magazine gave the new phenomenon of 'Throwaway Living' official status. They claimed that the products flying through the air, which include newly invented disposable diapers, foil pans, tablecloths, garbage bags, ashtrays and pet bowls, would save a housewife 40 hours of cleaning. (photo credit Peter Stackpole LIFE picture collection/Getty)

continuous programme of product innovation needed to maintain their market positions creates many opportunities to leverage this for more sustainable ends.

While many short-lived products once addressed basic 'needs' around food, drink and hygiene, today CPG companies have seduced their way into our everyday habits by creating 'wants' we never even imagined we had, and turning these into emotional 'needs'. It is also no secret that product designers have for a long time been instrumental in building brands by embodying their values through their physical touchpoints and experiences. This starts with a product's persuasive presence on the shelf (or

on screen) and later moves into the experience in use, which, if positive, cements a relationship with the product that leads to brand loyalty and repeat sales.

To change any of this, we need to understand the drivers that have contributed to the astounding rise of CPGs and the single-use disposable product. Four factors stand out from a sustainability point of view. The first is the development of materials and production technologies, mostly in plastics, that have made high-volume production extremely cheap while offering design flexibility, ideal for brand differentiation and a broad range of applications. This includes the introduction of the most used plastics in packaging, PET (1), HPDE (2), LDPE (4), and PP (5); the development of film and laminating technologies that have given us everything from the ubiquitous plastic bag, to film wraps, sticky tape, flexible pouches, beverage cartons, and all manner of wrappers and sleeves; the refinement of plastic moulding in the form of vacuum forming, blow moulding and injection moulding; and the invention of impact extrusion for producing high-volume thin-walled aluminium cans.

The second factor is the growth of the middle-class demographic. The rise of disposable incomes in the growing post-war middle classes became fertile ground for the introduction of a truly 'disruptive technology': throwaway products. This responded to and was also driven by a mood of liberation in which carefree convenience was a defining characteristic of modernity, before anyone really gave much thought to its consequences (fig 5.1). By the time the rampant resource and waste problem did catch up in any significant way, short-life and on-the-go products were a trillion-dollar industry firmly embedded in our lifestyles and across all retail platforms. Imagine a life without disposable pens, bottles, cans, chip bags, chocolate bar wrappers, nappies, sanitary towels, razors, rubber gloves, tapes, zip bags, shampoo bottles, deodorant cans, ear buds, foil, plastic wrap and plastic bags, not to mention your morning take-away coffee cup. Today the targets for embedding CPGs are the middle classes in emerging and developing markets growing at a rate of over 140 million per year, mostly in Asia.[7]

The third factor is the emotional hold many of these products and brands have over consumers by being an essential part of so many of our daily rituals, that provide us comfort, wellbeing and a sense of identity. These deep connections established over time are integral to many of our happiest memories, making it hard to question or change habits, let alone reject them altogether.

The final factor is simply because they can. The companies producing and selling these short-life disposable products are not yet required to take full responsibility for what happens to their goods after they have sold them on, despite Extended Producer Responsibility (EPR; see Chapter 2.4). Technically, these are externalities to their balance sheet, although some are beginning to discover that it may be costing them indirectly through loss of brand reputation.

5.1 in the balance: pros and cons of Consumer Packaged Goods (CPG)

The negative impacts of our 'throw-away' lifestyle and industry's relentless persuasion practices are well documented, but does

this mean that we can dismiss the world of CPG entirely as unsustainable? To avoid too simplistic a view of the industry and their products, we will consider the pros and cons of CPG through the three pillars of sustainability to ensure that new designs address their negative impacts without losing sight of their value.

environmental benefits

Despite their bad press, packaging and CPG do create many positives that are not always visible but deserve to be acknowledged. Beginning with food, not many people are aware that 30% of global GHGs come from food production and consumption. Of this, a staggering one-third of all food produced globally is wasted in post-harvest handling, processing, distribution or consumption phases.[8] A conservative estimate of the cost of this waste is US$400 billion annually.[9] This is a huge environmental, economic and humanitarian problem. Assuming that we could eliminate food waste in the system, we would not only reduce GHGs by a massive 10% but there would also be more than enough food for the 1 billion people who face hunger daily.

Extending the life of foods through processing and packaging innovations is one of CPG's biggest environmental and social contributions. Longlife aseptic pouches, cartons, tins, bottles and frozen food and drinks have given us access to prepared foods and seasonal staples straight from the fields all year long, improving the standard of diets and reducing domestic workloads. Packaging designs for fresh foods, meats, fish, dairy, fruit and vegetables can also significantly extend their longevity, cutting waste by as much as 75%.[10]

What people are even less aware of is that the GHG footprint of packaging is usually very small (<10%) compared to the footprint of producing its content, although to consumers it is the most visible.[11] Figure 5.2 illustrates this by comparing the GHG LCAs of two cheese products in Norway. It shows that the choice of packaging format (sliced or unsliced) has more impact than the packaging itself, by reducing food waste. This is not to say that reducing packaging is not important, but what it does point to is the fact that packaging has an important role to play in food waste reduction.

Both the food and packaging waste issues are also powerful arguments for local food production and consumption. Local networks can be more responsive, involve less intermediaries and shorter distances, so that packaging, transportation and food waste can all be reduced while boosting the local economy and strengthening social networks.

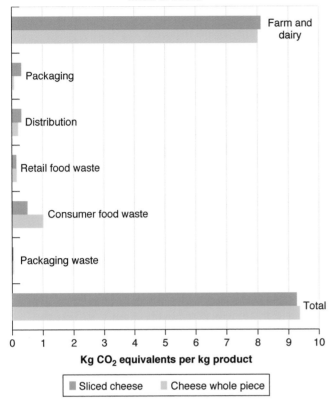

Comparison of GHG emissions for cheese packaged whole or sliced

- Farm and dairy
- Packaging
- Distribution
- Retail food waste
- Consumer food waste
- Packaging waste
- Total

Kg CO$_2$ equivalents per kg product

■ Sliced cheese ■ Cheese whole piece

Figure 5.2 By far the biggest impacts of food are in the production stage, but the design of different pack formats can directly reduce food waste and more than offset the impacts of the packaging itself. (source: Ostfold Forsning Norway 2016)

social benefits and challenges

Time-saving. Life-saving. Enabling. Liberating. These are all social benefits that can be ascribed to a number of consumables we use daily. Food packaging ensures that what we eat and drink is sterile and safe to consume. On-pack information helps us make healthier choices. Ready-to-eat foods, precooked meals and disposable diapers have decreased domestic workloads. Anti-bacterial wipes, soaps, cleaners, disposable gloves, dressings and masks protect us from the spread of infections at home, in public, in hospitals and in restaurants. Toiletries and make-up give us the tools for self-image and confidence. On-the-go food and drink enable greater mobility and opportunities for socialising and sharing.

The question is: Has the pendulum swung too far? Have 'convenience' and single-use products gone from life-saving and truly useful to wasteful and unnecessary? Do they in fact cultivate the lazier side of our nature, erode our self-discipline and self-confidence, hide from us our environmental impacts and alienate us from the origins of what we consume and our own

cultural roots? Or have they liberated the time-poor from drudgery to pursue more fulfilling activities?

Keeping in mind that social sustainability encompasses eco-justice and the strengthening of social capital, in developing and adapting new CPG products, we should consider how they contribute to these goals. And looking beyond the middle classes, how might CPG play a part in tackling some of the world's most challenging problems of social inequality?

economic benefits

Few industries personify the consumer economy better than CPG. Their business model is based on selling as many units as possible by tempting us with as many products as possible, ranging from staples to luxuries, for every second of our lives. In the words of the world's biggest brands: *"We [Nestlé Purina] make a product for every moment of every day, from morning to night, from birth to old age;"*[12] *"On any day, 2.5 billion people use Unilever products to look good, feel good and get more out of life."*[13]

The industry is remarkably successful at doing this. Global sales numbers currently exceed:

- 5 trillion plastic bags[14] and 160 billion disposable diapers yearly worldwide[15]
- 2 billion disposable razors in the USA yearly[16]
- 2 billion coffee cups per day, or over 700 billion a year[17]
- 1 million plastic drinks bottles a minute, or over half a trillion a year[18]
- and enough toilet paper to go around the planet every 2 minutes.[19]

Of these, only drinks bottles have any significant recovery and recycling rates.[20]

With these staggering numbers, it is no surprise that CPG and the packaging industry are a major employer and contributor to GDP globally. Millions of people work directly or indirectly for CPG companies in agriculture, manufacturing, R&D, engineering, innovation, marketing, retail, and of course design, to maintain the competitive edge and currency of their brands and thousands of product lines. It will also be no surprise that they have deep pockets for lobbying governments against any regulations that impact upon their bottom line and that NGOs keep a close watch on their activities.

CPG unsustainable models

Despite the CPG industry's enormous contribution to GDP and employment, this cannot entitle it to hold the planet to ransom by making profits at the expense of natural environments and resources. Average increase for shareholders across all CPG companies in the USA in the last 25 years to 2015 was 50%. Even without questioning the necessity or social value of many of their products, the CPG industry stands accused of using vast amounts of virgin renewable and non-renewable resources to produce its trillions of products while taking very little responsibility for the eye-watering amount of waste these generate. At present these are externalities to their business. Considering that the vast majority of CPG are consumed and discarded within minutes or at most months of purchase, and a high proportion end up as unrecycled waste in landfills, incinerators and oceans, it is probably high time to design a new business model and products to go with it.

Certainly the most highly publicised negative impact of consumer goods is the fate of its single-use packaging. While this is by no means the largest portion of the CPG footprint compared to the content, it is by far the most visible. Although the packaging industry uses a range of materials, including paper, board, plastic, glass and metal, it is the fate of plastic in all its forms that has reached crisis point. So much so that some countries such as France[21] and Costa Rica[22] are already phasing in bans on single-use plastics, including straws, bottles, cutlery, cups and bags, by

2020 and 2021. These are being replaced by either reusables or biologically based materials that can be composted domestically. This early action is being followed across Europe and many other cities and countries around the world.

plastics: the size of the problem

The existence of the Great Pacific Garbage Patch mentioned earlier was first officially documented in 1988. It now appears that this is only one of *five* gyres around the world that collectively equal the size of Russia.[23] Although we have known since the 1970s that we had a problem with waste plastic at sea, it is only very recently that we have known just how big a problem it is. A study in 2015 was the first to reliably estimate the amount of plastic pouring into our oceans and rivers at over 8 billion tons for 2010 alone.[24] Figure 5.3 shows the biggest sources of marine waste at the time of the report. If we could pull it all out (which we can't) this would be the equivalent of *lining up five shopping bags full of waste plastic along every foot of coastline around the world.*[25]

And because plastic does not biodegrade, the researchers also estimate that the cumulative quantity of plastic waste in the oceans will increase by 10 to 30 times by 2025 if consumption of plastic packaging continues to grow at its current rate and waste

Global ranking of top ocean-bound plastic waste contributors

Figure 5.3 The 20 largest sources of ocean plastic waste result from a combination of dense coastal populations and poorly managed or non-existent waste collection systems. (source: Jambeck *et al.*, *Science*, 2015)

Figure 5.4 From Labuan Bajo in Indonesia to Long Beach, California, will we allow more plastic waste to flow into the sea than fish by 2050? (left photo credit Don Mammoser / Shutterstock.com; right photo credit Don Mammoser / Shutterstock.com)

management practices don't improve. In the New Plastics Economy, the Ellen MacArthur Foundation predicts that by the mid-twenty-first century the oceans will contain more plastic waste than fish, ton for ton (fig 5.4). This highly quoted statistic together with the 'Blue Planet' effect have finally shocked the world into action, but will it be enough?[26]

That is the size of the problem at sea. Although less visible and emotive, the situation on land is even more concerning. The first-ever comprehensive survey of global plastics was conducted in 2017 quantifying the full extent of the problem based on data up until the end of 2015.[27] Here are some of the facts it found:

- plastic production has doubled every 15 years since 1960, growing 2.5 times faster than global GDP
- plastics are almost exclusively derived from fossil fuels; bio-based plastics are negligible
- packaging is the largest user of plastics accelerated by a global shift from reusable to single use. It accounts for 42% of non-fibre plastics, mostly PE, PP or PET (fig 5.5a)
- 50% of all plastic produced annually is discarded in less than a year (fig 5.5b)

The fate of all plastics ever produced is illustrated in figure 5.6 and summarised as follows:

- 30% are in use
- 9% are recycled (with only 10% recycled more than once)
- 12% are incinerated
- the remaining 59% of all plastics ever produced are accumulating in landfills or the natural environment

The report also found that recycling of plastics was negligible before 1980 and still is for all plastic-based clothing which

accounts for 12% of all plastics cumulatively, making packaging look good compared with the fashion industry. For non-fibre plastics, 42% of which is CPG packaging, recycling rates were better, at 18% globally, but still woefully low. The best recycling rates for non-fibre plastics as of 2015 were: Europe 30%, China 25% and the USA remaining static at 9% since 2012. At present rates, by 2050 there will be 12 billion metric tons of plastic in landfills, or 35,000 times the weight of the Empire State Building.

The authors of the study offer the following useful insights for designers:[28]

> *Gaining control of plastic waste is now such a large task that it calls for a comprehensive, global approach, that involves rethinking plastic chemistry, product design, recycling strategies, and consumer use.*
>
> Jenna Jambeck

> *We as a society need to consider whether it's worth trading off some convenience for a clean, healthy environment. For some products that are very problematic in the environment, maybe we [should] think about using different materials. Or phasing them out.*
>
> Roland Geyer

While there are a growing number of very positive collaborations between coastline communities (mostly in South East Asia) collecting shoreline plastics and defunct fishing nets and turning these in part into laptop casings (Dell), detergent and shampoo bottles (Ecover, Method, Head & Shoulders); office chair seating (Humasclae, Herman Miller); carpets (Interface); cycle seats (Trek); ink cartridges (HP), and skateboards (Bureo; see fig 4.30), removing the plastic from our oceans is already

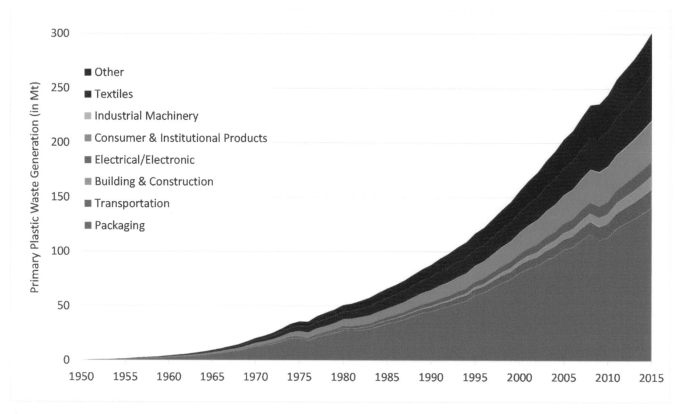

Figure 5.5a Global primary plastic waste generation by industrial sector, 1950 to 2015. (source: Geyer *et al.* 2017 *Science Advances*)

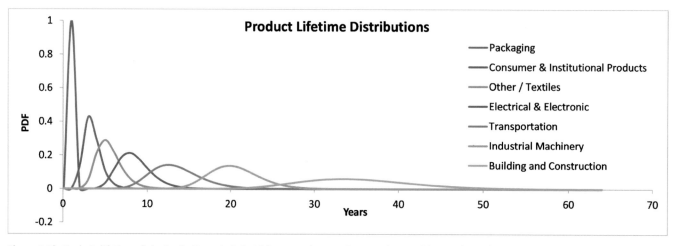

Figure 5.5b Product lifetime of plastics in the main industrial sectors. (source: Geyer *et al.* 2017 *Science Advances*)

an impossibility. That is because the plastics have deteriorated into smaller and smaller parts, creating a 'soup' covering immense areas. The time has come to design out any leakage and waste.

plastic waste: an environmental time bomb?
Apart from the unsightliness and persistence, scientists are only just beginning to understand how pervasive and serious the

effects of plastic waste are to humans and the environment. At a large scale, the slow and painful death by injury or starvation of hundreds of animal species by ingesting or become entangled in plastic debris is well documented.[29]

At a micro-scale, the picture is even more alarming because plastics do not biodegrade. Instead they accumulate over time, breaking down into smaller and smaller fragments that are easily

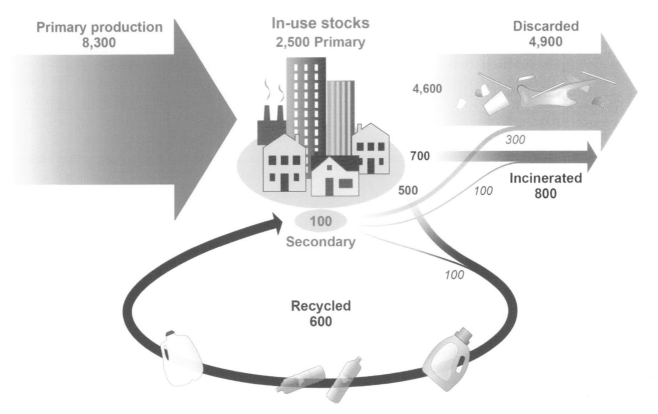

Figure 5.6 Global production, use and fate of polymer resins, synthetic fibres and additives, 1950 to 2015 (in million metric tons). (source: Geyer *et al.* 2017 *Science Advances*)

dispersed via water and land. More recently, we have discovered that they also travel by air in the form of micro-fibres shed from our clothing, carpets and upholstery, helped along by vacuuming, washing and drying. Tests around the world have found that 83% of our drinking water contains micro-fibres, with the highest incidence in the USA and Lebanon at 94%.[30]

The result is that micro-plastics are bio-accumulating across our food chain in the digestive tracks of zooplankton through to worms, fish, birds and humans. The smallest are only nano-metres, small enough to migrate through the intestinal wall and travel to the lymph nodes and other bodily organs.[31] The problem with this is that plastics are good at absorbing and releasing the chemicals that they come in contact with. These include toxic and carcinogenic substances such as persistent organic compounds (POPS), polyaromatic compounds and heavy metals, as well as the toxics that they are made from, including bisphenol A (BPA), phthalates and other plasticisers, brominated fire retardants and harmful monomers. They have also been found to carry dangerous microbes, making them new vectors in the spread of diseases.[32]

As this is being written, the effects on humans and other species of micro-plastics and especially micro-fibres is a topic of intense research and may have a serious impact on the materials we

specify and the systems to contain them. Just as micro-beads were successfully banned in many countries in 2015, industry, designers and society are being forced to take a fresh look at how plastics are used and reminded to apply the precautionary principle to our design strategies.

plastic's non-renewable footprint

Waste is not the only problem with using plastics in packaging. With over 90% of all plastics being produced from virgin fossil fuel feedstock, and accounting for over 6% of our global fossil fuel consumption, the plastics industry also has a very high carbon and non-renewable resource footprint. Putting it into perspective, it is equivalent to the whole global aviation sector's carbon footprint and is predicted to triple by 2050.[33]

Between high dependency on fossil fuels, serious environmental waste issues and new regulations banning single-use non-biodegradable plastics, there is now a big push to develop plastics from renewable sources in the form of bio-based and biodegradable plastics. But bio-plastics are not a straightforward solution and there is much debate on the pros and cons of using bio- vs. petroleum-based plastics. Some of it is caused by misunderstandings around the terminology used for the different types of bio-based plastics that Box 5.1 sets out to clarify.

Box 5.1 not all plastics are the same: understanding the difference between biodegradable and non-biodegradable bio-based and fossil fuel-based plastics

1. bio-based biodegradable plastics

These plastics are made from bio sources that can fully and safely biodegrade, although they often require industrial composting. They include cellulose acetate, thermoplastic starches, PLA, PHA and PBS. Some, like PLA, are also recyclable.

Examples: Natureworks' PLA Ingeo; Mango Materials bio-polyester and PHA made from waste methane.

2. bio-based or partly bio-based, non-biodegradable plastics

These thermoplastics are identical to their fossil fuel counterparts except that the ethylene is derived from plant sugars. They are recyclable but not biodegradable. Bio-derived PE, PP or PET versions are known as 'drop-ins', as they can be mixed in any proportion. On the other hand, thermosets, such as PU and casting resins, can never be wholly bio-based because only the main resin can be bio-based and recycling is difficult.

Examples: Coca-Cola's PlantBottle 30% PET; Ecover's Plantastic 100% HDPE.

3. fossil fuel-based biodegradable plastics

There are some fossil fuel-based plastics such as PBAT, PVA/PVOH that biodegrade fully. They often replace PE films and can also be mixed with bio-based plastics such as PLA starches.

Examples: Novamont's Origo-bi and Mater-bi; Bayer's Ecoflex and Ecovio; Wango; Ecoworld; Eastar Bio.

4. oxo-degradable fossil fuel-based plastics

These plastics are conventional polymers such as PE and PP which contain additives that accelerate their breakdown into smaller and smaller pieces with the help of oxygen and heat. Their use is controversial, as they do not biodegrade in composting or anaerobic digestion scenarios, and in the marine environment they can increase levels of micro-plastics and contaminate recycling waste streams. Based on these findings the EU is banning their use from 2021[34] and they are best avoided, as there are several fully bio-based biodegradable alternative plastics available.

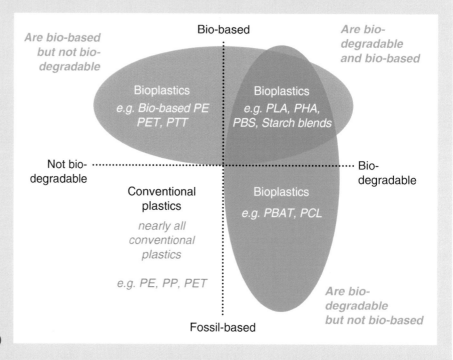

Figure 5.7 Map of bio-based, non-bio-based, biodegradable and non-biodegradable plastics. (source: European Bioplastics eV (EUBP) 2017)

Sources of bio-mass for plastics are evolving as follows:[35]

- first generation: food crops: sugar cane, corn, wheat, cassava
- second generation: non-food crops: waste vegetable oil, bagasse, corn stover, switchgrass
- third generation: bio-engineered algae, bacteria fermentation
- fourth generation: direct GHG capture: methane, CO_2

contentious issues with bio-plastics

1. in competition with food

The majority of bio-plastics are still being produced from first-generation sources, food crops, which drives up food costs and deforestation. Can this be sustainable as we move towards feeding another 2 billion people? Although it reduces plastics' CO_2 emissions, opponents argue that 100% recycling with maximum use of post-consumer waste would be a better strategy. This is leading to the push for second-, third- and fourth-generation bio-plastics made from non-food sources, with very promising GHG capture plastics being developed by companies such as Mango Plastics and PU foam alternatives for furniture and cars discussed in Chapter 7.2.

2. cross-contaminated recycling steams

Closed-loop recycling is the best way of securing the maximum recycled content back into new products. However, when biodegradable and non-biodegradable plastics are accidentally mixed, entire batches of recycling collections have to be discarded because of cross-contamination. Typical examples are non-biodegradable bags used for food waste compost collections and PLA bottles mixed with PET. Without better systems for differentiating biodegradable from non-biodegradable, they can be counterproductive. Innocent Drinks found this out when they introduced their compostable and recyclable PLA bottle in 2007, believing they were doing 'the right thing'. Instead, they had to make a quick retreat when they discovered that their PLA bottles where contaminating the PET recyclate. Undefeated, they went on to produce the world's first 100%rPET drinks bottle in 2008. (fig 5.9)

a way forward for plastics

In conclusion, bio-based and biodegradable plastics are showing promising signs of allowing us to continue enjoying many of the advantages of plastics while reducing their carbon footprint and environmental impacts. But in order for them not to create more unintended consequences than they are solving, the following will be important:

- shift away from arable land and food crops sources towards agro-waste, algae and GHG capture
- develop more bio-benign and intelligent plastics that respond to triggers for recycling and biodegrading
- design-in physical differentiators and develop global identification and traceability standards to achieve the separate bio- and techno-closed loops we need for biodegradable and non-degradable plastics to co-exist. (fig 5.8)

Figure 5.8 Biodegradable plastics need clear signalling to find their way into the right waste stream. (photo credit Voinakh/Shutterstock. com)

Figure 5.9 Innocent replaced their short-lived biodegradable PLA bottle (2007) with the first 100% rPET drinks bottle (2008). (photo credit Caziopeia)

5.2 key redesign strategies

The glaring issues surrounding plastics in CPG alone make it clear that the current design and consumption of short-use products is highly unsustainable. In this section we take a look at how a range of design strategies that address these issues are being put into practice alongside promising new materials, regulations and collaborative systems. This will broadly follow the anti-waste hierarchy that we looked at in Chapter 2 (fig 2.7), as it is particularly applicable to short-life, high-volume products.

asking the right question

Before we do this it may be helpful from a design perspective to take a moment to stand back and ask ourselves: Are short-use products the problem? Or is it that we have applied this *inappropriately* as a solution where there is no *real* need, or *irresponsibly* where there *is* a need?

If we look at nature, we find that it operates in short and long cycles that complement each other. For instance, a tree produces leaves to provide it with food through photosynthesis in the growing season and when this is over it sheds them, at which point the leaves become nutrients for the soil to feed the tree in the next season. The tree is a longlife product that grows over decades, but its leaves are effectively designed as short-use disposable products. Similarly, in designing our manmade products, we need to match the appropriate materials and technologies to the cycle length, long or short, and the infrastructure they feed into.

the anti-waste hierarchy for CPG

The beauty of the anti-waste hierarchy is that it offers us many routes for transitioning to more sustainable scenarios. Deciding which of the anti-waste strategies to apply successfully is a balance between what is most beneficial environmentally, socially acceptable, possible technologically and sufficiently profitable economically for the particular context of use. In the case of short-use products, the key question for the designer has to be: How can we meet short-use functionality differently and better? As a starting point, we need to break down the different 'needs' or justifications for current disposable products that will point the way towards the best strategy for designing different and better short-life or long-life, single or systemic alternatives:

1. temporary or transient usefulness: sales packaging and protection in transit ...
2. a means of consuming a product: containers or cartridges for everything from food, drink, toothpaste, shampoos, cosmetics, drugs, cleaners; coffee, ink ...
3. on-the-go consumption and convenience: take-out cups, meal trays, condiment sachets, cutlery, drinks bottles, travel wipes ...
4. saving cleaning time: disposable diapers, menstruation products, wipes, cleaning cloths, tableware, napkins, contact lenses ...
5. spent or worn-out: shavers, pens, tool blades and cutters, brushes, paper, pencils, lighters, batteries ...
6. hygiene, preventing spread of disease: gloves, masks, overalls, instruments, bandages ...
7. time-limited usefulness: ephemera, newspapers, magazines, tickets, cards ...

With only a few exceptions, these functions used to be and still can be delivered with non-disposables or electronically.

REFUSE: designing-out the need

At the top of the anti-waste hierarchy sits REFUSE, and in many ways this is the most challenging. As a design strategy, refuse is not about austerity or doing without. It is about gaining a deep understanding of users and the context that gives rise to a particular consumption 'need', what the negatives are around it and how these can be either bypassed, substituted or addressed differently.

In Chapter 3, we saw how dramatically the use of single use bags dropped by simply not giving them away and charging for them instead. While the trigger for this is regulation, it has led to the design and take-up of many reusable alternatives. Another good example of designing-out the problem is replacing liquid shampoo with solid bars. Until very recently clothing, body, hands and hair were all washed with solid bars until the industry persuaded us to change these for liquid versions that now mostly come in plastics bottles. Not only are we producing trillions of plastic bottles annually, we are also shipping its water content around the world, adding to GHG emissions. P&G alone produces over half a billion shampoo bottles a year for Europe.[36] Aware of this, Lush designed a range of solid shampoo bars. They estimate that each bar replaces three 250ml shampoo bottles, collectively eliminating up to 30 million bottles in five years[37] (fig 5.10).

Ecozone laundry balls are another example of addressing a need differently, by design. The balls contain mineral salts that clean clothes by producing ionised oxygen, last for over 1000 washes and are refillable. Not only are they better for the environment by eliminating the need for detergents and the cumulative packaging they come in, because they don't need a rinse cycle, they also reduce the water and energy needed and are kinder to sensitive skins (fig 5.11).

Figure 5.10 One Lush solid shampoo bar replaces three 250ml plastic bottles. (photo credit Jane Penty)

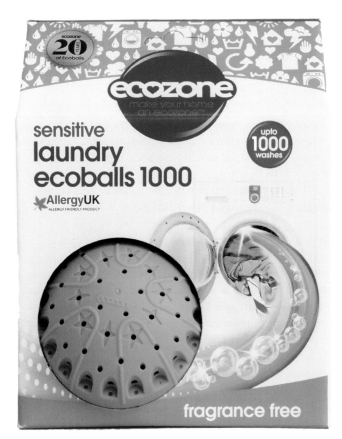

Figure 5.11 Refillable Ecozone laundry balls, first introduced in 1998, eliminate the need for detergents, bottles and rinse cycle, reducing water pollution, allergies, energy, water and material consumption. (photo credit Jane Penty)

These simple examples show that alternative designs can work. But how can change be scaled up across the system? If you enter most supermarkets in developed countries, you will see aisle upon aisle, shelf upon shelf of packaged products. Not only does

this add cost to the consumer, it also wastes a lot of material resources. While brands rely heavily on their shelf presence to sell their products and the packaging industry argues that it reduces food wastage, there are many products where this is harder to justify such as for dried foods and many long shelf life liquids.

Enter bulk foods. The concept of purchasing only the amount you needed or could afford was how all food was sold if you did not grow it yourself and is still the case in many countries around the world. In the 1970s this was revived through the alternative food movement, often through food cooperatives founded for ethical and environmental motives. The formula of selling from bulk bins spread to supermarkets, and it is still a common feature within many large stores and smaller wholefood shops across North America and Australia.[38]

Now, with a new focus on 'zero-waste' and 'zero-plastic' living, this concept is being revisited in different ways, and includes 'precycling' where users and retailers take action to anticipate and prevent waste in the first place. On a small scale, there are many new 'zero-packaging' shops opening across Europe, North America and Australia where customers bring in and fill their own containers. This low-packaging retail model presents plenty of opportunities for designing the food display and dispensing systems, as well as families of reusable containers that will work well in transit and in the kitchen. Unpackaged is an example of a company designing and producing retail refill systems that enable smaller or larger shops to transition to package-free selling (fig 5.12).

Dispensing machines are another way in which packaging is being eliminated. Across Europe, milk is now being sold via vending machines direct from the farmer into your own container, providing better incomes for producers (fig 5.13). On the other side of the globe, Algramo, an Indiegogo-funded company and Open IDEO Circular Design Challenge winner, has designed cycle-driven mobile vending machines aimed at low-income families across Chile. The machines can sell just the amount of dried or liquid goods needed at substantially reduced prices by eliminating packaging and retail space. For designers, the user interface, design language and experience of these vending machines poses an interesting challenge and opportunity.

Yet, despite being around for decades, the bulk food sales model has not yet succeeded in becoming the dominant format. It should not come as a surprise that CPG brands and retailers will resist changes that they feel threaten the basis of their lucrative business model. But could it also be that consumers are not yet ready to let go of their branded packaging either? This invites the question: Are there design solutions that could allow brands to flourish with near-zero packaging waste?

Figure 5.12 The bulk food Initiatives of the 1970s wholefood cooperatives are being revived through designs like Unpackaged's off-the-peg or bespoke retail refill systems enabling zero packaging solutions. (photo courtesy Unpackaged Innovations Ltd)

Figure 5.13 Milk dispensers in Ljubljana's central square are popular (Slovenia 2017). (photo credit Jane Penty)

Although still in testing phase, MIWA (MInimum Waste) is an example of a more radical redesign that could address this tension. They offer a whole new retail product ecology involving producers, distributors, retailers, e-retailers and consumers via connected containers. Their system consists of standardised and IoT-connected modular dispensing containers that goods are delivered in, direct to stores or e-retail warehouses. Shoppers order the product and quantity they want via an app, either instore or online. MIWA's staff then dispense the orders into smaller reusable containers ready to be picked up or delivered, eliminating primary, secondary and tertiary waste packaging in the system. Because customers can get information on the products online, instore or via the app, this lends itself to branded product sales without unnecessary packaging (fig 5.14).

In all the examples we have looked at, the new designs still address the essential need: clean clothes, clean hair, good food and profitability. What they demonstrate is that questioning *how* we meet a need can lead to simple or more complex systemic changes that effectively design-out the problem.

REUSE: changing systems and behaviours

After 'refuse', REUSE seems the natural antidote to disposability. The Lifecycle Assessment (LCA) example of the mug vs. disposable coffee cup shown in Box 2.3 demonstrated this point. Unless there is a very poor choice of material, an accidentally shortened lifespan or a highly inefficient cleaning regime, we may assume that there is a strong environmental case for substituting disposables with reusables and an energy-efficient cleaning routine.

Currently, the economic incentives for reusing and refilling are weak. From the user's point of view, there are some clear savings to be had from refilling your own water bottle, bringing your own shopping bag (where plastic bags are taxed), washing diapers and, where take-out coffee bars offer discounts, for bringing your own cup. But from the vendors' point of view, refilling is clearly not advantageous, as it reduces sales. The situation is a little better on the take-out front where food and drink are prepared on the premises, because the vendor will still make a sale when they fill a reusable. So overall across the sector, financial incentives for reuse are limited or negative compared with disposables.

From the social perspective, reusables are generally more inconvenient because you have to wash them and remember to carry them around. However, the health fears surrounding plastic additives such as BPA have proven to be quite motivating, leading to the design and take-up of many non-plastic or at least BPA-free reusables such as water bottles, coffee cups, lunch boxes and food storage containers. And yet sales of disposables have continued to rise around the world despite the availability of alternatives, and in many cases the knowledge that single-use is bad for the

Figure 5.14 MIWA's modularised bulk system works with brands and retailers right through from suppier to warehouse to shop or home. (photo courtesy MIWA Minimum Waste)

environment, hard on the budget and possibly worse for our health. Why is this?

To answer this question, we have to go back to the behaviour change theories in Chapter 3.1 to find some clues. Beginning with good choice architecture NUDGE, the first problem is that the incentives for reuse aren't aligned. We could go further and even say that the opposite is true. In the current business model, single-use is incentivised by being more convenient for buyers and sellers and financially advantageous to sellers. The second relevant NUDGE point is setting defaults to the preferred outcome. Again, the default here is the convenience of disposables. The few who reuse do so mostly from conviction rather than convenience or financial gain.

This brings us to the Value Modes system of pioneers, prospectors and settlers. Sustainable pioneers are driven by their conviction

to 'do the right thing'. They already use their own water canteens, coffee cups and tiffin boxes. They also bulk buy, wash their baby's diapers and replace the blade on their razor. Prospectors on the other hand are driven by external esteem. If having a particular reusable is seen to be cool, then they may join in, but generally convenience and speed will be stronger motivators and indicators of status. Finally, settlers will take part when reuse becomes the new normal, as we saw with plastic bags. Endorsement by their favourite brands will also be important to them.

We also know from BJ Fogg that changing habits, in this case the convenience of disposability, is hard. First there needs to be a strong motivation to buy into the change. This could be health, savings or simply reducing waste guilt. But for the behaviour change to stick, *the product and its ecosystem need to be designed for maximum convenience and satisfaction*. This means that designers must also anticipate the moments in their different stakeholders' use scenarios where their motivation will be most challenged and design-in ways to overcome these barriers.

With incentives to reuse virtually non-existent or negative in the system, behaviour change theory clearly tells us that a wonderfully designed reusable product or a few caring citizens will not be enough. Since the problem is systemic, it requires systemic solutions. On the one hand, we need regulations and industry standards to spur new collaborative business models where reuse or full take-back recycling become the most financially profitable and convenient option for all stakeholders. On the other hand, we also need reusable products to be highly practical and desirable: practical in terms of the logistics, longevity and maintenance, but also desirable by offering a much more pleasurable experience than their disposable alternatives. The right designs can help to build positive associations and overcome the psychological obstacles to changing habits. We will now look at a selection of individual products and product systems that illustrate some of the design challenges of replacing disposables and the ability of reusable designs to offer solutions to more than just environmental issues.

menstruation

The subject of female menstruation is surrounded by taboos: so much so that it has only recently been acknowledged as a social barrier in access to education and work across the globe for low-income women and girls. This is primarily because disposable menstruation products are unaffordable or unavailable to them. In India, 70% of women say they cannot afford pads and 23% of girls drop out of school after puberty, while many others around the world miss school when they have their periods.[39] One approach to solving this issue is to provide disposables through charity. However, this tends to create dependency as well as a waste problem. The alternatives are reusable designs, including washable pads and menstrual cups that are much more affordable and therefore empowering in the long term.

The design of the menstrual cup stands out as an example of using lateral rethinking to address important social and environmental issues by going to the source of the problem. Menstrual cups first appeared in the 1930s but the 'Tasette' which was marketed in the 1960s failed commercially against disposables which were being heavily pushed. With environmental concerns growing, it reappeared in a latex version, 'the Keeper', in 1987 in the USA. Finally, in 2002, the first hypoallergenic medical-grade silicone menstrual cup, the Mooncup®, was developed in the UK, and since then many design variations have been produced around the world (fig 5.15). Although it is by no means a solution for all women, there are many for whom it offers a viable alternative to disposables.

Figure 5.15 Mooncup® menstrual cup: a reusable alternative to disposables. (photo courtesy Mooncup®)

safer, cheaper, cleaner water

Water bottles are one of the most popular of all on-the-go reusables. Apart from the obvious environmental and money savings, their take-up has been spurred by health concerns around plastics, a reaction against plastic waste and more recently an increasing number of sales bans of plastic water bottles. For millennia water was carried in animal skins. Then came metal canteens made famous during the First World War, then glass to a limited extent and finally plastic in the 1980s, the most recent and controversial. The first plastic bottles made out of flexible HDPE were used for sports and outdoor pursuits from the 1980s onwards. Then came rigid polycarbonate (PC) bottles with better taste. These are still popular in their BPA-free form following its ban in Canada as a carcinogen in 2008.

While plastics have the benefit of being light, tough and cheap, as new findings continue to come to light beyond BPA about the substances they release and their effects on our health, designers have shifted to using inert materials such as stainless steel and glass. The diversity of styles, formats and features available catering to a wide range of use scenarios demonstrates that water bottles have gained the widest acceptance among

Figure 5.16 reusable water bottles continue to evolve in a wide range of materials and formats capable of addressing highly different contexts and tastes (Platypus, Bobble, Klean Kanteen, Memobottle, Eau Good). (photo courtesy Jet; Bobble; designed by Karim Rashid; Klean Kanteen; Memobottle; designed by Jesse Leeworthy; Black+Blum)

reusables and still have tremendous design possibilities (fig 5.16).

As one of the first to design a high-quality stainless steel bottle in 2004, Klean Kanteen is a good example of a B Corps in this field with a mission to address the 'insane' amounts of single-use waste. Their head of design Phil Notheis describes their design approach as one that *"factors health, safety, versatility, functionality, beauty and end of life into each product solution. If our products don't solve a problem around waste or health, we don't make them – period."*[40]

The other piece of the design jigsaw that needs to be in place for the mass uptake of reusable water bottles to happen is freely available safe water. While every town and hamlet in developed countries used to have a communal fountain or pump, these gradually disappeared with the installation of indoor plumbing. Recognising this as an obstacle to reusable bottles, the public 'fountain' is making a comeback through refill networks across cities, campuses, beaches and parks, and are now locatable through apps. The rise of shared fountains should be seen as a unique opportunity for designers to work with communities to consider what a twenty-first-century communal water point might be. Italy's network of Aqua di Sindaco, or 'Major's water', is one interpretation of this design opportunity (fig 5.17). Meanwhile, in the developing world, regular access to clean water is still a daily challenge for hundreds of millions of people as we saw in Chapter 3, Box 3.3.

coffee culture

Unlike water, the problems created by our coffee culture are not as simple as refilling from a tap. Our tastes have changed and it means that we prefer to spend our money on freshly made barista coffee rather than filling a flask at home before going out. This preference has led to a staggering 2 billion discarded single-use coffee cups worldwide every day. Despite increasing their discount for using personal cups and selling a reusable cup since 2011 at a cost of only $1, Starbucks have not managed to persuade more than 2% of their customers to bring in their reusable cup, failing to reach their 5% goal by 2015.[41] They report that:

> *We have found that bringing a mug or tumbler to a Starbucks store requires a change in personal behavior*[42] *[...] Despite these efforts, we have [also] learned that widespread behavior change is unlikely to be driven by one company alone.*[43]

The truth is that that compared to the zero responsibility and convenience of disposables, the reusable option requires effort. We either need designs that make it much easier or the incentives or penalties need to be much bigger. But making it 'easier' requires more than just a single product; it calls for a systemic approach through product service systems (PSS). This in turn involves collaboration among all the stakeholders, including governments, suppliers, owners, baristas, support services and coffee lovers. Around the world, circular economy solutions are beginning to emerge that include a combination of regulation, reusable,

Figure 5.17 Reinventing the public water fountain: ACEA water points in Rome provide free still and sparkling water as well as mobile charge points. (photo courtesy Tom Osborn 2018)

recyclable and compostable cup ecosystems alongside covetable personal designs.

In terms of regulation, France and Costa Rica are banning non-compostable disposable cups by 2020, and a tax on single-use

cups, or 'latte levy', now seems only a matter of time, as proposed legislation is waiting in the wings in many cities, states and countries. The experience of plastic bags has proven that the stick is much more effective than the carrot when it comes to reuse. Regulation would also bring a much-needed stimulus for alternative reusable designs and PSS solutions.

Although still in their early days, cup-share schemes designed to bring the convenience of disposability with the benefits of reusability are spreading rapidly. These PSSs essentially consist of a group of cafés and eateries in a locality or campus that all serve in a common reusable cup. After use, these can be dropped off in bins at participating businesses where they are collected, washed and redistributed. The main difference between schemes is whether you pay an initial deposit or membership fee and cups are tracked with bar codes or smart tags, or whether it is free. These have been used on many campuses and for events around the world but have only recently been trialled in urban contexts. German cities have taken the lead with several initiatives rolled out in 2016.[44, 45] Among these are the Freiburg Cup, Berlin's Recup and Just Swap It, Hamburg's Refill-it!, as well as Copenhagen's Coffee Collective, Perth's Go2cup and London's CupClub.

The design and material specification of the cups used for these schemes is another important consideration. Generally, the designs for the cups, lids and sleeves are very simple and generic to keep costs down, but they have taken different routes in material selection. Some schemes have opted for a recycled and recyclable approach using PP for cup and lid with a life of up to 500 dishwasher cycles. Others have favoured bio-based material composites using bamboo or lignin fibre mixed with bio-based resins that will biodegrade in industrial composters but have shorter lives. Up until this point, if the cups remain within the system, then both routes lead to circular solutions (fig 5.18). However, the lids and sleeves for the bio-based cups

Figure 5.18 Three levels of coffee cup product-service ecosystems: a. Coffee Collective (Copenhagen) sells customers their reusable compostable take-out Ecocoffeecup®, takes back the dirty one and refills in a clean one; b. Just Swap It (Berlin) supplies reusable compostable bamboo cups to cafés and events cup schemes; c. CupClub (London) offers a cups-as-service model providing cafés with clean scanable cups and customer drop-off points. (photos courtesy Jane Penty / cup courtesy Coffee Collective); ©JUST SWAP IT. www.justswapit.de; www.CupClub.com)

are often silicone, which is not biodegradable and rarely recycled unless in a closed-loop system. In recognition of this fact one manufacturer, Ecoffeecup®, has introduced a free take-back service to recycle the silicone lids and sleeves.

As with water bottles, one size does not fit all, so designing reusable cups to suit different tastes and use scenarios is also a very important factor in increasing reusable take-up. One company that has helped raise the profile of personal coffee cups to satisfy coffee aficionados in Australia and beyond is KeepCup. The interview with Cobalt Design (Box 5.2) explores some of the practical challenges of designing desirable products for behaviour change.

food on-the-go

In seeking inspiration for alternatives to our disposable culture, it is good to look back as well as forward. For over 100 years, Mumbai's Dabbawalas have successfully delivered millions of lunches every day to workers either made at home or in restaurants, as part of Mumbai's Tiffin Box system. Incredibly, they have an error rate of fewer than 1 in 6 million.[46] Not only are Dabbawalas and their system clever, so is the design of the tiffin boxes. These stacking metal tins are a durable, effective, portable, and fully reusable and recyclable design (fig 5.19). The whole system is an exemplar of a sustainable PSS based on human and social ingenuity, and bottom-up social entrepreneurship that new higher tech alternatives have failed to match.[47] The tiffin boxes also serve as inspiration for many alternative plastic-free reusable lunch containers by companies like Green Essentials (Australia) and Blum+Black (UK) (fig 5.20).

Although school children and workers are no strangers to lunch boxes, purchasing food away from home has been on the rise for many decades. Even in workplace and campus canteens, food is often served in disposables. One of the barriers to using personal reusables is food hygiene standards which only allow food to be served in containers that have been professionally sanitised. There are now a growing number of reusable to-go schemes that get around this barrier and work on an open or subscription basis on campuses and businesses.

Preserve's 2 Go and GET's Eco-takeout are two examples of reusable to-go container designs made of PP (no. 5) and in Preserve's case also 100% recycled with a full take-back service. However, these reusable containers can only work if they are part of well-designed PSS schemes where the boxes are returned and commercially sanitised (fig 5.21). One of the most ambitious is the GO Box scheme started in Portland, Oregon, now also in San Francisco, where users pay a subscription to have food from street vendors and local eateries served in a returnable GO Box (fig 5.22). Other approaches include Ozzi's

Figure 5.19 Dabbawalas in Mumbai. Not only are tiffin boxes clever product design but the Dabbawala system is an exemplar of human ingenuity and base of pyramid entrepreneurship. (photo credit Joe Sachs)

Figure 5.20 Blum+Black's 3-in-1 plastic-free stainless lunch box, oven dish and storage container. (photo courtesy Black+Blum)

Box 5.2 interview with Steve Martinuzzo on the design of KeepCup[48]

Steve Martinuzzo is co-founder of Cobalt Design, a product design consultancy in Melbourne that helps clients turn 'good ideas' into 'successful products'. In 2007 Abigail and Jamie Forsyth, owners of a small chain of cafés in Melbourne, approached Cobalt to design a reusable coffee cup. Along with expert branding and marketing input and a lot of determination, the first KeepCup went on sale in 2009 in Australia, sparking a new global product category for reusable espresso coffee cups.

JP. What brief did you start with and where did your research and insights take the design?

SM. Abigail and Jamie came to us asking for 'a plastic cup with a lid' that customers could buy and reuse for their regular coffees. At that point there was simply no alternative to disposable take-away cups, so in that sense we had a 'greenfield' opportunity.

We started by looking at what really happens from both the customer's and barista's point of view. That involved spending time in cafés, watching each step, to build a detailed understanding of user insights.

Early on we recognised that if people brought in their own cups there would be hygiene and ownership concerns. This insight led to KeepCup's signature-coloured bands and lids as a means to differentiate and personalise your cup.

Another conclusion from these observations was that it needed to look *similar but not the same* as a disposable cup. That led to introducing the subtle curve on the KeepCup that was also a nod to the classic cappuccino cup. And because you can't put a curve in a paper cup, it was just enough to say 'this is not a paper cup'.

We also wanted the experience of drinking from it to be better than from a disposable or mug-style cup. That meant avoiding the utilitarian look and feel of a disposable lid, and having the option of drinking from the rim without your lips brushing against mechanical screw threads.

From the café owner's point of view, we needed a product that cafés would be happy to promote, because initially that was seen as a prime channel to market. And for baristas, the cup had to fit under the coffee machine's group heads.

JP. Changing habitual behaviours is not easy. How did you deal with some of the obstacles to using a reusable cup on a regular basis?

SM. This was our biggest challenge and in the end, our greatest sense of achievement. Not diminishing the craft, but engineering a plastic cup and lid is well within a competent designer's skillset. But designing something that would change embedded habitual precedents was always going to require deeper empathy. We had to consider the cultural, emotional and functional barriers to regularly using a KeepCup. Our main approach was to add value to the experience, i.e. *I know I can have a take-away but if I*

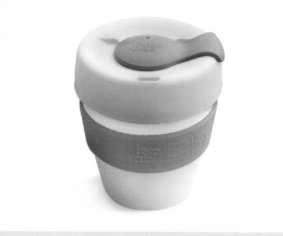

Figure 5.21a The original KeepCup. (photo courtesy Cobalt Design)

bring my KeepCup I'll feel better, and it's a nicer experience. We realised we needed to create an emotional connection to the cup as well as to the cause so that people would feel proud, but not self-conscious of their KeepCup. This linked back to the cup's form and colour choices, allowing owners to project their own personality rather than looking overtly 'green'.

In terms of the practical barriers, we worked through the whole user experience and designed the cup to address each scenario. Right from remembering to take it before going to a café, handing it to the barista and making sure their lid and cup come back correctly, to walking with a full cup to their workplace, drinking and enjoying their coffee, and then taking the cup back home to wash.

Figure 5.21b The later glass 'barista' KeepCup design. (photo courtesy Cobalt Design)

JP. I'm sure that there were many technical challenges in keeping hold of your design aesthetic while having a product that really worked. Can you tell us a little about these?

SM. You need to remember that in 2008 this was a new, unproven product. So the biggest technical challenge for KeepCup 1.0 was trying to get it into production on a budget that the client and product could support. Again, this challenge needed a multi-pronged solution. First, we designed the parts to suit simple open-and-shut tools which was tricky, as sealing and 'simple' functionality required some complex geometries and undercuts in the design.

Next, we needed to find the right supplier. In the end we recommended a local Melbourne moulder. Being local meant we could resolve teething issues easily, and the production process could keep up with the almost infinite number of colour and model variations which KeepCup pioneered. If production had gone offshore, these benefits would simply not have happened.

JP. KeepCup have now sold over 5 million products, but there are still billions of cups discarded every day. Do you think design can shift behaviours?

SM. That's the most satisfying part of working with KeepCup – it *is* changing behaviours, although there has to be a lot more of it. Even though as a designer you'd like to think that the design made all the difference, the reality is that it's also the branding, marketing, and a good dose of the right timing that have helped make KeepCup a success.

JP. Finally, in terms of the bigger picture across your practice, do you have these kinds of conversations with your clients?

SM. Thankfully the position is shifting, but historically for most of our clients sustainability was seen as 'nice-to-have' rather than a core driver. However, this is quickly changing, and I think the next generation of clients will include more and more people who genuinely care about products that reduce rather than add to the problems of waste, excess and social exclusion. This will shift the centre 'mainstream' into realising that they must deliver products with much better sustainability outcomes. This is when we will have those conversations and help these clients lift the bar.

And this is where KeepCup has been a much-valued exception. They came to us with 'the big sustainable idea' of designing a reusable cup for the coffee culture. Our job then was to make sure people *wanted* it and that it absolutely *works*.

Eco-Takeouts®

1. TAKE
users check out
a container

JOIN THE MOVEMENT

REUSABLE TO-GO CONTAINERS

3. RETURN
the empty container
for sanitizing

2. FILL
with their
favorite food

Figure 5.22 Being robust, stackable, single-piece, and having a secure closure and seal are important design details of Eco-take-outs, but they can only work with a well-designed PSS scheme. (source: G.E.T. Enterprises)

'reverse-vending' machines that act as collection points for reusable food containers on campuses[49] and Preserve's recycled Shareware Packs aimed at community events. All these, along with GoodToGo's imaginative adaptation of mason jars for cold drinks in Tainan, Taiwan,[50] are some of the very many ways that convenient reusables are being creatively 'reinvented' to wean us off on-the-go disposables.

Finally, with the growing crisis caused by one-way plastic waste, deposit schemes for reusing and recycling bottles are being reintroduced through regulation in a number of countries in Europe, and US and Australian states. As we saw in Chapter 2.4, with only a few exceptions – namely Denmark, Sweden, Norway, Germany, Canada and some US states – deposit schemes had all but disappeared by the 1990s. This was thanks to years of successful lobbying against them by the big drinks companies, despite deposit capture rates being above 90%, *twice* as high as for curbside collection.[51] Typically glass bottles can be refilled up to 50 times and plastic bottles 15 times. Not only do these schemes save taxpayers millions by reducing litter; figure 5.24 shows that deposit refillable glass and plastic have nearly half the CO_2 footprint of single-use bottles and two-thirds that of recycled PET bottles. This is without accounting for the environmental consequences of single-use litter.[52]

It is clear from all these examples that we are only just at the beginning of a return to reuse. As experience of designing and running new circular take-out ecosystems grows and is shared, the systems and design features will increasingly be refined and adapted to suit the particular circumstances of different localities, until one day their normality will have us wondering how it could ever be any different.

Figure 5.23 GO Box users enter a vendor code, show the app at a food stall or café, have their food served in a GO Box, and return it to a nearby drop-box. These are collected, commercially washed and returned to the vendors by bike. (photo courtesy Laura Weiss, GO Box)

REDUCE or REPLACE: beyond lightweighting

The concept of REDUCE can be and is interpreted in different ways. It can mean producing less and consuming less in real terms. However, most CPG businesses would consider this path suicidal, and instead they most commonly interpret it as doing more with less, or being 'less bad'. This is the eco-efficiency model we looked at in Chapter 2 which aims to reduce our impacts per functional unit – energy and resource use – while still increasing profits by selling more units. However, with the growth of middle-class markets in emerging economies, it will take quite a lot of efficiency gains to just stand still.

Design can push this much further by adding value and profitability with the same or fewer resources, effectively decoupling financial gain from environmental damage. Using resources efficiently will always be good practice and working within tight constraints leads to inventiveness. And so, at its most basic, 'reduce' is doing the same thing more efficiently, but at its most creative it means rethinking how and what we consume to deliver better things and experiences with less, to generate more value.

lightweighting, regulations and unintended consequences

The most popular strategy for 'reducing' CPG packaging impacts has been lightweighting. Lighter packages mean less material, less energy in production and transportation and less waste. Besides the cost savings, this has also been driven by Extended Producer Responsibility (EPR) regulation for packaging that we looked at in Chapter 2.4. The concept of EPR is that producers become responsible for the waste their packaging creates. Practically, they do this by contributing to the costs of collection and recycling services *based on the total weight of packaging sold*. It is quite easy to see how this has led to widespread substitution of glass, metal and card with plastics and composite laminates, especially for liquids. This serves as a good illustration of how regulation, in this case ERP, intended to reduce waste, has had the *unintended consequence* of contributing to the plastic waste crisis.

While lightweighting has undoubtedly led to lowering packaging's overall footprint, it is primarily driven by a single criterion: carbon emissions. While in some design sectors like air travel this may be top of the agenda, as we see for Virgin's on-board food service in Box 8.2, applying the single criterion of carbon emissions across the board more generally makes the choices facing packaging designers sometimes difficult. While a plastic pack is lighter and may have a smaller carbon footprint, if is comes from virgin non-renewable materials and cannot or is very unlikely to be recycled and could end up leaking into the environment, then a slightly bigger carbon footprint may be a better choice. Therefore lighter

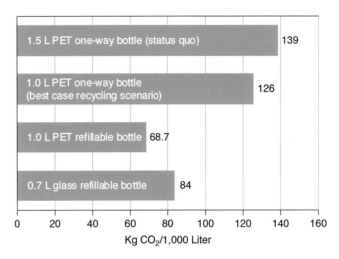

Figure 5.24 Annual CO_2 emissions for deposit scheme refillables vs. recycled single-use water bottles. (source: LCA from German Environmental Protection Agency IFEU)

Figure 5.25 Yeo Valley pot being 'unzipped' ready for recycling. The simple act of involving their customers in the recycling process raises awareness and creates a personal connection with the brand's values. (photo credit Jet)

Figure 5.26 Dissolvable solids: JAWS (just add water system) demonstrates how rethinking the product to eliminate the need for plastic bottles and transporting water can radically reduce impacts without compromising quality. (photo courtesy JAWS Canberra Corp)

may not always be better if we factor in its total environmental and economic costs.

For designers, the freedom to choose the material that best expresses the product and brand's ethos through its aesthetic qualities, functionality and overall environmental impacts is important. So rather than applying lightweighting as a hard-and-fast rule, they should instead design with the bigger product ecosystem in mind and aim to balance the different factors.

An example of a packaging design format that acknowledges this tension is Yeo Valley's yoghurt pot designed in 2001 that has since been replicated by many other brands. They needed a liquid resistant container but equally recognised that plastic pots were not being fully recycled. Keen to contribute to as little unrecycled, non-renewable waste as possible, they combined the thinnest possible inner plastic PP container with a recycled paper sleeve

for stiffness. When the pot is finished, the user unzips the sleeve to separate for recycling, connecting them to the brand's values (fig 5.25).

Taking a more holistic view, we could say that having a lighter bottle of water or handsoap actually misses the point. Why *are* we shipping water or liquid handsoap around in the first place? Equally, reminding ourselves that the footprint of packaging is very small compared to the content it delivers, designing more efficient packaging for unsustainable products does not make them sustainable.

This thinking leads to more radical interpretations of 'reduce' where the product content is redesigned to lessen or eliminate the need to package and ship water. Reducing water content is not a new concept – Campbell's has been selling concentrated soups for decades, halving their packaging and transportation impact. More recently there are some products that have gone all the way by removing water altogether, as we saw with Lush's solid shampoos. Isotonic tablets that you can pop into your sports bottle rather than buying a sports drink is one more example. Others are cleaning products like JAWS (Just Add Water System) (2011, US), Conserve and Splosh (2013) that sell dry concentrated tablets for their customers to dissolve either in their own spray bottles or ones supplied with their starter kit (fig 5.26).

The rise of e-commerce is another phenomenon creating big increases in waste packaging from the extra layers of secondary shipment packaging. Before e-commerce, packaging was an essential tool to sell the product on-shelf, keep it tamper proof and get it safely home. Now, with e-commerce, the online photographs, videos and product information sell the product, so much of this packaging is redundant. Using sustainability as a catalyst and its position as leader in online sales and distribution, Amazon has eliminated a whole layer of unnecessary and unrecyclable packaging through its Frustration Free Packaging (FFP) code. Not only has this increased recyclability, it has reduced waste, time, cost and customer frustration in unpacking. This is a clear win-win-win and a remarkable example of the power of systems rethinking. Amazon's FFP consists of the following simple rules:

- no clamshells
- no twist ties
- ships in own container
- right size
- recyclable

RECYCLE: better endings and new beginnings

Eventually, almost all manmade products come to the end of their useful life, beyond reuse, repair or remanufacture. In the case of

CPGs this usually happens within less than 12 months and often within seconds. At this point, the product has become a valuable material and energy store, and recycling is the best outcome for it. Trying to keep as much of this already processed material and embodied energy in the appropriate techno- or bio-system is the basis of the circular economy and C2C thinking that we saw in Chapter 2.2 and Chapter 4.5.

designing and specifying for CPG: materials, formats, scenarios and opportunities

The recyclability of a product is largely fixed by the choice of materials, its pack format and the context in which it is used and discarded. However, because the CPG market operates on such low margins, designers often have to make trade-offs between the most brand-appropriate format, the best environmental solution, and costs. With most packaging being an optimised compromise of these factors, it is important to be conversant with *actual* on-the-ground and *future* end-of-life scenarios for alternative materials and pack formats in order to make the best choices.

1. materials

Globally, paper and cardboard are the most-used packaging material by weight and value followed by flexible plastics (bags, pouches, films), rigid plastics, glass, metal and wood. However, in terms of number of units sold, flexible plastics have the biggest share, and together, rigid and flexible plastics account for the highest value.[53]

When we look at packaging materials used by weight, in Europe, paper and card account for 41%, plastics and glass 19% each, wood 16% and metal 6%. But when we look at recycling rates this is reversed, with glass at 83%, metal 69%, paper and card at 68% and plastic only 32%, *less than half of all the other main materials*.[54] Still worse, this is the highest regional rate in the world, with global plastic packaging recycling a dismal 18%.[55] This reinforces what we saw earlier. Despite being theoretically 'recyclable', thermoplastics stand out as the most problematic high-volume material to capture, separate and reprocess into a like-quality material. This is largely due to the multitude of formats and formulations, and the lack of incentivisation for a viable recycled plastics market.

glass

For short-life CPG products, metal and glass have high capture rates and stand out as the most infinitely recyclable. In addition, because glass is inert, it is the safest packaging for food and drink. However, in the drive to reduce carbon footprint and where shattering poses a danger, it has been heavily replaced with plastic, especially for drinks and toiletries, More recently, fears of chemical leaching from plastics and the return of reuse deposit

Figure 5.27 Mylkman is reviving doorstep milk deliveries in London, but this time around of the vegan variety. (photo courtesy Mylkman)

schemes is giving it new relevance. Glass can also communicate quality and timelessness, making it ideal for high-value packaging and for products produced and consumed relatively locally where carbon transport impacts are not significant. This can be seen in the return of some local milk deliveries we look at in Chapter 8.2, including new vegan versions such as Mylkman in London (fig 5.27).

aluminium

Aluminium is not only strong and light, but the energy input for recycling it is nine times less than for virgin stock (see fig 2.8). Therefore it is one of the most important packaging materials to capture for closed-loop recycling. This also means that formats that are easily recycled and have high return rates such as cans on deposit schemes, are the most appropriate for aluminium. On the other hand, aluminium used in thin foils, plastic laminates, and small separate parts such as those used for coffee capsules, chip bags, sealing lids, drink carton liners and pouches are almost impossible to capture and recover. Unless their functionality is irreplaceable, specifying formats with aluminium composites is best avoided. The aluminium coffee capsule format introduced by Nespresso is a glaring example of a product designed with no thought to recycling and much thought to repeat sales and convenience over responsibility. Fortunately, there are now competitor compostable versions and recycling schemes available. On the other hand, the redesign of the drinks can pull-tab with a stay-on version is a good example of how a small change can not only save millions of tons of aluminium but also the loss of lives from accidentally ingesting them.[56]

paper and cardboard

Despite being very traditional, paper and cardboard stand out as the most fully renewable and versatile materials for packaging and short-life products with universally high recycling rates. However, as virgin fibre can only be reprocessed between five to seven times because the fibres shorten and lose strength with each cycle, they are gradually downcycled or cascaded for less demanding uses. Hence virgin paper that starts off as office paper or prime beverage cartons is later turned into notepads, toilet paper and newsprint, while structural cardboard boxes later become shoe boxes, cereal boxes, moulded pulp and so on, after which point they can be simply composted.

In specifying card or paper products, the main pointers to ensure minimum environmental damage are:

- maximise recycled content for the performance required
- ensure 100% sustainable sourcing through certification such as FSC and PEFC for wood derivatives
- use non-chlorine bleach
- avoid coatings that make it unrecyclable such as non-biodegradable plastics, metallics and certain inks

While the most commonly used fibre for paper pulp is tree cellulose, consider specifying fibres from bamboo and high-volume agricultural by-products such as bagasse and different types of straw that have much lower footprints. Appropriate uses of these fibres are moulded biodegradable take-out food containers and other disposable dishes, especially for events and festivals where bio-composting can be controlled. Wasara's disposable tableware is an excellent example of how design can transform low-value, low-impact materials, such as bagasse and bamboo fibres, into high-value products that embody classic and timeless Japanese aesthetic values (fig 5.28).

Meanwhile, promising strides are being made in the development of pulp-based, compostable and recyclable materials that can hold liquids. An intermediate step towards this goal is Ecologic's (USA) packaging design based on a thermoformed pulp body with a removable recyclable plastic liner and pump.[57] This has been successfully used for L'Oreal's Seed Phytonutrients range and Seventh Generation's 4X laundry liquid, both launched in 2018 (fig 5.29). ecoXpak (Denmark) has taken the challenge a step further with its Green Fiber Bottle, a plastic-free alternative for carbonated drinks, designed with support from Carlsberg and packaging materials innovators BillarudKorsnäs (fig 5.30). Choose Water has also recently released their prototype of a plastic-free bottle with a pulp exterior and biodegradable waterproof structural liner made of biological by-products.

All these examples show that we are just at the cusp of a wave of design and production innovation that is pushing the boundaries of what is possible with moulded fibres. Not only will this help reduce our dependency on plastics, it will also open the door for designers to create new visual languages for the everyday.

plastics

As recycling figures demonstrate, plastics and plastic laminates are one of the most problematic materials to capture and recycle. Currently the most universally recycled are PET, HDPE and PP bottles. The New Plastics Economy estimates that 30% of plastic packaging is not recycled because it is either too small to capture, made of non-standard plastics or multi-material, or contaminated with food. In figure 5.31 they make clear recommendations on

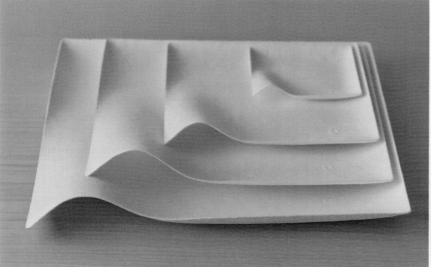
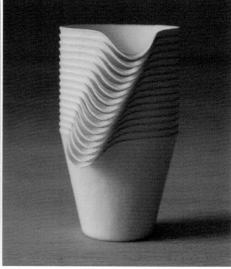

Figure 5.28 By instilling a sense of craftsmanship, WASARA tableware transforms low-impact materials into high-value products. (photo courtesy WASARA)

Figure 5.29 Ecologic has developed America's first moulded fibre bottles. The main structure is thermoformed fibre from recycled cardboard with an internal pouch and closure made of PE that uses 70% less plastic. (left photo credit Jane Penty; right render Ecologic packaging)

design steps to increase their capture and reduce the costs of recyclability.

The 5+Gyres *Better Alterative Now BAN list 2.0* report names the 20 most frequent products found in American coastlines.[58] These provide an excellent starting point of products that need to be

redesigned *today*. The EU has also announced a ban of non-degradable versions of the ten single-use plastic products and fishing gear that account for 70% of marine litter in Europe. This includes banning plastic cotton buds, cutlery, plates, straws, stir-sticks and balloon sticks, while drinks bottles will have to have caps attached and be part of deposit-return schemes, and the use of disposable food containers and drink cups will be vastly reduced.[59]

As we saw earlier, one approach to reducing the environmental problem of plastics has been the development of biodegradable bio-plastics, further incentivised by new bans on non-compostables (see Box 5.1). However, designers should take care when introducing new materials that there is infrastructure in place to match, or these materials may simply be adding to the problem in a different way. There are also promising signs that some of the enormous challenges facing plastic recycling may be lessened in the future through the development of chemical markers and trackers, reversible adhesives that will separate laminated layers,[60] and bacterial enzymes such as PETase that digest plastics, back into its original building blocks.[61]

disappearing problems: inventing benign, dissolvable and edible materials

The idea of packaging that simply disappears without any harmful effects is also gaining momentum. Thanks to the development of new materials that are dissolvable or edible, this is becoming much more plausible as an alternative to current plastics for some applications. In 2012 P&G popularised the use of dissolving plastics when it introduced dissolvable sachets for dishwasher tabs. This convenient format is now used across 70% of the market.

Figure 5.30 ecoXpac's Green Fiber Bottle is a fully biodegradable bottle thermoformed from pulp with a clay additive and is designed as an alternative for carbonated drinks. (courtesy ecoXpac)

30% of plastic packaging needs fundamental redesign before it can be reused or recycled

SMALL-FORMAT Lids, tear-offs, sweet wraps, sachets & generally all items smaller than 40 – 70mm

MULTI-MATERIAL Packaging with inseparable layers of different materials

>50% of plastic packaging (by no. of items)
>30% of plastic packaging (by weight)

UNCOMMON MATERIALS Uncommon plastic packaging materials like PVC, EPS, PS

NUTRIENT-CONTAMINATED Coffee capsules, organic waste bags, takeaway food packaging

Improvements in plastic packaging design would reduce cost of recycling

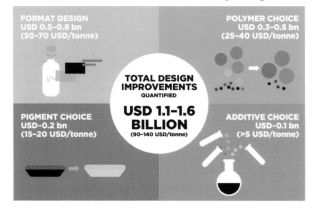

FORMAT DESIGN USD 0.5–0.8 bn (50–70 USD/tonne)

POLYMER CHOICE USD 0.3–0.5 bn (25–40 USD/tonne)

TOTAL DESIGN IMPROVEMENTS QUANTIFIED
USD 1.1–1.6 BILLION (90–140 USD/tonne)

PIGMENT CHOICE USD–0.2 bn (15–20 USD/tonne)

ADDITIVE CHOICE USD–0.1 bn (>5 USD/tonne)

NEW PLASTICS ECONOMY

ELLEN MACARTHUR FOUNDATION

Figure 5.31 World Economic Forum and Ellen MacArthur Foundation. (source: The New Plastics Economy – Catalysing action 2017, www.newplasticseconomy.org)

Other applications include dissolvable and edible films such as Monosol's Vivos films that allow convenient serving portion packs for porridge, spice mixes, hot drinks, etc. On a more radical tack, Skipping Rocks Lab (UK) caught the world's imagination in 2014 with Ooho, their alternative to water bottles. These spherical liquid pods made from a seaweed base dissolve when you pop them in your mouth. They are now extending this principle to challenge the billions of plastic condiment sachets discarded daily with Delta, their edible, dissolvable sachets for on-the-go eateries (fig 5.32).

In Indonesia, one of the countries with the worst plastic pollution in the world, Avani is producing a range of biodegradable disposables, including bags made from cassava that dissolve in water. Another Indonesian company, Evoware, has developed an edible biodegradable material from seaweed and damar, a local resin, to replace wet and dry small-pack formats such as noodle seasonings and food wraps (see Box 5.3, fig 5.35).

One of the most promising new materials for the large-scale substitution of polyethylene bags and films is polyvinyl alcohol PVOH (aka as PVA, or PVAl). Aquapak Polymer's PVOH Hydor-Pol has been shown to be twice as strong as PE, non-toxic, recyclable, compostable and benign to aquatic life when dissolved.[62] Going one step further towards a circular economy, Full Cycle's PHA is made from resin produced by bacteria feeding off food waste. It is also compostable, marine-degradable and food-safe.[63]

Pushing the boundaries of bio-materials from a different angle, Ecovative (US) has pioneered and refined a bio-benign alternative for producing protective packaging and other products. They do this by growing mycelium to bind a bio-medium that is

Figure 5.32 Ooho are liquid 'bites' contained in an edible seaweed-based material that makes them highly suitable for waste-free events and local production. (courtesy Skipping Rocks/photo CS Media)

custom-shaped to the application. The mycelium and medium biodegrade in any domestic composter, making it a perfect replacement for non-recycled expanded polystyrene coolboxes and protective packaging used daily in e-commerce (fig 5.33). With these and other bio-based material innovations coming on-stream, designers may soon have a whole new palette of 'safe' materials and plastics to choose from.

2. problematic formats

One of the most problematic formats for recycling are multi-material cartons and pouches. Despite this they are still the most popular format globally for fresh and longlife liquids because of their functionality. Tetrapak alone, the biggest manufacturer in the world, sells over 188 billion packs a year. They are typically made of a mix of virgin paperboard (74%), with layers of PE plastic (22–26%) and, in the case of longlife liquids, an added layer of aluminium (4%). Because they require special recycling facilities to separate out the carton fibres their recycling rates are below 25%, although this is gradually increasing. The argument in favour of these packs is that they are made of at least 74% renewable materials that are increasingly sustainably sourced, and are more convenient for handling compared with pouches. The longlife aseptic packs also save considerable amounts of food from wastage and energy for refrigeration. In addition, Tetrapak is among the RE100 companies committed to powering 100% from renewables by 2030.[64]

Meanwhile, pouches have been gaining popularity as an alternative to bottles and aseptic cartons because they are cheaper and lighter. Sadly, most of these, along with plastic foil bags used to keep food crisp and fresh, are not recycled. Although processes like microwave pyrolisis with aluminium recovery exist, they are not yet economic. New recyclable materials and facilities for pouch formats are desperately needed and a number are just beginning to appear on the market. Seventh Generation's pouch for dishwasher pods developed with Dupont, Accredo and the Sustainable Packaging Coalition is a step in the right direction. For this, the PE and PET layers have been substituted with only PE layers to make the pouch recyclable.[65] In Europe, the main industry players are joining forces under CEFLEX to find circular economy solutions for flexible pouches with design guidelines published by 2020 and a full recycling infrastructure by 2025.

Another example of material and design improvement is Ecolean's stand-up aseptic pouch. Made of a mix of PP and PE layers with an added 35% calcium carbonate (chalk) that reduces the plastic content, it is also 50 to 60% lighter than conventional cartons and bottles. From a design perspective, Ecolean's 'air' handle stands out as a small but ingenuous innovation that helps with pouring and ensures the pack stays upright, an excellent example of how design can add value at no additional environmental cost[66] (fig 5.34).

Figure 5.33 "Ecovative's pioneering mycelium based packaging is the perfect replacement for the notorious EPS used for one-way coolboxes and shipping fragile items. Shown here MycoFoam Packaging made from Ecovative Mushroom® Materials." (photo courtesy Ecovative Design)

Figure 5.34 Ecolean's ingenious use of air to create a pour handle and keep pouches up to 1 litre upright as they empty. They are extensively used by Tianrun in China. (courtesy Ecolean (Sweden) and Tianrun (China))

Box 5.3 Interview with Daniella Russo on the challenges of successful alternatives to disposable plastics[67]

Daniella Russo is founder and CEO of Think Beyond Plastic, an innovations accelerator advancing bio-benign materials, circular packaging design solutions, and innovative consumer and business products. By providing a path to commercialisation, access to materials innovation labs and support from multidisciplinary experts, they create a unique innovation ecosystem.

JP. *It's been a good number of years since you were inspired to set up Think Beyond Plastic. With the benefit of that experience, what do you consider to be the real challenges in shifting the status quo of plastic disposables and all its consequences?*

DR. Plastic is a challenge on so many fronts because it is so valuable and an immensely useful material: it is inexpensive, versatile and practically indestructible. The abundance of cheap oil, innovation in packaging and growing consumer purchasing power have made it the material of choice across many different sectors, providing great savings in CO_2, food safety, preservation, product delivery, etc. Yet at the same time, we have found out about its multiple negative externalities – human health and the environment as leading causes of concern.

So, the challenge is really: How do you replace something that is so pervasive and so useful? From the designer's point of view, it means finding alternatives that still meet the price-performance characteristics of plastic packaging that both consumers and manufacturers have come to expect.

And that leads into the other great challenge of balancing the ease of convenience and disposability with the need to conserve non-renewable resources such as petroleum – the feedstock for plastics.

JP. *You almost have to ask: How could we flip this around? Do we go for longer lasting reusable products or do we redesign the material so that it is temporal and benign?*

DR. Reusable products are a great alternative, but not always viable. There certainly is a school of thought that says that if we believe that all around the world we won't be able to collect every piece of packaging that is made, regardless of how valuable it is, then why not make it out of a material that when it enters the environment nourishes it? And if you were to do this where do you start? What product would be the first to target, and where would the high-priority areas be?

It sounds difficult to address, but actually we know that disposable plastics present the greatest danger to the environment, and we also know which ones tend to pollute the most.

This represents a terrific opportunity for designers to reinvent packaging choices that were made in the sixties and design around bio-benign materials that degrade into their natural components. And this brings us to the question: What if we get rid of packaging altogether, as we have seen in some of the Circular Design Challenge outcomes?

JP. *On one level it's not too difficult to imagine how we could eliminate a lot of disposable packaging practically, but how would 'no-packaging' work in the world of brands?*

DR. It does pose interesting challenges because of course packaging doesn't just have a functional purpose, it also has a marketing and informational purpose. So in the age of smartphones, where even the developing world relies on smartphones and Internet, can we deliver the product and the benefit of this information in a different way instead of printed on plastic packaging, as we've done for the last 50 years?

That also raises the fact that when you introduce a new material or delivery system you also force innovation along the entire value chain. Although most disruptions are driven by small companies, ultimately, they are not the ones that carry it forward. So, if you want to scale these innovations, you need to collaborate with the big brands, especially those who have communicated a sustainability agenda.

JP. *And presumably that's where Think Beyond Plastic comes in?*

DR. That's right. We identify early stage innovation with commercial potential and the capacity to meet the needs of some of these brands, as communicated to us. Advancing these early stage innovations has the capacity to de-risk innovation for major brands and to accelerate the path to solutions they need.

Our goal is to develop a thriving innovation ecosystem with hundreds of innovators and entrepreneurs competing with each other, thriving and strengthening the ecosystem. It's the competition that strengthens these start-ups and makes them better, more resilient and ultimately more desirable for investors.

JP. Could you share with us some examples that illustrate the sorts of innovations you are talking about?

DR. Each of the start-ups in our 2018 Accelerator class has the capacity to disrupt a key area of the supply chain. So starting from materials, we have benignly biodegradable alternatives made from agricultural waste for polythene films (Full Cycle Bioplastics, USA), food freshness barriers (Fraunhoffer Institute, Germany) and multilayer plastic pouches (VTT Research, Finland). Then in formats, there are algae- and seaweed-based edible or compostable substitutes for food

sachets and small packs (Delta, UK, and Evoware, Indonesia), and biodegradable (TrioCup, USA) and reusable packaging-as-service (CupClub, UK) coffee cups. Finally, at point of sale, we have Algramo (Chile) and MIWA (Czech Republic) developing systems for consumers to buy food in the quantities they need in their own reusable containers online or in-shop.

JP. Do you have any other thoughts for designers wanting to make a difference in this space?

DR. They should take what companies like Apple and Tesla have shown us to the world of plastics and packaging. That design should be amazing, beautiful and different. *Just different.* So that when you look at it on the shelf, you go, that is unlike anything I've ever seen and I want to *own* it. Maybe the change starts with higher-end products at the beginning but then it permeates down to cheaper fast-moving goods to finally reshape the whole sector.

Figure 5.35 Evoware in Indonesia has developed biodegradable seaweed-based packaging that extends into edible and dissolvable condiment sachets. (photo credit Evoware)

Figure 5.36 Two very different models for short-life products: a. BIC are proud to sell over 30 million disposable products every day; b. Preserve produce their products from recycled plastic and offer take-back for all their products. The retail packaging shown is also the postage-paid return pack. (photo credits pen: istock ID:154948399 iStock/PaoloGaetano; razor: istock ID:171364239 iStock/excentric_01 lighter: istock ID:528954388credit iStock/LeventKonuk Konoot ; tooth brush and razor courtesy Preserve)

Beyond packaging, billions of other CPG products that are designed to be disposable and fundamentally unrecyclable are being consumed each day in workplaces, homes, hospitals, etc. BIC, perhaps the most well-known brand in the world for disposables, proudly claimed in 2017 that *every day they sell over 30 million* of their disposable pens, shavers and lighters and *nearly 12 billion a year (2016)*.[68] For BIC alone, the total number of products they have brought into the world stands at *several hundred billion*.[69], [70] But they fail to mention that the overwhelming majority go unrecycled (fig 5.36a). It is hard to understand how this is still possible in the twenty-first century, but it is. On the other hand, Preserve, now a B Corps, operate a very different model for short-life products. They have been producing consumables, including toothbrushes, razors and tableware, from 100% recycled PP with full take-back of all their products for over two decades, demonstrating that a different model is possible in this market (fig 5.36b).

3. designing for context

The best and most sustainable design decisions usually depend on the context of use and what is possible or likely in terms of waste separation. If it is known that in a particular context very little material recovery is likely, then the short-term design choice may be to create as little post-use damage as possible, at the expense of a higher carbon footprint. Equally, there are some special situations where recovering short-life products for recycling into the same or a similar product is not feasible.

A particular case in point is packaging or products that are food-soiled. Normally, food-soiled paper or plastic cannot be recycled. In a domestic context this is not an issue, as they can generally be rinsed out ready for recycling, but in the case of street food, markets, festivals and other events, this is often not possible for users or vendors. In these scenarios, short-life biodegradable paper and plastic products used within a robust

Figure 5.37 Glastonbury: festivals and events are ideal for maximising recycling and composting. (photo credit antb.com/Shutterstock)

closed-loop composting collection system can be the best solution. Because cross-contamination is the biggest threat to composting and recycling, designing-in a very clear visual distinction between biodegradable and recyclable products and clear communication at collection points is essential for success. This approach is particularly appropriate at closed events where complete control of inputs and outputs makes it possible to manage composting and recycling waste streams to avoid cross-contamination (fig 5.37).

Single-use paper coffee cups, on the other hand, are a glaring example of a complete mismatch between material specification, recyclability and collection infrastructure in the to-go sector. To begin, the cups are almost exclusively made of virgin paper to meet food standards because of potential contact with the rim of the cup, although Starbucks manages 10% post-consumer content and a few cup designs are produced with non-food-contaminated recycled paper, like Huhtamaki's Bioware range. Next, this is typically coated with PE film that makes recycling or composting the paper very difficult. And the lids

are PS. Hence billions of cups and lids are simply landfilled or incinerated. It has taken persistent NGO and public campaigning to begin to shift the status quo. Cups made with recycled material, PLA biodegradable plastic liners and lids that are fully compostable are now available at a small premium. However, the corresponding infrastructure to collect these for industrial composting is *only just* being trialled. This is a classic example of the need for systemic solutions to the many issues around short-use products.

brand values: signalling intentions and collaborating

The anti-waste hierarchy is a good action guide for a more sustainable redesign of the very notion of CPG, but the cornerstone will always be the values of the company and brand behind them. In a sector with a growing number of consumers hungry for more sustainable alternatives, a brand's ethos and true achievements in this direction will create the loyalty that is crucial for success.

Pioneers from the 1980s and 1990s who understood this, such as Ecover, Seventh Generation, Body Shop and Preserve, are being joined by a growing number of companies that are genuinely and successfully offering products made in the best way possible for people and planet. They are generally characterised by transparency and an open and participatory relationship with their customers. Because they don't expect people to just take their word for it, they measure their performance and avoid greenwashing through independent certifications like B Corps, ethical trade, fair labour, cruelty-free, organic and other certifications specific to their product area.

It seems that most sustainable innovations are being generated by smaller companies and start-ups that are more agile, closer to the ground and are able to set a sustainable agenda from the outset. A serious commitment to sustainability often goes hand-in-hand with forming cross-industry collaborations like the Safer Chemical Coalition and the Sustainable Packaging Coalition that share design tools between members. Advocacy and campaigning to change regulations like LUSH's Go Naked and Animal Testing campaigns and Seventh Generation's Come Clean campaign for the Cleaning and Menstrual Products Right to Know Acts are also strong commitment indicators.

It is much more difficult for established companies, especially large ones, to change course. While it is possible with exceptional leadership and vision, as Paul Polman has shown at Unilever, it is certainly a much more challenging environment for the sustainably minded designer. Because of this, smaller sustainable companies are being bought by the larger ones with less ability to innovate but which are now interested in having a share of the sustainable market. These include the purchase of Tom's of Maine by Colgate Palmolive; The Body Shop by L'Oreal and now by Natura; Green & Black's by Cadbury Schweppes, now by Mondalez; Innocent by Coca-Cola; Ben and Jerry's and Seventh Generation by Unilever; Method by Ecover and now both by SC Johnson, to name a few. While these could be seen as a sell-out of values, depending on the terms negotiated, they can also be an opportunity for more sustainable products and approaches to reach larger markets and organisations. Having B Corps certification and/or benefit company legal status are also effective ways for companies to protect their original mission.

Above all, let us not forget the power of design to move environmentally sound products from the 'worthy' category to the 'desirable'. Method is an excellent example of a company that started in 2001 with two main objectives: to make cleaning products that would not harm the environment and bring these to the mass market. They achieved this by challenging the design language of cleaning products, from products to be kept out of

Figure 5.38 By challenging the out-of-sight aesthetics of cleaning products, Method made environmentally safe cleaning products desirable possessions. (photo credit Jet)

sight to products you would proudly display. They began this journey with a Karim Rashid design and then developed their in-house design team (fig 5.38). Method went on to demonstrate their commitment to sustainability by producing bottles from 100% post-consumer waste in 2007, having their products C2C certified in 2008, and becoming a public benefit corporation in 2013. Today many other smaller companies and designers are rising to the challenge of wooing users away from disposables and speed with seductive and well thought-out products like Morrama's angle shaver (fig 5.39). Both are excellent examples of how the design language of a product can induce behaviour change, reach a wider audience and indirectly lead to more sustainable consumption.

Weaning ourselves off unsustainable convenience will somewhat ironically not be quick or easy. As we have seen, there are many routes for transitioning to more sustainable

Figure 5.39 Morrama's Angle Razor uses only half a replaceable and recyclable standard safety blade and heralds a return to less speed and more skill in shaving. (photo courtesy Morrama)

scenarios. It can be part of an incremental approach or it could trigger a radical breakthrough which consumers have subconsciously been waiting for that completely disrupts the stranglehold of the existing business models and takes us ten steps forward. The only thing that is certain is that nothing will happen without systemic change involving all the actors and that it will require a large dose of behavioural understanding, environmentally informed design creativity and commercial ambition.

Chapter summary

1. More than any other product sector, consumer packaged goods epitomise the seamless integration of consumerism both physically and emotively in everyday life. They also account for over half of all consumer spending, and rising. The current CPG model thrives on high-volume repeat sales, short-lived products, overconsumption, constant novelty, resource depletion, and on taking little responsibility for the consequences of its waste and other externalities.

2. Product designers are inextricably involved in the cycle of constant product 'innovation' and novelty required to keep and attract new customers in this highly competitive market. They should leverage this close relationship to further genuine sustainable agendas.

3. In the much-needed redesign of the CPG industry, we should not lose sight of the fact that by far the biggest footprint associated with packaged goods is the content, not the packaging. Packaging provides many social and environmental benefits by contributing hugely to reducing damage to goods in transit and food waste, as well as delivering safe food and better hygiene. It is also an important employer globally. However, the proliferation of unnecessary consumption under the guise of convenience and the waste it creates offsets many of these advantages.

4. Selling billions of short-life products daily made of materials designed to last hundreds of years that are either unrecyclable or not recycled is a dead-end model. Plastic packaging waste in particular has reached a tipping point, threatening the entire planet's food chain.

5. The growing outrage against plastic waste supported by new regulations is spurring the development of a whole range of promising new bio-based materials coming on-stream for designers. As some fall into the techno-material category and others are biodegradable, they present designers with a new set of challenges to ensure that they find their way into the right recovery stream.

6. Resource overconsumption and waste remain the industry's worst offences. The anti-waste hierarchy – refuse, reuse, reduce and recycle – provides a number of jumping-off points for the much-needed redesign of CPG products. It demands that we seriously question existing 'needs' and how they are being met. It also requires that we tune in to the growing demand for products that support sustainable living whether overt or embedded.

7. The systemic lock-in of producers, retailers and consumers in the current CPG model makes it clear that no single product, however well designed, is capable of stemming the tide of negative impacts on its own. At the same time, the ground swell of public opinion spurred by NGO campaigning is finally giving governments the confidence to regulate. This is forcing companies into developing PSS that require multi-stakeholder engagement. Designers have an important contribution to make in the design of successful schemes by applying their understanding of behaviour change motivators to the user experience of all stakeholders and to the creation of desirable physical touchpoints as part of these new product service systems.

8. While the big conglomerates ensure they have maximum publicity for the smallest of sustainable improvements, the real heroes of sustainable innovation and disruption in CPG are smaller and often local companies or start-ups. By being close to consumers, they can share their frustrations and envision how it could be done differently without being shackled by investments in outdated models. They are typically characterised as entrepreneurial, open, responsive, responsible and often local.

Notes

1 Anon. (n.d.) Trash Isles | LADbible [online]. Available at www.ladbible.com/trashisles (accessed 21 May 2018).

2 First appearance of the term 'throw-away society' cited as the 1 August 1955 issue of *Life Magazine* article entitled 'Throwaway Living'.

3 Kenton, W. (2018) *Fast-moving Consumer Goods (FMCG)* [online, last update 1 April]. Available at www.investopedia.com/terms/f/fastmoving-consumer-goods-fmcg.asp (accessed 12 January 2019).

4 Hirose, R. *et al.* (2015) Three Myths about Growth in Consumer Packaged Goods | McKinsey & Company [online]. Available at www.mckinsey.com/industries/consumer-packaged-goods/our-insights/three-myths-about-growth-in-consumer-packaged-goods (accessed 22 September 2017).

5 While both terms are commonly used, this text will use CPG.

6 Anon. (2016) Invasion of the Bottle Snatchers. *The Economist* [online]. Available at www.economist.com/business/2016/07/09/invasion-of-the-bottle-snatchers (accessed 12 January 2019).

7 Kharas, H. (2017) *The Unprecedented Expansion of the Global Middle Class*, Washington, DC: Brookings Institution – Global Development and Economy: WP100, p. 5. Available at www.brookings.edu/wp-content/uploads/2017/02/global_20170228_global-middle-class.pdf.

8 FAO (2013) Food Wastage Footprint: Impact on Natural Resources [online]. Available at www.fao.org/docrep/018/i3347e/i3347e.pdf.

9 Parry, James and LeRoux (2015) *Strategies to Achieve Economic and Environmental Gains by Reducing Food Waste*, Banbury: WRAP Report, p. 14.

10 Gram-Hansse, I. (2016) Food Waste And Packaging. Innovations In Packaging That Have Allowed To Reduce Food Waste, Ostfoldforskning (Norway), presented at OECD food chain analysis network, Paris, June.

11 Ibid.

12 Nestlé Purina (n.d.) Understanding the Consumer Packaged Goods (CPG) Industry | Nestlé Purina Careers [online]. Available at www.nestlepurinacareers.com/blog/understanding-the-consumer-packaged-goods-cpg-industry/ (accessed 12 January 2019).

13 Anon (n.d.) About Unilever [online]. Available at www.unilever.co.uk/about/who-we-are/introduction-to-unilever/ (accessed 12 January 2019).

14 www.theworldcounts.com/counters/waste_pollution.../plastic_bags_used_per_year (accessed 14 May 2018).

15 $80billion@50¢ / avg. diaper cost= 160 billion. www.statista.com/statistics/617763/global-disposable-diapers-market-value/ (accessed 14 May 2018).

16 https://recyclenation.com/tag/epa/page/2/ (accessed 29 September 2017).

17 Fearnley-Whittingstall, H. (2016) The Waste Mountain of Coffee Cups [online, 27 July]. Available at www.bbc.co.uk/news/magazine-36882799 (accessed 12 January 2019).

18 Laville, S. and M. Taylor (2017) A Million Bottles a Minute: World's Plastic Binge 'As Dangerous As Climate Change'. *The Guardian*, 28 June [online]. Available at www.theguardian.com/environment/2017/jun/28/a-million-a-minute-worlds-plastic-bottle-binge-as-dangerous-as-climate-change (accessed 12 January 2019).

19 www.theworldcounts.com/counters/how_consumerism_affects_the_environment/toilet_paper_environmental_impact (accessed 14 May 2018).

20 Ellen MacArthur Foundation/World Economic Forum (2015) *The New Plastics Economy*, p. 49.

21 Martinko, K. (19/09/2016) France Leads the Charge against Single-use Plastics [online]. Available at www.treehugger.com/culture/france-leads-charge-against-single-use-plastics.html (accessed 12 January 2019).

22 Guitierrez *et al.* (2017) *Costa Rica Paves the Way to End Single-use Plastics* [online, 17 July]. Available at www.undp.org/content/undp/en/home/blog/2017/7/14/Costa-Rica-abre-el-camino-hacia-el-fin-de-los-pl-sticos-de-un-solo-uso.html (accessed 12 January 2019).

23 NASA (2015) SVS: Garbage Patch Visualization Experiment [online, 13 February]. Available at https://svs.gsfc.nasa.gov/cgi-bin/details.cgi?aid=4174 (accessed 14 May 2018).

24 Jambeck, G. et al. (13/02/2015) Plastic Waste Inputs from Land into the Ocean. *Science,* 13 February, 347(6223), pp. 768–771.

25 Parker, L. *et al.* (2015) Eight Million Tons of Plastic Dumped in Ocean Every Year [online]. Available at http://news.nationalgeographic.com/news/2015/02/150212-ocean-debris-plastic-garbage-patches-science/ (accessed 12 January 2019).

26 EMF/WEF (2015) *The New Plastics Economy*, p. 17.

27 Geyer, J. *et al.* (2017) Production, Use, and Fate of all Plastics Ever Made. *Science Advances*, 3(7), e1700782. doi: 10.1126/sciadv.1700782.

28 Parker, L. (2018) A Whopping 91% of Plastic Isn't Recycled. *National Geographic*, 12 December. Available at http://news.nationalgeographic.com/2017/07/plastic-produced-recycling-waste-ocean-trash-debris-environment/ (accessed 12 January 2019).

29 Thompson, R.C. *et al.* (2009) Plastics, the Environment and Human Health: Current Consensus and Future Trends. *Philosophical Transactions of the Royal Society*, B 364. doi:10.1098/rstb.2008.0304.

30 Tyree, C. and D. Morrison (2017) *Invisibles* [online, 8 October]. Available at http://orbmedia.org/stories/Invisibles_plastics (accessed 14 May 2018).

31 Ibid.

32 Wright, S. and, F. Kelly (2017) Plastic and Human Health: A Micro Issue? *Environmental Science Technology*, 51(12). doi: 10.1021/acs.est.7b00423.

33 EMF/WEF (2015) *The New Plastics Economy*, p. 28.

34 EU (16/01/2018) European Commission Report on the Impact of the Use of Oxo-degradable Plastic. COM(2018) 35 final [online]. Available at http://ec.europa.eu/environment/circular-economy/pdf/oxo-plastics.pdf.

35 EMF/WEF (2015) *The New Plastics Economy*, pp. 92–94.

36 P&G (19/01/2017) P&G's Head & Shoulders Creates World's First Recyclable Shampoo Bottle Made with Beach Plastic. Available at http://news.pg.com/press-release/head-shoulders/pgs-head-shoulders-creates-worlds-first-recyclable-shampoo-bottle-made- (accessed 12 October 2017).

37 Lush (17/03/2014) The Mighty Shampoo Bar [online, 17 March]. Available at https://uk.lush.com/article/mighty-shampoo-bar (accessed 12 January 2019).

38 Lockie, S., K. Lyons, G. Lawrence and D. Halpin (2006) *Going Organic: Mobilizing Networks for Environmentally Responsible Food Production*, Oxon: CABI, pp. 117–119.

39 Panigrahi, A. and A. Basu (2016) Breaking through the Menstruation Taboo. Nielsen Report [online]. Available at www.nielsen.com/content/dam/corporate/in/docs/reports/2016/nielsen-featured-insights-breaking-the-menstruation-taboo.pdf (accessed 20 October 2017.)

40 Anon (2016) An Interview With Klean Kanteen's Director of Product [online, 26 June]. Available at www.kleankanteen.com/blogs/blog/114355014-an-interview-with-klean-kanteens-director-of-product (accessed 21 May 2018).

41 Morales, M. (n.d.) www.sightline.org/2016/03/08/why-youre-still-not-bringing-a-reusable-mug-for-your-daily-coffee/ (accessed 22 October 2017).

42 Starbucks Global Sustainability Report, 2014, pp. 8–9.

43 Greener Cup (n.d.) Starbucks [online]. Available at www.starbucks.com/responsibility/environment/recycling (accessed 23 October 2017).

44 BBC News (22/11/2016) Germany Trials Reusable Coffee Cups. sec. Europe [online, 22 November]. Available at www.bbc.co.uk/news/world-europe-38066528 (accessed 23 October 2017).

45 Petit, M. (10/08/2017) RECUP: The Coffee Cup Share System Set to Take over Berlin | Green Living [online, 10 August]. Available at https://en.reset.org/blog/recup-coffee-cup-share-system-set-take-over-berlin-08102017 (accessed 23 October 2017).

46 Steve Marinuzzo of Cobalt Design, Melbourne, interviewed by Jane Penty, 8 Noember 2017.

47 Narayan, A. (2016) Startups Haven't Replaced India's 19th Century Food Delivery Service. [online, 3 February]. Available at www.bloomberg.com/news/articles/2016-02-03/india-food-apps-haven-t-replaced-traditional-dabbawalas-on-bikes (accessed 12 January 2019).

48 Anon (2008) The Cult of the Dabbawala. *The Economist* [online]. Available at www.economist.com/node/11707779 (accessed 12 January 2019).

49 Anon (n.d.) Welcome to OZZI [online]. Available at http://agreenozzi.com/ (accessed 12 January 2019).

50 Anon (n.d.) 好 盒 器 | 用玻璃杯取代免洗杯 [online]. Available at http://goodtogo.com.tw (accessed 12 January 2019).

51 Thornton, E. (2017) Global Deposit Return Schemes. Edie.net [online, 3 October]. Available at www.edie.net/blog/Global-deposit-return-schemes/6098359 (accessed 11 April 2019).

52 Simon, J.M. (2010) Beverage Packaging and Zero Waste. Zero Waste Europe [online]. Available at https://zerowasteeurope.eu/2010/09/beverage-packaging-and-zero-waste/ (accessed 12 January 2019).

53 Anon (2016) Packaging: Market and Challenges in 2016 – ALL4PACK Paris – Salon Emballage – Manutention, November [online]. Available at www.all4pack.com/The-Packaging-sector/Discover-the-packaging-sector/Packaging-market-challenges-2016 (accessed 29 October 2017).

54 eurostat (2019) *Packaging waste statistics – Statistics Explained* [online, January]. Available at https://ec.europa.eu/eurostat/statistics-explained/index.php/Packaging_waste_statistics#Recycling_and_recovery_rates (accessed 12 January 2019).

55 Geyer *et al.* (2017).

56 Vanderbilt, T. and J. Weissmann (2012) Pop Art. Slate [online]. Available at www.slate.com/articles/life/design/2012/09/

can_tabs_how_aluminum_pop_tabs_were_redesigned_to_make_drinking_soda_safer_and_the_world_a_cleaner_place_.html (accessed 30 October 2017).

57 www.ecoxpac.dk/green-fiber-bottle/ (accessed 17 May 2018).

58 5+Gyres *et al.* (2017) Better Alternatives Now. B.A.N. List 2.0, p. 6 [online, November]. Available at www.5gyres.org/publications/ (accessed 12 January 2019).

59 EU (2018/05/28) European Commission – PRESS RELEASES – Single-use Plastics: New EU Rules to Reduce Marine Litter [online]. Available at http://europa.eu/rapid/press-release_MEMO-18-3909_en.htm (accessed 03 June 2018).

60 EMF/WEF (2015) *The New Plastics Economy*, p. 20.

61 McGeehan, J.E. *et al.* (2018) Characterization and Engineering of a Plastic-degrading Aromatic Polyesterase. *PNAS* 201718804 [online, 17 May]. Available at doi.org/10.1073/pnas.1718804115.

62 www.adiltd.co.uk/aquapak/A_hold_page.htm (accessed 17 May 2018).

63 fullcyclebioplastics.com (n.d.) truly-compostable-marine-degradable-bioplastics-for-the-circular-economy [online]. Available at http://fullcyclebioplastics.com/ (accessed 12 January 2019).

64 Tetra Pak (2018) Sustainability Report, pp. 21–33 [online]. Available at https://assets.tetrapak.com/static/documents/sustainability/tetra-pak-sustainability-report-2018.pdf (accessed 12 January 2019).

65 Mohan, A.M. (2016) [online, 16 January]. Available at www.packworld.com/article/sustainability/recycling/seventh-generation-introduces-recyclable-flexible-sup (accessed 31 October 2017).

66 www.ecolean.com/media/3172/ecolean-environment-brochure.pdf (accessed 28 October 2017).

67 Daniella Russo of Think Beyond Plastics, California, interviewed by Jane Penty, 15 December 2017.

68 BIC (n.d.) BicWorld [online]. Available at www.bicworld.com/en/ (accessed 29 September 2017).

69 BIC (n.d.) Who We Are | BicWorld [online]. Available at www.bicworld.com/en/about-us/who-we-are (Accessed 12 January 2019).

70 Henley, J. (2005) Bic Over the Moon as Sales Top 100bn. *The Guardian*, 8 September [online]. Available at www.theguardian.com/world/2005/sep/09/france.jonhenley (accessed 31 October 2017).

CHAPTER 6

Electronic tools and digital gateways

Technology is both the source of environmental damage and our best hope to build a sustainable future.

UN Environment[1]

Devising and fashioning tools that extend our capabilities is one of humankind's distinguishing features. In fact, we have honed this process so well that the electronic tools we have developed are so powerful that we now have a digital universe parallel to the planet's own highly sophisticated and interconnected web of life. But while the bio-universe has evolved over billions of years through a process of trial and error, experimental risk-taking and consolidation, the digital universe has emerged in less than a century from our imaginations into a rapidly unfolding reality. From a sustainability point of view, we have to ask ourselves: Are these two realms set on a collision course or can they co-exist and become mutually beneficial?

For many decades product designers have been working closely with technologists in the conception and realisation of the electronic tools that act as our gateways to the digital world. This close association makes these very exciting times for product designers, and the nature of these products has also expanded the role of designers. Earlier on we saw how the discipline of ergonomics grew out of the need to understand human responses in highly critical man–machine interfaces to make them safer and more effective. Today, product designers are involved in designing whole-product ecosystems and user experiences across digital and physical interfaces, creating new design specialisms in user experience (UX), user interfaces (UI) and service design.

Although the whole field of electronic and digital products is rapidly evolving, enough is known about the effects of this industry on the environment and society to give us strong pointers towards more sustainable practices. This chapter will mostly focus on consumer electronic devices and digital experiences because these have become so universal and ubiquitous. However, most of what is discussed is equally applicable to B2B products, although the business models will allow for different strategies. We begin

with an overview of the environmental and ethical issues around their production, followed by looking at the design strategies that can be deployed directly in response to these. In the second part of the chapter we consider some of their social impacts and how their potential is being exploited from the perspective of social sustainability. Finally, we look into future technologies and trends together with the threats and opportunities they suggest with an eye to channelling these towards positive design directions.

6.1 the visible and invisible environmental impacts of the digital world and their causes

the global digital energy footprint

By its very nature, the digital world is mostly made up of intangibles rather than tangibles – that is, more bits than atoms. This makes most of its environmental impacts invisible to us, apart from the devices that we interact with directly. One of the least visible is the energy it consumes in the form of electricity and the rate at which this is growing. Most people would be very surprised to find out that, based on 2014 efficiencies, 4G streaming a two-hour film once a week for a year on a tablet or smartphone requires more energy (1.3x) than running an under-counter A+ refrigerator for the same year. If this was streamed over Wifi onto a TV you could watch five films a week for the same energy as the fridge.[2] With the worldwide online population exceeding 4 billion, it is estimated that in 2017 the whole information and communication technology (ICT) industry accounted for between 7 and 12% of global electricity and 2% of GHGs.[3] Looking ahead, a medium or 'expected' scenario for growth sees this rising to 21% by 2030, with a 'best' case at 7% and a 'worst' case at 51% of global electricity demand.[4] These are staggering growth predictions with equally staggering potential impacts.

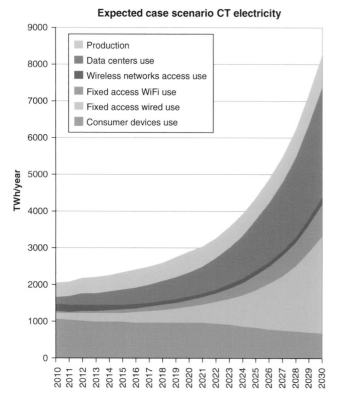

Figure 6.1 Current and future 'expected' case estimates for global ICT electricity demand. (source: Anders and Edler, *Challenges*, 2015, 6; doi:10.3390/challe6010117)

Figure 6.1 shows us the estimated electricity demand for the 'medium' or 'expected' scenario broken down into the components of the ICT ecosystem: transmission networks, data centres for storage and computation, and manufacturing and device use.

Figure 6.2 shows their relative share from 2010 to 2030. The first clear trend these projections show is that electricity demand for ICT is expected to continue to rise exponentially. The second is that ICT activity and therefore energy consumption is shifting from devices to the network and 'the cloud'. And the third is that despite the devices themselves becoming more efficient during use, the manufacture of their electronics is increasing in intensity. We will briefly look at the implications of these three trends and their relevance for sustainability and product design.

The exponential rise in the ICT energy footprint is primarily being driven by the enormous increases in data traffic from the growing use of mobile and connected devices, Internet access and the shift to cloud-based computing. To give a sense of scale, by 2014 the *hourly* traffic of Internet data had already surpassed the *yearly* traffic in 2000. Video streaming is a particularly data-hungry activity that is growing rapidly. In 2015, it accounted for 63% of global Internet traffic and is expected to rise to 80% by 2020 as more data-heavy formats come on-stream. Netflix alone generates over one-third of Internet traffic in North America and is expanding rapidly worldwide,[5] while in China, Tencent video and iQiyi each have over 400 million active mobile users.[6] All this requires ever-increasing amounts of energy to produce, store, transmit, process and display the zettabytes of data that we generate.

This surge in demand is not only due to billions more worldwide users and over 100 billion connected devices, but also to the rebound effect (or Jevons paradox) which we looked at in Chapter 3.1. As data becomes cheaper and cheaper and more and more services are on offer, we are generating and hoarding ever-more data that in turn is increasing our dependency on it (fig 6.3). "By

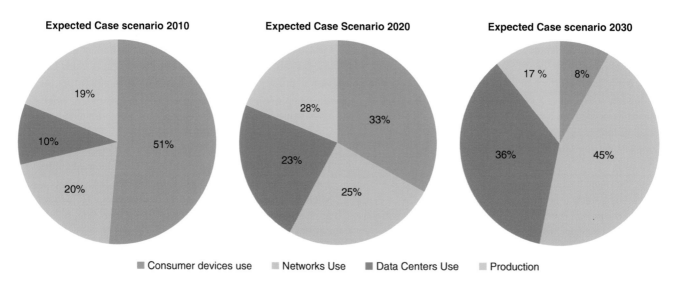

Figure 6.2 Breakdown of 'expected' ICT electricity demand showing energy for production growing in relation to energy for device use. (source: Anders and Edler, *Challenges*, 2015, 6; doi:10.3390/challe6010117)

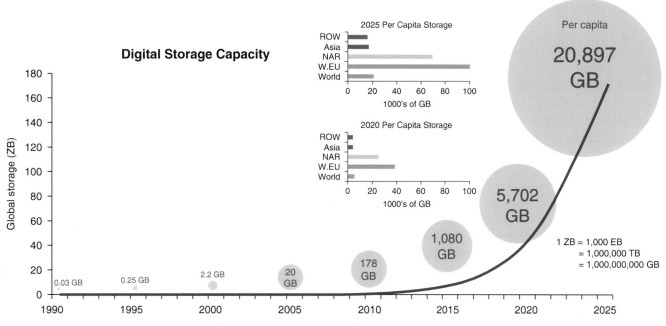

Figure 6.3 Humanity's increasing dependance on data and our tendency towards 'digital hoarding'. (graphic courtesy Marcus Weldon, *The Future X Network: A Bell Lab Perspective*, Boca Riton, FL: CRC Press, 2016)

2017 more than 5 trillion gigabytes of data will pass through the global communications network every year, which is the equivalent of everyone tweeting non-stop for more than 100 years."[7]

Fortunately, the companies engineering the ITC infrastructure are not standing still. By shifting their focus from performance to energy-efficiency, they believe that a *near-zero-power network* is achievable over the next decade.[8, 9] Despite this, most experts predict that these very ambitious efficiency gains in network delivery will not keep pace with the surge in demand anticipated, at least before 2030.

In the bigger picture of environmental sustainability, the expected growth in electricity demand from the ICT sector also has implications for GHG emissions and our ability to keep temperature rises below 2°C, let alone 1.5°C, given that most electricity is still being produced from coal and gas. The saving grace for the ICT sector is that unlike older industries such as manufacturing and transportation, it can run directly on clean electricity from renewables. This shift has already begun in earnest, with large cloud players like Apple, Box, Facebook, Google, Rackspace and Salesforce committed to 100% renewables.[10]

The second and third trends shown in figure 6.2 impact more directly upon the design of electronic devices. They are that the energy consumption in the *use phase* of most devices is falling partly because they have become more efficient and partly because processing and storage has shifted away from devices to the cloud. Against this trend we also have devices that are doing much more in smaller packages thanks to nano-technologies. While miniaturisation decreases the amount of material required, ever-more complex integrated circuits (ICs) require energy-intensive manufacturing processes in clean rooms, effectively making production a higher proportion of the device's overall footprint.

Not only is the intensity of production increasing as we pack in more and more speed and functionality, but the number of connected products being produced, particularly smartphones and tablets, is set to rise dramatically. Even medium or 'expected' scenarios forecast that the *net* amount of energy needed annually to produce devices will nearly double in real terms (+43%). To get a sense of the magnitude, the estimated positive and negative growth in the number of consumer devices produced annually between 2010 and 2030 is:[11]

* smartphones and phablets: 350 million to 4.6 billion units: +1200%
* tablets: 50 to 560 million units: +1000%
* mobile broadband modems: 100 to 900 million: + 800%
* Internet-connected TVs: 250 to 340 million: +36%
* laptops: 200 to 780 million by 2020, then 130 million by 2030: +69%, then -35%
* monitors: 160 to 120 million: -25%
* desktops: 146 to 100 million: -31%

the other hidden impacts of our devices

With predicted numbers like these, it would seem that we are *only just* entering the era of mass mobile connectivity and consumption. And because the environmental footprint of these billions of devices extends well beyond their energy consumption, we need to look at their *full* LCAs, not just at their global warming impacts, to know what particular aspects we should be targeting as designers. Figure 6.4 shows a Lifecycle Assessment (LCA) for the Fairphone 2 in detail. This data clearly demonstrates that the production phase of the electronic components is by far the most impactful and pinpoints the particular causes. It also finds that by comparison, the external "industrial design decisions such as housing materials have a minor impact". [12] This also concords with Apple's own GHG lifecycle assessments for iPads and iPhones that show manufacturing accounting for between 79 and 86% of their energy footprint[13] (fig 6.5).

For years, Greenpeace, Friends of the Earth, The Story of Stuff, Made in a Free World and many other NGOs have been casting

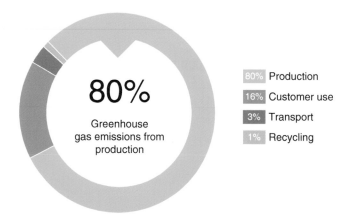

Figure 6.5 Greenhouse gas emissions over the life of an iPhone 8. (source: Greenpeace Guide to Greener Electronics 2017/iPhone 8-64GB)

light on the darker side of what goes into making and unmaking our electronics. These include devastating environmental and social practices in the mining, manufacturing and disposal of mobile electronic devices. In particular, Greenpeace's *Guide to Greener Electronics* has been holding the industry's main consumer electronics brands to account since 2006. Public pressure together with regulation is producing slow and steady progress. We will now look more closely at the worst impacts that arise during the physical production and disposal of electronics: mineral extraction, toxicity, hazardous working conditions, dirty energy and e-waste.

mineral extraction: human and environmental impacts

Electronic devices, particularly their integrated circuits (ICs), printed circuit boards (PCBs) and connectors, are among *the most resource-intensive products by weight on the planet.*[14] This is because they contain a large number of closely packed minerals, virtually all of which are virgin materials. In an openly available and ongoing study, Fairphone lists 38 different elements in a smartphone, giving us detailed insights into their usefulness and their ethical and environmental risks through the supply chain.[15] Their analysis identifies ten materials that have the most significant and persistent issues to address. These are: cobalt, copper, gallium, gold, indium, nickel, tantalum, tin, tungsten and rare earth elements.

The first glaring problem with current electronic production is their almost exclusive use of virgin minerals, because they all have to be mined, and mining has a huge environmental footprint. For each gram of purified mineral used, *340 times its weight in mineral ore* on average has to be extracted and processed.[16] Not only does this leave huge scars in the landscape, it also requires vast amounts of water and energy for processing, leaving behind toxic waste soil and water that poisons wildlife and affects local farmers and fishermen's livelihoods.[17]

(a) Fairphone 2 full LCA over three year use

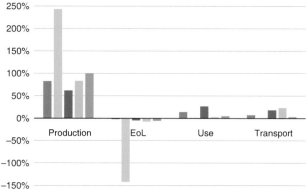

(b) Fairphone 2 LCA breakdown of component impacts

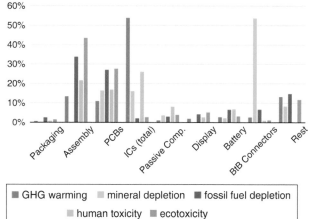

Figure 6.4 Fairphone 2 full LCA. (source: Fraunhofer IZM, Berlin Nov 2016)

Figure 6.6 A tin miner on Bangka Island, Indonesia (courtesy Friends of the Earth photo credit Ulet Ifansasti); 13-year-old boy sorting stones in artisanal cobalt mining in DRC (courtesy Amnesty International); and copper being washed in Katanga, DRC (courtesy Fairphone).

The mining required for electronics is also fraught with troubling social and human rights issues. These include the strong association between the mining of tin, tantalum, tungsten and gold (3TG) and the funding of armed groups, especially in the Democratic Republic of Congo (DRC), known as conflict minerals. There are also human rights issues connected to the hundreds of thousands of miners, including children, across the world, extracting minerals destined for our electronics who often work for very low wages in hazardous and unsafe conditions.[18]

As an illustration, 50% of the world's tin is used for solder and one-third is mined in Indonesia. Friends of the Earth exposed the challenging conditions that miners and their families live and work under on Bangka Island, where 90% of Indonesia's tin is mined. In 2011, Indonesian police estimated that one miner died every week in accidents, and the stories of environmental devastation from fishermen were on an industrial scale.[19] In southern DRC, UNICEF reported that approximately 40,000 children were working in mines in 2014. In 2016 Amnesty International's report ' "This is what we die for": Human rights abuses in the Democratic Republic of Congo' confirmed that cobalt from mines in the DRC where child labour is rife is making its way into electric vehicle and smartphone batteries[20] (fig 6.6).

toxicity and worker exposure
The issue of hazardous chemicals in electronics is not only about these substances leaching into the environment, particularly at their end of life (EoL). It is also about the human toxicity to which miners, factory and recycling workers and communities in proximity to factories find themselves exposed. While steady

progress is being made in substituting the worst, there are still 'substances of concern' associated with electrical and electronic products which designers should be aware of. Some of the most harmful are: heavy metals (lead, mercury, cadmium, hexavalent chromium); polybrominated fire retardants (BFRs), and a number of phthalates generally used as plasticisers for PVC.

As of July 2019, these substances have been banned in EEE products by the recast EU RoHS Directive. The EU regulations are mirrored by Korea RoHS, China RoHS (2016) less phthalates, and California RoHS, less phthalates and BFRs. Of the major producers, only Apple and Google have fully eliminated PVC, phthalates and BFRs to date.[21] Chapter 7.3 on furniture gives a fuller explanation of the issues surrounding PVC and BFRs. Although the phasing out of the worst substances is a very positive step forward, we should not forget that for some years to come, workers repairing or recycling e-waste in countries where there is little protection will continue to be exposed to these hazardous substances.

Beyond the materials in the products themselves, there is also the problem of the use of hazardous substances in the *production* and *assembly* of electronic products. Many workers in these factories are exposed on a daily basis to highly toxic substances in countries where regulations are not the most stringent. These include benzene, n-hexane, antimony trioxide and beryllium compounds. The LCA breakdown by component of the Fairphone 2 (fig 6.4b) confirms the high eco and human toxicity levels involved in making PCBs, ICs and their assembly (fig 6.7).

Figure 6.7 The Fairphone 2 assembled at Hi-P in Suzhou, China. Not all electronic assembly plants protect their workers from exposure to toxic substances. (photo courtesy Fairphone)

dirty energy

As we saw earlier, despite devices using less electricity locally, they are also becoming more complex and energy intensive to produce. This, together with the fact the demand is set to increase exponentially and lifespans are decreasing, means that the overall energy from manufacturing devices will continue to rise (see fig 6.1). *Where* this energy comes from matters hugely if we are to meet the Paris agreement targets of decreasing GHG emissions to keep temperature rises below 1.5°C.

Currently, most electronics production is concentrated in South East Asia, especially China, South Korea, Taiwan, Japan and Vietnam. Approximately 40% of electricity in these countries is generated from coal followed by natural gas, nuclear or hydro and less than 10% from solar and wind, although this is growing.[22] This tells us that with only a few exceptions, our electronic devices are being produced primarily with coal and other fossil fuels – effectively dirty energy.

Unfortunately, companies manufacturing electronics have not been as swift as ICT providers in moving to renewables. In fact 6 out of 17 of the biggest consumer electronics brands in the 2017 *Guide to Greener Electronics* do not even disclose the carbon footprint of their devices. This could in part be because transitioning to renewables requires manufacturers to *work with* their *whole supply chain* to reduce their carbon footprint. Unless that relationship is secure, suppliers are reluctant to invest in renewables. Apple however is leading the charge by reaching its target of using 100% renewable energy (RE) for its own operations in 2018 and working towards the same across its supply chain. Figure 6.8 shows one of Apple's component suppliers, Ibiden's solar installation in Japan. HP is also on board with 100% RE, albeit on a longer timescale for their own operations and supply chain. Achieving 100% RE is clearly achievable but remains work in progress.

e-waste

A great deal has been reported on the growing quantity and fate of hazardous e-waste. Latest figures available put the average e-waste generated each year *per person* at between 15 and 25kg in developed countries and 50 billion tons globally.[23] It stands to reason that if we are consuming ever more electrical and especially electronic products, then we must also be discarding an ever-growing amount. Perhaps this would not be such a big problem if all the electrical and electronic products that we discard had reached the end of their functioning life and then were safely collected and had all their valuable elements recovered. But this is far from the case.

Although this chapter focuses mainly on electronic products, e-waste as a term is largely used synonymously with WEEE (waste electrical and electronic equipment), a term introduced in Europe with the WEEE EPR directive of 2002. EEE includes "*any household or business items with circuitry or electrical components with power or battery supply*". And e-waste is defined as: "*all types of electrical and electronic equipment (EEE) and its parts that have been discarded by the owner as waste without the intention of reuse.*/"[24] The significant point for design is that *e-waste can include products that are still functional but are no longer wanted.*

There are three main causes for concern with e-waste that have implications for the design of electronic products. The first is that many WEEE products, especially older ones, contain toxic substances that require special handling. The list includes but does not end with: mercury in fluorescent bulbs; lead, cadmium, barium and yttrium in cathode-ray tube TVs and monitors; CFCs and HFCs in refrigerators and air conditioners; cadmium and lead in batteries; lead solder in circuit boards; PVC and phthalates in cables, and BFRs in circuit boards and plastic housings.

Figure 6.8 Floating solar farm built by Ibiden, Apple's IC and PCB supplier in Japan. (photo courtesy ©Ibiden Engineering Co. Japan)

Although these risks will be reduced in new products from 2019 through the RoHS phase-outs (see Table 2.2), most e-waste will still contain hazardous substances for some decades to come. With global collection rates estimated at only 40% of all WEEE, including the formal and informal sectors, this means that the other 60% is ending up in landfill or incineration with their valuable elements lost and the toxic substances leaching into land, water and air.[25] As for the e-waste that is collected, in 2014 only 16% came through official take-back schemes with the remaining 84% coming from the informal sector.[26] While the informal sector has many positives such as the extraction of equipment and components that are still working for reuse in secondary markets, it is mostly based in developing countries where the lack of regulation exposes recycling workers and the surrounding land, water and community to toxicity (fig 6.9). Despite the Basel Convention placing stringent restrictions on

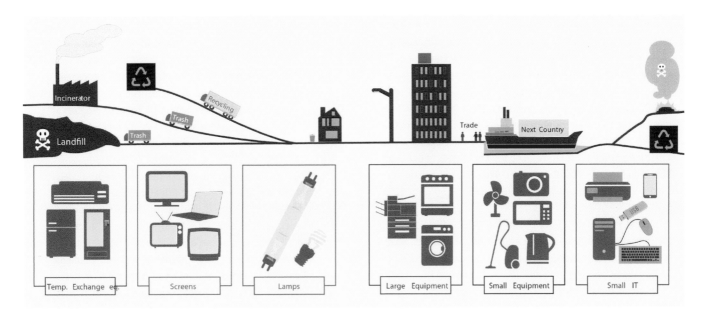

Figure 6.9 Diagram of e-waste journeys. (source: Baldé *et al.*/E-waste monitor 2014/United Nations University)

Figure 6.10 Reverse e-waste: Closing the Loop partners with Recell in Ghana to collect and ship mobile phone e-waste from Ghana back to Europe for safe recycling. (courtesy ©Closing the Loop/closingtheloop.eu)

the export of e-waste for this very reason, many EEE shipments slip through under the guise of reusable equipment. In a reverse move, the social enterprise Closing the Loop partners with local e-waste collectors to ship back used mobiles for safe recycling in Europe to protect the environment and create safe employment (fig 6.10).

The second problem is that although electronic e-waste is rich in valuable and scarce mineral elements, very little of this is actually being *recovered* and even less *recycled* back into new electronic products. To get an idea of the potential that is being lost, the gold content in all e-waste in 2014 was estimated at 11% (300 tonnes) of the *entire* gold production for 2013.[27] It is also estimated that there is more gold in a ton of computers than there is in 17 tons of gold ore. Looking at it a different way, the EPA calculates that 1 million cell phones would yield about 24kg (50lb) of gold, 250kg (550lb) of silver, 9kg (20lb) of palladium, and more than 9000kg (20,000lb) of copper.[28]

Smartphones in particular have one of the lowest official WEEE collection rates, even though they are one of the products most densely packed with valuable materials. In Europe, collection estimates range between 20% and 7%,[29] while in the USA it is 11% for cell phones compared with 40% for computers.[30] This is because they are often disposed of in household waste, passed on to friends and family, or simply forgotten in a drawer. The EU

calculates that in Europe alone, there were approximately 1.6 billion of these unused phones in 2012 and that this will double to 3.2 billion by 2020.[31]

Why is it then that this valuable 'urban mine' is so under-exploited? The reasons for this are, first, that current systems for collecting, handling, pre-processing and methods for recycling of e-waste are very inadequate. The second reason is that because electronics are made up of such a cocktail of materials and assemblies, they are very difficult and much more costly to recycle compared with simple mono-material products like consumer packaged goods. Despite these obstacles, the electronics industry, led by a few key companies, is beginning to make progress in moving to more circular models which we will look at in more detail in Section 6.2 on design strategies.

This brings us squarely to the third issue of concern, namely the trend towards shorter product life and usage times for EEE (shown in figure 6.11), particularly with smaller electronics like smartphones, laptops and tablets.[32] The premature shortening of a product's life is known as *obsolescence*. It appears to stem from different causes, be they material, functional, economic or psychological, that we will look at in more detail in design strategies. Regardless of its origin, what we do know is that obsolescence has significant environmental consequences, as it stimulates the production of new products, intensifies the

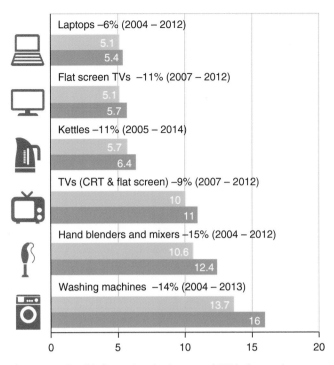

Laptops −6% (2004 − 2012)
5.1
5.4

Flat screen TVs −11% (2007 − 2012)
5.1
5.7

Kettles −11% (2005 − 2014)
5.7
6.4

TVs (CRT & flat screen) −9% (2007 − 2012)
10
11

Hand blenders and mixers −15% (2004 − 2012)
10.6
12.4

Washing machines −14% (2004 − 2013)
13.7
16

0   5   10   15   20

Figure 6.11 Trend in increasing obsolescence of EEE in Europe. (source: Prakesh et al. (2016), *Einfluss der Nutzungsdauer von Produkten auf ihre Umweltwirkung*, Umweltbundesamt (UBA), Dessau, Germany)

environmental footprint of devices by shortening their life and exacerbates the problem of e-waste.

6.2 design strategies for reducing the environmental impacts of electronic devices

Having exposed the causes and consequences of the environmental impacts of our existing electronics industry, we now turn to a range of design-specific strategies and challenges that address each of these directly or indirectly. How applicable these strategies are largely depends on what stage of the design process a designer is involved in – be it front-end concepts for new technology applications or back-end detail development. In addition, the particular business model and mission of the company or context they are working in or with, as well as the competitor landscape and regulatory framework, will constrain a designer's ability to 'do the best thing'.

Regardless of where this involvement begins in the design process of an electronic product, the first step is to have a good understanding of a typical LCA for the product category and then pinpoint the particular 'hot spots' that are most concerning. With these identified, the relevant design strategies can be selected to

shape or detail the product, depending on the design scope. The following are possible design strategies in response to the issues we have identified.

reducing energy consumption in use

We now know that the overall energy footprint of global digital operations is very substantial and will continue to rise for some time. While the local usage footprint of physical devices has been decreasing largely thanks to efficiency standards and labelling, the aggregated usage footprint is still rising because the number of devices and connected people is growing faster than the efficiency gains.

The direct energy consumption of a device is dependent on the inherent efficiency of the technology and components used, the time and intensity of use and how it is used. As designers are generally more involved in shaping *how a product is experienced and used*, they tend to influence the second half of the efficiency equation, although they are unquestionably interwoven. Certainly as a baseline in reducing in-use energy impacts, designers should include wherever feasible the ability of electrical and electronic products to self-power by integrating renewable and human-powering features (see fig 2.34).

behaviour change and defaults

As we saw in behaviour change (Chapter 3.1), best practice for nudging users into more efficient use habits is to set these as the product's operating defaults. The example of the hotel keycard demonstrates how creative thinking around how to design energy saving as the default mode can lead to very effective solutions (see fig 3.4). We also saw how feedback and prompts can help shape better habits. This approach is already very common in fitness-connected wearables and driving consoles, but in conceiving these interfaces, designers tread a thin line between being helpful and motivating or patronising and downright annoying. In the case of reducing our ICT footprint, most electronic devices now do this through software default settings and reminders. In fact, the ability to monitor behaviours through the Internet in conjunction with app interfaces is proving to be a powerful tool for prompting and motivating more energy-efficient behaviours.

IoT and AI solutions

With the rapid advances of the IoT and AI, decisions for optimising the energy efficiency of the products and systems that surround us are gradually being taken out of human hands and being determined by algorithms that feed off a range of data, including close observation of our usage patterns. The question for designers and technologists remains whether we will be able to design product ecosystems that on the one hand help us to

Figure 6.12 Desirable and smart thermostats by design: Nest designed with Bould Design, Hive designed with fuseproject and Netatmo with Philipp Starck, shown in situ and controllable radiator valves. (photos courtesy © Netatmo; Nest credit Constantine Pankin; Hive ©fuseproject)

live more efficiently and sustainably, yet on the other give users sufficient control and avoid infantilising, oversimplifying or creating undue dependencies. In short, will an all-pervasive IoT free us from the burden of too many interfaces, as Bruce Sterling suggested in *The Shape of Things*, and what will the price of this liberation be?

A good example is the role design has played in popularising and elevating energy-saving smart thermostats into highly desirable interior accessories. By working with top design studios – Nest with Bould design, Hive with fuseproject and Netatmo with Starck – the take-up and desirability of these products has increased enormously. Aside from producing energy savings in the order of 20 to 35% (see Chapter 2.5), they also demonstrate a good balance between the convenience of 'smart' control and personal control. On the back of the trust these products have established, these companies are now expanding their product ecosystem to become a one-stop home control app (fig 6.12).

countering rebound effects

As we saw in Chapter 3.1, improvements in the energy efficiency of technology are often partially negated by Jevon's paradox or the rebound effect. A very good example is the introduction of energy-efficient LED lighting. The most recent satellite tracking of light emissions across the globe between 2010 and 2016 shows that the rate of growth of light pollution worldwide continues

to increase and that the use and replacement of LED for outdoor lighting is not reducing the energy used for lighting as was initially anticipated[33] (fig 6.13). Essentially, as lighting has become cheaper, we are using more of it. Meanwhile, scientists are only just discovering the adverse effects that the loss of night darkness is having on the natural cycles and health of whole ecosystems, from the smallest organisms to human beings.[34]

Apart from the missed opportunity to save energy, this begs the question: How could the value of experiencing darkness come to be re-appreciated? More generally, the rebound effect remains a fascinating challenge for designers to take on. Are there ways to re-instil a sense of respect for the preciousness of the services our natural resources provide, such as light, warmth and mobility, through how we experience them? Or could design help to develop the quiet power of sufficiency and restraint even as technologies become more efficient and affordable?

The following points suggest some design challenges for reducing the impacts of electronic device in use:

- can we identify opportunities to save energy while adding value during use scenarios?
- how could more efficient use patterns become either the default or the most attractive, enjoyable and satisfying option?

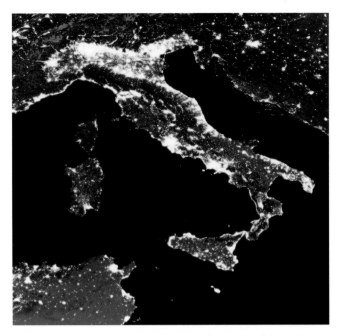

Figure 6.13 LED lighting rebound effect: satellite image of the Earth at Night from NOAA and NASA's Earth Observatory show increasing light pollution and loss of night sky. (source: NASA Earth Observatory/NOAA NGDC)

- how do we avoid overcomplicating or infantilising the relationship with products so that users still feel in control while being guided or prompted to 'best use' habits.
- can we step back and create the opportunities to design products around the most appropriate technologies as opposed to the newest technologies?
- are there creative ways that product design could help to counter rebound effects?

reducing production impacts

The production footprint of electronics is heavily burdened by its intense use of virgin materials, especially minerals, the ethical issues associated with working conditions in the supply chain and the impacts of toxic substances in production and EoL. The rising number of devices being produced then magnifies each of these.

convergent devices

Designing multifunctional or convergent products can be used as a strategy to reduce the overall number of devices being produced by cutting down on products that have functional overlaps. Looking at the ownership of electronic devices in the USA between 1992 and 2007, we see that the number per household increased by 300% and included a lot of redundancy in functionality[35] (fig 6.14). This is due in part to people holding onto older devices when newer ones are purchased, like televisions, as well as owning a large number of single-function products such as watches, clocks, cameras, recorders, desktop computers, stereos, speakers, MP3 players, satnavs, fitness trackers, game consoles and so on. This trend is already showing signs of reversing, as millennials, who have only ever known digital formats, are moving away from many single-function products. The new baseline for setting up 'home' now involves multifunctional devices like smartphones, tablets and notebooks.[36]

Currently device convergence centres on smartphones and tablets, but in the years ahead, designers will be involved in envisioning and creating a whole new generation of convergent and pervasive technologies. Newer technologies such as virtual reality (VR) and augmented reality (AR) combined with AI will supersede the smartphone as the mass personal device. Identifying opportunities for integrating functionality that truly simplifies life and reduces device and energy use requires deep user-centred research into a range of future scenarios. It also entails routing out and imagining the possible future technological hardware and software ecosystems that could support sustainably focused convergence with unexpected and inspiringly positive societal outcomes.

dematerialisation

While electronic devices have a heavy production footprint, they can offset this through the energy and resources saved by replacing the need for physical products, known as dematerialisation. The potential benefits of dematerialisation

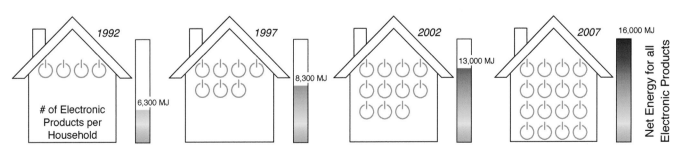

Figure 6.14 Increasing numbers of electronic products and the energy used to power them in US households, 1992 to 2007. (source: Ryen *et al.*, *Environmental Science Technology* 2015)

became very tangible when music consumption shifted from physical to digital MP3 formats in the first decade of the millennium, propelled by the winning combination of the iPod and iTunes music store (fig 6.15). Since then, digital formats have partially or wholly replaced print media, and all manner of person-to-person and paper-based personal and business communication and transactions.

At face value one might assume that this saves energy and resources, and on a like-for-like basis this is true. A comparison from 2009 of the carbon footprint associated with different modes of music delivery puts a simple digital download of an album stored locally with no CD backup at 80% lower than the best mode of purchasing a physical CD.[37] And even though the equation worsens somewhat with streaming depending on the number of times a track is listened to, this is a clear demonstration of the sustainable advantages of moving from products to digital PSSs.

However, digital dematerialisation also suffers from the rebound effect caused by the veritable explosion in the quantity of digital material produced and consumed thanks to the ease of generating, storing and distributing electronic content. Most consumers of digital material are unaware of the relative energy cost of different formats, as they pay by subscription rather than for what they consume. This is a clear case of where the business model does not incentivise culling stored data, and hence energy saving. It seems therefore that for us to reduce impacts in real

terms through dematerialisation may be just as much a matter of reaching social and cultural consensus on the notion of *digital sufficiency,* as it is a matter of increasing the technical efficiency of digital formats.[38]

supply chain ethics

The breakdown of ethics that we looked at in the electronic supply chain is largely a consequence of globalisation and the practice of subcontracting-out most production, often to distant countries. However, ignorance of what is happening on the ground is no longer an excuse for not taking responsibility for how every material and part of a product comes to be. Today's designers need to be informed about the challenges in their particular supply chain and become advocates for transparency and collaborators with their production partners in achieving common ethical and environmental objectives. HP, Dell and Fairphone are good examples of companies that have been working hard through all the layers of their supply chains to ensure common fair and safe labour practices.[39, 40] This includes establishing cross-industry collaborations such as the Electronics Industry Citizens Coalition (EICC) and benchmarks like 'KnowTheChain'.

Whether hazardous materials are being eliminated by choice or for compliance, designers can be actively involved together with engineers in solving the design and commercial challenges of substituting materials like PVC used for cables and accessories. They can also use materials more efficiently and continue to push for more recycled content in conjunction with designing products for optimal open- or closed-loop recyclability. However, capturing and including more recycled minerals extracted from electronic cores remains a big challenge for the industry that we shall look at in more detail in EoL strategies.

Designers can influence the *overall* and *relative* footprint of the manufacturing phase of devices directly and indirectly through the following actions:

- reducing electronics in absolute terms by number of devices or by weight for the same or additional functionality
- seeking beneficial applications for digital dematerialisation
- finding new opportunities for creative functional convergence
- substituting all hazardous materials
- ensuring ethical practices throughout the supply chain
- maximising recycled and minimising virgin content
- aiming for circular practices and achieving top certifications for safe and fair material content, emissions and supply chain

Figure 6.15 The winning combination of the Apple iPod design and iTunes digital music store started the rapid dematerialisation of music consumption. (photo credit Cesare Andrea Ferrari/Shutterstock.com)

reducing lifecycle intensity: extending product life

The most sustainable smartphone is the one that you already have and that you can keep using.[41]

For energy-consuming products, the *total* environmental impact and the *relative* impact of each phase as measured by an LCA depends on how long a product is in use. As an example, we saw that the extraction and production phase of connected electronic devices accounts for by far their greatest environmental impacts, while the local use phase is now relatively small[42] (see fig 6.4, Fairphone 2 LCA and fig 6.5, iPhone GHG LCA).

This means that extending the total time each product is used for can dramatically decrease the overall intensity of its impacts by delaying the production of a new device and spreading the burden of the existing one over more years. It also reduces the amount of e-waste. However, as we have also seen, the trend across all EEE since 2000 has been for products to be used for less time. In order to have effective strategies to counteract this trend, we need to define lifespan terminology and understand the causes of obsolescence.

Product obsolescence is the *premature shortening of the time a product is used for.* This may be because it is no longer functional or no longer desired and has been replaced. *Lifetime* is how long a product is *usable*. *Usage time* or *service life* is how long a product is *actually used*. *Residence time* is how long a product is kept but not necessarily used before being discarded. The main types of obsolescence are summarised and illustrated through smartphones:[43]

- *material obsolescence:* occurs when the failure or breakage of only one poorly designed, lower quality, unavailable or vulnerable part causes the whole product to become premature e-waste if it cannot be repaired or replaced. This is exacerbated when parts are difficult or impossible to repair, or are simply designed to be inaccessible (e.g. glued-in batteries, screens, soldered RAM).
- *economic obsolescence:* occurs when the cost of replacing a part such as a battery or screen is uneconomic compared to replacing the whole product with a new one. This is also closely connected to material obsolescence because products become too expensive to repair not only because of the cost of parts but also the difficulty of repairing due to lack of access and availability of parts and repair manuals.
- *functional obsolescence:* occurs when the device can no longer deliver the latest functionality or performance. This could be because the operating system is no longer supported, a key integrated circuit (IC) is no longer available, there is insufficient memory or processing speed to run new functionalities, or it lacks newer features. In this category, it is not uncommon to see hardware obsolescence caused by commercially driven software obsolescence.
- *psychological obsolescence:* occurs where the desire for 'newness', be this technological or aesthetic, leads to the premature replacement of products with new models. In the case of phones, notepads and laptops, because they are personal possessions, getting a new model is also connected to 'treating oneself' and self-esteem. This behaviour is actively encouraged by combined phone and service contracts that typically last two years, at which point the customer contract is renewed with a new shiny phone, starting the cycle all over again. This has led to typical 'usage' periods for smartphones in Europe to average 2.7 years.[44] Apart from this business model that is very conducive to obsolescence, Greenpeace suggests that with market saturation of phones in developed economies, manufacturers are increasingly adding features and making design changes to accelerate the replacement cycle. This practice is known as 'planned obsolescence'.[45]

Below are some key design strategies for tackling these different forms of obsolescence and extending product life for EEE.

addressing material and economic obsolescence: prevent damage and make products repairable

In the first instance, anticipating how a product might be damaged and preventing this through design comes before repair. Ethnographic observation of user behaviours to understand how products are *really* used or hacked in a range of contexts naturally leads to interesting design solutions that work *with* how people want to use products rather than *against* them. The design of Apple's MagSafe plug is a beautiful example of this, even though the feature has been replaced by the USB-C universal connector (fig 6.16). Its quick-release connection will have saved many laptops from serious damage when someone inevitably tripped over the cord while charging. This small but satisfying detail also created yet another positive connection between user, product and brand.

Figure 6.16 Apple's MagSafe: a beautifully simple detail that acknowledges the realities of everyday life and their consequences. (photo credit Pop Tika)

Box 6.1 Interview with Kyle Wiens on the importance of designing-in repairability[46]

Kyle Wiens is CEO and co-founder of iFixit, a leader of the global repair movement. Through their wiki-based site, they empower people to fix (their) products by sharing repair guides, teardowns and supplying parts. A firm advocate of the sustainable benefits of repair, he also campaigns for the right to repair through ifixit.org.

JP. Since you started iFixit in 2003, you'll have seen a lot of products and why they go wrong. In terms of design, do you consider 'unfixability' wilful or ignorance on the part of companies?

KW. Most of the time it's ignorance – it's design for manufacture without a thought for disassembly. What's interesting is that it actually turns out to be *bad* design for manufacturing because there's always rework that has to happen in the factory. You could think of design-for-repair and design-for-rework as the same thing.

In some cases though, it is intentional; for instance, when they design cell phones and electronics to be as thin as possible by gluing in the battery. My estimate is that making a product that has a removable battery adds about one-tenth of a millimetre, equivalent to a sheet of paper to the thickness of the device. So that is an *intentional* decision. Do we want to make it removable or not? I think it's worth it. They clearly disagree.

JP. Well, not all do.

KW. Sure, but you can't really buy a flagship cell phone with a removable battery anymore. So I would argue that Apple is intentionally and wilfully making it hard to repair. And you have to realise that there are environmental and social externalities as a result of that design, and because Apple was profiting from those externalities, all the other manufacturers had to follow suit and do the same thing.

JP What are the externalities connected to glued-in batteries?

KW. Glued-in batteries make recycling more expensive. And because the lithium batteries only last 400 charges, the product is disposable after 18 months. So that ends up costing the consumer more. And as we move to the IoT, we will be seeing more and more batteries included in products. Not only that, but glued-in batteries are also causing recycling safety

problems. Every recycler I know is having fires now as a direct result of this design decision.

JP. How are these devices being recycled if the battery is glued in – are they being shredded?

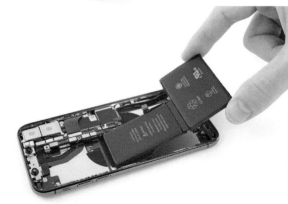

Figure 6.17a Steps 4, 35, 43 to replace an iPhone X battery. Estimated time: 1 to 2 hours. (photo courtesy ©iFixit/iFxit.com)

KW. You cannot run the battery through a shredder – there is no safe way of doing that – so they have to manually open the devices and prise them out, and in the process of doing this, 1 in 100 times they puncture the battery – which leads to fires.

Whereas a removable battery has a plastic shield around it, with an integrated battery that shield has been removed. That's the one-tenth of a millimetre they've shaved off that we talked about earlier. So there's just a thin sheet of foil and if it's punctured, the lithium comes in contact with air and we have a fire or explosion hazard. Even worse is when they miss a battery and it goes through the shredder because it doesn't combust immediately. The lithium gets sorted into the plastic fraction, and because there's moisture, it just sits there smouldering in the middle of a bunch of shredded plastic. And that's how you have a really big fire. It's either that, or there's an explosion in the shredder because of the lithium dust.

JP. So the message is that gluing, integrating or having non-replaceable batteries, or any other consumable for that matter, is a total no-go for product longevity and repairability but also for recyclability?

KW. Right. So my design advice is, *treat a consumable like a consumable*. Don't make the product disposable. And maybe

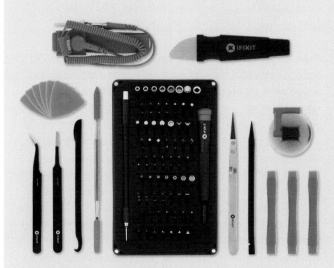

Figure 6.17b iFixit's Essential Electronics Toolkit. (photo courtesy ©iFixit/iFxit.com)

design long-lasting products and *build a business model around replacing parts and consumables, like the car industry*, rather than designing the device to be disposable when the consumable wears out.

JP. Whereas what is actually happening is that we have a model where disposables and durables are thrown in together?

KW. Yeah. They don't like the phrase *planned obsolescence*, but it sure seems to me that if you're designing the lifespan of a product around the lifetime of a battery that *is* the definition of planned obsolescence.

JP. Moving away from cell phones, in your experience, are there particular product areas, sectors or businesses that you think are especially problematic and you think designers should really be changing?

KW. What we see at the repair cafés are a lot of these very inexpensive kitchen gadgets – blenders, toasters, kettles. There's definitely been a race to the bottom in term of price on those – they're all made of plastic and they all snap together. So that is an area where I think there would be an opportunity for a mid-range brand that's long-lasting and repairable to come in.

Clearly the electronics side of many products is also frustrating. Nowadays you have to assume that any product you design may have electronics in it. So what we find is that when you integrate electronics into products that have traditionally had a reasonable lifespan, the electronics fail in new and exciting ways that are surprising to product designers and consumers. We've seen this with washing machines and home appliances where the lifespan has gone down to seven years, and usually it's the electronics that fail first. *So if you're going to build electronics into anything that is durable, design it so that the whole electronics module can be replaced several times during the lifetime of the product.*

JP. Finally Kyle, if you had magic wand, and you could redesign the way products are designed, manufactured and sold, what would you do?

KW. Just one thing. *You should not be able to sell a product without releasing a service manual and the electronic schematics for the product.* So I would change that ahead of any physical changes to the product. Product longevity is all about information flowing with the product.

But when a product does fail, ensuring they are repairable not only extends product life for the first user; it also means that it can go on to have multiple owners thanks to resale platforms. Repair also leads to greater economic sustainability by spreading financial benefit to more people through local employment and boosting secondary resale markets for affordable products. Given that products like smartphones and laptops have become an essential tool for most self-employed workers, many of whom are on low wages, extending the life of products by making them affordable to repair also becomes a matter of social equity and inclusion.

In the case of smartphones, the average failure rate across all brands was a staggering 14% in the first 12 months.[47] The most frequently replaced part by a long margin was the display, followed by water damage (accidental), camera and speaker modules (technical).[48] A good place to start in identifying the most common problems are repair and teardown blogs, including the repair platform iFixit that gives repairability scores for different product categories (see fig 4.20, iFixit manifesto). For smartphones and notepads, issues like LCD fused to the glass screen and soldered or glued components, especially batteries, are among the most common obstacles to repairability and life extension, and should be avoided. Brands like Fairphone, HP and Dell and more recently Apple have consciously moved towards greater access and repairability.

weakest link

A lesser-known cause of obsolescence is that the failure of a single tiny but essential integrated circuit (IC) unit determines the longevity of many large and small electronically controlled products due to the economics of producing ICs. Product manufacturers and brands often have to make educated guesses as to how many units they will need for the lifetime of the product, because the high set-up cost of producing IC modules makes small quantity orders later in the life of the product uneconomic.[49] To avoid this, design teams need to err on the high side in placing IC orders to include potential demand for replacement modules to keep otherwise functional equipment going.

Going forward, as we touched on in Chapter 4.3, the Maker Movement, regulations that will alter how products are planned and designed are now on the cusp of becoming a reality. In Europe, the Circular Economy Strategy includes moves to set standards of repairability and minimum or declared service life into the Eco-Design Directive for different product groups, and, in the USA, several states have legislation for the 'right-to-repair' EEE waiting to be passed.

Some product design 'dos' for repairability:

- know your product by familiarising yourself with the parts that most commonly break, fail or need replacing from normal wear and tear
- anticipate and prevent common causes of accidental damage (e.g. magsafe)
- in configuring the product, make parts accessible and replaceable with as few tools as possible and no proprietary fixings
- avoid gluing and soldering key components
- use standardised connectors
- create open repair instructions
- make reasonably priced spare parts available or locally printable

addressing functional and psychological obsolescence: make products upgradable and compatible

The ability to upgrade components in product categories where incremental technological improvements occur regularly not only extends the *functional* life but can also reduce *psychological* obsolescence by satisfying consumers who want or 'need' the latest performance from their devices. The demand for upgradability mostly revolves around performance, speed, capacity, quality and connective compatibility. Typical physical components that extend the life of smartphones and laptops are RAM, hard drives and batteries. The availability of software upgrades and extended software support are also essential for extending hardware longevity.

Physical modularity is one approach to extending product life but creating viable products designed from the ground up has proven more challenging than expected. Ara, PuzzlePhone and Fairphone all set out to do this for somewhat different motives, and to date only Fairphone has succeeded with a commercially viable product. The Ara phone, which started life as Phonebloks, was an ambitious Motorola ATAP/Google project which was sadly stopped in 2016. It set out to create 'extreme personalisation' by allowing phone owners to choose from any number of modules that they could pop on and off the base chassis.[50] In this sense Ara approached modularity purely from a user experience rather than sustainability. Given the level of public interest it raised, it would have been very informative to see whether this approach could create a powerful recipe for longevity and reduced e-waste through focusing on enhanced product experience (fig 6.18).

In contrast, PuzzlePhone designers, Circular Devices OY based in Finland, set out with the specific objective of creating a sustainable circular phone from the outset. Their design solution

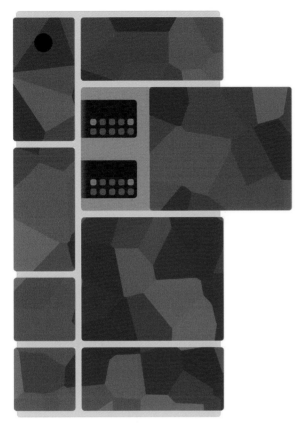

Figure 6.18 Illustration of the Ara phone, a development by Motorola ATAP, later Google, of the Phonebloks concept. (credit Martial Red)

Figure 6.19 The PuzzlePhone made up of three upgradable modules. (photo courtesy Circular Devices OY)

breaks the phone down into three key replaceable upgradable modules: the 'brain' (CPU, GPU and RAM), the structural 'spine' (screen), and the heart (battery and additional selected features) (fig 6.19). Although its development has been delayed, the phone is being designed to have ten years of usable life with the battery being replaced every three years.[51]

The third modular design, the Fairphone, grew out of a campaign to 'change the way products are made' and evolved into a social enterprise addressing the issues around the materials that go into making our phones, their longevity and our ever-increasing e-waste. After producing their first ethical phone that focused on a cleaner supply chain, they moved on to tackling life extension by designing the first ethical mass-market modular repairable smartphone, the Fairphone2, released in 2015. The design intention was that anyone would be able to repair their phone by simply replacing the damaged module. In an interview Olivier Hébert, their CTO, highlights some of the design challenges they encountered (Box 6.2).

The take-away from these three design adventures is that rethinking a product from the ground up is highly challenging, technically and commercially. But in the end it not only creates new product typologies; it also opens up the possibility of new relationships between owners and their electronic devices.

Some product design dos for upgradability and compatibility:

- be aware of the components that are likely to need upgrading and where possible make these accessible and changeable in the product architecture
- select software platforms that will continue to be supported for the longest time
- where relevant, design for personalisation through the physical and digital touchpoints to increase product bonding
- promote standardisation of connectors and interfaces to increase convergence and reduce redundant peripherals and accessories

addressing psychological and material obsolescence: give products long-term desirability and reliability

Although designers often have little say over the more technical specifications of a product, they have considerable input into shaping how we experience this technology through its digital and physical interfaces. While choices of form, detail, materials and finishes create a product's initial attraction, it is their ability to continue to please aesthetically, age well and delight functionally that contributes to longer ownership against the constant pull of newness.

Box 6.2 Interview with Olivier Hébert on challenging the status quo of smartphones and the electronics industry at Fairphone[52]

Fairphone is a social enterprise that designs and makes smartphones with a difference. They see themselves as part of a movement to show that the electronic products we use every day can be 'made better' and more ethically, right from mineral extraction to the end of their longer life. Their Fairphone2, the first mass-market ethical modular repairable smartphone, is a good demonstration of these principles in action.

As CTO, Olivier and team are responsible for everything that needs to happen from conception to production to get the 'right' Fairphone products into customers' hands.

JP. Starting from Fairphone's underlying principles of how to make electronics more sustainable, can you tell us about the key design decisions and insights that led to the Fairphone2 being what it is – inside and out?

OH. The Fairphone2 was all about importing the ambitions of Fairphone into a competitive product that would meet typical customer expectations. But we also wanted to build a smartphone that was as sustainable as possible driven by the fact that *the most sustainable phone is the one you already own and the one you can keep using.*

To achieve this we had to address the issues with the modern smartphone that go against longevity – that they are very fragile products, and very difficult and expensive to repair.

So we started by looking at the product from the inside out and asked ourselves: How can we re-engineer it in a way that:

- makes it easier to assemble
- easier to control waste

- uses fewer harmful processes
- can be a storytelling device

[...] and, crucially, still be a *fully competitive phone?*

Overall I think we've achieved this. When it was designed in 2014/2015, it was comparable with the Samsung S5 less a couple of features – wireless charging and NFC – which we felt were not essential at the time.

JP. Were there any design trade-offs in making it modular and less fragile?

OH. Our only design compromise was in adding a few millimetres to the thickness, which we are fine with because, as it turns out, that has the benefit of making the phone more robust, one of our key objectives. We also added a bezel to protect from screen breakages and the external case doubles as phone protection, which saves on extra covers or bumpers. So far, these features are working very well – we have had far fewer cracked displays than competing devices.

JP. And what about unforeseen design benefits to the modularity?

OH. Even though our main objective with the modular design was to create a phone that could be maintained for as long as possible, we found that we could use the modular construction to upgrade the camera module, as this is a technology that is still changing rapidly. Packing so much more functionality into the same dimensions was quite a test. But that's what is actually interesting about designing phones – the 3D challenge of fitting it all into the ridiculously small space you have.

Figure 6.20 Inside and behind the scenes of the Fairphone 2: fairly mined cobalt in Rwanda. (photos courtesy Fairphone)

JP. Making a phone that is completely accessible and repairable by its owner is quite a technical feat. Can you tell us how you approached this from the usability point of view?

OH. The way we see it, the entire product is a user interface, inside and out. So we took a lot of trouble to design it so that the user can service their own phone very simply without any instructions, training or special tools. It took quite a few user iterations to get the colour, design and placement of the graphics right. In the end we developed an iconography that clearly identifies the different modules and exactly which screws are user-serviceable.

JP. What role do you see aesthetics playing in product longevity to counteract people's temptation for the next newer and shinier phone, even if theirs still works?

OH. Yes, we certainly did consider aesthetics an important part of the strategy, because if you make the ugliest device ever, no one will want to buy it, let alone keep it! We also did some work around being able to update the look and feel of the product. The interchangeable slim case, for example, is one of those ideas that allows you to refresh the look without changing the entire device – which saves money and reduces environmental impacts.

We also experimented with ways people could connect more with their device via the software by showing how long they have owned it, but this has proved difficult to maintain when modules are refurbished or replaced. We like to try new things, but not all of them work.

JP. So far you are doing well in achieving three of Fairphone's objectives: fair materials, good working conditions and long-lasting products through your modular design. What about the fourth, reuse and recycling?

OH. Recycling of electronics, especially smartphones, remains a big challenge. At the moment the maximum recovery per phone is $1 to $2. For that money the recyclers can't spend time disassembling, even though they might recover a little more material through another process. So although the modular design lends itself to higher material recovery and we do have a take-back programme and refurbish modules, smartphones are still far from a circular economy, but we are working on this.

JP. What other factors stand in the way of a designer's good intentions in designing longer lived devices?

OH. Designers have to be aware that the mobile device industry is one of the key drivers of the entire electronics industry, simply because of the sheer volume. With about 2 billion devices a year, every cent and every competitive edge matters. So suppliers tend to shift their portfolios very, very quickly in order to cut costs in any way they can.

This means that designers have little control over how long the electronic IC components for their products will be available or how long the software will be supported, unless you are a large vertically integrated company like Apple. For smaller producers like us who depend on ODMs, you have to be good at estimating demand and base your design on the system platform that is likely to have greatest longevity. But there is no certainty, and these factors do in the end affect product longevity.

Figure 6.21 The Fairphone 2 assembled and disassembled into its modular components: display module, battery, main camera module, bottom module, core module, top module and selfie camera. (photos courtesy Fairphone)

Nokia's 3310 from 2000 and its re-launch in 2017 is an example of a design that became a classic through a combination of the Nokia signature aesthetics: supreme reliability, solidity and overall quality. It demonstrates very well the importance of what happens *after* the initial physical attraction of a product persuades us to bring it into our lives. As a product that we live with so intimately and rely on so closely, it is its dependability and familiarity that transforms the mobile phone from a *useful object* to a *trusted friend*. This can only be achieved if the attraction of the form factor is subsequently matched by the quality of the build, interface and product ecosystem (fig 6.22).

Today, with connected digital products, the deciding factor for repeat brand purchases has shifted from the physical form of a product to the whole experience and lock-in that product ecosystems create. This became clear after Apple introduced the iPod in 2001. While Apple did not invent MP3 technology, they did create a unique physical gateway to digital music that delighted its owners through its signature click wheel and clean aesthetics (see fig 6.14). Yet sales of iPods did not take off until *after* they introduced the iTunes store in 2003.[53] It needed a seamless download ecosystem for consumers to embrace digital music. Between the iPhone being the most-ever sold product and reaching the status of most profitable company in the world, Apple has amply demonstrated the impact that a clear design vision and an obsessive attention to design detail across all their digital and physical touchpoints can have on commercial success.

Below are some product design dos for long-term desirability and loyalty. Design products that:

- have seamless, intuitive and enjoyable digital and physical interfaces
- improve with age
- don't disappoint
- you don't want to part with
- you won't have to part with

optimal lifespan: extending life, but for how long?

Assuming products are used for longer by repairing and upgrading, how long *should* products be designed to last? Or, given that EEE products are continually becoming more efficient, at what point does extending product life become counterproductive? The point at which it is better to buy a newer product is when it reaches its *optimal lifespan*. This is when the cumulative impact of all the energy that could have been saved each year by using a newer model equals the impact of producing the latest, most efficient model.

As an example, figure 6.23 shows that between 1980 and 2020 the dynamic calculation for the *optimal* lifespan of fridge-freezers

grew longer, reaching 20 years from 2011. On the other hand, the optimal lifespan for laptops has remained a steady seven years from 1990 and 2010, although some studies suggest that it could be much longer.[54] However, *actual* lifespans are proving to be much shorter than the optimal. Fridge-freezers' lifespans in Germany dropped from 14.1 in 2004 to 12.6 years in 2012/2013, while laptops lifespans were 4 to 5 years between 2010 and 2012.[55] Ultimately, this suggests that designers and companies should be aiming to align their target *product design life* with *optimal lifespans*. For this they will have to use the best information available of future efficiency improvement regulations supported by the right PSS business models to keep their products in use for longer economically.

end-of-life (EoL) e-waste: reducing it, making it safe and getting more out of it

Some of the biggest problems associated with electronics are the rising volumes of e-waste being generated globally, their relatively low collection and material recovery rates and the unsafe handling and leakage of its hazardous materials. Several of the design strategies we have touched upon can contribute directly to cutting the quantity of e-waste because it is measured by weight. These include reducing the amount of material per product through material efficiency and miniaturisation and slowing down the number of products entering the waste stream through product life extension and digital convergence. On the other hand, increasing recovery rates, recyclability and safe handling of WEEE require that new circular systemic solutions be devised and implemented that encompass the whole PSS, including new business models (see Chapter 4.4).

In considering strategies that address e-waste, it is worth noting the fact that the EoL is the *only phase* of an environmental LCA where the negative effects from earlier phases can be mitigated by recovering and recycling its materials. This is clearly demonstrated in the Fairphone 2 LCA where full recycling was assumed. Recovering its precious metals, in this case gold, reduced resource-depletion impacts (ADP) by 60% (see fig 6.4a).

In an ideal world designers would design for the method of recycling their products are most likely to be fed into or, where there is a choice, for the most effective recycling method for their type of product. Yet, in most current EPR systems, companies and therefore designers have little control over how their products will be handled or recycled at their EoL, unless they are large enough to manage and control full closed-loop take-back systems such as the ones Dell, Apple and HP have begun to operate.

Figure 6.22 The original Nokia 3310 (2000) and the 2017 re-edition. (credits Hannah Kuprevich; bijutoha)

(a) Fridge-freezers

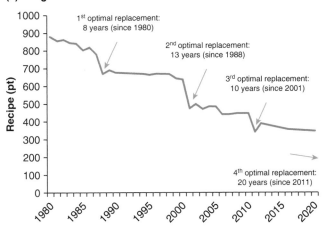

(b) Laptops

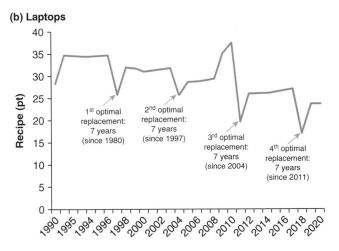

Figure 6.23 Optimal lifespans for fridge-freezers and laptops based on ReCiPe (Pt.) LCA impacts. (source: Bakker et al., *Journal of cleaner Production* 2014)

To better understand whether modularity contributes to better recyclability, Fairphone compared the effectiveness of recycling their modular product by the three most common processes used for smartphones (fig 6.24). The processes are:[56]

1. Smelting: the whole phone is fed into a metallurgical furnace with metals, alloys, inorganic compounds recovered and refined and plastics used as fuel.
2. Dismantling: the main components – battery, modules, casing – are separated and put though metal and plastic recovery processes.
3. Shredding: the battery is removed and the phone goes through a cutting mill and the scrap fractions are separated and processed accordingly.

The study found that for the Fairphone 2 modular design the dismantling route was marginally more effective. It produced more materials by weight than smelting as well as recovering the widest range of materials and using the least energy of the three. But even for these three standard recycling processes, the total material recovered for each was below 30%. In short, even if we managed to capture all our e-waste, *electronic products are unlikely to become 100% closed-loop recyclable in the very near future.*[57]

This is further evidenced by the fact that with very few exceptions, recycled minerals are almost non-existent in the production of new electronics. This may well be set to change with Apple's announcement in 2017 that their long-term aim is to close the loop and make all their products from recycled or renewable sources.[58] Although they have already started this journey with disassembly robots Liam (2016) followed by Daisy (2018)[59] that enable them to recover and recycle precious metals via their GiveBack programme, Apple have no fixed timeline for fully achieving this ambitious goal.[60] This is indeed uncharted and much-needed territory for electronic products (fig 6.25).

Meanwhile, as a member of the Circular Economy 100 (CE100), Dell is pioneering successful circular economy models for electronics plastics. Their Optiplex 3030 desktop (2014) containing up to 35% recycled ABS in the stand and back enclosure and their laptop packaging trays made from 25% ocean plastics from Haiti (2017) are both industry firsts. By 2017 they had surpassed their recycling targets for 2020, achieving 35% overall recycled plastic content across their product portfolio through their take-back and asset-resale schemes.[61]

While finding ways to reduce WEEE and increase the recyclability and the recycled content of electronics will remain a major challenge for designers and the whole industry in the years to come, the following actions can help:

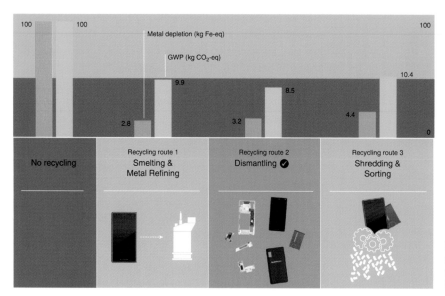

Figure 6.24 Comparison of GHG emissions and material recovery for the Fairphone 2 through the most common EPR recycling routes for smartphones in Europe. (courtesy Fairphone)

Figure 6.25 Apple's Daisy robot can disassemble up to 200 iPhone devices an hour and handle up to nine different versions of iPhone. Shown here: Daisy's disassembly table where sorted components are dropped ready for high-quality material recovery. (photo courtesy Apple Inc.)

- design products and services for the optimum lifespan and best EoL scenario
- persist in eliminating toxic substances by finding design solutions for substitutes
- be knowledgeable about the different EoL scenarios and recycling methods
- design products to be compatible with the most likely and most effective recycling methods, be they open- or closed-loop systems
- transition to include maximum recycled content in product specs to drive up demand for recycled materials

'green' and transient electronics: a greener future?

The design strategies we have looked at up until now have focused on mitigating the negative physical impacts of current consumer electronics. If we accept that the digital world is here to stay and that overall it is beneficial, the question we should be asking ourselves is: How could electronics be redesigned to be radically better for the environment rather than just 'less bad'?

To do this, we need to approach the design of electronics from a completely different mindset to what it was 60 years ago when electronics were first being developed to be durable and stable. This is the starting premise for the emerging fields of 'green' and 'transient' electronics. Their vision is to create a new class of high-performing and adaptable electronic devices that biodegrade safely when no longer needed.[62]

To achieve this, high-performance electronic components are being made from natural or nature-inspired bio-compatible materials that will not cause harm if released into the environment because they are either bio-benign or biodegradable. These include organic materials such as paper, nano-cellulose, silk, DNA, PVOH and other dissolving plastics, as well as many naturally occurring materials such as chitosan, collagen, melanin, waxes, gelatines and shellac. They are also being made from inorganic materials such as hydrolysable silicons and soluble metals and metal oxides. All these new possibilities for substrate materials also mean that electronics can take any form: rigid, flexible and even stretchable[63] (figs 6.26 and 6.27).

The successful demonstration of high-performance electronic components made of fully or partially biodegradable materials in the lab opens the door to a whole new generation of electronics that include:

- electronics printed onto flexible and even transparent paper and cellulose substrates for low-cost large-area displays and photovoltaic power cells

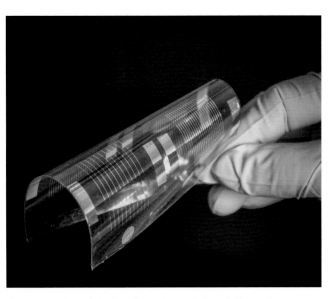

Figure 6.26 Towards benign electronics 1: Biodegradable conductor structures on biodegradable polymer film. This represents a potentially huge improvement over current printed flexible large area electronics. (courtesy ©Fraunhofer FEP/photo credit Jan Hesse)

- OLEDs an order of magnitude brighter with the addition of a thin DNA film, paving the way to ultra-effective and biodegradable optics, displays and living system interfaces
- bio-compatible and dissolvable silk protein used for electronic implants and intelligent clothing[64]

Meanwhile, the field of *transient electronics* is taking the idea of biodegradability a step further with fully bio-compatible and resorbable materials. All their components, including batteries, are designed to 'disappear' after a set time by fully dissolving in water or body fluids, or by disintegrating in response to a specific trigger such as light or temperature.[65] Successfully demonstrated applications for transient electronics include:

- consumer electronics that are fully biodegradable such that they can be safely disposed of and replaced when the technology needs upgrading, in response to the growing quantity of e-waste that is either unrecyclable or expensive and energy intensive to recycle and includes toxic substances
- bio-medical implants for diagnostics or therapies that are only needed for a short period of time like temporary heart stents, localised treatments, drug delivery or symptom monitoring
- environmental monitoring like animal and plant tags and water, soil and air quality sensors that don't need to be retrieved at the end of a study period
- memory devices that can self-destruct to keep sensitive information or personal data secure

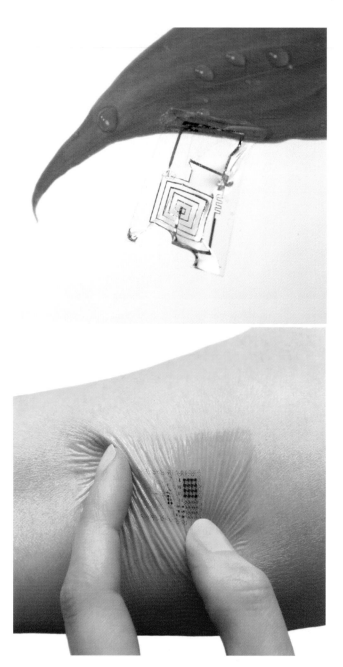

Figure 6.27 Towards benign electronics 2: transient electronic applications in medicine and environmental monitoring. (photos courtesy Professor John Rogers/Northwestern University and Univeristy of Illinois at Urbana Champaign)

With green and transient electronics at the stage of leaving the lab, product designers should seize the opportunity to be involved in envisioning and driving demand for a whole new era of digital devices that will 'blur the lines between physical, digital and biological spheres'.[66] Not only will these new electronics create completely new products and design languages, their biodegradability can make them compatible with the idea of programming in optimal lifespans.

We expect that in the future we will be as comfortable with highly flexible and degradable forms of electronics, embedded everywhere, in textiles, on skin and even within our body as we are now familiar with smartphones and table computers.[67]

6.3 the social value of digital tools

Taken on their own, the environmental costs of electrical and electronic devices suggest that we are simply creating yet another mass-production-consumption nightmare for ourselves and the planet. This can leave sustainably minded designers feeling frustrated by the fact that their products will at best be doing 'less harm' within the constraints of current production and disposal systems. But this would be ignoring their potential to create socially, economically and even environmentally beneficial and life-changing products.

At this point it would be good to remind ourselves of our definition of sustainable design as design that *enhances the wider human experience by meeting 'needs' more intelligently and creatively within the Earth's capacity supported by an enabling economic framework.* And sustainable products and services are those that *create net positive value socially, economically and environmentally.*

This definition of sustainable products ties in closely with the concept of 'net-positive' business that is gaining traction with a growing number of influential companies around the world. A 'net-positive' perspective that includes measuring social impacts is particularly useful for electrical, electronic and digital products because it allows us to set their negative physical impacts against their ability to be powerful instruments for both good across a spectrum of sectors.

In Chapter 2.5 on radical rethinks we touched on how digital and electronic tools are powering the IoT and big data to optimise energy, logistics and infrastructure efficiencies. In Chapter 8 we will see how digitally controlled drones are being used for environmental protection, monitoring and restoration projects as well as assisting with solar and wind farm maintenance and monitoring. We will also look at how connectivity and the digital control of electric vehicles are enabling the revolution that will transform mobility in the next two decades. All these applications demonstrate the positive environmental contribution that digital controls and electronics can make to offset some of their negative impacts.

The second half of the chapter explores some of the many instances where digital technologies channelled through physical products are being used positively to advance a sustainable agenda with people and planet at its centre. But first, we touch briefly on some of the criticisms levelled at digital technologies and the social threats they pose.

digital technology and society: criticism and debate

For the many millions of people with full access, the digital universe has become highly pervasive and even omnipresent. It increasingly mediates every aspect of how we conduct our personal and working lives, and how we experience the world around us. This is having disruptive and unsettling effects across all areas of society, from the loss of boundaries between private and public spheres to the very nature of our institutions, employment, education and democracy. We should also note that for large areas of the world where digital connectivity has not arrived, there are equally great concerns regarding the widening inequality of opportunities for development that this is creating.

As we find ourselves part of this live experiment, the subject of the social and economic effects of the 'tech' industry holds an immense fascination for us. Much has and is being written on this subject and there is a steadily growing body of research to support it. While it is beyond the scope of this book to explore these effects in any depth, John McNaughton's 95 Theses about Technology,[68] Doug Rushcoff and Jaron Lanier[69] are good starting points in appreciating some of the debates it is raising and the possible alternatives. For now we will recognise that there is much to question in how it is unfolding in society by summarising some key criticisms levelled against digital technology and its predicted direction of travel:

1. How digital technology's ubiquity and pervasiveness, supported by the asymmetrical relationships and business models of digital platforms, allows it to collect, generate and feed off people's data, creating a state of constant surveillance and manipulation that transgresses personal privacy and freedoms.
2. How the exponential speed at which technology is evolving and new business models and power structures are being created is testing to their limits the ability of individuals, social structures and institutions including democracy to adapt.
3. How its characteristic of always being 'on' and demanding attention by continuously generating and pushing information bites is, together with the other two points, creating ever-increasing levels of stress and mental health issues.

At the very least, the growing control of digital networks and platforms in the hands of a few powerful giants is raising questions. Is it too late for the Internet and its highly effective platforms to be wrestled back from the monopoly model to more equitable collaborative models?

Figure 6.28 Fully absorbed Pokémon Go players in Ho Chi Min City, Vietnam in August 2016, completely oblivious to their surroundings in Tao Dan Park. (photo credit xianhuongho)

From a design point of view, it is interesting to note the transformational effect that a single new product typology can have on society and how we experience life. The iPhone is one such product. As the first smartphone, it set the ubiquitous computing and connectivity revolution in motion in 2007 by providing the pocket-sized gateway that enables everyone to be constantly connected and tracked[70] (fig 6.28).

In the introduction to Chapter 3, we suggested some of the key challenges for product designers to further social sustainability. Among these were putting people at the centre of design and challenging the direction of technology to produce value for society. With this in mind, we will look at a few examples of tech-integrating products that keep humans at the centre while addressing some aspects of social and environmental equity and human dignity. These include tools for education and creativity, sustainable lifestyles, health, wellbeing and ageing, and empowerment for the base of the pyramid. It is also important to note that product design is not alone in pursuing these agendas. This is closely connected to the problems being addressed mostly through software by 'Digital Social Innovation',[71] a subset of Design for Social Innovation (DSI), and the 'Tech for Good' movement. Figure 6.29 shows the main areas that digital social innovation is engaged in and the most frequently used supporting technologies.[72]

education and learning

Ensuring inclusive and quality education for all and promoting lifelong learning is one of the UN's 17 Sustainable Development Goals and a core pillar of an equitable society. Education not only provides knowledge and skills for employment and personal

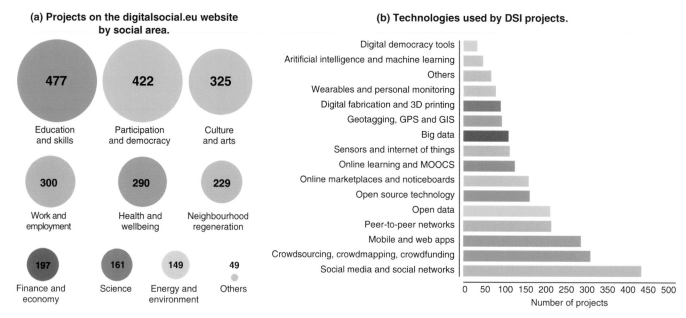

(a) Projects on the digitalsocial.eu website by social area.

477 Education and skills

422 Participation and democracy

325 Culture and arts

300 Work and employment

290 Health and wellbeing

229 Neighbourhood regeneration

197 Finance and economy

161 Science

149 Energy and environment

49 Others

(b) Technologies used by DSI projects.

Digital democracy tools
Aritificial intelligence and machine learning
Others
Wearables and personal monitoring
Digital fabrication and 3D printing
Geotagging, GPS and GIS
Big data
Sensors and internet of things
Online learning and MOOCS
Online marketplaces and noticeboards
Open source technology
Open data
Peer-to-peer networks
Mobile and web apps
Crowdsourcing, crowdmapping, crowdfunding
Social media and social networks

0 50 100 150 200 250 300 350 400 450 500
Number of projects

Figure 6.29 Problems addressed by digital social innovation projects and chief supporting technologies. (source: digitalsocial.eu 2017)

growth; crucially it also socialises and empowers people as citizens.[73] It is not difficult to see technology being used in education, for those with access to it. Or that technology is changing the *way* we learn through online material and tools. But how is it, or how could it contribute to *sustainable* education?

First, the Internet provides a point of entry to a global commons of knowledge as exemplified through platforms like Wikipedia. Leaving aside that the search engines through which we access this information have their own opaque and self-interested algorithm filters, it remains an extraordinary repository of open knowledge and understanding, and a live and dynamic tool for learning and dissemination. Our ancestors could only have imagined such a rich resource in their wildest dreams.

The Internet has also brought down the barriers to more formalised education by enhancing distance learning and enabling the creation of Massive Open Online Courses (MOOCS) that span cultures and continents. In addition, AI-assisted pedagogic methods and materials are increasingly allowing for personalised programmes to suit individual learning modes and speeds, potentially reducing exclusion by making learning more accessible.

While most of the learning content is software based, it is still primarily accessed through hardware that in turn is controlled through physical human interfaces, be they speech, gesture, touch, sight or, coming soon, thought. By designing tangible physical interfaces, there are a number of ways in which product design is actively contributing to the vast field of sustainable 'education and learning'. These include enabling access to and interaction with digital content, the creation of new digital content, and the design-and-build of tailored digital electronic tools and functionalities.

widening access to learning and digital literacy

By the end of 2018 just over half the world's population – 3.8 billion people – were using the Internet in one form or another.[74] While this is a wonderful milestone, it also highlights that the other half of the world's population is not accessing what is an increasingly essential tool for learning, employment and basic services. Among the possible reasons put forward for not using the Internet are: the fact that they may as yet have no need for it; they cannot afford a device; they don't have access to electricity or digital networks; and/or they are not digitally literate. Yet, in less than a generation, digital literacy has moved alongside literacy and numeracy as essential lifeskills, making this state of affairs deeply concerning.

With this in mind, the One Laptop Per Child (OLPC) NGO project founded in 2005 from the MIT Media Lab set out to provide children from the most disadvantaged backgrounds around the world with a computer as a tool for learning. In order to achieve this they designed a very rugged, low-energy and inexpensive laptop. Their aim was an all-in-one $100 computer by 2008.

The first version, the XO-1, launched in 2007, was both a technological and design feat. It operated and still does on an open source system with free software and was one of the earliest laptops to run on flash memory for increased reliability. It also featured a dual-mode display that is either transmissive in full

Figure 6.30 The original OLPC $100 OX beta-1 prototype (2006) and self-made charging racks in a classroom (2012). (photo credits Rudolf Simon; Mike McGregor)

colour or reflective in black and white, like an ebook, to reduce power consumption where electricity is in short supply. While Design Continuum shaped the initial physical concept, fuseproject under Yves Behar led the final design and have remained the project's lead industrial designers, overseeing its various upgrades, including the XO-4 touch 2013[75] (fig 6.30).

While OLPC succeeded in selling and distributing millions of laptops to countries around the world, in the early years they were far less successful in having these laptops integrated as effective teaching tools. Critics believe that their initial 'one-shot' approach of simply *hand[ing] out laptops failed because they ignored local contexts and discounted the importance of curriculum and ongoing social as well as technical support and training.*[76] There is now an understanding within the OLPC Association and other digital education programmes that their products need to be supported by a whole user-centred ecosystem that includes teacher training, support, and locally grounded and regularly updated curricula. *"Regrettably, there is no magic laptop that can solve the educational problems of the world's poor."*[77]

The ProFuturo education programme supported by Telefónica Foundation and 'La Caixa' Banking Foundation in Spain is an example of where a holistic approach was taken from the start. It has the ambition "to narrow the education gap in the world by providing quality digital education for children in vulnerable environments in Latin America, Sub-Saharan Africa and Asia". ProFuturo is an all-round solution that integrates a series of digital learning experiences for elementary school-aged children, itineraries for teachers' professional development and a system

Figure 6.31 Children in Central School, Puerto Galera, the Philippines, using their Profuturo tablets for lessons. (courtesy Fundación Profuturo)

for continuous assessment and impact measurement. When needed, the programme provides a hardware 'kit' that contains a laptop server, tablets, projector and power source. The unit is designed to be self-powered for a whole school day, and consists of a self-contained educational platform that only requires periodic Internet connection for content updates (fig 6.31). While the physical design elements are far more generic than the OLPC XO computer, the focus has been on whole-system design, building on more than a decade of local experience in delivering effective digital education programmes within these communities.[78]

code or be coded

The modern world is filled with billions of machines. But 1% of 1% of us can open them up, and change them.[79]

Kano

Our mission is to inspire kids everywhere to use technology to create new things, solve life-changing problems, and invent their own future in a world where 65% of kids in school today will have a job that doesn't exist yet. [80]

Tech Will Save Us

At littleBits, we believe we have to empower kids to be creators and inventors with technology, and not just consumers of it.[81]

littleBits

What do these mission statement extracts, Raspberry Pi, Arduino, Kano, littleBits, Tech Will Save Us, Makey Makey and others in this field have in common? That they are determined to demystify technology by providing the physical building blocks and systems for anyone, from children through to adults and companies to learn to code and create their own digital-physical applications (fig 6.32). In the case of Raspberry Pi, affordability was also fundamental. Eben Utpon and the team set out to sell a $25 computer in 2011. Since then they have designed models costing as little as $5 and have gone on to sell more than 25 million units (2019), becoming the third highest-selling general computer in the world.[82]

In this sense, these products may be considered to be the tools for democratising hardware, just as free and open-source codes are to software. By making coding and building accessible from a young age, they are empowering a wider and more diverse range of people with the skills and tools to shape what tech will do in the future, a sustainable achievement in itself.

But the success of these products goes beyond the physical artefacts, however well designed. As an extension of the hacker-and-maker movement, they are very much dependent on the supportive and sharing nature of their user communities. In the case of Raspberry Pi, a hybrid company structure ensures that the work of the Raspberry Pi Foundation is funded by the profits of Raspberry Pi Trading. This work includes generating research, educational material, training and supporting a network of school coding clubs to ensure that the movement grows at the grassroots.

Raspberry Pi and Arduino are also being put to good use directly as development tools in innumerable applications all over the globe, including on the International Space Station. More down-to-earth applications include Practical Action's use of Rasberry Pi computers run on open software and built with 3D printed components to act as autonomous rainfall sensors to help farmers in Peru. They have also been used in the First Light project initiated by Ensemble Pour la Difference and funded by the Fjord Innovation Fund that aims to help Congolese people build prosperous, sustainable businesses owned and run by local people. One of the first challenges was to design Internet services for the islanders of Idjwi in the Democratic Republic of Congo (DRC) in a form that would be useful and self-sustainable. The outcome is the Pamoja Net, a shared kiosked Internet service that runs a meshed wi-fi network off Raspberry Pi computers, where residents can now call, text and go online[83] (fig 6.33).

essential tech for the base of the pyramid

In Chapter 3, we saw that many of the most effective and successful designs for lifting the poorest people in the world out of poverty were low-cost and relatively low-tech solutions. However, there were two products that stood out as exceptions:

Figure 6.32 Part of Kano's kit computer with Raspberry Pi board in the early-build stage, one of several products that invite children to learn about and take control of technology through experimentation. (photos courtesy Kano)

Figure 6.33 Pamoja Net is a kiosked community Internet service running off Rasberry Pi computers. Shown here on Idjwi Island, Lake Kivu, there is a shared screen for news and weather and residents can text, call and get online. (DRC 2017). (photo courtesy Ensemble Pour la Difference)

Figure 6.34 Masai woman using her phone in Arusha, Tanzania: new technology complementing traditional Masai ways (2014). (photo credit franco lucato/ Shutterstock.com)

solar-powered LED lighting and smartphones. For people living hand-to-mouth on less than $2 a day, mobiles, cells and smartphones have become crucial tools for communicating, running businesses and making micro-payments for essential goods and services (fig 6.34). Equally, the availability of light results in better school outcomes and higher incomes by extending where and when people can study and work.

But both of these key products require electricity, which is only just becoming available in affordable forms for off-grid situations, mostly thanks to solar PV and micro-grids. For households still waiting for affordable electricity to reach them, solar-powered stand-alone lights with USB charging capacity such as d-light's S100 (see fig 3.23) and Greenplanet's Sun King range are already having a transformative effect (fig 6.35).

Figure 6.35 Greenplanet's Sun King Pro 400 solar light and USB charger. An essential tool for this fruit stall holder in Uttar Pradesh, India and fisherman in Siaya County, Kenya to earn their living off-grid. (courtesy Greenplanet/photo credits Michael Murage; Pankaj Anand)

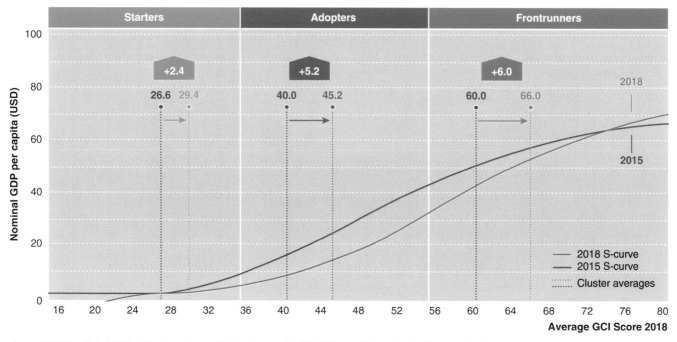

Figure 6.36 The digital divide risks becoming a digital chasm as the Global Connectivity Index (GCI) gap widens between countries with high and low GDP. (source: Huawei Global Connectivity Index 2018)

In addition, the smartphone requires connectivity, and there are many regions of the world where this is not yet available, particularly across the equatorial belt. The Huawei Global Connectivity Index shows a clear correlation between GDP and Internet access. More concerning, the digital inequality gap continues to grow, with over 84% of households in Europe having Internet access compared to Africa's 18% in 2018, making this more of a 'digital chasm' than a divide (fig 6.36). Not surprisingly, over time countries with well-established ICT infrastructures – the 'haves' – will leverage their head start to pull even further ahead over the 'have-nots' in what is known as the Matthew effect.[84] With social and economic inclusion one of the key premises of the UN SDGs, addressing the growing 'digital divide' is a very pressing issue.[85]

In response to the off-grid connectivity challenge, BuffaloGrid has set up vital connectivity and mobile charging services via its centrepiece, the solar-powered BuffaloGrid Hub. This is supported by its own network, local agents and a mobile pre-payment system designed for parts of the world where this is not otherwise available (fig 6.37). To complete the jigsaw, new nanosatellite networks such as the ones developed by Sky and Space Global are a ray of hope in achieving affordable universal connectivity in the near future.[86]

AI and robotics: tech for the 1% to control the 99%?

From simply gaining access to electricity and networks in order to benefit from the most basic technology we move to the other

Figure 6.37 A BuffaloGrid Hub at work charging phones in Utta Pradesh, India. (photo courtesy ©BuffaloGrid)

extreme: Artificial Intelligence (AI) and robotics. As our most advanced digital tool, AI conjures up scenarios that range from the utopian to the dystopian, fed by countless science fictions, fear and conjecture. Although nobody can say with certainty how or what it will develop into, what we do know is that AI is already with us and is actively being developed in different forms. However, the sense that it will affect our lives radically and that it is inevitable and unstoppable is causing fear and anxiety for many. From the mass job losses we are told to prepare for as people are replaced by more 'intelligent' systems and 'computer says' interfaces, to the existential threat of domination and even annihilation, there are many ethical issues surrounding AI and its consequences that are very relevant to sustainability.

In order to identify where the paths of AI, product design and sustainability may cross, we first need to understand what is meant by AI and its different levels. The AI we currently live with termed 'weak' or 'narrow' is AI focused on a single or a series of interconnected tasks. Typically this takes the form of making sense of data inputs, using these to generate responses and applying machine learning to adapt future responses based on the feedback loops these create. We currently experience this form of AI daily through the algorithms used in search engines, home automation, drones, driverless cars and 'virtual assistants' Siri, Alexa, Cortana, Watson, Xiaoyu Zaijia (Little Fish), and Google through our phone, computer, car or 'smart' speaker interfaces. It can also take the form of robots for manufacturing and carrying out a range of tasks, from butlers, vacuum cleaners and sex robots to care support for the elderly and family pets. Annual sales of industrial robots are already over 300,000, while household robots are expected to exceed 31 million in 2019.[87]

The goal of Artificial General Intelligence (AGI) on the other hand is the creation of machines that have the ability to deal independently with *any* problem without being specifically instructed. One step on from this is 'strong AI' that aims to create supra-human intelligent machines with consciousness and sentience. With sufficiently intelligent software involving neural networks and deep learning, this AI is capable of continuous self-improvement. This means it can get smarter and smarter, as demonstrated by Deep Mind's AlphaGo and later AlphaZero triumphs. Its creators found that AlphaGo was easily capable of defeating the top human Go player at the time, Ke Jie, by developing strategies beyond and better than human and computer tactics to date. The expectation is that programmes supported by neural networks will lead to 'super-intelligent' machines that far surpass the capacity of human intelligence. The point at which this happens is known as 'the singularity' because no human predictions can be made beyond it. Whether this super-intelligence is in pervasive computing, sentient robots or even coordinated nanobots in our cyborg bodies, it is not difficult to see why the goal of AGI and 'strong AI' raise concerns for the future of the human race and the entire planet.

The problem is not so much that AI inventions will turn against us through someone's will (although that would be possible), but rather through unintended consequences beyond our control or ability to predict given their supra-human intelligence. We only have to look at global warming and the unintended consequences that the use of fossil fuels has unleashed to appreciate that they are by their very nature unpredictable and probably inevitable. These very serious safety and ethical concerns of how AI is

developed have led to the creation of organisations like the Future of Life Institution (FLI) and OpenAI, a NFP co-founded by Elon Musk. Their purpose is for AI to be developed as a valuable social tool and to "ensure that AI's benefits are as widely and evenly distributed as possible".[88]

The importance of considering AI in relation to sustainable design cannot be understated. Over the next decade product designers will increasingly be involved in shaping a proliferation of products that embed AI or are based on new applications of AI as they emerge from the labs. And, depending upon how we choose to deploy them, these AI-led products will have significant societal implications.

As machines become able to do everything 'better' than humans and know us better than ourselves, there are many fundamental questions we need to ask ourselves and take a position on as citizens and as designers. Will humans find themselves deskilled, replaced and lacking a sense of purpose, or will AI extend our capabilities and provide access to wellbeing for a greater number? Will people have any real choice through collective decision-making, or will it simply 'happen' to them? Ethically, where and how do we draw the line between what is truly beneficial vs. developing technology 'just because we can' and then post-rationalising its usefulness?

Or, if we paraphrase Alan Kay and take the view that "the only way to predict a sustainable future is to invent it", might a supra-intelligence invested with an absolute respect for the environment and the highest human values solve the problem of human unsustainability for us?

health, wellbeing, technology and sustainability

Health and wellbeing for all through the equitable distribution of the planets resources is a central pillar of sustainability and a key SDG. This has also become a strong focus area for sustainably minded product design, often through the application of new technologies. Since the millennium, advances in medicine and how these reach people have led to very positive increases in the global average life expectancy to 72 years. In Africa between 2000 and 2016 it increased by 10.3 years to 61 years. However, despite the overall improvement, average life expectancy in several sub-Saharan countries is closer to 50 years, leaving a big gap between it and the highest average life expectancy of 77 in Europe. This highlights the very unequal distribution of health care resources across the globe.[89]

While developing countries are dealing with challenges around basic hygiene, living conditions, diet, safe water, sanitation and access to medical treatment, advanced economies face a very different set of challenges. Stress, loneliness, obesity, unhealthy lifestyle choices, substance dependencies and even increasing longevity of itself are growing contributors to chronic physical and mental illness. These two scenarios are truly worlds apart in terms of their needs and the appropriate forms of design interventions. However, selecting the most effective health care strategies is by no means only a question of money and technology. This point is demonstrated by the fact that Cubans and Americans have the same life expectancy, yet Cuba spends *11 times less* than the USA on health care.[90] Keeping this in mind, and recalling the power of frugal design (Chapter 3.3), sustainably minded designers should be prepared to question what approaches to health care and forms of technology are *really* beneficial and how best to apply them.

Without question in advanced economies, digital technology is rapidly changing how health and wellbeing is accessed, managed and delivered at home or in clinics. This is being enabled by the combination of remote access technologies and electronic bio-sensors that can be used for self- or professional diagnoses, monitoring, and managing chronic illnesses such as diabetes, asthma, epilepsy and hypertension (see fig 2.24).

People are also choosing to monitor themselves for fitness, weight loss, sleep quality and much more thanks to a plethora of wearable products that feed the fascination with the 'quantified self'. While many of these activity and health trackers have proven helpful in motivating users to embark upon fitness regimes and healthier lifestyles, research shows that many users rapidly lose enthusiasm.[91] Sadly, between the drop in motivation, general information overload and rapid introduction of newer sensing technologies, millions of these products are ending up forgotten in drawers or go down the unwanted gadget e-waste path. This suggests that these products could do with a thorough reconsideration of how to extend their longevity together with better closed-loop recyclability (see Chapter 2.5, IoT).

an ageing demographic meets AI and robots
As we can see from the 'quantified self' phenomena, the majority of tech applications deal with 'problems' of the richest 20%. There is however one problem that most 'rich' and 'poor' countries will share in the next decades and that is an ageing demographic. By 2050, 25% of the population in all regions of the world will be over the age of 60, except in Africa. This is already the case in Japan and Europe, with Australia, Russia, Canada, the USA, South Korea and Hong Kong close behind.[92] By 2030, China, Brazil and Thailand are expected to join the club. With people living longer, and more elderly people living on their own, the social and economic burden of senior care is growing. We will look at how some very different products that incorporate AI and robotics are helping older people live independently for longer and assisting in care homes.

As humans age they naturally lose muscle strength.[93] Gradually, it begins to limit their mobility which in turn causes more muscle loss and triggers other physical complications and psychological problems, including social isolation. The common response to this is to provide assistance with the daily tasks that have become difficult. Seismic's Powered Clothing™, initially designed as the Superflex Aura Powered Suit by fuseproject, takes a different approach. Instead it asks: *"What if technology and design could help us continue to move about the world and engage with it physically, socially and emotionally?"*[94]

Seismic's soft undergarment helps people remain active for longer by integrating electro-mechanical 'flex muscles', that support sitting and assist getting up and standing. Based on earlier exoskeleton technology developed for DARPA, it uses biomimicry to follow and learn from an individual's natural muscular movement to create a symbiotic technology seamlessly integrated into a garment.[95] Beyond the considerable technological challenge this poses, one of its biggest design merits is in making this a desirable *and* non-stigmatised piece of clothing. As it happens, the original purpose of maintaining our mobility as we age also has medical and industrial applications (fig 6.38).

Making the point that 82% of older people want to grow old at home but over half feel lonely, fuseproject and Intuition Robotics asked themselves: *"How do aging adults stay connected to the world when cognitive functions are diminishing, when technology is complex and intimidating, when family and friends are not close-by?"* Their design response is Elli•Q, an "emotionally-intelligent robotic companion" in the form of an elegant but familiar tabletop object. Elli•Q combines the functions of life coach and companion to help engage in activities, stay connected and feel safe. Its physical elements, the base, companion and screen, and the user interface (UI) and experience (UX) are carefully designed for intuitive and helpful interaction that can grow and adapt as the relationship develops[96] (fig 6.39).

Meanwhile across the Pacific, Japan has been leading the way in robotics for many years and regularly makes the news with captivating new applications for domestic and industrial droid and humanoid robots such as Honda's Asimo and Sony's Aibo. They have also been leaders in digital games and have demonstrated through these games the strong and caring relationships people can develop towards digital or robotic characters such as with Tamagochis (1996) (fig 6.40).

Japan also has the oldest population in the world and, with low immigration, not enough people to look after them.[97] Putting these two together has led the push to integrate AI and robotics for the benefit of the elderly and their carers that demonstrate

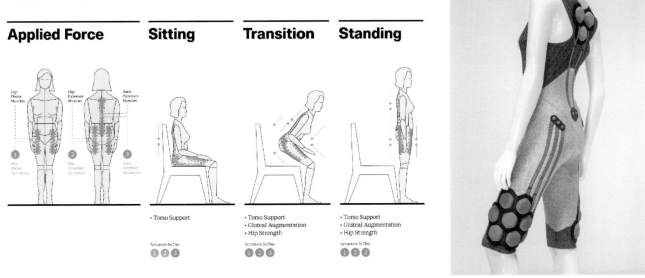

Figure 6.38 Seismic's Powered Clothing™ designed with Fuseproject integrates electro-mechanical muscles to create a symbiotic garment to help older people keep active for longer as well as having medical and industrial applications. (courtesy fuseproject)

Figure 6.39 AI technology as personal PA and social companion for the elderly. Intuition Robotics' ElliQ designed with fuseproject. (courtesy fuseproject)

Figure 6.40 Digital nurturing and caring through Bandai's Tamagotchi (Japan 1997). (photo credit Zeitblick)

their possible positive social uses. The most common type are carebots that help serve, fetch and communicate as well as offering additional companionship and emotional support. Pepper by Softbank is an example of a multipurpose robot that is gradually being introduced for these purposes by talking to patients, monitoring corridors, leading exercise classes, etc.[98] (fig 6.41).

In contrast, PARO is a therapeutic robotic baby harp seal made by Intelligent Systems (Japan) since 2003 that is being used in Japan, Europe and North America. It responds to touch and sound, turns towards and nuzzles patients who stroke or talk to it and will learn to behave as instructed.[99] Recognising the growing number of dementia patients, it was specifically designed to provide

the proven benefits of animal therapy for environments such as hospitals and care homes where live animals are problematic. Not only does it relax patients, it also helps more widely with social interaction between patients and between patients and carers (fig 6.42).

Designing robots that truly enhance life presents new challenges for product designers as the emphasis shifts from their physical presence and the digital tasks they will carry out to designing the whole 'personality' of the product. This will increasingly require inputs from multidisciplinary design and technical teams with no small dose of psychology and close user involvement.

These examples show AI and robotics being put to good use as more predictable and controllable alternatives to humans and animals. They also demonstrate what an attractive business and management proposition they can be by eliminating the need to deal with the tensions, flaws and variability inherent in humans and animals. But it also raises the question: Are robots the answer or instead should we be developing our abundant human capital and expanding our capacity for empathy and ability to deal with uncertainty and diversity?

speculative design fictions and sustainable futures

Earlier in the chapter we noted the feeling of inevitability and powerlessness many 'users' or citizens have in relation to the direction of technological development and therefore the products and systems they will be 'forced' to interface with, and be

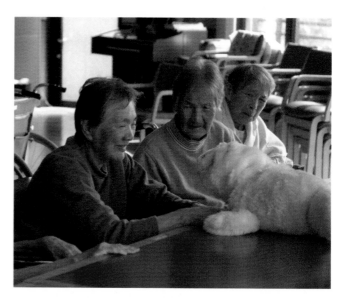

Figure 6.41 Softbank's Pepper helps lead a stretching class in a seniors' care home in Japan. (photo courtesy Softbank)

Figure 6.42 PARO, the therapeutic baby seal robot delighting dementia patients in Japan. (photo courtesy ©National Institute of Advanced industrial Science and Technology/AIST Japan)

Figure 6.43 A still from Superflux's Uninvited Guests design fiction video. (photo courtesy Superflux)

Figure 6.44 A scene from Curious Rituals, a design fiction film by the Near Future Lab that speculates about the evolution of our everyday digital gestures. (source: couretesy Near Future Lab)

surveilled by, on a daily basis. From the average citizen's point of view there appears to be little democracy or co-design in what and how technology is developed.

We saw in Chapter 3.4 how creating speculative design fictions can be used as a powerful tool to open the debate and introduce more voices in determining the future of the technologies we may one day be living with. *Uninvited Guests*, a short speculative design video by Superflux (UK), is a cautionary reminder of how, in our enthusiasm to design connected products, we should not allow the needs of the carer or 'care system' to infringe upon the privacy and rights of older people. As adults they should be able to make their own choices, even if these choices are not considered optimal for health or safety (fig 6.43).

The Near Future Laboratory (USA) is another group that uses the power of design fiction and narrative to "*swerve the present*

into new, more habitable near future worlds". They speculate on subjects such as the future evolution of our everyday digital gestures and habits in the highly entertaining 'Curious Rituals', prototype fictional apps that slow down social media consumption and have created a quick-start guide for a fictional self-driving car to help imagine a future with autonomous vehicles (fig 6.44).

But perhaps the darkest cautionary and thought-provoking tales of where technology may lead us to in the future, if we happen to take our eye off the ball, are to be found in the television series *Black Mirror* created by Charlie Brooker. Its portrayal of the many scenarios where new technologies have unanticipated consequences should provide ample motivation for designers and citizens across the world not to shrink back from taking an active role in shaping them for a positive future.

Chapter summary

1. Visibly and invisibly, the daily lives and experiences of at least half the population of the world are mediated, regulated and monitored through electronically controlled systems and connected digital tools. Their negative environmental impacts however are considerable and growing. Although these are mostly invisible at the point of consumption, designers need to apply all the strategies possible to lessen their negative impacts and increase their potential for distributed positive social and economic value.

2. The most invisible environmental impact of the electronic and ICT industry is its ever-growing energy consumption, which in 2017 was in the order of 7 to 12% of global electricity demand and 2% of GHGs and rising. This is driven by the exponential increase in the zettabytes of data we are storing and transmitting, alongside the energy intensity of manufacturing electronic components. While some large data service providers and manufacturers are committed to 100% renewables, the majority of the energy and electricity powering the industry still comes from 'dirty' fossil fuels.

3. Electronics are particularly resource-intensive and complex products to manufacture because of the cocktail of minerals and the special production facilities required. While electronic devices have become smaller and more energy-efficient in themselves, their overall manufacturing impact is still growing because the numbers being produced are also rising steeply. Mining for the 20+ different minerals found in the average electronic device is highly damaging environmentally and their supply chain is riddled with ethical issues that include poor working and safety conditions, unfair wages and child labour. This makes the need for clean supply chains, greater recycling and higher recycled content pressing.

4. Around the world electronic waste is growing exponentially. There are three main causes for concern with e-waste that have implications for the design of electronic products. The first is that many WEEE products, especially older ones, contain toxic substances that require special handling. The second is that although they include many precious and valuable mineral elements, because of their complexity and low collection rates (<40% globally), very little of this is being recovered and even less is being recycled back into new WEEE products. The third is that they have unnecessarily short lifespans, which exacerbates both the first two problems and intensifies the negative footprint of devices.

5. To counteract these negative environmental impacts, designers should address all forms of obsolescence and apply the following strategies:

   • reduce the number of devices needed through product convergence and dematerialisation
   • ensure that products and services are produced and operated by 100% renewable energy
   • ensure that ethical checks are carried out all the way up the supply chain
   • reduce the intensity of electronic lifecycles by extending the optimal life of EEE products through designing in repairability, upgradability, and physical and emotional durability
   • maximise recycled content within the product and ensure that it returns to a closed loop for maximum recovery.

6. 'Green electronics' in the form of biodegradable and transient electronics are just beginning to emerge from the laboratory. Made of benign bio-compatible materials and able to take any form, these advances point to a brighter waste-free future for electronics. Just for starters, they also suggest a whole new spectrum of applications in consumer electronics, bio-medical diagnostics, treatments and implants, and environmental monitoring.

7. Research and debate into the wider social impacts of the digital world are just beginning to unfold. What we do know is that the rate of change in how business and life is conducted is unprecedented and that its ubiquity and pervasiveness is transgressing hard-won freedoms and threatening democracy. Its constant demand for attention is also leading to increasing levels of stress and mental health issues. In addition, for the billions who are currently digitally excluded because they lack access to electricity or connectivity, the education and economic gap is widening.

8. At the same time we have only to look at the transformative social and economic benefits of smartphones to appreciate that we are only just scratching the surface of the social and environmental benefits that tech-integrated products could produce. Product design can closely align itself to social innovation and 'tech for good' where the delivery of the PSS requires both physical and digital interfaces and touchpoints.

9. Existing areas of positive tech interventions include but are not limited by:

   • tools for greater access to education and creativity, including demystifying the technology itself
   • tools that facilitate more sustainable lifestyles, control over personal health and wellbeing, and supported ageing
   • access to connectivity for the base of the pyramid through products that provide off-grid power and microsatellite network coverage
   • enhanced environmental performance of products and tools for ecological monitoring and restoration.

10. For all its mixed press and varied interpretations, 'weak' AI is already invisibly embedded in many of our interfaces and is becoming increasingly visible in the form of manufacturing, domestic and entertainment robots. The examples we looked at of AI-led products supporting independence and care of seniors demonstrates that carefully considered AI could have many beneficial applications. However, the prospect of 'strong' AI where machine learning goes on to create supra-human intelligence or even sentience is uncharted territory that some consider as great an existential threat to humanity as global warming. Sustainably minded designers must join their voice to the call for its development to be subject to the questioning of the precautionary principle and consensus on ethical boundaries. This calls for active engagement in designing the future we want.

Notes

1 UNenvironment.org (n.d.) Technology [online]. Available at www.unenvironment.org/ru/taxonomy/term/30 (accessed 19 November 2018).

2 Based on Mills, M., *The Cloud Begins with Coal*. An Overview of the Electricity Used by the Digital Global Ecosystem, and Recalculated by Terry, N. (2014) Mobile Energy in Fridge Unit [online]. Available at https://energy-surprises.blogspot.co.uk/2014/08/mobile-network-energy-in-fridge-units.html (accessed 13 November 2017).

3 Estimates vary depending on assumptions and what they include. These papers are a good illustration of how it is calculated. See Corcoran, P. and Andres Andrae (2013) Emerging Trends in Electricity Consumption for Consumer ICT, and Andrae, A. and Tomas Edler (2015)On Global Electricity Usage of Communication Technology: Trends to 2030. *Challenges*, 6, pp. 117–157. doi:10.3390/challe6010117.

4 Andrae and Edler (2015), pp. 137–142.

5 clickclean.org (2017), *Clicking Clean: Who is Winning the Race to Build a Clean Internet*, Washington, DC: Greenpeace. Available at www.clickclean.org/downloads/ClickClean2016%20HiRes.pdf.

6 South China Morning Post (2017) Tencent Video, iQiyi in Race to Lead China's Online Video Market [online, 3 October]. Available at www.scmp.com/tech/china-tech/article/2113720/tencent-video-iqiyi-race-lead-chinas-online-video-market (accessed 12 January 2019).

7 Weldon, M. (2016) *The Future X Network. A Bell Lab Perspective*, Boca Raton, FL: CRC Press, p. 441.

8 Ibid., pp. 82, 442.

9 Amazonaws.com (n.d.) GreenTouch [online]. Available at https://s3-us-west-2.amazonaws.com/belllabs-microsite-greentouch/index.html (accessed 12 January 2019).

10 clickclean.org (2017), p. 7.

11 Andrae and Edler (2015), p. 122.

12 Fraunhofer IZM (2016) *Life Cycle Assessment of the Fairphone 2*, Berlin: Fraunhofer, November, p.12. Available at www.fairphone.com/wp-content/uploads/2016/11/Fairphone_2_LCA_Final_20161122.pdf.

13 Oeko-Institut e.V (11/2016) *Resource Efficiency In the ICT Sector*, Freiburg, Germany: Greenpeace, November. Available at www.oeko.de/fileadmin/oekodoc/Resource_Efficiency_ICT_summary.pdf.

14 Greenpeace (17/11/2017) *Greenpeace Guide to Greener Electronics* 2017, 17 November, Washington, DC: Greenpeace USA, p. 6.

15 fairphone.com (2017) Why You Should Care about the Materials in Your Phone [online, January]. Available at www.fairphone.com/wp-content/uploads/2017/02/FairphoneScopingStudyMatrix_Final.pdf.

16 Merchant, B. (2013) Were the Raw Materials in your iPhone Mined by Children in Inhumane Conditions? *LA Times*, 23 July [online]. Available at www.latimes.com/opinion/op-ed/la-oe-merchant-iphone-supplychain-20170723-story.html.

17 Friends of the Earth (2012) *Mining for Smartphones; The True Cost of Tin*, London: FoE, November. Available at https://friendsoftheearth.uk/sites/default/files/downloads/tin_mining.pdf.

18 Merchant, B. (2017) *The One Device: The Secret History of the iPhone*, London: Bantom Press.

19 FoE (2012).

20 Amnesty International (2016) *"This Is What We Die For": Human Rights Abuses in the Democratic Republic of Congo Power the Global Trade in Cobalt*, London: Amnesty International. Available at www.amnesty.org/download/Documents/AFR6231832016ENGLISH.PDF.

21 Greenpeace (2017), pp. 17–18.

22 Ibid., pp. 11–13.

23 Baldé, C.P., F. Wang,R. Kuehr and J. Huisman (2015) *The Global e-waste Monitor – 2014*, Bonn, Germany: United Nations University, IAS–SCYCLE, pp. 37–47.

24 step-inititive.org (2014) One Global Definition of E-waste, Solving the E-waste (StEP). White Paper, 3 June, Bonn, Germany: UN University.

25 Baldé *et al.* (2015); Europa Eurostats WEEE statistics, July 2017. Available at http://ec.europa.eu/eurostat/statistics-explained/index.php/Waste_statistics_-_electrical_and_electronic_equipment; Electronics TakeBack Coalition, Facts and Figures on e-waste Recycling (2016). Available at http://electronicstakeback.com/wp- content/uploads/Facts_and_Figures_on_EWaste_and_Recycling.pdf.

26 Baldé *et al.* (2015), p. 23.

27 US Geological Survey (2014).

28 Electronics TakeBack Coalition (2014), p.7.

29 Oeko-Institut (2016), p. 41.

30 Electronics TakeBack Coalition (2014), p. 2.

31 EU (2016) *Ecodesign Working Plan 2016-2019*, European Commission Communication (COM (2016) 776, 30 November, Brussels: EU. Available as PDF at https://eur-lex.europa.eu/legal-content/EN/TXT/PDF/?uri=CELEX:52016DC0773&from=EN.

32 Prakesh *et al.* (2016) *Einfluss der Nutzungsdauer von Produkten auf ihre Umweltwirkung*, Dessau, Germany: Umwelt Bundesamt (UBA). Available at www.umweltbundesamt.de/sites/default/files/medien/378/publikationen/texte_10_2015_einfluss_der_nutzungsdauer_von_produkten_auf_ihre_umwelt_obsoleszenz.pdf.

33 Kyba *et al.* (2017) Artificially Lit Surface of Earth at Night Increasing Radiance and Extent. *Science Advances,* 22

November, 3(11), e1701528m; doi: 10.1126/sciadv.1701528 and https://gizmodo.com/the-switch-to-outdoor-led-lighting-has-completely-backf-1820652615.

34 Kwon, D. (2018) The Vanishing Night: Light Pollution Threatens Ecosystems [online, 1 October]. Available at www.the-scientist.com/features/the-vanishing-night--light-pollution-threatens-ecosystems-64803 (accessed 13 November 2018).

35 Ryen, E., C. Babbitt and E. Williams (2015) Consumption-weighted Life Cycle Assessment of a Consumer Electronic Product Community. *Environmental Science Technology*, 49(4), pp. 2549–2559.

36 Zickuhr, K. (2011) Generations and Their Gadgets. *Pew Research Center: Internet, Science & Tech* (blog, 3 February). Available at www.pewinternet.org/2011/02/03/generations-and-their-gadgets/.

37 Koomey, J., C. Weber and H. Matthews (24/08/2010) The Energy and Climate Change Impact of Different Music Delivery Methods. *Journal of Industrial Ecology*, 14(5), pp. 754–769. https://doi.org/10.1111/j.1530-9290.2010.00269.x.

38 Coroama, V.C., A. Moberg and L.M. Hilty (2015) Dematerialization Through Electronic Media? In Hilty, L. and Aebischer, B. (eds), *ICT Innovations for Sustainability*, New York: Springer. Available at https://doi.org/10.1007/978-3-319-09228-7_24.

39 HP (2016) *2016 Sustainability Report*, June, p.75, and Dell FY (2017) *Corporate Social Responsibility Report*.

40 Greenpeace (2017), p. 5.

41 The Fairphone variant of an often-used quote available at www.fairphone.com/en/2015/06/16/the-architecture-of-the-fairphone-2-designing-a-competitive-device-that-embodies-our-values/.

42 Greenpeace (2017), p. 6.

43 Oeko-Institut (2016), pp. 40-47.

44 Prakash *et al.* (2016), p. 36.

45 Greenpeace (2017), p. 4.

46 Penty, J. (2017) Kyle Wiens interview during the Restart Fixfest, LSE, London, 7 October.

47 Data from SquareTrade (2010) in Proske, Clemm and Richter (2016) *The Life Cycle Assessment of Fairphone,* Berlin: Fraunhofer IZM, p. 60.

48 Fraunhofer IZM (2016), p. 59.

49 Penty, J. (7/10/2017) Recorded interview with Chris Moller at Restart Fixfest, LSE, London, 7 October.

50 Webber, H. (2017) The Dream of Ara: Inside the Rise and Fall of the World's Most Revolutionary Phone | *VentureBeat*, January [online]. Available at https://venturebeat.com/2017/01/10/inside-project-ara-googles-revolutionary-modular-phone/ (accessed 12 January 2019).

51 puzzlephone (n.d.) PuzzlePhone [online]. Available at www.puzzlephone/ (accessed 12 January 2019).

52 Penty, J (2017) Skype interview with Olivier Hébert, Fairphone, Amsterdam, 19 December.

53 https://commons.wikimedia.org/wiki/File:Ipod_sales_per_quarter.svg based on Apple quarterly reports.

54 Bakker *et al.* (2014) Products That Go Round: Exploring Product Life Extension Through Design. *Journal of Cleaner Production*, 69, pp.13–14.

55 Prakash, S. *et al.* (2016), *Einfluss der Nutzungsdauer von Produkten auf ihre Umweltwirkung: Schaffung einer Informationsgrundlage und Entwicklung von Strategien gegen „Obsoleszenz"*, Dessau, Germany: Umwelt Bundesamt, February, pp. 90 and 128. Available at www.umweltbundesamt.de/sites/default/files/medien/378/publikationen/texte_11_2016_einfluss_der_nutzungsdauer_von_produkten_obsoleszenz.pdf.

56 Fairphone (2017) *Report on Recyclability. Does Modularity Contribute to Better Recovery of Materials?* Amsterdam: Fairphone. Available at www.fairphone.com/wp-content/uploads/2017/02/FairphoneRecyclabilityReport02 2017.pdf

57 Fairphone.com (2017) Examining the Environmental Footprint of Electronics Recycling [online, 8 August]. Available at www.fairphone.com/en/2017/08/08/examining-the-environmental-footprint-of-electronics-recycling/ (accessed 12 January 2019).

58 Duhaime-Ross, A. (2017) Apple Promises to Stop Mining Minerals to Make iPhones — It Just Isn't Sure How Yet. *Vice News*, 19 April [online]. Available at https://news.vice.com/en_us/article/xwv3yj/apple-promises-to-stop-mining-minerals-to-make-iphones-it-just-isnt-sure-how-yet (accessed 12 January 2019).

59 Apple.com (2018) Apple Adds Earth Day Donations to Trade-in and Recycling Program [online, 19 April]. Available at www.apple.com/newsroom/2018/04/apple-adds-earth-day-donations-to-trade-in-and-recycling-program/ (accessed 7 January 2019).

60 Apple (2018) Environmental Responsibility Report [online], pp. 19–22. Available at www.apple.com/environment/pdf/Apple_Environmental_Responsibility_Report_2018.pdf.

61 Dell, *FY17 Corporate Social Responsibility Report*, p. 25.

62 Professor John Rogers, (2013) quoted in New 'Transient Electronics' Disappear When No Longer Needed. *American Chemical Society*, 8 April [online]. Available at www.acs.org/content/acs/en/pressroom/newsreleases/2013/april/new-transient-electronics-disappear-when-no-longer-needed.html (accessed 12 January 2019).

63 Urimia-Vladu, M. (2014) 'Green' Electronics: Biodegradable and Biocompatible Materials and Devices for Sustainable Future. *Chemical Society Review*, 43, pp. 588–610. doi: 10.1039/C3CS60235D.

64 Irimia-Vladu, M., E. Glowacki N. Sariciftci and S. Bauer (eds) (2017) *Green Materials for Electronics*, Princeton, NJ: Wiley, pp. 2–15.

65 Fu *et al.* (2016) Transient Electronics: Materials and Devices. *Chemistry of Materials*, 28, pp. 3527–3539. doi: 10.1021/acs.chemmater.5b04931.

66 Irimia-Vladu *et al.* (2017) p. 1.

67 Baumgartner, M. *et al.* (2017) Emerging 'Green Materials' and Technologies for Electronics. In Irimia-Vladu *et al.* (2017), p. 2.

68 McNaughton, J. (n.d.) The Theses | 95 Theses about Technology [online]. Available at https://95theses.co.uk/?page_id=21 (accessed 7 January 2019).

69 Lanier, J. (2014) *Who Owns the Future,* and (2011) *You are not a Gadget*, New York: Penguin Books.

70 Merchant (2017).

71 see https://digitalsocial.eu/viz/ for an introduction.

72 Stokes, M. *et al.* (05/2017) *What Next for Digital Social Innovation?,* EU: Digital Social Innovation, May. Available at https://media.nesta.org.uk/documents/dsi_report.pdf.

73 Shipp, J. and I. Noula (05/09/2017) What's the Point of 'Digital Education'? Education, Citizenship and Sustainable Digital Lives in LSE Media Policy Blog. Available at http://blogs.lse.ac.uk/mediapolicyproject/2017/09/05/whats-the-point-of-digital-education-education-citizenship-and-sustainable-digital-lives/ (accessed 7 January 2019).

74 Broadband Commission for Sustainable Development (2018) *The State of Broadband 2018,* September, Geneva: ITU & Unesco, p.10 [online]. Available at www.itu.int/dms_pub/itu-s/opb/pol/S-POL-BROADBAND.19-2018-PDF-E.pdf.

75 Wikipedia OLPC and www.laptop.org (accessed 15 January 2018).

76 Warschauer, M. and M. Ames (2010) Can One Laptop Per Child Save the World's Poor? *Journal of International Affairs*, 64(1), p. 40.

77 Ibid., p. 46.

78 Fundacion Telefonica (2018) ProFuturo Information Dossier (EN) [online], 25 September. Available at https://profuturo.education/en/wp-content/uploads/sites/4/2018/10/Information_dossier_EN_VF.pdf with additional input from Sofia Fernandez de Mesa / Fundación Profuturo.

79 kano.me (n.d.) This is Kano [online]. Available at http://kano.me/blog/our-mission/ (accessed 17 November 2018).

80 techwillsaveus.com (n.d.) About Tech Will Save Us [online]. Available at https://about.techwillsaveus.com (accessed 15 January 2018).

81 littlebits.com (n.d.) About – Empowering Kids of all Ages to Create Inventions | littleBits [online]. Available at https://littlebits.com/about/ (accessed 7 January 2019).

82 Torrone, Phillip (2019) '25 Million + Raspberry Pi Computers Sold @Raspberry_Pi #raspberrypi'. *Adafruit Industries – Makers,* *Hackers, Artists, Designers and Engineers!* (blog) [online 16 March 2019]. https://blog.adafruit.com/2019/03/15/25-million-raspberry-pi-computers-sold-raspberry_pi-raspberrypi/. (accessed 2 July 2019).

83 Fjordnet.com (n.d.) Bringing the Internet to Africa's Forgotten Island [online]. Available at www.fjordnet.com/workdetail/bringing-the-internet-to-africas-forgotten-island/ (accessed 17 November 2018).

84 Huawei.com (2018) The GCI S-curve. Growing Inequality [online]. Available at www.huawei.com/minisite/gci/en/ (accessed 17 November 2018).

85 Broadband Commission for Sustainable Development [2017] *The State of Broadband 2017,* ITU & Unesco, pp.16–17.

86 www.skyandspace.global/smallsat-network-integrated-1-smartphone-sky-space-global-socialeco-plan/ (accessed 19 January 2018).

87 Cox, H. (2017) Are Robots Ready to Take Over the Household Chores? *Financial Times*, 17 March [online]. Available at www.ft.com/content/f5fb177c-04b5-11e7-aa5b-6bb07f5c8e12 (accessed 23 January 2018).

88 Dowd, M. (26/03/2017) Elon Musk's Billion-dollar Crusade to Stop the A.I. Apocalypse. *Vanity Fair*, 26 March [online]. Available at www.vanityfair.com/news/2017/03/elon-musk-billion-dollar-crusade-to-stop-ai-space-x.

89 WHO (2018) Global Health Observatory Data: Life Expectancy 2000–2016 [online]. Available at www.who.int/gho/mortality_burden_disease/life_tables/situation_trends_text/en/ (accessed 19 November 2018).

90 World Bank (2014) Health Expenditure Per Capita [online]. Available at https://data.worldbank.org/indicator/SH.XPD.PCAP (accessed 7 January 2019).

91 Research & America, N. (2015) Are Fitbits and Other Wearables Really Keeping Us Fit? [online, 17 July]. Available at http://knowledge.wharton.upenn.edu/article/are-fitbits-and-other-wearables-really-keeping-us-fit/ (accessed 19 November 2018).

92 UN ESA (2017) World Population Prospects, UN ESA [online]. Available at https://esa.un.org/unpd/wpp/Publications/Files/WPP2017_KeyFindings.pdf.

93 Keller, K. and M. Engelhardt (2013) Strength and Muscle Mass Loss with Aging Process. Age and Strength Loss. *Muscles, Ligaments, Tendons*, 3(4), pp. 346–350. Available at www.ncbi.nlm.nih.gov/pmc/articles/PMC3940510/.

94 fuseproject.com (2017) Aura Powered Suit – fuseproject [online]. Available at https://fuseproject.com/work/superflex/aura-powered-suit/?focus=overview (accessed 7 January 2019).

95 myseismic.com (2018) Seismic – Powered Clothing [online]. Available at www.myseismic.com/ (accessed 7 January 2019).

96 fuseproject.co (2017) *Elli•Q – fuseproject* [online]. Available at https://fuseproject.com/work/intuition-robotics/elliq/?focus=overview (accessed 7 January 2019).

97 UN ESA (2017).

98 Tarantola, A. (2017) Robot Caregivers Are Saving the Elderly from Lives of Loneliness [online, 29 August]. Available at www.engadget.com/2017/08/29/robot-caregivers-are-saving-the-elderly-from-lives-of-loneliness/ (accessed 7 January 2019).

99 PAROrobots.com (n.d.) PARO Therapeutic Robot [online]. Available at www.parorobots.com/index.asp (accessed 7 January 2019).

CHAPTER 7
Furniture and space-related products

In and out of doors, in our homes, at work and in public spaces, we are surrounded by and interact intimately on a moment-by-moment basis with furniture and space-related products. Furniture is also one of humankind's oldest artefacts with very rich cultural connections and regional variations. Given that in developed countries we spend an average of 90% of our time indoors,[1] these products also affect our health and shape the activities that take place in our spaces positively or negatively through the tone they set and the social opportunities they facilitate.

One step down in scale from buildings and architecture, furniture is human-sized and typically low-tech. It spans the local and traditionally handcrafted through to the global mass produced. While a few very large players exist, most furniture is still batch produced by small and medium-sized enterprises, although increasingly this is being made from mass-manufactured stock materials. However, more recent moves to integrate IoT capabilities, nanotech materials, computational analysis and experiments with digitally produced furniture are making inroads into some pockets of the industry. This chapter looks at recent trends in the production and consumption of furniture and space-related products, and the sustainable issues and design opportunities they present.

furniture as a social tool
In terms of social sustainability, furniture and interior spaces have long played a very significant role in giving material expression and meaning to our personal and collective social and cultural values. On the domestic front, the spaces we call 'home' support us in our private rituals and give us a sense of control over our lives. For those of us with the luxury of choice, the furniture with which we surround ourselves is increasingly considered an extension of our identity. It sets the scene – formal or casual, eclectic or orderly, sumptuous or minimal – for how we rest, work and play.

In the workplace, furniture and interiors do more than simply enable commercial activity. Businesses use their design as an outward expression of their corporate values and ethos. In this sense they have become an essential PR tool, particularly in the retail and service industries. Inwardly, furniture and interior layouts are designed to optimise worker productivity dating back to the first time-and-motion studies of the 1900s. Their design also plays an important role in worker safety and protecting long-term health by integrating the findings of ergonomic and health-and-safety research and regulations. Without a doubt, employers and workers alike are increasingly recognising the power of furniture and interiors to create a positive, productive and collaborative work atmosphere as demonstrated by the growth and growth of co-worker spaces and what is referred to as the 'Google office' effect.

In the civic arena, "*Public places play a key role in building community and placemaking, empowering local communities to create a sense of 'belonging' through place.*"[2] Whether on a large scale or at the micro-level, as we saw with Parklets in Design Activism (Chapter 3.4), designers can make an important contribution to the collaborative process of physically shaping public and community spaces that help build social capital, resilience and sustainability.

7.1 furniture trends and their sustainability implications

Some relatively recent and growing trends in the furniture market are having significant implications for sustainability. These include the rising number of urban dwellers living in smaller or shared spaces and furniture as consumable fashion and its growing contribution to our waste mountain through shorter lifespans. We will look at these trends and the drivers behind them together with the most important environmental impacts of the industry to identify design strategies for reducing their negative impacts and reinforcing positive trends.

market growth and demographics

Taken as a whole, the global furniture market has been growing steadily and is expected to continue to rise annually on average by over 4% until 2021.[3] While sales of furniture in developed markets have stabilised or even 'peaked',[4] most of the growth is now in emerging economies, notably in China and India, where expanding middle classes are moving from rural to urban areas.

This ongoing demographic shift to urban living is also leading to a global increase in smaller households of one or two persons.[5] This, coupled with the relatively high cost of housing for those moving from cheaper rural areas into cities, has led to the rising trend of people living in smaller units. Modularised micro-units are seen as one solution to the growing problem of affordable housing.[6]

Sitting at the intersection between product design, interiors and architecture, micro-living poses some very interesting new challenges for designers. In this new scenario, furniture will have to be cleverer and work harder to combine multiple user needs within a limited space envelope, leading to more built-in and customised furniture with greater functionality. Product designers will need to stretch their spatial skills and combine this with user-centred narratives to produce truly game-changing outcomes. At the mass-market flatpack end, design and solutions-driven companies like IKEA have already been exploring how *'to make small spaces big'* for some time with ever-increasing sales which we will be looking at in more detail.[7]

Designers are also working directly with architects and developers to produce custom designs for micro-space furniture. In 2013 nARCHITECTS won a New York City (NYC) competition for new solutions for the growing number of small households. Their design, Carmel Place (formerly My Micro NY), created the first high-rise affordable micro-living in NYC in 2016. They also introduced an innovative construction system of prefabricated modular living units that they hope will be a repeatable model for affordable housing. These units were built offsite and stacked by crane into tower blocks, and the interiors were especially fitted out with multifunctional furniture solutions for storage and day and night use (fig 7.1).

In 2018, Ori Systems, together with fuseproject, developed their high-end 'transformer' furniture product that also addresses the challenge of small space living. Initially targeted at developers, it consists of a multifunctional furniture unit that moves linearly with the help of 'robotics' to hide or reveal a bedroom or living space at the click of a button (fig 7.2).

The pressure of rising housing costs in cities has also led to the opposite trend of more unrelated people living in shared spaces, which has had much less design attention. Comparing these two trends in terms of sustainability, with less space per person, micro-living can mean a smaller space footprint per person compared with more traditional single units. However, shared living spaces have less duplication of furniture, rooms and appliances, and may create more social capital by fostering cooperation and resilience. Newer housing designs specifically intended for co-living are beginning to appear across the spectrum of budgets, presenting a different set of furniture design challenges. Figure 4.23 shows Opendesk's Lean Desk in use in a co-living/co-working development. Equally, some of the product duplication and pressure on storage space in both scenarios could be reduced through the use of the collaborative sharing platforms for infrequently used products that we looked at in Chapter 4.3.

Figure 7.1 Modular micro-living on the rise in New York. A prefab microliving unit for nARCHITECTS' Carmel Place (formerly My Micro NY) is lifted into place in 2015. View of interior unit by day and night demonstrating its highly adaptable furniture and integrated storage. (photos courtesy nARCHITECTS and Pablo Enriquez)

Figure 7.2 Ori Systems multi-functional furniture units, designed with fuseproject, glide along with the help of modular robotics to adapt a space to suit changing activities throughout the day and night. (photo courtesy fuseproject)

As finding solutions to affordable housing will continue to be a challenge in many cities across the world, designers should see these as a double opportunity to enable more sustainable ways of living.

furniture as consumable fashion

Another noticeable trend is that furniture is increasingly becoming a consumable product. A survey for a EU report across 10 countries found that 83% of people had either bought a furniture product over the past 3 years or were planning on buying one in the next 12 months. Higher purchasing frequency has also led to shorter product lifespans.[8] From the environmental point of view this is concerning, not only because it uses energy unnecessarily and stresses resources, but it also exacerbates our waste problem, as furniture is bulky. There seem to be two main drivers behind this trend.

The first is that home furnishings have moved into the realms of fashion. Driven partly by TV home makeover programmes, and the 'picture-bite' world of social media and Internet marketing, people feel compelled to update their furnishings regularly to keep up with new trends.[9] Not very long ago, young families would save up for new furniture that they planned to keep for life or would happily inherit items from family members, whereas today, furniture is 'refreshed' or changed much more frequently. Another factor leading to increasing sales and furniture waste is that people are moving more often, possibly exacerbated by the lack of affordability and rental security, and the fluidity in relationships.[10] With each move, the new inhabitants feel the need to put their 'personal' stamp on their new space to make it home, triggering new purchases.

The second major factor feeding the consumption of furniture is its relative affordability and cheapness since the advent of flatpack and mass-produced solutions. This has made buying and 'refreshing' furniture possible for many millions of households globally. Although IKEA, the world's largest furniture retailer, is deeply committed to sustainable production and designing-in more sustainable lifestyles for its customers, it is also aiming to double sales between 2013 and 2020.[11] Most of this growth is expected to come from the rising urban middle classes in China and India for whom the affordability of the furniture supermarket

Figure 7.3 A small part of IKEA's wall of spare bits for customers. (photo Jane Penty)

is compelling.[12] IKEA will be a good test of whether it is possible to have growth and dramatically reduce impacts at the same time, known as relative decoupling (see Chapter 4.1).

loss of quality and repairability

Along with a more fashion-oriented market and affordable prices has come a lowering of quality and the use of many materials, finishes and methods of joining that don't stand up well to wear or repair. Flatpacks are rarely designed to be disassembled or reassembled multiple times for moving, although IKEA are now revisiting this aspect of their designs and provide free replacement fittings (fig 7.3). Cheaper furniture and flatpacks are also renowned for damaging easily and are difficult to repair properly. Even when there is a desire to repair, similar to the problem of economic obsolescence with electronics, it is often cheaper in terms of cost and time to replace, although as we will see below, this is beginning to change.[13]

the furniture waste problem

Where refresh used to mean putting on a new coat of paint, revarnishing, repairing or reupholstering, now, with low prices and changing fashion, it has come to mean replacing. And more often than not, this also means discarding the unwanted furniture, as very little is, or can be, truly recycled. Up until now, waste and recycling statistics for furniture have been shameful.

According to EPA data for 2015, furniture is the least recycled household item in the USA, with over 9.8 million tons of furniture sent to landfill in one year alone and a pitiful 0.08% recycled.[14] With the exception of some metal office furniture, it considered furniture recycling to be negligible:

> *Actual recovery or remanufacture of either furniture or other products is generally not feasible due to the difficulty in removing wood finishes and stains on wood [...] [apart from some] metal furniture, and in particular, office furniture [and] material from [...] mattress recovery.*[15]

This may seem extreme, but the picture of furniture waste and recycling is not dissimilar across other developed countries. In the UK, 42% of municipal bulky waste is furniture but if you add mattresses it is over 50%. Of this, 32% by weight could be reused, rising to 51% with minor repairs.[16] WRAP estimated that nearly 6 million sofas and 1.4 million desks come to their end of life, with only 1 million sofas (16%) and 200,000 desks (14%) reused in 2009. The remainder went to landfill or incineration, with a very small proportion, mostly metal, being recycled (fig 7.4). In Chapter 4.3 on collaborative consumption we saw how a simple thing like having a safety label missing from sofas and mattresses makes them un-resalable and how designers can remedy this.

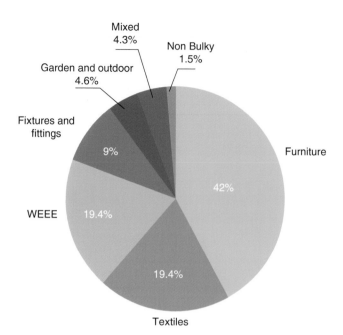

Figure 7.4 UK average composition of bulky waste by category. (source: WRAP)

More recent findings from a 2018 Australian furniture market survey confirm this trend. The report found that over half of Australians (56%) have thrown out furniture over the past year. The main reasons given were that it was: broken (55%); no longer needed (34%); and decluttering (26%). However, 1 in 4 Australians said they would keep their furniture if they knew how to repair or reuse it and 67% would be happy to buy pre-used furniture if it fitted the style of their home.[17]

Another strong contributory factor to our furniture waste problem is that unlike the electronics and packaging sectors, with the exception of France and Japan, there is currently no extended producer responsibility (EPR) for furniture. However, the big push for a more circular economy is beginning to have some positive effects in relation to furniture. As part of its Action Plan for a Circular Economy, the EU has plans to extend EPR to furniture and to ensure that manufacturers build in greater longevity and facilitate repair via its recast Ecodesign directive.

As we will see in Chapter 7.3, the higher end office furniture sector seems to be an exception to this rule with many companies pursuing C2C principles and certification for well over a decade. As the global furniture market leader, in 2016 IKEA also began to experiment with take-back, reselling and repair schemes for its furniture as part of its ambition to become 'people and planet positive' by 2030, which encompasses becoming 100% circular. These initiatives include exchanging new-for-old mattresses and appliances, and donating old items to charity for resale or full recycling. Their 'Secondlife for Furniture', first piloted in Japan, France, Belgium and Australia, is a voucher-based buy-back scheme for furniture that has resale potential and in 2019 they also began piloting office furniture leasing.[18]

changing perceptions: the creative repurposing and reuse of materials

Well before the term *circular economy* became a buzzword with governments and big business, some designers and grassroots movements were, and still are, engaged in countering the trend in the consumption and disposability of furniture. These include the repair and maker movement and online platforms that enable the reselling or gifting of furniture that we looked at in Chapter 4.3, over and above the existing network of charities that have been redistributing furniture and appliances for decades. Design has also made an important contribution to changing the negative perception of 'waste'. Many well-known and less well-known designers continue to work creatively with reused materials and repurposed furniture to create highly original objects of value.

Among these, the work by Piet Hein Eek, Tejo Remy (the Netherlands), and Umberto Campana (Brazil) developed in the late 1980s to early 1990s are representative of the desire to counter design's own contribution to thoughtless consumerism by celebrating the beauty and potential of discarded items. Piet Hein Eik pioneered the use of scrap wood to make unique pieces of furniture during his design studies in the late 1980s. He has since built a successful design business true to these early values that still produces his 1989 Scrapwood Cupboard among many more recent designs (fig 7.5). His 2018 collaboration with IKEA, the Industriell collection, explores the 'handmade – mass produced' and its multiple interpretations through low-impact materials.[19]

In 1991, Tejo Remy caught a generation's imagination with his take on a chest of drawers by repurposing and rearranging salvaged drawers to celebrate each drawer's individual story (fig 7.6). With a price tag of over €20k from Droog, the simplicity of the idea is almost an invitation for open and DIY variants. While none of these iconic pieces can be described as 'affordable', the ideas behind them have gone on to inspire more than one generation of designers with the power of the creative process to transform our perceptions of waste and create new narratives.

Many less well-known designers have demonstrated that it is possible to run viable furniture businesses based on designs that incorporate reused materials at more affordable prices (see figs 7.16 and 7.17). Mark Tuckey in Australia have been exploring and developing designs that incorporate recycled wood from different sources since 1990. As an example, for their Warehouse Desk range, they disassemble and rework ply from specialist shipping crates that intentionally feature the beauty of the wood markings and imperfections (fig 7.7).

Figure 7.5 A current edition of Piet Hein Eek's original pioneering Scrapwood Cupboard designed for his examination piece at Eindhoven Academy (1989). (photo courtesy Piet Ein Eek)

Figure 7.6 A recent version of Tejo Remy's original chest of drawers, 'You Can't Lay Down your Memory', (1991) available from Droog. (courtesy Tejo Remy/photo credit Ernst Moritz)

defying fashion

Designing furniture that defies fashion, makes use of existing materials stocks, improves with age, and is easily repairable, upgradable and reusable are fundamental elements that ensure product longevity for more sustainable furniture design. There are few designs that exemplify these good practices better than Peter Osvik's Tripp Trapp (Norway) (fig 7.8). The chair adapts to any age, growing up with the user from newborn to adult. It is made of sustainable materials that age well, is completely repairable and all parts are sold individually. Being fully dismantlable, it can easily be stored and passed on to siblings, friends and later generations. Perhaps most importantly, its inclusive nature welcomes children to the dinner table to develop their social skills from the moment they are born.

7.2 problematic materials and toxicity in furniture

A better understanding of the materials we specify and how best to design with these materials is an important element of reducing the negative impacts of furniture. Some of the worst culprits of

Figure 7.7 Reuse in the mainstream: Mark Tuckey (Australia) incorporate wood from used shipping crates in their Warehouse desk range that features the beauty of their imperfections. (photo courtesy Mark Tuckey)

Figure 7.8 The Tripp Trapp chair designed by Peter Opsvik in 1972 and produced by Stokke Norway. After over 45 years and more than 10 million sales, it remains highly popular and just as relevant today. (courtesy Stokke UK)

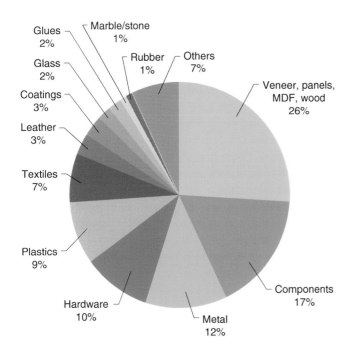

Figure 7.9 EU28 share of materials used in furniture production by value. (source: European Commisssion Furniture Market Report 2014)

furniture breakage and lack of repairability are the same materials and methods of construction that have made furniture easier to mass produce, cheaper, or, depending on how you look at it, more affordable. Almost all the problematic materials we have today were introduced after the Second World War. These include fibreboard wood panels faced in foils, plastic laminates and real wood veneers, as well as plastics, composites and foams. Not only do many of these materials not age well, they are also difficult or near-impossible to recycle as post-consumer waste. They are also responsible for most of the toxicity released by furniture during manufacture, in use and at the end of its functional life.

material issues

wood panels
Wood continues to be the top material by volume and value used for furniture globally, although panels far outstrip solid timber for furniture production, especially for built-in furniture like kitchens and storage[20] (fig 7.9). Between 1980 and 2016, the production of wood panels in the form of ply, particleboard and MDF increased by 310% and has more than doubled since 2000, with the biggest growth in Asia.[21] While these boards have transformed the design and production of furniture by providing a standardised product, they pose a number of environmental challenges that have not yet been fully addressed. Before specifying a panel product and its finish, designers should do their research and be aware of some of the key issues.

With deforestation still a major driver of global warming and biodiversity loss, the first of these challenges is ensuring that the wood or other fibres to make these boards comes from sustainable sources. Certification systems like FSC and PEFC provide chain of custody (COC) supply and are increasingly being recognised by consumers and required by procurement. While certification has grown dramatically over the past decade, covering nearly 40% of the world's production forests, there is still some way to go in terms of sustainability in wood supply.[22] As an illustration of this, in 2018, IKEA estimated that they alone use 1% of the world's wood resources. At the same time they have set themselves the goal of reaching 100% sustainable certification by 2020 while doubling their turnover. Given that in 2012 only 22.6% of their solid wood was FSC certified,[23] the fact that they are on track to reach their hugely ambitious goal is a testament to their determination and commitment to become planet positive by 2030.[24]

Recycling and recyclability is the next challenge for board products. As the world's forests come under increasing strain, recycling of wood products is a better strategy than constantly using virgin wood, even if it this comes from sustainable sources. Although wood panels are made from the part of trees that cannot be made into lumber, which is at least 60%, and other wood processing by-products, it is in competition with the paper pulp producers and increasingly wood pellet production for bio-mass energy as countries push to meet lower CO_2 targets. So this is not material that would otherwise go to waste.

In addition, particle and fibreboard are inherently difficult to recycle because they are made up of a mix of approximately 10% resin binders and are often finished with paints, plastic foils, laminates and other contaminants. This means that nearly all post-consumer furniture made of boards ends up in landfill or incineration. But as competition and prices increase in the wood by-products market, so are the incentives for manufacturers to develop recycling methods that overcome these difficulties. A case in point is D&R Henderson in Australia which produce particleboards from 100% recycled wood that are of equal quality to non-recycled boards through a process they developed that cleans contaminated shredded wood waste.[25] In the UK, a new process for separating MDF fibres from resin without chemicals could soon change the industry's outlook if it can be combined with closed-loop take-back programmes.[26] But, until a higher economic value is placed on protecting forests globally, it may be a while before these technologies become mainstream, and panel products are recycled as a matter of course.

The other route to reducing the strain on forests is to specify boards made from less impactful renewable resources such as bamboo, rattan and willow that are quick-growing and self-regenerating. There are also a number of companies in China, the

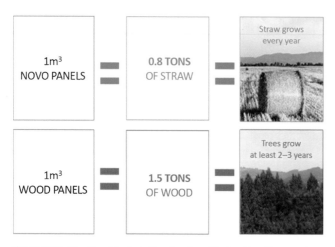

Figure 7.10 Novofibre illustrate the clear benefit of making fibre panels of waste agricultural straw vs wood in reducing the global stress on forest products. (courtesy ©2018 Novofibre Panel Board Holding / www.novofibre.com)

USA and Europe that are pioneering the commercial production of panel products made of agricultural and other waste. Feedstocks include waste reed, wheat, sorghum, rice straw and even fabrics. These come under commercial names such as Solid Textile Board, Kirei board, Wheatboard, Ecoboard and Novofibre to name a few. Figure 7.10 illustrates the environmental benefits of substituting wood for straw, while figure 7.11 shows Novo Deco boards made of waste straw being used in a project in Tianjin, China, and Really's Solid Textile Board used by the Bouroullecs for the Kvadrat Showroom in Copenhagen. These boards also have the health advantage of being formaldehyde free. Although these new, more sustainable panels are gaining traction, as with all new pioneering products, they come at a premium until demand for them increases.

plastics

Perhaps more than any other material, plastics have transformed the design language of furniture in the second half of the twentieth century and most especially the typology of the chair. Through its plasticity, mouldability, toughness, self-colouring and texturing qualities, it has made previously unimaginable designs possible and created pieces of great beauty. Robin Day's 1963 Polypropylene Side Chair, the first-ever mass-produced injection-moulded chair seat made from the new plastic 'polypropylene', heralded a new era of mass-affordable seating (fig 7.12). This was followed by Grosfillex in 1981 with the first 100% injection-moulded monobloc garden chair. Credited with democratising furniture, this iconic yet ubiquitous design has been copied in many variants and produced by the million. Every day, all over the world, they are facilitating cultural and social encounters in schools, communities, streets, markets, homes and gardens. They are also being repurposed and adapted for myriad other uses, from sports to bicycles, citizen bus stops to disabled mobility (fig 7.13).

However, plastics in furniture are also problematic. If we take the plastic chair, its first sin is that it continues to be made almost exclusively from virgin fossil fuel-based plastics. With less than 9% of the world's annual 8.3 billion tons of plastic production being recycled,[27] there can be no lack of material to recycle, and you would think no need to ever make another chair out of virgin plastic. Yet this is not the case. How can this be? In the absence of regulation and producer responsibility to support a circular economy infrastructure, the pricing of resources is skewed in favour of virgin material. This makes it cheaper to buy virgin plastics than recycled feedstocks because producers don't

Figure 7.11 Lower impact boards: Really's white Solid Textile Board used by Studio Bouroullec throughout the Kvadrat showroom (Copenhagen 2017); and Novofibre's Novo Deco formaldehyde-free strawboard used for shelving, acoustic ceilings and partitions in Tianjin Tenio Design Institute (2013). (photos courtesy ©Michel Giesbrecht – Studio Bouroullec; ©2018 Novofibre Panel Board Holding/www.novofibre.com)

Figure 7.12 Democratising seating 1: Robin Day's 1963 Polypropylene side chair was the world's first injection-moulded polypropylene seat that is still being used, produced and copied around the world. Shown here: the original series E School Chair launched in 1971 (Hille, UK) and 35,000 seats used at the 1968 Mexico Olympics. (photos courtesy ©Robin and Lucienne Day Foundation)

Figure 7.13 Democratising seating 2: the monobloc socially active around the world **a.** a monobloc chair (photo credit Coprid) **b.** playing cricket in Dharavi, Mumbai (courtesy Tours and Travel, Dharavi, India photo credit: Andreas Grosse-Halbuer) **c.** outdoor café in Oman (photo credit Thomas Weber) **d.** Intergenerational Forum in Velingara, Senegal. (photo courtesy The Grandmother Project)

have to pay directly for their upstream or downstream negative environmental impacts.

There are however a number of designers and companies around the world who are fully aware of the issue and are demonstrating by example how innovative combinations of post-consumer plastic recycled material can be used to create unique and successful mass-market designs. Figure 7.14 shows a sample of pioneering designs that illustrates the successful use of recycled plastics and more sustainable composites in commercial furniture production. An early torchbearer in this mission was Jane Atfield, who set up Made of Waste in 1992 to produce sheet material from waste HDPE shampoo, detergent and milk bottles that she used in her early furniture designs.[28]

Emeco stands out as a company that since its inception in 1944 has built its design narrative and business model around using recycled materials. Their classic designs and careful workmanship ensure a further degree of product longevity. Their first product was the now iconic 1006 chair made from recycled warship aluminium and in 2010 they produced the same design from 111 PET bottles combined with 35% glass fibre. In 2012 Philippe Starck continued this exploration in their Broom chair made of 100% post-industrial wood and polypropylene waste.[29]

Since 2005, Loll Designs in Minnesota have been producing sheet material, furniture and products made of 100% recycled post-consumer HDPE, including the iconic American Adirondack chair. Since then, Loll estimate that they have diverted over 95 million milk containers.[30] With his Green Eco design, produced by Mobles114 (Spain, 2011) and made of 100% recycle post-industrial polypropylene, Javier Mariscal set out to create an affordable and pleasant yet also sustainable and distinctive chair.[31]

The Tubo chair designed by Industrial Facility for TOG (Brazil, 2014) has a seat made of recycled PET bottles turned into a fleece mat that is thermoformed with low-cost compression moulds. The final material is reminiscent of wool felt, fully washable and recyclable, while the metal base focuses on elegant minimisation suggestive of George Nelson's DAF chair.[32] More recently, Pentatonic, a design group focused on circular economy solutions, has been working with Starbucks to decrease their environmental footprint by designing furniture made from their own waste. The result is a re-engineered 'Bean' chair (2019) made from a modular flatpack design that has an internal structure, upholstery and covering fabric entirely made from Starbuck's own waste PET bottles and cups.[33]

However, there is still a very long way to go in engaging the really big players of the plastic furniture industry such as Grosfillex and Allibert in moving to recycled plastic feedstocks, although the tide

may finally be turning on the unquestioned use of virgin plastic. In 2017 IKEA launched their first recycled plastic wood composite products. Their Kungbacka kitchen unit fronts are made from recycled wood and covered with a plastic foil made from recycled PET bottles (see fig 7.40). The Odger chair, similar to Emeco's Broom chair in style and composition, is made of 30% wood and at least 55% recycled plastic.[34] These early steps in weaning itself off virgin fossil fuel-based-materials are very promising and very necessary if furniture design is to become more sustainable.

While plastics have the advantage of making chairs light, flexible and all-weather, their second sin is that once broken or damaged, more often than not they are beyond repair. In addition, they do not wear or age well, and are frequently thrown out while still functional for aesthetic reasons. Although in theory chairs made of thermoplastics, most commonly polypropylene (PP) and high-density polyethylene (HDPE), are fully recyclable, they still end up in landfill or incinerators because there are extremely few specific take-back or recycling schemes in place. Figure 7.15a illustrates the reality on the ground with a dumpster full of mostly plastic furniture discarded from an institution. This includes over a dozen Matthew Hilton Wait chairs and several Ant chair lookalikes. It would seem that while most items were still functional, the main reason given for discarding was the visible ageing and scruffiness of the plastic surface. Another was that the style did not fit in with newer furniture purchases. Although in the case of this dumpster the metal would go on to be separated and recycled, the plastic and wood composites were destined for incineration.[35] In contrast, figure 7.15b shows one example among millions of the repair culture that pervades countries like India where money is tighter, forcing people to exercise their ingenuity and creativity.

Affronted by this daily reality, many designers are also turning their skills to the creative rehabilitation of plastic chairs as a circular economy social enterprise business proposition. In her b.a-ba project, Cyrille Candas worked with Emmaus companions in France to restore donated monobloc chairs in a range of coloured flocking. Although designed for outdoor use, monoblocs discolour and soon become unattractive. To fully close the loop and create further employment, the flocking itself was made of recycled waste clothing from the social enterprise Façon Relais (fig 7.16). In a different response to the issue, Urban Upholstery in London is redefining the art of upholstery by reinventing unloved furniture into uniquely desirable pieces (fig 7.17).

It bears mention here that the higher end office furniture sector seems to be an exception to the linear fate of most furniture, with many companies and products, especially office seating, achieving C2C certification. This is in large part driven by their need to meet the highest standards of 'green' procurement and competitive tenders. To achieve C2C certification, companies go through a

Figure 7.14 Pioneering chair designs made from recycled plastics and other waste **a.** Emeco chairs (USA): the original 1006 Navy chair (1944):100% recycled aluminium; 111 Navy chair (2010): 65% rPET (111 bottles) 35% glass fibre; Philippe Starck Broom chair (2012): 100% post-industrial wood and polypropylene **b.** Jane Atfield's RCP2 chair (UK 1992): 100% post-consumer HDPE bottles **c.** Loll's Adirondack chair (USA 2006): 100% recycled HDPE from either post-consumer milk bottles or post-industrial waste **d.** Mobles114 Green Eco designed by Javier Mariscal (2011): seat 100% recycled post-industrial polypropylene **e.** TOG Tubo designed by Industrial Facility (Brazil 2014): seat 100% recycled PET bottle thermoformed fleece **f.** Pentatonic's reengineered Bean chair for Starbucks (2019): 100% recycled Starbucks PET waste (photos courtesy Emeco; Jane Atfield; ©Loll Designs; Javier Mariscal; www.industrialfacility. co.uk; Pentatonic)

Figure 7.15a Functional furniture discarded as 'institutional waste' (London 2014). (photo Jane Penty)

Figure 7.16 Cyrille Candas' b.a-ba project has Emmaus companions restoring donated monobloc chairs with flocking made from recycled textile waste by Façon Relais (France 2011). (courtesy Cyrille Candas)

Figure 7.15b Where incomes are much lower, attitudes towards repair are very different and even the broken monobloc is worthy of attention. Shown here, a parking attendant's chair in an industrial park in Mumbai, India (2018). (photo credit Kenneth Rodrigues)

Figure 7.17 Pop, a discarded children's plastic school chair, is brought back to life in Urban Upholstery's 'Not Suitable for Adults' collection (UK 2014). (courtesy ©urbanupholstery www.urbanupholstery.com)

rigorous process of identifying and substituting toxic materials throughout their whole supply chain, maximising recyclate content in their products, shifting to renewable energy and offering closed-loop services with product repair and take-back.

Figure 7.18 shows task chairs from four pioneering C2C companies. Herman Miller's Mirra 1 chair designed with Studio 7.5 (Berlin) in 2003 was the first to fully integrate the C2C design process they developed with McDonough Braungart Design Chemistry (MBCD).

Figure 7.18 Cradle-to-cradle furniture firsts: **a.** Herman Miller's Mirra was the first office chair to fully integrate the C2C design process (USA 2003); **b.** Steelcase's Think™ chair was the first C2C certified product and demonstrates an extreme rationalisation of parts and materials (USA 2006); **c.** Orangebox's Ara was the first C2C certified task chair designed and manufactured in Europe (UK 2008); **d.** the 2020 chair is a product of Ahrend's whole-company C2C certification, not just the design (the Netherlands 2011). (photos courtesy the Chicago History Museum and Herman Miller; ©Steelcase; ©Orangebox; ©Koninklijke Ahrend)

Ninety-six per cent of its parts are recyclable by weight and of these 48% are made of recycled material. Studio 7.5 revisited the design a decade later to create the Mirra 2, a more agile and responsive chair without losing its C2C credentials. Steelcase's Think chair was the first C2C certified product in 2006. With 99% recyclable parts and 37% made of recycled materials, it also demonstrates an extreme rationalisation of parts and materials. In 2008, Orangebox's Ara Eba was the first office chair to be designed and manufactured in Europe with C2C accreditation. It includes an innovative moulding of the seat back and frame that eliminates fasteners or glue. It also features a single-piece base made of 100% recycled polished aluminium which reduces parts and simplifies recycling, and the chair is sold with a full repair, take-back and recycling service.

In 2011, Ahrend went a step further by integrating C2C certification throughout their whole business and service, not just their products. Their 2020 chair is made using 100% green energy,

contains no chrome, PVC or other toxic materials or processes, can be fully recycled and includes a unique way of fixing the upholstery without using any glue which enables the upholstery to be upgraded via their Next Life service. Interestingly, it seems that the benefits of whole-company C2C certification go far beyond the environment. In an interview, Diana Seijs, head of sustainability at Ahrend, described how the whole-company C2C certification process had had a surprisingly positive effect across their entire operations. By pursuing common and actionable goals, all the teams inside and outside the company – design, business, production and suppliers – developed much more collaborative working relationships.[36]

polyurethane foams

The third problematic mass-manufacture material is polyurethane (PU) foam made from petro-chemicals. This has largely replaced traditional renewable materials such as wool, horsehair, cotton, hemp and natural latex as the main material used in upholstery, cushions and mattresses. One of the problems with PU is that it has a limited life and starts to disintegrate after 20 or 30 years.[37] It is also not biodegradable and only truly recyclable through a relatively new process that reverses the chemical reaction but is rarely used, as it is still considered to be too expensive. The majority of PU foam recycling[38] is of post-industrial waste where factory trimmings are chipped and glued together into re-bonded foam products. Post-consumer foam, on the other hand, is primarily landfilled, incinerated or pyrolised owing to difficulties in separation and the high risk of these foams including unknown or banned toxic substances.[39]

The industry has tried to address the non-renewable nature of PU foam by using a percentage (5–30%) of vegetable oils (soya, cotton and so on) to create the base polyols and calling them bio-foams. While this improves the renewable footprint, substituting petroleum with useful crops is also a problematic solution. A more promising replacement material for manufacturing PU foams is CO_2 through carbon capture. In 2016, Covestro (Bayer) opened a factory alongside a coal-fired power station in Germany to make foam mattresses where sequestered CO_2 replaces 20% of the fossil fuel.[40] At the same time, in the USA, Ford and Novomer are jointly developing foams and plastics for car seating made from up to 50% polyols from sequestered CO_2 that they expect to commercialise by 2021.[41] Making foams and plastics from captured CO_2 is an obvious win-win and a growing area of R&D efforts (see Box 5.1, bio-plastics).

Another serious environmental issue in producing PU and most other foams is that they require a blowing agent, usually HFCs. These are powerful GHGs with global warming impacts up to 1000 times higher than CO_2. In recognition of this issue, the EU brought in the F-gas regulation in 2015 that will ban the use of HFCs with a GHG potential of over 150, but not until 2023 for PU foams.[42]

toxicity in furniture and its production

off-gassing

Perhaps more dangerous to the environment and human health are the highly toxic substances that are still permitted in furniture and furnishings that designers should be aware of and avoid. These toxins are released to indoor air slowly over the lifetime of the product in the form of volatile organic compounds (VOCs) by off-gassing or as dust particles, *making indoor air quality (IAQ) two to five times more polluted than outdoor air.*[43] Other pollutants are also released to air, land and water during production or disposal and bio-accumulate in the food chain. The worst among these are organobromine fire retardants, PVC with phthalate plasticisers and formaldehyde adhesives used in wood-based board products.[44] All three toxins are known to cause cancer and other respiratory problems, and the first two are classed as persistent

organic pollutants (POPS) that are being phased out by the 151 Stockholm Convention signatory countries.

brominated fire retardants

Fire retardants in upholstery have been a particular bone of contention with environmental campaigners. They were introduced in the 1980s as additives to PU foams and upholstery fabrics to pass specific fire regulations. Tragically, when these foams are involved in a fire or are incinerated, the flame retardants release highly toxic substances, dioxins and furans, leading to the deaths of some fire victims from toxic smoke rather than from flames.

In 2013, after years of campaigning, Arlene Blum of the Green Science Policy Institute, supported by a Chicago Tribune investigation, won a long, hard battle against the powerful chemical industry. California's TB117-2013 law, which took effect in 2015, makes the addition of these toxic chemicals to PU foam used in upholstery unnecessary by changing the standard flammability test for upholstery to reflect real conditions. With the new cigarette smouldering resistance test, the outer material can act as a fire barrier. Although the toxic substances have not been banned, this means that PU foams or other flammable fillings used inside furniture and cushions no longer need to be laced with toxic fire retardants in order to pass fire safety regulations, provided that the material they are covered in passes the test.[45]

California's new regulations have meant that most furniture manufacturers have eliminated the use of toxic flame retardants in the USA.[46] In Europe there are two levels of fire resistance tests for furniture: open flame or smoulder ignition. The former requires the addition of far higher levels of flame retardants to foams, similar to the older California regulation. In an effort to avoid the unnecessary use of potentially harmful flame retardants, the EC issued new EU Green Procurement guidelines in 2017 recommending that public bodies should not specify a level of fire protection beyond what is strictly required for the context of use.[47]

urea formaldehyde

Off-gassing of urea formaldehyde (UF) is a well-documented problem contributing to 'sick building syndrome'. Most commonly it is released from plywood, MDF and particleboards commonly used in kitchens, wardrobes, flatpack furniture and laminate flooring. UF is classified by the WHO as a carcinogen and respiratory irritant.[48] Since this problem was first recognised, there has been slow but steady regulation to decrease the amounts of UF permitted in boards classified as EU (E0,E1,E2), Japan (F*** and F****) and California (CARB - P2). These increasingly stringent reductions have forced manufacturers to reduce UF content and seek alternative adhesives.[49] If designers find themselves having to work with low-level UF boards, one way of reducing the risk of off-gassing is to create as few penetration points as possible and to seal off the boards wherever penetrations are necessary.

Many environmentally minded designers choose boards made without UF. These are usually termed NAF or NAUF (no added urea formaldehyde). The most commercial UF-free alternative resin used in these boards is MDI, and although this is toxic during application, unlike UF, once set it does not continue to release gasses.[50] Pure-bond plywood boards are another interesting UF-free alternative produced by Columbia Forest products based on biomimicry. They developed a soy protein-based adhesive that imitates a mussel's natural adhesive which is incredibly strong, water resistant, flexible – and non-toxic.[51]

PVC

PVC is another material still found in furniture, often used as a leather substitute in upholstery, inflatable mattresses, shower curtains and other products, which contains and releases toxic substances. As early as 1997, Greenpeace[52] exposed the serious toxicity of PVC over its lifecycle, making it clear that a phase-out was necessary. It also features on the C2C certified list of banned substances. But the sheer size of the PVC industry lobby, which includes the manufacturers of windows, doors and many building products, has meant that the PVC industry in Europe was granted a self-regulatory substance substitution programme to comply with the minimum EU REACH and other hazardous chemical regulations.

What is wrong with PVC? It contains and releases a series of compounds known to be bio-accumulative carcinogens and hormone disruptors in different ways over its lifecycle. Dioxins and furans created in the production of PVC are released during production and at their end-of-life if they are incinerated or burnt. In addition, phthalates used as plasticisers to make it flexible are released throughout their lifecycle, especially during the use phase, making them particularly dangerous to young children: so much so that they are now banned in children's toys and feeding products. In addition, lead, cadmium and organotins are used to stabilise PVC. Although the worst of these were phased out in Europe and the USA by 2015, there are still a huge number of PVC products in circulation that were produced with these ingredients before the phase-outs that continue to pose a risk in use and at their end-of-life. Many large furniture, sportswear, electronics, medical and baby product companies have taken the initiative of becoming PVC-free in the absence of stricter regulation. In short, despite its many useful properties, this is one material to avoid specifying, recycling or incinerating.

metals and their finishes

After wood products, metals are the second most commonly used material in furniture products. Since metals have very high environmental impacts in extraction and production, they should be treated as a precious resource. Their non-renewable nature and heavy energy footprint makes metals among the most important materials to recycle. Fortunately, they are highly recyclable without compromising their performance or appearance, and they have much higher recycling rates than wood or plastics. This makes 100% recycled metal stock available for product specification.

Their finishes are the next important environmental consideration. The most commonly used metals for furniture are mild steel, aluminium and stainless steel, in ascending order of environmental impacts. However, the overall impact for a metal needs to include its finish, as many are very damaging and energy-intensive. Whereas aluminium and stainless can be self-finished in polished or matt versions (see polished castings on C2C office chairs in figure 7.18), mild steel and, in some situations aluminium, requires coating for protection from corrosion or for aesthetic reasons. Common options include chroming, zinc galvanising, epoxy powder coating and anodising for aluminium. Of these, only powder coating provides solid colour, so this is frequently specified by designers, but it is high in energy use, much less durable and often includes toxic colour pigments. For outdoor applications, zinc coatings are much longer lived and overall less impactful than powder coating.[53] From the point of view of reducing toxic chemicals, chroming by physical vapour deposition (PVD) and thermal spraying for zinc are preferred environmental options. Thus, in specifying a metal from a shortlist of options that meet performance and aesthetic criteria, designers should consider the *total impact* of the base material together with its finish as well as its percentage of recycled content.

leather

Leather is the final material commonly used in furniture that needs close consideration before specifying, owing to its known environmental impacts. Leather is one of the oldest materials developed by humans for their clothing, furnishings, utensils, buildings and even transportation, but their increasing use in short-lived products in the fashion and furniture industries raises serious environmental and ethical concerns. By far the biggest issues related to leather arise in the preparation, tanning and finishing processes required to transform animal hides into a supple, useful and enduring material. This is due to the fate of its many toxic chemicals, the large volumes of water required and the risks associated with its waste by-products.

Despite the ban on the use of the highly carcinogenic hexavalent chrome (Cr6) for leather tanning, a true environmentally friendly 'eco-leather' from animal hide still seems difficult to come by, although footprints and impacts vary considerably depending on their origin.[54] A comparison of the full LCA of three of the most used tanning processes – chrome, aldehyde and vegetable – with the cleanest environmental controls shows that there is little to

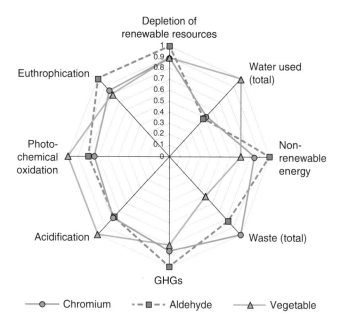

Figure 7.19 Comparison of LCA impacts for chromium, aldehyde and vegetable leather tanning. (source: Ecobilan report/BLC Leather Technology Centre)

choose between the processes when *all* impacts are considered, although the vegetable tanning had less toxic by-products[55] (fig 7.19). In its favour, most hides are biodegradable by-products of the meat and dairy industry, but because the milk and dairy industries have a high environmental footprint compared with other food sources, it is important that the demand for hides does not unduly subsidise the dairy industry.[56] Perhaps worse than the environmental dangers of traditional leather is the well-documented exposure of workers to a slow-killing cocktail of chemicals, particularly in South East Asia where most of the world's leather is processed and workplace safety regulations are scant[57] (fig 7.20).

Figure 7.20 Working conditions in many tanneries around the world put workers' health at risk. Leather worker in Fez, Morocco (2017). (photo credit TinasDreamworld)

Current substitutes for hide leather are synthetic 'leathers', also known as 'vegan' or 'faux' leather derived from a variety of base materials ranging from biodegradable to fossil fuel-based. The most common forms are produced by applying a textured coating of PU, or, less frequently these days, PVC, to a base fabric. The biggest problem with these materials is that they are effectively non-recyclable composites, or monstrous hybrids, made from virgin non-renewable materials and are generally not as tough or long-lasting as 'real' hide leather.

From the sustainability point of view, over the past few years promising alternatives have been emerging produced from waste products that are biodegradable and do not require the use of toxic chemicals. One such product is E-leather, a patented process of reworking waste leather fibres from the leather industry and bonding them to a fabric backing in a closed-loop system without adhesives. This is heavily specified in aircraft and car interiors. Piñatex is another recent leather substitute made by extracting the fibres from discarded pineapple leaves and transforming them into a leather-like non-woven material. The business model is also based on providing higher value employment to the pineapple-growing communities in countries like the Philippines. Piñatex is now being used for footwear, fashion and upholstery, including car interiors (fig 7.21).

A more radical approach to circumvent the environmental problems associated with natural leather is Modern Meadows' 'biofabrication' of leather from collagen fibres produced by genetically engineered yeasts. In 2017 they launched their first product Zoa™, a liquid leather that can be formed into stitch-less fabrications, with their first commercial products available from 2019[58] (fig 7.22). Once we can compare a full LCA of the biofabricated vs. traditional leathers, we will be closer to knowing whether this will one day become a sustainable alternative for traditional hide leather or even synthetic leathers.

Where does this leave the specification of leather in sustainable design? While our ancestors had a very limited number of materials to work with, in the twenty-first century designers are overwhelmed by choice. There is no question that few materials have the beauty, durability and ageing qualities of the best animal hide leathers. However, as with all design decisions based on sustainability, designers must weigh up the pros and cons of real leather against substitutes and alternatives. This should be based on matching the performance criteria and longevity against the impacts of production, use, and end-of-life scenarios. Certainly for short-lived products, natural leather is hard to justify, and if other criteria such as zero toxicity are essential as in C2C, then this may not be an option, but neither may many synthetic 'leathers'. For applications where product longevity is important and other materials cannot match its performance, natural leather becomes a

Figure 7.21 Sustainable leather alternative: (top) Waste pineapple leaf fibres drying after being decorticated and washed; (bottom) Piñatex sample in white. (photo courtesy Piñatex)

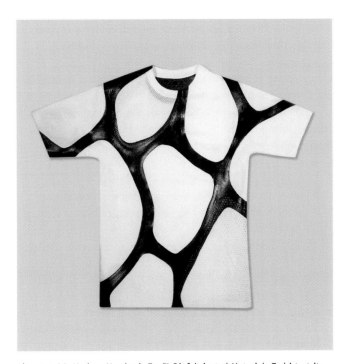

Figure 7.22 Modern Meadow's Zoa™ Biofabricated Materials T-shirt at its first public outing at MoMA New York (2017). (courtesy ©Modern Meadow Zoa™ / photo Sara Kinney)

strong contender. In this scenario, choosing the most sustainable natural leather is crucial. This should be based on careful scrutiny of the leather's provenance in terms of the highest environmental controls and worker conditions.

7.3 design strategies for more sustainable furniture

environmental design strategies

A good starting point for formulating design strategies is to identify the main environmental impacts or 'hotspots' from lifecycle assessments for your particular product type. LCAs in the form of EPDs (environmental product declarations) are now the norm for many contract furniture manufacturers who want to comply with eco-labelling and certification requirements such as ISO 14000, C2C and Greenguard. As we saw earlier, larger companies operating in the B2B contract and office sectors have been leaders in this area, in part due to their CSR commitments and increasingly to meet public 'green' procurement requirements.

In environmental strategies (see fig 2.4) we looked at a 'typical' LCA (lifecycle assessment) for furniture based on a single indicator: GHG potential. This clearly showed that furniture's biggest carbon emissions are by far in the material production phase. In 2005, Steelcase ran a full Simapro LCA comparison across all impact categories for a desk, chair and screen in the Answer office furniture range which gives us a much truer picture of furniture's impacts.[59] The results confirmed that the material production phase is still the most impactful, followed by production for all three products in terms of energy consumption, GHGs, acidification and pollutants. However, when it came to solid waste, end-of-life scenarios dominated.

In the 12 years since these LCAs were conducted, leading office furniture companies have reduced their solid waste and material production impacts considerably. Desking and chairs now have typically 50% recycled content and take-back schemes are in operation, ensuring near-full recycling. However, this is far from being the picture across the industry as yet, particularly in the consumer sector, although, as we have seen, the landscape is beginning to change with new circular economy initiatives by leading producers and retailers.

Looking ahead, new developments pushing the furniture industry towards integrating IoT technology do raise environmental concerns. Up until now, the impacts in the use phase of most furniture have been considered negligible, similar to buildings where the embodied energy of producing the materials is the main consideration. All this may be set to change as more and more digital technology becomes embedded in furniture. In these new scenarios, designers will have to consider the energy use footprint, reliability, as well as ease of repair, upgradability and separation of electronic components for effective recycling.

key lifecycle informed strategies

Below is a list of key strategies to adopt in making furniture more environmentally sustainable based on the main lifecycle issues discussed to date.

1. extend the product life by designing-in:
   * product resilience by anticipating usage scenarios, including sharing and serial ownership
   * similar longevity for all components to avoid the weakest link syndrome
   * good wearing qualities and low maintenance through the material and finish choices
   * damage proofing and repairability through the product architecture and the after-service offer, including information, advice and spare parts
   * upgradability that allows the product 'look' to change through different finishes and cover materials
   * flexibility of configuration for adaptability to different spaces, changing needs, frequent house moves and second-hand markets
   * disassembly with the same ease as assembly and reassembly for moving, storage and resale
2. select the lowest impact materials, finishes and processes that will achieve the functional and aesthetic qualities needed and desired by:
   * aiming for base materials from 100% recycled renewables or non-renewables followed by 100% sustainably certified renewables and avoiding monstrous hybrids (see fig 2.9, rules of thumb)
   * sourcing and engaging suppliers in increasing their recycled content
   * aiming for zero toxicity and VOCs by avoiding UF, chemical fire retardants, eliminating PVC and some colour pigments
   * selecting base materials and their finishes together based on their combined impacts
   * running LCA comparisons for material and design alternatives where possible or relevant (see box 2.3, fast-track LCA)
   * transforming low-impact materials into high-value products through creative exploration and experimentation
3. reduce the amount of material required to achieve the function by:
   * rethinking ways of achieving the same or multiple functions in less space
   * lightweighting through material substitution and pushing the boundaries of material properties
   * re-engineering the furniture structure
4. take full responsibility for the product at the end of its useful life by:
   * involving all the stakeholders in formulating an EoL strategy at the very beginning of the design process that builds in closed material and energy loops as part of the product service offer
   * only specifying materials that can and will be reused or recycled. Recyclable is not enough if you know that there is no infrastructure in place
   * designing-in re-manufacturing as a step better than recycling if offering take-back
   * making disassembly easy for the owner and recycler
   * minimising the number of different materials and fastener types
   * eliminating adhesives between different materials
   * designing-in features that can change behaviour norms at the end-of-life
   * clearly communicating the end-of-life options permanently on the product or through an electronic product 'passport'
5. ensure the most ethical and environmental supply chain by:
   * sourcing or developing local materials and skills wherever possible
   * researching and vetting the supply chain for employment and environmental standards, especially in specifying materials like leather and virgin metals
   * looking at transportation mode rather than just distance in assessing transport impacts
   * developing long-term collaborative relationships with suppliers to align values and practices
6. aim to power all operations and life stages with renewable energy
7. develop designs that:
   * are in tune with real and changing societal needs
   * stand the test of time and make lasting cultural connections
   * enable more socially and economically sustainable lifestyles

Furthermore, sustainable design is inextricably linked to 'good design', as Alberto Meda discusses (Box. 7.1). Many of these strategies are exemplified in a range of interpretations and furniture typologies throughout the chapter, and more particularly in figures 7.23 to 7.25. FNP, shown in figure 7.23a, is a modular, adaptable, fully dismantlable and lightweight shelving system by Axel Kufus (Moorman, 1989 to present). Only by thinking in systems and connecting detail can one achieve a truly modular

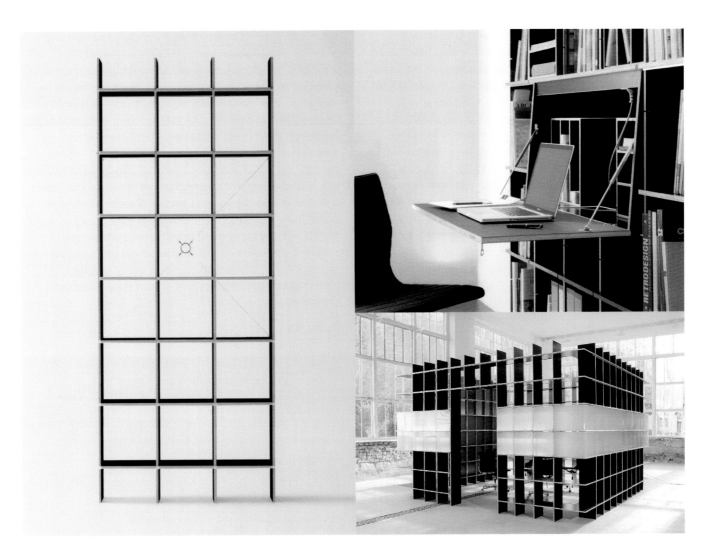

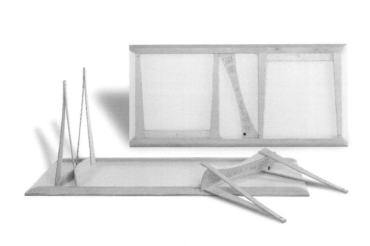

Figure 7.23 Flexibility and adaptability; **a.** FNP lightweight and modular shelving system by Axel Kufus (Moorman, Germany 1989); **b.** Spanoto table by Jakob Gebert (Moorman, Germany 1989). (courtesy Moorman: FNP photo JÑger & JÑger; Spanoto photo Lutz Bertram/JÑger & JÑger)

system that adapts to different situations and grows with changing needs and budgets. Jakob Gebert's Spanoto table, shown in figure 7.23b, cleverly exploits the flexible properties of thin ply to create these elegant, lightweight, flatpack and modular tables.

Figure 7.24 shows two contrasting examples of the use of low-impact materials. The Terra 2.0 outdoor seat by Nucleo is made of cardboard, soil, grass seed and sun. The original Terra armchair from 2000 won the Compasso D'Oro 'Product for the Community' award in 2001 (fig 7.24a). With continued demand and a successful Kickstarter campaign, Terra 2.0 was redesigned as a flatpack laser-cut cardboard kit in 2016. Figure 7.24b shows card furniture pioneer Olivier LeBlois' Desk-table. Made from a single sheet of card with near-zero waste, it is still selling after more than 20 years, along with armchairs and other card furniture.

The experimentation with materials and formats that lightweighting and dematerialising invites is demonstrated in

figure 7.25. Random chair by Bertjan Pot is an ultra-light chair of carbon fibre and epoxy resin. While the original material is not recyclable, its lightness, toughness and durability are reasonable compensations until it can be made as a bio-composite. Air is another material used to create light structures. The original Therm-a-Rest camping mat from 1972 set out to provide compact lightweight comfort and insulation for outdoor enthusiasts. By controlling the air in and out through a valve, it self-inflates and can be minimised in size for packing. With the addition of a simple harness, the camping mat can be transformed into a supportive seat. Snow Crash used the inflatable principle in Airbag, their informal chair-come-mattress made of air and sports fabrics. In Hechima, Ryuji Nakamura assembles repeat patterns of cut plywood (Hechima 1) and later vulcanised paper (Hechima 2) to create a chair that is both 'physically and visually light and porous' to defy our preconceptions of what these materials are capable of.

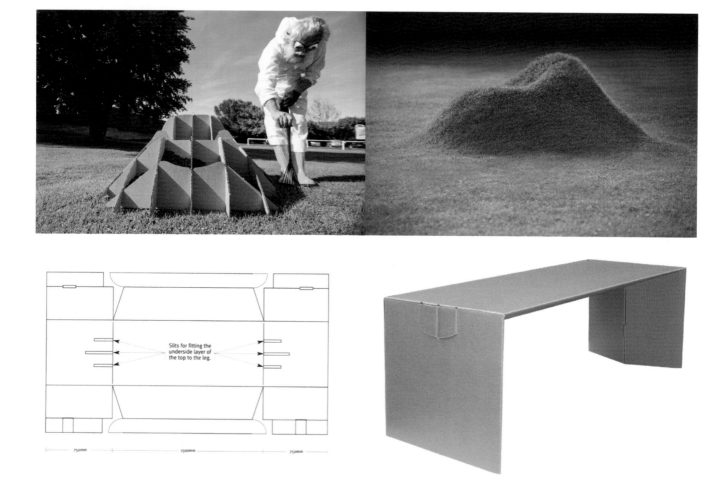

Figure 7.24 Low-impact materials: **a.** Nucleo 2 made of cardboard, soil, grass seed and sun (courtesy Nucleo_Andrea Sanna + Piergiorgio Robino/photo Twinpixelvideo.it, Nucleo, Italy 2016) **b.** Olivier Leblois' Desk-table, France 1995 made from a single sheet of card. (courtesy Quart de Poil)

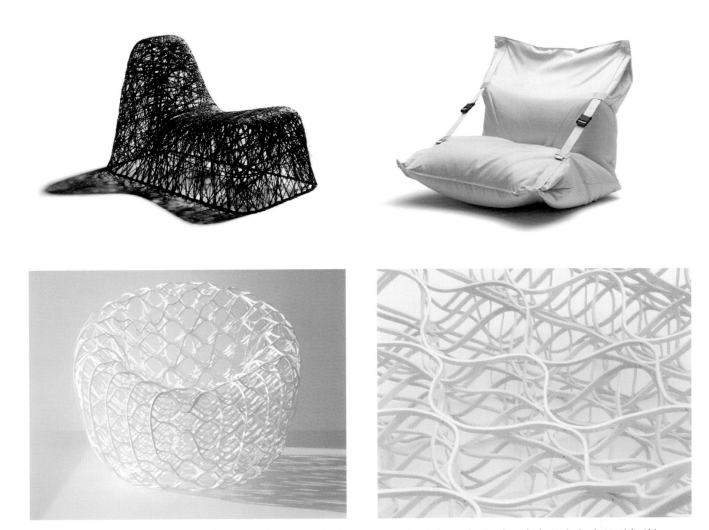

Figure 7.25 Lightweighting and dematerialising **a.** Random chair made of carbon fibre and resin by Bertjan Pot (Moooi, the Netherlands 2003) **b.** Airbag uses air and sports fabric to create an informal chair or mattress (Snow Crash with Pasi Kolhonen, Finland 1997) **c.** Hechima 2 by Ryuji Nakamura (Japan 2006) made of repeat patterns of vulcanised paper. (photos courtesy Berjran Pot; Iikka Suppanen; Ryuji Nakamura & Associates)

furniture and social sustainability

enduring material cultures

Earlier, we touched on the fact that furniture and space-related products are important socially and culturally as a material expression of our personal and shared values. For this reason, in producing designs that respond to current and changing societal needs, designers may find valuable inspiration by connecting with past material cultures. Figure 7.28 shows some examples of how designers have reinterpreted ancient and traditional designs to suit current needs with present-day material technologies to produce useful furniture with a lighter footprint.

Chairless was Alejandro Aravena's response when invited to design a chair for Vitra in 2010. He reinterpreted the Ayoreo Indians' use of a simple woven band to provide support for sitting on the ground for long periods of time, eliminating the need for a chair. In India, yogis also use similar straps for supportive seating. This dematerialisation suits many planned or impromptu situations in which we find ourselves today, including outdoor festivals, concerts, camping and indoor lounging. It is also surprisingly comfortable and relaxing (fig 7.28a).

Folding stools in different forms have been recorded in use since ancient times in Egypt. The same principle is still being used in such carefully crafted pieces as Kaare Klint's Propeller stool from 1930 (produced 1962, Denmark) and Poul Kjaerholm's PK91 stool, through to the common camping stool. The traditional leather tripod stool of the Mayan people of Mexico has also inspired many lightweight and versatile designs for outdoor activities. These range from drawing, walking, camping and fishing, through to folding stick seats for anyone not able to walk a long distance but wanting to keep active (fig 7.28b).

Box 7.1 Alberto Meda on the connection between 'good' design and sustainability[60]

Alberto Meda is the author of many highly successful furniture and lighting designs found in boardrooms, offices, airports and homes around the world. His designs are the expression of a determination to reduce complexity and deliver meaningful functionality by the simplest means possible. The results are both clever and timeless objects that speak of honesty and integrity.

JP. With your many years of experience designing successful products, what is your personal understanding of sustainability?

AM. I think it is a term that is very overused and now very commercialised as a selling point. For me a design is sustainable when the project makes sense. When it solves a problem or a need in a new way, when it is *really* useful – in that idea there is sustainability. It is also respectful of resources and will last a long time. It is the opposite of a gimmick or fashion. In this case design is a waste. In this sense it must have an ethical attitude.

JP. Can you give examples of successful products or initiatives that you have been involved in that meet your criteria for sustainability?

AM. I can give you two examples of good design. The first is the table lamp Berenice that Paolo Rizzatto and I designed

in 1985 for Luceplan. This design uses the structure of the lamp to conduct the electricity, so it has no redundant parts. Also this makes it easily repairable and dis-assemblable. In this way the structure is functional and aesthetic at the same time.

The second example is the Frame chair designed for Alias in 1989. It is made of only three simple components: the extruded aluminium frame, polyester mesh and castings. All the parts are removable and repairable.

JP. Do you have examples of initiatives that have not been so successful in sustainable terms? And could you explain the obstacles or reasons that got in the way?

AM. An example of a design that I consider is not so sustainable is the Lola light for Luceplan that I designed with Paolo Rizzatto in 1987. This design is made of three different materials. The reflector is made of glass-filled nylon (PA), the stem is carbon fibre and the base is a PU mould with a Zamac insert. It was very much an exploration of new materials to see how you could create unity with different functional materials. So in this sense it was about taking risks, experimenting and pushing boundaries. But the bad side is that it was glued ...

Figure 7.26 Berenice (1985) and Lola (1987) lamps designed by Alberto Meda and Paolo Rizzatto for Luceplan (Italy) and Meda's ground-breaking Frame mesh chair for Alias (1989). (photos courtesy Alberto Meda)

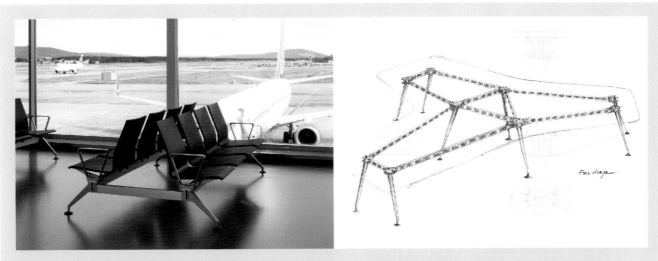

Figure 7.27 Meda Gate (2011) and Meda Morph (2007) designed by Alberto Meda with and for Vitra (Switzerland). (courtesy Alberto Meda)

The design is still pleasing, but I can now critique this decision. Repairability is an important aspect of sustainability – more than recyclability perhaps. Frustrating examples of this are mobile phones and cameras, etc. – the fact that we can't upgrade these products through a level of modularity. With furniture there can also be a relation to fashion, but if you look at how long we keep our sofas, the obsolescence is not comparable, although there is an intersection.

However, I think there is hope that the new technologies, like 3D printing on demand, will really change things. For example, if your bumper is damaged you could make a new one locally. Or thanks to the Internet, a repair is possible because you can identify and locate spare parts.

JP. Are there other key considerations in producing better products?

AM. Reducing complexity for everyone involved is important and easy to overlook. The Meda Gate seat is an example. I designed this with Vitra with whom I have had a long collaborative relationship over the last 20 years. It has the capability to be very easily disassembled – each seat is only attached with two screws so that airports and public places can easily change the layouts. So this means thinking about the airport management and the workers as well as the passengers. The earlier design had a separate seat and back, but this meant too many brackets and screws. It is only when you look at it from all their perspectives that it makes you, as designer, rethink the design.

Also the conference table MedaMorph that I designed for Vitra was about making it possible to have different layouts. The

installation of the cabling was another issue we addressed because these conference tables have to have a lot of electronic communication. MedaMorph allows the cabling to be installed before the tabletop is put on so that the fitters don't need to scrabble under the table. This is thinking about the worker as well.

JP. Can you share any aspects of the design process you follow that help arrive at 'good' designs that are ultimately more sustainable?

AM. With Vitra, for example, it is always a shared solution, a discussion with a lot of creative people working together where your idea is never dismissed. It is built on. So my role is to imagine a direction, to show the path. But even if you have a direction, like at sea, the wind can make you change course. So as a designer in a design team, you must have the capability to deal with issues as they arise. *This is the joy of the process.* Sometimes it can be quite frustrating, but this is good design. With experience, you know how to overcome these things to get a result.

Young designers are able to take risks but then they need to be cautious and they need to have good fortune on their side – this is very important also. Even after the creation there are so many other parameters to consider: sales, marketing, distribution, etc. The design is only successful when the whole process works. *So designers should not underestimate the complexity. But good design is complexity solved and good design is sustainable.*

Figure 7.28 Looking back to look forward: new 'furniture' based on ancient and traditional designs reinterpreted to suit current needs **a.** Chairless by Alejandro Aravena was inspired by Ayoreo Indian sitting strap (Vitra, Switzerland 2010) **b.** Folding and tripod stools: Arabian relief (second century BC); Poul Kjaerholm's PK91 stool (Republic of Fritz Hansen, Denmark 1961); Walkstool's occasional seat (Sweden 1997). (courtesy ©Vitra; Walters Art Museum; Fritz Hansen; ©Scandinavian touch)

wellbeing

As well as providing cultural connections, furniture contributes in many other ways to physical and mental wellbeing. The physical benefits of 'ergonomically' designed furniture are well documented and still provide a lot of scope for designers to challenge existing assumptions about how we *should* do things. It is this design thinking that has taken us from office chairs that lessen the physical problems associated with sitting for long periods of time, to standing desks that question whether we should even be sitting.

Although not all design innovation in this area is immediately appreciated, those that have become commercially successful amply demonstrate the power of user-led, ergonomically informed questioning to redefine furniture typologies and change people's lives. Figures 7.29 and 7.30 show two chairs designed by Peter Opsvik that illustrate where this thinking can lead. The iconic kneeling chair by Balans (1979) was one of the first designs to successfully challenge how we sit and work to support posture and is still in production today. The second, Capsico, produced by Håg (2001 and 2011), rethinks office seating to maximise mobility and flexibility in any activity and at any height. In keeping with Håg's established values, it also has outstanding environmental credentials, including a very low carbon footprint, high recycled content and Nordic Swan and Greenguard certification.

Designers can also help to spot and respond to 'unknown-unknown' needs. The workmate is a good example of this. It has

Figure 7.29 Variable Balans chair by Peter Opsvik (Stokke, Norway 1979/ Varier, Denmark since 2006). (photo courtesy ©Varier Furniture)

Figure 7.30 Capisco (2001) and Capisco Puls (2011), Peter Opsvik for Håg, Norway. (photos courtesy ©Håg Flokk)

and continues to facilitate all types of DIY, carpentry and repair work for millions of ordinary and professional people across the globe. Yet when Ron Hickman, its inventor, first showed the idea to Black & Decker and to Stanley in the mid-1960s, they said there was no market for it. He went on to produce and successfully sell it himself, prompting Black & Decker to finally take up the design in 1973. Since then they have sold over 30 million[61] (fig 7.31).

Perhaps less obvious is the role that interior products play in the quality of how we experience space. Poor acoustics, in the form of reverberation, are a growing problem caused by the hard acoustically reflective materials that have become popular in commercial buildings, open-plan workspaces, restaurants and contemporary homes. This causes discomfort for everyone at some level, as the brain unconsciously goes into overdrive trying to decipher what it is hearing over and over again. For some, however, particularly the elderly or hearing impaired, it can be socially excluding by making conversations impossible to follow. For others, it can be completely crippling, as continuous exposure causes severe headaches and tinnitus.

This state of affairs has led to the growth in the design of acoustic products. Figure 7.32 shows Flap designed by Alberto and Francesco Meda, winner of the 2016 Compasso d'Oro and one of several original acoustic products produced by Caimi Brevetti.

Figure 7.31 With over 30 million sold, the workmate came from nowhere in the mid 1960s to solve 'unknown-unknown' needs. (photo credit Fab Lab Carrefour Numerique, Paris)

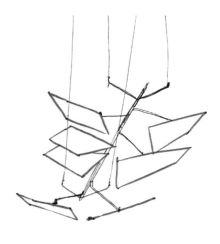

Figure 7.32 Improving how we experience space: Flap, designed by Alberto & Francesco Meda, winner of the 2016 Compasso d'Oro, is produced by Caimi Brevetti using their equally award-winning Snowsound acoustic technology. (courtesy ©Caimi Brevetti and Alberto Meda)

Their award-winning Snowsound acoustic technology is made of a single material, 100% polyester (PET),which cleverly provides both structure and sound absorption by varying its density. Using the same material for finish and structure also makes it easy to recycle and 30% of the core is already recycled PET. It also achieves Greenguard Gold certification, as polyester requires no fire retardants.

Regaining control over personal space in work environments is another important theme in interior products that we see in molo's Spacewall range (interview, box 7.2). It is also the main premise behind Ahrend's Comfort Workstation concept which we see in figure 7.33. Surveys of open-plan office workers found that that most are not comfortable: they feel either too hot or too cold, that air quality is lacking and they don't like the all-day, one-size-fits-all lighting. This new design concept gives open-plan office users control over their own heating, ventilation, desk height, acoustics and biodynamic lighting. It also saves up to 25% energy, as space temperatures can be maintained at their lowest settings.[62]

shared spaces
public space
Outdoor public spaces are known for building social capital and increasing wellbeing. In Chapter 3.4 we saw how reclaiming public spaces for people, especially those given over to the car, was an important focus of critical design and activism. In this sense, public furniture may be seen as a form of community generosity, inviting people to share with others, pause a moment, or to simply sit and watch the world go by. But with tight public budgets, it needs imagination to continue this long tradition

of civic amenity. People for Urban Progress' (PUP, a NFP social enterprise) PUPstops project in Indianapolis is an example of how designers with vision can instigate socially beneficial projects by spotting opportunities and brokering partnerships. Together with Ecolaborative they salvaged 9000 seats from a defunct local stadium in Indianapolis and persuaded the Indigo transit system to partner with them in repurposing the seats for bus stops. In the first two years, bus stop seats more than doubled in numbers in Indianapolis (fig 7.34).

In a different but highly creative vein, Tejo Remy and René Veenhuizen show us another way in which we can reshape street furniture by redefining what it is we want it to give us back. They transformed the idea of a school playground fence from an instrument of division and separation into a series of meeting points by design, connecting those inside and out to create a 'social fence'[63] (fig 7.35).

co-working
As we touched on in the collaborative economy in Chapter 4.3, the global phenomenon of shared or co-working spaces has radically transformed the landscape of workspaces. By creating a demand for designs better adapted to sharing and collaborating, it has triggered a rethink not only of how the space is used but also the nature of furniture, lighting and interior products (see fig 4.23, Opendesk). The overriding trend has been towards less formality and more adhocracy and flexibility by designing spaces and furniture that foster creative and collaborative practices. Interestingly, this trend is also feeding back into more traditional office designs and shaking up the whole sector. It is also important to point out that co-working spaces often contribute

Figure 7.33 Ahrend's Comfort Workstation saves energy on space heating and puts office workers back in control of temperature, ventilation, height and biodynamic lighting (the Netherlands 2018). (photo courtesy ©Koninklijke Ahrend/photo Stijn Poelestra)

Figure 7.34 Community enabling: People for Urban Progress repurposing seats for PUPstops in Indianapolis (2012 to 2014). (courtesy People for Urban progress/photo credit Michael Brciker)

Figure 7.35 A playground fence transformed into a place of meeting and regrouping rather than separation. Shown here in Dordrecht, the Netherlands, they have also been built in Utrecht and SanDiego, USA (2013). Design: Tejo Remy and Rene Veenhuizen, produced by Gelmo Helwerk (the Netherlands, from 2004). (courtesy ©RemyVeenhuizen/photo Hebert Wiggerman)

to reduced duplication of products and equipment and also to increased mental wellbeing.

home-away-from-home

The trend in 'sharing' home space that we touched on briefly in Chapter 4.3 has come in for much criticism because of the impact tourism is having upon local communities. Equally in terms of furnishing, sharing part of our personal spaces has inevitably influenced how we plan, design and choose furniture for these spaces. Is this also leading to less personalisation and more IKEAfication? Or could the likes of Couchsurfing and Airbnb also become vehicles for supporting the appreciation of regional cultures? Airbnb already promote some good practice in sustainable living with their hosts. Through their Samara studio, led by Joe Grebbia, they are taking this further by openly exploring how buildings, products and services can bring us closer to each other through design. Their Cedar House developed in collaboration with Go Hasegawa is an example of this thinking in action. The house is a community-run shared cottage available on Airbnb in Yoshino, Japan made of cedar from the local forests by local carpenters for the benefit of the village.[64]

furniture and economic sustainability

Having looked at how furniture can be more environmentally and socially sustainable, here we ask ourselves whether there are business models that inherently produce more sustainable furniture. As the furniture market spans everything from designs produced by the millions, to batch and one-off bespoke pieces, it is worth taking stock of the different design opportunities and limitations within these different business scenarios for greater sustainability, as well as understanding consumers' motivations.

consumer priorities

When surveyed about their priorities in buying furniture, European consumers listed functionality and style first, price second and environmental friendliness third. However, they also indicated that they would be willing to pay more for higher standards of durability, lower maintenance, zero toxicity, fair labour and environmentally friendly production[65] (fig 7.36). While this survey only covers Europe, there are two important lessons for designers to take away. First, that these results are consistent with the value modes analysis we looked at in Chapter 3.1 by pointing to the fact that apart from 'pioneers' or 'deep greens', for most people, sustainability credentials are not their top criterion in choosing furniture, yet they expect them to be there. This suggests that sustainable qualities should be embedded in products through voluntary or mandatory standards. The second lesson is that it is up to designers to create attractive products with compelling narratives that communicate to consumers the wider scope of sustainability. This should encompass pre-purchase information and post-purchase support in the important part they can play in product longevity and EoL after it leaves the showroom.

high-volume mass production

As we have seen with IKEA, high-volume producers have a big influence on the market's sustainable practices, as they can leverage economies of scale to keep their costs down and maximise energy and material efficiency. They can also leverage suppliers to drive through sustainable sourcing, new production methods and ethical employment practices. Because of the huge multiplier effect, comparative LCAs between alternative design and material options are especially important in this sector when making design decisions. As an example, Steelcase ran an LCA

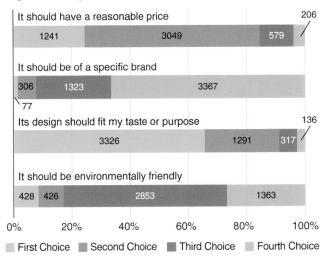

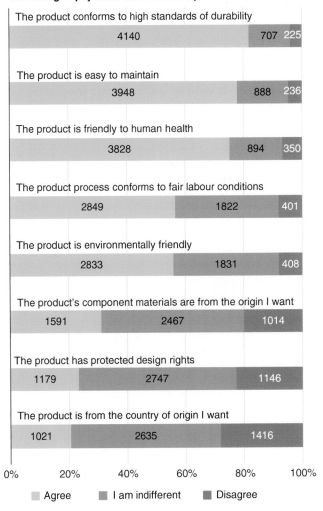

Figure 7.36 EU furniture report: results of two questions in a consumer survey. (source: EU Furniture Market Report November 2014)

Box 7.2 Interview with Stephanie Forsythe on molo's approach to design and sustainability[66]

Stephanie Forsythe and Todd MacAllen are the two architect designers behind Vancouver-based molo and their unique 'soft' collection. Stephanie discusses some of the real physical and commercial challenges in keeping their products true to their principles of sustainability, adaptability and surprise.

Their 'soft' collection is a range of paper and non-woven fabric, ultra-lightweight honeycomb structures that can be expanded and shaped to create spaces, partitions, lighting, seating and more. The collection is distinguished by minimal use of materials in relation to its function (one unit expands from 50mm (2") to over 4.5 m (15')), low-impact recycled and recyclable materials and the inherent flexibility and creative possibilities it affords users.

JP. softwall demonstrates that taking a completely different design approach to an existing need opens the door for more sustainable solutions on a physical and social level. But the commercial success of the soft collection is its ultimate endorsement. Can you tell us about its range of users and uses?

SF. We tend to create things that enable people to continue the design process. The fact that they can manipulate and change the shape of their own space in an ongoing way seems to appeal to a really diverse range of people.

We find our products used extensively for the events industry, from trade shows to community or family gatherings.

Connected to this are temporary exhibitions in museums and art galleries. For instance, softwall and softseating belong to the permanent collection of the MoMA in New York where they have also been used for cocktail bars, event backdrops and a temporary coat check.

Another group would be workspace, everything from small live/work studios to large, flexible open offices. *softwall* and *cloud softlight* have become a perfect fit for the informal flexible workspaces pioneered by California tech companies, along with co-working environments.

JP. In relation to open workspaces, lack of privacy and poor acoustics have increasingly become problematic. It is interesting that the very structure and material of softwall has the added benefit of being good acoustically – perhaps an unintended consequence?

SF. From the beginning, we knew that the cellular structure of softwall would help absorb sound and that the free form could be used to break up reflected noise that builds between parallel surfaces. Often people are selecting *softwall* to solve issues of privacy and acoustics after they realise it is a problem in their space, but increasingly these things are being planned from the beginning, so we help create things like phone booths or meeting areas in new construction too. Our cloud lighting is also being used for its acoustic qualities in large open spaces

Figure 7.37 molo's softblock in translucent white textile with LED lighting and kraft paper softwall taking shape. Magnetic connectors allow the expanding walls, blocks or seating to connect to each other and anchor to walls to shape any desired space. (photos courtesy ©molo)

Figure 7.38 cloud softlight pendants above softseating fanning stools and cantilever table in a temporary meeting space bounded by softwall. (photo courtesy ©molo)

like restaurants and foyers. So you can get three jobs out of one product: acoustics, light and intimacy.

JP. So you could say that in the wider sense of sustainability, your products inherently improve the quality of how a space is experienced. Can you tell us a bit about the development of softwall?

SF. Although we have been making them since 2003 there has been an evolution. When we started they were literally tissue paper. The next material we eventually decided on was a kraft paper made of new and recycled fibres. After playing with different combinations, we worked out that you need a mix of long new fibres with short recycled ones to make it strong enough and avoid it shedding small fibres that get into the air.

JP. How did you evolve into the non-woven fabric?

SF. We wanted a translucent white to work with light. But as white paper yellows over time, shows dirt and requires chemicals for bleaching, we quickly decided it wasn't going to work. Instead we chose the textile, a 100% polyethylene non-woven fabric that we were familiar with because it's used

for building wraps. We also see the textile as something that has lightness, not only because it weighs half as much as paper, but also its gentle aesthetic quality and how beautifully it takes light.

JP. How do non-woven textile and kraft paper compare in longevity?

SF. If you take water damage out of the equation, I would say that they are very equal in terms of longevity. What we tend to tell people is that they can expect to get a good five years. If less people are handling it more gently, they might just live with it forever. Every few months we hear from people who still have original tissue paper walls 12 years on and are thinking about recycling them and looking for a replacement.

JP. What about repairing damage?

SF. The paper will occasionally get a tear – especially in public spaces because people wonder what it is, then go up and find out. [...] We recommend the textile wall for these situations. But in any case, tears can be repaired by splitting the wall, removing the torn layer and re-laminating it. As an aside, we spent a lot of time in Japan and have seen how beautiful Shoji screens look over time as they are repaired by their owners with little patches that gradually create a pattern of their own.

Repair also has an interesting cultural dimension, particularly in North America where there is this belief that building materials need to be bulletproof. In Japan we observed that what appears to be light and delicate also has a structure that 'anybody can fix', whereas things that are very hard, like concrete and steel, have different types of wear and tear that can't be fixed by the person living with it.

JP. I suppose that really demonstrates the difference between strength and resilience.

SF. Yes, we talk about resilience a lot.

JP. What do you think is the most satisfying about what you have achieved with molo?

SF. Early on, as recently graduated architects experimenting and playing around with all this, we suddenly had the ah-ha moment where we felt, 'This is something worth sharing'. This continues to be a satisfying thing. We also enjoy the idea of putting things into the world that allow people to engage in the process of design themselves. Seeing the different ways that people apply creativity to shape their own space is very rewarding.

to compare the use of PP vs. ABS for their tabletop edges. They found that across all LCA categories, human health, ecosystem quality, GHG emissions and resources PP has between 40 and 75% less impact than ABS. Multiplied up, this is a very significant impact reduction. Despite these findings, many companies still use PVC and ABS edging either through ignorance or a blinkered drive to shave off a few cents from their cost sheet (fig 7.39).

Reducing bulk and weight through flatpacking and lightweighting, as well as rationalising the transportation distances, is especially important for high-volume producers, as most furniture components are not produced locally. When Steelcase ran a comparison LCA of different supply chain options for the Steelcase Think® back frame for their European production, they found that transporting the parts from the USA increased the GHG emissions of the part by nearly 25%. This reinforces the importance for high-volume manufacturers of running rigorous comparison LCAs as part of their design decision-making process.

The downside of the high-volume model is that it offers limited opportunity for the continuity or integration of regional traditions and skills, use of local materials or individualisation. It

is also based on the premise of high levels of consumption and depends on continued growth in turnover, the impacts of which giants like IKEA are only just beginning to offset through the inclusion of recycled material content in their designs as well as piloting closed-loop and furniture take-back and leasing schemes. IKEA's ambition to become people and planet positive by 2030 will be the real test of the ability of the high-volume model to be more sustainable by decoupling sales growth from negative impacts.

small to medium-sized enterprises (SMEs)

The sustainability potential and credentials of SMEs vary widely because they cover the full spectrum of the market – from luxury to low-budget. The enormous added value that high-end designer and luxury goods can command makes more sustainable provenance of materials and employment conditions economically feasible, although more often than not this is not fully embraced. With some of the most world-renowned brands and designers in this group, the luxury end can also offer a more bespoke service and higher quality, ensuring product longevity and good resale value. Introducing more sustainable alternatives that shift the traditional perceptions of luxury is an interesting creative challenge for designers.

At the lower end are companies with very tight margins that usually outsource production at cut-throat prices where environmental concerns are not a priority. Transportation impacts can also be significant here if they are outsourcing from long distances. This group will tend to be followers that will respond to mandatory regulations.

Perhaps the biggest opportunity for sustainable innovation in furniture in this category comes from an array of smaller niche producers, including some very interesting new hybrid and distributed manufacturing models that can cater to more environmentally aware and individually minded consumers. The flexible mix of digital machining with handcrafting has enhanced what small designer-makers can offer in terms of personalised multiple one-offs and bespoke customisation. Internet platforms have also been instrumental in breathing new life into more specialist and individual production by expanding their markets and ensuring viable businesses.

As discussed in Chapter 4.3, innovative companies like Opendesk have pioneered a new model of furniture production that combines open design with distributed production by local workshops via a common platform (see fig 4.23). Piet Hein Eik in Eindhoven (see fig 7.5) and Unto This Last in London are two further examples of businesses that are leveraging their smaller size to engage customers through their in-house making process by opening their combined workshop and salesroom to customers.

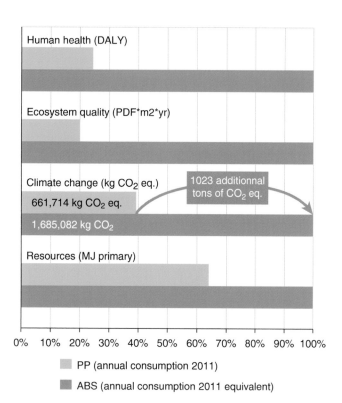

PP (annual consumption 2011)

ABS (annual consumption 2011 equivalent)

Figure 7.39 LCA comparison showing the avoided environmental impacts over a year by using PP over ABS for Steelcase's table-top edges. (source: S. Zinck/Aero Montreal)

Figure 7.40 IKEA's Kungsbakca kitchen fronts made from recycled wood and covered with a plastic foil made from recycled PET bottles represents a promising step towards making mass-manufacture panel products more sustainable. It suggests that we are only just beginning to explore the possibilities for sustainable design innovation in mass-market furniture (2017). (photo courtesy ©Inter IKEA systems)

Figure 7.41 In contrast to IKEA, the design language and detail of Sebastian Cox's kitchen for deVOL emerges from a smaller scale craft practice closely linked to its local sustainable woodland timber supply. (photo courtesy Sebastian Cox)

Seeing the furniture being made first-hand and personally selecting the model is a way of ensuring greater product longevity and customer loyalty. The Internet has also created a new lifeline for the long tradition of smaller craft-makers who work with local materials to produce unique designs that connect with regional material culture and strengthen local economies. Sebastian Cox is one example of a new generation of makers who believe that "a traditional approach can be radical and that the past can be used to design and make the future".[67] His designs combine inventiveness with the best qualities of timber from sustainably managed British woodlands (fig 7.41).

Regardless of the business model, producers should signal their positive actions through good communication and voluntary accreditation from the supply chain with FSC, PFC, Greenguard and C2C certification or Eco-labelling. These labelling systems not only help consumers and institutional buyers to make better choices, they also inform and keep checks on the whole product process, starting with design.

sustainable futures and the pull of new tech

Design thrives on new materials, processes and evolving societal demands. Each time a new material or process emerges, the designer's palette expands and new design languages and possibilities emerge. This certainly holds true for furniture. Thonet's refinement of bentwood techniques allowed him to produce the first really mass-market flatpack furniture in the 1800s. Its popularity went on to make it inextricably associated with the intellectual life of the nineteenth-century café culture across Europe. We also saw how the Bauhaus used new materials like steel tubing, wood panels and plate glass as a way of redefining furniture typologies to break away from their existing connotations in the hope of shaping a more egalitarian material culture. In parallel, Alvar Aalto pushed the technical possibilities of wood through bent ply to redefine wood furniture forms in the 1920s, creating pieces of great beauty and efficiency (see fig 2.12).

These pre-war innovations were followed after the Second World War by new processes from the aerospace industries. GRP moulding embraced by the Eames, Nelson and Bertoa in the 1950s, injection moulding in the 1960s and 1970s, and later lightweight carbon and nano-composite mouldings. In the later decades of the twentieth century digital processes like CNC and laser cutting have introduced yet another dimension to design interpretations for furniture and related products made from traditional and new sheet materials, from the one-off to customised mass production.

As we progress into the twenty-first century, several new technologies are finding their way into furniture, and we have already touched on several that also offer more sustainable options for designers (see chapters 2.3 and 4.3) Open design and distributed manufacturing is new territory for local production, materials and customisation (see fig 4.23), and 3D printing and responsive algorithms can enable the production of highly optimised design (see figs 2.14 and 2.28). On the bio side we have seen that growing furniture is possible and, while it is not a mass-market solution, it certainly achieves a very low footprint (see fig 2.16). Bio-engineered materials such as leather (see fig 7.22) and plastics from algae are only just emerging from the laboratory, potentially expanding the palette of sustainable options over the next decades if these can be proven to be safe. Nano-materials are also enabling reactive and sensing furniture

that may reduce energy usage (see fig 2.20) or support an ageing population (see fig 2.29). Finally, the IoT is already being used by companies like Ahrend for their circular Furniture as a Service (FaaS) model to track office furniture usage, optimise maintenance and adjust furniture to match demand. It may also be one of the key ingredients in creating product passports that make one of the furniture industry's biggest challenges possible: closed-loop systems.

As we have seen, the function of most furniture can effectively be achieved through low-tech, small-scale, local production. However, through the combination of meeting the demand for affordable furniture for growing urban populations and the ongoing pressure to introduce and embed digital, nano- and bio-technologies into furniture, designers will face important decisions in relation to sustainability in the decades to come. End-of-life scenarios in particular will need careful consideration before new combinations of materials like electronics and nano-materials are integrated into furniture to avoid the creation of unintented consequences including new monstrous hybrids and unrecyclable products. While new technology can either feel highly seductive or disturbingly inevitable, it is for designers to explore and assess their potential to create more sustainable outcomes in terms of social and environmental value. They should then be prepared to stand back and either reject or be actively involved in adapting and developing them for sustainable ends.

Chapter summary

1. Few product sectors still have the freedom of expression and range of processes that furniture and space-related products have. Because of this freedom, they remain some of the most culturally evocative and personally defining products that we share our lives with. If we set ourselves the challenge of designing within the natural boundaries of a circular economy, grounded in a collaborative exploration of real or as yet unarticulated needs, then the designs which emerge will bring daily enjoyment in ways that are surprising yet quietly satisfying, empowering and sustainable.

2. The ongoing demographic shift from rural to urban living across the globe coupled with the prohibitive cost of housing has led to people living and working in micro- and shared spaces. In both of these scenarios, furniture will have to be cleverer and work harder to combine multiple user activities and storage within a limited envelope. This is leading to more built-in and customised furniture with increased functionality. The counterpoint to a smaller space footprint is

how to reduce duplication of furniture and products through communal sharing facilities and platforms.

3. Furniture and mattresses constitute the largest element of post-consumer waste by volume and weight in industrialised countries, as very little is recycled and much of it is barely recyclable. This is in part a result of the increased frequency of home moving together with furniture becoming a fashion-conscious consumable, causing shorter lifespans and more production and waste. This trend has also been enabled by affordable prices largely made possible by lowering the quality and increasing the use of many materials, finishes and methods of joining that don't stand up well to wear, repair, dis- or re-assembly.

4. Consciously weaning our designs off virgin materials and fossil fuels is a necessary step towards sustainable furniture. In this regard, three of the most heavily specified materials in furniture – wood-based panels, plastics and PU-based foams – are environmentally problematic. This is due to the

provenance of these materials and the fact that they are rarely recycled and difficult to recycle. Designers should look to substitute any toxic, virgin and non-recyclable materials in their furniture and maximise the recycled or sustainable renewable waste content. This will drive up demand and reduce prices for circular recycling processes and feedstocks, transforming these into products that can and will be recycled or composted again and again.

5. We spend 90% of our time indoors, and indoor air quality (IAQ) can be two to five times more polluted than outdoor air due to toxic releases from furniture and interior products. These releases include off-gassing of urea formaldehyde from wood-based panels, brominated fire retardants from PU foams, and phthalates from PVC as well as the environmentally hazardous releases at their end-of-life. In addition, chroming, zincking and powder coating of metals and leather production involve the use of highly toxic ingredients during production that can have serious environmental and worker health implications. This means that specifying materials and finishes requires informed considerations and in many cases identifying safe substitutes in product specifications.

6. The environmental lifecycle analysis of furniture tells us that its main impacts are from the nature and amount of materials used and the end-of-life scenario. This challenges designers to create furniture that defies fashion, makes use of circular non-toxic material stocks, is both beautiful and functional, improves with age, and is easily repairable, upgradable and reusable to ensure product longevity and lower impacts.

7. Furniture and interior products have the important role of setting the scene for most of our cultural and interpersonal activities. In this regard, our past material cultures can offer valuable insights and inspiration for designers dealing with current 'needs'. As well as being tools for socialising, furniture and interior design can contribute in many ways to improved physical and mental wellbeing by challenging existing assumptions that condition our lifestyles. Designers can also use their skills to spot and respond to 'unknown-unknown' needs and help shape the nature and opportunities for creative collaboration, supportive communities and ad-hoc encounters across shared work, living and public spaces.

8. The size and nature of a furniture business plays a large part in dictating what designs are possible and sets many of the parameters for how sustainable it can be. Large mass production can transform the whole industry through its influence over the supply chain and market but it also demands very careful detailing and rigorous LCAs before scaling design decisions up to millions of units. The high-end designer sector has the margins to ensure the highest standards of sustainability in production and the creative latitude for new interpretations of sustainable luxury. Finally, SMEs are potentially the most fertile ground for the emergence of new sustainable models of production through a combination of flexible digital technologies, craft skills and Internet platforms that can connect them to local and globally distributed audiences.

Notes

1 Although often quoted without a source, the NHAPS survey for the EPA is the only clear source I have been able to trace. It concludes that there is very little variation in the figure across the population in USA and into Canada. The same figure is accepted and used in European reports.
N. Klepeis *et al.* (2001) The National Human Activity Pattern Survey (NHAPS): A Resource for Assessing Exposure to Environmental Pollutants. *Journal of Exposure Analysis and Environmental Epidemiology*, 11, pp. 231–252. doi10.1038/sj.jea.7500165.

2 Silberberg, S. *et al.* (2013) *Places in the Making. How Placemaking Builds Places and Communities,* MIT White Paper. Available at https://dusp.mit.edu/cdd/project/placemaking.

3 Research and Markets (n.d.) Global Furniture Market 2017–2021 [online]. Available at www.researchandmarkets.com/ reports/4368933/global-furniture-market-2017-2021 (accessed 12 January 2019).

4 Farrell, S. (2016) We've Hit Peak Home Furnishings, Says IKEA Boss. *The Guardian*, Business Section, 18 January. Available at www.theguardian.com/business/2016/jan/18/weve-hit-peak-home-furnishings-says-ikea-boss-consumerism (accessed 12 January 2019).

5 Marceux, P. (2016) A World of Smaller Homes: Causes and Effect on Consumption. Euromonitor International – Analysis, 18 January. Available at www.portal.euromonitor.com/portal/analysis/latestresearchindex# (accessed 7 August 2016).

6 Brake, A. (2016) NArchitects Complete New York's First Micro-apartment Tower [online]. Available at www.dezeen.com/2016/02/01/carmell-place-micro-apartment-tower-new-york-city-narchitects-photos/ (accessed 12/01/2019).

7   IKEA.com (11/07/2013) Make Small Spaces Big – IKEA. 11 July. Available at www.ikea.com/gb/en/ikea_family/ small_space_living.html (accessed 8 August 2016).

8   Centre for European Policy Studies (11/2014) The EU Furniture Market Situation and a Possible Furniture Products Initiative. Final Report_en.pdf.Available at www.ceps.eu/system/files/ Final%20report_en.pdf.

9   Zutshi, A., A. Creed, M. Holmes and J. Brain (2016), Reflections of Environmental Management Implementation in Furniture. *International Journal of Retail & Distribution Management*, 44(8), p.4. http://dx.doi.org/10.1108/IJRDM-10-2015-0154.

10 Bingham, J. (2014) Britain's Flat-pack Recovery: Record Surge in Furniture Sales as Property Market Heats Up. *Telegraph*, 18 September. Available at www.telegraph.co.uk/finance/ newsbysector/retailandconsumer/11105858/Britains-flat-pack-recovery-record-surge-in-furniture-sales-as-property-market-heats-up.html (accessed 5 January 2019).

11 Gustafsson, K. (n.d.) Ikea Gains Global Furniture Market Share on Price Cuts. Bloomberg.com. Available at www.bloomberg.com/news/articles/2015-01-28/ikea-gains-global-furniture-market-share-on-price-reductions.

12 Kumar, S. (2010) *Gandhi Meets Primetime*, Chicago: University of Illinois Press.

13 RSA (2015) *Rearranging the Furniture. A Great Recovery Report*, London: RSA, p. 9. Available at RSA_ Great_Recovery_ Rearranging_the_Furniture_Report _090915.pdf (accessed 5 January 2019).

14 US EPA (2017) Durable Goods: Product-Specific Data [online]. Available at www.epa.gov/facts-and-figures-about-materials-waste-and-recycling/durable-goods-product-specific-data (accessed 5 January 2019).

15 EPA.Gov (2014) *Municipal Solid Waste Generation, Recycling, and Disposal in the United States: Facts and Figures. A Methodology Document*, EPA Office of Resource Conservation and Recovery, April, pp. 8–9. Available at www.epa.gov/sites/production/files/2015-12/documents/ methodolgy_document_for_selected_municipal_solid_waste_ products.pdf.

16 WRAP (2016) Study into the Re-use Potential of Household Bulky Items | WRAP UK [online]. Furniture summary. Available at www.wrap.org.uk/sites/files/wrap/Furniture%20-%20 bulky%20waste%20summary.pdf (accessed 12 November 2018).

17 Ringvall, K. (2018) *IKEA Australia and Sustainability Report*, IKEA quoting IBISworld, 6 June, Furniture Retailing – Australia Market Research Report. Available at https:// www.ikea.com/ms/en_AU/media/pdf/sustainability/ IKEAPeoplePlanetBrochureFINALAPPROVEDSinglePagesFile.pdf (accessed 5 January 2019).

18 Ibid., p. 14.

19 Anon (n.d.) The IKEA story | PIET HEIN EEK [online]. Available at https://pietheineek.nl/en/blogmessages/the-or-my-ikea-story (accessed 8 January 2019).

20 Centre for European Policy Studies (2014).

21 FAO (2018) Forest Products Statistics 2016 [online, 3 April]. Available at www.fao.org/forestry/statistics/80938/en/ (accessed 12 November /2018).

22 Based on FSC having 16% cover of the world's production forests (2016) with 190m ha and the PEFC 23% 275m ha (2016), making this a total of 39%. Ref FSC/IUCN paper, August 2016.

23 Kelly, A. (2016) Ikea to Go 'Forest Positive' – But Serious Challenges Lie Ahead. *The Guardian*, Sustainable Business, 14 December. Available at www.theguardian.com/sustainable-business/ikea-sustainability-forest-positive-karelia.

24 Rigvall (2018), p. 28.

25 Sustainability Victoria (12/2015) Giving Recycled Wood a New Lease of Life. Case study, December [online]. Available at www.drhenderson.com.au/wp-content/uploads/2016/04/ Investment-Case-Study-D-R-Henderson-December-2015.pdf (accessed 5 August 2016).

26 Mdfrecovery.co.uk (n.d.) Home – MDF Recovery [online]. Available at www.mdfrecovery.co.uk/ (accessed 5 January 2019).

27 Geyer *et al.* (2017) Production, Use, and Fate of All Plastics Ever Made. *Science Advances*, July, 3(7), p. e1700782. doi: 10.1126/sciadv.1700782.

28 www.janeatfield.com (accessed 5 January 2019).

29 Emeco.net (n.d.) Story [online]. Available at www.emeco.net/ story (accessed 5 January 2019).

30 Lolldesigns.com (n.d.) Eco Initiatives. Loll Designs – Recycled, Modern, Outdoor Furniture [online]. Available at https:// lolldesigns.com/eco-initiatives/ (accessed 8 November 2018).

31 Mobles114.com (n.d.) Ecological Chairs | mobles 114 [online]. Available at http://mobles114.com/en/furniture/chairs/green-wooden.html (accessed 5 January 2019).

32 Industrial Facility.co.uk (n.d.) Tubo Chair/Industrial Facility [online]. Available at www.industrialfacility.co.uk/page/ projects/furniture/tubo-chair (accessed 10 August 2016).

33 Pentatonic.com (n.d.) The Circular Revolution [online]. Available at www.pentatonic.com/ (accessed 30 October 2018).

34 Techinsider.io (2016) IKEA's New Kitchen Cabinets Are Made from Plastic Bottles [online, June]. Available at www. techinsider.io/ikeas-new-kitchen-cabinets-are-made-from-plastic-bottles-2016-6.

35 On-site interviews, London, October 2014.

36 Penty, J. (2016) Interview with Diana Seijs, Head of Sustainability Ahrend, 11 August.

37 Pellizzi, E., A. Lattuati-Derieux, B. Lavédrine and H. Cheradame (2014)Degradation of Polyurethane Ester Foam Artifacts: Chemical Properties, Mechanical Properties and Comparison

between Accelerated and Natural Degradation. *Polymer Degradation and Stability*, September, 107, pp. 255–261. doi:10.1016/j.polymdegradstab.2013.12.018.

38 Communications, C. A. (n.d.) Rebonded Foam [online]. Available at www.polyurethanes.covestro.com/en/Technologies/Processing/Rebonded-Foam (accessed 3 January 2019).

39 Europur (n.d.) Flexible Polyeurathane Foam in Mattresses. An Overview of Possible End of Life Solutions. Factsheet [online] Europur. Available at www.europur.org/sustainabilty/recycling. www.europur.org/publications/item/44-facsheet-eol-foam-from-matresses-and-furniture (accessed 3 January 2019).

40 Chem Park (2016) Covestro Launches Industrial Production of Plastics Using CO_2. *Latest news*, 17 June [online]. Available at www.chempark.com/en/latest-news/items/2016-06-17-covestro-launches-industrial-production-of-plastics-using-carbon-dioxide.html (accessed 3 January 2019).

41 Ford (2016) Preserving Mother Earth: Ford First Automaker to Use Captured CO_2 to Develop Foam and Plastic for Vehicles | France | Français | Ford Media Center [online, 17 May]. Available at https://media.ford.com/content/fordmedia/feu/fr/fr/news/2016/05/17/preserving-mother-earth-ford-first-automaker-captured-co2.html (accessed 13 January 2019).

42 gluckmanconsulting.com (2015) EU F-Gas Regulation Guidance. Information Sheet 27: Foam Insulation Products [online]. Available at www.gluckmanconsulting.com/wp-content/uploads/2015/02/IS-7-Insulating-Foam-v3.pdf.

43 Greenguard.org (n.d.) The Importance of Healthy Air in the Home - Indoor Air Quality Information for Consumers [online] Available at http://greenguard.org/en/consumers/consumers_iaq.aspx (accessed 3 January 2019).

44 Sarigiannis, D.A. (ed.), WHO (2014) *Combined or Multiple Exposure to Health Stressors in Indoor Built Environments. An Evidence-based Review Prepared for the WHO Training Workshop "Multiple Environmental Exposures and iRsks"*, 16–18 October 2013, Copenhagen: WHO Regional Office for Europe.

45 Technical bulletin 117-2013 State of California Department of Consumer Affairs, FAQ, 2014. Available at www.bearhfti.ca.gov/about_us/tb117_faqs.pdf.

46 Chicago Tribune (2015) Furniture Firms Shun Flame Retardants but Some Toxic Couches Still for Sale [online, 23 May]. Available at www.chicagotribune.com/news/watchdog/ct-flame-retardants-furniture-20150123-story.html (accessed 2 August 2016).

47 Chemical Watch.com (2017) Furniture Trade Body Welcomes EU Warning on Flame Retardants [online, 23 November]. Available at https://chemicalwatch.com/61983/furniture-trade-body-welcomes-eu-warning-on-flame-retardants (accessed 2 November 2018).

48 IARC Monographs on the Evaluation of Carcinogenic Risks to Humans Volume 88 (2006) Formaldehyde, 2-Butoxyethanol and 1-tert-Butoxypropan-2-ol (pdf, html), WHO Press.

49 CWC furniture group (2016) Comparison of International Composite Board Emission Standards [online]. Available at http://cwcfurnituregroup.ca/CWCV11/index.php?option=com_content&view=article&id=177&Itemid=343 (accessed 4 August 2018).

50 Healthy Building Network (2008) Fact Sheet: Alternative Resin Binders for Particleboard, MDF and Wheatboard [online]. Available at http://healthybuilding.net/uploads/files/alternative-resin-binders-for-particleboard-medium-density-fiberboard-mdf-and-wheatboard.pdf (accessed 2 November 2018).

51 Columbia Forest Products (2014) Purebond. Formaldahyde-free Hardwood Plywood. CFP106 [online]. Available at www.columbiaforestproducts.com/wp-content/uploads/2014/02/CFP106_PureBond_Brochureweb1.pdf (accessed 3 January 2019).

52 Greenpeace (1997) What's Wrong with PVC? The Science behind a Phase Out of Polyvinyl Chloride Products [online]. Available at www.greenpeace.org.uk/MultimediaFiles/Live/FullReport/5575.pdf.

53 galvanising.org (2016) Why Galvanizing is Sustainable | Galvanizers Association [online]. Available at www.galvanizing.org.uk/sustainable-construction/galvanizing-is-sustainable/ (accessed 13 January 2019).

54 Current chrome leather tanning uses Cr3 and no longer involves the very toxic Cr6, as it is banned in the EU and USA.

55 Ecobilan. BLC Report 002 (n.d.) [online]. Available atwww.blcleathertech.com/images/db/dt_leather-journal/32/Nov-Dec07%20(300650).pdf (accessed 6 August 2016). See also summary of Ecobilan. BLC Report 002 [online]. Available at www.all-about-leather.co.uk/what-is-leather/the-eco-leather-story.htm (accessed 1 November 2018).

56 Redwood, M. (2018) A White Paper View of the Sustainability of Responsibly Made Leather. Leather Naturally [online]. Available at www.leathernaturally.org/Resources/Useful-Articles/White-Paper-Explores-Sustainability-of-Leather.aspx (accessed 7 January 2019).

57 Tarantola, A. (2014) How Leather Is Slowly Killing the People and Places That Make It. *Gizmodo*, 6 March. Available at http://gizmodo.com/how-leather-is-slowly-killing-the-people-and-places-tha-1572678618 (accessed 6 August 2016).

58 Dormehl, L. (2017) Modern Meadow's Animal-free Leather Is Finally Here, And It's Awesome [online, 2 October]. Available at www.digitaltrends.com/cool-tech/modern-meadow-leather-here/ (accessed 3 January 2019).

59 Dietz, B. (5/04/2005) *Life Cycle Assessment of Office Furniture Products*, Center for Sustainable Systems, Report No. CSS05-08, University of Michigan, Ann Arbor. http://css.umich.edu/sites/default/files/css_doc/CSS05-08.pdf (accessed 03/01/2019)

60 Penty, J. (2014/2018) Skype interview with Alberto Meda, Milan, Italy, 16 August 2014, updated 29 May 2018.

61 Hanson, J. (2017) History of the Great Workmate Workbench
• Tools First [online, updated 15 August 2018]. Available at
https://toolsfirst.com/workmate-workbench-history/ (accessed
3 January 2019).

62 Ahrend (2018) Comfort Workstation [online]. Available at
www.ahrend.com/en/innovationlab/comfort-workstation/
(accessed 10 November 2018).

63 Remy, T. and René Veenhuizen (n.d.) Playground Fence, Social
Fence. Text sent by studio, 1 May 2018.

64 Tucker, J. (2017) *Yoshino Cedar House by Airbnb and Go
Hasegawa – DesignCurial* [online, 6 June]. Available at www.
designcurial.com/news/yoshino-cedar-house-by-airbnb-and-
go-hasegawa-5834132/2 (accessed 3 January 2019).

65 EU Furniture Market Report (2014). *The EU Furniture Market
Situation and a Possible Furniture Products Initiative*,
November, pp.144–145 [online]. Available at www.ceps.eu/
system/files/Final%20report_en.pdf.

66 Penty, J. (2016) Skype interview with Stephanie Forsythe,
Vancouver, 26 July.

67 Sebastiancox.co.uk (n.d.) HOME [online]. Available at www.
sebastiancox.co.uk/ (accessed 3 January 2019).

CHAPTER 8

Transportation and mobility: products and services

From a purely logistical point of view, transportation is the system of products, services and infrastructure that moves people and goods about. And yet, for individuals and society, it is so much more. Driven by people's desire to interact socially, expand their cultural horizons, embark on adventures as well as the need to earn a living and for businesses to operate, it forms the backbone of our economy and contemporary culture. But how much mobility do we need for our wellbeing and prosperity, and can we make it sustainable?

Few developments define the twentieth century more than the expansion of mass mobility and the globalisation of business and culture that this has engendered. The inventions of new ways to travel over land, sea, air and space have truly made the world much 'smaller' and more connected for those with access to them. The products of mobility are also among the most iconic of all manmade artefacts and hold a deep fascination for designers and consumers alike, not least for the status and freedom that they represent.

But mass mobility has come at a price. As a sector, transportation is one of the world's leading contributors to air pollution, global warming and premature deaths, while for individuals, personal travel choices often make up the largest share of their carbon footprints.[1] From 1990 to 2015, transportation's carbon emissions grew more than any other sector's.[2] And as a vital ingredient of economic development, it is expected to continue expanding globally, at least until 2050.[3]

It is clear that the mobility models we have inherited from the twentieth century are highly unsustainable. This challenges designers and society in the twenty-first century to seize the opportunity of cleaner and smarter technologies to transform mobility and reshape cities and towns into healthier, more inclusive and liveable spaces. It also challenges us to find ways to extend effective transport infrastructures to underserved communities and countries, and to respond to the impacts of unbridled tourism that are being felt around the world.

Designing for sustainable mobility should embrace the appetite for real positive change in this sector, beyond another 'business opportunity'. There are many different ways in which designers can be involved in more sustainable transportation. This could range from the design of elements for new urban landscapes right through to entire user experiences on mass-transit systems. Or it might be designing lighter aircraft interiors, highly accessible wheelchairs and buggies or one of the myriad accessories that make cleaner travel options safer, easier to use and more enjoyable.

Starting from an understanding of the environmental, social and economic impacts of the transport sector, we will explore some of the design strategies and technologies that have the most potential to lessen its environmental impacts and produce maximum social and economic benefits. Ultimately, the design challenge of sustainable transportation is just as much about *how we want to live* as it is about finding the economic models and technologies that will make this possible.

8.1 the environmental, social and economic impacts of transportation and mobility

environmental impacts

By far the biggest and, it has to be said, most negative impacts of transportation are environmental. To the average person, some of these impacts are invisible and intangible, such as greenhouse gas (GHG) emissions and non-renewable resources. Some are mostly invisible but tangible in their health impacts, such as air pollution and noise. Others are very visible and very tangible, such as land use and the visual degradation and physical barriers that transport infrastructures create.

invisible and intangible: GHG emissions and non-renewable energy

The transportation sector as a whole is almost exclusively powered by non-renewable fuels, either directly in engines or indirectly by electricity generated from non-renewables. It burns over 65% of the world's oil and is growing at a faster rate than any other energy-using sector.[4] Not only does this make it a major source of GHGs, it is also depleting irreplaceable resources and pushing oil exploration to ever more fragile environments. Although the electrification of transport is beginning in earnest, as of 2017 it was still less than 1% of vehicles[5] and its electricity was largely powered by different forms of non-renewable energy, although the renewables share is growing.

Activity in transportation accounts for more than 18% of the world's GHGs[6] and its emissions are growing at a faster rate than any other energy-using sector, up a staggering 68% since 1990, the Kyoto baseline year for measuring emissions. In industrialised countries, its share of GHG emissions is much higher. In the USA, transportation was the largest contributor of GHG emissions at 31% when agricultural, construction and off-road vehicles are included.[7] For the EU28, it was 26% (2015), up 23% on 1990 levels with international aviation increasing by 105%.[8] In the UK, transport became the largest contributor of GHG emissions for the first time in 2016 at 26%.[9] In addition, the highly potent HFCs used for air-conditioning and refrigerated trucks also contribute to a significant amount of GHGs.

Looking ahead to 2050, the International Transport Forum predicts that total carbon emissions from transportation will rise by 60% between 2015 and 2050 based on a baseline scenario of current trends and policy developments. Although the efficiency of travel is expected to improve considerably, this is and will continue to be overtaken by the predicted *doubling* of global passenger miles and freight.

The biggest rise in demand will continue to come from international air travel, growing rapidly at 5% annually, and the increased use of cars and goods vehicles, especially in Asia, as middle classes expand in the world's fastest growing economies[10] (fig 8.1). This will cause carbon emissions from road transport to rise by 70% and those from international aviation and maritime activity to *treble* by 2050. Unless much more radical low-carbon solutions are implemented, transportation will substantially overshoot the targets set by the Paris Agreement to limit global temperature rise to 2°C, let alone the strongly recommended 1.5°C (fig 8.2).

visible, invisible and intangible: air pollution

Of the 65% of worldwide oil used by the transport industry, 90% of this is used to power road transport.[11] Of this, 61% is used

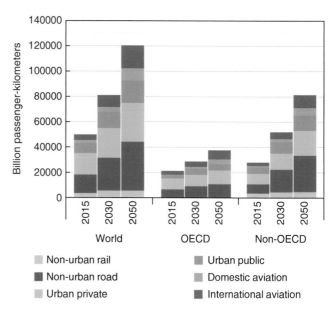

Figure 8.1 Global forecast for passenger demand by transport mode up until 2050 based on current trends and policy directions. (source: ITF Transport Outlook 2017)

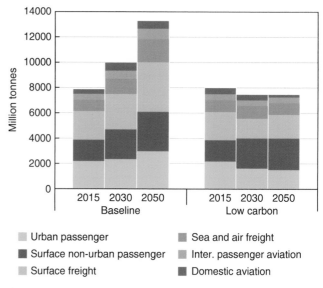

Figure 8.2 Global forecasts for CO_2 emissions by transport sector and scenario. (source: ITF Transport Outlook 2017)

by passenger cars and 27% by freight.[12] Besides being a major producer of GHGs, the gasoline and diesel fuels burnt by internal combustion engines also emit a range of very toxic air pollutants that have a highly detrimental effect on human health and the environment. The worst of these are: particulate matter (PM) below 10 and 2.5 microns from diesel, nitrogen oxides (NO_2, NOx), ozone as ground smog, carbon monoxide (CO), benzene, polycyclic aromatic hydrocarbons (PAHs), sulphur dioxide (SO_2) and metals, including lead.[13]

The World Health Organisation (WHO) estimates that this cocktail of air pollutants causes 3.7 million premature deaths worldwide, as well as decreasing the quality of life for millions from respiratory and cardiovascular diseases, including asthma, cancer and adverse birth outcomes.[14] We also know that children and the elderly are most affected.

Air pollution problems from transportation are especially severe in urban areas where concentration levels are highest and local geographic and climatic conditions can also exacerbate the problem. A quick look at the WHO data and map of air pollution levels from particulate matter (PM2.5) in cities across the world shows that the highest levels are all in cities in emerging and developing economies[15] (fig 8.3). Sadly this aligns with the UN/World Bank's findings that the richest countries with the highest per capita energy consumption also have the lowest levels of air pollution.[16] This is a clear indication of the need for more affordable clean technologies in developing countries.

Similarly, the idea that electric- or hydrogen-powered cars might be the panacea for urban air pollution is flawed if it merely displaces the pollution and emissions. Unless the electricity is powered by renewable energy, electric vehicles (EVs) can in fact be up to four times more polluting, depending on how dirty or clean the energy mix used to generate the electricity is.[17]

invisible but tangible: noise
Noise from traffic is another insidious reality for people living in busy congested urban areas, close to fast roads or under aeroplane flight paths, and predictions are that this will get worse. While most noise is connected with road traffic (90%),[18] aircraft produce the highest levels of noise and annoyance over road and rail.[19] High levels of ambient noise are known to reduce quality of life by affecting our ability to work, learn, relax and sleep. Studies have directly correlated them to disturbed sleep patterns, inability to concentrate especially in children, and to heart disease, primarily through the stress levels they induce.[20]

The effects of transport noise are so great that the social cost to human health has been estimated at 40 billion per year (0.4% of total GDP),[21] with well over 1 million healthy life-years lost annually to traffic-related noise in Western European countries, according to the WHO.[22] Sadly, transport-related noise is also very much a NIMBY (not in my back yard) problem where everyone wants to have quick access to airports and better, faster roads, but no one wants to live next to them (fig 8.4). Solutions to the noise issue need to come from a range of sources which include reduced traffic speeds, electrification, innovation in tyre and surfacing materials, to individuals changing their driving styles, automation and better town planning and investment in infrastructure for quieter transport modes.

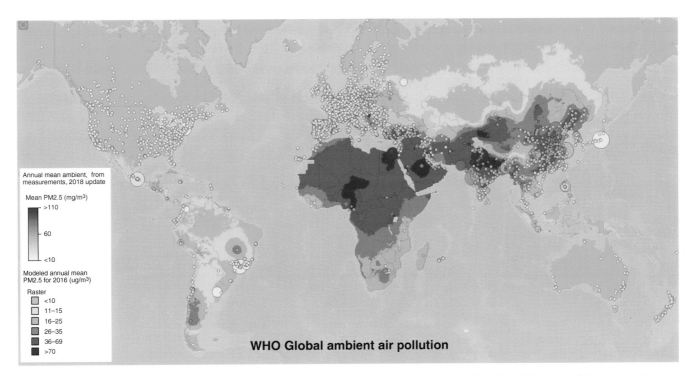

WHO Global ambient air pollution

Annual mean ambient, from measurements, 2018 update

Mean PM2.5 (mg/m³)
>110
60
<10

Modeled annual mean PM2.5 for 2016 (ug/m³)
Raster
<10
11–15
16–25
26–35
36–69
>70

Figure 8.3 This map shows annual mean particulate matter (PM2.5), measured for over 3000 urban areas indicated by circles and modelled across regions. (source: WHO 2018 update http://maps.who.int/airpollution/)

Figure 8.4 The NIMBY effect: living under a flightpath (UK, 2014). (photo credit Steve Mann/Shutterstock.com)

highly visible and tangible: land use and visual landscape

One aspect of transport and mobility that is not often considered is just how much land it occupies. It is estimated that transport infrastructure covers between 1.5 to 2% of the world's total land area, mostly for roads and parking lots with much of it on arable land.[23] These paved areas also cause run-off of chemically polluted water and increase the risk of flooding.[24] In industrialised countries this rises to over 3.5% of land area and coverage in urban areas is between 30 and 60%. For cities that have been planned around the car, such as Los Angeles, this can reach a staggering 70%.[25] Besides being very land hungry, roads also create barriers to natural animal movements, so much so that motorised vehicles are *the leading cause of death for wild animals* in many countries such as Brazil, overtaking pollution, illegal hunting and deforestation.[26]

As Paul Hawken and the Lovins put it in *Natural Capitalism*, even if we solve the problem of GHGs, pollution and noise, *"A fleet of 200 mpg roomy, clean, safe, recyclable, renewably fuelled cars might keep drivers from running out of oil, climate or clean air, but instead they'd run out of roads, land and patience"*.[27] All these negatives are causing the dominance of the motorised vehicle to be contested and a greater priority given to public transport, cycling and walking in sustainably oriented cities. Not only do these occupy less space, they can radically improve mobility while making cities more human-centred and its citizens healthier (fig 8.5). With the desire to own a car in emerging economies such as India, China and Brazil catching up with rising incomes, it will be increasingly challenging for these countries to balance priorities for land use and quality of life in urban areas.

economic impacts

> [S]ustainable transport enables sustainable development.
>
> ITF Transport Outlook 2017

transport infrastructure as an economic lifeline

In contrast to the environmental picture, transportation provides hugely positive economic benefits and is a crucial driver of poverty reduction.[28] This is because the economic development of a country is very closely linked to the effectiveness of its transportation infrastructure by providing access to markets and employment, and lowering business costs and goods. But for countries with low GDP, this becomes a chicken-and-egg situation, as they don't have the means of investing in the transport infrastructure that would improve opportunities and the growth of internal markets. Therefore, access to a basic level of mobility becomes an issue of equity and a cornerstone of a sustainable

Figure 8.5 Contrasting priorities: car-centric and non-car centric approaches to urban mobility (Shanghai 2015/Freiburg 2017). (photo credits GDAE2015, Ekapong/Shutterstock.com)

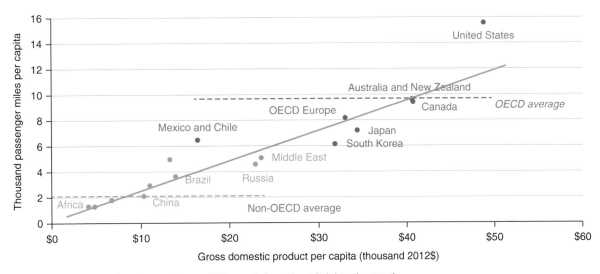

Figure 8.6 Annual passenger travel vs. income. (source: US Energy Information Administration 2016)

economy, not only between countries but also between regions and even neighbourhoods.

access to mobility

Figure 8.6 shows how the level of personal mobility is directly proportional to income. In wealthier economies, people travel on *average* between 10 and 16,000 miles a year (16 to 25,000km/ year), while in the least developed non-OECD economies the figure is below 2000 miles (3200km/year).[29] In Africa and the poorest countries in Asia this drops to as low as 1600 miles (2560km/year), which is not surprising when you consider that this is where the majority of those at the bottom of the pyramid live (see Box 3.7).

The contrast in daily life between the richest and poorest economies could not be greater. For billions in the world today, even a bicycle or cart are unaffordable and walking is their only mode of travel, be it to get to schools, markets or medical care, or the daily quest for water and wood. Designing and building sustainable transport networks that are appropriate and viable in these countries must be a priority in breaking through the cycle of poverty. The positive side to this is that emerging economies have an opportunity to leapfrog into smarter and cleaner technologies and avoid the problems of existing scenarios in planning their new transport and mobility systems.

the rise of tourism and the travel industry

A combination of tumbling air travel prices, growing middle classes, Internet connectedness and the increasing desire to consume 'experiences' has unleashed what seems to be an insatiable appetite for travel. The tourist industry now accounts for one in ten jobs globally and for some countries it is their main source of foreign income.[30] While the tourist industry provides

employment where there might otherwise be very little, what these numbers belie is that the majority of the local employment it creates is low paid. In addition, many of the tourist facilities in developing countries are foreign-owned, with little of the profits being reinvested in the local community.

We also know that global tourism combined with the rise of cruise ships and the Airbnb effect is taking its toll on the environment and deeply affecting the social fabric of neighbourhoods, making the notion of sustainable tourism more urgent than ever. The problem has reached such a peak that residents are taking to the streets in cities affected, such as Barcelona, Venice, Dubrovnik and Prague[31] (fig 8.7). The question has to be: Could tourism be redesigned such that the growing appetite for experiences is satisfied in a way that supports and

Figure 8.7 Anti-tourist protest graffiti Barcelona (2015). (photo credit ONA_PLANAS/iStock)

protects natural environments, brings maximum benefit back
into the local community and continues to build intercultural
understanding?

social impacts

*There is a growing recognition that better transport is not about
increased mobility and tonne–kilometres but about providing
equitable access to jobs, opportunities, social interactions and
markets, contributing to healthy and fulfilled lives.*

ITF Transport Outlook 2017

empowerment and freedom

A high level of mobility has become a hallmark of twenty-first-
century 'modern life' in developed economies and increasingly so
in emerging economies. This unprecedented degree of mobility and
even hypermobility has had, and will continue to have, a profound
effect on social structures, life choices and how we experience the
day-to-day. However, compared with environmental and economic
impacts, the social impacts of transportation are much more
balanced between positives and negatives.

Beginning with the positives, the proximity to good transport
infrastructure provides access to employment, education and a
broad range of cultural and leisure activities. Conversely, because
people on lower incomes have far less choice about where they
live, whether or not their communities are served by good and
affordable transport has a greater impact on their employment
and education opportunities (see fig 2.33, example of Medellin,
Colombia). The UN's Sustainable Development Goal SDG 11.2,
*"providing access to safe, affordable, accessible and sustainable
transport systems for all"*, spells out just how important this is
(fig 8.8).

Psychologically, access to mobility also has many positives. It
gives people a strong sense of empowerment and associated
perceptions of freedom. Growing international travel and
tourism also contribute to greater cultural understanding
globally, although, as we have seen, tourism is not without its
environmental and social downsides.

what price mobility? deaths, injuries and health

However, the freedom and speed that current transport modes
provide comes at a human cost. The extremely high toll of
accidental deaths and injuries, reduced quality of life from
unhealthy lifestyles and pollution, as well as social isolation, loss
of community cohesion and cultural identity, are part of the price
we pay.

The number of deaths caused by transport is staggering. According
to the WHO, globally there are *1.35 million* road accident deaths

Figure 8.8 People's access to mobility is worlds apart: a. head-carrying on
foot in rural India; b. high-speed train in China. (photo credits cornfield;
gui jun peng)

a year. There are also another 20 to 50 million non-fatal injuries,
many of which result in permanent disabilities.[32] But it is not just
humans who are being killed – a study in Brazil estimated that 1.3
million wild animals are killed *every day* on roads. That is nearly
half a billion a year in one country alone.[33]

To put these figures into perspective, 97% of all transport-related
deaths are on roads. Of these, 93% occur in low- and middle-
income countries, with Africa having by far the highest toll
and Europe the lowest by two-thirds. Motorised road vehicles
are also the biggest killer of 5- to 29-year-olds globally and
over half involve vulnerable road users: pedestrians, cyclists
and motorcyclists. On top of the loss of life, road accidents are
estimated to cost 3% of a country's GDP.[34] Not surprisingly, two
SDG targets are focused on road safety. Target 3.6 aims to *halve
the number of global deaths and injuries from road accidents by
2020*, and target 11.2 aims to *improve road safety by expanding
public transport*. Safety and reduced accidents are certainly one
area where design and behaviour change have proven to have a
significant impact.

life in highly mobile societies
> *Prosperity raises fences: as we become richer we can travel
> further, but there are fewer places into which we can venture.*
> George Mombiot, *Heat*

How much more mobile are we, and what effect is this having
on us and on society? Although we still spend a similar amount
of time travelling than we did 60 years ago, we travel much
greater distances as we have shifted from walking and bicycling
to motorised modes. Within the UK alone, where distances are
relatively small compared with bigger countries, there was a
ten-fold (1000%) increase in the distance travelled per person
between 1952 and 2016.[35] And this excludes international travel.

The shift to high mobility via motorised travel is also taking
a significant toll on our health. We have seen that the noise
caused by road traffic and aircraft increases stress levels for
those living and working close to it, while the air pollution it
produces triggers long-term and chronic respiratory problems
and premature deaths for millions of people. We also know that
traffic congestion and delays outside of our control, something
that millions of commuters face every day on public and private
transport, is another significant source of stress. Although by no
means the only factor, high car dependency has also been linked
to unhealthy lifestyles and correlated to increased obesity.[36,37]
In contrast, studies confirm that active modes of travel have
beneficial effects on physical and mental health.[38]

Being able to travel greater distances has meant that we construct
our working and social lives around what is possible, not what
is local. While this has widened the catchment for work and
allows us to maintain contact with friends and family around the
world, it inevitably means that we have less time to invest in our
communities and neighbourhoods, decreasing their social capital.
As John Adams put it: "*As we spread ourselves ever wider, we must
spread ourselves thinner. If we spend more time interacting with
people at a distance, we must spend less time with those closer
to home.*"[39] This loss of immediate social contact is exacerbated
when towns and cities are built around the car. In contrast, when
communities are planned around people rather than around cars,
and walking and cycling is facilitated, building and maintaining
social ties locally comes naturally as people inevitably cross paths
going about their daily business.[40]

When we add the steep rise in air travel of the past two decades,
and the increased appetite for travel and experiences fed by
the Internet and social networks, we see the phenomenon of
hypermobility emerge. In hypermobile scenarios, all the effects
of high mobility are pushed to the extreme as time and money,
not distance, become the limiting factors. While we can hop on
a plane and arrive at almost any destination in the world in a

day, do we know our next-door neighbours, or have they become
virtual? The combination of hypermobility and digital technology
is leading to a form of modern-day nomadism of no fixed abode.
Known as 'digital nomads', their virtually connected 'communities'
are spread physically across the globe. Wealth and the right
passport have become the essential criteria for membership to the
club.

8.2 design for more sustainable transport modes

We have now built up a picture of just how significant our
transportation systems are to all human undertakings and the
environment. From the largest corporations to individual citizens,
long-term strategies through to day-to-day decisions are strongly
affected by the transportation systems that are physically
accessible and financially viable to them.

We also know that in the past 70 years, mobility has increased
exponentially in industrialised economies, creating changes
in social and working patterns as well as land use and the
environment. In the meantime, it is has remained quite static
for several billion people in poorer countries and communities,
severely restricting their opportunities for better lives.

Given all the pros and cons currently embedded across our
transportation systems, how can we design these to be more
sustainable? As we embark on another three decades of continued
urban and middle-class growth to 2050, this is a huge global
challenge, where one-size does not fit-all. For transport systems to
have any hope of being sustainable they will need to be designed
collectively around a new vision of how communities want to
live and run their businesses. Designers are there to support
communities, urban planners and industry to imaginatively
develop transport modes and infrastructure that connect with
these visions. In the process they should look to enhance the
quality of life and the environment for the greatest number of
people and species.

An ambitious sustainable transport and mobility design agenda
should aim to:

- be 100% human or renewably powered
- be human- and environment-centred
- provide fair accessibility for all
- provide people with viable sustainable choices
- use the most appropriate efficient, clean, safe technologies
- find creative ways to get maximum utility out of the
  infrastructure and resources

- reduce the distances people and goods need to travel
- radically reduce accidents and deaths
- make sustainable communities and lifestyles possible

Achieving these goals involves designing all aspects of the travel and transport systems and experiences, from the macro-systems level to micro-detail level, including the software and hardware design of products and interfaces. With the merging of electric mobility technologies, P2P connectivity and autonomous control systems, we stand poised at a pivotal moment in the development of new mobility and distribution systems linked to mobility and business models. At the same time it is clear that simply moving to less polluting and resource consuming modes, or 'techno-fixes', will not produce sustainable solutions on their own, because the problem is also about how we want to live. We will now look in more detail at the key strategies and examples of design interventions that are leading to more sustainable transport.

avoid, shift, improve: aligning design with policy
The IPAT equation that we looked at in Chapter 2.1 points us to the levers that can be used to reduce the environmental impacts of transportation. They are:

- *demand* in the form of the number of **Passenger** miles/km travelled
- impact per mile travelled of the different **Technologies** or transport modes

- *Affluence*, or wealth of those travelling or having goods transported

The third lever, *affluence*, has been demonstrated to have a direct correlation with the number of miles travelled, both at a country and individual level (see fig 8.6). Research also confirms that *how much* and by *what modes* individuals choose to travel has by far the biggest impact on their personal footprint, after the choice of whether or not to have children.[41] (fig 8.9).

This analysis leads directly to the key strategies used in sustainable transportation design: *avoid, shift* and *improve*.[42] This means reducing the distances travelled and, wherever possible, shifting these to lower impact modes known as *modal shift*. For designers, modal shift is about finding creative ways for people and goods to travel fewer miles and to move from the most environmentally and socially damaging to the least; from unhealthy to healthy; from unsafe to safe; and from vehicle-centred to human-centred modes of travel.

One strategy for achieving this is through planning and supporting strong local and regional economies in denser developments. Denser conurbations reduce the distances people need to travel and make it economically viable to building the infrastructure that enables people to travel these distances safely via the lowest impact modes.[43] In this way urban planning, policy, design

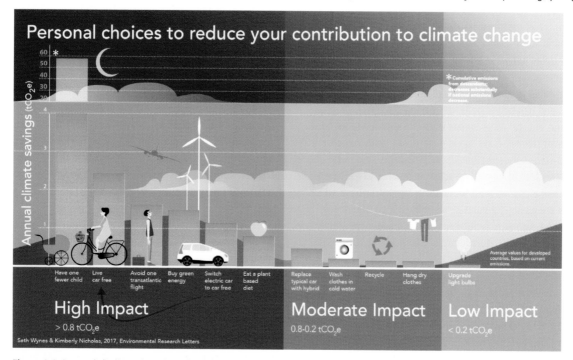

Figure 8.9 Research findings show that after raising children, how, and how much, we travel has the greatest impact on our footprint. (infographic courtesy Wynes and Nicholson (2017) Envrion.Res. Lett. 12 074024/infographic C. Jakobsson, Lund University)

and technology all play their part in creating the modal shifts necessary for more sustainable transport which we will look at in more detail.

promising technologies: comparing modes

The first step in designing for shifts to more beneficial transport modes is to understand their relative impacts. In the rules of thumb set out in Chapter 2, figure 2.9, we compared the impact of different modes of transport for goods and people. In **figure 8.10** we take these a step further by comparing modes of transport by whole lifecycle eco-costs for passenger/km and ton/km.

The headline results are that motorised road transport and air travel are the most energy- and resource-intensive, while

human- and electric-powered bicycles, walking, water and rail are the least intensive modes. However, the values are bracketed to show that factors such as occupancy rates, vehicle weight, aerodynamics, fuel type, style of use and distances covered can create very wide variations in energy intensity and environmental impacts for similar vehicles. With these comparative data in mind, we will review the potential of new technologies within different modes by air, land and water. We will then explore the best ways to connect these up through new business models across the public and private sectors to deliver more sustainable transport models.

air transport

Human flight is the newest and one of the most awe-inspiring feats of modern engineering. However, it is also one of most – and in some cases *the* most – impactful travel mode in terms of global warming and noise. This is because the effects of emissions at altitude are amplified. Research shows that aviation's non-CO_2 climate effects can equal or exceed the climate impact of its CO_2 emissions, more than doubling the overall GHG effect.[44] These include NOx emissions, contrails, cirrus cloud formation, soot and water vapour at altitude. At the same time, as we have seen, aviation is the fastest-growing mode of travel, especially in Asia, and is expected to continue to grow until 2050. With three-quarters of air travel being for personal and recreational purposes,[45] it has clearly become a major facilitator of longer distance travel leading to the rise of mass tourism and hypermobility.

Together, these factors make reducing the number and impact of air miles very urgent. Design strategies to reduce these impacts include lightweighting, electrification, and new aircraft typologies, including airships, blended wing body forms and drones. Ambitious goals, set by the EU's Flightpath 2050 to reduce CO_2 emissions by 75%, NO_x by 90% and perceived noise by 65% from a baseline of 2000 are also helping to drive design innovation.[46] In parallel, strategies to reduce the need for air travel include the greater use of virtual meeting technologies, promoting local tourism, or 'stacationning', and diverting demand to less impactful modes such as high-speed trains (HSTs) for long distances.

Against the efforts to lower impacts is the fact that internationally aviation fuel is untaxed, effectively acting as a subsidy and keeping prices artificially low. International aviation is also outside of national carbon emission targets. In response, the ICAO is aiming to level out the carbon emissions of air travel from 2020 through a carbon-offset scheme called CORSIA which has been voluntary since 2016 and will be phased in as mandatory, but not until 2027.[47]

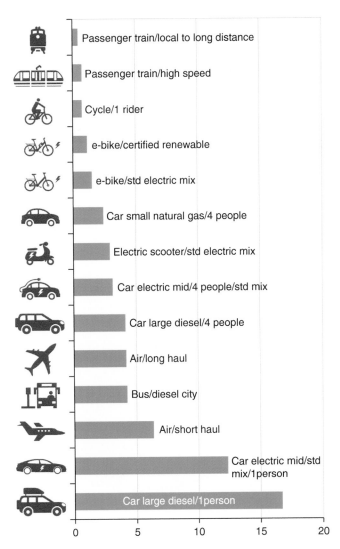

Figure 8.10 Lifecycle € ecocosts comparison of different transport modes per passenger km. (source: Idematapp2018 using Simapro v.3.5 LCI data + depletion of fossil fuels, 80 euro cents per kg oil by ecocosts method J. Vogtländer)

Figure 8.11 Solar Impulse 2 on second test flight over Abu Dhabi, UAE: inspiring a new vision for 100% renewably self-powered flight (Mar 2015). (courtesy ©Solar Impulse/photo Jean Revillard/Rezo.ch.)

electrification of flight

One way to reduce the environmental impacts of flying is to electrify aviation, provided the electricity is generated by renewables. As it turns out, electrifying travel by air is much more challenging than on land. This is because the power density of a battery is lower than that of hydrocarbon fuel, which means that it adds to the weight the aircraft has to lift. Despite its challenges, the dream of 100% clean air travel has begun. One of the most inspiring designs to demonstrate its possibility is the Solar Impulse 2, which flew around the world in 2016 entirely powered by its own solar energy (fig 8.11).

The vision of flying entirely on renewables has now also made a commercial debut. The Taurus Electro G2 glider made by Pipistrel in Slovakia is not only the first fully electric production two-seat aircraft; it also comes with a solar trailer that recharges the batteries (fig 8.12). Other small electric aircraft and multicopters are also just coming onto the market. They include Pipistrel's second commercial all-electric aircraft, a two-seat trainer, the Alpha-electro and China's RGAC's RX1E-A, a two-seater electric light-sport aircraft soon to be joined by a four-seater.

Thus far, these examples of electrified winged aircraft are all in the exclusive market of private micro-aircraft. Although much more challenging and still a few years off, the electrification of commercial airlines has begun in earnest. The initial focus is on introducing hybrid-electric engines to short-haul airliners. This is because most of the energy for flying goes into getting aircraft up rather than cruising, so the shorter the flight, the greater the

Figure 8.12 Flying for free: the Pipstrel Taurus-E glider, the world's first two-seater all-electric glider and its solar-charging trailer. (courtesy Pipistrel.si/photo Matjaz Milavec)

Figure 8.13 First steps towards the electrification of commercial short-haul airliners: Airbus' e-Fan-X demonstrator and Zunum Aero's 2022 12-seater hybrid electric regional aircraft expected by the early 2020s. (photos courtesy ©Airbus and ©Zunum Aero)

impact. Zunum Aero, backed by Boeing in the USA, is hoping to have its 12-seat hybrid-electric regional airliner ready to fly by 2022. They claim that this will have 80% less CO_2 emissions and be 80% quieter. In Europe, Airbus, Rolls-Royce and Siemens are developing a fully hybrid-electric regional 50- to 100-seat aircraft. Their next step is to have a demonstrator aircraft fitted with the e-Fan-X technology flying by 2020 (fig 8.13).

lightweighting

Lightweighting and better aerodynamics are essential design aspects of making flying more energy-efficient and electrification viable. All the small electric aircraft we have looked at are made of composites for this very reason. Boeing's 787 Dreamliner, launched in 2011, pioneered the use of composites in the design of commercial long-haul aircraft, inside and out. It is made of 80% composites by volume and designed to reduce fuel consumption by 20%.

With every gram counting, lightweighting has become a top priority for all aspects of aircraft interior design. This pushes product designers to constantly innovate through new materials and configurations. Taking a more holistic view of sustainability, one of the main design challenges for commercial aircraft

interiors is how to optimise the use of space while maximising passenger comfort and numbers. Minimising the weight of waste generated on board is also important. Although a lot of design effort and PR goes into the exclusive first and business class areas, designing for economy class is much more challenging and impactful in terms of sustainability.

Figure 8.14 shows an evolution of RECARO's ground-breaking economy seating that led the way in lightweighting and slimming aircraft seats, creating space for extra seat rows in the process. Iacobucchi's ReTrolley (fig 8.15), a concept that emerged from Airbus's Bizlab accelerator, shows how redesigning existing onboard systems with sustainability in mind can reduce cabin footprints. Launched in 2018, ReTrolley allows cabin crew to sort waste as it is collected, ensuring the highest possible recycling rates. With 5.2 billion tons of waste generated onboard aircraft in 2016 alone, this is no small matter.[48]

hybrid airships

In the search for more efficient air travel, airships have been re-engineered into helium-filled hybrid aircraft such as Hybrid Air Vehicles' (HAV) Airlander10. Aside from being 70% more fuel-efficient than jets, airships don't need expensive runways for landing – a field will do. This means they can fly people and cargo direct to where they are needed, including reaching remote sites or for emergency relief. Their efficiency comes from the fact

Figure 8.14 The highly successful RECARO BL3710 short- and mid-haul economy seats were developed as the lightest in their class with an ultra-slim profile, adaptable head and neck support, a foot rest and modularity (Germany). (photo courtesy ©RECARO)

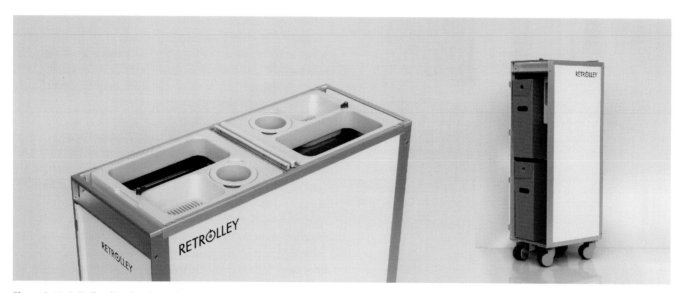

Figure 8.15 ReTrolley (Iacobucci 2018), a rethink of onboard services, sorts waste as its collected into cassettes ready for recycling on land. (courtesy Iacobucci HF Aerospace)

that they travel at much slower speeds than jets, can stay in the air for up to five days and fly direct to destination without the need for a runway.

These qualities inspired designers Seymour Powell to create a new vision for sustainable luxury travel with their zero-emission Aircruise concept in 2011. *'In a world where speed is an almost universal obsession, the idea of making a leisurely journey in comfort is a welcome contrast.'* [49] Picking up on Seymour Powell's inspirational concept, HAV joined forces with Design-Q to propose a version of luxury air cruising for the Airlander 10 (fig 8.16).

Part of the challenge of making the return of airships viable is safety. This means constantly inspecting and repairing any damage to their membrane's envelope. A small team at Lockheed Martin's Skunk Works have created an ingenious product to do just that. Spiders are autonomous robots that crawl in pairs all over the airship surface, one in and one out, locating, recording and patching any pinholes as they find them (fig 8.17). It demonstrates how, as we develop new and more efficient travel typologies, there will also be a need to design supporting products that ensure safety and reliability.

Figure 8.16 The hybrid aircraft Airlander 10 on a test flight (UK 2017) and Design Q's concept for the Airlander 10 Infinity Lounge for zero-emission sustainable travel where time becomes the ultimate luxury (2018). (courtesy Hydrid Air Vehicles Ltd/Design Q)

eVTOL drones

Drones are another form of electrified flight that is revolutionising the use of air space. They are increasingly being used to bypass traffic congestion as well as carrying out a whole range of aerial tasks that are impossible from the ground, including surveillance, rescues, mapping, monitoring and conservation work. Officially known as unmanned air vehicles (UAVs), they were first developed for the military. New designs, ranging in size from fireflies to air taxis, are appearing thick and fast, and their uses are only limited by the imagination. Urban skies and rooftops are likely to change dramatically in the coming decade as drones are increasingly used for deliveries and drone air taxis become the norm for the more affluent to sidestep traffic on the ground.

From the sustainability point of view, smaller drones are already being used for unique environmental and humanitarian tasks. Examples include aerial monitoring and inspections of wind turbine blades, solar farms, pipelines, power cables, as well as damage assessment after natural disasters and rescue operations (fig 8.18). They are also being put to good use for environmental monitoring and protection missions such as: policing illegal logging; monitoring threatened species; safeguarding wildlife from poachers; spotting diseases; and precision farming to reduce the use of pesticides and fertilisers. Taking environmental work a step further into large-scale ecosystem restoration, BioCarbon Engineering has designed drones that survey and fire germinated tree seed-pods into the ground. They can plant up to 5000 trees a day in difficult-to-reach reforestation terrain.[50]

Another use of drones that has caught the imagination in the field of humanitarian work is Zipline, an ingenious fixed-wing drone that flies much faster and further than quadcopters. Having proven itself in Rwanda by saving thousands of lives by airdropping blood and other critical drugs to remote medical facilities, it is now scaling up in Tanzania and the USA. Their long-term mission is to deliver super-fast, low-cost, on-demand medicines and other products without using a drop of gasoline[51] (fig 8.19). Still under development but also very inspiring is Pouncer, an edible single-use drone that can be precision dropped into difficult-to-reach disaster zones.[52] Made from a food composite structure, its body is filled with emergency food and water portions (fig 8.20).

Meanwhile there is a race between the on-demand mobility companies to be the first to have their autonomous air taxis up and running. China's EHang 184 (fig 8.21) and German Volocopter are leading this field with test flights under their belts in 2017 and impressive technology. However, the sustainability of eVTOLs for mobility and deliveries as opposed to difficult-to-access monitoring services needs close questioning. This is because helicopters, and even more so multicopters, are inherently less efficient than winged aircraft and land vehicles. Thus, although

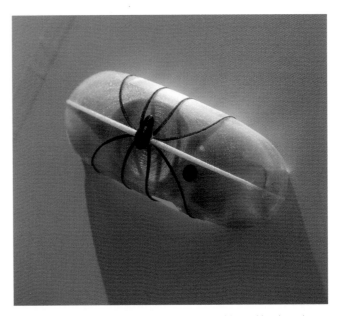

Figure 8.17 Spiders are ingenious robots designed by Lockheed Martin that crawl round in pairs inside and outside the surface of airships inspecting, recording and repairing any damage (US, 2016). (courtesy ©LM Aero)

Figure 8.18 Atlas Dynamic's Atlas Pro drone inspecting electric infrastructure. Their UAV design won a Red Dot Award in 2018 and when it's not flying it folds down into a suitcase. (courtesy AtlasDynamics.eu)

Figure 8.19 Zipline's ingenious fixed-wing drones first began air dropping payloads with life-saving drugs and blood bags to difficult-to-reach medical centres in Rwanda in 2016 (USA). (photos courtesy Zipline)

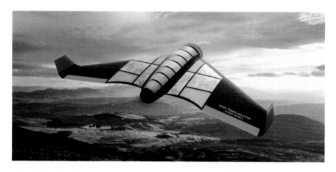

Figure 8.20 The Pouncer is an entirely edible single-use drone concept by Windhorse Aerospace filled with food and water portions for up to 50 people for difficult-to-reach disaster relief. (courtesy ©Winchourse Aerospace)

electric air taxis could be powered by renewables, they still require up to 100 times more energy to cover the same distance.[53] Perhaps an even bigger critique of the development of eVTOLs for mobility is their exclusivity, which stands to widen even further the mobility access gap.

last mile: drone or van?

The same question needs to be asked of the full-scale use of drones for deliveries once they have regulation go-ahead. The last mile of a journey, especially for goods, is usually the most impact-intensive. That is because the small goods vehicles normally used for the final doorstep delivery are less fuel-efficient and get caught in stop-start traffic, making them far less efficient per ton

Figure 8.21 Render and reality: China's EHang184 autonomous aerial vehicles (AAV) will soon make Blade Runner scenes a reality following over 1000 test flights (China 2017). (courtesy EHANG)

hauled compared with rail or larger long-distance trucks. A recent study compared the CO_2 emissions and vehicle miles travelled by drone and truck deliveries in ten different, real-world scenarios in the Los Angeles area. They found that drones fared better for single dispersed light parcel deliveries but vans were much more efficient for routes with many deliveries in close proximity, such as in towns and cities, and were the only option for heavier goods.[54] Despite their relative inefficiency, there can be no doubt that the push to certify drones, big and small, will certainly impact upon our visual landscape and privacy in the decades to come.

Anne Goodwin, the main researcher, was highly impressed by the speed and sophistication drone design has achieved in such a short time. She reflects: *"If we took the same amount of energy we've put into making drones light and efficient, applied that to trucks and got them on the street, we could do so much good for the transportation industry and the environment."*[55]

motorised road transport

Road transport and especially the private car have been blamed for much of what is most unsustainable about our current transportation system. Without repeating all that has been said up to this point, road transport, particularly in the form of fossil fuel-driven vehicles:

- accounts for 90% of all miles travelled
- burns 50% of the world's annual oil consumption
- is noisy, polluting and land hungry, blighting whole areas and segregating communities
- accounts for 95% of all transport deaths, killing and disabling millions of people and billions of animals annually
- cannot keep up with demand for road use, creating gridlock, congestion and daily stress for commuters
- contributes to unhealthy lifestyles, social isolation and weaker communities

Against this, the car still holds many strong psychological and practical attractions:

- gives a sense of personal control and independence
- provides a unique personal space
- is a significant symbol of status and personal identity
- can be highly enabling, convenient and, in certain contexts, may be the only viable transport option available

Despite the negatives of motorised road transport, a combination of the growth in global populations and middle classes is expected to drive up demand for goods and mobility at least up until 2050. Predictions are for global freight, mainly on roads, to treble by 2050 and motorised mobility in cities to double between 2015

and 2050. Alongside this, the overall number of private cars is expected to double overall, rising significantly in emerging economies while decreasing slightly in developed economies.[56]

These rises in passenger and freight demand will increase transport emissions by 70% between 2015 and 2050 if we continue with current transport models (a baseline scenario), despite large vehicle efficiency gains.[57] This would fail dismally to meet the Paris Agreement goal for 2050 transport emissions to remain at 2015 levels and barely begin to address the UN SDG goals of *reducing pollution, halving road deaths and increasing equitable access to transport*.

alternative emerging scenarios

While it is quite clear that the business-as-usual option falls very short of delivering sustainable transportation, there are much more optimistic alternative scenarios emerging for decarbonising transport and increasing its accessibility by design. These include a combination of modal shift strategies, cleaner, more efficient technologies, optimisation and vehicle-sharing measures for freight fleets and mobility, as well as infrastructure investment in developing countries.[58] In particular, we will look at examples of positive design interventions in some of the most promising technologies and business models. These include electric vehicles (EV), active mobility, autonomous vehicles (AV), shared, on-demand mobility and MAAS (Mobility as a Service).

In doing so, let us remind ourselves of what more environmentally sustainable road transport should be aiming for:

- eliminate air pollution: power from 100% renewables
- reduce noise pollution
- maximise efficiency of propulsion, weight and aerodynamics
- build from recycled and recyclable materials and be fully recycled
- increase utilisation rates of infrastructure and vehicles
- make clean technologies affordable
- reduce land usage
- radically reduce accidents, deaths and injuries

electrifying road transport

One of the big hopes for decarbonising all road transport and reducing air and noise pollution is the move to electric vehicles (EVs). Over the past decade, big technical and commercial advances in electrification are pivoting the whole automotive industry away from the internal combustion engine. Although electrification on its own will not resolve everything that is wrong with automobility or transportation, it is one of the essential ingredients towards making it more environmentally sustainable. More importantly, as we will see at the end of this chapter, EVs' ability to connect and be controlled autonomously presents designers, business and policy strategists with an opportunity to radically redesign mobility to overcome many of its other drawbacks.

Currently there are two competing technologies to supply the electric power for EVs: hydrogen fuel cells or batteries. As with all emerging technologies, it is much too early to say if one will ultimately dominate or whether they will co-exist. While battery electric vehicles (BEVs) have a head start in the car market, hydrogen fuel cell electric vehicles (FCEVs) are primarily being used for larger vehicles, such as buses and trucks.

The history of electric vehicles goes back to the early days of the automobile when they were being developed and produced in parallel with the combustion engine in the early 1900s. Although electric drive trains are far simpler mechanically and therefore require less maintenance, ultimately they lost out, as they could not compete on distance or speed. Despite not being mainstream, BEVs continued to be designed and used throughout the 1900s for several niche purposes, particularly as low-speed neighbourhood, factory or campus utility vehicles (NEVs).

One particularly good example of a NEV being used for a circular model is the milk-float, the electric milk delivery vans used across Britain. Designed to be very quiet for night and early morning drop-offs, they deliver fresh milk from local dairies to the doorstep in time for breakfast and take back the empty glass bottles for refill. When most milk was delivered this way, milkmen also played a social role by keeping an eye on their customers, particularly the elderly, and were another watchful eye in preventing neighbourhood crime (fig 8.22). Unable to compete with aggressive supermarket pricing, doorstep milk's share of the market fell from 95% in 1975 to less than 3% in the 1990s in the UK. However, helped by the plastic waste crisis, or 'Blue Planet' effect, demand for milk deliveries in glass bottles is growing again across Britain.[59]

Although milk-floats have almost disappeared, NEVs certainly have not. Since these are typically customised and produced to order, distributed manufacturing and open design platforms like Local Motors and Open Motors that we saw in Chapter 4 (see figures 4.22 and 23) are making the design and production of EVs for many niche markets more viable than ever by facilitating customisation and small-batch production.

It has to be said that the current transition away from the combustion engine is not thanks to the vision of the big car manufacturers. Although all the major car companies developed commercial EVs under duress by California's zero-emissions vehicle laws in the 1990s, mostly at the taxpayers' expense,

Figure 8.22 Milk floats and doorstep deliveries return: a circular model built around a neighbourhood electric vehicle or NEV, (UK, 1971 to present). (photo courtesy ParkerDairies.co.uk)

they fought and won against having to offer electric models and then sat on the technology for over two decades. We owe it instead to a combination of consumer appetite for cleaner vehicles demonstrated through the commercial success of Toyota's Prius hybrid cars (1997–), growing public awareness of climate change, and Tesla's inspiring and ambitious vision of an all-electric and renewable mobility future led by Elon Musk (fig 8.23).

Today, Prius vehicles are very popular as taxis and service vehicles all over the world while the Roadster, now in its second incarnation, has become a status symbol, proving that electric vehicles are not an aesthetic or performance compromise. The commercial success of this new vision has finally made the industry wake up. In under a decade, there is not one major car manufacturer that does not have electric models available, is pouring money into research on EV and automation, and is talking about phase-out dates for fossil fuel-powered vehicles within the next 30 years.

lifecycle thinking: the infrastructure and network

As we transition to electrification, now more than ever, designers need to approach it from a holistic lifecycle perspective. While EVs can considerably reduce the impact of the use phase if they are powered by renewables, the relative vehicle efficiency, materials, production and end-of-life impacts are still very important design considerations. As it happens, electric motors are considerably more energy-efficient than internal combustion engines. Based on EPA data, electric drive trains convert 59 to 62% of their energy to wheel power compared with 17 to 21% for gasoline engines.[60] This translates into EVs having an equivalent MPG or KPL three times better than gasoline engines.

Figure 8.23 The popularity of the Toyota Prius hybrid (from 1997) and the desirability of Tesla Roadster BEV (2008) woke up the car industry to people's appetite for cleaner cars. (photo credits Stuart Monk/Shutterstock.com; VanderVolf Images/Shutterstock.com)

The other important element of making electrification sustainable is how the electricity is generated. If it comes from highly polluting, toxic and CO_2 emitting sources, EVs merely displace the problem. In fact, in some countries like India and China where in 2015 75 and 67% respectively of their electricity was generated from coal,[61] it will most certainly be worse overall environmentally unless vehicles are charged directly from renewables. However, given that India and China are among the countries with the highest levels of urban pollution and where car ownership is set to grow the most, it will at least be a local relief to urban dwellers.

Taking an integrated lifecycle approach, the design of EVs, battery charging and hydrogen production should be part of a holistic renewable energy infrastructure. The combination of Tesla's Powerwall and Solar Roofs with car charging is a clear example of this systemic thinking in action across their product offer (fig 8.24). On a mass scale, car batteries and hydrogen fuel plants are now seen as an integral part of balancing a distributed renewable energy system known as vehicle-to-grid (V2G). By plugging cars into two-way charging points, they can act as an energy store when there is energy overproduction and a supply at peak demand times. Examples of enabling products include the first mass-market domestic smart V2G charger (2018) by OVO, a UK energy provider, together with Nissan and Indra Renewable Technologies. It optimises charging to take advantage of cheaper electricity when there is an oversupply of renewable energy in the system and gives customers the option of selling power back to the grid at peak times[62] (fig 8.25). Sion's integral solar cells have

taken this a step further by making the car itself a mobile power station through bidirectional charging (see fig 4.19d).

As cities all over the world are working out how to transition to EV, developing the new charging infrastructure is a growing area of design activity that involves new product architecture, typologies, interfaces and services. How well these are designed and implemented is important, as they will shape the overall experience, and impact upon the successful transition to EVs. Approaches to make charging as ubiquitous and frictionless as possible include Ubitricity's (Germany) SmartCable that meters and automatically pays for your car charging wherever you plug in.

Figure 8.24 Tesla's integration of Solar Tiles for home power generation, Powerwall smart storage and cars demonstrate the circular renewable energy thinking behind their family of products. (courtesy Tesla)

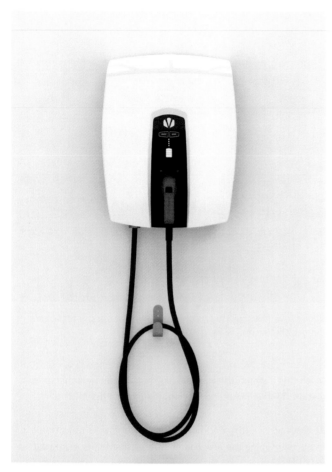

Figure 8.25 The first domestic vehicle-to-grid (V2G) charger developed by OVO energy creates a new two-way relationship between electricity consumer and supplier. (photo courtesy OVO energy)

Figure 8.26 Ubitricity's SmartCable and streetlight conversion designs are just some of the many EV infrastructure products being developed to make charging as frictionless as possible. (photo courtesy Ubitricity)

These are a good complement to their simple design for converting street lamps into charge points that are being rolled out in a number of European cities (fig 8.26). Other charging options are wireless induction pads that the vehicle drives over for rapid charging. These are especially useful for trucks and all-electric buses to recharge in minutes at either end of their routes.

new materials and production

Beyond designing new infrastructure, EVs also present a number of opportunities for the redesign of the physical vehicle itself for new use scenarios, through to rethinking whole transport systems. Here we will look at some of the more inspiring advances in making vehicle production and materials more sustainable.

Given that the number of cars globally is expected to double by 2040,[63] optimising the efficiency of EVs is no less important than it is for fossil-fuel-powered cars if we are to minimise their strain on electricity demand globally. As with aircraft, this is principally achieved through lightweighting and aerodynamics that lead to new design possibilities. There are a number of designs from pioneering companies that deserve to be mentioned for their early technical and commercial contributions in bringing electric automobility to different mass-market audiences. These include the Nissan Leaf (2010), whose accessibility made EVs popular with the mainstream market, as well as BMW's i3 (2012), Tesla's Model S(2012) and the Hyundai Ioniq (2016), a later arrival, which has set new standards in efficiency with its exceptional aerodynamics.

Tesla's bold marketing and seductive design of the Model S has probably done more to make EVs an enviable status symbol among car lovers than any other brand. This was done on the basis of delivering enhanced performance together with tech and design appeal without any compromises on distance range (see fig. 4.11d). From the outset, Tesla have been committed to producing cars from 100% renewable energy, which also lowers their production footprint. Their early investment in BEV infrastructure and the design of their iconic charging points powered by renewables not only increased their viability; it also increased their brand visibility and helped them take a lead in the market (fig 8.27).

In terms of pure design concept and detail, BMW's i3 is the most innovative of the pioneers. With the i3, BMW set out to redesign the configuration, materials and production methods used for cars, leading to a number of firsts and exemplars for the industry. These innovations include: a high-strength carbon fibre passenger module that creates a single, open, flexible space and the lightest production car in its class; interior composite panels made from renewable and sustainable kenaf fibres that replace plastic and are 30% lighter; 100% recycled polyester fabrics; leather tanned by an environmentally friendly process from waste olive leaves;

Figure 8.27 Tesla's iconic charge point design supports the viability of their cars as well as increasing the brand's visibility. (photo credit Sheila Fitsgerald/Shutterstock.com)

and sustainable fast-growing eucalyptus wood for the dash that requires 90% less finishing chemicals (fig 8.28). In addition, production of the i3 uses half the energy of other BMW models and is entirely wind powered. And when it reaches its EoL, the i3 is 95% recyclable, including using the batteries for solar farm energy storage, following BMW's leadership in materials recovery.

designing the EV transition: infrastructure and business models

Although EVs are generating a great deal of design excitement, they still made up only 0.35% of the global vehicle sales at the end of September 2018. However, total sales passed the 4 million mark in 2018,[64] and their growth continues to be sharply exponential. In this, China is now the leader in the total number of EVs and charge points, while Norway has the highest per capita EV ownership by a considerable margin at 60/1000 Inhabitants, ahead of California and the Netherlands at 13 and 8/1000 respectively (2018).[65]

As we have seen, the success of any sustainable innovation is not only down to great designs and technology but also to the whole supporting product ecosystem and business model. Some of the biggest barriers to EV adoption are cost, lack of infrastructure and the rapid improvements in technology that make some weary of buying into it. Countries with the highest rates of adoption have achieved this through a combination of measures to support the growth of infrastructure, technology and new vehicle purchase. Car manufacturers have also introduced creative new business models that reduce the cost and risk element of purchasing an EV. In particular, several have adopted the performance model that we introduced in Chapter 4.5. That is, you either lease or purchase the car, but pay-as-you-use on the battery. This reduces the initial outlay considerably and lessens the risk by allowing for upgrades as the technology develops.

EVs demonstrate how new, more environmentally sustainable technologies present a broader opportunity for designers to question every aspect of vehicle design and business models. Riversimple's hydrogen fuel cell car Rasa is an example of where the prime objective of maximum efficiency through lightness and aerodynamics led to creating a new design language using carbon fibre. They have also consciously built the business around a sale-of-service model where customers pay a monthly fee that covers the car, maintenance, insurance and fuel. This incentivises Riversimple, the manufacturer, to design for maximum reliability and efficiency, effectively linking their profits directly to sustainability while the user has the benefit of an 'affordable, hassle free, fun-to-drive eco car'[66] (fig 8.29).

motorised transport for developing countries

Up until now we have considered road mobility largely in the context of urban industrialised and emerging economies. The scenario of getting people and goods around in areas where incomes are extremely low and roads are unpaved and largely

Figure 8.28 BMW redesigned the i3 from the bottom up, including an open and light carbon fibre passenger module and more sustainable interior materials. Shown here: kenaf panels, eucalyptus wood and vegetable tanned leather. (courtesy BMW)

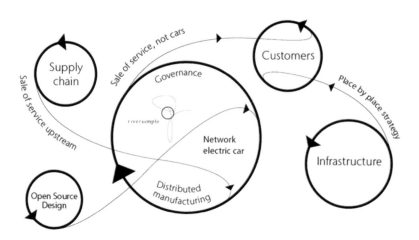

Figure 8.29 The innovative Rasa hydrogen fuel-cell car from Riversimple aims to deliver an affordable fun-to-drive eco car as a complete product service. (courtesy Riversimple/photo Anthony Dawton)

impassable by ordinary vehicles is worlds away, as are the most appropriate design solutions. In this context, the greatest energy-efficiency and smartest control systems give way to providing essential transport for delivering services, getting goods to market, and people to work and to school effectively and affordably.

Global Vehicle Trust's OX is an example of disruptive design that addresses all of these challenges. As the world's first flatpack vehicle, it allows for simple local self-assembly while reducing transport costs. Its clever pared-down design keeps it lightweight but highly manoeuvrable in difficult conditions. Ruggedness, affordability, reliability, repairability and adaptability have been top considerations in every detail of its innovative engineering and configuration. All parts that may need maintenance are easily accessible. Features include interchangeable panels and components from left and right sides with simple fasteners, making it quick to adapt from carrying big payloads to up to 13 passengers. Field trials in India and Africa in 2018 are the first step in bringing this low-cost all-terrain mobility to rural communities[67] (fig 8.30).

Figure 8.30 Developed by Global Vehicle Trust, the OX is a vehicle designed for African conditions that can be shipped as a flatpack and easily adapted to local needs (UK 2016). (courtesy OX Global Vehicle Trust/3D render Peter Robain/photo Gordon Murray)

Figure 8.31 The SMATI Turtle 1 concept car for Africa built from the ground up by 30 mechanics out of used parts in the Suame Magazine car recycling district of Kumasi (Ghana-Netherlands 2013). (courtesy AARDSCHAP Foundation; photos Teum Vonk 2013)

The S.M.A.T.I. Turtle1 takes a grassroots, open-design approach to designing a vehicle suitable for African needs. It originates in the Suame Magazine district of Kumasi, Ghana where approximately 200,000 craftspeople work with car scrap. Here, 30 local mechanics collaborated with Dutch and Ghanaian universities to produce a car suitable for Africa. It is brand-free, has a one-fits-all chassis, all working parts are mechanical, easily repairable with simple tools and interchangeable second-hand parts. The upper body can be custom designed for any purpose. The Turtle does not do speed. Instead it is a robust and functional boneshaker that can be kept running for a very long time[68] (fig 8.31).

active road transport: cycling, walking and wheelchairs

The bicycle is one of the main heroes of sustainable mobility. As we saw in the lifecycle comparison (see fig 8.9), it is the mode of transport with the lowest ecocosts, outstripping even walking. This is because overall cycling requires less energy and therefore food calories to travel the same distance, even including the ecocosts of producing the bicycle and its maintenance . It manages to do this through an ingenious human-powered design developed in the nineteenth century. To get a sense of their usefulness and popularity, well over 2 billion bicycles have been produced worldwide,[69] and since 1980 annual production has more than doubled that of cars.[70] Over half of these are in China where the classic Flying Pigeon PA-02 alone, a design based on the 1932 Raleigh Roadster, has sold more units than any other vehicle model in the world[71] (fig 8.32).

The development of the bicycle is a beautiful example of how good ideas get better through the collective effort of inventors, tinkerers and enthusiasts. In a matter of a few decades, it evolved

from the fun but lethal velocipede designed by Karl von Drais in 1817 (Germany), via the penny farthing, to finally settle on the 'safety bicycle' designed by John Kemp Starley in 1885 (UK). This design defined the frame geometry, chain-drive and pneumatic tyres still used for the manufacture of most bicycles in use around the world today (fig 8.33).

Not only does cycling come out on top as the most environmentally sustainable form of transport we have, it also has many social and economic benefits that make it particularly appropriate for many twenty-first-century scenarios. For cities and towns in wealthy and developing countries alike, it presents the most cost-effective solution for reducing congestion, air and noise pollution as well as taking pressure off public transport and health services. As an industry, cycling also creates three times

Figure 8.32 Based on the 1932 Raleigh Roadster, the Chinese Flying Pigeon, made in Tianjin, is the bestselling vehicle in the world, deservedly making China the 'Kingdom of Bicycles'. (photo credit Tim Quijano)

Figure 8.33 A Rover ladies' safety bicycle from an advertisement in a beauty book from 1889, a variant on John Kemp Starley's 1885 design that established the geometry and mechanics of today's bicycles. (illustration public domain)

EU BENEFITS OF CYCLING - SUMMARY
(BILLION EUROS)

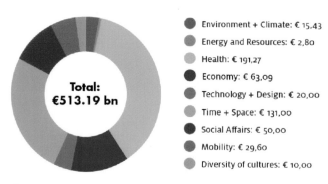

**Total:
€513.19 bn**

- Environment + Climate: € 15,43
- Energy and Resources: € 2,80
- Health: € 191,27
- Economy: € 63,09
- Technology + Design: € 20,00
- Time + Space: € 131,00
- Social Affairs: € 50,00
- Mobility: € 29,60
- Diversity of cultures: € 10,00

Figure 8.34 The socio-environmental-economic case for cycling. (2016) (courtesy European Cycling Federation)

more jobs than the automotive industry per unit invested, and much of this employment is at a local level in tourism, sales, infrastructure, manufacturing and repairs.[72] According to the European Cyclists Federation (ECF), *"Investing in cycling provides a better economic return than almost any other transport option"*[73] (fig 8.34).

For city dwellers and commuters, young and old, choosing to cycle is the nearest thing there is to a win-win-win. It is cheaper, healthier and generally faster and more reliable. For people living in underserved rural and urban communities around the globe where walking is their only other option, bicycles are no less than a lifeline. This also makes it potentially one of the most socially equalising forms of mobility after walking. Yet for many of the rural and urban poor in developing economies, they are simply

unaffordable. We will look at how design can help in these two contrasting scenarios.

With such a clear environmental, health and economic case, increasing cycling's modal share, especially in cities, has become an important objective of sustainable transport policy alongside walking and public transport. A key measure of modal share is based on what mode of transport people use most regularly to get to work or study. Although modal share varies hugely between regions and cities, the overall trend around the world shows that cycling has been steadily increasing in cities and towns since the millennium.

For some years Copenhagen has been leading the way as the world's bicycle-friendly capital, with 41% commuter share as of 2017.[74] Although the average EU cycle mode share is 8%, a number of European cities, including Amsterdam, Utrecht and Strasbourg, are not far behind Copenhagen.[75] In the USA, cycle commuting grew 51% between 2000 and 2016 with some cities in California, Oregon and Colorado having rates between 6 and 16%, although regional city averages are closer to 2 and 3%, and overall it is 1% across the USA.[76] In China, the 'Kingdom of Cycling', cycling has declined from rates as high as 30% in Beijing as prosperity has increased over the past decades. That is, until very recently. The boom in dockless bike-share schemes is reversing this trend, with cities like Shenzhen replacing nearly 10% of private car travel with a fleet of 500,000 bikes.[77]

For sustainably minded designers, understanding what lies behind these statistics is important. While cities around the world wake up to the benefits of increasing cycling over cars, what are the barriers and enablers for more people to take up cycling? Although bicycles are a very effective means of getting around, they do have their limitations and constraints that need to be understood if uptake is to increase by design. These include: a limited distance range, exposure to the weather, fear of accidents and vulnerability, theft, maintenance, and limitations on passengers and cargo-carrying capacity. We will look at each one of these as a design opportunity and demonstrate some of the best solutions and ongoing challenges.

the bicycle: an inherently sustainable design

Before we delve into these issues, let us first consider what makes the design of the bicycle itself inherently sustainable, aside from being a means of clean and efficient mobility. The bicycle stands out as one of the best examples of the sustainable advantages of a standardised modular parts system. By having standardised parts, bicycles can be assembled and components easily repaired, replaced or upgraded with universal tools all around the world, ensuring product longevity (fig 8.35). Equally, accessories that make cycles versatile, such as carriers, lights, trailers, child seats,

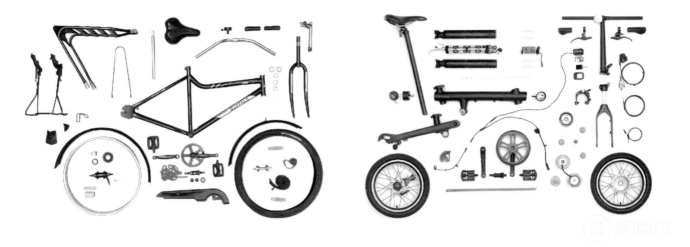

Figure 8.35 From the robust and basic African Buffalo bicycle to Xiaomi's sophisticated folding e-bike, bicycle components are highly standardised and interchangeable around the world. (photos courtesy World Bicycle Relief and iFixit)

locks, water bottles, panniers, bells and whistles, can be added or removed to suit owners' changing needs.

Designs that stray from these standard elements or have too much integration and too many proprietary complex components invariably lead to lower repairability and shorter product life. Another important aspect of most bicycles is that apart from their tyres and some parts of their seats, they have until recently been wholly recyclable. The introduction of carbon fibre to frames and forks to lighten them reduces its recyclability and repairability and should be reserved for applications where it is required for performance rather than as a tool to create new form factors and higher margins, as tempting as this is for designers.

While there are many types of bicycles and price tags to match, including touring, track, mountain, downhill, cross, hybrid, folding, stunt … if a bicycle is to be the main means of transport, it must above all be reliable, easy to use and low maintenance, even when left outdoors – and preferably not too attractive for thieves. Aside from the Flying Pigeon mentioned earlier, the design of the classic 'Dutch-style' urban bicycle that has been used for decades and is still being used by millions across Europe deserves to be toasted. With its sturdy frame, covered chain, internal gears, integrated dynamo lights and inbuilt lock, it is beautifully designed for minimal maintenance, maximum reliability and the sedate cycling style necessary for high-density urban cycling.

extending the bicycle's range

For the average user, bicycles have an upper commuting range of around 8 to 16km (5 to 10 miles) one-way, depending on terrain and fitness levels.[78] This distance is perfect in smaller towns and cities, but in larger conurbations commutes are often longer,

Figure 8.36 Design opportunities for safe cycle storage: on-street bike storage for space-constrained apartment dwellers in London and a Cycle Hub at commuter station. (photo credit Jane Penty)

making distances impractical for cycling. Extending the viable travel distance by bicycle can be tackled through a number of different design interventions.

The first is to make cycling an integral part of what is known as multimodal travel. In plain language, this means making it as easy as possible to combine cycling with other modes of travel, especially public transport. This can be done by either designing and providing generous amounts of (secure) bicycle storage at stations or allowing cycles to be transported on trains and buses. Figure 8.36 shows one of the many new street cycle storage designs that replace a parking space and a more service-oriented bike park at a commuter station which acknowledge the need for secure bicycle storage and servicing. Figure 8.37 shows a bus with a front cycle carrier thoughtfully designed for quick deployment, loading, securing and unloading of bicycles which is now quite common across North American public transit systems.

Bike-share schemes, which we explore in 8.3, are an alternative solution that are proving very popular. Finally, folding bicycles are another option, not only for mixing travel modes but also to address the problem of bicycle theft and storage. Andrew Ritchie designed the now iconic Brompton folding bicycle with multimodal use in mind in the late 1970s. The Brompton is also an example of how focusing on solving a functional problem and refining the solution can lead to an unselfconscious, timeless, well-thought-out, robust and ultimately sustainable design[79] (fig 8.38).

The second approach to extending a bicycle's range is to reduce the physical effort required by adding an electric motor that

Figure 8.37 A bus in Santa Cruz, California loaded with a Schwinn Tailwind e-assist bicycle. (photo credit Richard Masoner)

assists the pedalling. These are known as e-bikes, pedal-assist bicycles or pedelecs. Not only do they extend the distance which bicycles can cover; they also make cycling much more accessible to a broader range of physical abilities and ages. Studies in Norway confirm that e-bikes do increase modal share, distance travelled and also female uptake.[80] Of course pedal-assisted bikes (top speed of 25km/15.5mph in the EU) do use power, and as with cars, their footprint will depend on the source of the electricity. In figure 8.10 we saw that compared with traditional bicycles, e-bikes powered by renewables increase whole lifecycle ecocosts by 60%, while an e-bike charged on the Swiss grid doubles the ecocosts, making it comparable to a tram ride.

Figure 8.38 Folding bicycles like the classic Brompton are one approach to integrating sustainable modes of transport while reducing issues of storage and theft. (photo courtesy Brompton)

Figure 8.39 The Faraday Porteur commuter e-bike has a discrete front hub electric assist motor with integrated electronic sensing controls and battery pack (USA 2018). (courtesy Faraday Bicycles)

Figure 8.40 Beijing cyclists wear special duvet-like covers to keep warm in winter as well as smog masks. (photo credit Spondylolithesis)

E-bikes have been popular in China for many years and over 200,000 of them provide an important means of mobility, especially for the lower middle classes. However, a lack of regulation enforcement and their misuse is making them a serious danger on China's urban roads and the cause of many fatalities. This has led to bans and restrictions in a number of cities, including Beijing, Shanghai, Guangzhou, Xiamen and Shenzhen.[81] This should be a warning for Europe and North America, where their use is rapidly growing, not to allow the line between bicycles and motorcycles to be blurred. In our enthusiasm for clean mobility, we should not put at risk the many qualities of cycling, top of which are not speed or power.

With the rising popularity of pedelecs, it is very tempting for designers and manufacturers to want to make their mark with new distinctive designs. But just as with the mobile phone, the most sustainable bicycle is the one you already own. This makes the electric conversion kits not only the cheapest but also the most sustainable solution as a first step (and maybe the only step required) in transitioning from traditional to motor-assisted cycling. These motors can be fitted to front or rear hubs, mid-drives, or even as wheel drives as in the case of Michelin's e-drive, and only require additional battery packs and controls. The Faraday Porteur demonstrates how these three elements can be discretely integrated into classic bicycle designs. In any case, the principles of modularity, repairability and upgradability should be firmly embedded in new e-bike designs (fig 8.39).

mitigating exposure to air pollution and the weather
Another reason people are put off cycling and walking is exposure to the weather. In some areas of the world extreme heat, snow

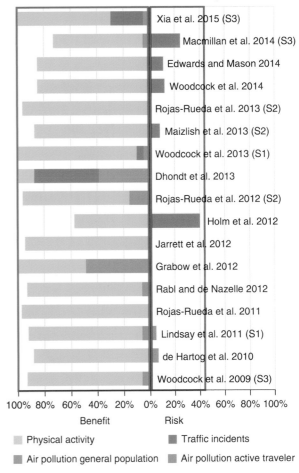

Figure 8.41 Research review: health benefits of active travel outweigh risks. (source: *Mueller et al.* (2015) *Preventative Medicine* 76)

Figure 8.42 One-size does not fit all in persuading people at risk to wear masks: a. Respro Ultralight urban sport mask (UK 2015); b. Cambridge Mask's (China/UK 2016) personalised fashion mask; c. Airmotion Laboratories' (China 2017) Woobi Play mask kit; d. Aetheris' Airpop smart mask and collaboration with XiangNui electric scooters (China 2018) (courtesy Respro; Cambridge Mask; Airmotion Laboratories; Aertheris)

Figure 8.43 Studio Roosgarde's Smog-free Bicycle that sucks in smog and delivers clean air for rider and city is a truly inspiring vision of how products could be restorative (Netherlands/China 2017) (courtesy Studio Roosgarde)

and ice can make cycling impossible for part of the year. While it is hard to avoid sweating, getting wet, too hot or too cold on a bicycle, where there is a strong bicycle culture, this is all taken in its stride. The development of high-performing all-weather outdoor clothing and materials has helped this aspect of cycling tremendously, but low-tech solutions also work, as we see in Beijing (fig 8.40). Aside from investing in the right clothing and weather protection, facilities at work are a help to those whose cycling style or work dress code require showering and changing.

Exposure to high levels of pollution is another potential deterrent to cycling and other active travel modes such as jogging and walking. And rightly so, as the WHO ranks air pollution as the world's largest single environmental health risk. However, a review of research studies (fig 8.41) shows that on balance there are still far more benefits to be gained from active transport in all but the most polluted cities of the world.[82, 83] Although the worst pollution levels are generally found in cities in emerging and developing economies due to lower vehicle emissions standards, WHO guidelines are still exceeded regularly in many cities around the world.[84]

Growing public awareness of poor air quality has led to a whole range of new personal air monitoring and purifying products, as we saw in Chapters 2 and 3 (see figs 2.25 and 3.32). Although very much end-of-pipe solutions, masks that filter particulate, NO_x and smog can be very important for people's health, especially

the elderly, the young and the physically active. Figure 8.42 shows four different design approaches to anti-air pollution masks aimed at engaging different users. Respro's (UK) long-established urban and sports masks focus on breathability and performance. Airmotion Laboratories' (China) Woobi Play mask comes in kit form that puts kids in control and makes wearing a mask 'cool'. Cambridge Mask (China/UK) approaches it as a fashion accessory that normalises and personalises their use. Finally, AirPop has introduced a smart mask, or 'Air Wearable', with a sensing valve that monitors both external conditions and internal breathing biodata. By pairing the Halo Sensor valve to your phone it can give you personal health insights and, if desired, be linked to bigger public health diagnostics and data. Its data-capture capabilities have spurred collaborations with Mobike and XiangNui electric scooters, leading to the development of future products and user insights. Designing comfortable, effective and socially acceptable masks is challenging but important where air quality puts health at risk.

Air pollution on the streets is also of particular concern for babies and young children, as concentrations are highest close to the ground. This has led to designs such as Buggy Air, involving citizen and open data collection that we saw in Chapter 3 (fig 3.33) and Brizi. Nestled by a child's head, Brizi deals with this by tracking air quality and activating its air filter when needed. The Brizi app also shows local live data to help carers choose better walking routes (fig 8.45). Finally, Daan

Box 8.1 Interview with Alex Hulme on the challenges of integrating sustainable thinking into mainstream industrial design[85]

Alex Hulme is a Director at Map Project Office, a team of industrial designers based in London who work with an impressive portfolio of local and global clients. They believe great design can do great things and love making things that make a material difference.

JP. Before we discuss some of Map's design work, could you share with us what sustainability means to you and how it impacts upon your practice?

AH. I think we're living in a way that we can't maintain – which can be at conflict with what we do as industrial designers because we're essentially involved in the production of new physical stuff. This means that we also have an interesting responsibility and opportunity to affect it in some way. From my experience, the key in any project is to what extent sustainable thinking is baked into the proposition before a client approaches us. The big change we've seen in our practice has been that along with the public perception of sustainability increasing exponentially, it's becoming one of the first things that clients bring up. The rate of change is really quite astonishing.

As an example, we've been working on packaging in the health and beauty area with a client where sustainability is built into their business model. It's wonderful to work on a project where every aesthetic decision and every production decision we make is run through this thought process because everyone's on board. The process just flows.

JP. Could you tell us about any projects where you've specifically tackled some aspect of sustainability?

AH. Probably one of the best examples is the meal service we redesigned for Virgin Atlantic. We worked with an environmental consultant to understand the issues and try to make genuinely more sustainable decisions. Without an expert, from a designer's point of view, it can be frankly quite confusing to navigate your way through all the information that's out there.

The advice we were given was to aim for incremental improvements focused on embodied carbon. This led us to explore weight and reusability as key opportunities. As part of this strategy we replaced a bowl that was disposable with one that could be reused several times, which gave a genuine carbon saving over one being binned straight away. The service was also lighter and more compact, producing a saving of

Figure 8.44 BeeLine cycle compass gives a real-time indication of direction that offers the cyclist freedom to vary the route. Its utlra-low power e-paper display keeps it working for months of normal use. (photo courtesy ©Map Project Office/photo Clare Lewington)

Figure 8.45 Brizi and Map Project partnered to design a headrest for babies that tracks air quality and purifies it when needed. (photo courtesy ©Map Project Office)

over 129kg over its lifecycle. This added up to a 46% overall improvement on its previous carbon footprint. The reason why projects like this are interesting as case studies is that they show how sustainability can make sense commercially because for an airline, cutting down weight and space translates directly into cost savings.

JP. That's a good example of aligning environmental and economic sustainability. Are there any products you've designed that you think have also added social value?

AH. Yes, an interesting example in that space would be Brizi, an air purifier for kids' buggies. This is a project where the client came to us extremely switched on and ahead of the curve. He really opened our eyes to the scale and effects of air pollution on the street. The reason why it's a real problem is that air quality is officially measured at several metres above street level, but if you look at how the particles are distributed on a streetscape, they tend to sit towards the edges of the street at low level – which is exactly where you'd be pushing a buggy. And on top of that, babies' and toddlers' lungs aren't fully developed, so the particulates they breathe stay in their lungs.

What makes Brizi even more interesting is that it has another social dimension. As well as being open source and open access, it's building an air pollution monitoring network. By having air quality monitors built in, all the products out there become mobile monitoring stations helping to build up a real-time map of local air pollution.

JP. You've also designed another product that uses technology to support more active mobility: cycling. Can you explain the thinking behind Beeline?

AH. Beeline is a new type of cycle navigation device. It's an interesting project because it sits in a space that people are really passionate about and tries to facilitate more sustainable behaviours. In this project we identified a group of people we called 'third-wave cyclists'. These are people who are either lapsed cyclists, or people just struggling to do it regularly. Beeline was designed specifically for this large group of people who just want to get around, not for the avid cyclist or Lycra brigade. Beeline is about saying, "you want to get from the supermarket to the pub, or from A to B? Here's the product for you." It doesn't have to be a sports device, it just has to be a really great simple product.

One of the other things that's particularly interesting about Kickstarter projects like Beeline is that they're quite a nice way to test the market. With smaller start-ups, the first production runs are usually small batches of a few thousand or so to

Figure 8.46 Honda. Great Journey. (courtesy ©Map Project Office photo Petr Krejčí)

establish a demand and later, when they've caught on, this can be ramped up. This avoids the pitfall industrial designers get drawn into of designing products made in huge volumes that don't end up selling.

JP. In terms of mobility more widely, do you see any opportunities for more sustainable products or systems? For instance, where did the Honda project take you?

AH. The Honda Great Journey project is about an alternative viewpoint on a new technology: autonomous driving. If you look at what's going on at the moment, it's all about the technology and how it can be interpreted in a very practical way. For us what was missing was the storytelling – we worked with a Japanese film director, Morihiro Harano, to take a slightly dreamy approach to what it could be. For us, projects like this are about inspiring people to go and do something new and exciting in this space. So in the same way that Beeline is about 'Oh, I could do that', the whole point of the Honda Great Journey project is that it's about taking a new, potentially more sustainable technology, and getting people to engage with it in a way that gets them excited.

Roosgarde's Smog-free Bicycle turns the problem on its head by having the bicycle absorb smog and expel clean air, a truly inspiring vision of how products could be restorative. The concept is being developed further in collaboration with Ofo Bicycles in Beijing as a handlebar attachment that sucks in polluted air and delivers clean air to riders and their immediate surroundings[86] (fig 8.43).

feeling safe and being safe

Fear of accidents and lack of confidence in dealing with heavy traffic situations is another common reason people give for not cycling, especially females.[87] Statistically, however, urban cyclists have a lower probability of being killed *per mile travelled* than pedestrians and about three times less likely than the driver of a powered two-wheeler.[88] Countrywide, motorcycles remain by far the most risky mode of travel, followed by walking and cycling, while the safest are air, ferry and rail[89] (fig 8.47).

Although cycling is less dangerous than walking, any road accident is one too many and there are a number of measures that have proven results. The first is increasing the number of cyclists or its mode share. Although this may seem counter-intuitive, research shows that the number of cycle accidents per mile pedalled goes down the more miles cycled (fig 8.48). Statistics also show that

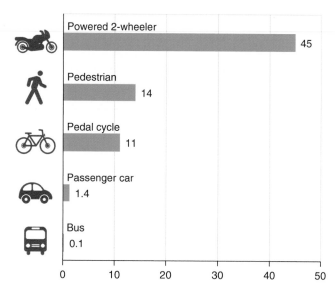

Figure 8.47 Urban fatalities per billion passenger kms. Median 2011 to 2015 for Auckland, Barcelona, Berlin, London, Paris. (source: Santacreus/ITF Safer City Streets database)

cycling numbers go up in cities where there is investment in cycle infrastructure, such as cycle lanes and bike-share schemes.[90] Segregating bicycle lanes is one design intervention that has proven to increase cycling numbers by making cyclists feel safer,

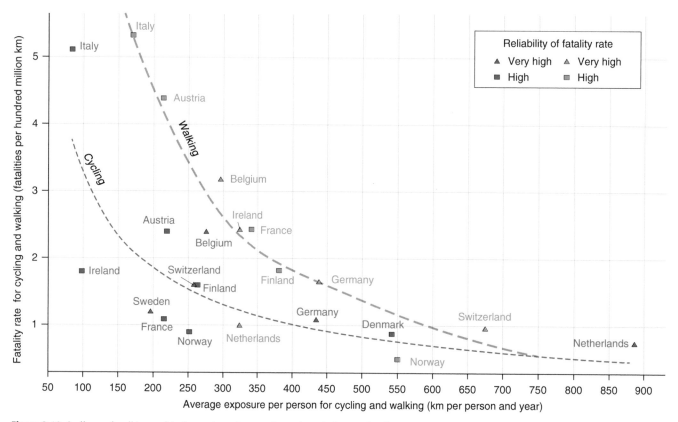

Figure 8.48 Cycling and walking: safety in numbers. (source: Castro (2018), International Transport Forum)

Figure 8.49 Urban landscape products around cycling and walking present a design opportunity for simple, effective and potentially iconic street products with positive associations. (photo courtesy ©Christopher Martin, Urban Movement, UK)

and reduce accidents.[91] There are a range of products specifically designed for doing just this – segregating lanes. These take the form of either low-level bumps such as armadillos, lacasitos or orcas, or mid-height fixed or flexible posts and even planters (fig 8.49).

Since not all cycling can happen in segregated cycle lanes, finding the best cycle route and being visible are other factors that improve safety. This is where app connectivity has helped a great deal in planning safer routes. Combining this with navigation products like Beeline's Cycle Compass are additional ways to make cycle journeys easier and less stressful (see fig 8.44).

Helmets are another product related to cycle safety – but a controversial one in terms of making them mandatory. In Northern Europe where cycling is most popular, helmet use is low; yet there are the least accidents in the world. Some countries have chosen to make them mandatory, especially for children, but opponents argue that they have reduced the number of cyclists, and, as we have seen, fewer cyclists means an increased risk of accidents. The argument against, supported by research, shows that cyclists with helmets tend to take more risks and cars drive closer to them. The reasoning is that car drivers perceive them as less vulnerable and cyclists feel safer. The argument 'for' maintains that helmets reduce the severity of head injuries and fatalities. While opponents do not dispute this, they argue that making them mandatory puts the onus on the cyclist and shifts the focus away from motorists and investing in the known solutions for reducing accidents, which are more segregation from motor traffic, slower driving speeds and greater driver awareness.[92]

Eco Friendly Index

Figure 8.50 Urge's SupaTrail helmet scores 6 out of 7 on their eco-friendly index with 100% recycled EPS inner shell and 100% recycled PET straps (France). (courtesy Urge Bike Products, France)

In contrast to the urban cycling scenario, for more intentionally risk-taking activities like mountain biking, stunt riding and downhilling, helmets seem almost universally accepted. From the sustainability perspective, what matters is that design interventions act to increase cycling numbers and make it safer while applying sustainable design principles. Cycle helmets are typically made of virgin non-renewable expanded polystyrene (EPS) moulded into hard plastic shells with polyester straps. Very few make any serious attempt at recyclability. One rare exception is Urge. Each of their helmets is given an eco-friendly index and is made of as much recycled content as possible (fig 8.50).

passengers, cargo and all things practical

The final major barrier to making cycling one's main mode of urban transport is ferrying passengers and 'stuff' around. This could be getting children to nursery or school before work or bringing the weekly groceries or DIY materials home. The design of child seats, baskets, panniers and many other accessories is a rich area for designers, both from the enabling and practical point of view but also materiality and personalisation. Figure 8.51 shows contrasting design approaches to a child's cycle seat, from the prevailing injection moulded designs good for all weathers to the more traditional Dutch wicker seat that challenges this materiality and is 100% recyclable and compostable as well as easily detachable.

However, there comes a point when attaching accessories reaches its limit. Enter an amazing array of ingenious trailers, tricycles and cargobike designs, often assisted by small electric motors. These are the real workhorses of the bicycle world that have been and still are heavily used around the world, from Asia's rickshaws to street vendors and car-free family living. In developing countries these are often custom fabricated locally, while in wealthier economies some well-established brands have been designing these for years, such as Thule and Hamax for seats and trailers, and Nihola, Bullit, Babboe, and more recently, Urban Arrow, for

Figure 8.51 Contrasting approaches to child seat design: a. easily detachable traditional Dutch rear child seat made of ply, wicker and a metal bracket; b. front handlebar injection-moulded plastic seat and visor for babies in use in Amsterdam. (photo credits: a. Rob Williams b. Sam Cliff)

cargobikes. Today, the rapidly expanding demand for pollution-free last-mile urban deliveries and multi-user family bikes is opening up many opportunities for custom- and batch-production for designers and makers(fig 8.52). Besides making car-free living as easy as possible, modularity, adaptability and recyclability should be high up on the design agenda.

cycling as the new normal: establishing a cycle culture
Making cycling the number one choice over driving takes much more than the design of a good bicycle or accessory. It requires a year-on-year commitment to overcoming all the barriers of safety and convenience by designing and investing in the right infrastructure. When this happens, as Copenhagen has

Figure 8.52 Some of the many designs of trailers and cargobikes: a. car-free family life in Amsterdam with an Urban Arrow (2018); b. new business models in London: fabricated trailer attached to e-bike for bakery supplies and customer deliveries (2018). (photo credits: a. Rachel Perry b. Jane Penty)

ROOM FOR THE WHOLE FAMILY

25% of families in Copenhagen with 2 children have a cargobike and, in 30% of households with a cargobike, they replace cars

COPENHAGENERS' REASONS FOR CYCLING

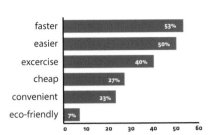

faster 53%
easier 50%
excercise 40%
cheap 27%
convenient 23%
eco-friendly 7%

TRAFFIC CROSSING CITY CENTRE 1970-2016

Car
Bicycle

Figure 8.53 Copenhagen statistics show that understanding users and investment are what it takes to get people on bikes. (source: City of Copenhagen 2017)

proven, people choose cycling first because 'it's faster', 'it's easier', 'it's good exercise', 'it's cheaper', 'it's more convenient', and lastly, 'it's eco-friendly'[93] (fig 8.53). As well as designing out the barriers, it is also about establishing a positive cycle culture as the norm that starts from when babies are taken by bicycle to nursery (see fig 3.9). These findings completely align with our earlier observations in Chapter 3 that sustainable behaviour change happens when the most sustainable option is the easiest and most rewarding and eventually becomes the norm, embraced even by 'settlers'. Many cities around the world are demonstrating that increasing active transport and making cities healthier and more liveable is achievable by design.

Within and beyond the bounds of our local communities cyclists also tend to form supportive communities. This extends across national boundaries and is helping to make more sustainable tourism possible through P2P networks like Spinlisters and Warm Showers that let you arrange local bike hire and exchange free accommodation.

the bicycle as a tool for prosperity
Up until now we have focused on product and infrastructure designs that get people in relatively rich cities out of their cars by making cycling the best option for travel alongside public transport. Interestingly, cycling is often the best option for people at the base of the economic pyramid, who mostly live in rural areas. In this context, bicycles enable medical services to be reached and delivered, children to attend school regularly, and act as workhorses for getting products and services to market for much-needed income (see Box 3.7). However, there are two main obstacles to this happening. The first is that most people in this situation cannot afford the initial outlay for a bicycle. The second is that bicycles used in these contexts need to be very robust and reliable to keep maintenance costs down to a minimum and to cope with very poor roads and tracks.

These are exactly the problems identified and addressed by a number of NGOs, including World Bicycle Relief (WBR) set up by

one of the co-founders of SRAM. WBR operate a hybrid company structure in Africa where their commercial arm Buffalo Bicycles has designed a robust and reliable bicycle specifically suited to African conditions. The bicycle parts are produced in China and assembled in Africa. Half are sold directly to local users and the other half to WBR and other charities to distribute where need is identified (fig 8.54). WBR also operate a training programme for field mechanics, so that a local repair network keeps the bicycles rolling.[94] On a different tack, Craig Calfee, an innovator and pioneer designer of performance bicycles, talks about how he has shared his bicycle design expertise and set up social enterprises around the world to build bamboo bikes made by local craftspeople for local needs (box 8.2).

Figure 8.54 The Buffalo Bicycle and its local repair network make it possible for children to attend school regularly, for medical services to reach villagers and local businesses to trade. (photo courtesy World Bicycle Relief)

Box 8.2 Interview with Craig Calfee on the development of bamboo bicycles and local fabrication projects around the world[95]

Craig Calfee has always been an innovator in materials and processes. From his first experiences of working with carbon fibre for Olympic class kayaks in the 1980s, he went on to pioneer the use of carbon fibre for bicycle frames. In 1991 he built the first all-carbon fibre bike used in the Tour de France for three-times winner Greg LeMond. At Calfee Design he has continued designing top-performance bicycles and more recently developed bamboo as a viable material for frames. Since his first bamboo bike in 1996, he has gone on to share his expertise in fabricating bamboo frames, assisting social enterprises to train and produce them for the benefit of communities in Africa, Asia and Latin America.

JP. You have years of experience designing very special bicycles and have earned a reputation as an innovator and master craftsman in this field. Can you tell us about how you got there and what connection you think there might be between sustainable design and having a deep understanding of materials, production and performance?

CC. At some point in my youth, I was advised to choose a career doing what you love. My only guideline at the time was that I knew that I really enjoyed making things with my hands. Through that, I decided to go to art school and major in sculpture. There, I worked with a variety of materials and learnt that each material seemed to have a specialty in terms of its most suitable uses. Later, I discovered carbon fibre epoxy composites and found it outperformed most other materials in so many ways. When I built my first bicycle with it, I realised it was the best material for bicycles. Being one

of the few who recognised it at the time gave me a huge head start in that industry, so I decided to focus on bicycles. Later, I discovered that bamboo is an excellent material for bicycles, too. It's also sustainable and low cost. And the seemingly universal attraction to a bicycle made of bamboo can be explained by the combination of the efficiency of a bicycle with the obvious sustainability of bamboo. Not many products do this so well.

JP. As a pioneer of modern bamboo bicycles, how did you first become interested in bamboo as a material for bicycles? And what do you think they offer in the context of sustainable design and sustainable transportation?

CC. In 1995, I was looking for a material to build a bike that would get a lot of attention at the Interbike trade show. As soon as I settled on bamboo, I realised the potential it had as a legitimate material for making bicycles. After selling a few of them and noticing how people became enamoured with them, I came up with the idea of bamboo bikes in developing countries as a way to solve transportation problems. So, in 2006, I put a notice on my website that I wanted to try building bamboo bikes in Africa. I had travelled across central Africa as a backpacker 22 years previous, so I already knew there was plenty of bamboo and that people valued bicycles. And it was pretty clear that they needed more employment and self-reliance. It also seemed to me that it was more sustainable to extract bamboo from the forests rather than dig more open pit mines or clear cutting trees.

Figure 8.55 Calfee Designs' Dragonfly carbon fibre and Bamboo Road bikes. (photos courtesy Calfee Designs)

JP. From producing your own specialist bamboo bicycles, how did you come to setup Bamboosero?

CC. In providing a technical solution for joining bamboo tubes together into a bicycle, I was able to promote it on four fronts: transportation, employment, sustainable agriculture and tourism. That last one, tourism, solved a problem of not having good, interesting bikes for tourists to rent. And some of the shops where the bikes were made became tourist attractions unto themselves. This was all in the interest of having the projects be economically sustainable. We even tried exporting the bikes to the USA and we did sell some under the Bamboosero name. But the demand was not strong enough for Bamboosero to continue as a bicycle brand.

JP. Can you tell us how Bamboosero evolved and what its main challenges were?

CC. It proved to be difficult to convince people that a new material was strong enough and would last. People were also sceptical about where they were made. But enough were sold so the builders could branch off and start their own brands, finding a bigger market in Europe, where there is a closer connection to Africa. These include Boomers and Danso in Ghana, Booganda and Boogaali in Uganda and Bambikes in the Philippines.

JP. What are your current and future projects?

CC. Projects are still running in Ghana, Uganda, Zambia, the Philippines, India and the Congo (DRC). Another one in Cuba is producing bamboo bikes for tourist rentals and may develop further with e-bikes. New ones are in planning and market research stages in Liberia, Kenya, Ethiopia and Rwanda. We hope to scale up and start importing bicycle parts into Africa in larger volume. This will need some financing mechanisms to allow people to buy them over time. In the Congo, an agricultural cooperative rents bamboo cargo bikes to farmers so they can transport their produce to the market town and get better prices. Financially, this works out for everyone, although it takes a year to pay for the bikes.

JP. Based on your own business and design journey, what advice would you give young designers with aspirations to put their design skills to good use and earn a living?

CC. One must consider so many factors when designing solutions. The product itself is just part of the challenge. Aside from it needing to work well, look good, and solve a problem that actually exists, it must also be economically sustainable. That doesn't mean it has to be cheap. It just has to demonstrate value over the life of the product and not be a burden to dispose of at the end of its lifecycle. And if a product can be attractive on multiple fronts, that makes adoption a lot easier.

Figure 8.56 A fleet of bamboo bicycles ready for hire in Khoma (DRC) and a bamboo cargo bike in process of assembly. (photos courtesy Calfee Designs)

Figure 8.57 Motivation's hand-powered tricycle in use in India and Rough Terrain's three-wheeler design in Uganda are based on their design philosophy: robust, affordable, repairable, adjustable and, most importantly, *fitted*. (source: ©David Constantine, Motivation)

Figure 8.58 COGY is a radically transformative wheelchair design that allows people with no lower limb movement to activate the pedals by triggering motion reflex (TESS, Japan 2019). (photo courtesy COGY Japan)

wheelchairs: levelling the playing field

When we talk about access to mobility we often forget that there are over 130 million people worldwide – that is, nearly 1 in 50 - who have no access to the most basic mobility: walking. For them, wheels are the same as a pair of legs - their lifeline to independent living. In developed economies, 95% of the 10 million people who need wheelchairs have access to one, while in developing economies the numbers reverse to 90%; that is, 100 million who do not have wheelchairs because they cannot afford one.[96] As a result, they miss out on schooling and employment, condemning them to a cycle of poverty.

Two social enterprises that stand out for their design work in this field are Whirlwind and Motivation. Whirlwind's founder Ralf Hotchkiss started working with users in developing countries in 1980 on a small scale to build their own customised chairs. This eventually evolved into a social enterprise, Whirlwind, in 2008, which produces and sells their Rough Rider chair primarily to charities. A chair sale includes a full customised fitting and training programme so that users can get the most out of their chairs.[97] Similarly, Motivation, started in 1991, produces and supplies a number of chair designs especially adapted to real needs and conditions in developing countries. This includes their signature three-wheel rough terrain design, a number of adaptive chairs for children, sports chairs and their hand-powered tricycles that are especially useful in urban areas[98] (fig 8.57).

One of the universal issues for wheelchair users is the lack of adaptability and personalisation. With this in mind, Disrupt Disability was set up to use the power of hackathons, open source design and 3D printing to create an open library of standardised parts for modular, affordable and customisable "wheels that people want to wear".[99] Meanwhile, in Japan, COGY has developed a truly transformative design that demonstrates there is still a lot of room for true innovation in disabled mobility. COGY is ingeniously designed to trigger a response known as *motion reflex*, such that people with no movement in their lower limbs can activate the front pedals to propel themselves. For these people, being able to use their legs again to assist mobility is truly amazing[100] (fig 8.58). While these demonstrate positive progress, there is still a long way to go. As designers, we often unwittingly hamper wheelchair users' access, forgetting to challenge our preconceptions of disability or realising that at some point in our lives we may well be using one.

travel and transport by water

Travelling and moving goods by water is humankind's oldest mode of transport after walking and running. Today, boats are mostly used for shipping billions of tons of goods around the world,

Figure 8.59 The exquisitely detailed Hamburg solar shuttle (Germany 2000) and India's first working solar ferry, the down-to-earth Aditya in Kerala (India-France 2017) are raising hopes of clean passenger ferry travel. (courtesy Christoph Behling and ©Navaltboats.com)

ferrying island and river dwellers, leisure pursuits and cruise tourism. Up until the eighteenth century, boat travel was either human-powered with paddles and oars, or wind-powered by sails. As the servant of global trade, maritime transport accounts for over 2% of global GHGs,[101] and is set to triple between 2015 and 2050.[102] Luckily, the International Maritime Organisation has at last set the goal to decarbonise shipping by at least 50% by 2050 and there are a number of clean technologies waiting to be deployed for big ships. These revolve around electrification using a combination of onboard solar and wind power via fixed sails, or vertical turbines to run the motors directly or produce hydrogen for fuel cells.[103]

Despite using the dregs of the oil industry as fuel, the ecocosts per ton/km of shipping by water are in the order of ten times less than by road and similar to or better than rail, although slower (see fig 8.10). Understanding the relative footprints of different forms of freight transportation is important to product design. This is because *where* goods are produced, assembled and consumed geographically dictates *how* they can be transported, and significantly impacts upon a product's lifecycle assessment (LCA).

Many riverside and island communities are completely dependent on ferries for their travel and supplies. Up until the present these have mainly burned marine diesel, causing local water, air and

noise pollution. Tilla Goldberg and Christoph Behling's original Solar Shuttle built for Lake Constance in 1999 was an inspiration for how this could be done differently. Behling's SolarLab has gone on to build many more solar ferries and yachts, including the Hamburg and London Serpentine shuttles. NavAlt Boats (India–France) is applying this principle to working ferries on much smaller budgets. They designed India's first operational solar ferry, the Adytia, in Kerala, India (2017), leading the way for a new generation of accessible, clean and quiet ferries (fig 8.59).

The popularity of cruise holidays has been increasing exponentially over the past two decades, to a point where they are having serious sociocultural impacts on the cities and towns they stop at, as we discussed earlier in the chapter. Cruise ships also have a very high per-passenger footprint, with a single cruise ship polluting as much as 5 million cars going in the same direction.[104] Another deeply troubling development are 'last-chance' cruises that offer trips to 'pristine' and ever-more fragile natural environments such as the Galapagos Islands and Antarctica, yet they are adversely affecting the very nature they set out to admire (fig 8.60). Is there scope for designers to re-envision cruise liners as floating micro-eco-communities that produce net environmental benefits and develop new relationships with the communities they visit?

Figure 8.60 'Last chance' to visit Antarctica's pristine landscapes in a polluting cruise ship before it disappears. (photo steve estvanik)

8.3 systems thinking: new technologies and business models for mass personalised mobility

We complete this chapter with a look at how instrumental connected platforms will be in realising more sustainable transport. Having looked at the pros and cons of different travel modes and current technological developments, it is quite clear that design and investment in active travel, mass transit and the electrification of all modes, if powered by renewables, are indisputably necessary and desirable targets for sustainable mobility. But it is also clear that electrification alone will not be enough to avoid system gridlock. With over 2.5 billion more city dwellers expected in Asia and Africa by 2030,[105] certainly the dream of everyone owning and using their own car, even if electric, is not only physically impossible on a spatial level; it is also undesirable on many social and environmental levels. Beijing and a number of other cities across China already restrict car use to certain days through their End-number License Plate policies to try to keep pollution and congestion levels manageable.

To achieve anything like sustainable transport will require systemic thinking and collaboration. This means that the preferred modes, namely active travel and mass transit, must be open to radical redesign if they are to solve the mobility challenges and become the top choices for urbanites. Enter the mobile phone, connected data, collaborative business models, and eventually autonomous vehicles (AV), and we have the tools to create a very different system. A picture is now emerging of how these new technologies can combine with physical infrastructure to provide people with the on-demand flexibility, personalisation and control that automobility originally promised but failed to deliver, at least

in dense urban contexts. This places designers and citizens at a pivotal moment in shaping the future of mobility to reflect our values and how we want to live.

In United Micro-Kingdoms, Dunne and Raby demonstrated the use of speculative design (Chapter 3.4) as a tool to explore how mobility might evolve under different political ideologies and value systems when fossil fuels run out.[106] Figure 8.61 shows just how different the vehicles and systems resulting from each Micro-Kingdom's own set of priorities and objectives could be.

The politics of mobility suggested in United Micro-Kingdoms is not so far from the current over-simplistic ideological divide between 'private' and 'public' transport where the first is stereotyped by the private automobile and the latter by publicly owned mass-transit systems. Even before on-demand platforms, the distinction between public and private is already inextricably blurred. The 'private' car or bicycle depends on 'publicly' owned road infrastructure and often rail and transit systems are mixtures of public–private ownership. This points to the real divide being between individual and collective modes and competing

Figure 8.61 Two ideological responses to mobility from 'United Micro-Kingdoms': Communo-nuclearists' 3km-long mobile paradise home and landscape, and below, self-driving digicars programmed to constantly calculate the best and most economic route for digitarians ruled entirely by market forces. (courtesy Dunne and Raby; CGI Tommaso Lanze)

Figure 8.62 Docking public bike schemes: a. Paris' early and inspiring Vélib (2008); b. Hanzhou's impressive scale and organisation (2011). (photo credits Payton Chung, Jane Penty)

commercial interests that aren't necessarily aligned with public interests. From the perspective of sustainability, the objective would be for collectively owned space and infrastructure to be used to provide mobility in the best interests of the community, including business and the environment.

With new connected technologies, these relationships are becoming yet more fluid. As car ownership becomes more of a handicap than an asset in urban areas, access to mobility is becoming more important than car ownership. This has led to the growth of collaborative mobility platforms for cars, vans and bicycles over the past decade that are effectively extending mobility services where mass transit systems leave off. These fall within the *'access-over-ownership'* model we looked at in Chapter 4.3 where getting from A to B by the most effective means trumps ownership. But how sustainable are these platforms? We consider the current scenarios for bicycles and car sharing and later extend this to future autonomous vehicle scenarios and Mobility as a Service (MaaS).

bicycle sharing

The concept of the shared public bicycle started with the tentative but brave Freeriders in Amsterdam (1965), which was later improved by Bycyklen in Copenhagen (1995). Portsmouth University's Bikeabout was the first to use swipe cards and Rennes' Vélo-à-la-Carte was the first city-wide card and RFID tracking system (1996). However, it was not until payment interfaces, tracking technologies and bicycles were developed further that it could prove itself on a large scale thanks to leading schemes like Paris' Vélib and Barcelona's Bicing in 2007, and Hangzhou's public bicycle scheme in 2010.[107] Bicycle sharing now forms an integral part of mass-mobility strategies in over 700 cities across the world and has a surprisingly long list of benefits (fig 8.62).

In summary, shared bicycle schemes have been found to:[108, 109, 110]

- increase cycling miles and reduce pollution, GHGs and congestion
- make cycling more accessible: proven to increase overall cycling miles, uptake by previous non-cyclists, returners and females, with many moving on to purchase their own bicycles
- provide considerable personal benefits for health and wellbeing which also translate into economic benefits, costed in the UK at £370 per cyclist p.a. in 2016/2017[111]
- relieve the stress on public transport systems and help to solve 'last mile' problems as many trips are integrated with bus or rail travel journeys
- lead to an increase in cycling infrastructure investment through more cycling take-up
- increase awareness of cyclists' vulnerability
- offer convenience, fresh air, exercise, time saving, and avoiding congestion and parking, as cited by users in order of response
- support greener tourism

There are now two competing design models of cycle schemes: docking and dockless. Docking versions have fixed pick-up and carefully planned locations that are usually subsidised by local authorities, as they require investment in infrastructure, logistics and staff to redistribute the cycles. With the more recent dockless systems championed by Ofo and Mobike in China and many others that can now be found in cities around the world, cyclists simply sign up with a deposit to the app, locate a bicycle, use it and leave it nearly anywhere. This operates on the assumption that supply-and-demand will more or less even out. It will be interesting to watch how this theory works out in the long run, as bicycles obstructing public pavements and bike stores have led to some cities banning them altogether[112] (fig 8.63).

Figure 8.63 Two faces of dockless bike-sharing schemes: a. pedestrians, Ofo and Mobike bicycles battling it out for sidewalk space in Shanghai (2017); b. local urban convenience (Victoria, Canada 2018). (photo credits Philip Cohen, Jane Penty)

With rentals costing just pennies, the dockless business model is based not on rental income but on the commercial value of the profile and tracking data generated by users. However, the downside of the dockless 'free-market' model is that heavily funded start-ups are competing head-to-head. In their attempt to win market share, they have massively overproduced and flooded the streets with their bicycles. This has led to the highly unsustainable graveyards of tens and possibly hundreds of thousands of cleared bicycles[113] and the demise of China's number three, Bluegogo, along with their 700,000 bicycles.[114]

From the point of view of the physical design itself, both the docked and dockless have challenged designers to rethink and innovate many aspects of the physical bicycle, making them much more reliable and robust while also developing and integrating sophisticated UX, tagging, locking and navigation technologies.

The main design challenges for shared bicycle schemes remain:

- lowering the barrier to cycling and maximising uptake through the design of the whole system, including pricing, convenience, density and usability
- closely integrating with public transport and solving the last mile issue – how close can this come to being a door-to-door service?
- preventing loss, vandalism, theft and damage through tamper-proof mechanics
- encouraging responsible user behaviour through a combination of rewards and penalties
- keeping scheme owner maintenance costs low through a highly reliable choice of technologies, easy problem diagnosis and quick modular repairability

- ensuring safety through rider adjustability, visibility, monitoring of critical components and disabling of faulty bicycles
- creating as accessible and seamless an experience as possible by integrating systems information, payment, identification, locking, locating, tracking [,] and using

By making cycling highly affordable, convenient and 'modern', bike-share schemes are proving very successful. In China cycle miles reportedly doubled in two years since their introduction.[115] These schemes are a true demonstration of the benefits and design challenges of moving from a stand-alone product to a product service system. Beyond the usability and safety of the bicycle, the shared bicycle needs to integrate with local infrastructure and services, a system of logistics and user interface based on an understanding of users' needs. Although the majority of schemes have been successful, not all have had the same level of take-up and some have closed altogether, making it important for designers to understand the success factors and obstacles. These include the cost to the user and scheme provider, density and coverage, and the effect of mandatory helmet laws that reportedly contributed to the demise of the Melbourne and Seattle schemes.[116]

car sharing

For cars, there are several models of shared and on-demand mobility that fall broadly under collaborative consumption. Listing these in order from the most environmentally and socially beneficial to least, they are:

- carpooling and ride sharing (*BlaBlacar, Rideshare, LyftLine, Didi Chuxing*)

- P2P and B2P car 'sharing' or renting (*Zipcar, Snappcar, Car2Go, Autolib, Drivy, Goryd*)
- ride sourcing, ride hailing, or simply taxis (*Uber, Lyft, Sidecar, Didi Chuxing*)

Studies from US, Chinese, European and Australian cities consistently show that carpooling and ride sharing generate net benefits which include:[117, 118, 119, 120]

- directly reducing vehicle miles/kms travelled through higher occupancy levels, typically between 20 and 45%
- reducing car ownership because car sharers either opt not to purchase a car (25–65%), or sell their car on (15–30%). Every shared car substitutes between 9 and 13 cars
- reducing additional car miles and unnecessary journeys, as not owning a car or a second car changes travel mode and usage patterns
- reducing overall GHGs associated with car usage and ownership by 15 to 50%, in part because shared cars are generally more fuel-efficient or electric
- greater socio-economic benefits than car sharing and ride hailing, such as building community and widening social horizons by sharing with people you would otherwise not meet, leading to the associated benefit of wellbeing while reducing travel costs

Ride sourcing, on the other hand, has similar or worse negative impacts than taxi use, as the ease of access and lower costs offered by these app-based services are increasing car miles/kms travelled for these particular users.[121] At best, it may substitute car ownership and create employment if we don't look too closely at the socio-sustainability effects on employment rights and safety regulations.

MaaS

The environmental and social benefits of collaborative schemes for cycling and ride sharing are only the tip of the iceberg. Alongside the relative efficiency of different travel modes is the intensity with which it and its infrastructure is utilised. A full five-person vehicle is four times (400%) more efficient per passenger distance travelled than single occupancy. And the same is true when applying occupancy rates to buses, trains, planes and boats. Thus maximising utilisation without increasing passenger or freight miles travelled on the most efficient modes is a winning strategy after choosing the most sustainable mode.

In this respect, the smartphone and data-connected mobility platforms are proving to be the most revolutionary tools for enabling this aspect of sustainable transport. The ability of their algorithms to orchestrate and match the complex demands from passengers and goods with available capacity across all modes

means that the use of existing infrastructure and vehicles can be optimised.[122] The ultimate expression of this connectivity is MaaS, an integrated ecosystem of mobility services that provides travellers with real-time options across all modes and services via a single transit and journey-planning app. One of its biggest challenges is to connect all the service providers via open data networks and offer a single payment ticketing system to make the service as seamless as possible. Further sophistication, such as different levels of service, individual travel preferences, budget, time constraints and weather conditions, can all be thrown in to provide highly personalised solutions.[123]

Finland's transport agency has pioneered the concept of MaaS by creating the necessary regulatory framework and supporting the development and operation of the world's first MaaS apps, Whim and Kyyti, initially piloted in Helsinki and Turku (2016). Whim is now established in other cities in the UK, the Netherlands and Belgium. By maintaining a central regulatory role, public agencies play a crucial part in directing the mix of services towards the most sustainably optimal combinations.

At the centre of MaaS is a flourishing of shared on-demand vehicles and services combining last-mile connections to rapid mass-transit and active travel modes like cycling that could push private car ownership into redundancy. Simulations by the International Transport Forum (ITF) for Lisbon and Helsinki show the dramatic impact of taking this scenario all the way by replacing all existing private cars, buses and taxis with a combination of shared taxis, bookable taxi buses and rapid mass transit. The headline benefits are:[124, 125]

- only 3% (Lisbon) and 4% (Helsinki) of current vehicles would be required for a full mobility service
- CO_2 emissions drop by 62% (Lisbon) and 28% (Helsinki) even without adding in electrification
- 95% of prime land used for parking is freed up for other public uses

And all this without making door-to-door travel more difficult for users. MaaS also promises more sociability, lower travel costs and greater equality of access, as near-door-to-door service can reach less well-served areas and become affordable. At a smaller scale, especially in developing economies where there is little money for publicly funded public transit, shared informal transport has been the norm for many decades in the form of jeepneys, collectivos, matatus, car rapides and so on. The development of MaaS platforms brings the hope that many informal and formal micro-transit systems may interconnect to offer a more cohesive service without the need for huge investment.

autonomous vehicles

Alongside connectivity and MaaS, the development of autonomous vehicles (AVs) is the next element of the transport revolution that stands to have the most profound and far-reaching social and economic implications.[126] Although automation is a logical progression of connected AI capabilities and electrification, it will be highly disruptive due to the sheer size of the transport sector and how integral it is to our built environments and life choices. At the same time, it has the potential to enable much more sustainable movement of people and goods if it is harnessed with this intention.

Apart from being an enormous and highly competitive business opportunity, what are the implications and design opportunities of AVs for more sustainable transport? Just as with MaaS, the full benefits of AVs do not kick in until they reach substantial (90%) market penetration. In this scenario, AVs promise:[127]

- much greater safety and reduced road deaths and injuries
- highly efficient and optimised movement of people and automated freight
- vastly reduced pollution by being fully electric
- lower travel costs, enabling a more socially, physically and geographically inclusive service

In a context such as MaaS where private ownership becomes virtually redundant, AVs are perfectly suited for:

- shared use for people and goods and maximum utilisation rates
- reduced congestion through optimisation algorithms and pricing
- local personalised services feeding into automated busways
- high-speed, high-capacity smart lanes and expressways created by 'platooning' vehicles
- repurposing large areas of redundant parking land
- the constructive use of travel time
- vastly reduced vehicle numbers and therefore production

The pitfalls to guard against in the implementation of autonomy include:

- lower costs and 'productive' time, leading to increased demand and travel miles (a rebound effect)
- longer commutes and travel time becoming more accepted
- susceptibility to cyber attacks
- continuous movement surveillance
- affordable only by wealthy economies or the wealthiest individuals within them

While there are still many technical, economic and social challenges before AVs become the norm, the intermediate step of partial AVs is already with us and rapidly expanding. This is taking the form of automated industrial mining vehicles, shuttle buses for campuses such as Olli from Local Motors (see fig 4.22), self-driving taxis, as well as soon-to-be licensed delivery drones and air taxis. Today there is not a serious manufacturer of transport vehicles, tech company or mobility service provider that is not deeply involved in the development of driverless vehicles. As designers we are indeed at a privileged moment where we can be involved in imagining the different directions this could take before options close down.

designing for shared mobility and driverless transport

As a sector, mobility and transportation are second only to electronic and digital tools in the scale of the changes that lie ahead in the next decade. The hold that big car companies have had for the past decades on the design of mobility products is being seriously challenged. If they are to survive the onslaught of new players like Tesla, and soon-to-come Dyson and possibly Apple, they must transform themselves into mobility companies through partnerships with service and tech companies as seen between Chrysler and Waymo, Volvo and Uber, Daimler and BMW, and VW and Apple. In addition, as and when MaaS and AVs achieve critical mass, and only a fraction of the number of current vehicles are needed, competition will be even stiffer, although their higher utilisation rates means that they will be replaced more frequently and availability will be critical.

It's not just *what* the new vehicle designs will be, it's *how* they are designed and produced that is changing. In Chapter 4 we saw this with crowd-funded cars like the solar Sion (see fig 4.19), open source modular designs like Open Motor's Edit (see fig 4.23) that can easily be customised and Local Motor's driverless Olli that is being co-created for maximum accessibility (see fig 4.22). Tech and mobility companies are also designing-in and producing their own purpose-built vehicles, such as Easy Mile's EZ10 driverless shuttle already on the roads in Europe.[128]

It would be impossible to predict exactly what the motorised vehicles we will be using in 10 or 20 years' time will be like, but we do know that a sustainable future is *renewably electric* and *shared*. Of those elements, the 'shared' aspect is the least well addressed by current vehicle offer and where near-term design should be focused to make the transition to shared mobility successful. This leads to the following design prompts:

- how can vehicle configuration and accessibility be rethought for passenger drop-offs and pickups?
- as we move to driverless/autonomous cars, how can the shared car be seen as an opportunity to catch up on personal activities or a convivial space for more social interaction?
- how could controls and interfaces become simple, robust and self-explanatory?

Figure 8.64 London's iconic black cab, with its signature roominess and hop-on hop-off ease of access, is now produced as a hybrid electric vehicle, the LEVC TX. (UK 2017). (photos courtesy London EV Company LEVC)

- how could simple modularity be designed-in for ease of upgrading, repairing and replacing parts subject to wear and tear?
- could interior layouts, detailing and materials specification become virtually self-cleaning and self-maintaining to avoid the 'other person's mess' syndrome for multi-user scenarios?

London's Black Cab stands out as a rare yet decades old example of a vehicle that was designed for sharing and ease of access from the off (see fig 8.64). Now in its new EV incarnation, it continues to be quick and easy to get in and out of, has generous space for luggage buggies and wheelchairs, fold-down seats, hand grabs and integral wheelchair access. Although built for ride hailing rather than ride sharing, it still demonstrates how differently access and space can be approached.

With the shift to autonomous control and shared use, the design of motorised vehicles, as opposed to 'cars', is at last getting a long-awaited shake-up, with many design agencies and mobility companies introducing new concepts. Among these, Renault's EZ-GO (fig 8.65) shown in 2018 begins to set the scene for AVs as convivial and convenient travel spaces. IDEO's exploration of autonomous mobility brings alive possibilities for a range of scenarios, including vehicles as mobile workspaces, autonomous robotic delivery trucks, autonomous commute vehicles platooning on expressways and the fully integrated ride-share car with bookable pods (fig 8.66).[129]

Mobility is not the only use that designers are exploring for AVs. As IDEOs, Toyotas and a number of other design concepts demonstrate, AV vehicles are being seen as mobile spaces that

Figure 8.65 Renault's EZ-GO concept car suggest what life with more convivial and convenient driverless vehicles might be like (France 2018). (photos courtesy Renault and Julien Oppenheim)

Figure 8.66 IDEO's Future of Automobility explores how we may move people, things and spaces over the next decade. Shown here: a. the autonomous vehicle as office space on the expressway commute; b. autonomous bookable ride-share vehicles with customisable pods; c. curbside deliveries with the roboticised CODY trucks; d. mobile meeting spaces. (courtesy ©IDEO)

can be designed to adapt to any number of commercial and community services offered en route or taken to where they are needed. There will also be a lot of creative energy devoted to the re-appropriation of public and private land previously occupied by the many cars that remained static 95% of the time. Hopefully this will be embraced as an opportunity for building community spaces and much-needed affordable housing. And of course it is also a chance to reimagine what we do about the useful 'stuff' we used to cart around in the trunk. Do we really need it, and if so, do we need to own it? Or can this also be available on demand?

As we have seen, mobility and transportation have a profound effect on business, social structures, life choices and how we experience day-to-day life. Viewed critically, the mobility models we have inherited from the twentieth century come at a high environmental and health cost. Yet somehow, collectively, society has accepted this price. It would be wonderful to think that a combination of the urgency of global warming, the growing awareness of the health effects of pollution, the increase in numbers and density of urban populations and new connected technologies could herald a new agenda for mobility. With so much potential and so much at stake, certainly for designers this is a critical time to engage in shaping these new models of mobility and applying their sustainable values and creative skills to collaboratively reimagine liveable cities and convivial transport.

Chapter summary

1. Modern transportation and the high levels of mobility that it affords is a defining element of our economy and culture. It also creates very polarised negative and positive impacts. Through mass mobility and ever-greater speed, it has shrunk distance and time, effectively making the world smaller and more connected. Together with digital connectivity, it is also the sector that will undergo the most radical changes in the decades ahead, making it a very important focus for sustainably minded designers.

2. Our current mobility systems are a very tangible expression of the accelerating entropy that is stoking global warming. While transportation designs undoubtedly represent some of humankind's most impressive and iconic engineering achievements, the models we have inherited from the twentieth century are increasingly unsustainable. However, with the help of renewable electrification, connected technologies and sharing economy models, the design of our mobility systems stands at a pivotal point where they can be radically reshaped to prioritise better quality of life, equitable access and a healthy environment for all.

3. On the positive side of the balance, a good transport infrastructure:

   - provides essential access to services and social interactions
   - widens opportunities for self-development through access to employment and education
   - affords a sense of freedom and control
   - enables the trade of local and global goods and services to thrive
   - broadens intercultural exchanges through travel, making the world more physically and emotionally connected

4. On the negative side of the balance, as a sector, the mobility of goods and people:

   - is the single biggest consumer of petroleum oil in the world
   - is one of the biggest contributors to climate change and air pollution, seriously impacting upon the quality of life and health of billions of people and species
   - makes up the biggest part of an affluent individual's environmental footprint
   - is widening the gap between rich and poor countries
   - threatens local economies and communities through asymmetric global trade and tourism

   - will continue to grow exponentially, making it the only sector expected to increase CO_2 emissions by 2050, putting the Paris Accord targets in jeopardy

5. In its current form, motorised road transport, especially in the form of automobility and haulage:

   - is land hungry, noisy, highly polluting, and its infrastructure creates physical and visual barriers, blighting whole communities
   - kills over 1.35 million people annually and permanently disables tens of millions more
   - is the number one cause of wild animal deaths in many countries, killing billions worldwide
   - cannot meet demand in its present form, creating gridlock, congestion and daily stress for commuters

6. to address these issues, design for sustainable transport should aim to:

   - be 100% human or renewably powered
   - reduce the distances people and goods need to travel
   - be human- and environment-centred
   - provide fair accessibility for all
   - actively work to create viable choices for people to willingly shift to the most efficient, clean and safe modes
   - radically reduce accidents and deaths
   - improve the urban environment and make sustainable communities and lifestyles possible

7. One of the key strategies for achieving greater sustainability in transport is 'modal shift'. This is about getting more people to use cleaner, safer and more efficient modes for the same travel. Comparing the whole lifecycle assessments of different modes, low-occupancy motorised road transport and air travel are the most energy- and resource-intensive, while human- and electric-powered bicycles, walking and rail are the least intensive modes. In order to achieve the desired modal shift, designers need to focus on making the whole experience of healthier, cleaner, more efficient ways to travel the easiest and most enjoyable options.

8. Although electric trains have been operating for decades, the electrification of all other transport modes is only just underway in earnest in an effort to get urban pollution and carbon emissions under control. Bicycles, cars, buses and trucks are leading this new wave, followed by aircraft, including drones, and ships. However, electric vehicles (EVs) must be charged with renewable energy if GHG emissions are to be reduced significantly. A major challenge for the

positive transition to EVs is designing the new charging systems and interfaces to make the transition as frictionless as possible. EVs should be seen as an integral part of a balanced renewables network.

9. Active modes – walking and cycling – are by far the most beneficial forms of mobility in terms of health, costs and the environment – a true case of win-win-win. Lessons learned from cities that have achieved consistently high cycling rates point to two main interventions. These are year-on-year investment in cycle-only lanes to make riders feel safe, and generous bicycle storage, especially at key mass-transit nodes. Once cycling reaches a critical mass and becomes the norm, more day-to-day activities will move onto bikes, including last-mile deliveries and child transport. This creates a creative and entrepreneurial opportunity for the design of specialist cargobikes, trailers and all manner of cycling accessories to flourish. Cycle-share schemes around the world are also helping to increase uptake by giving bicycling a new status as low-cost, modern and convenient, and will require considerable design input to ensure their continued success.

10. Alongside the resurgence of cycling and electrification, collaborative platforms for shared mobility are the most

revolutionary change to come to transportation. The ultimate expression of this connectivity is Mobility as a Service (MaaS), an integrated ecosystem of mobility services providing travellers with real-time options via a single booking and payment interface. With sufficient coordination it is capable of making private vehicle ownership redundant. This also paves the way for a sustainable use scenario for autonomous vehicles. Together, MaaS and AVs open the door to a whole new typology of vehicles for travel and a raft of other shared uses and possibilities.

11. An important aspect of sustainable transport is accessibility and affordability. Most of the focus of mobility and transport design is centred on solutions for wealthy economies that can invest in new infrastructure and stock. For those living in developing economies, especially in rural areas, design must focus on the most appropriate, low-cost, robust, repairable, reliable, safe and imaginative transport solutions. There is still a very big market for the right products that can address this question of inequity and create the snowball effect that will enable economic development for the billions currently at the bottom of the economic pyramid.

Notes

1 Wynes, S. and K.A. Nicholas (2017) The Climate Mitigation Gap: Education and Government Recommendations Miss the Most Effective Individual Actions. *Environmental Research Letters,* 12 074024. https://doi.org/10.1088/1748-9326/aa7541.

2 EPA (2017) Fast Facts, USA Transportation Sector GHG Emission. EPA-420–F-7-013 [online, July]. Available at https://nepis.epa.gov/Exe/ZyPDF.cgi?Dockey=P100S7NK.pdf.

3 International Transport Forum (ITF) (2017) *ITF Transport Outlook 2017,* Paris: OECD Publishing, p. 107. http://dx.doi.org/10.1787/9789282108000-en.

4 International Energy Agency (IEA) (2017) *Key World Energy Statistics 2017,* Paris: IEA, p. 39: 49.7% road; 7.5% air; 6.7% navigation; 0.8% rail.

5 Bonte, D. (2017) Vehicle Electrification and Wireless Charging | ABI Research [online]. Available at www.abiresearch.com/market-research/product/1029572-vehicle-electrification-and-wireless-charg/ (accessed 20 November 2018).

6 IEA (2018) CO_2 *Emissions from Fuel Combustion 2017 Highlights,* Paris: OECD/IEA, p. 12; and IPCC (2014) *Fifth Assessment Report, Summary for Policymakers,* p. 10.

7 EPA (2017) *USA Transportation Sector GHG Emission,* July.

8 Including international maritime and aviation: European Environment Agency (2017) *Greenhouse Gas Emissions from Transport,* Copenhagen: EU EEA, July. Available at www.eea.europa.eu/data-and-maps/indicators/transport-emissions-of-greenhouse-gases/transport-emissions-of-greenhouse-gases-10.

9 Excluding international maritime and aviation; UK Department BEIS (2018) *2016 UK Greenhouse Gas Emissions, Final Figures,* February London: Office of National Statistics, pp. 4, 17.

10 ITF (2017) *ITF Transport Outlook 2017,* p. 60.

11 IEA (2017) *Energy Efficiency Indicators,* Paris: OECD/IEA, p. 9.

12 Ibid.

13 Health Effects Institute (Jan 2010) *Traffic-related Air Pollution: A Critical Review of the Literature on Emissions, Exposure, and Health Effects. Executive Summary.* January, Boston, MA: HEI, p. 3. Available at www.healtheffects.org/system/files/SR17TrafficReview_Exec_Summary.pdf (accessed 27 February 2018).

14 WHO.int (n.d.) *WHO | Health and Sustainable Development. Air Pollution* [online]. Available at www.who.int/sustainable-development/transport/health-risks/air-pollution/en/ (accessed 04 January 2019).

15 WHO.int (n.d.) WHO | WHO Global Ambient Air Quality Database (update 2018)[online]. Available at www.who.int/airpollution/data/cities/en/ (accessed 04 January 2019).

16 Gorham, R. (2002) *Air Pollution from Ground Transportation: An Assessment of the Causes, Strategies and Tactics and Proposed Actions for the International Community*, World Bank/UN Division of Sustainable Development. Available at www.un.org/esa/gite/csd/gorham.pdf (accessed 27 February 2018).

17 Wilson, L. (2013) Shades of Green. Electric car's Carbon Emissions Around the Globe. Shrink that Footprint [online]. Available at http://shrinkthatfootprint.com/wp-content/uploads/2013/02/Shades-of-Green-Full-Report.pdf (accessed 27 February 2018).

18 Boer, L.C. and A. Schroten (March 2007) *Traffic Noise Reduction in Europe. Health Effects, Social Costs and Technical and Policy Options to Reduce Road and Rail Traffic Noise*, Delft: CE Delft. Available at www.transportenvironment.org/sites/te/files/media/2008-02_traffic_noise_ce_delft_report.pdf.

19 Miedema, H.M.E. and C.G. Oudshoorn (2001) Annoyance from Transportation Noise: Relationships with Exposure Metrics DNL and DENL and Their Confidence Intervals. *Environmental Health Perspectives*, 109(4), pp. 409–441.

20 Sørensen, M., Z.J. Andersen, R.B. Nordsborg *et al.* (2012) Road Traffic Noise and Incident Myocardial Infarction: A Prospective Cohort Study. *PLoS One*, 20 June. doi. org/10.1371/journal.pone.0039283.

21 Boer and Schroten. (2007).

22 WHO Bonn Centre (2011) *Burden of Disease from Environmental Noise. Quantification of Healthy Life Years Lost in Europe*, Copenhagen: WHO Regional Office for Europe,. p. xvii. Available at www.euro.who.int/__data/assets/pdf_file/0008/136466/e94888.pdf (accessed 27 February 2018).

23 Monbiot, G. (2006) *Heat*, London: Penguin, p.150.

24 Schiller, P. and J. Kenworthy (2018) *Sustainable Transportation. Policy, Planning and Implementation* (2nd edn), Abingdon, Oxon, and New York: Earthscan Routledge, p. 20.

25 Rodrigue, J-P. *et al.* (2017) *The Geography of Transport Systems* (4th edn), New York: Routledge, ch. 2.

26 Clevenger, A. and J. Wierzchowski (2006) Maintaining and Restoring Connectivity in Landscapes Fragmented by Roads. In *Connectivity Conservation*, ed. Crooks, R. and M. Sanjayan, Cambridge: Cambridge University Press.

27 Hawken, P., H. Lovins and A. Lovins (1999) *Natural Capitalism. The Next Industrial Revolution*, Boston, MA: Little Brown, p. 41.

28 World Bank (2014) Transport: Sector Results Profile [online, 14 April]. Available at www.worldbank.org/en/results/2013/04/14/transport-results-profile (accessed 13 January 2019).

29 U.S. Energy Information Administration (EIA) (2016) Annual Passenger Travel Tends to Increase with Income – Today in Energy [online, 11 May]. Available at www.eia.gov/todayinenergy/detail.php?id=26192 (accessed 26 March 2018).

30 World Travel and Tourism Council (2017) Global Economic Impact and Issues [online]. Available at www.wttc.org/-/media/files/reports/economic-impact-research/2017-documents/global-economic-impact-and-issues-2017.pdf (accessed 30 March 2018).

31 Coldwell, W. (2017) First Venice and Barcelona: Now Anti-tourism Marches Spread across Europe. *The Guardian*, 10 August [online]. Available at www.theguardian.com/travel/2017/aug/10/anti-tourism-marches-spread-across-europe-venice-barcelona.

32 WHO (2018) Road Traffic Injuries [online, updated 7 December]. Available at www.who.int/news-room/fact-sheets/detail/road-traffic-injuries (accessed 3 January 2019).

33 Guimareis, T (2015) A principal causa da morte de animais silvestres no Brasil. BBC, 2 October [online]. Available at www.bbc.com/portuguese/noticias/2015/10/150924_atropelamentos_fauna_tg (accessed 27 March 2018). Also available at doi: 10.1007/s10531-015-0988-3.

34 WHO (2018).

35 UK Department for Transport (2016) Road Use Statistics, Great Britain 2016 [online]. Available at https://assets.publishing.service.gov.uk/government/uploads/system/uploads/attachment_data/file/514912/road-use-statistics.pdf (accessed 28 November 2018).

36 Price, A. and A. Godwin (2012) Mapping Transportation and Health in the United States [online, 16 January]. Available at www.planetizen.com/node/53728 (accessed 28 March 2018).

37 Gramenos, F. (2011) Healthy Travel Modes: Correlations, Causality and Caution [online, 13 November]. Available at www.planetizen.com/node/51851 (accessed 28 March 2018).

38 Pucher, J. *et al.* (2010) Walking and Cycling to Health: A Comparative Analysis of City, State, and International Data. *American Journal of Public Health*, 100(10), pp. 1986–1992 [online]. doi: 10.2105/AJPH.2009.189324.

39 Adams, J. (2000) Hypermobility [online, 20 March]. Available at www.prospectmagazine.co.uk/magazine/hypermobility (accessed 26 March 2018).

40 Schiller, P. and J.R. Kenworthy (2018) *An Introduction to Sustainable Transportation* (2nd edn). Abingdon, Oxon, and New York: Routledge, pp. 290–337.

41 Wynes and Nicholas (2017).

42 *ITF Transport Outlook* (2017), p. 3.

43 Schiller and Kenworthy (2018), p. 139.

44 Delft, C.E. (2017) Towards Addressing Aviations Non-CO_2 Climate Impacts, p. 3 [online, May]. www.cedelft.eu/en/

publicatie/towards_addressing_aviations_non-co2_climate_impacts/1961 (accessed 04 January 2019).

45 ITF (2017) *ITF Transport Outlook* (2017), p. 60.

46 Acare (n.d.) FlightPath 2050 Goals | Acare [online]. Available at www.acare4europe.org/sria/flightpath-2050-goals (accessed 8 April 2018).

47 icao.int (n.d.) Carbon Offsetting and Reduction Scheme for International Aviation (CORSIA) [online]. Available at www.icao.int/environmental-protection/Pages/market-based-measures.aspx (accessed 8 April 2018).

48 IATA statistic for 2016 onboard waste.

49 or Airlander PR/Nick Talbot, Design Director at Seymourpowell in Aircruise: Giant Hydrogen Airships could Herald a New Era in Luxury Travel. *Telegraph* [online]. Available at www.telegraph.co.uk/travel/picturegalleries/7139342/Aircruise-giant-hydrogen-airships-could-herald-a-new-era-in-luxury-travel.html?image=5 (accessed 13 March 2018).

50 BioCarbon Engineering (n.d.) Industrial-scale Ecosystem Restoration [online]. Available at www.biocarbonengineering.com/ (accessed 4 January 2019).

51 Zipline (2018) US Delivery Press Release, 3 April.

52 Anon (n.d.) Windhorse Aero [online]. Available at https://windhorse.aero/ (accessed 04 January 2019).

53 Rez, P. (2018) Energy Use by Air Taxis and Drones for Parcel Delivery, Is It Practical? Is It Sustainable? *MRS Energy & Sustainability*, 5. [online]. Available at www.cambridge.org/core/product/identifier/S2329222918000053/type/journal_article (accessed 04 January 2019).

54 Goodchild, A. and J. Toy (2017) Delivery by Drone: An Evaluation of Unmanned Aerial Vehicle Technology in Reducing CO_2 Emissions in the Delivery Service Industry. *Transport Research Part D*. Available at http://dx.doi.org/10.1016/j.trd.2017.02.017.

55 Langston, J. (2017) Drone vs. Truck Deliveries: Which Create Less Carbon Pollution? *UW News*, May [online]. Available at www.washington.edu/news/2017/05/30/drone-vs-truck-deliveries-which-create-less-carbon-pollution/ (accessed 23 March 2018).

56 *ITF Transport Outlook* (2017), p. 13.

57 Ibid., pp. 60–61.

58 Mohieldin, M. and N. Vandycke (2017) Sustainable Mobility for the 21st Century [online, 10 July]. Available at www.worldbank.org/en/news/feature/2017/07/10/sustainable-mobility-for-the-21st-century (accessed 24 April 2018).

59 Turns, A. (2018) Best in Glass – Can the Return of the Milkround Help Squash our Plastic Problem? [online]. Available at www.theguardian.com/lifeandstyle/2018/feb/07/return-milkround-plastic-problem-glass-bottle-deliveries (accessed 15 April 2018).

60 EPA (n.d.) All-electric Vehicles [online]. Available at www.fueleconomy.gov/feg/evtech.shtml (accessed 24 November 2018).

61 Latest IEA data: 2015. Available at www.iea.org/stats/WebGraphs (accessed 14 April 2018).

62 OVO Energy (2018) OVO Vehicle-to-Grid Product Information Data Sheet, April.

63 Nitch Smaith, M. (2016) The Number of Cars Worldwide is Set to Double by 2040 [online, 26 April]. Available at www.weforum.org/agenda/2016/04/the-number-of-cars-worldwide-is-set-to-double-by-2040/ (accessed 21 April 2018).

64 Hanley, S. (2018) 4 Million Electrified Vehicles Sold Globally, 5 Million Expected In 6 Months (BNEF) [online, 3 September]. Available at https://cleantechnica.com/2018/09/03/4-million-electrified-vehicles-sold-globally-5-million-expected-in-6-months-bnef/ (accessed 4 January 2019).

65 IEA (2018) *Global EV Outlook 2018*, IEA/OECD, p. 6. Available at www.iea.org/publications/freepublications/publication/GlobalEVOutlook2018.pdf (accessed 4 January 2019).

66 Riversimple.com (n.d.) How the Business Works – Riversimple Hydrogen Car Company [online]. Available at www.riversimple.com/how-the-business-works/ (accessed 4 January 2019).

67 OXGVT.com (n.d.) THE OX • OX Global Vehicle Trust [online]. Available at http://oxgvt.com/the-ox-all-terrain-vehicle/ (accessed 3 June 2018).

68 Smets, M. and J. van Onna (2015) *Turtle 1. Building a Car in Africa*, Dortmund: Paradox and Verlag Kettler.

69 Sibilski, L.J. (2015) Cycling Is Everyone's Business [online]. Available at https://blogs.worldbank.org/publicsphere/cycling-everyone-s-business (accessed 24 April 2018).

70 Anon (n.d.) *Bicycles Produced in the World – Worldometers* [online]. Available at www.worldometers.info/bicycles/ (accessed 23 May 2018).

71 Newson, A. (2013) *Fifty Bicycles that Changed the World*, London: Octopus Books, p. 40.

72 Blondiau, T. and Bruno van Zeebroeck (2015) Jobs and Job Creation in the European Cycling Sector. European Cyclists Federation [online]. Available at https://ecf.com/sites/ecf.com/files/141125-Cycling-Works-Jobs-and-Job-Creation-in-the-Cycling-Economy.pdf.

73 Neun, M. and H. Haubold (2016) *The EU Cycling Economy – Arguments for an Integrated EU Cycling Policy,* Brussels: European Cycling Federation, 1 December. Available at https://ecf.com/sites/ecf.com/files/FINAL%20THE%20EU%20CYCLING%20ECONOMY_low%20res.pdf.

74 Anon (2017) *Copenhagen City of Cyclists. Facts and Figures 2017*, City of Copenhagen. Available at www.cycling-embassy.dk/wp-content/uploads/2017/07/Velo-city_handout.pdf.

75 Coleville-Andersen, M. (2017) The Best Biking Cities on the Planet [online, 16 June]. Available at www.wired.com/story/

world-best-cycling-cities-copenhagenize/ (accessed 24 April 2018).

76 League of American Bicyclists (2017) Where We Ride. Analysis of Bicycle Commuting in American Cities [online]. Available at http://bikeleague.org/sites/default/files/LAB_Where_We_Ride_2016.pdf.

77 Reid, C. (2018) Dockless Bike-share Leads to Quick Spike in Bike Use in Chinese Cities [online, 26 January]. Available at www.bikebiz.com/news/dockless-booming-in-china (accessed 24 April 2018).

78 McLeash, M. (2017) How Far Is Too Far to Bike to Work? Mobility Lab [online, 27 February]. Available at https://mobilitylab.org/2017/02/27/how-far-bike-work/ (accessed 4/January 2019).

79 Penty, J. (2013) Interview with Andrew Ritchie at Brompton Bicycles, London, 10 June.

80 Fyhry, A. and N. Fearnley (2015) Effects of e-bikes on Bicycle Use and Mode Share. *Transport Research Part D*, 36, pp. 45–52. Available at http://dx.doi.org/10.1016/j.trd.2015.02.005.

81 Shepard, W. (2016) Why Chinese Cities Are Banning The Biggest Adoption Of Green Transportation In History [online, 18 April]. Available at www.forbes.com/sites/wadeshepard/2016/05/18/as-china-chokes-on-smog-the-biggest-adoption-of-green-transportation-in-history-is-being-banned/ (accessed 25 April 2018).

82 These are cities with PM2.5 above 160μg/1000 and do not include smog or NOx. Tainio, M. *et al.* (2016) Can Air Pollution Negate the Health Benefits of Cycling and Walking? *Preventative Medicine*, 87(June), pp. 233–237. Available at https://doi.org/10.1016/j.ypmed.2016.02.002.

83 Mueller, N. *et al.* (2015) Health Impact Assessment of Active Transportation: A Systematic Review. *Preventative Medicine*, 76. pp. 103–114. Available at http://dx.doi.org/10.1016/j.ypmed.2015.04.010.

84 Mead, N.V. (2017) Tipping Point: Revealing the Cities Where Exercise Does More Harm than Good. *The Guardian* [online]. Available at www.theguardian.com/cities/2017/feb/13/tipping-point-cities-exercise-more-harm-than-good (accessed 26 April 2018).

85 Penty, J. (2018) Interview with Alex Hulme, Map Project Office, London, 1 February.

86 studioroosegaarde.net (2018) Smog Free Bicycle | Smog Free Project | Studio Roosegaarde [online]. Available at www.studioroosegaarde.net/project/smog-free-bicycle (accessed 26 November 2018).

87 Feleke, R. *et al.* (2018) Comparative Fatality Risk for Different Travel Modes by Age, Sex, and Deprivation. *Journal of Transport and Health*, 8(March), pp. 307–320. https://doi.org/10.1016/j.jth.2017.08.007.

88 Santacreu, A. (2018) Cycling Safety in World Cities: Measuring Exposure and Risk [online, 29 January]. Available at www.

itf-oecd.org/cycling-safety-world-cities-measuring-exposure-and-risk (accessed 26 April 2018).

89 European Transport Safety Council (2003) *Transport Safety Performance in the EU: A Statistical Overview*, Brussels: The Council.

90 Robinson, D. (2018) Bike-share Schemes Improve Safety – Helmet Laws Do Not. In reponse to Hu, G. and D. Yin (2018) China: A Return to the 'Kingdom of Bicycles'? *British Medical Journal*, 24 January [online], 360k94. Available at www.bmj.com/content/360/bmj.k94/rr-2 (accessed 26 April 2018).

91 Deegan, B. (2018) Cycle Lane Protection: A State of the Art Review [online pdf, 30 January]. Available at www.itf-oecd.org/sites/default/files/docs/cycle-lane-protection-deegan.pdf (accessed 26 April 2018).

92 Walker, P. (2017) The Big Bike Helmet Debate: 'You Don't Make it Safe by Forcing Cyclists to Dress for Urban Warfare'. *The Guardian*, 21 March [online]. Available at www.theguardian.com/lifeandstyle/2017/mar/21/bike-helmet-cyclists-safe-urban-warfare-wheels (accessed 27 April 2018).

93 Anon (2013) *Copenhagen City of Cyclists. Facts and Figures 2017*, City of Copenhagen. Available at www.cycling-embassy.dk/wp-content/uploads/2017/07/Velo-city_handout.pdf.

94 worldbicyclerelief.org (2018) Buffalo Bicycles – Strong, Simple to Fix & Good for the Long Haul [online]. Available at https://worldbicyclerelief.org/en/bike/ (accessed 2 December 2018).

95 Penty, J. (2018) Craig Calfee email interview, 9–29 May.

96 Wheelchair Foundation (n.d.) Analysis of Wheelchair Need [online]. Available at www.wheelchairfoundation.org/programs/from-the-heart-schools-program/materials-and-supplies/analysis-of-wheelchair-need/ (accessed 8 May 2018).

97 Whirlwind (n.d.) Our History. Whirlwind Wheelchair [online]. Available at https://whirlwindwheelchair.org/our-history/ (accessed 4 January 2019).

98 motivation.org.uk (n.d.) Our Story [online]. Available at www.motivation.org.uk/our-story (accessed 4 January 2019).

99 disruptdisability.org (2018) Disrupt Disability [online]. Available at www.disruptdisability.org/ (accessed 04 January 2019).

100 cogycogy.com (2018) *COGY | The Wheelchair for Those Who Still Believe* [online]. Available at http://cogycogy.com/en/ (accessed 4 January 2019).

101 Pearce, F. (2018) The Race is on to Decarbonize the 50,000-plus Ships that Carry Our Stuff around the World. Ensia [online, 3 May]. Available at https://ensia.com/features/ship-carbon/ (accessed 8 May 2018).

102 ITF, *International Transport Outlook 2017*, IFT/OECD, p. 56.

103 Pearce (2018).

104 McVeigh, T. (2017) As British Tourists Take to the Seas, Giant Cruise Ships Spread Pollution Misery. *The Guardian*, 8 January [online]. Available at www.theguardian.com/

environment/2017/jan/08/ports-pollution-cruising-ships-freight-sea (accessed 8 April 2018).

105 UN DESA (2018) Revision of World Urbanization Prospects | United Nations Department of Economic and Social Affairs [online, 16 May]. Available at www.un.org/development/desa/publications/2018-revision-of-world-urbanization-prospects.html (accessed 6 June 2018).

106 Dunne, A. and F. Raby (2013) *Speculative Everything*, Cambridge, MA, and London: MIT Press, pp.173–189.

107 Goodyear, S. (2015) The Real Story Behind the Global Bike-share Boom [online]. Available at www.citylab.com (accessed 4 December 2018).

108 Ricci, M. (2015) Bike Sharing: A Review of Evidence on Impacts and Processes of Implementation and Operation. *Research in Transportation Business & Management,* 15, pp. 28–38. http://dx.doi.org/10.1016/j.rtbm.2015.03.003.

109 Bikeplus (2017) Bike Share Benefits. Statistics on the Contribution to Eight Key Policy Areas [online]. Available at www.carplusbikeplus.org.uk/wp-content/uploads/2016/02/Smarter-Travel-Conference-Bike-Share-Benefits-A4-AW.pdf (accessed 31 July 2017).

110 Bikeplus (2017) Public Bike Share User Survey Results [online, September]. Available at https://como.org.uk/wp-content/uploads/2018/06/Public-Bike-Share-User-Survey-2017-A4-WEB-1.pdf (accessed 6 June 2018).

111 UK Department for Transport Guidance for 2016/2017 on 2010 prices.

112 Reid, C. (2017) Amsterdam Bans Dockless Bikes [online, 8 August]. Available at www.bikebiz.com/news/amsterdam-bans-dockless-bikes (accessed 23 August 2017).

113 Haas, B. (2017) Chinese Bike Share Graveyard a Monument to Industry's 'Arrogance'. *The Guardian*, 25 November [online]. Available at www.theguardian.com/uk-news/2017/nov/25/chinas-bike-share-graveyard-a-monument-to-industrys-arrogance (accessed 11 May 2018).

114 Chandler, C. (2017) China's Bike-sharing Bubble Goes Bust [online, 17 November]. Available at http://fortune.com/2017/11/18/chinas-bike-sharing-bubble-goes-bust/ (accessed 11 May 2018).

115 Reid (2018).

116 Collinson, P. (2017) On Your Bike: The Best and the Worst of City Cycle Schemes. *The Guardian*, 25 February [online]. Available at www.theguardian.com/money/2017/feb/25/best-and-worst-city-cycle-schemes-bike-sharing-london (accessed 11 May 2018).

117 Nijland, H. and J. van Meerkerk (2017) Mobility and Environmental Impacts of Car Sharing in the Netherlands. *Environmental and Societal Transitions*, 23(22 January), pp. 84–91, Elsevier. https://doi.org/10.1016/j.eist.2017.02.001.

118 TSRC (2015) Mobility and the Sharing Economy: Impacts Synopsis | TSRC - Transportation Sustainability Research Center [online]. Available at http://tsrc.berkeley.edu/node/1004 (accessed 5 July 2017).

119 Bergren Miller, A. (2016) Two New Reports Confirm Social, Environmental Benefits of Carsharing. *Shareable*, 20 October. Available at www.shareable.net/blog/two-new-reports-confirm-social-environmental-benefits-of-carsharing (accessed 5 July 2017).

120 Chi, M. (2017) Carpooling Brings Benefit to Beijing and Neighbouring Cities – China – Chinadaily.com.cn [online, 19 April]. Available at www.chinadaily.com.cn/china/2017-04/19/content_28997348.htm (accessed 29 July 2017).

121 TSRC (2015).

122 Lindsay, G. (2016) Now Arriving: A Connected Mobility Roadmap for Public Transport. New Cities Foundation [online]. Available at http://bit.ly/NCFConnectedMobility.

123 Schiller and Kenworthy (2018), pp. 259–262.

124 Furtado, F. (2017) Shared Mobility Simulations for Helsinki. OECD-ITF [online, 12 October]. Available at www.itf-oecd.org/sites/default/files/docs/transition-shared-mobility.pdf (accessed 8 June 2018).

125 ITF (2017) *Transition to Shared Mobility*. ITF Corporate Partnership Report, 31 May [online]. Available at www.itf-oecd.org/sites/default/files/docs/transition-shared-mobility.pdf (accessed 8 June 2018).

126 Nesnow, G. (2018) 73 Mind Blowing Implications of a Driverless Future. Medium, 9 February [online]. Available at https://medium.com/@DonotInnovate/73-mind-blowing-implications-of-a-driverless-future-58d23d1f338d (accessed 24 May 2018).

127 Schiller and Kenworthy (2018), pp.144–148.

128 Easymile press (2019) Another Milestone for EasyMile: The First Fully Driverless Service of our EZ10 Driverless Shuttle. EasyMile [online]. Available at www.easymile.com/another-milestone-for-easymile-the-first-fully-driverless-service-of-our-ez10-driverless-shuttle/ (accessed 13 January 2019).

129 IDEO (n.d.) The Future of Automobility [online]. Available at https://automobility.ideo.com/moving-together/intro (accessed 4 January 2019).

Conclusion

Some of the things we now know, and some that are still to be discovered about sustainability and product design, by way of a conclusion.

about humans and the state of the planet

We know:
- that humans dominate the planet
- that our population has more than doubled and our consumption quadrupled since 1970 when we surpassed the Earth's bio-capacity
- that climate change has escalated into an emergency that threatens all life on Earth as we know it
- that ecosystems are being destroyed at such a rate that we are heading towards the sixth mass extinction of species
- that we are busy working our way through known reserves of irreplaceable non-renewable materials that have taken billions of years to create

and that these existential crises are caused primarily by the scale of human activity and the systems, technologies and choices we have made and continue to make every day to meet our physical and emotional needs.

We know:
- that the current measure of economic success is continuous financial growth
- that our dominant economic systems indirectly reward environmental destruction and inequality by not including social and environmental capital on their balance sheets
- that the planet's natural wealth and economic power are very unequally distributed, leading to billions of people failing to live dignified lives let alone reach their potential
- that human capital is one of the most abundant yet neglected resources on the planet

and that we could meet our needs and share the planet's wealth much more fairly and effectively.

We also know:
- that the solution – *one-planet living* – while a simple concept, involves a change of mindsets at all levels and by all people
- that designers have a key role to play in the process of co-creating this new way of living

although no one yet knows how we will get there, nor what it will look or feel like.

about designing products for sustainable living

We know:
- that we already have most of the technological and non-technological answers to solve our environmental problems
- but that we lack sufficient political, economic and behavioural will to support these

and we also know:
- that collectively rethinking and reframing the nature of how we produce and what and why we consume lies at the heart of living more sustainably
- and that this also means redesigning how, why and what we design.

We know

that to be more *environmentally sustainable,* products should:
- take into account whole lifecycle impacts
- be produced with and run on renewable energy
- not create or use substances that are toxic to life
- be part of circular bio- or techno-material loops
- be made from materials that are either recycled or from sustainable renewable sources

- embrace opportunities to be restorative
- question needs and explore new and less impactful ways of satisfying these needs
- look for solutions in old as well as new tech
- deliver functionality with ever less energy, resources and materials
- favour longevity over newness, quality over quantity, simplicity over complexity
- provide positive feedback loops for the most sustainable behaviours
- lower the psychological barriers to change by being persuasive and compelling

that to be more *socially sustainable,* products should:
- be meaningful and enabling tools for sustainable lives
- seek to improve the quality of life for the greatest number of people but not at the expense of the environment
- build cultural capital and celebrate diversity
- strengthen positive and supportive relationships between people to build social capital
- be responsible and anticipate unintended consequences
- use design to actively challenge social and economic injustice and demonstrate more equitable models
- trigger ethical debates about emerging technologies to engage citizens in shaping these 'for good'

that to be more *economically* sustainable, products should:
- operate within the most equitable business structures possible to achieve their purpose
- emerge from a process that has a clear vision, actionable goals, measures its impacts and builds in responsive feedback loops
- be equitably produced through fair and safe labour practices
- be supported and informed by the shared knowledge and sustainable practices of cross-industry alliances
- empower the base of the pyramid to meet their own needs and live dignified lives
- offer the best, most sustainable and viable proposition.

about sustainably minded designers

We know

that sustainably minded product designers have never had as many opportunities or been in such high demand thanks to:
- open design and collaborative co-creation platforms

- direct access to finance and customers through crowd-funding
- digital and distributed manufacturing and maker spaces
- the breadth of roles open to designers across physical and virtual domains, from meta-designers to entrepreneurs, global strategists to local crafters.

We also know

that to tackle the complex issues and causes around unsustainability and come to solutions that are 'functionally relevant and emotionally resonant' designers will need to:
- be sustainably literate and informed
- understand the constraints they are operating within
- question existing assumptions
- build reflective feedback loops into their practice
- employ their whole design process tool chest, including:
  - creating a culture of openness, empathy, freshness and optimism
  - employing collaborative and co-design methods
  - engaging audiences through storytelling and narrative
  - experimenting and having the courage to take risks
  - making ideas 'real' through visualisations, early prototyping and tireless testing
  - using the power of convergent and divergent creative thinking processes to generate, expand, analyse and synthesise new ideas.

about product-specific challenges and opportunities

We know

that the design of short-life products should:
- think in systems to question single-use consumption models and revisit reusables
- explore and develop new benign materials and effective short- and longlife solutions
- reconsider the use of plastics to match end-of life scenarios with the most appropriate materials, formats and product service models

that the design of electronic and digital tools should:
- push for recovery, repairability and upgradability
- seek to create social value and anticipate negative consequences
- actively engage in shaping a positive direction for emerging technologies

that the design of furniture should:
- increase usefulness, flexibility and perceived value
- eliminate toxics, maximise renewables and recyclability, and extend life
- consider furniture's power to create social and cultural capital in both private and public spaces

that the design of transportation and mobility should:
- make active and low-impact modes safer and more attractive than high-impact motorised travel
- include the redesign of communities to reduce the distances people need to travel and increase quality of life
- maximise the use of renewable energy where motorisation is needed
- maximise infrastructure and vehicle utilisation rates through connected sharing platforms.

about the 'big picture' of what we are aiming for and how we might get there

We think

that sustainable living will involve:
- a shift to compact, more self-sufficient urban clusters with people living closer together travelling on foot, by bicycle, public transit or shared electric vehicles
- protecting approximately 50% of the planet from human activity to allow natural ecosystems to rebalance themselves

- obtaining all our energy from renewable sources and locally distributed networks
- aligning our consumption and production with the natural world's capacity and circular systems
- developing new forms of governance and a new economic rulebook that values and rewards the building of social and environmental capital
- finding a balance between localism and globalism that benefits the maximum number of people and enables a reflourishing of local cultures and values

but that it will take all our most creative and collaborative efforts to find our way there.

Finally, and perhaps most importantly, we also know that sustainability presents us with the biggest opportunity to redesign how humans will live alongside their fellow species, and:
- that designers are in a good position to catalyse tangible change
- that products for sustainable living must be rewarding, motivating, enjoyable and fulfilling
- that sustainability is not a place but a constant process of setting and resetting our course
- that with the sense of urgency growing we are pushing at an open door

And, that *today* is the perfect day to act.

Glossary

3Ps	good for people, profit and planet, closely connected to the triple bottom line (TBL)
AM	the generic term for additive manufacturing, including all forms of 3D printing, as opposed to subtractive manufacturing
B Corps	abbreviation for corporations that achieve certification by the non-profit B Labs. For certification, a company must achieve a minimum B Impact score measured across their entire social and environmental performance. B Corps certification can also signal an organisation's commitment to creating a positive impact for their employees, communities and the environment.
B2B	business-to-business
B2C	business-to-customer
benefit corporation	a company that has the creation of stated social and/or environmental benefits enshrined in its articles of incorporation (BC)
BEV	battery electric vehicle
BioBricks	in synthetic biology, the trademarked name for standard interchangeable DNA sequence parts for designing and building synthetic biological circuits that can be incorporated into living cells
biodegradable	any organic material that can be broken down naturally into basic organic molecules, gases and water, and reabsorbed into the environment for use as nutrients by other organisms
biological cycle /bio-cycle	in circular or cradle-to-cradle systems, the continuous cycles within which bio-based materials can and should circulate
biosphere	the sum of all the parts of the Earth – land, water and atmosphere – where life exists
bluewashing	a variation on greenwashing used to describe companies that endorse the UN Global Compact to implement ten universal sustainability principles and support UN goals while largely continuing with business as usual
BoP	base (or bottom) of the pyramid: refers to the group of people at the bottom of the economic income pyramid globally. This is commonly calculated on the basis of $/day earnings. In this book it includes those earning less than < $10/day 2011ppp, made up of the 'extremely poor', the 'poor' and those on a 'low income'
BRIC/BRIICS	emerging economies: Brazil, Russia, India and China (Goldman Sachs term) + Indonesia (OECD term)
bycatch	fish and marine animals accidentally caught and killed when fishing for specific species, often discarded at sea
C2C	cradle-to-cradle: a lifecycle approach to design, production and consumption that seeks restorative opportunities and eliminates waste through closed-loop bio- and techno-cycles
cascading loops	recycled material that is downgraded to a function requiring a lower performance due to impurity or loss of original properties; for example, office paper being used for making notepads, then newsprint. Also known as downcycling.

CC	creative commons: an intellectual property licensing system that enables stipulated levels of sharing
CCS	carbon capture and storage systems and technologies
CFCs / HCFCs	Chlorofluorocarbons and Hydrofluorocarbons: gases most commonly used as refrigerants, propellants in aerosols and solvents in dry cleaning, largely responsible for ozone depletion
circular economy	an economy based on the principles of industrial ecology and C2C that aims to keep resources in use for as long as possible; to extract the maximum value from them while in use; and then to recover and regenerate products and materials at the end of each service life through separate bio- and techno-recycling loops
closed-loop recycling	where recycled materials go on to produce the same products or products of a similar functionality and level of performance
CNT	carbon nanotubes
conflict minerals or resources	resources whose purchase serves to fund armed conflict groups directly or indirectly. The Frank-Dodds Act in US and EU legislation puts the responsibility for 'due diligence' on companies to ensure that their supply chains are 'conflict free'. Particularly associated with minerals for electrical and electronic products.
COP	Conference of the Parties, supreme decision-making body of the UN Framework Convention on Climate Change (UNFCCC)
CPG	consumer packaged goods: also known as fast-moving consumer goods (FMCG). Generally consumables and disposable products, including food and drink, characterised by short-life, low-value, high turnover where brand and packaging design play key roles.
CSR	corporate social responsibility encompasses an organisation's actions to achieve regulatory compliance or higher self-imposed targets in environmental protection, social value and ethical practices across their business. This is typically reported on annually.
declared unit	in lifecycle assessments, the specification of a product per meaningful unit of output or functionality which may include the scenario of use
decoupling (eco-economic)	eco-economic decoupling means having economic growth without corresponding increases in environmental damage
design activism	using design, with its many tools and disciplines, to draw attention to injustices, and to catalyse social, political, environmental and economic change directly or indirectly
design thinking	the thinking behind human-centred, convergent-divergent design processes and skillsets used to generate and develop innovative concepts for product and services, and capable of finding synergies between technological, human and business needs
DfE	design for environment (also ecodesign, green design): design approach that seeks to reduce the impacts of products and services on human health and the environmental over their whole lifecycle
DfS/D4S	design for sustainability: goes beyond DfE to include the social component of sustainability and how consumer needs could be met differently and less impactfully
downcycling	recycling material that is then used to produce lower performing products because of impurity or loss of original properties (e.g. food grade plastic used for horticulture/plant pots or garbage bags). Also known as cascading.
e-waste	electrical and electronic waste equipment: discarded electronic and electrical products and parts, including products that may still be functioning; also referred to as WEEE
ecodesign	see DfE
ecological footprint	a measure of human pressure on ecosystems expressed in global hectares, that quantifies the amount of regenerative biosphere capacity needed to supply and absorb the waste from human activities against existing bio-capacity

ecosystem services	the services provided by the natural environment, including food, water, materials, soil, medicines, crop pollination, climate regulation, flood defences, carbon storage, waste absorption, nature's cultural services and many more
electronics, green	high-performance electronics made from natural or nature-inspired materials that are either bio-benign or biodegradable
electronics, transient	electronics made of materials that are fully bio-compatible and resorbable
EMAS	Environmental Management and Assessment System: the EU Eco-Management and Audit Scheme for organisations to track, improve and be certified for their environmental performance
EoL	end-of-life: in product lifecycles, when a product is discarded either because it is unwanted or no longer functional
EPA	USA Environmental Protection Agency (founded 1970)
EPD	environmental product declaration: a standardised method for reporting verified lifecycle assessments (LCA) of environmental impacts of products and services to ISO 14025 international standards. An established practice in industries, such as building and public sector green procurement, with rules for new product categories (PCR) coming on stream every year.
EPR	extended producer responsibility: a strategy to reduce the environmental impacts of products by making manufacturers responsible for their entire lifecycle, especially the end-of-life stage, through take-back, recycling and final disposal
EPS	expanded polystyrene
ErP	energy-related products: a term created by the EU ErP Directive (2009) for products that use energy or that have an indirect impact on energy consumption, such as water-consuming devices, building insulation products, windows, etc. Products that comply with these regulations are CE marked.
existential threat	a threat to human survival
FMCG	Fast-moving consumer goods: *see* CPG
FoE	Friends of the Earth – international grassroots environmental organisation based in 75 countries
FP	a for-profit company or business
frugal design and innovation	closely associated to design for the base of the pyramid, an approach to designing products and services that solve essential problems with the least resources and cost, and appropriate longevity and reliability, that are affordable to the largest number of people on very low incomes
FSC/PEFC	Forestry Stewardship Council and Programme for the Endorsement of Forest Certification: the first and largest independent 'chain of custody certification' (COC) programmes for tracking wood sourced from responsibly managed forests
FU	functional unit: the essential function that a product or system delivers per relevant unit and set time, used for LCAs
GDP	gross domestic product: the value of the total production in a country, usually for a given year, calculated by adding together total consumer, government and business spending, and the value of net exports
GHGs	greenhouse gases: gases causing global warming, the main ones being carbon dioxide (CO_2), methane (MH_4) and nitrous oxide (N_2O)
Gini coefficient (or index)	a measure of the spread in income or consumption among individuals or households in an economy, where zero represents perfect equality and 100 maximum inequality
GPI	genuine progress indicator: an alternative metric to GDP, calculated by subtracting the negative and adding the positive social and environmental effects of economic activity from the GDP
green design	*see* DfE

greenwashing	using untrue or misleading claims of care for the environment to increase sales and consumption, causing greater environmental harm
GWP	global warming potential of a gas measured in CO_2 equivalents
HCD	human-centred design, also known as user-centred design
HEV	hybrid electric vehicle
IAQ	indoor air quality: an assessment of air quality inside buildings, especially in relation to pollutants that have long-term health implications
ILO	UN, International Labour Organisation
IoT	the Internet of Things: refers to the network of digitally connected sensing objects able to generate, transmit or receive data that provide the feedback and monitoring loops for big data for 'smart' AI systems to operate
IP	intellectual property: refers to the legal ownership over creations of the mind, including inventions, literary and artistic works, symbols, names, images, photographs, and designs used commercially. This can take the form of copyright or industrial property rights such as patents
IPCC	Intergovernmental Panel on Climate Change (IPCC), the leading international body for the assessment of climate change. Established by the UNEP and the World Meteorological Organization (WMO) in 1988
IUCN	International Union for the Conservation of Nature: monitors and produces the Red List of Endangered Species
LCA	lifecycle assessment: a quantitative tool that analyses the impact on humans and the environment of a product or activity across its lifecycle, measuring multiple indicators supported by extensive datasets (LCIs). It is increasingly being used to compare products through environmental product declarations (EPDs)
LCD	lifecycle design: design that takes into consideration all the phases of a product or service's life
LCI	lifecycle inventory: a database of quantified inputs and outputs associated with all forms of human activities used for LCAs
LCIA	interprets the quantified LCI data for the substances generated or extracted within an LCA systems boundary into damage or prevention scores across human health, resource depletion and ecosystem quality
leapfrogging	in the context of developing countries, leapfrogging is when new technologies are adopted, bypassing intermediate stages, such as having mobile communication without ever having had landlines or electricity without a main grid
MDG	Millennium Development Goals: a set of eight goals agreed by all UN member countries to improve the lives of the world's poorest between 2000 and 2015
MEPS	minimum energy performance standards: typically set for products or systems that use energy or water in their use phase, such as appliances and lighting
modal shift	in sustainable transportation a strategy to move people and goods from high- to low-impact modes
monstrous hybrids	manmade materials that cannot be recycled either because the materials cannot be separated for appropriate recycling or because the materials have undergone a one-way chemical reaction, such as rubber vulcanisation or chemically activated resins in composites and foams
natural capital	the valued sum of all the stocks of natural assets that provide the ecosystem services that make life possible on Earth
NFP	not-for-profit company or organisation
obsolescence	the premature shortening of a product's life from material, functional, economic or psychological causes

one-planet living	the concept whereby all humans can meet their needs for healthy and meaningful lives within the boundaries of what the planet can sustainability supply, including sufficient space for wildlife to thrive
open-loop recycling	where the materials recovered go on to produce products of lesser value or lower performance than their original function because the mixing of materials in the recyclate stream lowers their performance characteristics
optimal product lifespan	the point at which the total impact of all the energy that could have been saved each year by using a newer model equals the impact of producing the latest, most efficient model
P2P	peer-to-peer networks, particularly facilitated through Internet platforms
PE/HDPE//MLDP/LDPE/LLDPE	polyethylene in high-, medium-, low- and very low-density formulations, from rigid to highly flexible
PET	polyethylene terephthalate
PHEV	plug-in hybrid vehicle
PP	polypropylene
precautionary principle	avoiding or diminishing any human activities that may plausibly cause harm now and in the future to human and all other life forms based on scientific analysis
precycling	seeking to reduce consumer waste by avoiding waste in the first place, such as buying unpackaged, reusable or recyclable products
product ecosystem	connected to product service systems, the recognition that a product is not a stand-alone but emerges from and relies on a whole system, from its conception to manufacture, and distribution, sales, after-sales and end-of-life services
product lifespan	the time between when a product is bought and when it is discarded (also called product lifetime)
PSS	product service system: the combination of physical products and the services to support these to meet users needs
PVOH	polyvinyl alcohol, also acronymed as PVA and PVAI, not be confused with the adhesive
pyrolysis	the chemical decomposition of materials at very elevated temperatures in an inert atmosphere. Useful for converting plastics that would otherwise not be realistically recycled back into their original constituents.
RE	renewable energy
ROI	return on investment
S-LCA	social lifecycle assessment: aims to measure the social impacts of products through their whole lifecycle on all their different stakeholders. Categories include human rights, worker conditions, health and safety, cultural heritage, governance, and socio-economic repercussions
SDG	Sustainable Development Goals: 17 goals agreed by all UN members (2015–2030). They aim to tackle poverty through strategies that improve health and education, reduce inequality, and spur economic growth while tackling climate change and preserving natural habitats through partnerships between businesses, governments and civil society.
social capital	the collective yet intangible wealth created through supportive relationships and networks, be they families, friends, colleagues, communities, workplaces or associations
social innovation	the process of developing and implementing effective solutions to challenging and often systemic social issues
stakeholder	individuals or organisations affected by, or involved in, the production and use of a product or service
steady state economy	an economy where consumption demands are stabilised and roughly constant to match the ability of the environment to provide and absorb them

sustainable product design	design that meets human needs more sustainably by creatively balancing the planet's health and bio-capacity while enhancing the human experience within a viable economic framework
sustainable products	products that create net value socially, economically and environmentally through their entire product ecosystem
sustainable thinking	underpinning all strategies, decisions and processes with sustainable principles and objectives
systems thinking	a way of understanding everything, from the universe through to the behaviour of the tiniest of organisms or events as interconnected parts of a whole, governed by action–reaction feedback loops that helps us analyse and solve problems at any scale
TBL	triple bottom line: business accounting that includes economic, social and environmental profits and losses
technical material cycle/techno-cycle	in circular or cradle-to-cradle systems, the continuous cycle of use, recycling and reuse within which manmade materials should circulate
TEEB	The Economics of Ecosystems and Biodiversity under UNEP: has established ecosystem accounting systems to assess the value of Natural Capital stocks
the commons	the natural resources held and shared for common use, such as air, water and land. Since digitalisation, this has also come to include shared culture, information and knowledge.
tipping point	a point of no return caused by small cumulative inputs that lead to a sudden event or change of far greater consequence than the sum of its parts. One of the potential existential threats of climate change
UF	urea formaldehyde: a known carcinogen released through off-gassing used in the adhesive formulation of many furniture and construction board products, such MDF, ply and particleboards. To be free of UF, boards must be specifically classed as zero UF
UNEP	United Nations Environment Programme established in 1972, now known as UN Environment
VOCs	volatile organic compounds: any organic compound that turns gaseous or evaporates. Used in the context of materials and processes in design, it usually refers to gases that are released and are considered harmful to human health and the environment in the making or use phases, such as formaldehyde from boards
WBCSD	World Business Council for Sustainable Development
WEEE	waste electrical and electronic equipment: all types of electrical and electronic equipment (EEE) and their parts that have been discarded as waste without the intention of reuse
WEF	World Economic Forum
WHO	World Health Organisation
WMO	World Meteorological Organisation
WWF	World Wildlife Fund for Nature

Index